S0-AUE-795

COMPLETE COURSE Fourth Edition

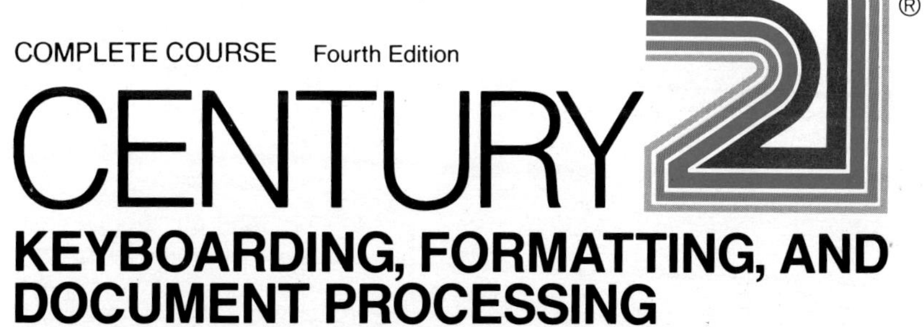

CENTURY 21 KEYBOARDING, FORMATTING, AND DOCUMENT PROCESSING

T. James Crawford, Ph.D.

Professor of Business
and of Education
Indiana University

Lee R. Beaumont, Ed.D.

Professor of Business, Emeritus
Indiana University of Pennsylvania

Lawrence W. Erickson, Ed.D.

Professor of Education, Emeritus
University of California (LA)

Jerry W. Robinson, Ed.D.

Senior Editor
South-Western Publishing Co.

Arnola C. Ownby, Ed.D.

Professor of Office Administration
and Business Education
Southwest Missouri State University

Published by

SOUTH-WESTERN PUBLISHING CO.

T55 CINCINNATI WEST CHICAGO, IL DALLAS PELHAM MANOR, NY LIVERMORE, CA

ACKNOWLEDGMENTS

Contributing Authors

Several teachers prepared selected materials for this textbook and correlating laboratory materials and tests. Their names are listed here as evidence of our appreciation of their helpful participation.

Jack P. Hoggatt, Ed.D.
Associate Professor of Business Education and Administrative Management
University of Wisconsin, Eau Claire

John J. Olivo, Jr., Ph.D.
Assistant Professor of Business Education and Office Administration
Bloomsburg (PA) University

Sharon Lund O'Neil, Ph.D.
Associate Professor of Business Education
University of Houston

Jon A. Shank, Ed.D.
Professor of Administrative Management and Business Education
Robert Morris College, Coraopolis (PA)

Donna L. Willard, M.S.
Instructor of Business Education
Great Oaks Joint Vocational School District, Cincinnati

Other Contributors

In addition to the authorship team and editorial staff who prepare and process the manuscript that becomes a textbook, thousands of others contribute in vital ways to the quality of the final product. Among these are teachers and students too numerous to thank individually. We mention these groups here as an expression of appreciation and thanks.

In preparation for this new fourth edition of *Century 21 Keyboarding, Formatting, and Document Processing,* over 5,000 teachers responded to a comprehensive questionnaire sent to a stratified sample of keyboarding/typewriting teachers throughout the country. Their responses weighed heavily in deciding the major changes that have been made in the revision.

Planned changes in course titling and course content were obtained by questionnaire responses from all state and selected city supervisors. The responses helped to guide the changes in the book's title, content, and sequence.

Almost 2,000 teacher interview reports prepared by marketers, editors, and authors during interviews with users of the previous edition were helpful in identifying for revision specific materials that appeared to cause some learning difficulty.

A more limited sample of teachers and students reported specific feedback on selected segments of the textual and teaching/learning support materials in a formal learner verification revision (LVR) study.

Photo Credits

COVER PHOTO and photo in heads on pages iii and RG 1: © Richard Fukahara/West Light

PHOTO, p. xi, top: IBM Corporation
PHOTO, p. 243: Photo courtesy Colorado Tourism Board
PHOTO, p. 298: Courtesy of NCR Corporation
PHOTO, p. 362: Kerr-McGee Corporation
PHOTO, p. 447: Photo courtesy of Varityper
PHOTO, p. 463: Courtesy of: Computer Consoles, Inc. ("CCI"), Rochester, N.Y.
PHOTO, p. 484: The 3M Company
PHOTO, p. 490: © Joel Gordon 1984

PHOTOS FOR ALL PHASE OPENERS: Melvin L. Prueitt, IS-2, Los Alamos National Laboratory, author of *Art and the Computer,* 1984.

ISBN: 0-538-20550-4

Library of Congress Catalog Card Number: 85-50269

6 7 8 9 10 11 12 13 14 H 2 1 0 9

Printed in the United States of America

PREFACE

If one were asked to list the terms which best represent the changes that have occurred in the workplace during the past decade, these would likely be among the top twenty: information processing, automation, personal computers, word/data processing, electronics, technology, communication, keyboard (ing), format(ting), text-editing, and document processing. Thus, the information and electronic age has ushered in a whole new vocabulary that permeates personal, professional, and business communication.

At the center of the many changes which the information and electronic age has brought are a wide variety of typewriter-like keyboards and an equal variety of people who operate them. Any learning program designed to prepare students to function knowledgeably and efficiently in the modern world must give attention to the concepts, terminology, and processes that those who use that program are expected to know.

From its title to its index, *Century 21 Keyboarding, Formatting, and Document Processing*, Fourth Edition, reflects the changes that are taking place in school curriculums as well as in office systems throughout the country -- and the world. The words in this book's title and contents are deliberately chosen to mirror the language of the modern workplace; for until one understands the language of change, one can only reluctantly accept change itself. Some of the terms are merely different words applied to familiar concepts and processes. Others are new words to name new methods of handling familiar functions.

But whatever the changes in vocabulary, the course of study this book is designed to serve -- keyboarding, typewriting, word processing, or some variant of these -- still has three major thrusts or areas of emphasis: keyboarding (manipulative skill development), formatting (arrangement, placement, and spacing of documents), and document processing (skilled production of letters, reports, tables, and other communication forms). *Century 21* develops each of these skill components in a timely, educationally sound way.

Keyboarding

Keyboarding is the manipulative skill required and used in completing a task on a keyboard. It is also an essential prerequisite for the development of document formatting and processing skills. Thus, keyboarding is not only the first but also a continuing emphasis in the development of document processing competence.

Century 21 has long been the recognized leader in developing keyboarding skill according to widely accepted skill-building principles which are supported by a strong research base. This new edition is no exception.

The major change in initial keyboarding skill development in this new edition is the presentation of only two new keys in each lesson to provide more intensive and comprehensive practice on new learnings before other new learnings are presented. In addition, more review/reinforcement lessons are provided to assure keyboard mastery. Both changes resulted from learner verification revision (LVR) feedback from users of the previous edition.

The first phase of 25 lessons is devoted almost exclusively to alphabetic keyboarding skill development. Thereafter, emphasis on keyboarding skill is provided mainly in periodic units of intensive practice. Again, LVR feedback led to the removal of much of the keyboarding skill activity from formatting and document processing units and to the placing of such materials in separate units. Doing so focuses the attention and effort of teachers and students on one major goal at a time.

Keyboarding on the top row is delayed until correct technique has been developed on the alphabetic keyboard and an essential level of keyboarding skill has been demonstrated. LVR feedback supports this delay.

This new edition places first emphasis on technique of keyboard operation (*without* time pressure) and second emphasis on speed of manipulative performance (*with* strategic timed writings). Then, when appropriate, it emphasizes accuracy of copy produced (with restricted-speed paced practice). This plan of emphasis is in harmony with generally accepted principles of skill learning and with a large body of keyboarding research.

Supporting the structure of the skill-building materials are two other important learning principles: work from the known to the unknown; and progress from the simple to the more complex.

Formatting

Formatting includes arranging, spacing, and placing copy according to accepted conventions for specific documents (letters, reports, tables, forms, and so on). It involves learning and following efficient, orderly steps for making machine adjustments, for making within-document decisions, and for evaluating final format acceptability.

Whether one learns to format on a typewriter, computer, or word processor, the concepts and principles are the same. What does differ are the machine-specific procedural steps for accomplishing the task.

Century 21 begins format learning with the simplest formats in the first cycle. For example, only block style letters, unbound reports, and simple tables with blocked columnar headings are presented. Later cycles present the other letter and report formats and introduce the more complex formats for tables.

What is learned in one cycle is reviewed and reinforced in the next cycle before new formats or variants of familiar ones are presented.

Special drills are provided on those parts of documents that emphasize the format features (opening and closing lines of a letter style, for example).

Students work first from model typescript, then from semi-arranged print, and later from handwritten and rough-draft copy. Each progression in difficulty of format features and copy source leads the learner increasingly nearer the actual conditions of final performance.

This plan of simple-to-complex presentation and periodic review and expansion has received the endorsement of users for almost forty years.

Document Processing

Document processing is the culmination of keyboarding and formatting training. It results from the integration of these prerequisite skills and is greater than either alone. It also includes:

1. job task planning;
2. external formatting (machine adjustments);
3. internal formatting (sequencing, arranging, and spacing document parts);
4. language skills (application of accepted conventions of written English);
5. supplying information that is missing from source documents;
6. transferring (with modification) concepts, principles, and procedures to similar but variant job tasks;
7. detecting and correcting errors and evaluating final copy for acceptability.

All these subtasks are done while producing a series of similar or dissimilar documents over extended periods of time.

Century 21 helps students acquire document processing competence by providing training activities on specific subtasks, time-pressure production writings, and a variety of office job simulations in which the student is responsible for the satisfactory completion of all facets of the work.

To prepare students for the modern workplace in the most efficient way is why this fourth edition of *Century 21 Keyboarding, Formatting, and Document Processing* has been written.

CONTENTS

Cycle 3 Lessons 151-225
Formatting/Processing Business Documents

Cycle 4 Lessons 226-300
Modern Office Simulations

KNOW YOUR TYPEWRITER

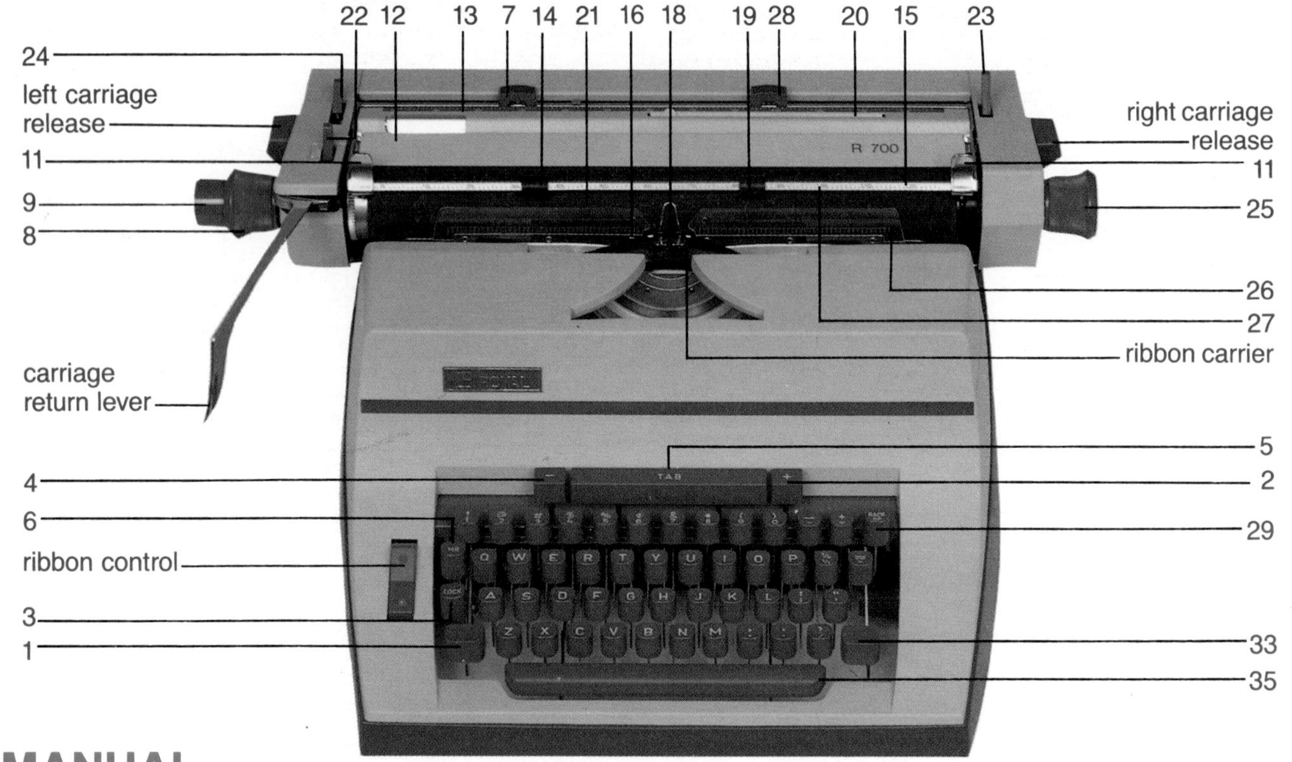

22 12 13 7 14 21 16 18 19 28 20 15 23
24
left carriage release
11
9
8
carriage return lever
4
6
ribbon control
3
1
right carriage release
11
25
26
27
ribbon carrier
5
2
29
33
35
R 700

MANUAL

17
10 11 12 13 14 15 16 18 19 20 21 22 23
half-backspace key
9
8
7
6
5
4
3
2
1
24
25
26
27
28
29
30
31
32
33
34
35

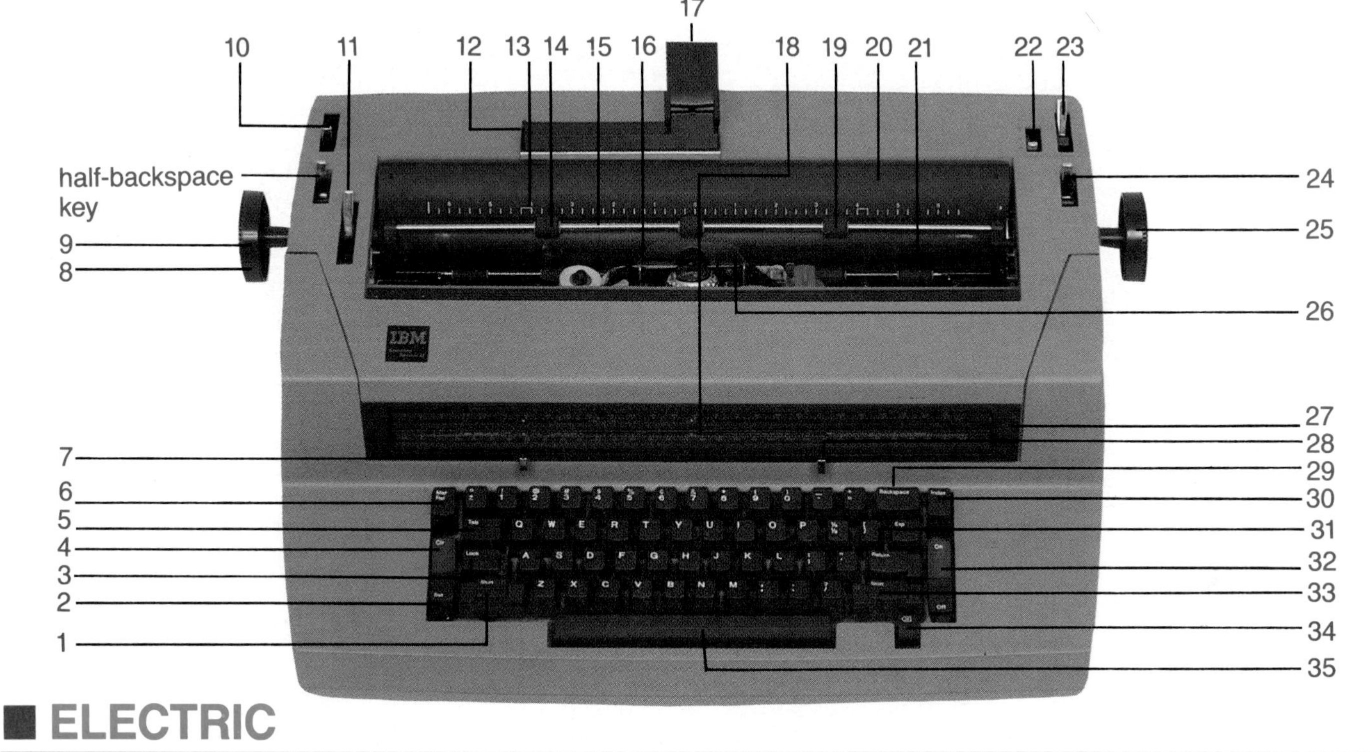

ELECTRIC

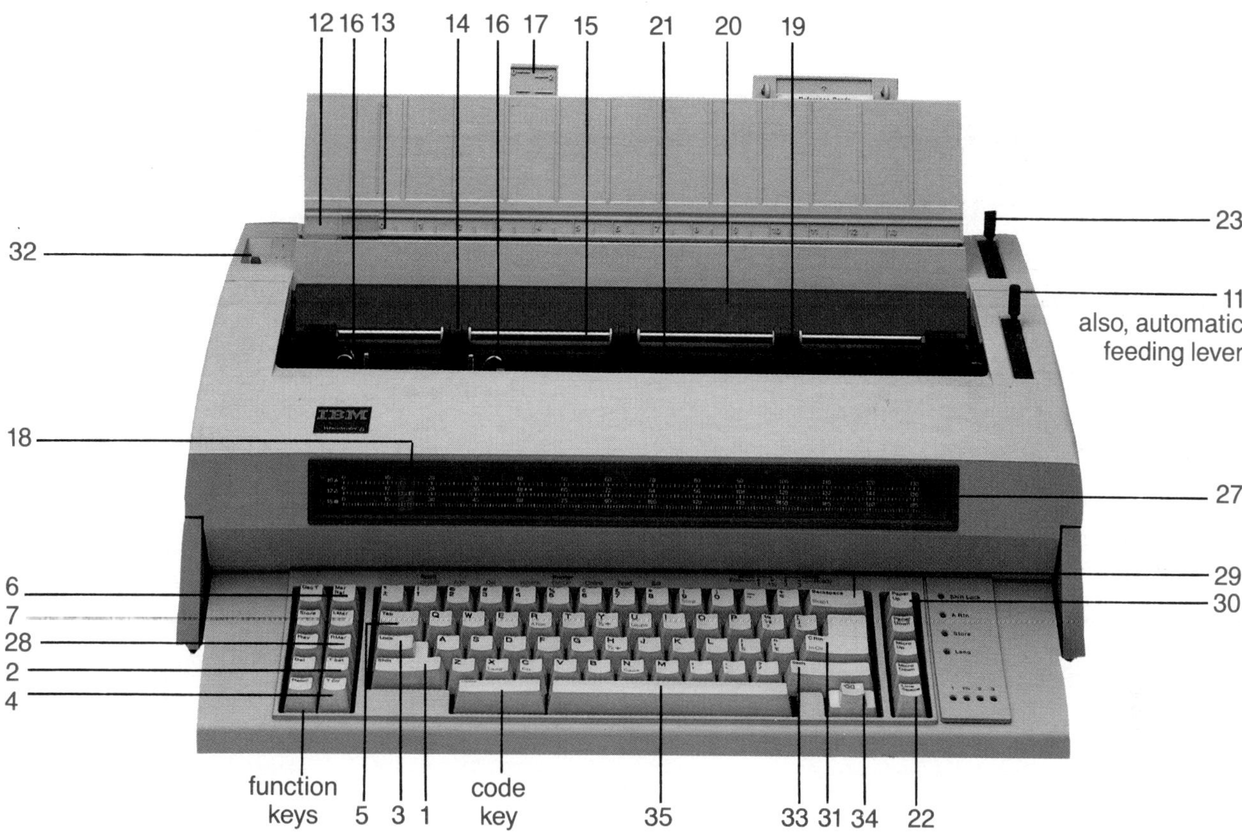

■ ELECTRONIC

The diagram above shows the parts of an electronic typewriter; the diagrams on page vi show the parts of a manual typewriter and an electric typewriter.

Since all typewriters have similar parts, you will probably be able to locate the parts on your typewriter from one of these diagrams. However, if you have the instructional booklet that comes with your machine, use it to identify the exact location of each operative part, including special parts that may be on one machine but not on another.

Illustrated on page viii is an array of microcomputers to which your keyboarding skills will transfer.

1. Left shift key: used to type capitals of letter keys controlled by right hand

2. Tab set: used to set tabulator stops

3. Shift lock: used to lock shift mechanism so that all letters are capitalized

4. Tab clear: used to clear tab stops

5. Tabulator: used to move carriage (carrier) to tab stops

6. Margin release key: used to move carriage (carrier) beyond margin stops

7. Left margin set: used to set left margin stop

8. Left platen knob: used to activate variable line spacer (not on some electronic models)

9. Variable line spacer: used to change writing line setting permanently (not on electronic machines)

10. Pitch selector: used to select 10-pitch (pica), 12-pitch (elite), or 15-pitch spacing (on some electronics, pitch changes automatically when you change daisy wheels; not on manual machines)

11. Paper bail lever: used to pull paper bail away from platen

12. Paper guide: used to position paper for insertion

13. Paper guide scale: used to set paper guide at desired position

14/19. Paper bail rolls: used to hold paper against platen

15. Paper bail: used to hold paper against platen

16. Card/envelope holders: used to hold cards, labels, and envelopes against platen

17. Page end indicator: used to check distance from typing line to lower edge of paper (not on manual machines)

18. Printing point indicator: used to position carriage (or element carrier) at desired point

19. (See 14)

20. Paper table: supports paper when it is in typewriter

21. Platen (cylinder): provides a hard surface against which type element or bars strike

22. Line-space selector: sets machine to advance the paper 1, 2, or 3 lines for single, double, or triple spacing when return lever or key is used

23. Paper release lever: used to allow paper to be removed or aligned

24. Automatic line finder: used to change line spacing temporarily, then refind the line (not on electronic machines)

25. Right platen knob: used to turn platen as paper is being inserted (not on some electronic machines)

26. Aligning scale: used to align copy that has been reinserted (not shown on electronic machine)

27. Line-of-writing (margin) scale: used when setting margin and tab stops and in horizontal centering

28. Right margin set: used to set right margin stop

29. Backspace key: used to move printing point to left one space at a time

30. Index key: used to advance paper one line at a time without returning to left margin (called "paper up" on some electronic machines; not on manual machines)

31. Carriage (carrier) return key: used to return carriage (carrier) to left margin and to move paper up (carriage return lever serves same function on manual)

32. ON/OFF control: used to turn electric-powered machines on or off

33. Right shift key: used to type capitals of letter keys controlled by left hand

34. Correcting key: used to erase a character (not on manual machines)

35. Space bar: used to move printing point to right one space at a time

KNOW YOUR COMPUTER

Typical components of a microcomputer are:

1. Alpha-numeric keyboard
2. Display screen
3. Disk drive(s)
4. Numeric keypad

Often a printer is attached to the computer so that a "hard" or printed copy of stored information or documents can be made.

GET READY TO KEYBOARD

Operators of computers should learn from the Operator's Manual for specific machines how to power up the equipment and how to set margins and spacing. The procedures vary from brand to brand.

The procedures for making machine adjustments and getting ready to keyboard given here are primarily for the use of operators of typewriters.

1 Adjust paper guide

Move **paper guide (12)** left or right so that it lines up with 0 (zero) on the **paper guide scale (13)** or the **line-of-writing** or **margin scale (27)**.

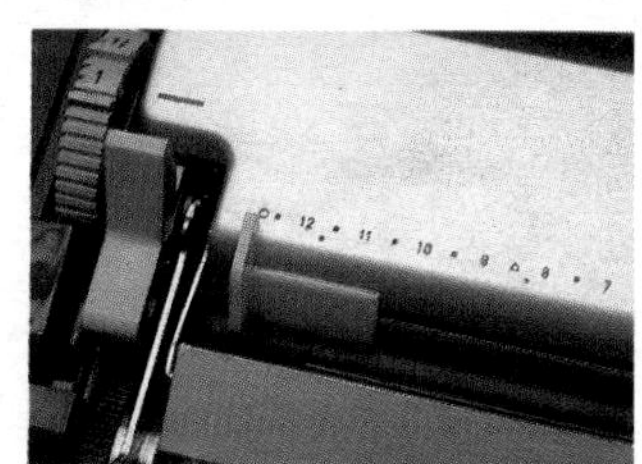

2 Insert paper

Take a sheet of paper in your left hand and follow the directions and illustrations below.

1. Pull **paper bail (15)** forward (or up on some machines).

2. Place paper against **paper guide (12)**, behind the **platen (21)**.

3. Turn paper into machine, using **right platen knob (25)** or **index key (30)**.

4. Stop when paper is about 1½ inches above **aligning scale (26)**.

5. If paper is not straight, pull **paper release lever (23)** forward.

6. Straighten paper, then push paper release lever back.

7. Push paper bail back so that it holds paper against platen.

8. Slide **paper bail rolls (14/19)** into position, dividing paper into fourths.

3 Set line-space selector

Many machines offer 3 choices for line spacing--1, 1½, and 2 indicated by bars or numbers on the **line-space selector (22)**.

Set the line-space selector on (−) or 1 to single-space (SS) or on (=) or 2 to double-space (DS) as directed for lines in Phase 1. To quadruple-space, set line-space selector on (=) or 2 to double-space, then operate return twice.

1 Lines 1 and 2 are single-spaced (SS).
2 A double space (DS) separates lines 2 and 4.
3 1 blank line space
4 A triple space (TS) separates lines 4 and 7.
5
2 blank line spaces
6
7 Set the selector on "1" for single spacing.

GET READY TO KEYBOARD, continued

4 Plan margin settings

A machine may have pica type (10-pitch type -- 10 spaces to a horizontal inch) or may have elite type (12-pitch type -- 12 spaces to a horizontal inch).

Machines have at least one **line-of-writing scale (27)** that reads from 0 to *at least* 110 for machines with *elite* type, from 0 to *at least* 90 for machines with *pica* type.

When 8½- by 11-inch paper is inserted into the machine (short side at top) with left edge of paper at 0 on the line-of-writing scale, the exact center point is 51 for elite, 42½ for pica machines. Use 51 for elite center, 42 for pica center.

To center typed lines, set left and right margin stops the same number of spaces left and right from center point. Diagrams at the right show margin settings for 50-, 60-, and 70-space lines. When you begin to use the warning bell, 5 or 6 spaces may be added to the right margin.

Set left margin stop for a 50-space line for each lesson in Phase 1; set right margin stop at right end of line-of-writing scale.

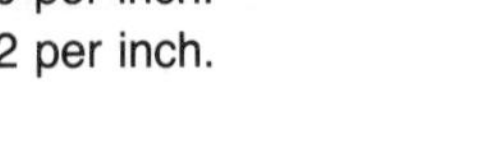

Pica, 10 per inch.
Elite, 12 per inch.

Elite center

Pica center

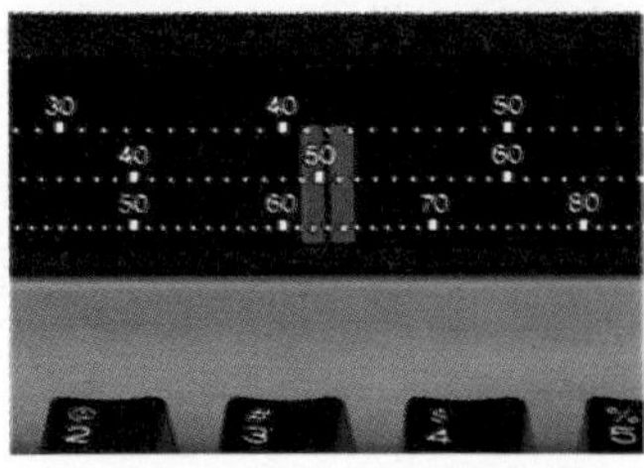

Elite (12-pitch)

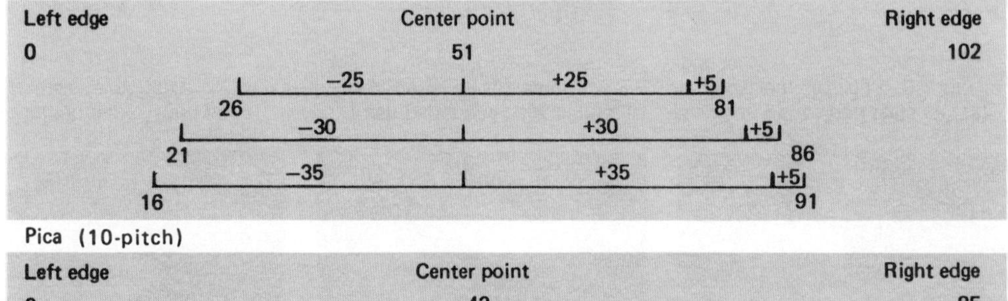

Pica (10-pitch)

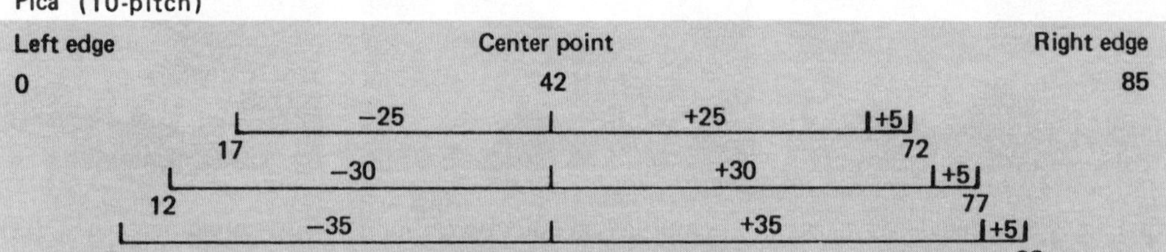

5 Set margin stops

Type A

Push-button set

Adler, Olympia, Remington, Royal, and Smith-Corona manuals

1. Press down on the left margin set button.
2. Slide it to desired position on the line-of-writing (margin) scale.
3. Release the margin set button.
4. Using the right margin set button, set the right margin stop in the same way.

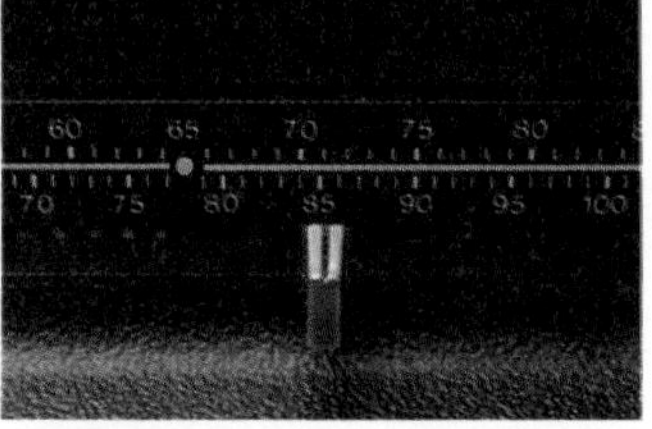

Type B

Push-lever set

Single element typewriters, such as Adler, Olivetti, Remington Rand, Royal, Selectric

1. Push in on the left margin set lever.
2. Slide it to desired position on the line-of-writing (margin) scale.
3. Release the margin set lever.
4. Using the right margin set lever, set the right margin stop in the same way.

Type C

Key set

IBM typebar, Olivetti electric

1. Move carriage to the left margin stop by depressing the return key.
2. Depress and hold down the margin set (IBM reset) key as you move carriage to desired left margin stop position.
3. Release the margin set (IBM reset) key.
4. Move carriage to the right margin stop.
5. Depress and hold down the margin set (IBM reset) key as you move carriage to desired right margin stop position.
6. Release the margin set (IBM reset) key.

Type D

Electronic set

To set margins on some electronic machines, such as Xerox and Silver-Reed, space to the desired margin position and strike the appropriate (left or right) margin key.

On other machines, such as some models of IBM, space to the desired margin position and strike the CODE key and the appropriate (left or right) margin key *at the same time*.

General information for setting margin stops is given here. If you have the manufacturer's booklet for your typewriter, however, use it; the procedure for your particular model may be slightly different.

GLOSSARY

Circuit board (including the CPU)

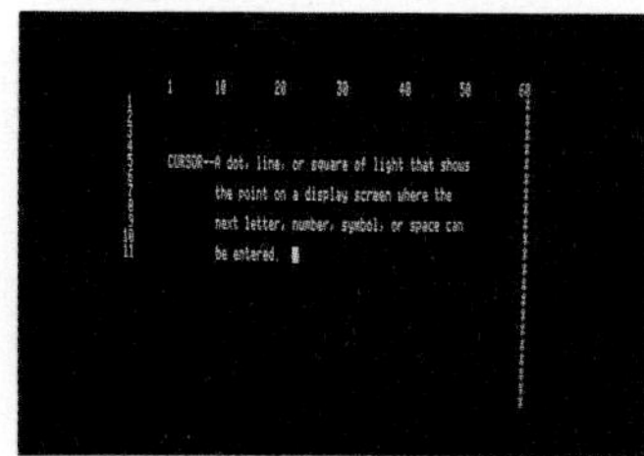

Cursor

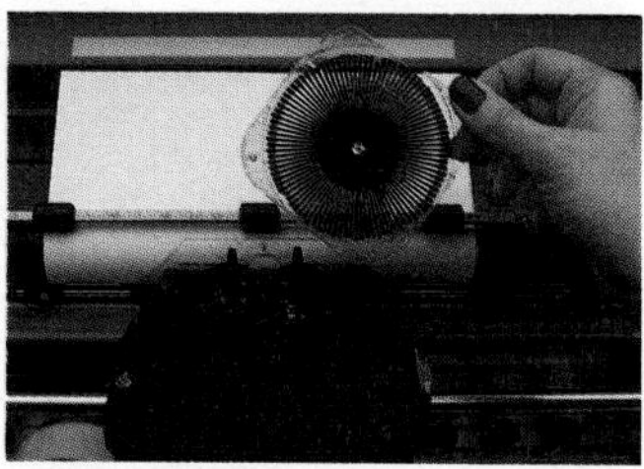

Daisy wheel

Disk drive and diskette

Defined below are some special terms you may encounter as you complete the activities in this textbook on a typewriter, computer, or word processor. These are terms you need to learn as you prepare yourself for the world of tomorrow.

ACCURACY degree of freedom from errors (mistakes) measured from zero--usually expressed as 1 error, 2 errors, etc.; sometimes as *errors a minute (eam)* or *percent of error.*

BACKSPACE to move printing or enter point (element, daisy wheel, or cursor) to the left one space at a time by striking the backspace or *back arrow* key once for each character or space.

CPU (central processing unit) the internal operating unit or "brains" of an electronic computer system; *also* "the little black box."

CRT (cathode-ray tube) *see* **VDT**.

CONTROL the power to cause the hands and fingers to make correct motions; *also* the ability to hold keystroking speed down so that errors (mistakes) are kept to an expected or acceptable number.

CONTROL KEY (CTRL) a special key that is pressed at the same time another key is struck, causing that key to perform a special function.

CURSOR a dot, line, or square of light that shows the point on a display screen where the next letter, number, symbol, or space can be entered.

DAISY WHEEL a printing wheel shaped like a daisy used on some typewriters and printers.

DELETE to remove from text a segment of copy (a character, a word, a phrase, a line, a sentence, a page).

DISK (DISKETTE) DRIVE the unit into which a diskette is inserted to be read or written by the CPU (central processing unit).

DISKETTE (DISK) a magnetic, Mylar-coated record-like disk (encased in a square protective envelope) used for recording, reading, and writing by the CPU (central processing unit).

DISPLAY SCREEN *see* **VDT**.

DOUBLE-SPACE (DS) to use vertical line spacing which leaves one blank line space between displayed or printed lines of text (copy).

EDIT to rearrange, change, and correct existing text; editing includes proofreading but is not limited to it.

ELEMENT a ball-shaped printing device on many electric and electronic typewriters.

ENTER to input keystrokes; *see* **KEY**

ENTER KEY *see* **RETURN KEY**

ERROR any misstroke of a key; *also* any variation between source copy and displayed or printed copy; departure from acceptable format (arrangement, placement, and spacing).

ESCAPE KEY (ESC) a key on some computers which lets the user leave one segment of a program and go to another.

FORMAT the style (arrangement, placement, and spacing) of a document.

FORMATTING the process of arranging a document in proper form.

FUNCTION KEYS special keys on typewriters, computers, and word processors that when used alone or in combination with other keys perform special functions such as setting margins, centering copy, and so on.

GLOBAL SEARCH AND REPLACE to direct a computer or word processor to find a repeated series of characters and replace it with a different series of characters automatically throughout a document (for example, find and replace Co. with Company).

GWAM (gross words a minute) a measure of the rate of keyboarding speed; GWAM = total standard 5-stroke words keyed divided by the time required to key or type those words.

HARDWARE the physical equipment that makes up a computer or word processing system.

INDENT to set in from the margin, as the first line of a paragraph.

INFORMATION PROCESSING the job of putting text and data into usable form (documents).

INPUT text and data that enter an information system; the process of entering text and data.

INSERT (INSERTION) new text that is added to existing text; *also* the process of adding new text to existing text.

KEY to strike keys to record or display text and data; *also called* enter, key in, keyboard, input, and type.

Detached keyboard

Microcomputer

Computer printer

Video display terminal (VDT)

KEYBOARD an arrangement of keys on a "board" that is attached to or apart from a machine such as a typewriter, computer, or word processor; *also* the act of keyboarding or typing.

MEMORY storage location in a computer, word processor, or electronic typewriter.

MENU a list of options from which a keyboard operator may (or must) choose when using a word or data processing machine.

MERGE to assemble new documents from stored text such as form paragraphs; to combine stored text such as a form letter with newly keyboarded text (names, addresses, inserts).

MICROCOMPUTER a small-sized computer with a keyboard, screen, and auxiliary storage; its central processor is usually a single CPU chip; *also* "computer on a chip."

MONITOR *see* VDT.

MOVE to reposition a heading or text up or down the video screen; when a block of copy (paragraph) is moved, it is a "block move."

OUTPUT useful information that leaves an information system, usually presented to the user as a screen display or a printout.

PRINT to produce, using a printer, a paper copy of information displayed on a screen or stored in computer or word processor memory.

PRINTER a unit attached to a computer or a word processor that produces copy on paper.

PRINTOUT the printed paper output of a computer, word processor, or electronic typewriter.

PROMPT a message displayed in the window of an electronic typewriter or on the screen of a computer or word processor telling the user that the machine is awaiting a specific response.

PROOFREAD to read copy on a display screen or on a printout against the original or source copy and to correct errors (or mark them for correction); *also* one of the steps in editing text.

QUADRUPLE-SPACE (QS) to use vertical line spacing which leaves 3 blank line spaces between displayed or printed lines of text (copy); equals 4 single spaces, 2 double spaces.

RATE the speed of doing a task, as *keyboarding* or *typing rate* -- usually expressed in words a minute or lines per hour.

RETRIEVE to make stored information available when needed.

RETURN to strike the RETURN or ENTER key to cause the cursor (or enter point) to move to the left margin and down to the next line.

RETURN KEY a key that when struck causes the cursor (or enter point) to move to the left margin and down to the next line; *also* ENTER KEY.

SEARCH to locate an editing or correcting point within a document by matching a series of characters or words.

SHIFT KEY a key used to make capital letters and certain symbols when struck at the same time as another key.

SHIFT LOCK (CAPS Lock) a key that when depressed causes all letters to be capitalized (ALL-CAPPED).

SINGLE-SPACE (SS) to use vertical line spacing which leaves no blank space between printed or displayed lines of text.

SOFTWARE instructions, or programs, that tell a computer or word processor what to do.

SOURCE DOCUMENTS forms on which raw text or data are written and from which a machine operator keys and formats.

SPACE BAR a long bar at the bottom of a keyboard used to move the cursor (enter point) to the right one space at a time.

STORE to save information on magnetic media so that it may be used later.

TAB KEY a key that when struck causes the cursor (enter point) to skip to a preset position, as in indenting paragraphs.

TECHNIQUE the degree of expertness with which a task is performed; *also* good form, style.

TEXT (DATA) ENTRY the process of getting text and data from the writer's mind or from a written or voice-recorded document into the computer or word processing system.

VDT (video display terminal) a TV-like picture tube used to display text, data, and graphic images; *also called* CRT, display screen, and monitor.

WORD PROCESSING the writing and storing of letters, reports, and other documents on a computer, electronic typewriter, or word processor; may also include printing of the final document.

Lessons 1-25

PHASE 1

Learn Alphabetic Keyboarding Technique

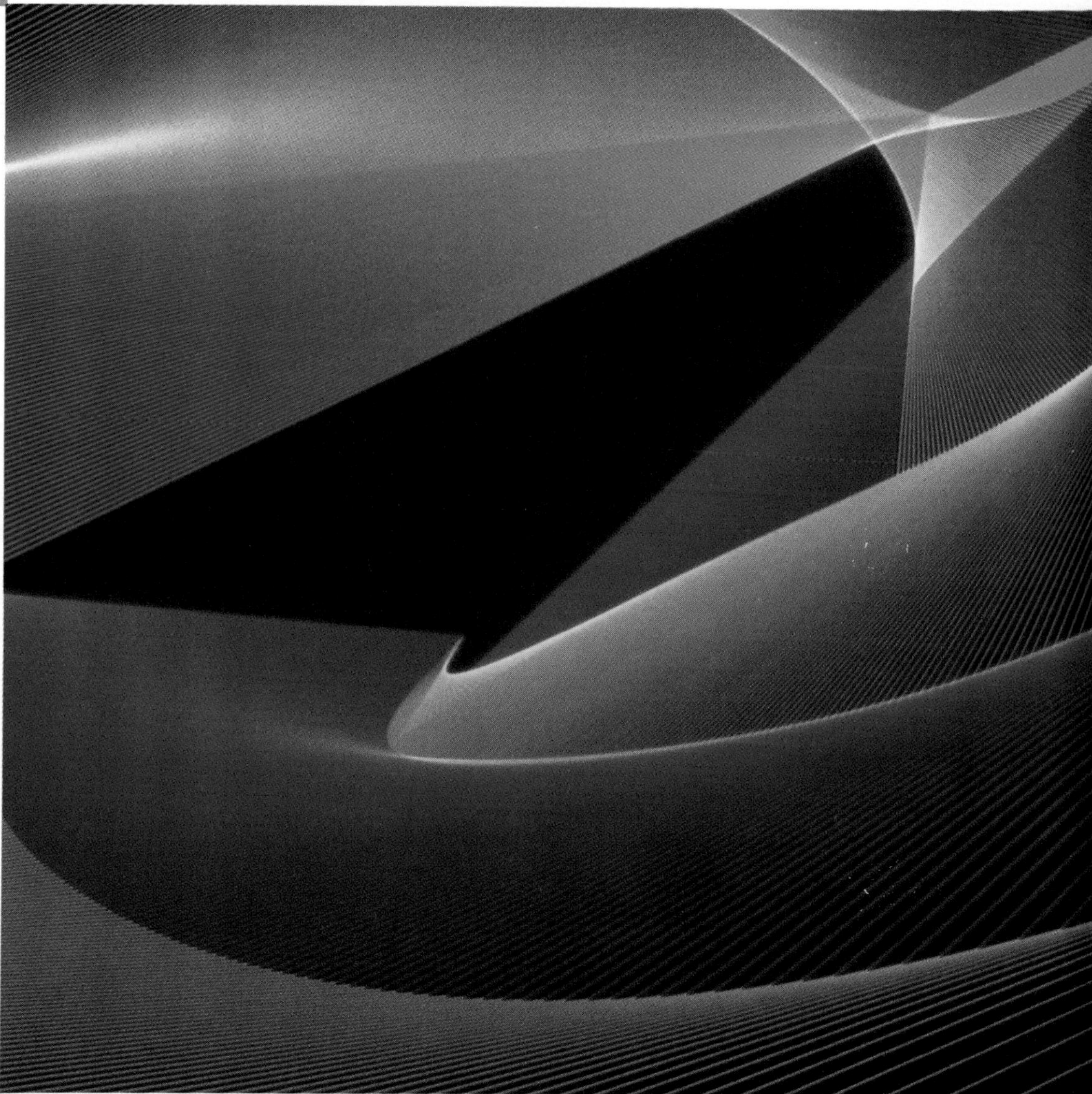

A typewriter-like keyboard is the modern means of entering data, retrieving information, and communicating facts and ideas. To be a successful participant in the business and professional world of today and tomorrow, you must be able to use a keyboard -- on a typewriter, on a computer, and on a word processor or text-editor.

The letter keyboards on these kinds of machines are quite similar. Therefore, if you learn to operate the keyboard on one kind of machine, you can readily transfer your skill to other keyboarding machines.

Your goal during the next few weeks is to learn to operate a letter keyboard with good technique and reasonable speed.

The 25 lessons of Phase 1 are designed to help you learn:

1. To adjust your machine for correct margins and spacing.
2. To operate the letter keyboard by touch (without looking).
3. To use the basic parts of your machine with skill: space bar, shift keys, the return, and the tabulator.
4. To key words, sentences, and paragraphs without time-wasting pauses and with good keyboarding technique.
5. To apply capitalization guides correctly as you key.

words

Teleconferencing. According to White (White, Bonnie 472
Roe. "Teleconferencing: Its Potential in the Modern Office 472
(Part 1)." Century 21 Reporter, Fall, 1984, 4.), teleconfer- 476
encing is "the meeting of three or more people at two or 488
more locations using telecommunication (television) systems." 498
These meetings help to reduce travel costs considerable. At 510
the same time, communication, understanding, and cooperation 522
among employees in an organization at different locations 534
can be greatly ~~xxxx~~ enhanced. As companies become more cost 545
conscious, ~~using~~ the use of teleconferencing ~~will~~ is expected to grow. 557

Document 3
Reference Page

Prepare a reference page for the report completed in Document 2.

Total words in reference page: 136.

Document 4
Schedule of Tour

Place the schedule attractively on the page, DS.

words

TRADEWINDS TRAVEL AGENCY 5

Spe~~ical~~cial Escorted Tour to Yokohama via SS ~~Olympia~~ Columbia 15

PORT	ARRIVE	DEPART	words
~~New York City~~ Baltimore		August ~~7~~ 8, ~~7:00 p.m.~~ 11:45 a.m.	28
Fort Lauderdale	August 8, ~~5:30~~ 5:45 p.m.	August 8, ~~6:45~~ 7:00 p.m.	39
Cancun	August 10, ~~7:30~~ 8:00 a.m.	August 10, ~~6:15~~ 6:30 p.m.	49
Cristobal	August 11, 6:30 a.m.	August 11, 7:00 a.m.	60
Panama Canal	August 11, ~~7:30~~ 8:00 a.m.	August 11, ~~4:30~~ 5:00 p.m.	71
Balboa	August 11, ~~6:00~~ 6:30 p.m.	August 11, ~~11:00~~ 11:30 p.m.	81
Acapulco	August 15, ~~7:30~~ 8:00 a.m.	August 16, ~~7:45~~ 7:30 a.m.	91
Los Angeles	August 19, ~~8:00~~ 9:00 a.m.	August 19, ~~6:30~~ 7:00 p.m.	101
Honolulu	August 24, ~~7:30~~ 8:30 a.m.	August 25, ~~5:15~~ 6:30 p.m.	112
Yokohama	August 27, ~~7:30~~ 10:00 a.m.	August 29, ~~9:30~~ 9:40 a.m.*	122

*Via Trans-Pacific Airways to Baltimore 130

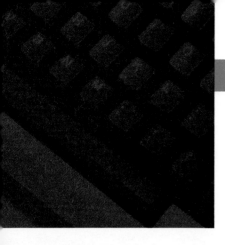

Unit 1 Lessons 1-20

Learning Goals

1. To learn to operate letter keys and punctuation by touch.

2. To learn to operate basic service keys (space bar, shift keys, return, shift lock, and tab key) by touch.

3. To build correct techniques.

4. To learn to type (key) sentences and paragraphs with good technique and speed.

Machine Adjustments

1. Paper guide at *0*.

2. Ribbon control to use top half of ribbon.

3. Margin sets: left margin (center - 25); right margin (move to right end of scale).

4. Line-space selector set to single-space (SS) drills.

5. Line-space selector set to double-space (DS) paragraphs.

Lesson 1 Home Keys (ASDF JKL;)

Line length: 50 spaces
Spacing: single-space (SS)

1a ▶ Get Ready to Keyboard

1. Arrange your work area as illustrated at the right:

- front frame of machine even with front edge of desk
- book at right of machine, top raised for easy reading
- paper, if needed, at left of machine
- unneeded books and other materials stored or placed out of the way

2. Get to know your machine by studying pages vi-viii.

3. Make needed machine adjustments and insert paper (if necessary) as directed on pages ix-x.

4. Take keyboarding position as illustrated at the right:

- fingers curved and upright
- wrists low, but not touching frame of machine
- forearms parallel to slant of keyboard
- sit back in chair; body erect
- feet on floor for balance

Position at computer

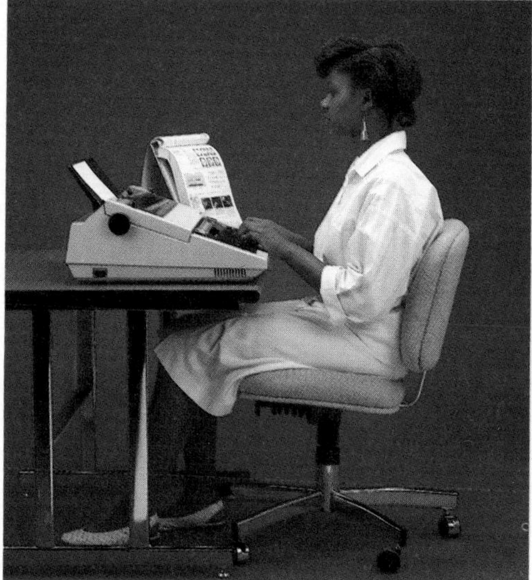

Position at typewriter

300b (continued)

Document 2
Unbound Report with Textual Citations

1. Prepare the material at the right as an unbound report DS with textual citations, using the title: NEW DEVELOPMENTS IN TELECOMMUNICATIONS.

2. For each citation, the complete reference information has been included in the report for your convenience in preparing the reference page. As you prepare the report, insert the proper textual citation and make note of the complete reference for the reference page.

words

heading 8

the field of
What is included in telecommunications? The answer to 21
this ~~query~~ question depends upon which "expert" is consulted. 33
Waterhouse takes a narrow view when she writes, ". . . elec- 44
tronic mail or <u>telecommunications</u> is ~~is~~ simply sending and 59
receiving typewritten messages over telephone lines." (Water- 70
house, Shirley, A. <u>Word Processing Fundamentals</u>. San Fran- 70
cisco: Canfield Press, 1979, 147.) The instruments of this 77
form of telecommunication are the teletypewriter and the 89
telegram. Casady and Sandburg (Casady, Mona J. and Dorothy 95
C. Sandburg. <u>Word Information Processing</u>. Cincinnati: 95
South-Western Publishing Co., 1985, 22), on the other hand, 101
take a broader view. "Actually," they write, "telecommuni- 113
cations means communicating electronically over a distance." 125
This view ~~has~~ includes more modern developements such as 136
electronic mail, facsimile machines, and teleconferencing, 147
which use not only telephone lines but microwave links, sat- 159
telites, and television. 164

<u>Electronic Mail</u>. It has been estimated that more than 178
50% of all telephone calls made daily go unasnwered. Return 193
calls often find the originel caller "out" or "busy." This leads 206
to what is known as "telephone tag." Using electronic mail 218
is one way to ~~avoid~~ eliminate this costly and time consuming 229
game. Electronic mail is sent and recieved via a computer 241
or word processor. As the <u>Small Business Report</u> ("Applica- 255
tions of Electronic Mail." <u>Small Business Report</u>, December 255
1984, 74.) pints out, there are two basic types of electronic 267
mail: Print and Voice. Using print electronic mail, messages 280
are sent from one copmuter to another. The message is stored 292
in the ~~the~~ receivers' computer and can be reviewed on the 303
screen and answered, if necessary. If desired, a ~~har~~ ~~ca~~ copy 315
can be produced. Voice mail sends messages in the caller's 327
own voice which is converted to numberical code. Then the 339
code is sent to the receiver's computer where it is stored. 351
Both print and ~~xxx~~ voice systems can be ~~xxxxx~~ used to send 361
the same message to a number of individuals simultaneously. hard 373

<u>Facsimile</u>. Sending a copy of an original document elec- 386
tronically is known as facsimile. Foulton and Hanks (Foulton, 396
Patsy J. and Joanna D. Hanks. <u>Procedures for the Professional</u> 396
<u>Secretary</u>. Cincinnati: South-Western Publishing Co., 1985, 397
459.) describe the procedures: "A special copying machne 409
called a facsimile unit or copier, sends the images of a 421
document over telephone lines to a simialr copying machine 432
in another location." Facsimile is capable of sending graphic 445
material as well as words. It is possible this may be the "mail of
the future." 461

(continued on page 500)

1b ▶ Place Your Fingers in Home-Key Position

1. Locate on the chart **a s d f** (home keys for left hand) and **j k l ;** (home keys for right hand).

2. Locate the home keys on your keyboard. Place fingers of your left hand on **a s d f** and of your right hand on **j k l ;** *with your fingers well curved and upright (not slanting).*

3. Remove your fingers from the keyboard; then place them in home-key position again, curving and holding them *lightly* on the keys.

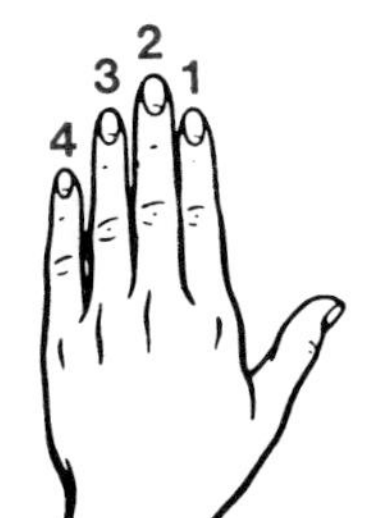

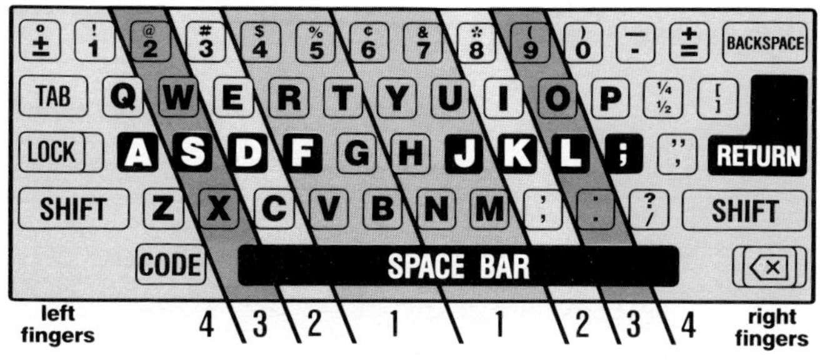

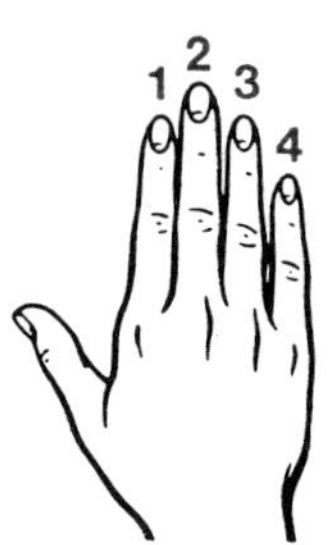

1c ▶ Learn How to Strike Home Keys

1. Study the keystroking illustrations at the right.

2. Place your fingers in home-key position as directed above.

3. Strike each of the following keys once:

fdsajkl;

Strike the key with a quick, sharp finger stroke; snap the finger slightly toward the palm of the hand as the keystroke is made.

If you are using an electric or electronic machine, strike each key with a light tap with the tip of the finger; otherwise, keystroking technique is the same as for a manual typewriter.

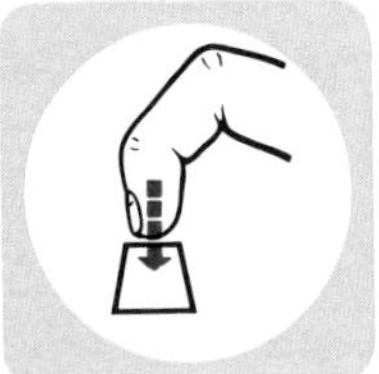

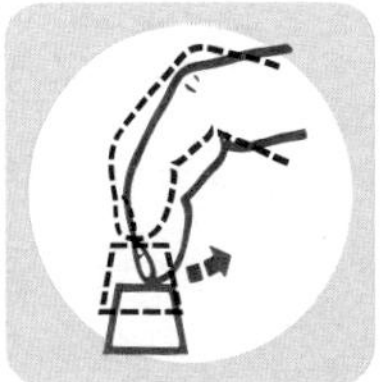

1d ▶ Learn How to Return at Line Endings

To return the printing point of a typewriter or the cursor of a computer to the left margin and move down to the next line:

- strike return key (31) on electric and electronic typewriters
- strike RETURN or ENTER key on computers
- operate return lever on manual typewriters

Study the illustrations at the right; and **return** 3 times (triple-space) below the line you completed in 1c above.

Electric typewriter return
Reach with the little finger of the right hand to the return key, tap the key, and return the finger quickly to its typing position.

Microcomputer return
Reach with the little finger of the right hand to the RETURN or ENTER key, tap the key, and return the finger quickly to home-key position.

Manual typewriter return
Move left hand, fingers braced, to return lever; return carriage with quick inward flick-of-the-hand motion. Drop hand quickly to typing position; do not let it follow the carriage across.

1e ▶ Learn How to Space Between Letters

1. Study the spacing illustrations at the right.

2. As you type (key) the following letters, strike the space bar once after each letter:

f d s a j k l ;

Strike the space bar with the right thumb; use a quick down-and-in motion (toward palm). Avoid pauses before or after spacing.

300b ▶ 45
Evaluate Document Processing Skills

Time Schedule

Plan and Prepare .... 5′
Timed Production .... 30′
Proofread; compute *n-pram* .... 10′

Note: To find *n-pram* (net production rate per minute), deduct 15 words for each uncorrected error; divide remainder by 30 (time).

1. Prepare the document beginning at the right and Documents 2, 3, and 4 on pages 499 and 500 in order given for 30 minutes. Correct all errors.

2. At the end of 30 minutes, proofread the documents you prepared and correct any errors you may have missed, but do not redo any problems. After you have done so, compute *n-pram*.

Document 1
Letter
(LM p. 217)

Prepare the letter at the right in block style with open punctuation. Use the company name **Franklin Legal Services** in the closing lines.

opening lines

Please prepare the following letter, dated August 10, to Mr. and Mrs. Ray- 25
mond T. Andrews, 4140 N. Henderson Road, Arlington,
VA 22203-8102 for my signature as Attorney-at-Law.
¶ As you requested, we have completed ~~wills~~ revised wills 35
for ~~you and your wife~~ Raymond T. and Caroline A. Andrews, based on 44
copies of your previous wills and the changes that you indicated. 58
¶ As we agreed, we have included your son, Arthur L. Andrews, 70
as the alternate executor in both wills. This was done so 82
that your son may dispose of your estate when both of you 102
are deceased. rather than the Commonwealth of Virginia. 105
In addition, we have added tertiary heirs in the event 116
that your son should predecease you without issue. 126
¶ May we suggest that you meet in our office at 2:30 p.m. on 138
August 17 to sign your wills. At that time, we shall have 150
two ~~individuals~~ persons present to witness your signa- 158
tures. We shall also have a notary public present to 169
notarize the wills. This is done to simplify the execution 181
of the estate ~~since~~ so that it will not be necesary to recall the 193
witnesses when the will is recorded. 201
¶ Since it is possible that your safe-deposit box may be 212
sealed upon the death of one of the renters, we suggest that 224
you retain your wills at home. If you wish, we can keep 235
them in our files and ~~make~~ provide copies for you. 247
To facilitate the ~~fiscal~~ financal arrangements, and your son 256
we have enclosed an invoice covering the fee for 265
~~making~~ the wills. 268

Sincerely
Nancy Merriman

closing lines 283/**299**

1f ▶ Practice Home-Key Letters

1. Place your hands in home-key position (left fingers on **asdf** and right fingers on **jkl;**).

2. Type (key) the lines as shown: single-spaced (SS) with a double space (DS) between pairs of lines.

Do not type (key) the line numbers.

Spacing hint
With the **line-space selector (22)** set for single spacing, return twice at the end of the line to double-space.

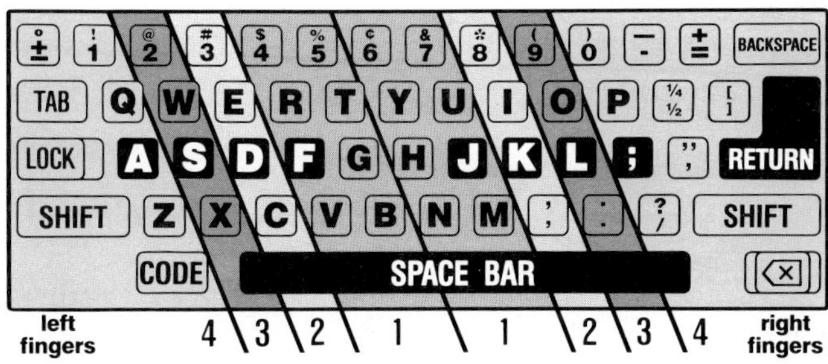

Fingers curved and upright

Strike space bar once to space

```
1 f ff j jj d dd k kk s ss l ll a aa ; ;; fdsa jkl;
2 f ff j jj d dd k kk s ss l ll a aa ; ;; fdsa jkl;
```
DS
```
3 a aa ; ;; s ss l ll d dd k kk f ff j jj fjdk sla;
4 a aa ; ;; s ss l ll d dd k kk f ff j jj fjdk sla;
```
DS
```
5 a;a sls dkd fjf ;a; lsl kdk jfj asdf jkl; a;sl fj
6 a;a sls dkd fjf ;a; lsl kdk jfj asdf jkl; a;sl fj
```
Return 3 times to triple-space (TS)

1g ▶ Type (Key) Letters, Words, and Phrases

Type (key) the lines as shown; return twice to double-space (DS) between lines. If time permits, repeat the drill.

Down-and-in spacing motion

```
1 f f ff j j jj d d dd k k kk s s ss l l ll a a aa;
```
Return twice to double-space (DS)
```
2 fj dk sl a; jf kd ls ;a ds kl df kj sd lk sa ;l j
```
DS
```
3 sa as ld dl af fa ls sl fl lf al la ja aj sk ks a
```
DS
```
4 a a as as ad ad ask ask lad lad fad fad jak jak j
```
DS
```
5 all all fad fad jak jak add add ask ask ads ads a
```
DS
```
6 a jak; as all; ask dad; all ads; ask all; a lass;
```
At end of drill, return 3 times to triple-space (TS)

1h ▶ End of Lesson: Typewriter

1. Raise **paper bail (15)** or pull it toward you. Pull **paper release lever (23)** toward you.

2. Remove paper with your left hand. Push paper release lever back to its normal position.

3. On movable carriage typewriters, depress **right carriage release**; hold **right platen knob (25)** firmly and center the carriage.

4. Turn electric-powered machines OFF.

299c ▶ 30 Evaluate Language Skills

1. In each sentence at the right, items have been underlined. The underlines indicate that there *may* be an error in spelling, punctuation, capitalization, grammar, or in the use of words or figures.

2. Study each sentence carefully. Keyboard the sentence DS. If an underlined item is correct, keyboard it as it is; if the item is incorrect, correct it. Also correct any errors you may make as you work.

3. When you have completed the sentences and *before* you remove the paper from the machine, study each sentence carefully and correct any errors you may have missed. If necessary, you may keyboard a sentence a second time immediately below your original sentence in order to correct a major error.

4. You may not correct errors once you have removed the paper from the machine.

1. Neither of the salesmen expect to excede the months' quota.
2. She complained; "The nineth items on both lists are ilegible".
3. We are commited to the slogan, "A days pay for a days work."
4. I wish I were able to develope a likeing for classicle music.
5. This and similer models come in six colers: but red is favored more.
6. We can't determine a reason to fulfill our firms' commitment.
7. It occured to us that the affect of his action benefitted us to.
8. It will be necesary to publish the book, "Daggers", on June 6th.
9. The amount of cars acomodated by the Parking lot was small.
10. To match his Den, we used a similer shade of blue as he had asked us.
11. We can't separate the good reciepts from the bad one's.
12. "Help," he cried, "you're financiall papers are blowing away."
13. Please acknowlege our frieght shipment of 10 55-gallon drums.
14. We gave the order to the latter of the two elligible bids received.
15. Their permanant address is 4505 6th Avenue, Atlanta, GA, 30901-2422.
16. The room was all most empty, however, almost everyone came to the show.
17. Just between you and I, he choose the wrong catagory.
18. The bank pays 6 percentage on mortgages--a rise of 1%.
19. Refer to Page 37 for the differences between the three theories.
20. Of the two, who is most qualified for the benifits?
21. In my judgment, his principle residents is in Garden city.
22. 6 of the 15 men are inelligible for the current raise.
23. "Do you know? he asked, "Which book pictures the capital."
24. In this instants, we shall indemnify him for the lightening damege.
25. Neither Helen nor her deputies believe the worker's moral is low.

Review Lesson 1

Line length: 50 spaces
Spacing: single-space (SS)

R1a ▶ Get Ready to Keyboard

1. Arrange your work area (see page 2).

2. Get to know your machine (see pages vi-viii).

3. Make needed machine adjustments and insert paper if necessary (see pages ix-x).

4. Take keyboarding position (see page 2).

Margin settings for a 50-space line (paper guide at *0*):
pica, 42 − 25 = 17
elite, 51 − 25 = 26

Move right margin stop to the right end of the margin scale.

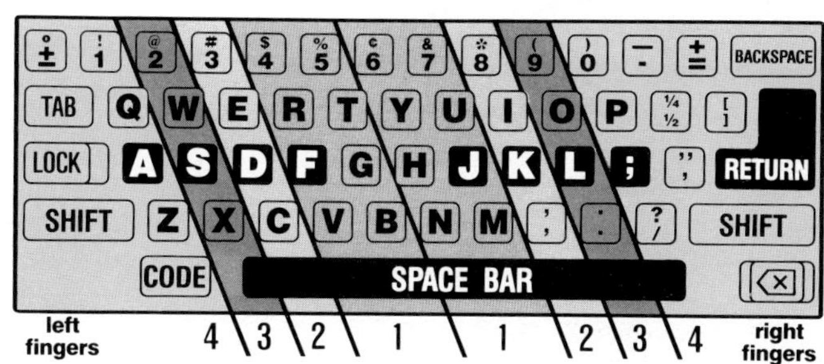

R1b ▶ Review Keystroking, Spacing, and Return Technique

Keystroke
Curve fingers of your left hand and place them over **a s d f** keys. Curve fingers of your right hand and place them over **j k l ;** keys. Strike each key with a quick-snap stroke; release key quickly.

Space
To space after letters, words, and punctuation marks, strike the space bar with a quick down-and-in motion of the right thumb. Do not pause before or after spacing stroke.

Typewriter return
Electric: Reach the little finger to RETURN key, strike the key, and release it quickly.

Manual: Reach to lever and return the carriage with a quick flick-of-the-hand motion.

Microcomputer return
Reach the little finger of the right hand to RETURN or ENTER key, strike the key, and release it quickly.

Type (key) the lines once as shown. Do not type the line numbers.

Space once

```
1 ff jj ff jj aa ;; aa ;; dd kk dd kk ss ll ss ll a;
2 ff jj ff jj aa ;; aa ;; dd kk dd kk ss ll ss ll a;
```
Return twice to double-space (DS)
```
3 a aa ; ;; s ss l ll d dd k kk f ff j jj fj dk sl a
4 a aa ; ;; s ss l ll d dd k kk f ff j jj fj dk sl a
```
DS
```
5 f j fj d k dk s l sl a ; a; fj dk sl a; fj dk sl a
6 f j fj d k dk s l sl a ; a; fj dk sl a; fj dk sl a
```
Return 3 times to triple-space (TS)

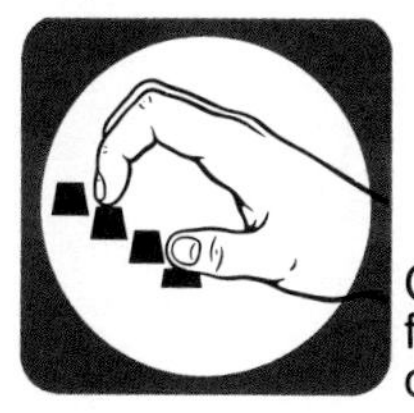
Correct finger curvature

R1c ▶ Improve Home-Key Stroking

Type (key) the lines once as shown.

Goals
- curved, upright fingers
- quick-snap keystrokes
- down-and-in spacing

```
1 fj fj dk dk sl sl a; a; jf jf kd kd ls ls ;a ;a fj
2 fj fj dk dk sl sl a; a; jf jf kd kd ls ls ;a ;a fj
```
Return twice to double-space (DS)
```
3 a al ak aj s sl sk sj d dl dk dj f fl fk fj a; fj;
4 a al ak aj s sl sk sj d dl dk dj f fl fk fj a; fj;
```
DS
```
5 j ja js jd jf k ka ks kd kf l la ls ld lf a; fj a;
6 j ja js jd jf k ka ks kd kf l la ls ld lf a; fj a;
```
DS
```
7 fdsa jkl; asdf ;lkj a;sldkfj fjdksla; fdsa jkl; a;
8 fdsa jkl; asdf ;lkj a;sldkfj fjdksla; fdsa jkl; a;
```
Return 3 times to triple-space (TS)

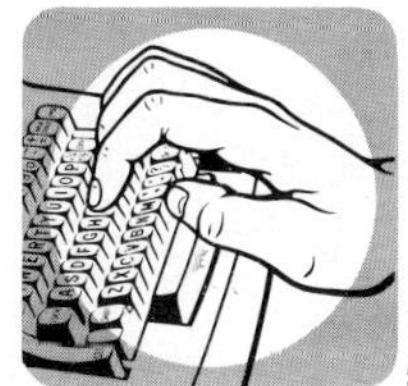
Down-and-in spacing motion

SOUTH-WESTERN PUBLISHING CO.

Unit 68 Lessons 299-300

Performance Evaluated

1. To measure your skill in keyboarding straight-copy material.
2. To measure your language skills.
3. To evaluate your ability to produce usable business documents.

Machine Adjustments

1. 65-space line for Check Equipment; 70-space line for sentences and timed writings; as directed or necessary for documents.
2. 75-space line for Language Skills.
3. DS sentences and timed writings; space problems as directed or as necessary.

Lessons 299-300

299a-300a ▶ 5 Check Equipment

Before you begin the evaluation material each day, check your machine to see that it is in good working order by keyboarding the paragraph at the right at least twice (first slowly, then faster).

all letters/figures used

Jacky Maxwell developed her unique metric zipper for the new packing bags. It will come in sizes of 6 cm (#40), 12 cm (#172), and 18 cm (#95). With the profit she may make for the proficient work, she may enrich both chapels downtown with a tidy endowment.

| 1 | 2 | 3 | 4 | 5 | 6 | 7 | 8 | 9 | 10 | 11 | 12 | 13 |

299b ▶ 15 Evaluate Straight Copy

Take two 5′ writings on the ¶s at the right. Record *gwam* and errors on better writing.

all letters used | A | 1.5 si | 5.7 awl | 80% hfw |

	gwam 1′	5′	
The ability to use a keyboard quickly and efficiently is a helpful	13	3	60
tool at any level of an organization. Office employees may use a key-	27	5	63
board to take orders, make reservations, or check an account; a manager	42	8	65
may use a keyboard to send and receive mail, obtain data, or plan for	56	11	68
the future. A major use of the keyboard is to process documents. With	70	14	71
a display, storage unit, and printer, it is relatively simple to enter,	85	17	74
revise, and produce business documents of all types.	95	19	76
Any person who enters the office as a keyboard operator has found	13	22	79
that the job can be a stepping stone to bigger and better jobs. From a	28	25	82
position as an operator, one can progress to a specialist or trainer and	42	27	85
then to the job of a supervisor or manager. The manager is responsible	57	30	87
for all the work completed in the center. He or she selects equipment,	71	33	90
develops procedures, provides a favorable place to work, and supervises	86	36	93
the people who process the documents.	93	38	95
The specific duties of a manager differ from place to place. Most	13	40	97
experts agree, in general terms, that all managers plan, organize, direct	28	43	100
and control the activities of their units. Since a manager can only at-	42	46	103
tain goals through others, his or her most basic function concerns per-	57	49	106
sonnel. In other words, he or she must be skilled in the art of getting	71	52	109
along with others, including the talent to communicate with others and to	85	55	112
motivate them to do their jobs to the best of their abilities.	97	57	114

gwam 1′ | 1 | 2 | 3 | 4 | 5 | 6 | 7 | 8 | 9 | 10 | 11 | 12 | 13 | 14 |
5′ | 1 | 2 | 3 |

R1d ▶ Type (Key) Home-Key Words

each line twice single-spaced (SS); DS between 2-line groups

Goals

- space quickly between letters and words
- return without spacing at line endings
- begin the new line quickly after return

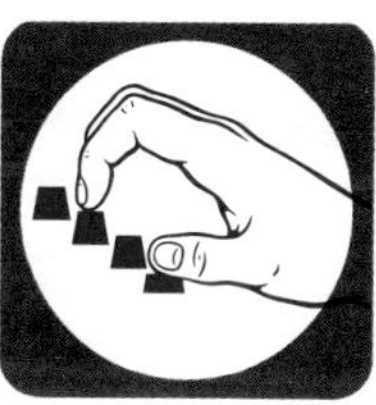

Correct finger curvature

Correct finger alignment

1 l la lad j ja jak f fa fad s sa sad f fa fall fall
Return twice to DS

2 a a as as ask ask a a ad ad lad lad all all ad ads
DS

3 a a ad ad as as lad lad all all ask ask fall falls
DS

4 as as jak jak ads ads lass lass fall fall add adds
DS

5 ad ad fad fad jak jak all all fall fall as as asks
DS

6 a as ask asks a ad lad lads a ad add adds all fall
Return 3 times to TS

R1e ▶ Type (Key) Home-Key Phrases

each line twice single-spaced (SS); DS between 2-line groups

Goals

- curved, upright fingers
- eyes on copy in book
- quick-snap keystrokes
- steady pace

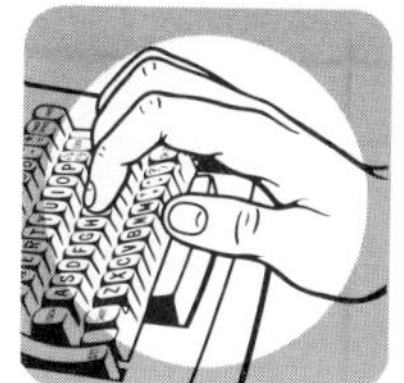

Space with right thumb

Use down-and-in motion

1 a jak; a jak; ask dad; ask dad; as all; as all ads
Return twice to DS

2 a fad; a fad; as a lad; as a lad; all ads; all ads
DS

3 as a fad; as a fad; a sad lass; a sad lass; a fall
DS

4 ask a lad; ask a lad; all jaks fall; all jaks fall
DS

5 a sad fall; a sad fall; all fall ads; all fall ads
DS

6 add a jak; a lad asks a lass; as a jak ad all fall
Return 3 times to TS

R1f ▶ End of Lesson: Typewriter

1. Raise **paper bail (15)** or pull it toward you. Pull **paper release lever (23)** toward you.

2. Remove paper with your left hand. Push paper release lever back to its normal position.

3. On movable carriage typewriters, depress **right carriage release**; hold **right platen knob (25)** firmly and center the carriage.

4. Turn electric-powered machines OFF.

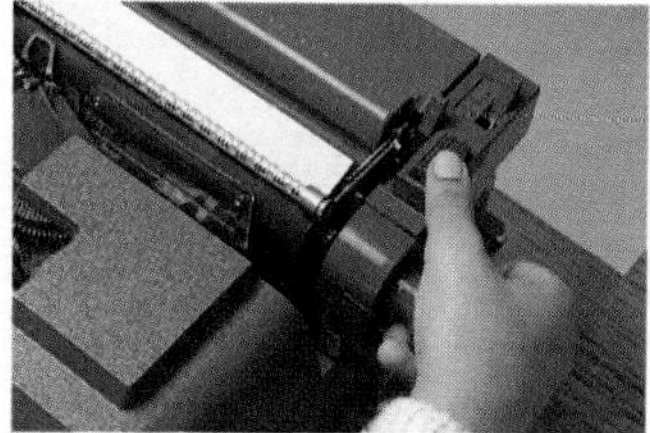

294b-298b (continued)

Document 6
Table of Airports

Mr. Tyler's instructions: "Keyboard the table at the right in final form. Add a third column between *Airport* and *Designation* with a heading of *Tag*. Beneath *Tag*, keyboard the letters which follow each airport."

BUSIEST COMMERCIAL AIRPORTS IN THE UNITED STATES IN THE 1980s*

Based on Total Take offs and Landings

Airport	Designation
Chicago CHI	O'Hare International
Atlanta ATL	International
Los Angeles LA	International
Denver DEN	Stapleton International
Orange County (Cal.) SNA	John Wayne Airport
Dallas/Fort Worth ~~Regional~~ DAL	International
Long Beach LGB	
Seattle SEA	Boeing
San Francisco SFO	International
St. Louis STL	International
Oakland OAK	International
Denver DEN	Araphahoe County
Boston BOS	Logan
NY/La Guardia LGA	
NY/J. F. Kennedy JFK	International
Phoenix PHX	Sky Harbor
Miami MIA	International
Honolulu HNL	International
Anchorage ANC	International

Source: Federal Aviation Administration.

Read Before Beginning Lesson 2

Standard Procedures for Getting Ready to Keyboard

DO at the beginning of each practice session:

Arrange your work area as directed and illustrated on page 2. Keeping your work area clear of everything except your textbook, paper, and machine will make your practice more efficient and productive.

Adjust the paper guide (if the machine has one) so that it lines up with 0 (zero) on the paper-bail scale or the line-of-writing or margin scale. Doing this will help you in setting margin stops. See page ix.

Adjust the ribbon control (if the machine has one) to use the top half of the ribbon. Ask your teacher to show you how.

Insert paper with short edge at top (long edge against the paper guide) unless your machine has a display screen. See page ix.

Set line-space selector (if your machine has one) to single-space (SS) your practice lines. Move lever opposite 1 or – for single spacing, opposite 2 or = for double spacing. See page ix.

Set margin stops for a 50-space line: left stop = center – 25; right stop at right end of the scale. Since pica center is 42, 25 left of center is 17. Since elite center is 51, 25 left of center is 26. See page x.

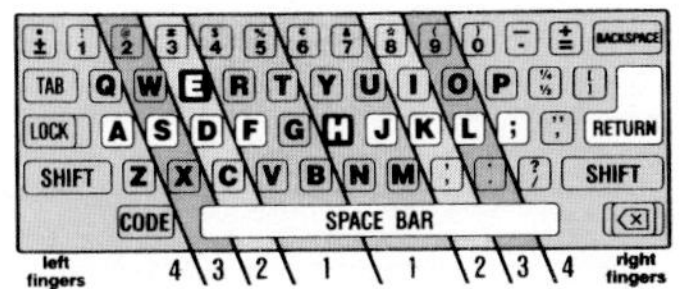

Standard Plan for Learning New Keys

All keys except the *home keys* (ASDF JKL;) require the fingers to reach in order to strike them. Follow these steps in learning the reach-stroke for each new key:

1. Find the new key on the keyboard chart given with the new key introduction.
2. *Look* at your own keyboard and find the new key on it.
3. Study the reach-technique drawing at the left of the practice lines for the new key. (See page 8 for illustrations.) Read the printed instructions in it.
4. Identify the finger to be used to strike the new key.
5. Curve your fingers; place them in home-key position (over ASDF JKL;).
6. *Watch* your finger as you reach it to the new key and back to home position a few times (keep it curved).
7. Practice twice SS each of the 3 lines at the right of the reach-technique drawing:
   slowly, to learn the new reach;
   faster, to get a quick-snap stroke.

Technique Emphasis During Practice

Of all the factors of proper position at the keyboard, the position of the hands and fingers is most important because they do the work.

Position the body in front of the keyboard so that you can place the fingers in a vertical (upright) position over the home keys with the fingertips just touching the face of the keys. Move your chair forward or backward or your elbows in or out a bit to place your fingers in this upright position. Do not let your fingers lean over onto one another toward the little fingers.

Curve the fingers so that there is about a 90-degree angle at the second joint of the index fingers. In this position, the fingers can make quick, direct reaches to the keys and snap toward the palm as reaches are completed. A quick-snap stroke is essential for proper keystroking.

Place the thumbs *lightly* on the space bar, the tip of the right thumb pointing toward the *n* key; tuck the tip of the left thumb slightly into the palm to keep it out of the way. Strike the space bar with a quick down-and-in motion of the right thumb.

Body properly positioned

Fingers properly upright

Fingers properly curved

Thumb properly positioned

294b-298b (continued)

Document 5
Itinerary
(LM p. 207-209)

Mr. Tyler gives you the following instructions: "One of our travel consultants, Mr. Jim Oswald, asks that you keyboard the itineraries at the right in final form."

TRADEWINDS TRAVEL AGENCY
1919 Jefferson Davis Hwy.
Arlington, VA 22202-6170
(202) 478-6300

ITINERARY FOR Phillip T. Nacarelli

FROM	TO	DATE	AIRLINE	SEAT	DEPART	ARRIVE	MEAL
Washington	Los Angeles	Aug. 12	TransC	3A	5:20p	8:00p	D
Los Angeles	Las Vegas	Aug. 16	Coastal	14B	12:30p	1:15p	
Las Vegas	Washington	Aug. 19	Trans C	7B	10:25a	7:07p	L, D

TRADEWINDS TRAVEL AGENCY
1919 Jefferson Davis Hwy.
Arlington, VA 22202-6170
(202) 478-6300

ITINERARY FOR Marcia L. Conners

FROM	TO	DATE	AIRLINE	SEAT	DEPART	ARRIVE	MEAL
Washington	Boston	Aug. 13	North E	12C	4:55p	6:10p	D
Boston	Chicago	Aug. 16	Central	24D	9:05a	12:02p	S
Chicago	Washington	Aug. 18	Trans C	6F	9:59a	4:17p	L

TRADEWINDS TRAVEL AGENCY
1919 Jefferson Davis Hwy.
Arlington, VA 22202-6170
(202) 478-6300

ITINERARY FOR Connie M. Benson

FROM	TO	DATE	AIRLINE	SEAT	DEPART	ARRIVE	MEAL
Washington	Rome	Aug. 14	Oceanic	6A	3:35p	7:05a	D, B
Rome	Amsterdam	Aug. 16	Cont. P	8D	10:30a	2:35p	L
Amsterdam	London	Aug. 21	HOA	2C	9:05a	10:10a	
London	Washington	Aug. 26	Concorde	3A	1:30p	11:45a	D

Lesson 2 — E and H

Line length: 50 spaces
Spacing: single-space (SS)

2a ▶ Get Ready to Keyboard

1. Arrange your work area as directed on page 7.

2. Make needed machine adjustments as directed on page 7.

3. Insert paper (if necessary) as directed on page 7.

Your teacher may guide you through the steps appropriate for your machine.

2b ▶ Review Home Keys

each line twice single-spaced (SS): once slowly; again, at a faster pace; double-space (DS) between 2-line groups

all keystrokes learned

```
1 al ks ja fl ds lk fa ll sk as sl da lf sa ff aj ss
2 ad ad as as jak jak fad fad all all fall fall lass
3 ask dad; ask dad; flak falls; flak falls; as a jak
```

Return 3 times to leave a triple space (TS) between lesson parts.

2c ▶ Learn E and H

For each key to be learned in this lesson and lessons that follow, use the Standard Plan for Learning New Keys given on page 7.

Study the plan now, relating each step to the illustrations and copy at right and below. Your teacher may guide you in these early lessons.

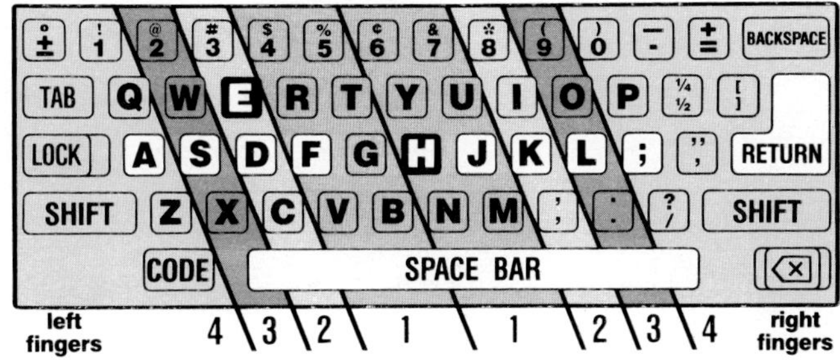

Reach technique for e

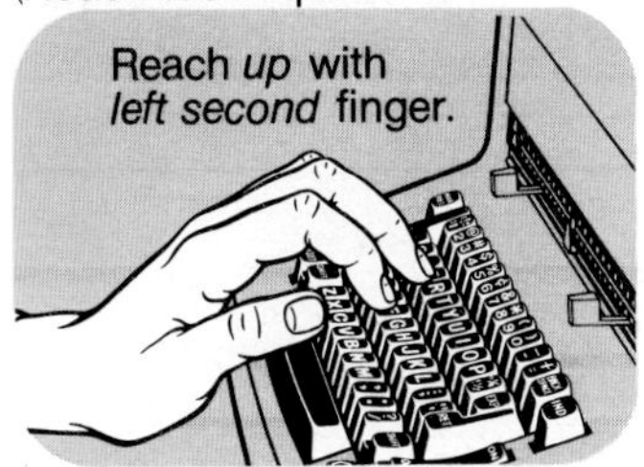

Reach technique for h

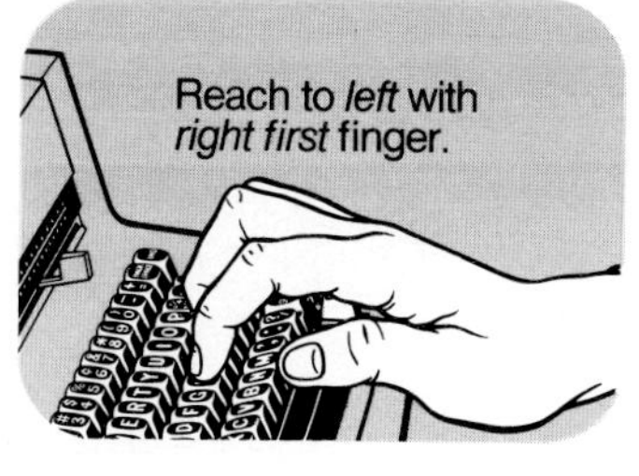

Learn e

```
1 d e ed ed el el led led eel eel lee lee ed el de d
2 ed ed el el led led eel eel fed fed lee lee eke ed
3 a lake; a jade; a jade sale; a desk sale; as a fee
```

Return twice to double-space (DS) after you complete the set of 3 lines.

Learn h

```
4 j h hj hj ha ha ah ah had had has has hj hj ha had
5 hj hj ah ah ha ha has has had had ash ash had hash
6 ah ha; has had; had ash; has half; has had a flash
```

Combine e and h

Do not attempt to type the color verticals separating word groups in Line 7.

```
7 he he he|she she she|shed shed|held held|heed heed
8 a shed; a lash; he held; has jade; she held a sash
9 she has jell; he held a jade; she had a shelf sale
```

Return 3 times to leave a triple space (TS) between lesson parts.

294b-298b (continued)

Document 4
Advertising Leaflet

Mr. Tyler gives you the following instructions: "Arrange attractively in final form this information about our new land, sea, and air tours."

Land, Sea, and Air Tours) — All Caps

London on a Budget

Enjoy 7 days in London for as low as \$749 per person, double occupancy. Tour includes round-trip airfare, hotel acomodations, continental breakfast ~~each day~~ daily, a guided tour of London, and lunch at a British Pub. (Tour No. 457)

Acapulco Vacation

Spend 4 days and 3 nights in Acapulco for as little as \$371 per person, double occupancy. Tour includes round-trip air transportation; lodgings ~~acomodations~~ for 3 nights at a ~~first class~~ premier hotel, and a [tour] ~~by~~ [bus] of Acapulco, including a visit to see the world-famous cliff divers. (Tour No. 62)

Bermuda by Sea

From \$395 per person, double occupancy, you can enjoy a 4-day cruise to Bermuda abroad the Royal Sun. Tour includes port taxes and all meals. Enjoy a Broadway revue each night; dance under the stars; swim indoors or out; try your luck in the casino; ~~and~~ enjoy numerous activities designed for all ages. (Tour No. 540) (Guided tours available in Bermuda).

Williamsburg on Wheels

Deluxe 4-day coach trip to Williamsburg and Busch Gardens. Includes 3 nights at the Williamsburg Inn, all meals, a ~~tour~~ guided tour of historic Williamsburg, an exciting day at "The Old Country" in Busch Gardens, and a visit to a pottery factory. Price per person: \$275 twin. (Tour No. 761)

2d ▶ Improve Keyboarding Technique

each pair of lines twice SS (slowly, then faster); DS between 4-line groups; if time permits, retype the drill.

Do not attempt to type the line identifications, the line numbers, or the color verticals separating word groups.

Space once after ; used as punctuation.

Fingers curved

Fingers upright

home row
1 lad lad|ask ask|jak jak|has has|all all|fall falls
2 a lad; a lass; a jak; had all; all fall; has a jak

e
3 he he he|el el|led led|elf elf|self self|jell jell
4 she led; he fell; she had; a jade ad; a desk shelf

all keys learned
5 she she|elf elf|all all|ask ask|led led|hall halls
6 she had a flask; he had a jell sale; he asked half

all keys learned
7 he fell; a lad fell; she has a desk; he has a sled
8 he asked a lass; she led all fall; he had a jak ad

Lesson 3 O and R

Line length: 50 spaces
Spacing: single-space (SS)

Time schedule

A time schedule for the parts of this lesson and lessons that follow is given as a guide for your minimum practice. The figure following the triangle in the lesson part heading indicates the number of minutes suggested for the activity. If time permits, however, retype selected lines from the various drills of the lessons.

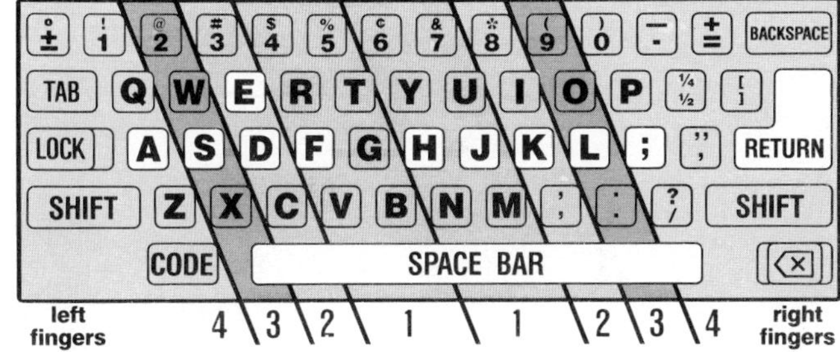

3a ▶ 5 Get Ready to Keyboard

Follow the steps on page 7.

3b ▶ 7 Conditioning Practice

each line twice SS;
DS between 2-line groups

Goals

First time: Slow, easy pace, but strike and release each key quickly.

Second time: Faster pace; move from key to key quickly; keep element, carriage, or cursor moving steadily.

Technique hints

1. Keep fingers upright and well curved.
2. Try to make each key reach without moving hand or other fingers forward or downward.

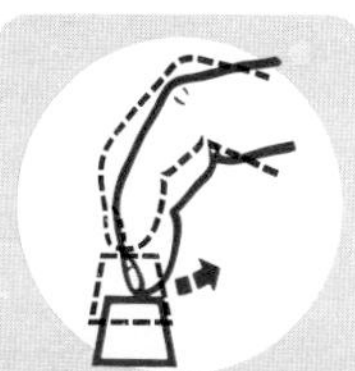

home row
1 ah ah|jak jak|has has|lad lad|ask ask|all all|fad;

e/h
2 he he he|ah ah ah|el el el|she she she|elf elf elf

all keys learned
3 all ask; a jade sale; he had half; she has a lead;

Return 3 times to leave a triple space (TS) between lesson parts.

294b-298b (continued)

Document 3
Itinerary

Mr. Tyler gives you the following instructions: "Prepare in final form this itinerary for Mr. and Mrs. Leon Houston. Arrange it attractively on the page.

AN ITINERARY PREPARED FOR

Nora and Leon Houston

August 15

9:00 a.m.* Depart Washington on Amtrak--Train #567 for NYC.

12:10 p.m. Arrive New York City

2:00 p.m. Embarkation begins on the Queen Victoria; ship sails at ~~5:00~~ 4:30 p.m.

August 20

5:00 p.m. Arrive Southhampton; disembarkation at approximately 7 p.m. Confirmed reservations for eight nights at the Fairfax Hotel, Berkley Street, London W1A 2AN; telephone (01) 629-7777.

August 22 Two tickets in the Stalls, Globe Theater, for comedy, "Shake a Tail." **

August 24 Two tickets in the Dress Circle, Victoria Palace Theater, for musical "Ivor!"

August 25 8:50 a.m. Check in Waterloo Station for Brit-Rail tour to Salisbury and Bath at Platform 11.

August 26 Two tickets in the Stalls, Covent Garden Theater, for the opera "Carmen."

August 28 8:10 a.m. Check in Euston Station for Brit-Rail Tour to Avon and Canterbury at Platform 14.

August 29

5:00 p.m. Embarkation begins on the Queen Victoria; ship sales at 7:30 p.m.

September 6

10:00 a.m. Arrive New York; disembarkation at approximately 11:30 a.m.

* All times given are local.

** Theater tickets will be delivered to your hotel by Keith-Prowse, Ltd.

3c ▶ 18 Learn O and R

each line twice SS (slowly, then faster); DS between 2-line groups; if time permits, key each line once more

Follow Standard Plan for Learning New Keys, page 7.

Goals

- curved, upright fingers
- finger-action keystrokes
- quick return, your eyes on textbook copy

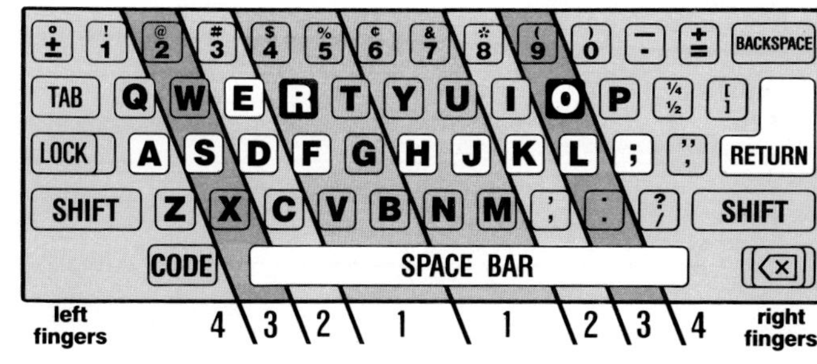

Reach technique for o

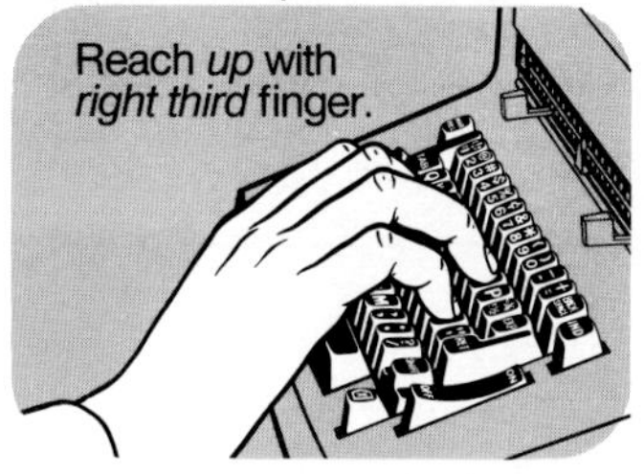

Reach technique for r

Learn o

1 l o ol ol lo lo so so of of do do old old foe foes
2 ol ol so so old old doe doe foe foe oak oak of off
3 do so; a doe; of old; of oak; old foe; of old oak;

Learn r

4 f r rf rf fr fr jar jar her her ark ark lark larks
5 rf rf fr fr her her rah rah jar jar jerk jerk rake
6 a lark; a rake; a jerk; has a jar; had a jell jar;

Combine o and r

7 or or or | for for for | fork fork | door door | food food
8 a rod; a roll; a door; he rode; for her; he or she
9 for her; he has oak; she sold jade; she had a rose

Triple-space (TS) between lesson parts.

3d ▶ 20 Improve Keyboarding Technique

each pair of lines twice SS (slowly, then faster); DS between 4-line groups; if time permits, key selected lines again

Goals

- curved, upright fingers
- finger-action keystrokes
- down-and-in spacing
- quick return, your eyes on textbook copy

reach review
1 hj ed ol rf hj de lo fr hj ed ol rf jh de lo fr hj
2 ah ah el el or or he he she she for for hold holds

e/h
3 he he he | she she she | eel eel | elf elf | her her | shell
4 he had a sled; she has jak jell; she held a shell;

o/r
5 or or or | for for | rod rod | fork fork | rode rode | doors
6 for food; her fork; oak door; her doll; ash or oak

all keys learned
7 ask for; ask for her; sold a jar; has jak for sale
8 she had hash for food; so he asked her for a fork;

all keys learned
9 of old jade; half a loaf; has a rash; old oak keel
10 she asked for a jar of jell; he had asked for hash

294b-298b (continued)

Document 1 (continued)

NAME	ADDRESS	TELEPHONE	INQUIRY
Mrs. Luanne Greene	14 Elm Street	479-6351	Spain
	Annandale, VA 22003-4850		Oct. 4
Miss Ruth C. Davis	237 Belvoir Street	982-6462	London Air
	Alexandria, VA 22314-4961		Oct. 2
Mr. + Mrs. Roy E. Thomas	1807 Malta Ln.	871-5373	Bermuda cruise
	McLean, VA 22101-5072		Sept. 10
Miss Stephanie Gold	1815 N. Lynn Street	478-9981	Mexico cruise
	Arlington, VA 22209-6183		Oct. 2
Dr. Charles F. Zerby	P.O. Box 890 A	512-7463	Orlando
	Springfield, VA 22150-3100		Oct. 8
Mrs. Lila D. Roberts	2001 N. Adam St.	478-1072	Hawaii
	Arlington, VA 22201-4837		Date open
Col. Mark E. Goldman	Quarters 1502 B	980-4500 Ext. 631	Paris via Concorde
	Ft. Myer, VA 22211-5020		Oct. 14

Document 2
Letter
(LM p. 205)

Mr. Tyler gives you the following instructions: "We have received a complaint by telephone from Dr. Charles F. Zerby regarding his recent trip from Washington, DC to San Francisco on Trans-Continental Airlines. Dr. Zerby is one of our best clients.

"Draft a letter to Dr. Zerby, dated August 5, telling him that we regret the difficulties he encountered on his flight and that we have had no complaints in the past about this airline.

"Ask him to write us a letter giving us specific information about his difficulties so that we can report the matter to the airline's home office in Atlanta. If we do not receive a satisfactory reply, we can present the matter to the American Society of Airline Passengers, if he wishes. Close by telling him that we value his patronage, and in the future we shall not book him on another Trans-Continental flight as he requested.

"Make any corrections necessary in the draft of the letter and then prepare it in final form for my signature as Manager."

Line length: 50 spaces
Spacing: single-space (SS)

4a ▶ 26
Review What You Have Learned

1. Review the steps for arranging your work area (see page 2).

2. Review the steps required to ready your machine for keyboarding (see pages ix-x for typewriters; see the appropriate User's Guide for computers).

3. Review the steps for inserting paper into a typewriter (see page ix).

4. Take good keyboarding position:

- fingers curved and upright
- wrists low, but not touching frame of machine
- forearms parallel to slant of keyboard
- sit back in chair; body erect
- feet on the floor for balance

5. Type (key) each line twice SS: first, slowly; again, at a faster speed. DS between 2-line groups.

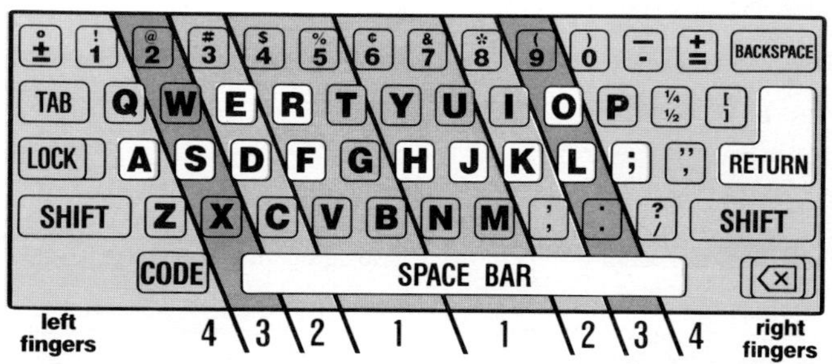

Fingers curved

Fingers upright

Home-row emphasis (Keep unused fingers on home keys.)

```
1 a;sldkfj a;sldkfj fjdksla; fjdksla; fj dk sl a; fj
2 a ah as ha ad all ask jak lad had fad has sad fall
3 ask a lass; had a fall; all had hash; a jak salad;
4 a fall ad; has a sash; a jak falls; had a sad fall
                                                   TS
```

Third-row emphasis (*Reach* up without moving the hands.)

```
5 ed ol rf de lo fr ded lol frf ed ol rf de lo fr hj
6 he or of so do for she off doe foe led odd she rod
7 he led her; a jade jar; ask for her; a jar of jell
8 for a hero; hoe for her; off her desk; a fake jade
                                                   TS
```

All keystrokes learned (Curved, upright fingers; steady pace.)

```
9  a la do ha so ah of he or el as fa jak sod foe for
10 lo old she off jar her led roe rod ark doe eke elk
11 held flak half hero desk road jerk load lead shelf
12 ask her for a jade jar; he sold oak desks for half
                                                    TS
```

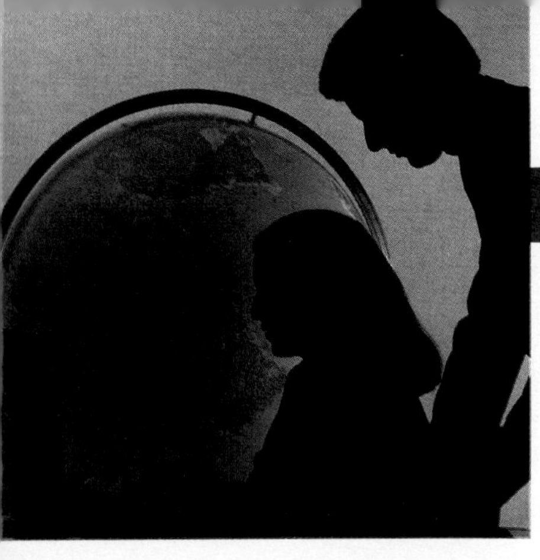

Unit 67 Lessons 294-298

Learning Goals

1. To acquaint you with some of the typical documents produced in a travel agency.

2. To increase your skill in planning, organizing, and producing acceptable business documents.

3. To illustrate some of the problems found in a "people-oriented" business.

Documents Produced

1. Reference Cards
2. Letter (composition)
3. Itinerary
4. Advertising Leaflet
5. Itineraries on Printed Forms
6. Table of Airports

Lessons 294-298

294a-298a ▶ 5
Check Equipment

Before you begin work each day, check your machine to see that it is in good working order by keyboarding the paragraph at the right at least twice (first slowly, then faster).

all letters/figures used

The Wexco preferred stock, in very heavy trading, made quite a sizable jump. It rose from 245 7/8 on 4/30 to 268 on 5/1 (a 9% increase of 22 1/8). If an audit of the profit is held this May, it may dispel the skepticism and end the risks of a big downturn.

| 1 | 2 | 3 | 4 | 5 | 6 | 7 | 8 | 9 | 10 | 11 | 12 | 13 |

294b-298b ▶ 45
Document Processing

Modern Office Tempos has assigned you to work temporarily at the **Tradewinds Travel Agency, 1919 Jefferson Davis Highway, Arlington, VA 22202-6170.** The travel agency consists of ten travel consultants, under the direction of Martin C. Tyler. They provide travel services for individuals, corporations, government agencies, and other organizations.

Document 1
Card File
(LM pp. 201-203)

Mr. Tyler gives you the following instructions: "Each agent maintains a daily log of inquiries as shown below. Prepare a 5″ × 3″ card for each inquiry as follows: name on second line from top edge of card 2 spaces from left edge in inverse order (Lee, Kim) followed by a title in parentheses; date on the same line, ending 2 spaces from the right edge; name and address a DS below in postal order:

Mr. Kim Lee
203 Kent Street, N
Arlington, VA 22209-5723

DS and type telephone number. Place inquiry a DS below, followed by date of travel, if given.

TELEPHONE LOG FOR *August 5, 19- -*

NAME	ADDRESS	TELEPHONE	INQUIRY
Mr. + Mrs. Ray Staltz	*870 Glebe Rd., S*	*478-2361*	*Cancun Special*
	Arlington, VA 22204-5610		*Sept. 16*
Ms. Lois L. Flint	*310 Park Avenue*	*561-3452*	*NYC Theater*
	Falls Church, VA 22046-8326		*Sept. 23*
Mr. & Mrs. F. Hardy	*14 North Street*	*982-4563*	*Carib. Cruise*
	Alexandria, VA 22314-7198		*Sept. 30*

(continued on page 491)

4b ▶ 8
Build Keystroking Speed by Repeating Words

Each word in each line is shown twice. Practice a word the first time at an easy speed; repeat it at a faster speed.

1. Type (key) each line once SS; DS when you finish the drill. Use the plan suggested above.

2. Type (key) each line again. Try to keep the printing point or cursor moving at a steady speed. TS at the end of the drill.

Technique hint
Think and say the word; key it with quick-snap strokes using the fingertips.

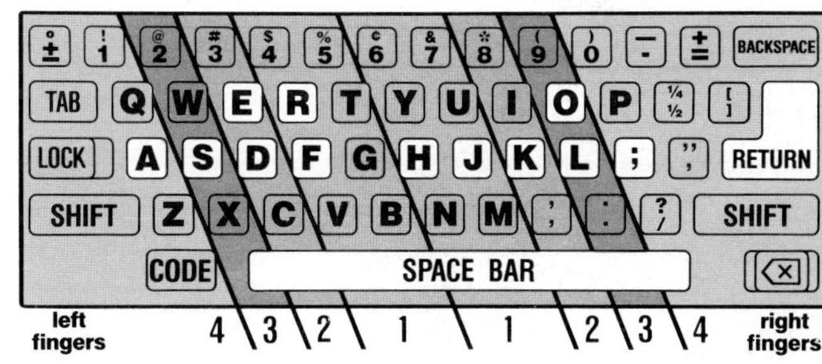

GOAL: To speed up the combining of letters

1 do do|so so|sod sod|or or|of of|for for|fork forks

2 of of|off off|or or|rod rod|re re|ore ore|are hare

3 ad ad|had had|he he|she she|as as|has has|jak jaks

4 ha ha|has has|el el|eel eel|lo lo|old old|ark arks

TS

4c ▶ 8
Build Keystroking Speed by Repeating Phrases

1. Type (key) each line once SS. Speed up the second try on each phrase. DS when you finish the lines.

2. Type (key) the lines once more to improve your speed. TS when you finish.

Space with right thumb

Use down-and-in motion

GOAL: To speed up spacing between words

1 do a|do a|do so|do so|or as|or as|as he|as he fell

2 ah so|ah so|ah ha|ah ha|a jar|a jar|or all|or fall

3 as he|as he|a jak|a jak|a rod|a rod|as old|as sold

4 he held|he held|she rode|she rode|for all|for fall

TS

4d ▶ 8
Build Keystroking Speed by Striking Keys at a Steady Pace

1. Type (key) each line DS. Try to keep the printing point or cursor moving steadily.

2. Type (key) each line again. Try to finish each line without slowing down or stopping.

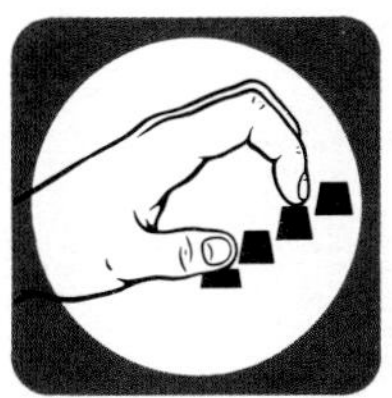
Curved, upright fingers

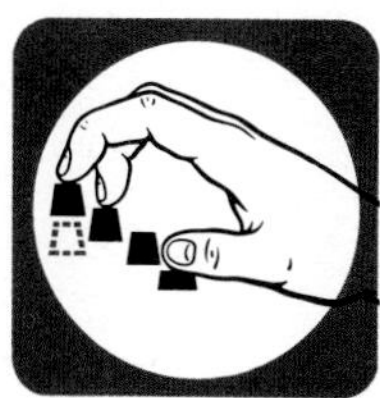
Finger-action keystroking

GOAL: To keep printing point or cursor moving steadily

1 he had a fall jade sale; she asked for a jade doll

2 she held a jar of salad; she asked for half a jar;

3 she has a sales lead; her dad had a lead all fall;

4 he has a sled load of leeks for her fall lake sale

290b-293b (continued)

Document 4
Program for Conference

O U R   E X H I B I T O R S

Allied Reprographics

Barlow Publications, Inc.

Computype Inc.

Eastern Research Corporation

Hamilton Information Systems Group

ITN Telecommunications

Metropolitan Office Technology

Modern Office Tempos, Inc.

North-Eastern Publishing Co.

ORTEC Microfiche, Inc.

Seaboard Telephone Company

Sumida Computers, Inc.

TELENET Communications Systems

THE MODERN OFFICE MAGAZINE

United Data Systems, Ltd.

Video Hut

Voice Mail Services, Inc.

Word Processing Professional Services

Fold

AMERICAN INFORMATION PROCESSING ASSOCIATION

Proudly Presents

The First Annual

****

OFFICE AUTOMATION CONFERENCE

****

May 5, 19--

Carlton Arms Hotel
1919 Connecticut Avenue, NW
Washington, DC

P R O G R A M

"Today's Office in Transition"

(All meetings will be held in the Adams Room)

9:00 - 10:15	-	"Office Workstations," by Ron Bowman, Crystal City Management Institute
10:15 - 10:30	-	Coffee Break
10:30 - 11:15	-	"Planning for Office Automation" by Marsha T. Abrams, T&L Consultants, Ind.
11:15 - 2:00		Visit Our Exhibitors
2:00 - 3:15		"Ergonomics in the Office Environment," by Gordon L. Collins, Maryland Institute of Technology
3:15 - 3:30	-	Coffee Break
3:30 - 4:15	-	"Office Automation--A World of Change," by Patty O. Clark, Automatrix, Inc.
4:15 - 5:30	-	Visit Our Exhibitors
6:00 - 7:00	-	Hospitality Hour in the Ballroom Foyer
7:00		Dinner in the Crystal Chandelier Ballroom

Conference Chairperson: T. Jeffrey Mullins, President of the American Information Processing Association

Fold

D I N N E R

M E N U

Shrimp Cocktail

Broiled Rib Eye Steak

Baked Idaho Potato

Asparagus Spears

Tossed Green Salad

Assorted Dressings

Strawberry Sundae

Rolls and Butter

Coffee, Tea, or Milk

Assorted Mints

Dinner Speaker: Oki Toyohiki
Professor of Commerce
Tokyo University

Subject: "A Japanese View of Office Automation"

Entertainment: "The Old Dominions"
Country-Western Group

Line length: 50 spaces
Spacing: single-space (SS)

5a ▶ 8 Conditioning Practice

each line twice SS (first, slowly; again, at a faster speed); DS between 2-line groups

In this lesson and remaining lessons in this unit, the time for the Conditioning Practice is changed to 8 minutes. In this time you are to arrange your work area, ready your machine for keyboarding, and practice the lines of the Conditioning Practice.

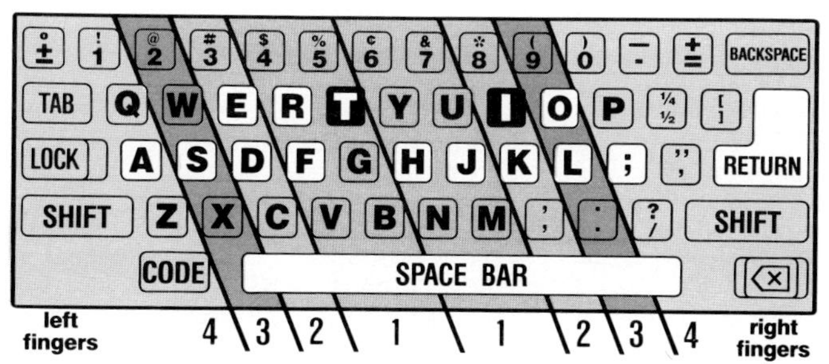

1 as has ask jak rod led off she had elf oak for her
2 do so|so he|ask her|led off|had roe|has oak|of all
3 he had roe; for a jar; she led off; ask for a fork
TS

5b ▶ 18 Learn I and T

each line twice SS (slowly, then faster); DS between 2-line groups; if time permits, key lines 7-9 again

Follow the Standard Plan for Learning New Keys outlined on page 7.

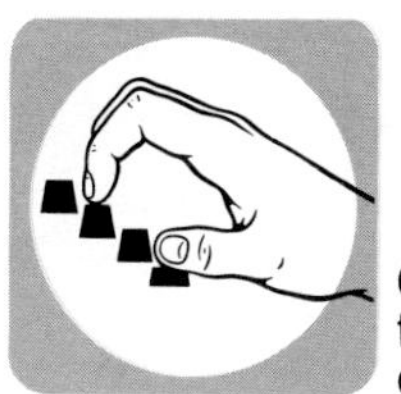

Correct finger curvature

Correct finger alignment

Reach technique for i

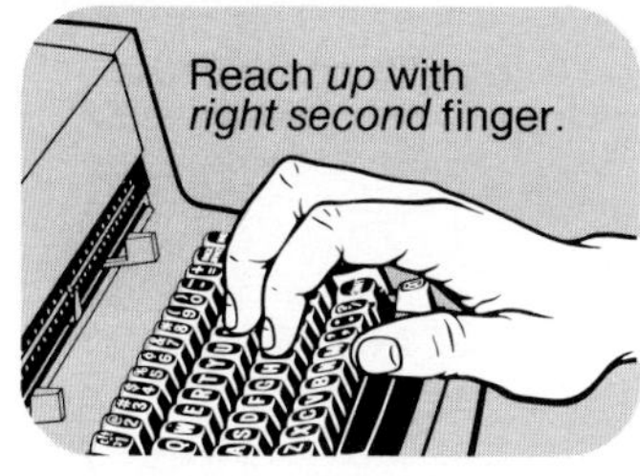

Reach technique for t

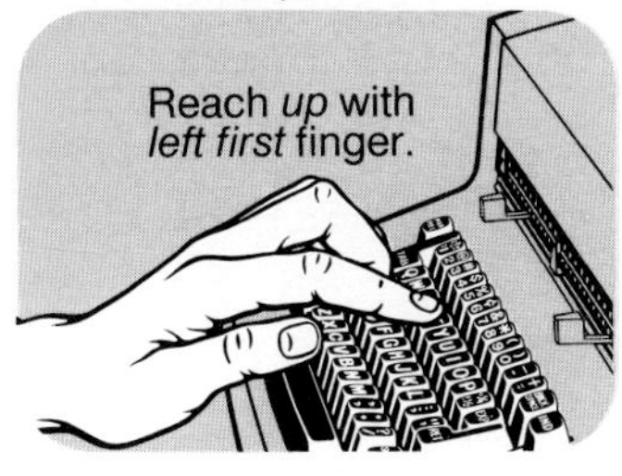

Learn i ▼

1 k i ik ik is is if if fir fir die die did did side
2 i ik ik ki ki if if is is kid kid ski ski hid hide
3 a ski; a kid; a fir; he is; if she is; he did ride
TS

Learn t ▼

4 f t tf tf to to at at the the toe toe dot dot loft
5 t tf tf to to tot tot dot dot the the too too toot
6 to do; to the; to dot; the toe; to toss; to do the
TS

Combine i and t

7 i t it it fit fit sit sit tie tie hit hit kit kite
8 if it is; it is his; dot the i; if the tie is his;
9 she is fit; if the toe; the hat fits; it is a jet;
TS

290b-293b (continued)

Document 4

Program for Conference

Miss Brooks provides the following instructions: "Mr. T. Jeffrey Mullins, President of the American Information Processing Association, has requested us to prepare a model copy of the program for the Second Annual Office Automation Conference to be held at the Carlton Arms Hotel on August 27.

"On the following page is a reduced copy of the program from the first conference. At the right is an enclosure to Mr. Mullin's letter indicating the changes to be made in this year's program. Either make a photocopy of the enclosure or make notes of the changes that must be incorporated into this year's program.

"Using the model copy for last year's conference (p. 489), prepare a model for this year's conference. Make the changes that Mr. Mullins requested."

Note: To keyboard spread headings, such as P R O G R A M:

1. Backspace from center *once* for each letter, character, and space except for the last letter or character in the heading. Begin keyboarding at this point.

2. To keyboard a spread heading, space once after each letter or character and three times between words.

Enclosure: Changes for conference program

Page 1:

Change "The First Annual" to "The Second Annual" and the date to August 27. Also change the graphics (asterisks) to give the page a "new look."

Page 2:

The theme of the program will be "What's New in Office Automation?" Insert the following times, speakers, and topics indicated:

9:00 - 10:15 - "What's New in Word Processing?" by Joan Weber, DC Office Services

10:30 - 11:15 - "What's New in Communications?" by Ronald T. Wilcox, Delaware Institute of Business

2:00 - 3:15 - "What's New in Personal Computers?" by Michael C. Green, ECM Corporation

3:30 - 4:15 - "What's New in Reprographics?" by Theresa L. Santos, National Repro-Tech, Inc.

Page 3:

The menu will be as follows: Fruit Cocktail; Stuffed Turkey Breast; Mashed Potatoes with Gravy; Buttered Asparagus; Lettuce and Tomatoes; Assorted Dressings; Rolls and Butter; Raspberry Supreme; Coffee, Tea, or Milk; and After-Dinner Mints.

The dinner speaker will be Philip B. Murphy, Director of Vocational Education, U.S. Office of Education, who will speak on the topic: "Preparing Students for the Office of the Future."

Entertainment will be provided by "The Misfits," a musical variety group.

Page 4:

Most of the same exhibitors will participate in this year's conference. Make the following changes: eliminate Video Hut and Computype, Inc.; add General Data Company, Ace Computers, Inc., and Universal Automation Products, Inc.

5c ▶ 24 Improve Keyboarding Technique

each line twice SS (slowly, then faster); DS between 2-line groups; if time permits, key the lines again

Fingers properly curved

Fingers properly aligned

Home-row emphasis (Keep unused fingers on home keys.)

1 a add lad had all as ask jak ha has jaks asks lads
2 a fall hall dash sash half flash shall salad salsa
3 a lad; a fall; a dash; a jak salad; has a fall ad;
TS

Third-row emphasis (*Reach* up without moving hands.)

4 ed led ol old rf for ik kid tf fit it or he so off
5 so do of or is it if to he she the toe fit sir for
6 of it; if it is; he or she; it is she; for the jet
TS

All keystrokes learned (Strike keys at a steady, brisk pace.)

7 he said it is her jade jar; he also has a jade jar
8 she took a jet to the lake; he is to see her there
9 she asked if all the jade is at this old lake fort
TS

Space-bar emphasis (Space quickly between words and phrases.)

10 it so if do he to of as oh or ha is re ah at id hi
11 if it|to do|he is|of it|do so|or if|ah so|to do it
12 he is to do it for a fee; the jet took to the air;

Lesson 6 Left Shift and . (period)

Line length: 50 spaces
Spacing: single-space (SS)

6a ▶ 8 Conditioning Practice

each line twice SS (first, slowly; again, at a faster speed); DS between 2-line groups

Recall
Space once after ; used as punctuation except at line endings. Do not space at the end of *any* line. Instead, return and start the new line.

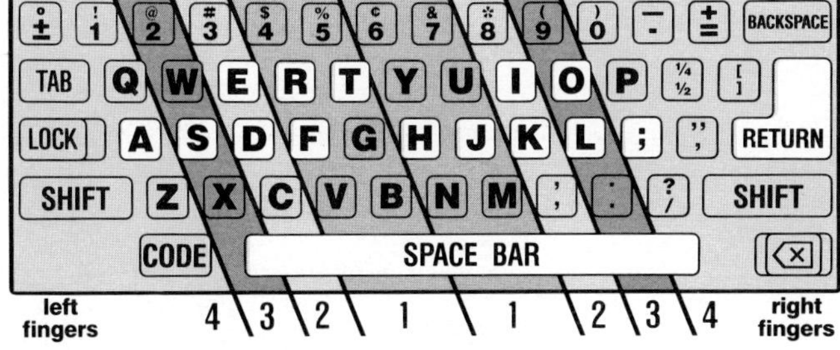

Technique hint
Eyes on copy in book; look at keyboard only when lost.

1 hj ed ol rf ik tf jh de lo fr ki ft hj ed ol rf ik
2 a kid led fir for dot fit held sift half loft jerk
3 she took the oak oars; she has a skiff at the lake
TS

290b-293b (continued)

Document 3

Rough Draft of Instructional Materials

See p. 486 for instructions.

THE STENCIL DUPLICATION PROCESS

Thousands of copies of programs, bulletins, newsletters, and other publications can be reproduced in a short time through the use of the stencil duplication process. A stencil consists of three basic parts: the stencil sheet, the backing sheet, and the cushion sheet. When a key strikes the stencil sheet, it "cuts" an impression in the shape of the type. A cushion sheet is placed between the stencil and the backing sheet to absorb the impact of the striking keys. A film sheet may be placed over the stencil sheet if darker print is desired. This film also protects the stencil sheet from letter cutout when the type face is extremely sharp.

Before keyboarding the stencil, follow these steps:

2~~1~~. If your machine has a cloth ribbon, clean the type thoroughly, paying close attention to the letters where ink tends to accumulate, such as the o and the e. Adjust the ribbon lever to "stencil" position.

3~~2~~. Insert the cushion sheet between the stencil sheet and the backing sheet. Place the top edge of the model copy at the corner marks of the stencil to see where to position the first line. The scales at the top and sides of the stencil will help you place the copy correctly.

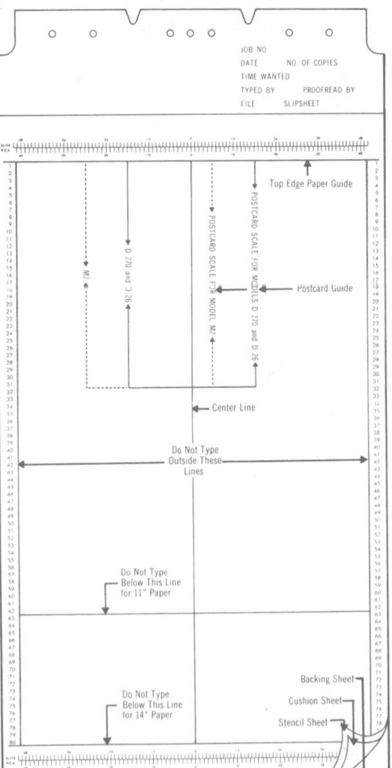

4~~3~~. Insert the s~~e~~tencil assembly into the machine. If you are using a manual machine, use a firm, uniform touch. Some keys that are completely closed such as d and p must be struck more lightly. Capitals and letters such as m and w must be struck with greater force. On electric and electronic machines, which provide even pressure automatically, keyboard as usual.

5. If you make an error, it can be corrected easily with correction fluid. If there is a film over the stencil, this must be detached until you resume keyboarding. Use a smooth paper clip to rub the surface of the error on the stencil sheet. Place a pencil between the stencil sheet and the cushion sheet and apply a light coat of correction fluid over the error. Let it dry; then make the correction, using a light touch.

1. Prepare a model copy of the material to be reproduced. Check it for accuracy of format and keyboarding. Be certain that you place the copy on the page so that it will be within the stencil guide marks (see illustration).

6b ▶ 20 Learn Left Shift and . (Period)

each line twice SS (slowly, then faster); DS between 2-line groups; if time permits, repeat each line

Follow the Standard Plan for Learning New Keys outlined on page 7.

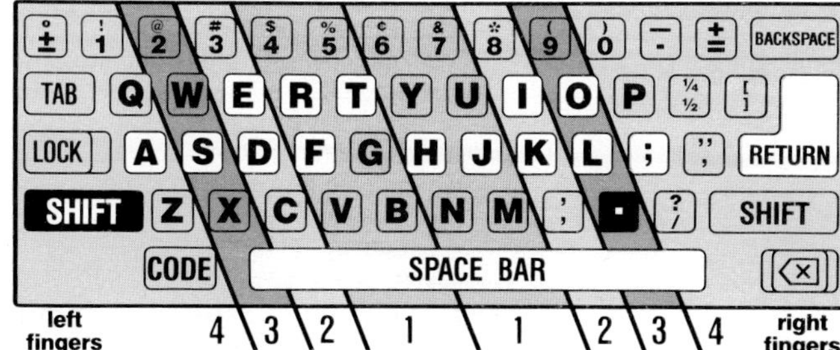

Control of left shift key

Reach *down* with *left little* finger; shift, type, release.

Reach technique for . (period)

Reach *down* with *right third* finger; space twice after . at end of sentence.

Learn Left Shift Key (Shift, strike key, release both.)

1 Ja Ja Ha Ha Ka Ka La La Hal Hal Kae Kae Jae Jae Jo
2 Ida fell; Jae did it; Hal has jade; Kae had a fall
3 I see that Jake is to aid Kae at the Oak Lake sale
TS

Learn . (Period)

4 l . . .l .l ed. ed. fl. fl. rd. rd. ft. ft. asstd.
5 . .l .l ed. ed. fl. fl. off. off. ord. ord. dissd.
6 fl. ed. rd. hr. ft. rt. ord. fed. off. alt. theol.
TS

Combine Left Shift and .

7 I do. Jo is. I did. Ola is ill. I shall do it.
8 Hal did it. Jae said so. Jake has left the lake.
9 I shall ask Kae if she left her skis at Oats Lake.
TS

6c ▶ 22 Improve Keyboarding Technique

each pair of lines twice SS (slowly, then faster); DS between 4-line groups; if time permits, practice selected lines again

Spacing hints

Space *once* after ; and after . used with abbreviations and initials.

Space *twice* after . at the end of a sentence except at line endings. There, return without spacing.

3d row emphasis
1 Jo is to ask at the old store for a kite for Kier.
2 Ike said he is to take the old road to Lake Heidi.

abbrev./initials
3 He said ft. for feet; rd. for road; fl. for floor.
4 Lt. Oats let O. J. take the old skiff to Lake Ord.

key words
5 a or he to if ha of do it so is as led jet old for
6 ah off the aid dot ask jar she fit oak are had rod

key phrases
7 it is|to do|if so|if it|do so|he is|is so|to do it
8 to the|do the|is the|if the|for it|for the|ask for

all keys learned
9 J. L. said he took fish; Karla said she had salad.
10 Jake is to fish at the lake if Odie is also there.

290b-293b (continued)

Documents 2 and 3

Rough Drafts of Instructional Materials

Miss Brooks gives the following instructions: "On this and the following page are two sheets of instructional material that I usually distribute to educators when I give my presentation on reprographics.

"I am in the process of revising both sheets. So that I can make changes more easily, please keyboard each handout DS in unbound report format. Backspace and strike over errors or, if necessary, X out errors and repeat the material. Be certain, however, that the copy is readable.

"You do not have to reproduce the illustrations."

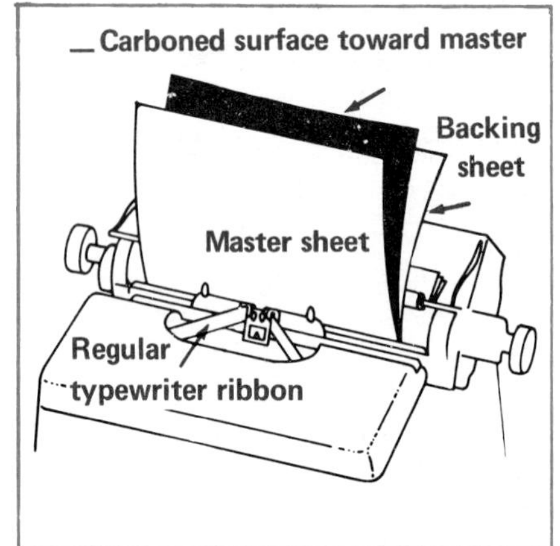

THE SPIRIT DUPLICATION RPOCESS

When the quality of the copy is not of primary importance, the spirit duplication process is used for making copies quickly and at a low cost. As many as 300 copies can be made from a single master, although the number of copies from one master usually ranges from 11 to 150.

The spirit master set consists of two basic parts: the master sheet and a sheet of special carbon that can only be used once. A backing sheet may also be used to improve the consistency of the print. If a specially prepared master is not available, simply place the carbon paper between the master sheet and the backing sheet, with the glossy side of the carbon toward you. When you keyboard, the carbon copy will be on the back of the master sheet. Follow these directions for a better masters:

2 1. If you do not have a carbon ribbon, you can avoid "fuzzy" type and filled-in characters by preparing the copy with the ribbon indicated in the "stencil" position. This procedure, makes it difficult to proofread the copy, however.

3 2. Use a firm, even stroke on a nonelectric machine; keyboard capitals a little heavier than usual and punctuation marks a little lighter. On electric and electronic machines, which provide even pressure automatically, keyboard as usual.

4 3. Insert the open end of the spirit master into the machine first so that you can make corrections easily (see the illustration below). If you make an error, scrape off with a razor blade or knife the incorrect letter or word on the reverse side of the master sheet. Before correcting the error, tear off an unused portion of the carbon and slip it under the part to be corrected. Correct the error and remove the torn portion as soon as you have done so.

5 4. Proofread the copy and correct any errors you may have missed before you remove the master from the machine.

1. Prepare a model copy of the material to be duplicated. Leave at least a one-half inch margin at the top of the master. Proofread the model copy for accuracy.

Lesson 7 U and C

Line length: 50 spaces
Spacing: single-space (SS)

7a ▶ 8 Conditioning Practice

each line twice SS (first, slowly; then faster); DS between 2-line groups

```
1 ik rf ol ed hj tf .l ki fr lo de jh ft l. La. Ltd.
2 he to jet ash rid she jot fled jerk half tore fork
3 Karla has the first slot; Jeff is to ride for her.
```
TS

7b ▶ 18 Learn U and C

each line twice SS (slowly, then faster); DS between 2-line groups; if time permits, repeat selected lines

Follow the Standard Plan for Learning New Keys outlined on page 7.

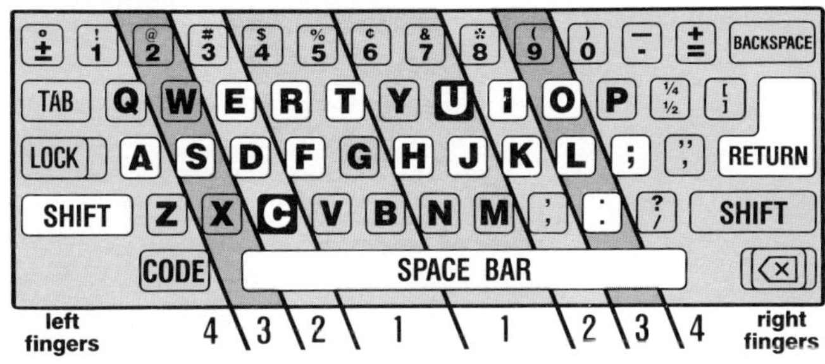

Reach technique for u

Reach technique for c

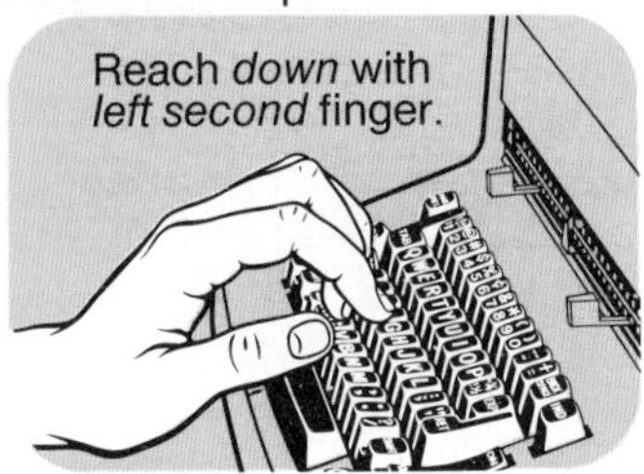

Learn U

```
1 j u u uj uj us us jut jut due due sue sue fur furs
2 u uj uj ju ju us us jut jut hue hue fur fur us use
3 a jut; is due; sue us; due us; is rude; it is just
```
TS

Learn C

```
4 d cd cd dc dc cod cod; ice ice cot cots code codes
5 cd cd dc dc cod cod cot cot tic tic dock dock kick
6 a cod; a cot; a code; to dock; to cite; for a code
```
TS

Combine U and C

```
7 c u cud cud cue cue cut cut cur cur cure cure duck
8 a cud; a cur; to cut; the cue; the cure; for luck;
9 of the cue; use the clue; cut the cake; a fur coat
```
TS

7c ▶ 4 Review Spacing with Punctuation

each line once DS

Spacing hint
Do not space after an internal period in an abbreviation.

```
1 Use i.e. for that is; ck. for check; cs. for case.
2 Lt. Houck said to use fl. for fluid; hr. for hour.
3 K. J. Loft has used ed. for editor; Ir. for Irish.
```
TS

Document 1
Speech (continued)

Choosinge the right mehtod of reproducing a document xexixes
depends upon a number of faxtorxs criteria including the purpose
of the document, the quality desired, and the num ber of copies
required. There are quitexaxfew a number of machines available
for reproducing copies. The following are the ones most commonly found in the office.

Spirit Duplicator. The spiit duplicator, some times
called a Ditto (a trade name), is the most inexpensive way of
reproducing up to 200 several hundred copies. Although purple
is the primary color used, pale sahdes of red, blue, green, and
black are also available. Copies, however, are not usually as
clear and attractive as those produced by other duplicators.
This machine is found chiefly primarily by churches, schools
and small business firms.

Mimeograph. Using a stencil process, the mimeograph can
reproduce thousands of copies in black and white or color at a
low price cost. Stnecils are easy to make keyboard, but trac
illustrations or other graphic materials on the stencil may
prove difficult. Although the price is relatively inexpensive
for copies of 200 or more, the quality is not as good as other
duplicators available. This machine is also found mostly in
churches, schools, and small businesses.

Offset. One of the machines frequently found in business
offices are is the offset duplicator. Literally hundreds of
thousands of copies in black and white or coloer can be reproduced quickly from a special master at a small cost. If properly done prepared, the quality of the copies is excellent.
Although the machine is expensive, the cost per copy is fairly
low for long runs.

Copiers. Copiers of various kinds can be found in the
modern business office. Most of them can be put placed in one
of two categories: xerographic or thermographic. Xerographic
machines use a light sourse to produce copies; where as,
thermographic machines use heat. Sin the copies from these
devices machines are produced from the original, the quality
depends upon how well the original hasxbeen was made. Machines that produce copies in color are available, but they
are quite expensive. Although expensive, copier are considered cost affect for one to ten copies.

Printers. A product of the computer age, high-speed
printers are used by many companies to make produce hundreds
of thousands of documents at less than a cent a page. At
speeds of 75 characters per second (cps) and higher, an
average one-page letter can be made produced in less than 15
seconds. If the printer is connected interfaced with a memory
storage unit, usually a computer, documents can be individualized by the inclusion of different items or variables in
each document, such as names, and addresses

7d ▶ 20
Improve Keyboarding Technique

each pair of lines twice SS (slowly, then faster); DS between 4-line groups; if time permits, practice selected lines again

Goals

- reach *up* without moving hands away from you
- reach *down* without moving hands toward your body
- quick-snap keystrokes

3d/1st rows
1 cod fir cot for ice led cut sit due call rule duel
2 for sure; cash is due; off the cuff; just her luck

abbrev./initials
3 He used Ut. for Utah; Oh. for Ohio; Id. for Idaho.
4 Lori Koch had a lot of luck as she led J. O. Hull.

key words
5 led cue for jut hut kid fit old ice just half coed
6 us cut due such rich fuss lack juke dock turf coil

key phrases
7 to use|to cut|for us|is due|use it|cut off|call us
8 such a|is sure|like to|just as|curl it|lot of luck

all keys learned
9 Lisa said it is a just cause; Katie is sure of it.
10 Jack said he is sure he left for the lake at four.

Lesson 8 Review

Line length: 50 spaces
Spacing: single-space (SS)

8a ▶ 8
Conditioning Practice

each line twice SS (slowly, then faster); DS between 2-line groups; if time permits, practice each line again

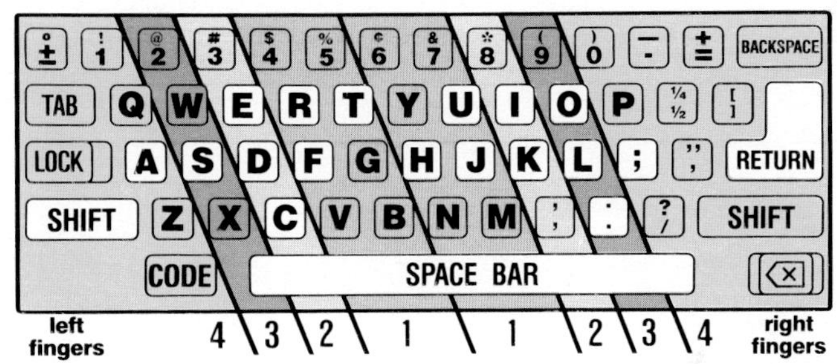

1 u uj ed ik rf ol ed hj tf cd .l; do us if ah or it
2 a for did sit due toe cut just such tusk half fuel
3 Jud is sure to share the cash if he cuts the lead.
TS

8b ▶ 8
Improve Return Technique

each pair of lines once as shown (SS); DS between pairs

> **Return hint**
> Keep up your pace to the end of the line; return immediately; start the new line without pausing.

Eyes on copy as you return

1 Ora asked us to take her;
2 I had a ski race set for four.

3 Jacki left a file at the desk
4 for us to use at the old lake dock.

5 Hal asked her to talk to all of us
6 to see if there is just cause for a cut.

7 Lora said that she has a hut at the old
8 lake site for the use of all the late skiers.
TS

Unit 66 Lessons 290-293

Learning Goals

1. To familiarize you with the field of reprographics.
2. To acquaint you with various methods used to reproduce materials in business and other organizations.
3. To teach you how to prepare materials that are to be reproduced by spirit duplication, stencil duplication, and photo or thermal reproduction.

Documents Produced

1. Partial Text of Speech
2. Rough Draft of Handout -- Spirit Duplication
3. Rough Draft of Handout -- Stencil Duplication
4. Conference Program

Lessons 290-293

290a-293a
Check Equipment

Before you begin work each day, check your machine to see that it is in good working order by keyboarding the paragraph at the right at least twice (first slowly, then faster).

all letters/figures used

Jorgio quickly expressed our views at the big meeting of all citizens. Bill #58420 would raise water rates by 16.3% and taxes by 14 mills (9.7%). To the dismay and fury of the town, both the auditor and the haughty civic panel held firm to their handiwork.

| 1 | 2 | 3 | 4 | 5 | 6 | 7 | 8 | 9 | 10 | 11 | 12 | 13 |

290b-293b
Document Processing

Modern Office Tempos has assigned you to work temporarily in the office of **National Repro-Tech, Inc., located at 6 Dupont Circle, NW, Washington, DC 20036-4512.** National Repro-Tech provides reprographic services for business, government, educational and other organizations. You will work for Miss Irene T. Brooks, Manager of the DC office. If you are not given specific directions for preparing a document, use your best judgment.

Document 1

Miss Brooks gives you the manuscript at the right with her instructions:

"I am revising a speech on reprographics that I give at business and educational conferences. Before she went on vacation, Kim Masami, my assistant, completed a draft of the first part of the speech from machine dictation. Prepare this material as an unbound report DS. Look for uncorrected errors."

REPROGRAPHICS IN ~~TODAY'S~~ THE MODERN OFFICE — Center

Reprographics is a ~~term~~ word that is so new that it is found only in the very latest reference books. Webster's Ninth New Collegiate Dictionary indicates that reprographics ~~are~~ is the plural of reprography which is defined as the "facsimile reproduction (as by photocopying) of graphic matter." In a narrow sense, the field of reprographics includes only the process of makeing copies of all ~~sorts~~ kinds of materials. In a broad~~er~~ sense, however, it includes planing and organizing the material to be reproduced as well as deciding the most affective and efficeint means of doing ~~so.~~ it

There are ~~a number of factors~~ numerous items to be considered when planning and organizing material for duplication. ~~An~~ One impro-tant factor~~, of course,~~ is cost. The objective is to ~~use~~ select a duplication process that will provide the material at the lowest ~~possible~~ cost per copy ~~asxwellxas~~. The appearence of the copy in terms of ~~clearness~~ clarity and eye appeal~~, as well as the~~ format, size, and make up must also be considered. Since time available to do the work may affect quality and cost, time is an impr0tant factor.

(continued on page 485)

8c ▶ 10
Build Keyboarding Skill: Space Bar/Shift Key

each line twice SS; DS after each 2-line group

Goals

- to reduce the pause between words
- to reduce the time taken to shift/type/release when making capital letters

Down-and-in spacing

Out-and-down shifting

Space bar (Space *immediately* after each word.)

1 if he is to do so or us if ah of ha it el id la ti
2 if he|he is|is to|to do|do so|so it|it is|is to us
3 if he is|is to do|to do so|so it is to|it is to us

Left shift key (Shift; strike key; release both quickly.)

4 Lt. Ho said she left the skiff at Ute Lake for us.
5 Jae or Hal is to hike to Oak Lake to see Kate Orr.
6 He is to call for J. O. Hess at Luft Hall at four.

TS

8d ▶ 24
Improve Keystroking Skill

each line twice SS (slowly, then faster); DS after each 2-line group

Correct finger curvature

Correct finger alignment

Direct downward stroke

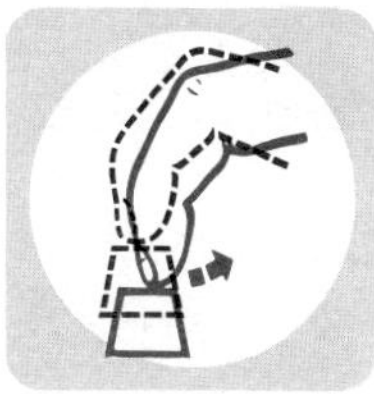
Quick-snap release of key

Third/bottom rows (Reach with *fingers*; not the hands.)

1 us she cut for due ode use tic dot oak fit cue sit
2 coal tick lock cite said coat sock cuff sick thick
3 code jack luck jute suit duet soft froth etc. Ltd.

Key words (*Think, say,* and *key* the words.)

4 as the did oak she for off tie cut has led jar all
5 re ore air cue her his aid rid sit had fir ask jet
6 talk side fold just fled call stir fork hurt route

Key phrases (*Think, say,* and *key* the phrases.)

7 to do|it is|of us|if he|is to|or us|to it|if he is
8 if she|for us|he did|of the|to all|aid us|is a fur
9 he or she|if she did|is to aid|to cut it|is to ask

Easy sentences (Strike keys at a brisk, steady pace.)

10 Jo said she left her old fur coat at the ski lake.
11 Jack asked us for a list of all the furs she sold.
12 Joel said he did code four tests left at his desk.

Lesson 289

289a ▶ 5
Check Equipment

Before you begin the drills which follow, check your machine to see that it is in good working order by keyboarding the paragraph at the right at least twice (first slowly, then faster).

all letters/figures used

Moves to block the funds I requested will jeopardize the six highway projects. When HB489027 is approved, costs will rise 16% and taxes will increase 13.5%. Also, the panel may suspend their goal to fix the signals downtown and risk the problem with autos.

| 1 | 2 | 3 | 4 | 5 | 6 | 7 | 8 | 9 | 10 | 11 | 12 | 13 |

289b ▶ 19
Improve Language Skills: Proofread/Correct

1. In each sentence at the right, items have been underlined. The underlines indicate that there *may* be an error in spelling, punctuation, grammar, capitalization, or in the use of words or figures.

2. Study each sentence carefully. Keyboard the sentence number. If an underlined item is incorrect, correct it as you work. In addition, correct any typographical errors you may make.

1. Only one of the girls are planning to persue a carreer in medecine.
2. Everyone on the board anticipate changes in benefits for personnell.
3. Neither the advise nor the judgement of the attorney were good.
4. A number of admendments was refered to the companys' president.
5. Three quarters of the furniture are subject to the tarriff.
6. Secretarys who prepare letters find you must know how to spell.
7. Allmost six percent of the group was in favor of there new salery scale.
8. The student counsel voted to summerize president Jone's plan.
9. They could not hardly understand the 9th sentence in the journel.
10. He said it was alright to go, however, we weren't ready to procede.
11. The well used dictionery was lying on the nineth shelve.
12. If every one worked as well as myself, we would of finished fast.
13. 2 of the three Agents siezed the liscenses at 1 Vine Street.
14. "It maybe," she said, "The amount of people here will decrese.

289c ▶ 14
Improve Keystroking Skills

60-space line

Keyboard each sentence twice; once for speed, then slower for accuracy; key difficult sentences again as time permits.

289d ▶ 12
Improve Basic Keyboarding Skills

1. Take two 1′ writings on each ¶ of 288d, p. 482.

2. Take one 5′ writing on the three ¶s combined.

double letters 1. *Di Webb keeps all her letters and school books in my office.*

top row 2. *We were quite sure you would tell us to try your typewriter.*

bottom row 3. *Evan can have my extra razor if he cannot buy a new one now.*

long words 4. *Universities provide advantageous educational opportunities.*

short words 5. *If it is up to me, they will do the job as soon as they can.*

direct reaches 6. *My brother has many great new scenes as an eccentric hunter.*

balanced hand 7. *Did she make both men pay for all the work she did for them?*

Lesson 9 — N and W

Line length: 50 spaces
Spacing: single-space (SS)

9a ▶ 8
Conditioning Practice

each line twice SS (first, slowly; again, at a faster speed); DS between 2-line groups; if time permits, repeat selected lines

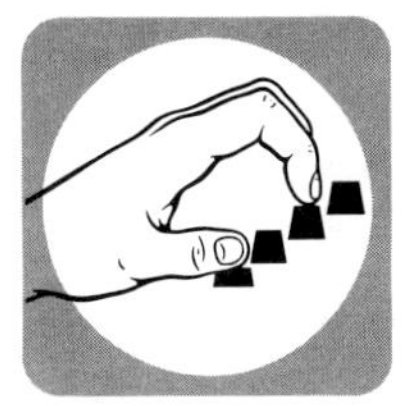
Curved, upright fingers

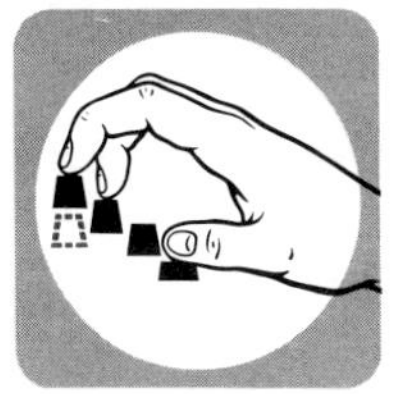
Finger-action keystroking

All keys learned

1 ed uj rf ik tf ol cd hj rt hu do if so us or it he
2 a risk; a cook; is just; to take; if this; of that
3 Lt. Li has just sold us four fish to cook at dusk.

TS

9b ▶ 20
Learn N and W

each line twice SS (slowly, then faster); DS between 2-line groups; if time permits, repeat each line

Follow the Standard Plan for Learning New Keys outlined on page 7.

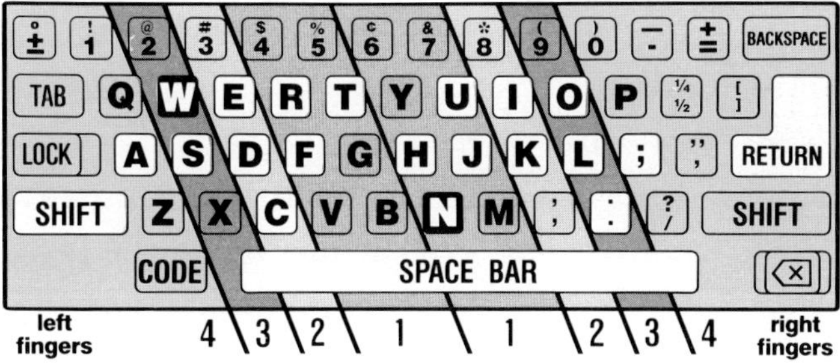

Reach technique for n

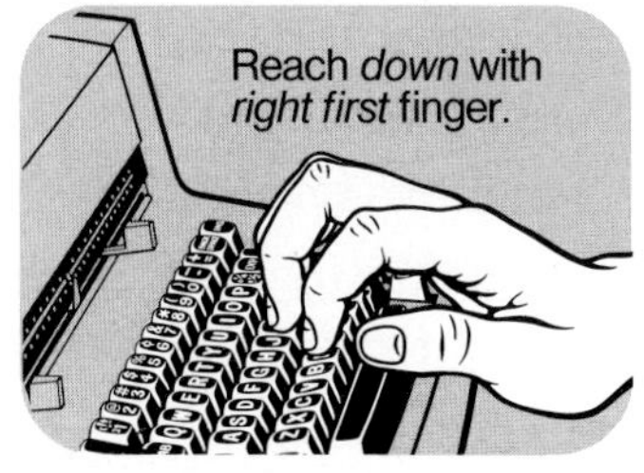

Learn n

1 j n nj nj an an and and ant ant end end land lands
2 n nj nj an an en en in in on on and and hand hands
3 an oak; an ant; an end; and so; the end; she is in

Reach technique for w

Learn w

4 s w ws ws sw sw ow ow wow wow sow sow cow cow owes
5 w ws ws ow ow low low owe owe how how sow sow sows
6 so low; we sow; to owe; is how; too low; is to row

Combine n and w

7 n w own own win win won won now now when when news
8 to win; to own; is low; of now; she won; to own it
9 Lou owns an inn in the town; she won it on a show.

TS

288c ▶ 18 Improve Language Skills: Proofread/Correct

1. In each sentence at the right, items have been underlined. The underlines indicate that there *may* be an error in spelling punctuation, capitalization, grammar, or in the use of words or figures.

2. Study each sentence carefully. Keyboard the line number. If an underlined item is incorrect, correct it as you work. In addition, correct any typographical errors you may make.

1. Exersises for the book, "Information Today" will be included.
2. The newspaper correspondant asked, "are you older than he"?
3. Even if eligible, she don't think she will ask for assistence.
4. Either the attorney or his aids have worked on the ordnance.
5. The comittee agreed that the use of drugs are dangerous.
6. Neither the first or the second choice are acceptible.
7. If he drives slow and careful, he may accompany me.
8. On this ocassion, the prominant author answered incorrect.
9. He will escort his nieghbor to the Church alter at 8:30 A. M.
10. I expected to acompany him to the quite class room.
11. The new commission beleives that we may find it's policys to radicle.
12. She said; "I do not like these kind of surprise"!

288d ▶ 15 Improve Basic Keyboarding Skills

Take two 5′ writings on the ¶s at the right. Record *gwam* and errors.

all letters used | A | 1.5 si | 5.7 awl | 80% hfw

gwam 1′ | 5′

What is word processing? Is it a novel concept? Is it difficult? 14 | 3
The answer to the last two queries is "no." Ever since humans began to 28 | 6
convey their ideas in writing, we have been processing words. In its 42 | 8
simplest form, word processing is nothing more than forming a record 56 | 11
of ideas. The function of word processing is not new to business or 70 | 14
other enterprises because office workers have been processing words for 84 | 17
many years. Thousands of people have proven that it is not a hard job. 98 | 20

Some people believe that the pencil is the ultimate word processor. 14 | 22
It is easy to move from place to place, it can produce documents in any 28 | 25
language, it can be fixed easily if it breaks, and it needs only human 42 | 28
energy to make it work. Writing by hand, unfortunately, is very slow, 57 | 31
often difficult to understand, and very expensive in terms of time when 71 | 34
it is used to produce business documents. Until the invention of the 85 | 37
typewriter, though, all documents in an office were processed by hand. 99 | 39

The typewriter was hailed as the "amazing writing machine," and it 13 | 42
did improve the speed and quality of work in the office. Unfortunately, 28 | 45
even this machine was too slow to keep up with the huge increase in 42 | 48
data. This led to the birth of modern word processing, which is now a 57 | 51
vital part of information processing. What is word processing? It is 70 | 53
simply a system of producing documents of all types at higher speeds, 84 | 56
lower costs, and with less effort by the use of electronic equipment. 98 | 59

gwam 1′ | 1 | 2 | 3 | 4 | 5 | 6 | 7 | 8 | 9 | 10 | 11 | 12 | 13 | 14
5′ | 1 | 2 | 3

9c ▶ 22
Improve Keyboarding Technique

each line twice SS (slowly, then faster); DS between 2-line groups; if time permits, practice selected lines again

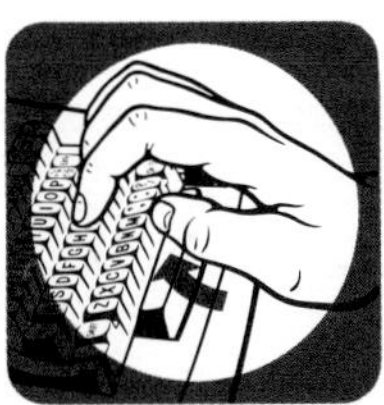

Down-and-in spacing

Out-and-down shifting

Reach-out-and-tap returning

New-key emphasis (*Think, say,* and *key* the letters.)

```
1  is we on ow no an jaw own and owl end now win down
2  we do|an end|to owe|an owl|and won|was due|the new
3  I now know that a new skill takes the will to win.
```

Shift-key emphasis (Shift; strike key; release quickly.)

```
4  Nan or Jena; Jan. or Oct.; Lew and I are in Haiti.
5  Nell and Hew; see Lt. Lowe; Jan asked to see N. K.
6  Newt and Lana can work for the new chef at Hainan.
```

Key words (*Think, say,* and *key* the words.)

```
7  a an is do if to el or the cut own and she due jak
8  we ran owe one win den sow new won nor tin awl sun
9  wish then work corn jack down land lend thus cloth
```

All letters learned (Strike keys at a steady, brisk pace.)

```
10 Janis had won just one set of three when luck hit.
11 Les can do the work if he will just use his skill.
12 Jacki knew she owned the land where oil was found.
```

Lesson 10 | G and Right Shift Key

Line length: 50 spaces
Spacing: single-space (SS)

10a ▶ 8
Conditioning Practice

each line twice SS (first, slowly; again, at a faster speed); DS between 2-line groups; if time permits, practice selected lines again

Goals

- quick-snap keystrokes
- brisk, steady pace
- down-and-in spacing

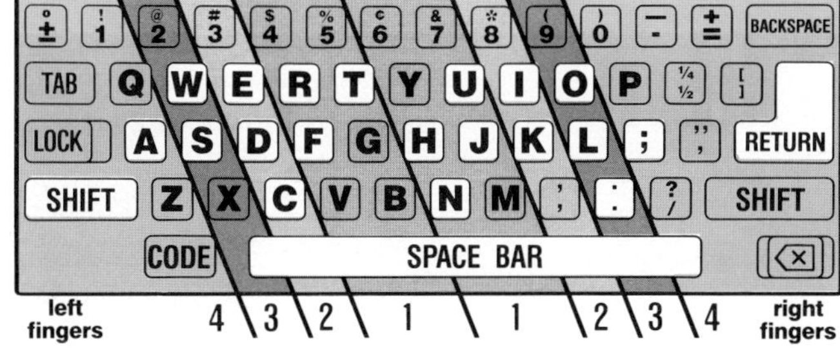

All keystrokes learned

```
1  nj ws hj rf ol tf ik ed uj cd; I now know I own it.
2  if we|so as|is in|as is|he saw|an art|is nul|we cut
3  Kirt had just taken the race of the week at school.
```

TS

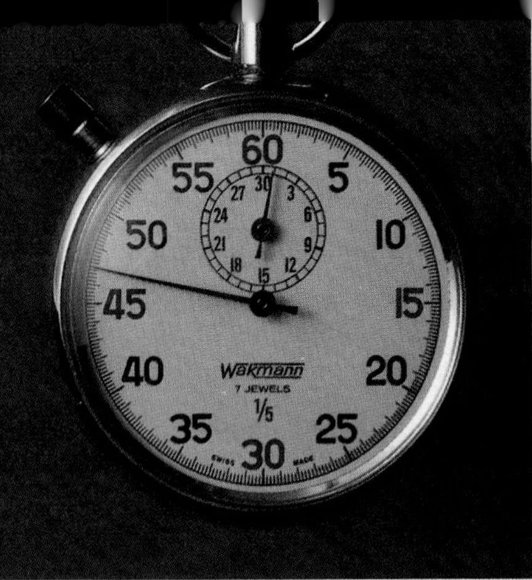

Unit 65 Lessons 288-289

Learning Goals

1. To improve basic keyboarding techniques.
2. To increase keystroking speed and to improve accuracy on straight copy.
3. To improve language skills.

Machine Adjustments

1. 65-space line for Check Equipment exercises.
2. 75-space line for Language Skills.
3. 70-space line for drills unless otherwise indicated.
4. SS sentence drills with a DS between groups; DS writings; DS language skills sentences.

Lesson 288

288a ▶ 5 Check Equipment

Before you begin the drills which follow, check your machine to see that it is in good working order by keyboarding the paragraph at the right at least twice (first slowly, then faster).

all letters/figures used

Wilma Zinji quickly booked an exceptional rock group for the festivals. She hopes to gross $540,000 (14,600 × $37) on April 9 and $680,200 (17,900 × $38) on May 30. Their sorority paid for a fuchsia gown for the woman and a fuchsia paisley tie for the man.

| 1 | 2 | 3 | 4 | 5 | 6 | 7 | 8 | 9 | 10 | 11 | 12 | 13 |

288b ▶ 12 Skill-Comparison Keyboard

1. Take three 1′ writings on ¶ 1. Note highest *gwam*.
2. Take three 1′ writings on ¶ 2. Note highest *gwam*.
3. Take three 1′ writings on the ¶ on which you had the lowest *gwam*.

Goal: Increased speed.

all letters used

E | 1.2 si | 5.1 awl | 90% hfw   D | 1.8 si | 6.3 awl | 70% hfw

	gwam 1′	3′
The work in an office varies from firm to firm. A few of the more	13	4
common jobs you can expect to do are to type letters, memos, and forms,	28	9
use the phone, process mail, and use office machines of all types. You	42	14
can also expect to keyboard a wide range of work from labels and file	56	19
cards to long and quite complex forms, reports, and records.	68	23
The administrative office is often called the nerve center of a	13	27
firm. The office carries out duties that are vital for the smooth,	26	32
organized working of a company. The usual jobs given to an administra-	41	36
tive office call for superior skills in communication, record keeping,	55	41
accounting, data and word processing, and in reprographics.	67	45

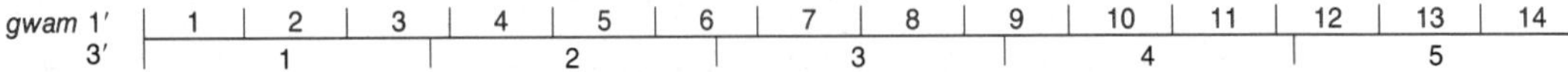

10b ▶ 20
Learn G and Right Shift Key

each line twice SS (slowly, then faster); DS between 2-line groups; if time permits, practice selected lines again

Follow the Standard Plan for Learning New Keys outlined on page 7.

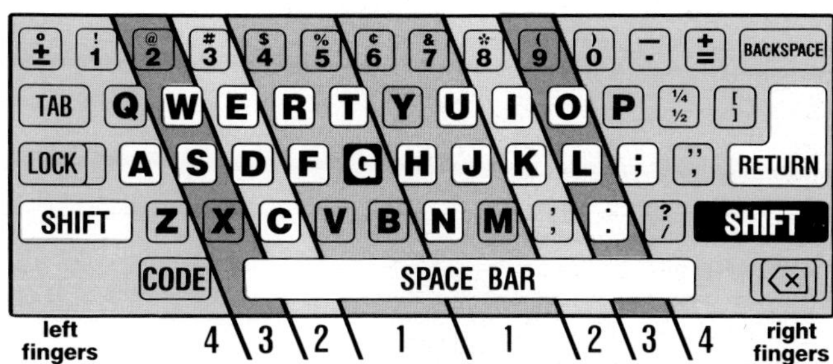

Reach technique for g

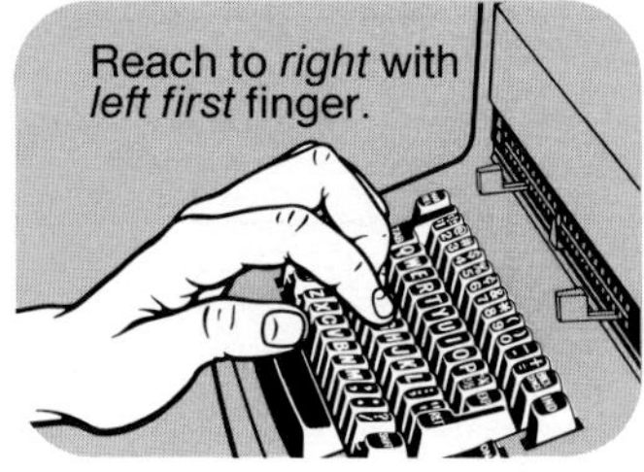

Learn g

```
1 f g g gf gf go go fog fog fig fig got got jog jogs
2 g gf gf go go got got jog jog fig fig log log golf
3 to go; he got; to jog; to jig; the fog; he is gone
```

Control of right shift key

Reach *down* with *right little* finger; shift, type, release.

Learn Right Shift

```
4 A; A; Al Al; Cal Cal; Ali or Flo; Di and Sol left.
5 Dale lost to Wes; Elsa lost to Cal; I lost to Del.
6 Tish has left for Tulsa; Rich is to see her there.
```

Technique hint
Shift, strike key, and release both in a quick 1-2-3 count.

Combine g and Right Shift

```
7 Gig has gone to Rio on a golf tour with Gene Soto.
8 Golda got an A for her win; Rog got a C for fifth.
9 Gilda is to sign for Reggie; I can sign for Signe.
```

TS

10c ▶ 22
Improve Keyboarding Technique

each pair of lines twice SS (slowly, then faster); DS between 4-line groups; if time permits, practice selected lines again

Goals

- Reach *up* without moving hands away from you
- Reach *down* without moving hands toward your body
- quick-snap keystrokes

3d row emphasis
```
1 or sow got for due the sit low dot rug owe fir law
2 he is; to go; of us; is low; he got it; if we owe;
```

1st row emphasis
```
3 an can nag and cash land call hand dank lack slack
4 a fan; a can; a nag; an ad; an ash; a call; a jack
```

key words
```
5 if all rug her cot and dig fur the cut own jet ask
6 us an this wore disk that cook just lend sign work
```

key phrases
```
7 to go|a foot|an inch|to sign|at work|is just|a dog
8 to ask|the jet|the lawn|her disk|and sign|too high
```

all keys learned
```
9 Jan and Chris are here; Di and Rick are also here.
10 Doug walked two hours in the fog to get to Newton.
```

284b-287b (continued)

Document 7
Income Tax Form: Schedules A and B
(LM p. 191)

Bernard H. Goodman, one of the accounting assistants, has submitted to Mr. Mason this personal income tax worksheet that shows the incomes of Phyllis and Fred W. Poole. Mr. Mason's instructions: "Using the information provided on the worksheet, complete Schedules A and B (illustrated below).

"Be sure to fill in all necessary information and to record the figures in the proper columns. You may have to use the variable line spacer to accurately place the figures on the lines."

Note: The salaries listed on the worksheet will not be entered on Schedules A or B.

INDIVIDUAL INCOME TAX

Income Work Sheet

For Phyllis and Fred W. Poole SSN 141-02-4224

Source	Type	Amount
Davis & Hall, Inc.	Salary	24,600
Martin Industries, Inc.	Salary	18,120
UT&T	Div.	1,350
EE Bonds	Int.	510
Fidelity Bank	Int.	460
EVVON Corporation	Div.	3,000
United Cash Reserve	Div.	675
United Savings and Loan	Int.	795
Teletex Co.	Div.	630

1987 COMMONWEALTH OF VIRGINIA VA-40 A,B (9-87) DEPARTMENT OF REVENUE

Name as shown on form VA-40 | Social Security Number

SCHEDULE A INTEREST			SCHEDULE B DIVIDENDS		
LIST PAYERS AND AMOUNTS IF OVER $400 INCLUDE INTEREST FROM SAVINGS AND LOAN ASSOCIATIONS, CREDIT UNIONS, BANK DEPOSITS, BONDS, ETC. If additional space is required, attach separate sheet			LIST PAYERS AND AMOUNTS IF OVER $400 If additional space is required, attach separate sheet		
Subtotal			Subtotal		
Interest from Partnerships			Dividends from Partnerships		
Interest from VA S corporations			Dividends from VA S corporations		
Enter total here			Enter total here		

Lesson 11 B and P

Line length: 50 spaces
Spacing: single-space (SS)

11a ▶ 8
Conditioning Practice

each line twice SS (first, slowly; again, at a faster speed); DS between 2-line groups; if time permits, practice selected lines again

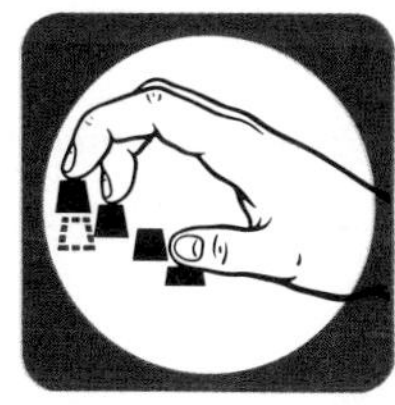

Finger-action keystroking

Down-and-in thumb motion

All letters learned

1 go as of or to and cut jot irk the own for cog all
2 of it|go for it|jot it down|take a cut|she will go
3 A kid had a jag of fruit on his cart in New Delhi.

TS

11b ▶ 20
Learn B and P

each line twice SS (slowly, then faster); DS between 2-line groups; if time permits, practice selected lines again

Follow the Standard Plan for Learning New Keys outlined on page 7.

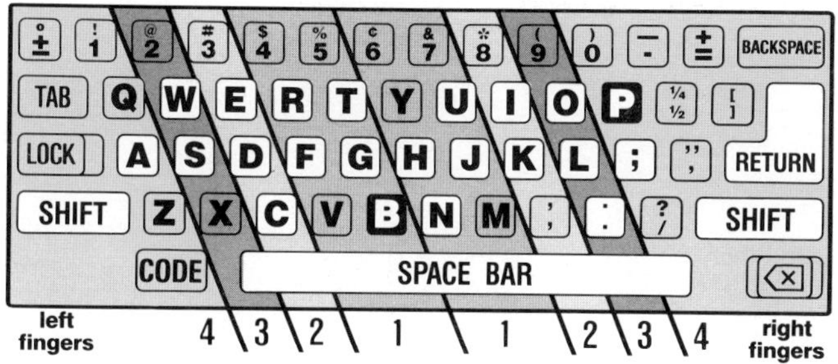

Reach technique for b

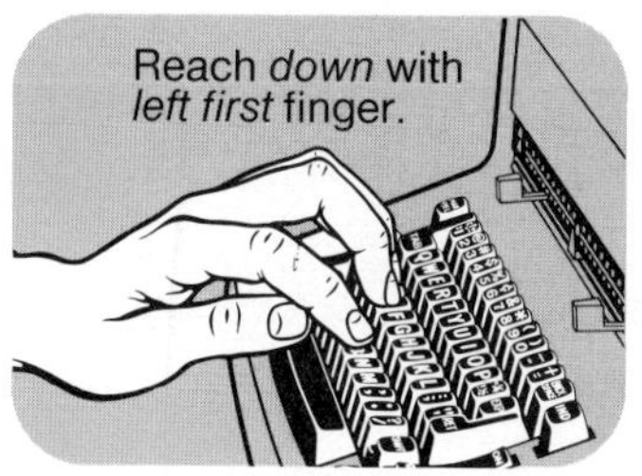

Reach technique for p

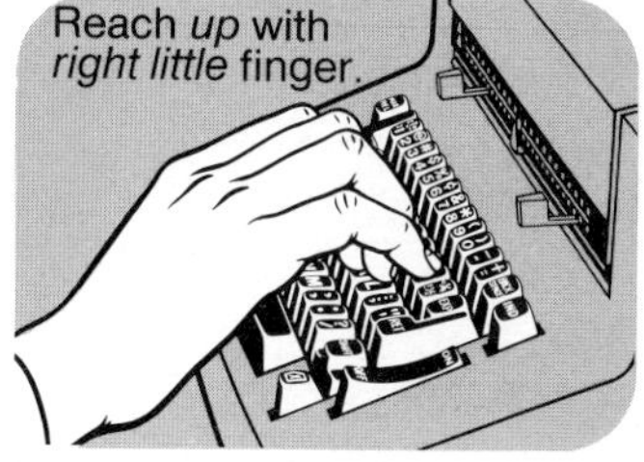

Learn b

1 f b b bf bf fb fib fib rib rib big big rob rob but
2 bf bf fib fib fob fob but but lob lob bib bib ribs
3 a bud; to fib; but us; lob it; too big; to buff it

Learn p

4 ; p p p; p; pa pa; up up; apt apt pen pen nap naps
5 p p; p; pa pa paw paw pan pan lap lap pen pen kept
6 apt to keep; pick it up; take a nap; pack the pans

Combine b and p

7 b p up but put bit pit rib rip bid dip pub sup sub
8 a bus; a pan; to dip; to pit; the bid; put both up
9 Peg put both pans in a bin at the back of the pub.

TS

284b-287b (continued)

Document 6
Letter of Audit
(LM p. 189)

Mr. Raymond L. Roberts, President of **Crystal Industries, Inc., 2520 Jefferson Davis Highway, Arlington, VA 22220-6631,** has contracted with Temple Accounting Services to audit his firm. Mr. Mason's instructions: "Prepare the letter in final form for the signature of Frank T. Davis, CPA. Date the letter July 27, 19--."

We have *examined* ~~audited~~ the balance sheets, statements of income, stock holder's equity, and *financial* changes made by the Rosslyn Wholesale Company, a fully-owned subsid*i*ary of Crystal Industries, Inc., for the year ended June 30, 19--. Our examination was made in accordance with generally excepted *auditing* ~~accounting~~ standards and, *accordingly,* included such *tests* ~~checks~~ of the accounting records and such other audi*t*ing *procedures* ~~methods~~ as we *deemed* ~~considered~~ necessary *in* ~~under~~ the circumstances.

In our opinion, the *financial* ~~consolidated~~ statements *mentioned above* present fairly the financial position of the Rosslyn Wholesale Company as of June 30, 19--. These statements, in accordance with *generally* accepted and consistently *applied* ~~held~~ accounting principals, present the results of Rosslyn Wholesale *Company's* operations and changes in their financial position for the *fiscal* year.

During *this fiscal* ~~the~~ year ~~ended June 30, 19--~~, the *Rosslyn Wholesale* Company changed its method of accounting for adjusting fees. This income is now *recognized* ~~recorded~~ when earned rather than when *invoiced* ~~established~~. The affect of the change for this *fiscal* year was *immaterial* ~~minimal~~. *A pro forma* calculation of net income and earnings *per share* for *prior* ~~previous~~ periods was not included in ~~the~~ financial statements since the affect of the change on these *periods* ~~years~~ would not have been material.

The for*e*going statement may be reproduced, under our signature and appended to *the* ~~your~~ financial statements *of the Rosslyn Wholesale Company* for the year ended June 30, 19--.

11c ▶ 22
Improve Keyboarding Technique

each pair of lines twice SS (slowly, then faster); DS between 4-line groups; if time permits, practice selected lines again

Goals
- Reach *up* without moving hands away from you
- Reach *down* without moving hands toward your body
- quick-snap keystrokes

reach review
1 cd nj ws uj ed ol gf ik bf hj rf .l tf ce un rb p;
2 jut led gift cold turf lows bike herb pace Bif Jan

1st/3rd rows
3 an win cut fan bus pad new cog hen cub tan cup pen
4 curt plan want curb wisp torn pick cost high clips

key words
5 go bid can jet pen rub pep own for nap his irk all
6 lend pack high wish club jest gold silk fold court

key phrases
7 to put|an old|of use|is all|go for|to irk|the jets
8 a wire|to know|on land|big bus|the cord|a new chip

all keys learned
9 Peg can take a bus at one; Cal gets a jet at four.
10 Chloe used to work for a big pet shop in San Juan.

Lesson 12 Review

Line length: 50 spaces
Spacing: single-space (SS)

12a ▶ 8
Conditioning Practice

each line twice SS (slowly, then faster); DS between 2-line groups; if time permits, practice each line again

Goals
- curved, upright fingers
- quiet hands and arms
- steady keystroking pace

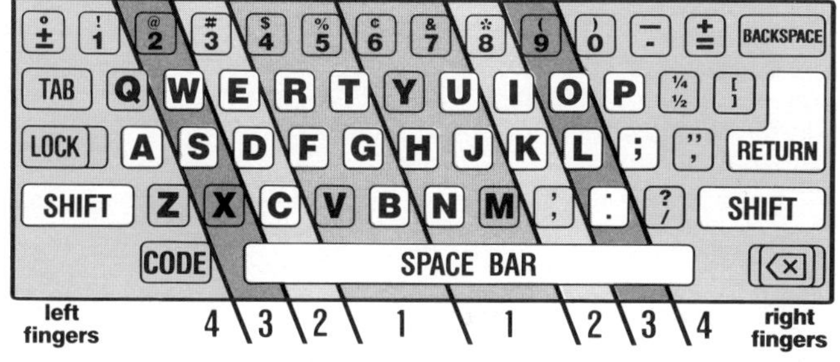

All keys learned

1 we up as in be on re ok no us if la do ah go C. J.
2 up to us; get a cup; the bid is; in a jet; to work
3 Fran now knows it is her job to take the gold cup.
TS

12b ▶ 12
Improve Return Technique

1. Key each 2-line sentence once as teacher calls "Return" each 30 seconds (30″).

Goal: To reach the end of each line just as the 30″ guide ("Return") is called.

2. Repeat the drill.

Note: The 30″ *gwam* scale at right shows gross words a minute if you reach the end of each line as the 30″ guide is called.

Eyes on copy as you return

		gwam 30″	20″
1	Deb wants to see the old globe	12	18
2	that he has to sell this fall.	12	18
3	Jack will take the first train into	14	21
4	town to see the big car show there.	14	21
5	Keisha will ask her to talk with all the	16	24
6	workers who are here for the first week.	16	24
7	Peg will add to her skill when she learns not	18	27
8	to look up or pause at the ends of the lines.	18	27

TS

284b-287b (continued)

Document 4
Schedule of Depreciation

Mr. Mason gives this schedule to you with these instructions: "This Schedule of Depreciation was prepared by Colleen R. Patrick, an accounting assistant, at the request of Ryan T. Zuccheralli, one of the major partners. Prepare the schedule in final form. Keyboard the horizontal rules above and below the columnar headings and at the end of the table, but do not key any other rules. Also, do not include the instructions written at the end of the schedule."

Document 5
Letter of Transmittal
(LM p. 187)

Mr. Mason's instructions: "Miss Patrick has left a note on the bottom of the Schedule of Depreciation requesting that you compose a letter of transmittal in draft form for her approval. Prepare the letter dated July 26, 19-- to **Miss Catherine M. Ling, Finance Officer of the Troy Manufacturing Co., 2396 Pinecrest Road, Annandale, VA 22003-4170.**"

SCHEDULE OF DEPRECIATION

ITEM: Lathe, Serial # 1394-06

TERM OF DEPRECIATION: 5 years

DATE PURCHASED: July 1, 19--

COST: $ 42,000

TERM OF USE: 5 years

SALVAGE OR TRADE-IN VALUE: $ 2,000

METHOD OF DEPRECIATION: Straight line

Year	Depreciation Expense	Accumulated Depreciation	Book Value
First*	$ 4,000	$ 4,000	$ 38,000
Second	8,000	12,000	30,000
Third	8,000	20,000	22,000
Fourth	8,000	28,000	14,000
Fifth	8,000	36,000	6,000
Sixth*	4,000	40,000	2,000

*Six-months' depreciation

Prepare letter, for Mr. Zuccheralli's signature transmitting this schedule to Miss Catherine M. Ling, Finance Officer of the Troy Manufacturing Co. Tell Miss Ling that legislation now pending in the U. S. Congress may require us to amend this schedule in the next fiscal year.

C. R. Patrick

12c ▶ 10
Build Keyboarding Skill: Space Bar/Shift Keys

each line twice SS; DS between 2-line groups

Goals

- to reduce the time used between words
- to reduce the time taken to shift/type/release when making capital letters

Down-and-in spacing

Out-and-down shifting

Space bar (Space *immediately* after each word.)

1 Pat saw an old gold urn she wants for the new den.
2 Cleo is to go to work as a clerk at the town hall.
3 I know she is to be here soon to talk to the club.

Shift keys (Shift; strike key; release both quickly.)

4 Janet Pell left the file on the desk for Lana Orr.
5 Rod and Coila went to the lake with Sig and Bodie.
6 Nita Salas and Luis Rios work for us in Los Gatos.
TS

12d ▶ 10
Improve Keystroking Skill

each line twice SS (slowly, then faster); DS after each 2-line group

Goals

- quick-snap keystrokes
- quick joining of letters to form words
- quick joining of words to form phrases

Key words and phrases (*Think, say,* and *key* words and phrases.)

1 ah cub pan dog all jak got rid the off sit own irk
2 of us|do the|to rub|all of|he got|for the|to do it
3 if we do|is to be|as it is|in all the|if we own it

All letters learned (Strike keys at a brisk, steady pace.)

4 Prudence just left for work up at the big ski tow.
5 Jacob said that all of us can pick the right work.
6 June had gone for the big ice show at Lake Placid.
TS

12e ▶ 10
Check Keyboarding Skill

1. Take a 20-second (20") timed writing on each line. Your rate in gross words a minute (*gwam*) is shown word for word above the lines.

2. Take another 20" writing on each line. Try to increase your keystroking speed.

Goal

At least 15 *gwam.*

20" *gwam*

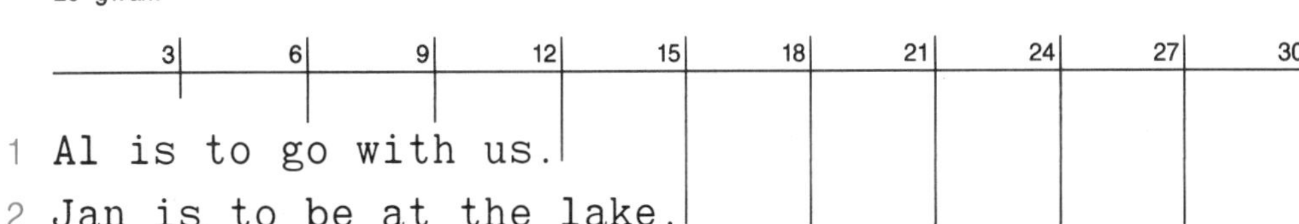

1 Al is to go with us.
2 Jan is to be at the lake.
3 Cal said he will take his dog.
4 Olga sold an old pair of ski boots.
5 She told us to set a goal and go for it.
6 It is now up to us to see how high we can go.
7 Jake is to go to town to work with the rich girls.

284b-287b (continued)

Document 3
Budget Projection

Eileen S. Wilhelm, an accounting assistant to Frank T. Davis, has given this budget projection to Mr. Mason. His instructions: "Please prepare the spreadsheet of budget projections in final form. DS all entries."

BUDGET PROJECTIONS PREPARED FOR THE CAMERON CORPORATION

	Previous Period	Scenario A	Scenario B
Gross sales	$850,000	$935,000	$977,500
Cost of sales			
Salaries and wages	130,000	136,500	140,400
Materials and supplies	80,000	84,800	88,000
Manufacturing overhead	60,000	61,200	61,800
Total	270,000	282,500	290,200
Gross profit on sales	580,000	652,500	687,300
Selling expenses	30,000	30,900	31,200
Administrative overhead	55,000	56,100	56,650
	85,000	87,000	87,850
Net operating profit	$495,000	$565,500	$599,450

Assumptions:

Scenario A: Sales will increase by 10%; salaries and wages will increase 5%; the cost of materials and supplies will increase by 6%; manufacturing overhead will increase 2%; selling expenses will increase 3%, and administrative overhead costs will increase by 2% over the previous period.

Scenario B: Sales will increase by 15%; salaries and wages will increase 8%; the cost of materials and supplies will increase by 10%; manufacturing overhead costs will increase 4%, and administrative overhead costs will increase by 3% over the previous period.

Lesson 13 — M and X

Line length: 50 spaces
Spacing: single-space (SS)

13a ▶ 8 Conditioning Practice

each line twice SS (slowly, then faster); DS between 2-line groups; if time permits, practice each line again

1 bf nj cd ik ws ol rf p; tf hj gf an be up we on of
2 up cup but own can sub pep ran tic bit owe run ice
3 Bick will win a gold if he just runs at top speed.

TS

13b ▶ 18 Learn M and X

each line twice SS (slowly, then faster); DS between 2-line groups; if time permits, practice selected lines again

Follow the Standard Plan for Learning New Keys outlined on page 7.

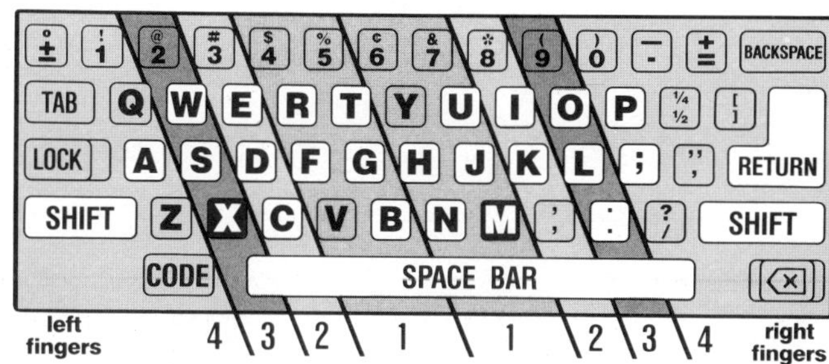

Reach technique for m

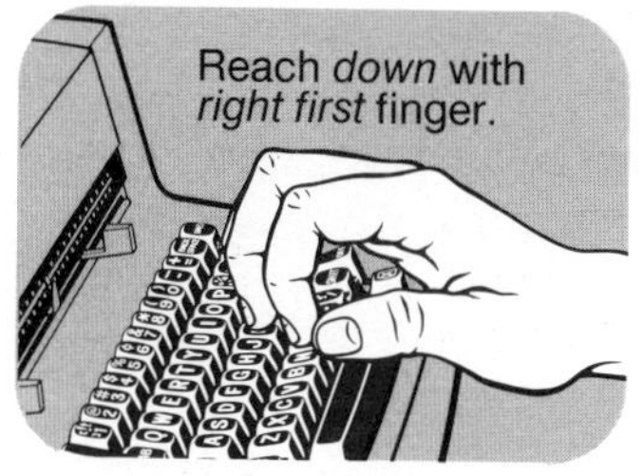

Reach technique for x

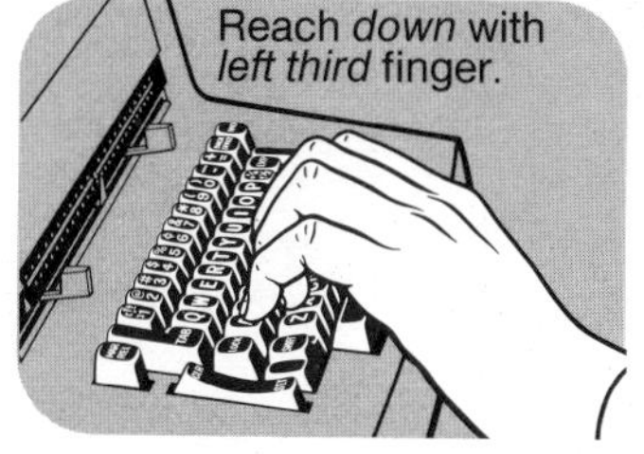

Learn m

1 j m m mj mj me me am am ma ma jam jam ham ham make
2 m mj mj am am jam jam ham ham dam dam map map same
3 to me; am to; a ham; a man; a map; an amp; has jam

Learn x

4 s x x xs xs sx ox ox ax ax six six fix fix fox fox
5 xs xs sx sx ox ox fix fix nix nix fox fox lax flax
6 a fox; an ox; to fix; is lax; at six; to fix an ax

Combine m and x

7 m x mx am ox me ax jam six ham fox men lax fix mix
8 a fox; a jam; a mix; am lax; six men; to me at six
9 Pam can mix a ham salad; Max can fix soup for six.

TS

13c ▶ 4 Review Spacing with Punctuation

each line once DS

▽ Do not space after an internal period in an abbreviation.

1 Mae has a Ph.D. from Miami; Dex will get his Ed.D.
2 J. D. Marx will go to St. Croix in March with Lex.
3 Ms. Fox is to send to me this week six maps c.o.d.

TS

284b-287b (continued)

Document 2
General Guidelines

Mr. Mason gives you the following instructions: "These guidelines were prepared by Mark P. Byers, an accounting assistant, at the request of Faith D. Leary, one of the major partners.

"The guidelines will become page 37 of the firm's *Standard Operating Procedures Manual*, which is bound at the left."

GENERAL GUIDELINES FOR ANALYZING AN ACCOUNTING SYSTEM

1. Has the authority and responsibility for the system been clearly ~~designed~~ defined and assigned to one ~~person~~ individual in a major organizational ~~element~~ unit?

2. Is the system an ~~important~~ integral part of the overall ~~or~~ organizational structure?

3. Does the system provide ~~executives~~ managers with the data they need to make ~~efficient~~ effective decisions?

4. Does the system make an important contribution to the financial ~~aims~~ objectives of the organization?

5. Is the system relatively simple, easy to understand, and easy to ~~use~~ utilize?

6. Have standard accounting methods been established?

7. Have written procedures been ~~devised~~ developed to guide all personnel in the performance of there duties?

8. Does the system ~~provide for~~ include a training program to insure that all personel understand ~~and follow~~ standard accounting methods?

9. Does the system include checks and balances so that deviations from established practice will be detected quickly?

10. Is the system the most affective one for ~~the~~ current operations?

11. Will the system meet the future ~~demands~~ needs of the organization?

12. What suggestions do managerial and operational pesonnel have for improving the system?

13d ▶ 20
Improve Keyboarding Technique

each pair of lines twice SS (slowly, then faster); DS between 4-line groups; if time permits, practice selected lines again

Goals

- reach *up* without moving hands away from you
- reach *down* without moving hands toward your body
- quick-snap keystrokes

3d/1st rows

```
1 ox me ax ma be fix can box map but six man hex hem
2 am nix cut bomb name fans came gnat plan form comb
```

space bar

```
3 am to an is of me us do if ma or en em bun sum gem
4 an and lob hem din fob sum fun rob man cab fan lab
```

key words

```
5 us do if an me big cut sow pep has jam oak rub lax
6 just work name form born flax curl high dope rough
```

key phrases

```
7 is big|to jam|if she|for me|an end|or lap|is to be
8 to cut|and fix|the call|for work|and such|big firm
```

all keys learned

```
9 Bix left for camp last week; Judith is to go soon.
10 Jamie knew he could fix an old speed bike for Peg.
```

Lesson 14 Y and Z

Line length: 50 spaces
Spacing: single-space (SS)

14a ▶ 8
Conditioning Practice

each line twice SS (slowly, then faster); DS between 2-line groups; if time permits, practice each line again

Goals

- curved, upright fingers
- quiet hands and arms
- steady keystroking pace

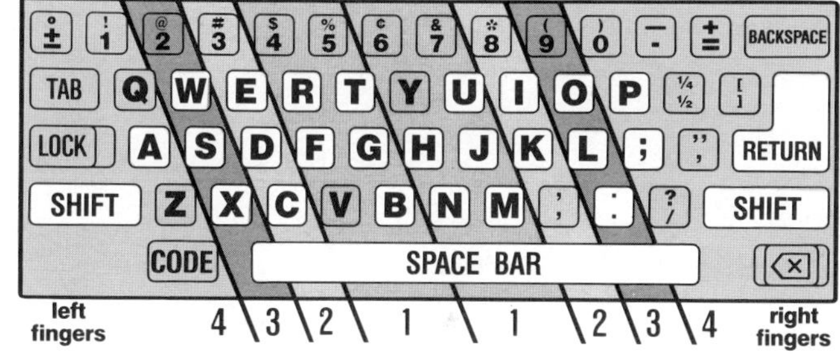

All letters learned

```
1 if do us pa go me an is to he am or in we no be ax
2 of lace|so when|or just|of work|to sign|is to form
3 Herb Roe can win a gold cup for the six ski jumps.
```

TS

14b ▶ 6
Improve Return Technique

Each 2-line sentence once as "Return" is called each 30 seconds (30″).

Goal: To reach the end of each line just as the 30″ guide ("Return") is called.

Note: The 30″ *gwam* scale shows gross words a minute if you reach the end of each line as the 30″ guide is called.

Eyes on copy as you return

	gwam 30″	20″
1 Amber was to pick a slow pace	12	18
2 and then work up to top speed.	12	18
3 Alex has worked for her as a sales	14	21
4 clerk in the shop since last March.	14	21
5 Mae sang a solo at the last music show;	16	24
6 Cam joins her in a duet in the next one.	16	24
7 Bo is to work for a big auto firm this fall;	18	27
8 his job is to check cars coming off the line.	18	27

TS

Unit 64 Lessons 284-287

Learning Goals

1. To acquaint you with some of the special documents produced in an accounting office.

2. To improve your skill in keyboarding figures and commonly used symbols.

Documents Processed

1. Letter
2. General Guidelines (leftbound report)
3. Budget Projections
4. Schedule of Depreciation
5. Letter of Transmittal
6. Letter of Audit
7. Income Tax Form: Schedules A & B

Lessons 284-287

284a-287a Check Equipment

65-space line

Before you begin work each day, check your machine to see that it is in good working order by keyboarding the paragraph at the right at least twice (first slowly, then faster).

all letters/figures used

Vera will adjust and fix prices quickly if the embargo is set on zinc oxide. On 9/21, the price was $16.59; on 10/17, the price was $18.34 -- a difference of $1.75. If the audit of the proficient panel is right, they may then suspend the penalty of the provisos.

| 1 | 2 | 3 | 4 | 5 | 6 | 7 | 8 | 9 | 10 | 11 | 12 | 13 |

284b-287b ▶ 45 Document Processing

You have been assigned by Modern Office Tempos to work in the Information Processing Department of **Temple Accounting Services, 3540 King Street, Alexandria, VA 22302-6187.** Temple Accounting Services prepares taxes, budgets, audits, and financial statements for individuals and businesses. You will work under the direct supervision of Vincent C. Mason, Chief of the Department. If you are not given specific directions for preparing a document, use your best judgment.

Document 1
Letter
(LM p. 185)

Instructions from Mr. Mason: "Ms. Stephanie Mihalic, President of **Old Dominion Corporation, 1200 S. Court House Road, Arlington, VA 22204-2126,** in a letter dated July 20, has requested information about the services we provide.

"Prepare the letter at the right in reply dated July 25. List numbered items. Frank T. Davis, CPA, will sign the letter."

Temple Accounting Services appreciates your interest in our firm, and we are prepared ~~qualified~~ to assist you in any aspect ~~area~~ of the accounting field. Here are a few of the majer services we offer: 1. Devise and impliment a general accounting system tailored to meet your needs 2. Audit your present accounting system to insure complience with State state and federal ~~lations~~ regulations 3. Devise and install a tax system and prepare all necessary ~~essential~~ tax returns 4. Develope and install a budget ing system ~~procedure~~ to help insure effective use of yoeur resources 5. Devise and impliment a system which will provide ~~determine~~ detailed data costs as a basis for increasing operational efficiency

The resources of our entire staff are ready to meet your accounting needs. Our costs are moderate and are based on the time ~~hours~~ and complexety of the service ~~work~~ we provide ~~perform~~.

Please tell us ~~let us know~~ which services you require, ~~need~~ and we shall develop a system for you. Simply ~~Just~~ dial 415-7000 and ask for me.

14c ▶ 18
Learn Y and Z

each line twice SS (slowly, then faster); DS between 2-line groups; if time permits, practice selected lines again

Follow the Standard Plan for Learning New Keys outlined on page 7.

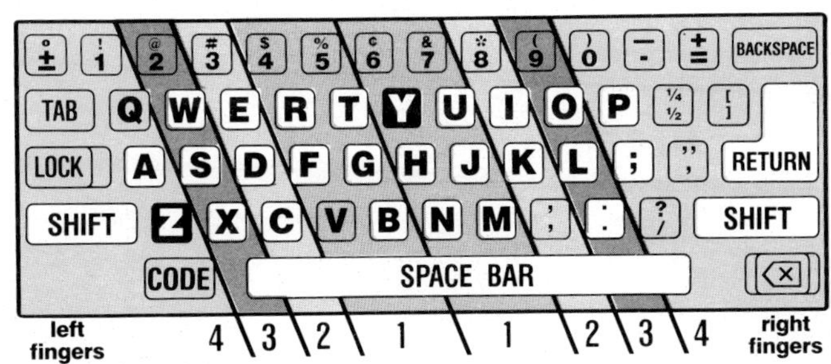

Reach technique for y

Reach technique for z

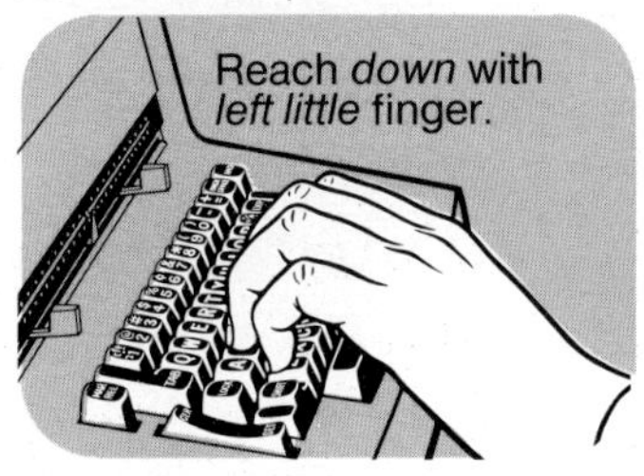

Learn y

1 j y y yj yj jy jay jay lay lay hay hay day day may
2 y yj yj ja jay jay eye eye yes yes yet yet dye dye
3 a jay; an eye; to pay; he may; you say; you may be

Learn z

4 a z z za za zoo zoo zap zap oz. oz. zone zone maze
5 z z za za zap zap zoo zoo zed zed zag zag zip zips
6 an adz; to zap; zip it; the zoo; zap it; eight oz.

Combine y and z

7 y z zy jay zap eye zoo yes zip boy zag you adz yet
8 to zip; an eye; an adz; to you; the boy; by a zoo;
9 Liz likes a hazy day for a lazy trip to buy pizza.

TS

14d ▶ 18
Improve Keyboarding Technique

each pair of lines twice SS (slowly, then faster); DS between 4-line groups; if time permits, practice selected lines again

Goals

- Reach *up* without moving hands away from you
- Reach *down* without moving hands toward your body
- use quick-snap keystrokes

1st/3d rows
1 ox an oz. mix net may cut buy zoo ten icy win size
2 Roz and Pixie may catch a bus; you can go by bike.

space bar
3 an by ran buy dim any sky form sign corn many from
4 Ann is to jog with me to the city park by the zoo.

key words
5 an the for own six you led zoo but jam cup got irk
6 city firm next zone both land work turn pick eight

key phrases
7 to be | is dim | to zip | fix it | of coal | if both | to lend
8 is to pay | buy the lamp | owns the land | does the work

all letters learned
9 Doug will pack sixty pints of prize jams for Beth.
10 Makuzi has sixty jobs he can get done for low pay.

280b-283b (continued)

Document 6
Medical Insurance
Claim Form
(LM p. 183)

Dr. Karl L. Mayes, Suite 301 of the Doctors' Annex, has sent the following message:

"Lee C. Tait was admitted to the Emergency Room on July 17 (see Admissions Register) complaining of severe pains in the lower right quadrant. After an extensive examination, the diagnosis was acute appendicitis.

"The patient was taken immediately to the OR, where I removed the diseased appendix.

"On July 20, after a limited medical examination in his hospital room, I discharged him.

"Please submit the necessary claim to his insurer, DELTA, 4239 Farnam Street, Omaha, NE 68131-1403 for the extensive examination ($150), and the operation ($680)."

Note: ER, OR, and other charges will be billed by the hospital. Refer to previous documents for information necessary to complete this form.

MEDICAL INSURANCE CLAIM FORM

_____ ALPHAMED _____ AMCARE OTHER: DELTA

1. PATIENT'S NAME (Last, First and Initial): TAIT, LEE C.
2. DATE OF BIRTH Mo. Day Yr.: 9 7 72
3. SEX (1) M X (2) F ____
4. GROUP NUMBER: C-723049
5. AGREEMENT NO., (Including Alpha Prefix): DELTA 8706-1
6. APPLICANT- SUBSCRIBER'S NAME (Last, First and Initial) ADDRESS (Including City, State and ZIP Code)
7. RELATIONSHIP OF PATIENT TO APPLICANT- SUBSCRIBER (1) Self X (2) Spouse ____ (3) Dependent ____ (4) Other ____
8. WAS INJURY OR CONDITION RELATED TO: (1) PATIENT'S EMPLOYMENT ____ (3) AUTO ACCIDENT ____ (2) NEITHER EMPLOYMENT NOR AUTO X (4) BOTH EMPLOYMENT AND AUTO ____
9. DOES THIS PATIENT HAVE OTHER HEALTH INSURANCE? (1) Yes ____ (2) No X
MEDICARE PART B? (1) Yes ____ (2) No X
10. TYPE OF SERVICE Specify by Code 532 901
11A. DIAGNOSIS / SYMPTOMS (if more than one, relate each by reference to line 1,2,3, etc. in Description of Services)
11B. DATE OF INJURY OR ONSET OF ILLNESS IF APPLICABLE / IF MATERNITY LMP Mo. Day Yr.

12A. DATES OF SERVICE Mo. Day Yr.	12B. PLACE CODE	12C. KEY CODE	12D. PROCEDURE CODE	DESCRIPTION OF SERVICES - ITEMIZE (if unusual or complicated describe in detail)	12E. ITEMIZED CHARGES
(1)					
(2)					
(3)					
(4)					
(5)					

PLACE CODES: 01- Hospital (Inpatient) ____ 02- Clinical (Outpatient) ____ 03- Doctor's Office ____ 04- Ambulance ____ 05- Emergency Room ____ 06- Laboratory ____ 07- Physical Therapy ____ 08- Operating Room ____

13. HOME/OFFICE VISIT IF PATIENT ABSENT FROM WORK DUE TO ABOVE CONDITION PLEASE INDICATE
Last Day Worked MO / DAY / YR ____
Date Patient Returned To Work MO / DAY / YR ____
Did Condition Leave Patient Totally Disabled? Yes ____ No ____

14. FOR HOSPITAL CASES
Date Admitted MO / DAY / YR ____
Date Discharged MO / DAY / YR ____

15. HAS FEE BEEN PAID? (1) Yes ____ (2) No ____

16. DID ANOTHER DOCTOR PARTICIPATE IN THIS CASE? (1) Yes ____ (2) No ____ If Yes, Complete Applicable Items Below
(1) Surgeon ____ Name of Operation ____ Date Mo Day Yr
(2) Consultant ____ Specialty ____
(3) Medical ____ Medical Diagnosis ____
(4) Other WAYNE C. WALSH, R.N. Type of Service OR NURSE 7/17/19--

17. DOCTOR'S NAME, ADDRESS AND ZIP CODE

18. I CERTIFY THAT I AM LEGALLY QUALIFIED TO PERFORM THE REPORTED SERVICES AND THAT THEY WERE PERFORMED:
(1) A. X By Me Personally
(2) B. ____ By Me And My Associate in This Case, Dr. ____, personally
C. X Under My Supervision And in My Presence By A
____ (3) Resident ____ (4) Intern X (5) Registered Nurse ____ (6) Registered Nurse Anesthetist
(7) D. ____ Under My Supervision, But Not in My Presence By A
____ Resident ____ Intern ____ Registered Nurse ____ Registered Nurse Anesthetist
(No payment will be made for services listed in Section D)

I agree that I will accept as full payment the lesser of my charge as shown hereon, or the amount payable according to the applicable Fee Schedule Program (for under-income Subscribers) or Prevailing Fee Program

19. SIGNED ____ DPM ____ DDS ____ DO ____ MD ____

20. TELEPHONE NUMBER (Including Area Code)

FOR INSURER'S USE ONLY

Eff. Date	Plan	Type	Cov.		Procedure	Vis-Tr	Action	Diag.	App. Amt.
BASIC				(1)					
DIAGNOSTIC				(2)					
AMT. OF ADJ.	Date	Clerk	Control	(3)					
Explanation:				(4)					
Medical Director:			7A- 1/86	(5)					

Lesson 15 — Q and , (Comma)

Line length: 50 spaces
Spacing: single-space (SS)

15a ▶ 8
Conditioning Practice

each line twice SS (slowly, then faster); DS between 2-line groups; if time permits, practice each line again

All letters learned

1 ox had zoo but jam ski got for men pay low sic you
2 by the oz.; pay the zoo; buy the adz; the hazy day
3 Marj had kept a sly tab on cut wages of six zones.
TS

15b ▶ 18
Learn Q and ,

each line twice SS (slowly, then faster); DS between 2-line groups; if time permits, practice selected lines again

Follow the Standard Plan for Learning New Keys outlined on page 7.

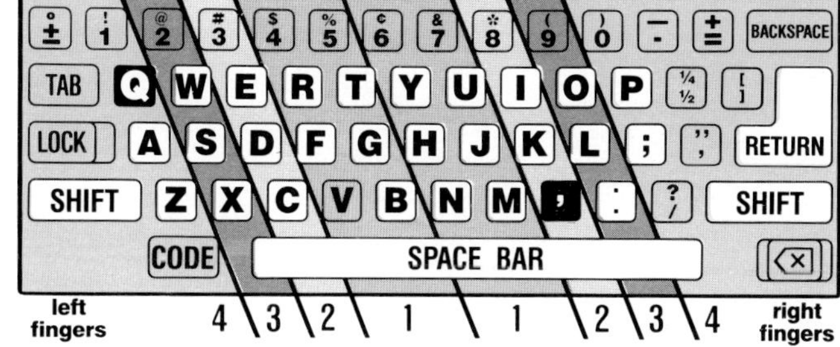

Reach technique for q

Reach technique for , (comma)

Reach *down* with *right second* finger; space once after , used as punctuation.

Learn Q

1 a q q qa qa aq quo quo qt. qt. quit quit quay quay
2 q q qa qa qw quo quo quit quit aqua aqua quiz quiz
3 a qt.; a quiz; to quit; pro quo; the quay; to quiz

Learn , (comma)

4 k , , ,k ,k kit, kit; Jan, Kit, or I will go, too.
5 a ski, a ski; a kit, a kit; a bike, a bike; to ski
6 Ike, go to work with Shep; Sue, stay here with me.

Combine Q and ,

7 Key in the words quo, quit, quiz, quay, and quite.
8 I quit the quiz show, Quen. Jaques has quit, too.
9 Quig, Raquel, and Quincy will quit the squad soon.
TS

15c ▶ 4
Review Spacing with Punctuation

each line once DS

▽ Space once after comma used as punctuation.

1 Aqua means water, Rico; it is a unique blue, also.

2 R. J. used oz. for ounce and qt. for quart, I see.

3 Send the books c.o.d. to Dr. Su at the Quinta Inn.
TS

280b-283b (continued)

Document 4
Medical Letter (continued)

Mr. Ryan T. Winslow
Page 2 9
July 17, 19--

On August 7, I shall meet with you to discuss review in detail the findings of the tests and the recomendations of the physicians who examined you. We shall consider at that tiem the treatment recomended and any surgexical procedures that may be necessary. You will be free, of course, to obtain a second opinion on these recommendations if you so desire.

I have provided you with a detailed explaination of the treatment you will recieve at the Center in order to alleviate any apprehension you may have regarding the examination. If you should have any questions regarding any of the procedures, please call Dr. Joel M. Rafferty, one of my assistants, who is familier with your case. In the meantime, will you sign please sign the inclosed Authorization and Release Form and return it to me by mail.

Sincerely yours

Joseph Palmiscino, M.D.

Document 5
Authorization and Release Form
(LM p. 181)

The General Medical Center is awaiting the delivery of a shipment of *Authorization and Release Forms* from the printer. In the meantime, Mrs. Upcraft provides these instructions: "Keyboard a master copy of the *Authorization and Release Form* on General Medical Center letterhead. Start on line 12; DS the body of the form. Use a 6-inch line; DS twice after the body and then keyboard the lines for the date and the signature. Enclose a copy in Dr. Palmiscino's letter (Document 4)."

I, (leave about 25 spaces for name), hereby authorize the General Medical Center to perform any and all tests deemed medically necessary for the comprehensive physical examination I shall undergo from (leave about 20 spaces for date). I hereby release the General Medical Center from all legal consequences as the result of any inadvertent negative reactions which may occur as a result of any test which is properly conducted.

I hereby authorize my insurance benefits to be paid directly to the General Medical Center and certify that I am financially responsible for any service that is not covered by my insurance. I also authorize the Center to release any information necessary to process claims for reimbursement.

__________________ ________________________
Date Signature

15d ▶ 20 Improve Keyboarding Technique

each pair of lines twice SS (slowly, then faster); DS between 4-line groups; if time permits, practice selected lines again

Goals

- keep fingers curved, upright
- reach the third and fourth fingers without twisting the wrists outward
- use quick down-and-in spacing

1st/2d fingers	1	fit her met dim bin tic but bug yet city kick rich
	2	if he|in it|my fur|the jet|met her|cut him|but get
3d/4th fingers	3	ap. aq. oz. ox as lox pal was zap paw all low also
	4	a zoo; a paw; lax law; all saw; so slow; was also;
key phrases	5	of us|of all|is to go|if he is|it is due|to pay us
	6	if we did|up to you|if we aid|is of age|she saw me
space bar	7	Al is to go to the firm for the pay due the clerk.
	8	Jan is to go by bus to the town to audit the firm.
all letters learned	9	Zampf did log quick trips by jet to the six towns.
	10	Jantz will fix my pool deck if the big rain quits.

Lesson 16 Review

Line length: 50 spaces
Spacing: single-space (SS)

16a ▶ 8 Conditioning Practice

each line twice SS (slowly, then faster); DS between 2-line groups; if time permits, practice each line again

Goals

- curved, upright fingers
- quiet hands and arms
- steady keystroking pace

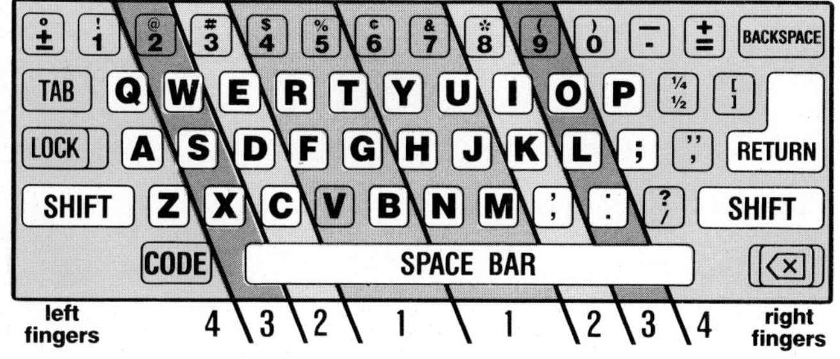

all letters learned	1	Jorgie plans to find that mosque by six with Zack.
shift keys	2	Maria Paso had a tea for Dr. and Mrs. Ruiz in Rio.
easy sentence	3	He is to work with us if he is right for the work.
5-stroke words		| 1 | 2 | 3 | 4 | 5 | 6 | 7 | 8 | 9 | 10 |

TS

16b ▶ 10 Type (Key) Block Paragraphs

each paragraph (¶) once SS as shown; DS between ¶s; at your teacher's direction, take a 1-minute (1′) writing on each ¶; find your rate in *gwam*

> To determine your speed in *gwam* (gross words a minute):
>
> **1.** Note the figure at the end of your last complete line.
>
> **2.** Note from the scale under the ¶s the figure below where you stopped in a partial line.
>
> **3.** Add the two figures; the resulting number is your *gwam*.

Paragraph 1 *gwam 1′*

Do not stop at the end of the line before you make 10
a return. Keep up your pace at the end of a line, 20
and return quickly after you strike the final key. 30

DS

Paragraph 2

Make the return with a quick motion, and begin the 10
next line with almost no pause. Keep your eyes on 20
your copy as you return to cut time between lines. 30

gwam 1′ | 1 | 2 | 3 | 4 | 5 | 6 | 7 | 8 | 9 | 10 |

280b-283b (continued)

Document 4
Medical Letter
(LM p. 179)

Instructions from Mrs. Upcraft: "Dr. Palmiscino, who is Chief of Professional Services, prefers to have his correspondence prepared in the modified block style with paragraphs indented using a 6-inch line. Prepare the letter for his signature; date the letter July 19, 19--."

Mr. Ryan T. Winslow
6901 Old Keene Mill Road
Springfield, VA 22150-5038

Dear Mr. Winslow

As we agreed in our telephone conversation on July 17, you will begin your ~~complete~~ comprehensive physical examinatoin at the General Medical Center on August 4. We ~~expect~~ anticipate that the examination will ~~consume~~ take at least ~~three~~ four days so that we shall be able to ~~determine~~ ascertain your overall physical, mental, and emotional ~~condition~~ status and to determine presisely the cause of the problems you have been ~~having~~ experiencing.

Please report to the Admissions office of the Center no later than ~~3~~ 2 p. m. on August 4. After you have been admitted, a member of our staff will ~~ask you for~~ record your complete medical history. If you have any previuos Medical records or reports, please bring them with you. The remainder of the day will be spent preparing you for the tests, which will be administered the following day.

On August 5, you will ~~take~~ under go a series of laboratory tests including an EKG, EEG, a CAT Scan, and a complete series of X rays and blood tests. The results of these tests will be entered in to the computer and will be examined seperately by the specialists in radiology, gastroenterology, and internal medecine. Each specialist will perpare an analysis of the reports.

On August 6, you will be interviewed and examined by three ~~experts~~ specialists. After these physicians have completed their separate examinations, they will synthesize their findings and enter the data into the computer. That after noon, they will hold a staff conference to ~~study~~ review the results of the tests and their examinations. At that time, they will decide ~~if~~ whether ~~or not~~ additional tests or examinations are ~~considered~~ necesary.

On August 7, you will undergo a complete series of tests and examinations by a team of clinical phycholoigsts who will compile a profile of your mental and emotional condition. You will also undergo any aditional physical tests that the specialists decide are necessary. All of these data will be entered into the computer. The computer will then prepare a detailed analysis of your condition and, based on a special program, will reach a consensus regarding your condition and make specific recomendations for further treatment.

16c ▶ 12
Build Keyboarding Skill: Space Bar/ Shift Keys

each line twice SS; DS between 2-line groups

Goals

- to reduce the time used between words
- to reduce the time taken to shift/ type/release when making capital letters

Down-and-in spacing

Out-and-down shifting

Space bar (Space *immediately* after each word.)

1 of an if us to me is am so pan urn may own buy jam

2 am to pay|he may own|for a day|is to buy|a new law

3 I may go to the city to pay the firm for the sign.

Shift keys (Shift; strike key; release both quickly.)

4 Cory and Lara went with Jose and Rosa to San Juan.

5 Maria Eppel is at school in Miami with Susie Quan.

6 Max, Raul, and I may see Aida or Luis in San Jose.

TS

16d ▶ 10
Improve Keystroking Skill

each line twice SS (slowly, then faster); DS after each 2-line group

Goals

- quick-snap keystrokes
- quick joining of letters to form words
- quick joining of words to form phrases

Key words and phrases (*Think, say,* and *key* words and phrases.)

1 them with they make than such when both then their

2 to risk|both of|sign it|but then|and when|too busy

3 an oak box|for the city|such a risk|six of the men

All letters learned (Strike keys at a brisk, steady pace.)

4 size next help jack went same form quit body signs

5 Gus Zia packed the box with quail and jam for you.

6 Quig can ski with Lex Zemp but just for four days.

TS

16e ▶ 10
Check Keyboarding Skill

1. Take a 30-second (30") timed writing on each line. Your rate in gross words a minute (*gwam*) is shown word for word above the lines.

2. If time permits, take another 30" writing on each line. Try to increase your keyboarding speed.

Goal

At least 18 *gwam*.

30" *gwam*

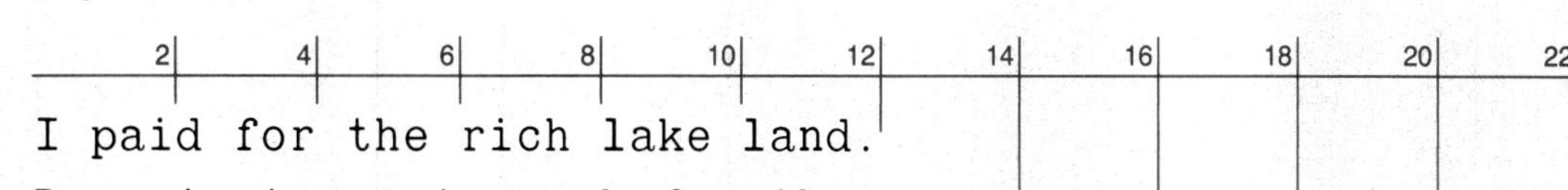

1 I paid for the rich lake land.

2 Dana is to go to work for them now.

3 Zoe is to pay half price for an old urn.

4 Jack docks his boat next to ours at the quay.

5 You must keep up the good work if you want to win.

6 Size up a job and work at it with all the zeal you can.

| 2 | 4 | 6 | 8 | 10 | 12 | 14 | 16 | 18 | 20 | 22

If you finish a line before time is called and start over, your *gwam* is the figure at the end of the line PLUS the figure above or below the point at which you stopped.

280b-283b (continued)

Document 3
Patient Evaluation
(LM p. 177)

Directions from Dr. Ortiz: "Keyboard the patient evaluation in final form DS."

DATE: *July 18, 19--*

PATIENT: *Elizabeth L. Taylor*

PHYSICIAN: *Lisa J. Ortiz, Chief of Ophthalmology*

Patient is an 85-year old *Caucasian* ~~white~~ female in *excellent* ~~good~~ health who complained that she was having reading difficulty. A complete evalation *including refraction* revealed that her best correctabled vision *is* ~~was~~ 20/400 in *the* ~~her~~ right eye and 20/200 in the left eye. She is astigmatic, but was adviced that she did not need new glasses *because of a prescription change.*

A slit lamp microscopic examination *revealed* ~~showed~~ early cataracts due to age rather than disease, medecation, radiation, etc. They should ripen slowly and surgery will not *be required* ~~indicated~~ for quiet a few years.

Fundus examination of the back of the eye revealed a *mild* degree of macular degeneration compatable with age. Patient was *advised* ~~told~~ that this condition might make it difficult to read, but that her mobility or independance would not be impared. No treatment is *available* ~~needed~~ fort this common finding.

A glaucoma pressure test was normal.

In summary, patients' over-all eye health has been good. The findings *cited* ~~mentioned~~ above are not unusual and should not interfere with her normal activities such as painting, sewing, television, and reading *with the aid of a magnifying glass for small print.*

Follow-up will be made in *approximately* ~~about~~ 2 years.

Lesson 17 V and : (Colon)

Line length: 50 spaces
Spacing: single-space (SS)

17a ▶ 8 Conditioning Practice

1. Each line twice SS (slowly; then faster); DS between 2-line groups.

2. If time permits, take three 1′ writings on line 3; find *gwam* (total 5-stroke words typed or keyed): words in complete line PLUS words in a partial line.

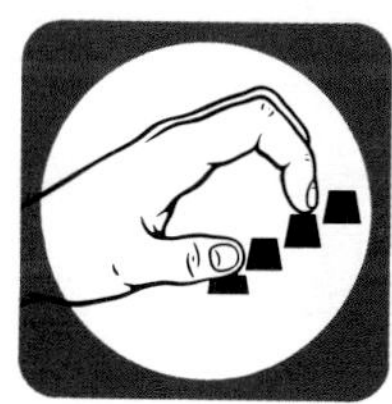

Curved, upright fingers

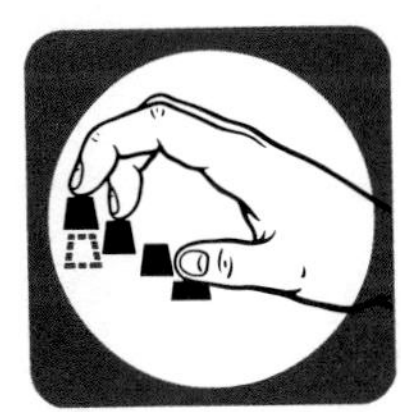

Finger-action keystroking

all letters learned	1	Lyn was quick to get the next major prize for Deb.
space bar	2	to own|is busy|if they|to town|by them|to the city
easy sentence	3	She is to go to the city with us to sign the form.

5-stroke words | 1 | 2 | 3 | 4 | 5 | 6 | 7 | 8 | 9 | 10 |

17b ▶ 20 Learn V and : (colon)

each line twice SS (slowly; then faster); DS between 2-line groups; if time permits practice selected lines again

Follow the Standard Plan for Learning New Keys outlined on page 7.

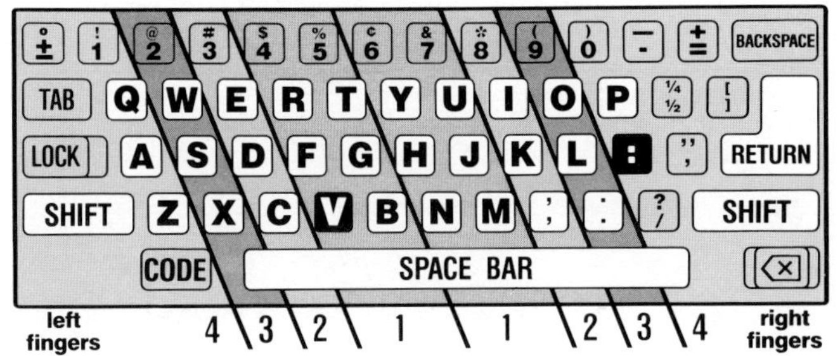

Reach technique for v

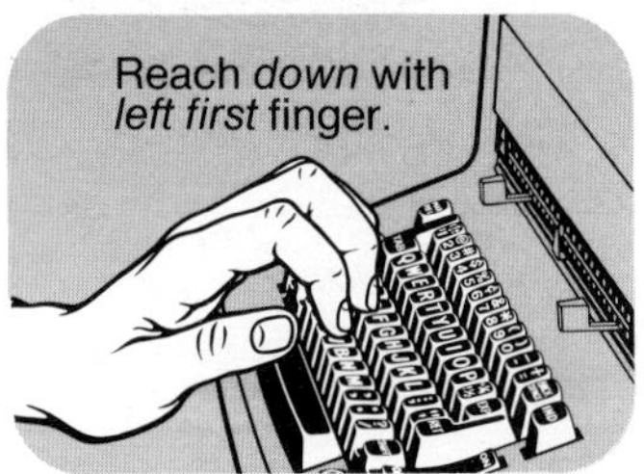

Reach technique for : (colon)

Left shift and strike ; key; space twice after : used as punctuation.

Learn V

1 f v v vf vf fv via via vie vie have have five five

2 v v vf vf live live have have view view dive dives

3 go via; vie for; has vim; a view; or have; to live

Learn : (colon)

4 ; : : :; :; To: From: Date: Name: Time: File:

5 ; :; :; In re: Reply to: Dear Jo: Shift for a :

6 Two spaces follow a colon, thus: Try these steps:

Combine V and :

7 Vic: Enter via, view, and have five times for me.

8 Marv read: Shift to enter : and then space twice.

9 Vi, key the right word: let or leave; then go on.

10 Vida has a micro with the : where the ; should be.

Language Skills Notes

- Space twice after : used as punctuation.
- Capitalize the first word of a complete sentence following a colon.

280b-283b (continued)

Document 2
Medical Forms
(LM pp. 171-175)

Mrs. Upcraft has given you a sample copy of a Patient Identification Card and a part of a computer printout which shows the names of some of the patients admitted on July 17, 19--. Her directions: "Using the sample copy as a guide, please keyboard an ID Card for each patient on the printout. Use the service codes to determine the place and type of service.

GENERAL MEDICAL CENTER
1600 16th Street NW
Washington, DC 20009-4500

IDENTIFICATION NO. 841-402 DATE OF ADMISSION July 17, 19--

NAME OF PATIENT Kuhn (Last) Arlene (First) M. (MI)

ADDRESS 2103 H Street, NW (Street) Washington, (City) DC (State) 20037-3410 (Zip)

PLACE OF SERVICE Hospital (Inpatient)

TYPE OF SERVICE(S) Major Surgery

NAME OF PHYSICIAN Carla L. Quinn, MD

MEDICAL INSURER Federal Ins. Co. AGREEMENT NUMBER CX90921

GROUP NUMBER 14-1-276

REMARKS: allergic to penicillin

ADMISSIONS REGISTER FOR JULY 17, 19--

I.D. NO.	NAME/ADDRESS	PLACE	SVC	PHYSICIAN	INSURER/NUMBER
94-1	RAY T. BURNS 80 MONROE ST ROCKVILLE, MD 20850-2319	06	852	LEVI T. GROSS, MD	AMCARE 90145 GROUP: T5610
94-2	MARY T. MILLS P.O. Box 276 WHEATON, MD 20902-3415	03	531 603	JEAN L. BARNES, MD	ALPHAMED 6-4520 GROUP: 798-A-21
94-3	LEE C. TAIT 20 ELM ST SUITLAND, MD 20746-3200	05 08	532 901	KARL L. MAYES, MD	DELTA 8706-1 GROUP: C-723049
94-4	RALPH M. KING 1120 MILL RD, NW WASHINGTON, DC 20007-3252	02	603	NOLA C. SHAW, OD	AMCARE 89536 GROUP: 12876X
94-5	VERA K. ROSE 10102 FOREST AVE FAIRFAX, VA 22032-4870	01	533 602	ALI N. AMADI, MD	METCO 61952A GROUP: TC-457L
94-6	ALICE L. DUPONT 18 LANGLEY CT, NW WASHINGTON, DC 20016-6549	02	840	KAREN N. SILVER, MD	AMCARE 90345 GROUP: T7390

17c ▶ 22
Improve Keyboarding Technique

each pair of lines twice SS (slowly; then faster); DS between 4-line groups; if time permits, practice selected lines again

q/v
1 via qua vow quo have quit move quiz vote aqua live
2 Viva has quit the squad to move to Quebec to live.

y/x
3 by ox you fix yes mix any six try fox say lax boys
4 Xica, you and the boys are to fix my mixer by six.

key words
5 by bid map key bit fix die end tie apt ivy ale wig
6 paid fuel maps soap born laid rush duty pens chair

key phrases
7 key it|apt to|lay it|to fix|an end|to tie|due them
8 she got it|key the name|fix the sign|boot the disk

easy sentences
9 He is to pay the man for the work and sign a form.
10 Lana is due by six and may go to the city with us.

all letters
11 am quo box can via jar zoo sip owl the dug oak fly
12 Glenda saw a quick red fox jump over the lazy cub.

Lesson 18 — SHIFT LOCK and ? (Question Mark)

Line length: 50 spaces
Spacing: single-space (SS)

18a ▶ 8
Conditioning Practice

each line twice SS (slowly; then faster); DS between 2-line groups; if time permits, practice selected lines again

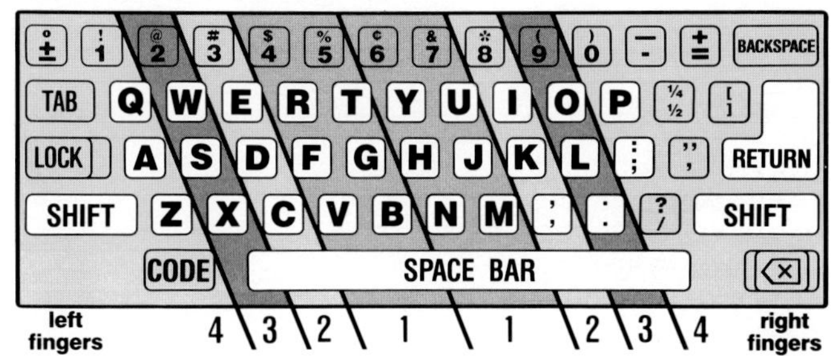

all letters 1 Bev aims next to play a quick game with Jud Fritz.

v and : 2 To: Miss Val Devlin; From: Dr. Silvia J. Vicars.

easy sentence 3 He is to go to the town and to do the work for me.

18b ▶ 5
Type (Key) Block Paragraphs

each paragraph (¶) once SS as shown; DS between ¶s; if time permits, practice ¶ 1 again

If you take a 1′ timed writing, see 16b, page 29, for the steps to find *gwam*.

Paragraph 1 *gwam 1′*

You know all the letters now, so keep up the good 10
work. Just pick a new goal each day, and work in 20
the correct way to gain it. Good form is the way. 30

Paragraph 2

First, set a goal that is easy to gain; next, try 10
one that will push you a bit to reach. Speed can 20
grow only if you force the rate and use good form. 30

gwam 1′ | 1 | 2 | 3 | 4 | 5 | 6 | 7 | 8 | 9 | 10 |

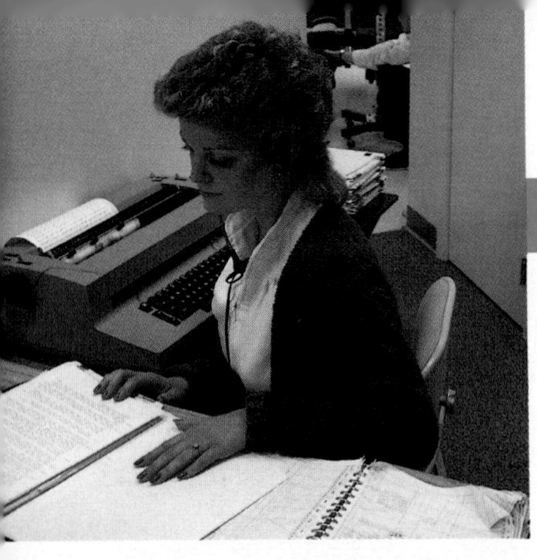

Unit 63 Lessons 280-283

Learning Goals

1. To familiarize you with duties performed in a medical facility.
2. To improve your skill in planning, organizing, and preparing special documents.

Documents Processed

1. Table of Service Codes
2. Medical Forms
3. Patient Evaluation
4. Medical Letter
5. Authorization and Release Forms
6. Medical Insurance Claim Form

Lessons 280-283

280a-283a ▶ 5 Check Equipment

Before you begin work each day, check your machine to see that it is in good working order by keyboarding the paragraph at the right at least twice (first slowly, then faster).

all letters/figures used

Jacques explained why he memorized the various passages from the book. For his presentations on March 19 and 20, he wants six quotes from pages 136, 157, and 184. With a vivid title and formal theme, he may dispel the skepticism of the men of this panel.

| 1 | 2 | 3 | 4 | 5 | 6 | 7 | 8 | 9 | 10 | 11 | 12 | 13 |

280b-283b ▶ 45 Document Processing

You have been assigned by Modern Office Tempos to work temporarily in the **General Medical Center, 1600 16th Street, NW, Washington, DC 20009-4500**. The Center includes a hospital for inpatient treatment, a large clinic for outpatient services, and an annex for doctors' offices.

You will work in the Patient Information Section of the Administrative Division under the direction of Mrs. Lillian Upcraft, the Word Processing Supervisor. If you are not given specific directions for preparing a document, use your best judgment.

Document 1
Service Codes

Mrs. Upcraft asks you to prepare in final form the new service codes which will be used to identify the type of service and the location where service is provided to patients. Mrs. Upcraft says, "DS the material; keyboard the secondary headings as side headings."

SERVICE CODES

Place ~~Location~~ of Service

01 - Hospital (Inpatient)
02 - Clinic (Outpatient)
03 - Doctor's Office
04 - Ambulence
05 - Emergency Room
06 - Labratory
08 - Operating Room
07 - Physical Therapy

Type of Service

530 - Limited Medical
531 - Intermediate Medical
532 - Extended Medical
533 - Comprehensive Medical
601 - Hospital Facilities
602 - Nurseing Care
603 - Injections
840 - X ray
850 - Blood Analysis
534 - Consultation
851 - EKG
852 - Urinalysis
853 - Culture
900 - Minor Surgery
901 - Major Surgery
902 - Anesthesia
903 - Medication Intravenous
904 - Oral ~~Medicale~~ Medication
905 - Blood Transfusion
999 - Other

18c ▶ 15
Learn SHIFT LOCK and ? (question)

each line twice SS (slowly; then faster); DS between 2-line groups; if time permits, practice each line again

Follow the Standard Plan for Learning New Keys outlined on page 7.

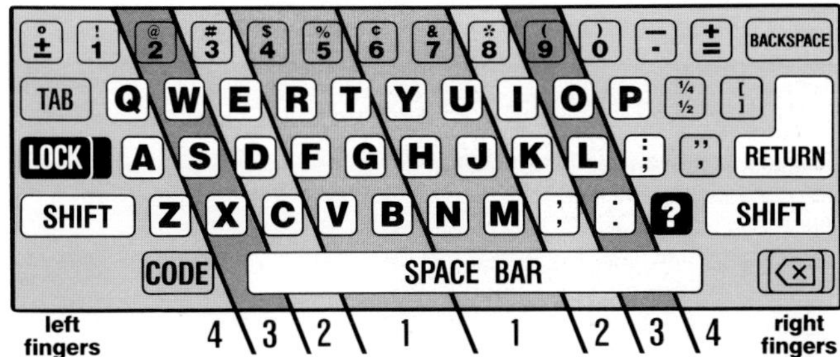

Reach technique for shift lock

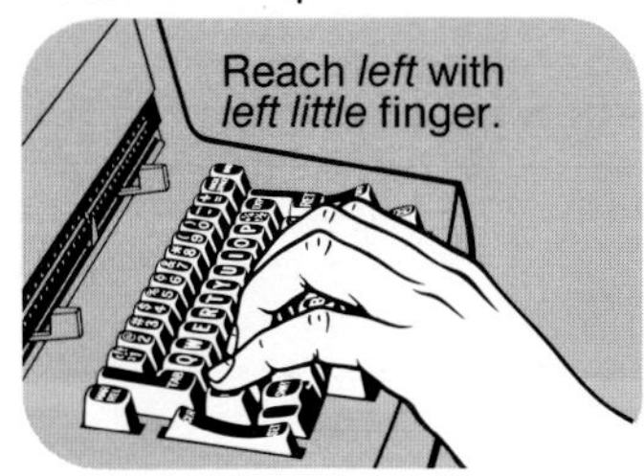

Reach technique for ? (question)

Left shift; reach *down* with *right little* finger; space twice after ? at end of sentence.

Learn SHIFT LOCK

1 The CPA firm said we should explore IRA and Keogh.
2 Jo Ann is sure the VDT showed UPS instead of USPS.
3 Oki joined FBLA when her sister joined PBL at MSU.

Learn ? (question)

Space twice

4 ; ?; ?; Who? Who is? Who is it? Did she not go?
5 Why not? Was it he? Shall we go? Are they here?
6 Is it up to me? Do you have it? Can you do this?

18d ▶ 22
Improving Keyboarding Technique

1. Each pair of lines twice SS (slowly; then faster); DS between 4-line groups.
2. As time permits, take two or three 1′ timed writings on line 12; find *gwam*.

Goals

- reach *up* without moving hands away from you
- reach *down* without moving hands toward your body
- use SHIFT LOCK to make ALL CAPS; strike either shift key to release lock.

LOCK and ?
1 Did she join AMS? Did she also join OEA and DECA?
2 Do you know the ARMA rules? Are they used by TVA?

v and :
3 Harv, look up these words: vex, vial, shiv, cove.
4 Show state names with ZIP Codes thus: VA, WV, VT.

q and ,
5 I missed the words quay, aqua, mosque, and quince.
6 Quentin, Quig, and Jacques passed the quiz, I see.

key words
7 pick they next just bone more wove quiz code flags
8 flax plug quit name wore jack zinc busy vine third

key phrases
9 to aid us | is to pay | or to cut | to fix it | apt to own
10 if we did | to be fit | is on the | to my pay | due at six

all letters
11 Bix Glanz packed my bag with five quarts of juice.

easy sentence
12 He or she is to go to the lake to do the map work.

5-stroke words | 1 | 2 | 3 | 4 | 5 | 6 | 7 | 8 | 9 | 10 |

To find 1′ *gwam*: Add 10 for each line you completed to the scale figure beneath the point at which you stopped in a partial line. The total is your 1′ *gwam*.

276b-279b (continued)

Document 6
Simple Family Will
(LM p. 163)

Mrs. Sherry Myers of Gore, Virginia has requested Mr. Franklin to have a will prepared for her with the following bequests:

"To my son, Jon T. Myers, the sum of $10,000, with the remainder to my husband, Albert C. Myers. In the event my husband should predecease me, my estate shall be distributed to my son."

Using the form at the right as a model, prepare the will as requested. On July 29, Mrs. Myers will visit our office to sign the document.

LAST WILL AND TESTAMENT OF (give full name)

I, (full name) of the City of ______, Commonwealth of ______, being of sound mind and body, make this my last Will and Testament, hereby revoking all former Wills and Codicils.

FIRST: I direct that all my just debts be paid.

SECOND: I give and bequeath to (name of legatee and specific bequest, followed by other legatees, if any, and specific bequests).

THIRD: All the rest, residue and remainder of my estate, real, personal, or mixed, I bequeath to my (husband/wife, followed by name). In the event my husband/wife should predecease me, I declare that my estate shall be distributed (as specified).

FOURTH: I hereby appoint as Executor of my Will the firm of Franklin Legal Services, Arlington, Virginia, to serve without bond.

IN WITNESS WHEREOF, I have hereunto subscribed my name and affixed my seal the _____ day of _________, 19--.

________________________________ (L.S.)

SIGNED, SEALED, PUBLISHED, AND DECLARED BY (name) as (his/her) Last Will and Testament in the presence of us, and we, in (his/her) presence and the presence of each other have hereunto set our names as witnesses.

____

____

Document 7
Form Letters
(LM pp. 165-169)

David T. Schmitt, an attorney on the staff, has requested that you prepare the letter at the right for his signature dated July 12, 19-- to the following people.

Miss Rose T. Channing
7057 Braddock Road
Springfield, VA 22151-4137
Appointment at 9 a.m., July 21.

Mr. Bryan F. Gilbert
4207 Contry Squire Lane
Fairfax, VA 22032-8193
Appointment at 11 a.m., July 21.

Mrs. Alberta T. Irving
7270 Lee Highway
Falls Church, VA 22046-2601
Appointment at 1 p.m., July 21.

The case of Marcy T. Evans vs. Katherine E. Jones is scheduled to begin in Courtroom 2 of Arlington County Courthouse on July 29, 19--. You have been subpoenaed as a witness for the plaintiff, Marcy T. Evans.

Your testimony is extremely important to the outcome of this case. For this reason, we feel it would be advisable for us to meet with you and to review the pertinent points of your testimony.

Will you please meet with us at (time) on (date) in our office in the Lincoln Building. If this time is not a convenient one, please call me so that we can make alternate arrangements.

Lesson 19 Tabulator

Line length: 50 spaces
Spacing: single-space (SS)

19a ▶ 8
Conditioning Practice

each line twice SS (slowly; then faster); DS between 2-line groups; if time permits, practice the lines again

Spacing summary

Space once after , and ; and once after . at end of an abbreviation or following an initial. Space twice after . and **?** at end of sentence. *Do not* space after any punctuation mark that ends a line.

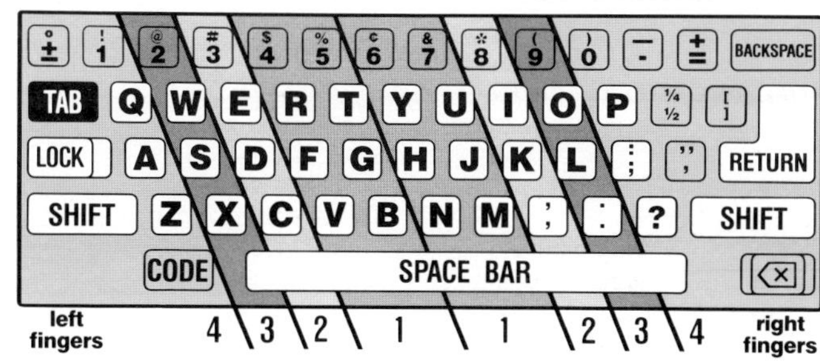

alphabet 1 Buck Zahn will vex the judge if he quits my group.

space bar 2 than busy them city then many sign duty when proxy

easy sentence 3 I am to go to the dock, and he is to work with me.

5-stroke words | 1 | 2 | 3 | 4 | 5 | 6 | 7 | 8 | 9 | 10 |

19b ▶ 12
Learn Tabulator

To clear electric/manual tabs

1. Move carrier to extreme *right* (or carriage to extreme *left*).
2. Hold **clear key (4)** down as you return carrier to extreme *left* (or carriage to extreme *right*) to remove all tab stops.

To clear electronic tabs

1. Depress tab key to move carrier to the tab stop to be cleared.
2. Depress tab clear key to clear the stop.
3. To clear all stops, depress tab clear key, then the repeat key.

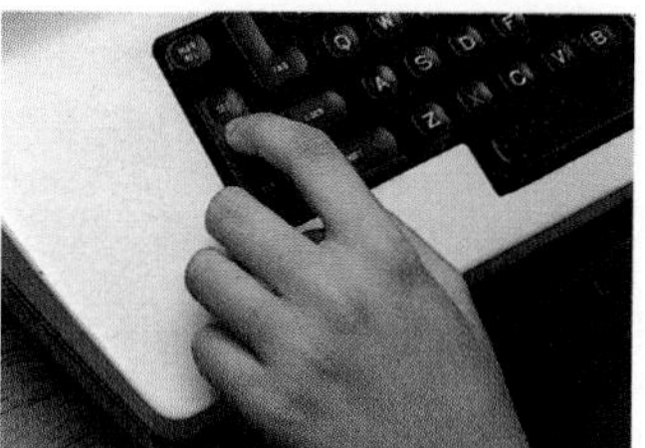

To set tabs (all machines)

1. Move carrier (carriage) to desired tab position by striking space bar or backspace key.
2. Depress **tab set key (2)**. Repeat this procedure for each stop needed.

Tabulating procedure

Strike the **tab key (5)** with the nearer little finger or the **tab bar (5)** with the right index finger; release it quickly and return the finger to home-key position.

Drill procedure

1. Clear all tab stops, as directed above.
2. Set a tab stop 5 spaces to the right of left margin stop.
3. Set the **line-space selector (22)** on "2" for DS (double spacing).
4. Type (key) the paragraphs once DS as shown, indenting the first line of each paragraph.

Tab ⟶ To indent the first line of a block of copy,

use the tab key or bar.

Tab ⟶ On electrics, just strike the key or bar and

release it at once.

Tab ⟶ On some manuals, though, you must strike and

hold down the key or bar.

276b-279b (continued)

Document 5
Legal Letter
(LM p. 161)
Prepare the letter in final form as requested by Miss Morales in her note at the bottom of the letter.

Letter to District Enterprises, Inc., 5701A Connecticut Avenue, NW, Washington, DC 20015-6349 from Miss Maria D. Morales, Attorney-at-Law.

¶ McNeill Relaty Company, lessors of the property you occupy ~~utilize~~ at 5701A Connecticut Avenue, NW, Washington, DC, has referred to us the matter of overdue rents you owe ~~owing~~ to them. As of July 1, you are 3 months in arrears, and you owe our client $3,440 for past ~~previous~~ rents plus $1,460 for rent during the month of July. Attempts ~~Efforts~~ made by our client to collect the rent due ~~them~~ has been unusccessful.

¶ Under the provisions ~~terms~~ of your lease, your tenency is terminated automatically if the specified rent is not paid within 10 days of the due date, which is the first day of each month. Our client is willing, however, to waive this provision on this one occasion if the total amount due--$4,900--is payed within ten days after the reciept of this letter. If payment is not made at that time, legal action will be initiated ~~instituted~~ to have you evicted form the premises and a suit filed to obtain the money due plus court costs and interest.

¶ Our client would prefer not to take legal action ~~steps~~ as a means of collection, and ~~but~~ feels you should have a final opportunity to meet this obligation. If, however, you do not remit the rent due under the provisions outlined ~~spelled out~~ above, we will be forced to resort to legal action.

NOTE: Date letter July 11. Send it by CERTIFIED MAIL—RETURN RECEIPT REQUESTED. Use company name in the closing lines followed by my name and title. M. D. M.

19c ▶ 12
Improve Keyboarding Technique

each pair of lines twice SS; DS between 4-line groups

Lines 1-2

Clear tab stops; beginning at left margin, set a tab stop every 9 spaces until you have set 5 tab stops. Type (key) the first word in Column 1; tab to Column 2 and type the first word in that column; and so on. There will be 5 blank spaces between the columns.

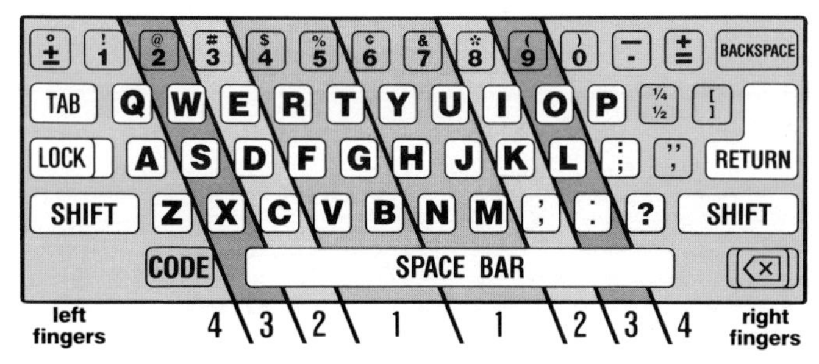

tabulator
1 pair Tab auto Tab kept Tab goal Tab worn Tab their
2 body fuel sick born soap risks

space bar
3 go am he me so do an us if by or it is of fur keys
4 an we me as am re us my if on by pi he no the join

shift keys
5 The winners are: Elena and Juan; Masami and Bing.
6 Did Miss Quadnau send us the report of Dr. Lamont?

shift lock
7 The FHA meeting is on Monday; the FFA, on Tuesday.
8 Luis watched the game on HBO; Nana saw it on WKRC.

19d ▶ 18
Build Keyboarding Speed

Lines 1-4

each line twice SS; DS between 2-line groups; speed up the second attempt at the line

Key words and phrases (*Think, say,* and *key* words and phrases.)

1 in we on be as no at up ad my are you was him gets
2 my ad|at no|as we|be in|we are|was him|you get set
3 turn rush duty girl maps rich laid down held spend
4 to rush|if they|by them|the duty|she kept|and paid

Lines 5-8

a 1′ timed writing on each line; find *gwam* on each writing (see bottom of page 33)

Goal: *At least* 21 *gwam*

Easy sentences (Key the words at a brisk, steady pace.)

5 Did they go by bus to visit six of the lake towns?
6 To do the work right is the duty of the six of us.
7 He is to do all the field forms for the usual pay.
8 She did lend all the audit forms to the six girls.

5-stroke words | 1 | 2 | 3 | 4 | 5 | 6 | 7 | 8 | 9 | 10 |

Easy paragraph

1. Type (key) the paragraph once DS as shown.

2. Two 1′ timed writings on the paragraph; find *gwam* on each writing.

Goal: *At least* 19 *gwam*

Alphabetic paragraph (all letters used)

. 2 . 4 . 6 . 8 .
Tab In just a few weeks, you have found the keys
10 . 12 . 14 . 16 . 18 .
to a top job. You know you need good form in the
20 . 22 . 24 . 26 . 28 .
next plan for a high speed. Be quick to prize it.

276b-279b (continued)

Document 4
Power of Attorney
(LM p. 159)

Mr. Bernard T. Franklin, the senior member of Franklin Legal Services, asks you to prepare a power of attorney similar to the form at the right. Include the following information:

Enoch C. Wooten (the principal) of Montgomery County, Maryland, wishes to appoint Julian C. Lopez of the same county and state to be his agent, "to manage and operate during my absence, my business, The Dorset Boutique, located at 6901 Wisconsin Avenue, Bethesda, Maryland."

1. Space the document as specified in the *Office Procedures Manual* (as revised by Ms. Jen).

2. The document will be signed and witnessed on July 11.

Legal Endorsement: In many law offices, a description of a legal document (called the *endorsement*) is placed on the outside cover of a backing sheet and prepared in a special way for storage in a safe-deposit box or special filing cabinet.

Make a 1½" fold at the top of the backing sheet. Fold the backing sheet into equal thirds and type the endorsement in the middle third as shown on the illustration below. Insert the typed document under the fold and staple it in place.

POWER OF ATTORNEY

KNOW ALL MEN BY THESE PRESENTS: that

I, (name of principal) of the County of ________, State of ________, by these presents do make, constitute, and appoint (name of agent) of the County of ________, State of ________, my true and lawful attorney for me and in my name, place, and stead (state responsibilities), giving and granting unto said attorney full power and authority to do and perform all and every act and thing whatsoever requisite and necessary to be done in and about the premises, as I might or could do if personally present with full power of substitution and revocation, hereby ratifying and confirming all that my said attorney shall lawfully do or cause to be done by virtue thereof.

IN WITNESS WHEREOF, I have hereunto set my hand and seal the ____ day of _________, 19--.

______________________________ (L. S.)

STATE OF MARYLAND)
: ss.
County of Montgomery)

The foregoing instrument was acknowledged before me this _____day of __________, by ____________________.

______________________________ (L. S.)
Notary Public

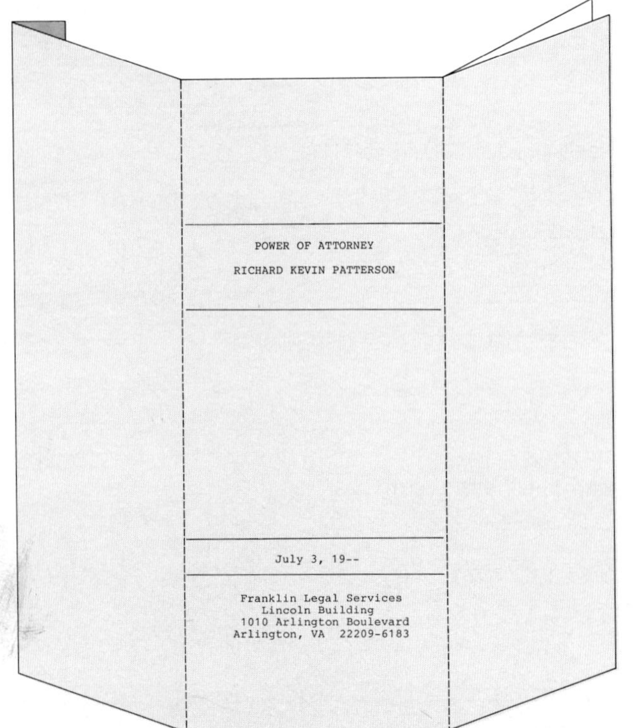

POWER OF ATTORNEY

KNOW ALL MEN BY THESE PRESENTS: that

I, Richard Kevin Patterson of the County of Montgomery, State of Maryland, by these presents do make, constitute, and appoint Meredith Patterson of the County of Montgomery, State of Maryland, my true and lawful attorney for me and in my name, place, and stead to manage and operate during my absence, my business, Walton Electric, located at 5702 Aberdeen Road, Bethesda, Maryland 20814-6378, giving and granting unto said attorney full power and authority to do and perform all and every act and thing whatsoever requisite and necessary to be done in and about the premises, as I might or could do if personally present with full power of substitution and revocation, hereby ratifying and confirming all that my said attorney shall lawfully do or cause to be done by virtue thereof.

IN WITNESS WHEREOF, I have hereunto set my hand and seal the 3d day of July, 19--.

______________________________ (L.S.)

STATE OF MARYLAND)
: ss.
County of Montgomery)

The foregoing instrument was acknowledged before me this 3d day of July, by Richard Kevin Patterson.

______________________________ (L.S.)
Notary Public

Line length: 50 spaces
Spacing: single-space (SS)

20a ▶ 8
Conditioning Practice

1. Each line twice SS (slowly; then faster); DS between 2-line groups.

2. If time permits, take three 1′ writings on line 3; find *gwam* (total 5-stroke words typed or keyed): words in complete line(s) PLUS words in a partial line.

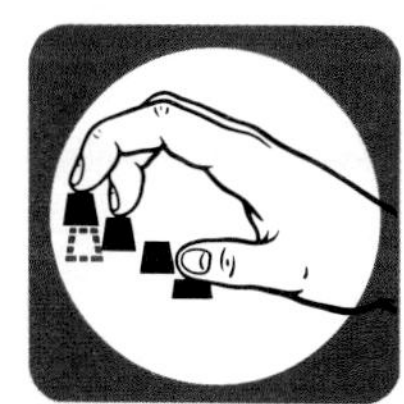

Finger-action keystroking

Down-and-in spacing

alphabet 1 Jo Fox made five quick plays to win the big prize.
space bar 2 a of to is it or if an do so he go she the and for
easy sentence 3 Pay them for the sign work they do if it is right.

5-stroke words | 1 | 2 | 3 | 4 | 5 | 6 | 7 | 8 | 9 | 10 |

20b ▶ 22
Check Keystroking Technique

each set of lines twice SS; DS between 6-line groups; on the second attempt, try to increase your speed

Ask your teacher to check your keystroking technique as you type (key) the following lines.

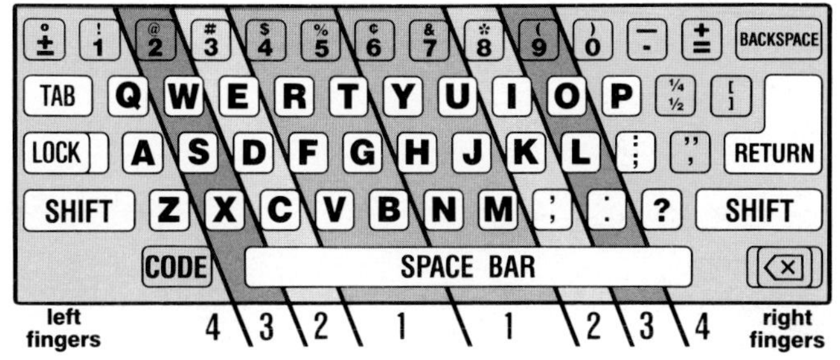

Fingers upright

Rows (Reach *up*, reach *down* without moving the hands.)

home/3d 1 pay got law jar lap rod dug sit hue risk four aqua
home/1st 2 an ax jab can zag ham van cash lack hand flax glad
3d/1st 3 Beryl is apt to win the gold cup in the next race.

Fingers (Keep on home row the fingers not used for reaching.)

1st/2d 4 it dig cut run den net fur yet vie jet fib rub the
3d/4th 5 so pal zoo lax low zap sow sap also slaw laws wasp
all 6 A judge will next read the laws to the open court.

Fingers curved

One-hand words (*Think*, *say*, and *key* words at a steady pace.)

words 7 pi as on at in we on re oh are oil was ink gas nil
words 8 ax up ad no be you saw him get ilk tax mop bad pun
sentence 9 As you see, we aced a pop test on a poll tax case.

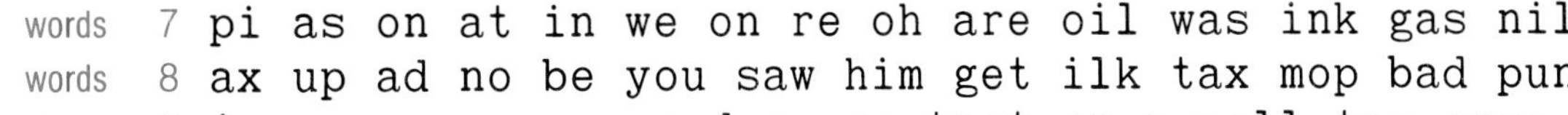

Balanced-hand words (*Think*, *say*, and *key* the words as *words*.)

words 10 am us own bus lay fix but key big pay due cut half
phrases 11 to pay half | if the city | of the maps | is to pay them
sentence 12 Aisha did fix the dock sign; the city paid for it.

5-stroke words | 1 | 2 | 3 | 4 | 5 | 6 | 7 | 8 | 9 | 10 |

276b-279b (continued)

Document 3
Simple Partnership Agreement with Acknowledgments
(LM p. 157)

Nancy Merriman, one of the group's attorneys, has filled in the necessary information for the partnership agreement at the right. Ms. Merriman asks you "to prepare the document which will be dated and signed on July 7, 19--."

PARTNERSHIP AGREEMENT

THIS AGREEMENT made on this _______ day of _______ 19--, by and between Emi T. Soga and Lee M. Katz of Arlington, Virginia.

WHEREIN IT IS MUTUALLY AGREED, AS FOLLOWS:

1. That the parties hereto shall, as equal partners, engage and conduct the business of renting and selling videocassettes under the name of Emilee Videos.

2. That the capital of the partnership shall be the sum of fifty-thousand dollars ($50,000); and each party shall contribute thereto, with the execution of this agreement, the sum of twenty-five thousand dollars ($25,000) in cash.

3. That at the end of each calendar year the net profit or ~~net~~ loss shall be divided equally between the parties.

____

____

COMMONWEALTH OF VIRGINIA)
: ss.
County of Arlington)

On this _____ day of ________, 19--, before me personally appeared the above-named individual(s), to me known to be the person(s) described in and who executed the foregoing instrument and acknowledged that he/she/they executed the same in his/her/their own free act and deed.

In testimony whereof, I have hereunto subscribed my name and affixed my seal of office the day and year last above written.

______________________________(L. S.)

20c ▶ 10
Check/Improve Keyboarding Speed

1. Take a 30-second (30″) timed writing on each line. Your rate in *gwam* is shown word for word above the lines.

2. If time permits, take another 30″ writing on each line. Try to increase your keyboarding speed.

Goal

At least 22 gwam.

30″ *gwam* | 2 | 4 | 6 | 8 | 10 | 12 | 14 | 16 | 18 | 20 | 22

1 Aida is to fix their gold urn.
2 Jay is to pay all six for the work.
3 Did the queen also visit the lake towns?
4 The theme for the panel is world fuel profit.
5 Buzz works for the big map firm for the usual pay.
6 Elena is to fix the sign then go to the lake with Rick.

| 2 | 4 | 6 | 8 | 10 | 12 | 14 | 16 | 18 | 20 | 22

If you finish a line before time is called and start over, your *gwam* is the figure at the end of the line PLUS the figure above or below the point at which you stopped.

20d ▶ 10
Check/Improve Keyboarding Speed

1. A 1′ writing on each ¶; find *gwam* on each writing.

2. Using your better *gwam* as a base rate, select a *goal rate* and take two 1′ guided writings on each ¶ as directed at the bottom of the page.

Copy used to measure skill is triple-controlled for difficulty:

E = easy HA = high average
LA = low average D = difficult
A = average

Difficulty index (shown above copy)

E	1.0 si	4.4 awl	95% hfw
	1 Syllable intensity	2 Average word length	3 High-frequency words

Difficulty index

all letters used | E | 1.0 si | 4.4 awl | 95% hfw |

gwam 2′

¶ 1 Good form means to move with speed and quiet 5
control. My next step will be to size up the job 10
and to do the work in the right way each day. 14

¶ 2 To reach my goal of top speed, I have to try 19
to build good form. I will try for the right key 24
each time, but I must do so in the right way. 28

gwam 2′ | 1 | 2 | 3 | 4 | 5 |

Guided (Paced) Writing Procedure

Select a practice goal:

1. Take a 1′ writing on ¶ 1 of a set of ¶s that contain superior figures for guided writings, as in 20d above.

2. Using the *gwam* as a base, add 4 *gwam* to determine your goal rate.

3. Choose from Column 1 of the table at the right the speed nearest your goal rate. At the right of that speed, note the 1/4′ points in the copy you must reach to maintain your goal rate.

Quarter-minute checkpoints

gwam	1/4′	1/2′	3/4′	Time
16	4	8	12	16
20	5	10	15	20
24	6	12	18	24
28	7	14	21	28
32	8	16	24	32
36	9	18	27	36
40	10	20	30	40

4. Note from the word-count dots and figures above the lines in ¶ 1 the checkpoint for each quarter minute. (Example: Checkpoints for 24 *gwam* are 6, 12, 18, and 24.)

Practice procedure

1. Take two 1′ writings on ¶ 1 at your goal rate guided by the quarter-minute calls (1/4, 1/2, 3/4, time).

Goal: To reach each of your checkpoints just as the guide is called.

2. Take two 1′ writings on ¶ 2 of a set of ¶s in the same way.

3. If time permits, take a 2′ writing on the set of ¶s combined, without the guides.

Speed level of practice

When the purpose of practice is to reach out into new speed areas, use the *speed* level. Take the brakes off your fingers and experiment with new stroking patterns and new speeds. Do this by:

1. Reading 2 or 3 letters ahead of your typing to foresee stroking patterns.

2. Getting the fingers ready for the combinations of letters to be typed.

3. Keeping your eyes on the copy in the book.

276b-279b (continued)

Document 2
Office Procedures Manual

Ms. Jen has been revising the *Office Procedures Manual*. A part of her revision is shown at the right. Ms. Jen says, "Prepare the page in final form. Place the title on line 6, and position the material on the page so that it can be bound at the left."

PREPARATION OF LEGAL ~~PAPERS~~ DOCUMENTS — CENTERED

Paper

Legal documents ~~are~~ may be prepared on 8½" x 11" plain paper or ruled paper 8 1/2" x 13", or 14".

Margins

Left margin, 1 1/2"; right margin, ~~1"~~ 1/2"; top margin, begin copy on line 12; bottom margin, at least 1". On ruled paper, leave one space between the left rule and the copy and at least one space before the right rule.

Spacing

DS body of doucment; SS acknowledgements, quoted material, and land descriptions. Indent paragraphs ~~5 or~~ 10 spaces.

Titles

Center title in all caps between ruled or margins lines. DS twice (quadruple-space) after ~~entering~~ keyboarding the title.

Pagination

Except for a will, do not number the first page. number other pages 1/2" from bottom of the page (line 63).

Signature Lines

Place signeture lines for the maker or makers of the document on the right side of the page. Place the lines for the signatures of witnesses (if any) on the left side of the page. Place the first signature line a quadruple space below the last line of the document. If there is more than one line, ~~quadruple~~ double-space between them. Lines should be approximately 3" in length.

Accuracy/Corrections

Accuracy in legal documents is ~~very important~~ of the utmost importance. Correct figures, dates, names, and places carefully. Any obvious correction of an important item should be initialed by all parties concerned to indicate their agreement with the change. (Insert sentence below.)

Latin Abbreviations

The abbreviation "ss." represents the Latin word scilicet, wich means "namely." "L.S." is the abbreviation for the Latin phrase locus sigilli and is used in place of a seal.

To insure absolute accuracy, keyboard important figures and sums of money in both figures and words.

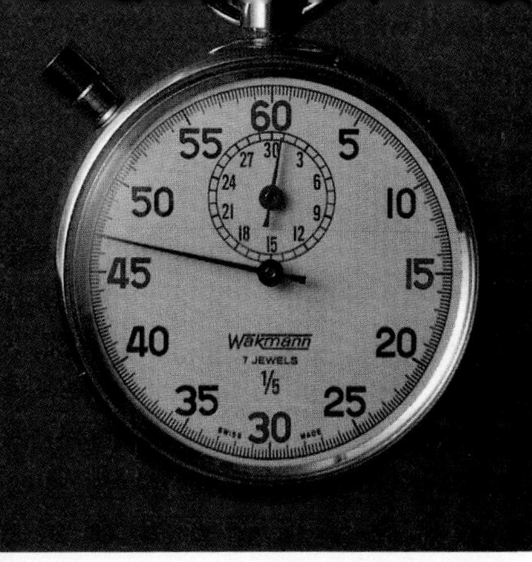

Unit 2 Lessons 21-25

Learning Goals

1. To improve keyboarding techniques.

2. To improve speed on sentence and paragraph copy.

3. To review and improve language skills: capitalization.

Machine Adjustments

1. Paper guide at *0*.

2. Ribbon control to use top half of ribbon.

3. Margin sets: left margin (center - 25); right margin (move to right end of scale).

4. Line-space selector set to single-space (SS) drills.

5. Line-space selector set to double-space (DS) ¶s.

Lesson 21 Basic/Language Skills

Line length: 50 spaces
Spacing: single-space (SS)

21a ▶ 6 Conditioning Practice

1. Each line twice SS.

2. A 1′ writing on line 3; find *gwam*.

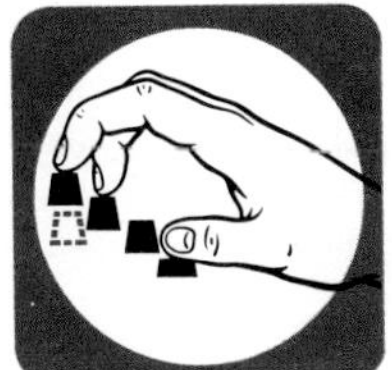

alphabet	1	Jewel amazed Vic by escaping quickly from the box.
punctuation	2	Have we used these words: view, vote, five, gave?
easy sentence	3	He is to do social work for the city if they wish.

5-stroke words | 1 | 2 | 3 | 4 | 5 | 6 | 7 | 8 | 9 | 10 |

21b ▶ 22 Improve Keyboarding Technique

each set of lines twice SS (slowly; then faster); DS between 4-line groups; if time permits, practice selected lines again

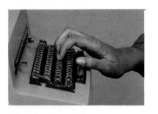

Fingers curved

Reach review (Keep hands and arms quiet, almost motionless.)

ol/lo	1	old lot lox loan told long hold local whole school
	2	Lou told me that her local school loans old books.
za/az	3	zap maze lazy jazz hazy zany raze haze amaze crazy
	4	A jazz band played with pizzazz at my pizza stand.
ik/ki	5	kite bike kind like kilt kick pike kiwi hike skill
	6	The striking pink kite skimmed over the ski trail.
ed/de	7	led side heed used made need wide idea guide delay
	8	Ned said the guide used a slide film for her talk.
ws/sw	9	was saw laws rows swan swam sway flaws shows swing
	10	Wes said the first two rows saw flaws in the show.
ft/ju	11	oft jug sift just left jury lift judge often juice
	12	Jud left fifty jugs of juice on a raft for a gift.

Unit 62 Lessons 276-279

General Goals

1. To prepare in an acceptable form with all errors corrected a series of documents found in a legal office.
2. To increase your skill in planning, organizing, and preparing a variety of realistic production materials.
3. To familiarize you with some of the terms and forms used in a legal office.

Documents Processed

1. Tentative Court Calendar
2. Office Procedures Manual
3. Simple Partnership Agreement
4. Power of Attorney
5. Legal Letter
6. Simple Family Will
7. Form Letters with Fill-Ins

Lessons 276-279

276a-279a ▶ 5
Check Equipment

Before you begin work each day, check your machine to see that it is in good working order by keyboarding the paragraph at the right at least twice (first slowly, then faster).

all letters/figures used

They may jeopardize this next bill which gives equal pay for equal work. If not passed by May 31, Ordinance #4890 (equal pay) will be replaced by #27560 (equal opportunity). The amendment to codify the work proviso may dispel the skepticism of the auditor.

| 1 | 2 | 3 | 4 | 5 | 6 | 7 | 8 | 9 | 10 | 11 | 12 | 13 |

276b-279b
Document Production

Your first assignment as a Modern Office Tempos employee is in the Data Services Branch of Franklin Legal Services, a group of attorneys who practice both civil and criminal law. Franklin Legal Services is located in the **Lincoln Building, 1010 Arlington Boulevard, Arlington, VA 22209-6183.**

As a keyboarding specialist, you will prepare a variety of documents under the direction of Ms. Suzy Jen, Chief of the Data Services Branch. If you are not given specific directions for preparing a document, use your best judgment.

Document 1
Court Calendar

Ms. Jen tells you, "Please prepare the court calendar in final form. Be sure to place the cases in chronological order."

TENTATIVE COURT CALENDAR

DATE (lc)	Client	Charge	Docket No.
7/2	Jon E. Gruen (Def)	DUI	1459-C-42
7/2	Margaret C. Tyler (Def)	Unlawful Entry	2560-C-51
7/3	Carl E. West (Def)	Slander	2782-I-72
7/4	Justin M. Laird (Plaint)	Manslaughter	3671-C-83
7/4	Roy T. Wolf (Def)	Larceny	4071-C-74
~~7/5~~ 7/10	Sean C. Bixler (Def)	DUI	4782-C-37
7/5	Marian T. Jones (Plaint)	Illegal Entry	5891-C-90
7/6	Otto C. Kern (Plaint)	Breach of Contract	2385-I-30
7/9	Robert L. Cox (Def)	Assault & Battery	6902-C-18
7/11	~~Gertrude~~ Trudy M. Hooper (Def)	~~Suborning~~ Perjury	7013-C-46
7/12	Jean C. Webb (Def)	Theft	7904-C-25
7/13	Alonzo C. Shaw (Plaint)	Divorce	3496-I-27
~~7/13~~ 7/16	Diane R. Stevens~~ons~~ (Def)	Trespass	4507-I-55
7/17	Anita G. Ennis (Plaint)	Child Custody	5109-I-91

21c ▶ 12 Check/Improve Keyboarding Speed

1. Take one 1′ timed writing and two 1′ *guided* writings on ¶ 1 as directed on page 37.

2. Take one 1′ timed writing and two 1′ *guided* writings on ¶ 2 in the same way.

3. As time permits, take one or two 2′ timed writings on ¶s 1 and 2 combined *without* the call of the guide; find *gwam*.

1′ *Gwam* Goals

▽ 17 = acceptable
□ 21 = average
○ 25 = good
◇ 29 = excellent

all letters used | E | 1.2 si | 5.0 awl | 95% hfw | — *gwam* 2′

```
    It is important for me to learn to force two      4
to four letters close together in time.  If I can     9
cut the time between them, my skill will increase.   14
    The size of the word and the sequence of its     19
letters may determine just how fast I can move to    24
handle it.  To cut time should get next attention.   29
```

gwam 2′ | 1 | 2 | 3 | 4 | 5 |

21d ▶ 10 Improve Language Skills: Capitalization

1. Read the first rule highlighted in color at the right.

2. Type (key) the *Learn* sentence below it, noting how the rule has been applied.

3. Type (key) the *Apply* sentence, supplying the needed capital letters.

4. Read and practice the other rules in the same way.

5. If time permits, type (key) the three *Apply* sentences again to increase decision-making speed.

Capitalize the first word in a sentence.

Learn 1 You left your book here. Shall I bring it to you?
Apply 2 do you plan to go? the bus will get here at noon.

Capitalize personal titles and names of people.

Learn 3 Did Mrs. Hickman say that Mr. Mazla would take us?
Apply 4 ask if alma and suzan took the trip with ms. diaz.

Capitalize names of cities, states, and other important places.

Learn 5 While in New York, they saw the Statue of Liberty.
Apply 6 she will visit the white house in washington, d.c.

Lesson 22 Basic/Language Skills

Line length: 50 spaces
Spacing: single-space (SS)

22a ▶ 6 Conditioning Practice

1. Each line twice SS.

2. A 1′ writing on line 3; find *gwam*.

alphabet 1 Have my long quiz boxed when Jack stops by for it.
space bar 2 to do it|go to the|and to do|if she is|he may work
easy 3 He may do all the work if he works with good form.

5-stroke words | 1 | 2 | 3 | 4 | 5 | 6 | 7 | 8 | 9 | 10 |

22b ▶ 12 Check/Improve Keyboarding Speed

1. Take one 1′ timed writing and two 1′ *guided* writings on ¶ 1 of 21c, above, as directed at the bottom of page 37.

2. Type (key) ¶ 2 of 21c, above, in the same way.
Goal: To increase speed.

3. As time permits, take one or two 2′ timed writings on ¶s 1 and 2 combined; find *gwam*.

MODERN OFFICE TEMPOS

After you register with Modern Office Tempos, you are interviewed by Mrs. Frances P. Rafferty, a Personnel Specialist, who gives you a series of tests to determine the kind of jobs for which you may be qualified. After you sign a contract, she gives you a copy of the *Personal and Professional Standards of Conduct* for Modern Office Tempos and asks you to review it carefully.

MODERN OFFICE TEMPOS
Personal and Professional Standards of Conduct

Job Responsibilities. You will be required to perform a variety of tasks including receiving visitors, making and receiving telephone calls, filing, duplicating materials, and processing documents. Most offices will provide you with a job description which outlines your duties. Study it carefully so that you will know exactly what is expected of you.

Personal Qualities. "The ability to get along with others" tops the list of the desirable qualities of an office worker. Remember, you will need the help of others to adjust quickly to each new job assignment. You will gain a great deal if you are friendly, cooperative, and mannerly. Other essential personal qualities include loyalty, honesty, and reliability.

Attendance. The absence of an employee can affect the efficiency of an entire office. You will be expected to be on the job during the hours prescribed unless you cannot do so because of illness, death in the family, or another valid reason. If you cannot be at work, notify your immediate supervisor at the earliest possible moment. Also, call our Employee Service Unit (565-6400, Extension 201) and explain why you cannot report to work. Remember, your contract may be voided by excessive absenteeism or chronic tardiness.

Appearance. Office workers are required to present a neat, orderly, and attractive appearance. If you are uncertain about the appropriate standard of dress, and you are not given any suggestions about clothing and hairstyles by your supervisor, be on the safe side and dress conservatively. The dress and grooming of your fellow workers may give you an idea of how to dress.

Standard Operating Procedures. Some companies publish a manual which contains uniform procedures to be followed in performing repetitive, routine tasks. Use the manual as a guide in performing your job. If instructions for the task you are asked to do are not included in the manual, do not be afraid to ask your supervisor or a fellow worker for help.

Processing Documents. The Standard Operating Procedures Manual may include specific information on processing documents. If so, follow the directions given. If no specific instructions are provided, use your best judgment. Be sure your completed work is neat, free of errors, placed attractively on the page, and serves the purpose for which it was intended. As one who has been trained in document processing, you will be expected to

1. Supply the date for correspondence.
2. In a letter, include an appropriate salutation, complimentary close, signature block (typed name and title of the person who originated the letter), and your initials as reference.
3. If the content of a document indicates there are enclosures or attachments, provide the proper notation.
4. Use the proper document format.
5. Correct any errors made by the originator of a document (check spelling, punctuation, and grammar).
6. Correct errors you make as you prepare a document in final form.
7. Proofread all documents and correct any errors you may have missed.
8. Complete all documents quickly and neatly.
9. Meet all deadlines for the preparation of documents.

22c ▶ 20
Improve Keyboarding Technique: Response Patterns

1. Each pair of lines twice SS; DS between 4-line groups.

2. A 1′ writing on line 11 and then on line 12 to increase speed; find *gwam* on each.

Practice hints

One-hand lines: *Think*, *say*, and *key* the words by letter response at a steady but unhurried pace.

Balanced-hand lines: *Think*, *say*, and *key* the words by word response at a fast pace.

Letter response
Many one-hand words (as in lines 1-2) are not easy to key. Such words may be keyed *letter by letter* with continuity (steadily, without pauses).

Word response
Short, balanced-hand words (as in lines 3-4) are so easy to key they can be keyed as words. Think and key them at your top speed.

one-hand words	1	at up as in we on be no ax oh ex my pi are you was
	2	ad him get ink few pin tax pop set ilk far pup car
balanced-hand words	3	us do if an so am go he to me or is of ah it by ox
	4	el the and for may but pay due own men did box map
one-hand phrases	5	as in|at no|be up|as my|be in|at my|we hum|see you
	6	get set|get him|you are|pop art|red ink|my oil tax
balanced-hand phrases	7	of us|if he|do so|it is|to us|or by|an ox|to do it
	8	he did|the map|and for|she may|the six|got the bus
one-hand sentences	9	You set my tax only after I gave you my wage data.
	10	As you saw up at my mill, my rate was up on water.
balanced-hand sentences	11	He is to go to the city and to do the work for me.
	12	I am to pay the six men if they do the work right.
5-stroke words		| 1 | 2 | 3 | 4 | 5 | 6 | 7 | 8 | 9 | 10 |

22d ▶ 12
Improve Language Skills: Capitalization

1. Read each rule and type (key) the Learn and Apply sentences beneath it.

2. If time permits, practice the Apply lines again to increase decision-making speed.

Capitalize the days of the week.

Learn 1 Are you sure the FBLA contest is to be on Tuesday?
Apply 2 the joggers meet on monday, wednesday, and friday.

Capitalize the months of the year.

Learn 3 April was quite chilly, but May has been pleasant.
Apply 4 from june to september seems like a long vacation.

Capitalize names of holidays.

Learn 5 We usually picnic in the park on Independence Day.
Apply 6 bev plans to visit her family on thanksgiving day.

Capitalize the names of historic periods and events and special events.

Learn 7 Bastille Day is in honor of the French Revolution.
Apply 8 the fourth of july honors the american revolution.

Lessons 276-300

PHASE 12

Modern Office Tempos: Professional Office Situations

You have registered with **Modern Office Tempos, 1024 17th Street, NW, Washington, DC**. Modern Tempos provides temporary office employees for businesses and U.S. Government agencies in the Greater Washington Area, which includes parts of Virginia and Maryland.

Temporary employees are in great demand to fill in for employees who are sick, on vacation, or absent temporarily. Temporary workers are also employed to help an office that has an occasional heavy workload, or to assist an employer who does not need a full-time worker.

As a temporary employee, you will broaden your knowledge of the jobs performed in an office; gain valuable experience in a variety of office situations; improve your personal and professional skills; and meet a large number of people who may help you in your career. You will experience a "taste" of different jobs which may help you decide exactly the kind of work you want to do. Finally, many *temporary* positions often turn into permanent ones.

Line length: 50 spaces
Spacing: single-space (SS)

23a ▶ 6 Conditioning Practice

1. Each line twice SS.
2. A 1′ writing on line 3; find *gwam*.

alphabet 1 Aquela Javicz kept the new forms by the tax guide.
shift lock 2 Did you OK this show for ABC, for NBC, or for CBS?
easy 3 They may cut the fish down by the end of the dock.

5-stroke words | 1 | 2 | 3 | 4 | 5 | 6 | 7 | 8 | 9 | 10 |

23b ▶ 20 Improve Keyboarding Technique: Response Patterns

1. Each set of lines twice SS (slowly; then faster); DS between 6-line groups.
2. A 1′ writing on line 10, next on line 11, then on line 12; find *gwam* on each; compare rates.

Combination response
Normal copy (as in lines 7-9) includes both word- and letter-response sequences. *Use top speed for easy words, lower speed for more difficult ones.*

letter response
1 as no we in be you far him few oil get pin age kin
2 you set|oil car|see him|few kin|bad pun|set my tax
3 As you were in a tax case, we set up rates on gas.

word response
4 is to if am ox own and but did she may air end big
5 if so|to own|if she|of six|did own|but she|the air
6 Vi is to go with them to the quay by the big lake.

combination response
7 if on so as or we of no us up go my to be am at by
8 is in|go on|if no|to be|is up|so as|is my|am up to
9 If we are to be in the city, she may see him then.

letter 10 You gave only a few facts in my case on oil taxes.
word 11 Dick is to make a visit to the eight island towns.
combination 12 Daq may be paid extra if he works on my big barge.

5-stroke words | 1 | 2 | 3 | 4 | 5 | 6 | 7 | 8 | 9 | 10 |

23c ▶ 12 Improve Language Skills: Capitalization

1. Read each rule and type (key) the Learn and Apply sentences beneath it.
2. If time permits, practice the Apply lines again to increase decision-making speed.

Capitalize names of clubs, organizations, and companies.

Learn 1 The Beaux Arts Club did a show at Jewish Hospital.
Apply 2 apex corp. aids our chapter of junior achievement.

Capitalize geographic names, regions, and locations.

Learn 3 Texas and Mexico share the Rio Grande as a border.
Apply 4 i viewed the grand canyon as we flew over arizona.

Capitalize names of streets, avenues, and buildings.

Learn 5 Suzi Quan has moved to Croix Towers on Park Place.
Apply 6 their office is in gulf plaza on san pedro avenue.

275b (continued)

Document 2 (continued)

words

remote location. But, for now, the most popu- 208
lar form of electronic mail requires generating 217
a letter by computer, remotely printing ~~it~~ the 226
letter and snding it by either the U.S. mail 235
or a private courier service. 242

According to the Small Business Report ("Applica- 254
tions of Electronic Mail." Small Business Report 254
December 1984, 74), "Electronic mail is no longer an 262
exclusive communication tool for large corporatoins." 273
The report ~~goes on to say~~ also says, "Reasonably priced systems 283
are now developed to meet the needs and budgets of 293
samll ~~companies~~ firms as well." It appears, therefore, that 304
telecommunications will help all business firms keep pace with the "information 320
explosion." 322

Document 3
Reference Page

Prepare a reference page for the report completed in Document 2.

Total words in reference page 141.

Document 4
Table

Prepare the table at the right on a full sheet DS.

ELECTRO-TECHNOLOGIES, LTD. 5

Salary Schedule for Administrators 12

(As of ~~September~~ July, 19--) 16

Grade	Minimum	Maximum	
1	$~~13,200~~ 14,520	$~~17,550~~ 19,305	28
2	~~13,950~~ 15,345	~~19,050~~ 20,955	31
3	~~14,050~~ 16,335	~~20,805~~ 22,885	34
4	~~16,050~~ 17,655	~~23,250~~ 25,575	38
5	~~17,700~~ 19,470	~~18,100~~ 27,417	41
6	~~19,500~~ 21,450	~~30,450~~ 33,495	44
7	~~21,450~~ 23,595	~~34,500~~ 37,950	47
8	~~28,050~~ 30,855	~~39,750~~ 43,725	50
9	~~34,890~~ 38,379	~~46,500~~ 51,150	54
10	~~41,640~~ 45,804	~~53,250~~ 58,575	57

23d ▶ 12
Check/Improve Keyboarding Speed

1. Take one 1′ timed writing and two 1′ *guided* writings on ¶ 1 as directed on page 37.

2. Take one 1′ timed writing and two 1′ *guided* writings on ¶ 2 in the same way.

3. As time permits, take one or two 2′ timed writings on ¶s 1 and 2 combined *without* the call of the guide; find *gwam*.

1′ *Gwam* Goals

▽ 19 = acceptable
□ 23 = average
○ 27 = good
◇ 31 = excellent

all letters used | E | 1.2 si | 4.5 awl | 91% hfw |

	gwam 2′
¶ 1 Now it is up to me to build a major skill to	4
prize. I will develop my speed if I will key the ▽	9
copy in the right □ way. To reach the next ○ goal, I	14
must ◇ move quickly from one letter to another.	19
¶ 2 A step to which I must give attention in the	23
days just ahead is reading. The size of the word ▽	28
can limit how I □ read and key it. I must ○ focus on	33
a short, ◇ easy word and then key it as a unit.	38

gwam 2′ | 1 | 2 | 3 | 4 | 5 |

Lesson 24 Basic/Language Skills

Line length: 50 spaces
Spacing: single-space (SS)

24a ▶ 6
Conditioning Practice

1. Each line twice SS.

2. A 1′ writing on line 3; find *gwam*.

alphabet 1 By solving the tax quiz, Jud Mack won first prize.
? 2 Where is Yuri? Who can say? Is he to go with us?
easy 3 Title to all of the lake land is held by the city.

5-stroke words | 1 | 2 | 3 | 4 | 5 | 6 | 7 | 8 | 9 | 10 |

24b ▶ 12
Improve Language Skills: Capitalization

1. Read each rule and type (key) the Learn and Apply sentences beneath it.

2. If time permits, practice the Apply lines again to increase decision-making speed.

Capitalize an official title when it precedes a name, and elsewhere if it is a title of high distinction.

Learn 1 Our company president spoke with President Reagan.
Learn 2 The Vice President asked to speak with the doctor.
Apply 3 in what year did juan carlos become king of spain?
Apply 4 masami chou, our class president, made the awards.

Capitalize initials; also letters in abbreviations if the letters would be capitalized when the words were spelled out.

Learn 5 We have a report from Ms. R. J. Buckley of London.
Learn 6 M.D. means Doctor of Medicine, not medical doctor.
Apply 7 does dr. j. t. Peterson have a ph.d., or an ed.d.?
Apply 8 he said that UPS stands for united parcel service.

24c ▶ 12
Check/Improve Keyboarding Speed

Using the directions of 23d, practice ¶s at top of page.

Goal: An increase of *at least* 2 *gwam*.

275b (continued)

Document 2
Unbound Report with Textual Citations

1. Prepare the copy at the right as an unbound report DS.

2. For each citation, the complete reference information has been included in the text of the report for your convenience in preparing the reference page. As you prepare the report, insert the proper textual citation and reference for the reference page. Check carefully for uncorrected errors.

words

ELECTRONIC MESSAGE SYSTEMS Center 5

The "information explosion" has had a ripple affect 16
upon almost every aspect of work ~~in the~~ office, particu- 25
larly in the area of communications. Dispite predictions 37
of a "paperless office" in the future, the number of com- 48
munications continues to expand at an annual ~~a yearly~~ rate of ~~about~~ 59
approximately 10 percent (U.S. Bureau of Census. Statis- 64
tical Abstracts of the United States: 1984. 104th ed. 64
Washington, D.C.: U.S. Government Printing Office, 1983 4, 554). Because of ~~Due to~~ the tremendous 72
growth in communications, many companies are now aban- 83
doning the traditional ~~usual~~ means of communication in favor of elec- 95
tronic mail. Henry Fersko-Weiss (Fersko-Weiss, Henry. 102
"Electronic Mail: The Emerging Conection." Personal 102
Computing, January 1985, 71-79) states ~~says~~, "Companies of all 110
sizes are using electronic mail because of its ability 121
to save time and increase the flow of infomation across 132
the confines of corporate sturcture." 140

According to Casady and Sandburg (Casady, Mona J. 147
and Dorothy C. Sandburg. Word/Information Procesing. 147
Cincinnati: South-Western Publishing Co., 1958, 21), 149
"Electronic mail involves machine-to-machine communica- 160
tions". Neill Borowski (Borowski, Neill. "Business 165
Starting to Surge in Electronic-mail Market." Philadelphia 165
Inquirer, 9 July 1984, 5c), on the other hand, indicates ~~states~~: 173

> Electronic mail in its purest form would 181
> be a message written on a computer terminal 190
> and sent to another computer terminal in a 199

(continued on page 460)

24d ▶ 20
Improve Keyboarding Technique

1. Each set of lines twice SS (slowly; then faster); DS between 8-line groups.

2. Note the lines that caused you difficulty; practice them again to develop a steady pace (no pauses between letters).

> Adjacent (side-by-side) keys (as in lines 1-4) can cause many errors unless the fingers are kept in an upright position and precise motions are used.
>
> Long direct reaches (as in lines 5-8) reduce speed unless they are made without moving the hands forward and downward.
>
> Reaches with the outside fingers (as in lines 9-12) are troublesome unless made without twisting the hands in and out at the wrist.

Adjacent-key letter combinations

ew/we 1 The news is that we may view a new film next week.
ui/iu 2 The genius quickly drank fruit juice after a quiz.
er/re 3 The terms of her sale are there on the other side.
oi/io 4 Eloise may join the oil firm; she has that option.

Long direct reaches with same finger

un/nu 5 Our unit may not have its annual bonus until June.
ec/ce 6 Once we receive the pacer, you may expect a check.
um/mu 7 I must assume that sales volume is our mutual aim.
ny/yn 8 Lyn says a smile turns a rainy day sunny for many.

Reaches with 3d and 4th fingers

op/po 9 The poet will opt for a top spot in our port town.
as/sa 10 Sam said the cash price for gas went up last week.
az/za 11 Zane played a zany tune that amazed the jazz band.
q/a 12 My squad set a quarter quota to equal our request.

Lesson 25 Basic/Language Skills

Line length: 50 spaces
Spacing: single-space (SS)

25a ▶ 6
Conditioning Practice

1. Each line twice SS.

2. A 1′ writing on line 3; find *gwam*.

alphabet 1 Virgil Quin has packed twenty boxes of prize jams.
capitalization 2 Rule: When : precedes a sentence, cap first word.
easy 3 When she got such a profit, she paid for the land.

5-stroke words | 1 | 2 | 3 | 4 | 5 | 6 | 7 | 8 | 9 | 10 |

25b ▶ 14
Improve Keyboarding Response Patterns

1. Each set of lines twice SS; DS between 6-line groups.

2. A 1′ writing on line 10, next on line 11, then on line 12 to increase speed; find *gwam* on each.

Goal: *At least* 24 *gwam* on line 12.

letter response
1 were only date upon rate join gave milk gets jumps
2 my tax|saw him|bad oil|raw milk|you beat|get a fee
3 Zac gave only a few facts in a case on wage taxes.

word response
4 goal town iris pens turn risk coal fuel auto elbow
5 the risk|pay them|for both|six girls|but rush them
6 They did lend the formal gowns to the eight girls.

combination response
7 so ink she are for him own far tie mop apt war and
8 for him|due you|did zag|may set|and get|she saw me
9 You may join their union only if you pay the fees.

letter 10 You served poppy seed bread as a sweet noon treat.
combination 11 Vi read a theory on the state of art in the world.
word 12 The firm also owns the big sign by the town field.

5-stroke words | 1 | 2 | 3 | 4 | 5 | 6 | 7 | 8 | 9 | 10 |

275b ▶ 45
Evaluate Document Processing Skills

Time Schedule

Plan and Prepare .... 5′
Timed Production .... 30′
Proofread; compute *n-pram* .... 10′

1. Prepare the document on the right and the documents on pages 459 and 460 in the order given for 30 minutes. Correct all errors.

2. At the end of 30 minutes, proofread the documents you prepared and correct any errors you may have missed, but do not redo any problems. After you have done so, compute *n-pram*.

Note: To find *n-pram* (net production rate per minute), deduct 15 words for each uncorrected error; divide remainder by 30 (time).

Document 1
Letter
(LM p. 155)
Prepare the letter as directed. Check carefully for uncorrected errors.

opening lines

Please prepare the following letter dated June 27, 19-- 28
(block style, open punctuation) to
Mrs. Rebecca T. Counds, Chief of Supplies
James & Oliver Co., 23 S. Charles Street
Baltimore, MD 21201-3796

Thank you, Mrs. Counds, for your recent ~~letter~~ inquiry 37
about our outstanding ~~new~~ line of LASER Copiers. The 47
enclosed brochure ~~shows~~ illustrates our inventory of this 58
item. 59

All of our products have been engineered, tested, and im- 70
proved to ensure that they will help you to operate your 82
business more efficiently. Through strict quality control in 94
our plants, we have ~~earned~~ won a reputation for ~~always~~ 102
providing ~~prompt service~~ superior products at low 109
prices. 111

Words and pictures do not always provide the ~~data~~ 120
esential information you need to make decisions. At 131
ELECTRO-TECHNOLOGIES, we sell more than hardware. 141
Our goal is to help you make better, more affective use 152
of your facilities. Through our management professionals, 164
we can give you a ~~new~~ fresh outlook on your organiza- 174
tion, provide innovative suggestions for saving time 184
and money, and increase your over all efficiency. 194

For ~~more~~ further information, please call 202
Michael Young, one of our specialists, at 1-800- 211
555-6452. You have nothing to lose--but a great 221
deal to gain. 224

Sincerely yours   Mary Ann Jock
Director of Marketing Operations
xx Enclosure

closing lines 239/**256**

25c ▶ 20
Check/Improve Keyboarding Speed

1. A 1′ writing on each ¶; find *gwam* on each; record the best *gwam*.

2. A 2′ writing on ¶s 1-3 combined; find *gwam*.

3. Using your best *gwam* in Step 1 as a base rate, take a 1′ *guided* writing on ¶ 1 as directed on page 37.

4. Take a 1′ writing on ¶ 2 and on ¶ 3 in the same way.

5. If time permits, take another 2′ writing on ¶s 1-3 combined; find *gwam*.

1′ Goal: At least 22 *gwam*
2′ Goal: At least 20 *gwam*

all letters used | E | 1.2 si | 4.9 awl | 92% hfw | *gwam 2′*

```
          .    2    .    4    .    6    .    8    .
     As you key copy, read it with care.  Do more      4
10   .   12    .   14    .   16    .   18    .
than that, though; think each word, too.  You can      9
20   .   22    .   24    .   26    .   28    .
key the word as a unit if you think it and say it.    14
          .    2    .    4    .    6    .    8    .
     You must realize that some words have letter     19
10   .   12    .   14    .   16    .   18    .
sequences that are hard to type.  These are often     24
20   .   22    .   24    .   26    .   28    .
traps for a new person who does not yet know them.    29
          .    2    .    4    .    6    .    8    .
     Your major purpose now should be to learn to     33
10   .   12    .   14    .   16    .   18    .
key the easy words quickly and to drop your speed     38
20   .   22    .   24    .   26    .   28    .
for hard ones.  Learn next to vary the speed rate.    43
```

gwam 2′ | 1 | 2 | 3 | 4 | 5 |

25d ▶ 10
Check Language Skills: Capitalization

1. Type (key) each sentence once, capitalizing words according to the rules you have learned in this unit.

2. Check with your teacher the accuracy of your application of the rules.

3. As time permits, do again the lines in which you made errors in capitalization.

The references refer to previous lesson parts containing capitalization rules.

all letters used

Reference		
21d	1	is this your coat? it was left here this morning.
21d	2	is enrique going with mrs. dover to the book sale?
21d, 23c	3	did you tour the black hills when in south dakota?
21d, 24b	4	alice has gone to work for nasa in houston, texas.
22d	5	all term reports are due the last friday in april.
22d	6	labor day is always the first monday in september.
22d, 24b	7	l. k. syke may go to the hula bowl game this year.
23c	8	do you know if the zorn building is on oak street?
23c, 24b	9	does fbla mean future business leaders of america?
24b	10	tomas garcia is an m.d.; joann markham is a d.d.s.
24b	11	ms. lincoln is a manager in our office in phoenix.
24b	12	was margaret thatcher a prime minister of england?

274c ▶ 30 Evaluate Language Skills: Proofread/Correct

1. In each sentence at the right, items have been underlined. The underlines indicate that there may be an error in spelling, punctuation, capitalization, grammar, or in the use of words or figures.

2. Study each sentence carefully; then keyboard it, including the number. If an underlined item is correct, keyboard it as it is; if the item is incorrect, correct it. Also correct any errors you may make as you work.

3. When you have completed the sentences and *before* you remove the paper from the machine, study each sentence carefully and correct any errors you may have missed. If necessary, you may keyboard a sentence a second time immediately below your original sentence in order to correct a major error.

4. You may *not* correct errors once you have removed the paper from the machine.

1. Some one from maintenance must vacuum all of this companys' floors.
2. She_ as well as her supervisor were pleased with the eficiency report.
3. The Benificial Insurance company is different than any other Company.
4. According to Table 7 (see Page 15), our receipts went up in Febuary.
5. He will discribe the architecture of our east and west coast offices.
6. We devided the dividends between the stockholders on the forth of May.
7. If the loan is refused_ we must file immediately for bankruptsy.
8. We payed this bill last week_ therefore_ we shall not pay it again.
9. Locate these cities; Boise, Idaho, Bangor, Maine, and Lima, Ohio.
10. This calender is your's, but it is similer to my assistant's.
11. The general principles are in chapter 11, "Administrative Procedures".
12. Untill the firm gets it's money, we can not impliment our plans.
13. 75 of the ninty eligable workers recieved the annual bonus.
14. Can they develope the valuable new medecine in there labratory?
15. My division was alotted the highest of the two special allocations.
16. The extrordinary project may jepardize our financial reputation.
17. During your liesure, read the new novel, "Murder by Computer."
18. He asked, "Do you recommend a carreer in medicine"?
19. On May 6th and 7th, we shall analyze the usable questionnaires.
20. Did they except his ordnance to make the devise illegal?
21. He, among others, don't believe the foreign venture will suceed.
22. Any farther cancelations will have an averse effect on us, to.
23. Neither the consultent or the manager were eficient.
24. Everyone of the 8 investigators in the agency were indispensable.
25. In his speech he said, "This Project is all together unecessary".

Lessons 26-50

PHASE 2

Learn Numeric Keyboarding Technique and Correspondence Formatting

In the 25 lessons of this phase, you will:

1. Learn to type (key) figures and basic symbols by touch and with good technique.

2. Improve speed/control on straight copy, script (handwritten) copy, rough-draft (corrected) copy, and statistical copy (copy containing figures and some symbols).

3. Review/improve language skills.

4. Apply your keyboarding skill in preparing simple personal and business papers.

The copy from which you have typed (keyed) up to now has been shown in pica (10-pitch) typewriter type. In Phase 2 much of the copy is shown in large easy-to-read printer's type.

All drill lines are written to an exact 60-space line to simplify checking. Some paragraphs and problem activities, however, contain lines of variable length. Continue to key them line for line as shown until you are directed to do otherwise.

SOUTH-WESTERN PUBLISHING CO.

Unit 61 Lessons 274-275

Performance Evaluated

1. To measure your skill in keyboarding straight-copy material.
2. To measure your language skills.
3. To evaluate your ability to produce usable business documents.

Machine Adjustments

1. 65-space line for Check Equipment exercise.
2. 70-space line for timed writing.
3. 75-space line for Language Skills activity.
4. As required for documents.
5. DS sentences and timed writings.

Lessons 274-275

274a-275a ▶ 5 Check Equipment

Before you begin the evaluation material each day, check your machine to see that it is in good working order by keyboarding the paragraph at the right at least twice (first slowly, then faster).

Jack expects the increase of heavy smoke will be quite a big
hazard. We will close Plants #32, #47, and #59 if this pollution
increases more than 10% within 6 to 8 days. The firm may suspend
the work of the coalfield if the panels blame it for the problem.

| 1 | 2 | 3 | 4 | 5 | 6 | 7 | 8 | 9 | 10 | 11 | 12 | 13 |

274b ▶ 15 Evaluate Straight Copy

Take two 5′ writings on the ¶s at the right. Record *gwam* and errors on the better writing.

all letters used | A | 1.5 si | 5.7 awl | 80% hfw |

	gwam 1′	5′
As our society grows in size and complexity, there is a great need for	13	3
information--data on which to base decisions. Many experts say we	28	6
are in the midst of an "information explosion" which will play a very	42	8
important role in the way we live and work. A wave of new electronic	56	11
equipment has given us new tools to produce, process, store, retrieve,	70	14
and utilize information so that work can be done better and faster.	84	17
One of the vital steps in this process, of course, is communication.	98	20
The value of office employees is rated, in large measure, on the	13	22
basis of their communication skills. The number of positions for those	27	25
who can operate a keyboard continues to grow, but the demand is for	41	28
those who can take the ideas of others and express them correctly. Many	56	31
accountants are in great demand, but they must be able to do more than	70	33
just enter figures in a column; they must be able to interpret clearly	84	36
and concisely the meaning of figures on a spreadsheet.	95	39
Business places a premium on individuals who are adept in the use	13	41
of language. People who are well trained to work in an office can earn	28	44
good salaries, but those who have also developed the talent to express	42	47
ideas quickly and concisely will gain success more rapidly. If you	55	50
have developed a high skill in communication, there is no doubt that	69	52
you will find your skill rewarded in terms of better pay. If you excel	84	55
in communication, you can expect a better job in your future.	96	58

gwam 1′ | 1 | 2 | 3 | 4 | 5 | 6 | 7 | 8 | 9 | 10 | 11 | 12 | 13 | 14 |
5′ | 1 | 2 | 3 |

Unit 3 Lessons 26-30

Learning Goals

1. To learn the location of each figure key.
2. To learn how to strike each figure key properly with the correct finger.
3. To build keyboarding speed and technique on copy containing figures.
4. To improve keyboarding speed and technique on alphabetic copy.

Machine Adjustments

1. Paper guide at *0*.
2. Ribbon control to use top half of ribbon.
3. Margin sets: left margin (center - 30); right margin (move to right end of scale).
4. Line-space selector set to single-space (SS) drills.
5. Line-space selector set to double-space (DS) paragraphs.

Lesson 26 — 1 and 7

Line length: 60 spaces
Spacing: single-space (SS)

26a ▶ 6
Conditioning Practice

1. Each line twice SS.
2. A 1′ writing on line 3; find *gwam* (total 5-stroke words completed).

alphabet 1 Vida was quick to get the next bus to Juarez to play for me.
space bar 2 to row|is to row|is to|is to fix|to the|to the lake|the sign
easy 3 Keith is to row with us to the lake to fix six of the signs.

5-stroke words | 1 | 2 | 3 | 4 | 5 | 6 | 7 | 8 | 9 | 10 | 11 | 12 |

26b ▶ 18
Learn 1 and 7

each line twice SS (slowly, then faster); DS between 2-line groups; if time permits, practice each line again

Follow the Standard Plan for Learning New Keys outlined on page 7.

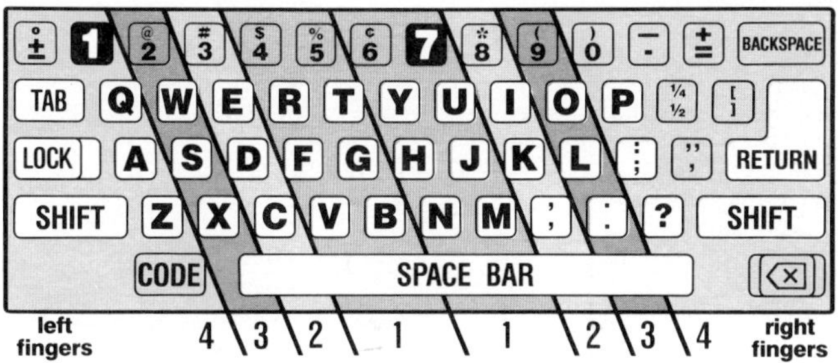

Reach technique for 1

Learn figure 1

1 a 1 a 1 aa 11 aa 11 a1a a1a 11a Reach up for 1, 11, and 111.
2 Key the figures 1, 11, and 111. Please study pages 1 to 11.

Reach technique for 7

Learn 7

3 j 7 j 7 jj 77 jj 77 j7j j7j 77j Reach up for 7, 77, and 777.
4 Add the figures 7, 77, and 777. Have just 7 of 77 finished?

Combine 1 and 7

5 Key 11, 17, 71, and 77. Only 11 of the 17 joggers are here.
6 Do you want a size 7 or 11? I have 17 of each one in stock.
7 The stock person counted 11 coats, 17 slacks, and 77 shirts.

SS
Time out?

Minutes?

Lines?

DS

Indent enumerated items 5 spaces from each margin.

NOTES:

1. If the document originator's name or number contains punctuation, it must be ~~entered~~ enclosed in double quotation marks as described previously. this also applies to the storage number~~ed~~.

2. The input form must be entered as "SC" (straight copy), "RD" (rough draft), "SCRIPT" (script), or "STAT" (statistical). It is not necesary to key in the double quotation marks, but the entries must be made in all capitols. If an invalid entry is made, the program will display the ~~legal alternatives~~ correct forms and re-prompt for input.

3. The time in and time out fields should be entered as ("hhmm") or ("hh:mm"). Some BASICs ~~may~~ require the former format to be enclosed in double quotation marks. The program makes no check on the validity of ~~these fields.~~ the times

4. The minutes must be entered as an integer in the range ~~of~~ 1-32767. thus, a task requiring 1 hour and 27 minutes must be entered as 87. The program does not verify that "time out" ~~less the~~ minus "time in" equals the number of minutes specified.

5. The total lines must be entered as an integer in the range 1-32767.

After the last log sheet item has been entered, key~~ing~~ END (in uppercase) when the program asks for ~~the~~ "Document originator?" The report for this operator ~~now prints~~ will then print in this format:

Report for (operator's name)

Total weighted lines:

Total time:

Lines Per minute:

The program will then terminate. If another operator's statistics are to be computed, key~~ing~~ RUN~~should~~ to restart the program.

26c ▶ 14 Improve Keyboarding Technique

1. Each pair of lines (1-6) twice SS (slowly, then faster); DS between 4-line groups.

2. A 1′ writing on line 7, then on line 8; find *gwam* on each writing.

Technique hints

- Make *upward* reaches without moving the hand forward.
- Make *downward* reaches without twisting the wrists or moving the elbows in or out.

Row emphasis

home/3d
1 just try|will keep|they quit|you would|play golf|did ship it
2 Pat always tries to keep her eyes off the keys as she works.

home/1st
3 can call|hand ax|can land|lava gas|small flag|jazz band ball
4 Hannah had a small van all fall. Max has a small jazz band.

figures
5 Just 17 of the 71 boys got 77 of the 117 quiz answers right.
6 The test on the 17th will cover pages 11 to 17 and 71 to 77.

easy
7 Alan may make a bid on the ivory forks they got in the city.
8 Tien may fix the bus panel for the city if the pay is right.

5-stroke words | 1 | 2 | 3 | 4 | 5 | 6 | 7 | 8 | 9 | 10 | 11 | 12 |

26d ▶ 12 Improve Keyboarding Speed: Guided Writing

1. A 1′ writing on each ¶; find *gwam* on each writing.

2. Using your better *gwam* as a base rate, select a *goal rate* 2-4 *gwam* higher than your base rate, and take three 1′ writings on each ¶ with the call of the quarter-minute guide (see p. 37 for routine).

Quarter-minute checkpoints

gwam	1/4′	1/2′	3/4′	Time
16	4	8	12	16
20	5	10	15	20
24	6	12	18	24
28	7	14	21	28
32	8	16	24	32
36	9	18	27	36
40	10	20	30	40

all letters used | E | 1.2 si | 4.8 awl | 90% hfw |

gwam 2′

I am now trying to learn to vary my keying rate to fit 5
the job of keying the words. When I learn to speed up more 11
of the easy words, I can take time to break the longer ones 17
into small parts and handle them quickly. 22

With a bit more practice, I shall be able to handle by 27
word response more of the shorter ones that just now I must 33
analyze and key letter by letter. As I learn to do more of 39
these words as units, I shall become more expert. 44

gwam 2′ | 1 | 2 | 3 | 4 | 5 | 6 |

Lesson 27 4 and 8

Line length: 60 spaces
Spacing: single-space (SS)

27a ▶ 6 Conditioning Practice

1. Each line twice SS.

2. A 1′ writing on line 3; find *gwam* (total 5-stroke words completed).

alphabet 1 Marv wanted a quiet place, but Felix kept playing show jazz.
figure 2 Please review Figure 11 on page 17 and Figure 17 on page 77.
easy 3 Iris is to go to the lake towns to do the map work for them.

5-stroke words | 1 | 2 | 3 | 4 | 5 | 6 | 7 | 8 | 9 | 10 | 11 | 12 |

27b ▶ 12 Improve Keyboarding Speed: Guided Writing

Practice again the 2 ¶s above, using the directions in 26d.

Goal: To improve your speed by at least 2-4 *gwam*.

268b-273b (continued)

Document 7
User Documentation
for Computer Program

Prepare as an unbound report.
Use storage number: 7003.

PROGRAM TO COMPUTE WP LINES PER MINUTE

User Documentation

~~The operator should~~ key the program into the BASIC interpreter ~~available on his/her system~~ or recall it form storage if it has been previously *entered* ~~put there~~. The line numbers must be keyed ~~precisely~~ exactly as indicated. Many BASICs require that the keywords, such as (PRINT) and (IF), be keyed in upper case. The *text* inclosed within pairs of double quotation marks (") is user communication, which may be keyed in uppercase, lowercase, mixed cases, or modified as desired.

When the ~~programmer~~ program has been successfully keyed into the BASIC interpreter, ~~the operator should~~ type "RUN" to *execute* ~~make~~ the program ~~execute~~. If everything has been done properly, the program will then print: Operator's name?

~~The user should~~ key in the operator's name form the top of the log sheet. *The program performs calculations for only one operator at a time.* Note: If the operator's name contains spaces or punctuation ("Smith, John"), it must be entered enclosed in double quotation*s* ~~marks~~. If only a single name is to be entered (Carson), *it need not be enclosed in quotation marks.*

The program will then ~~continue~~ proceed to cycle through the following prompts. ~~The operator should~~ key in the information from the log sheet in the order in which it is prompted, working across the page:

DS

SS

Type END when done.

Document originator?

Storage number?

Input form?

Time in?

(continued on page 455)

27c ▶ 18
Learn 4 and 8

each line twice SS (slowly, then faster); DS between 2-line groups; if time permits, practice each line again

Follow the Standard Plan for Learning New Keys outlined on page 7.

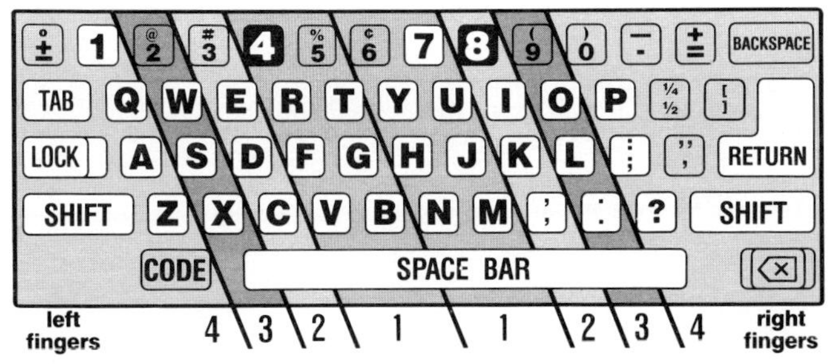

Reach technique for 4

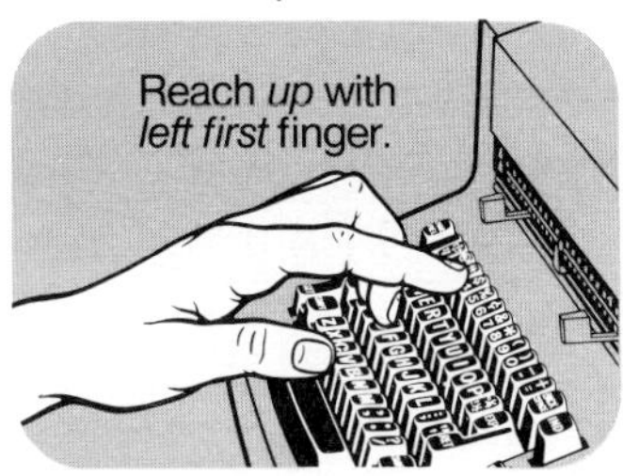

Learn 4

1 f 4 f 4 ff 44 ff 44 f4f f4f 44f Reach up for 4, 44, and 444.

2 Key the figures 4, 44, and 444. Please study pages 4 to 44.

Reach technique for 8

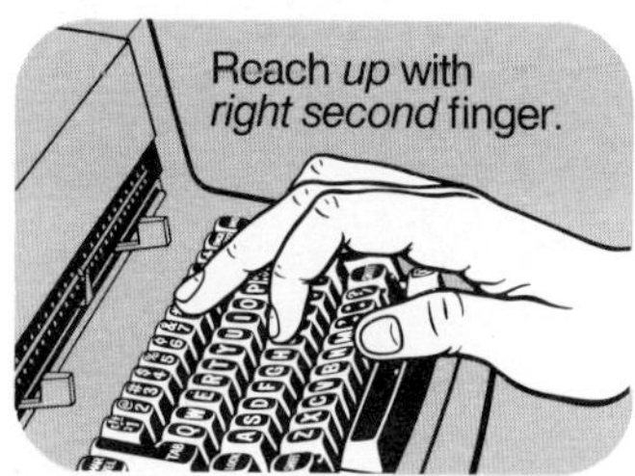

Learn 8

3 k 8 k 8 kk 88 kk 88 k8k k8k 88k Reach up for 8, 88, and 888.

4 Add the figures 8, 88, and 888. Have just 8 of 88 finished?

Combine 4 and 8

5 Key 44, 48, 84, and 88. Just 48 of the 88 skiers have come.

6 Reach with the fingers to key 48 and 488 as well as 4 and 8.

7 On October 8, the 4 hikers left on a long hike of 448 miles.

27d ▶ 14
Improve Keyboarding Technique

1. Each of lines 1-6 twice SS (slowly, then faster); DS between 2-line groups.

2. Two 1′ writings on the ¶ which contains all the letters; find *gwam* on each writing.

Goal: *At least* 22 *gwam*.

Figure sentences

1 Key 1 and 7 and 4 and 8. Add 4, 11, 17, 44, 48, 78, and 88.

2 I based my April 4 report on pages 447 to 488 of Chapter 17.

3 Just 17 of the boys and 18 of the girls passed all 47 tests.

Alphabetic sentences

4 Elena may have Jack rekey parts two and six of the big quiz.

5 Vic Kibold may win quite a just prize for his next pop song.

6 Peg can have a jeweler size my antique ring to fit Burk Dix.

Fingers upright

Alphabetic paragraph | E | 1.1 si | 4.9 awl | 92% hfw |

. 2 . 4 . 6 . 8 . 10 .

Seize the chance to build your speed to the quite high

12 . 14 . 16 . 18 . 20 . 22 .

level you want. If you will just try harder for a new high

24 . 26 . 28 . 30 . 32 . 34 .

speed each week, you can gain in speed more than you expect.

268b-273b (continued)

Document 6
Computer Program

1. Keyboard the program (prepared by Arthur Franklin) on plain paper *exactly* as shown. Each individual block on the form is equal to one horizontal space. Use a top margin of 1½" and a 1½" left margin.

2. Head the program: PROGRAM TO COMPUTE WP LINES PER MINUTE.

3. Be sure all zeros are keyboarded with a diagonal (Ø) so that the data processing operator will not mistake them for the letter O.

4. Proofread the program carefully to insure that it is spaced and punctuated exactly as shown. Record as "STAT" under storage number 6083.

Note: Print the greater than symbol (>) on lines 300, 370, and 420 in pencil.

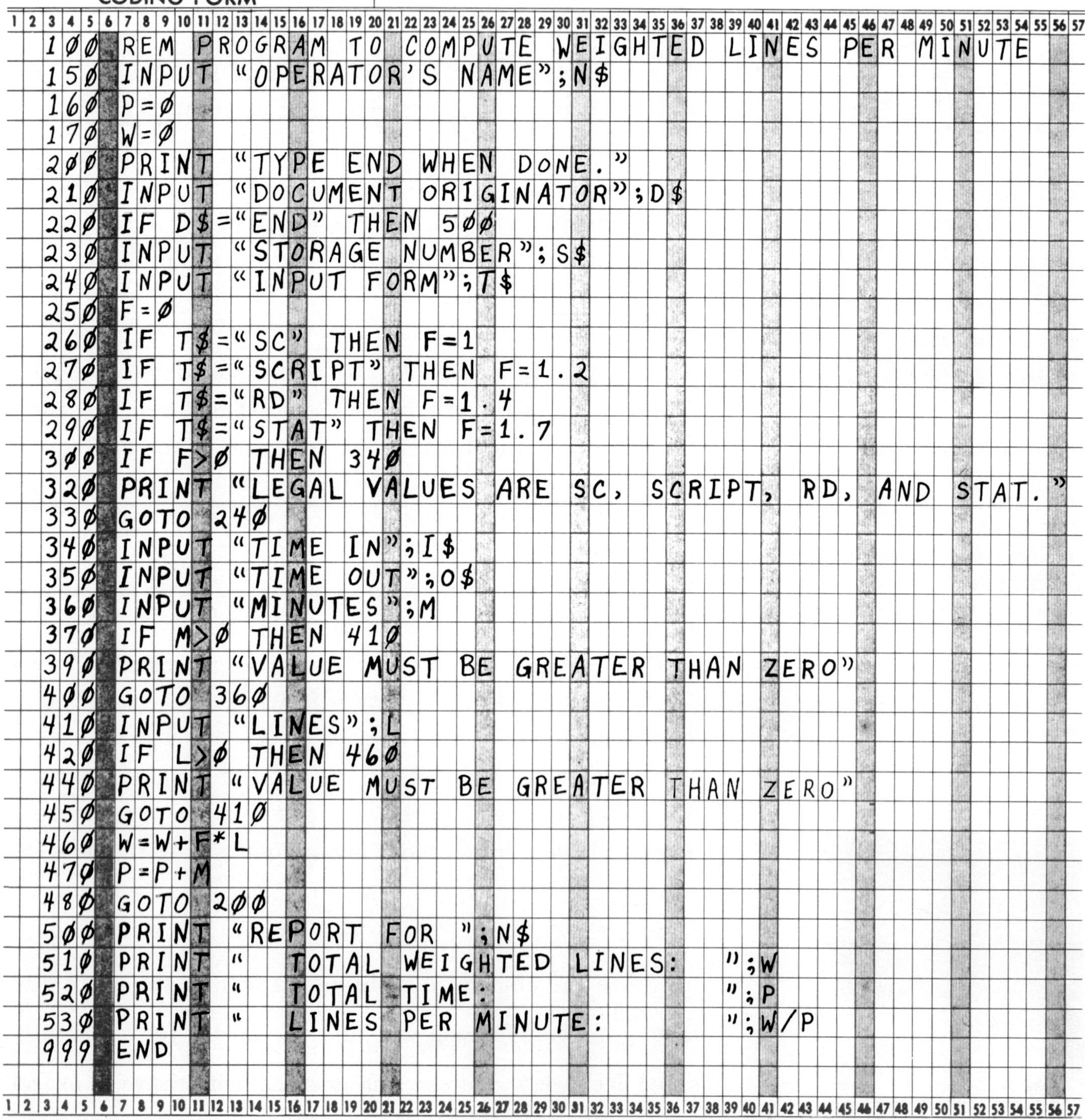

GENERAL PURPOSE CODING FORM

```
1ØØ REM PROGRAM TO COMPUTE WEIGHTED LINES PER MINUTE
15Ø INPUT "OPERATOR'S NAME";N$
16Ø P=Ø
17Ø W=Ø
2ØØ PRINT "TYPE END WHEN DONE."
21Ø INPUT "DOCUMENT ORIGINATOR";D$
22Ø IF D$="END" THEN 5ØØ
23Ø INPUT "STORAGE NUMBER"; S$
24Ø INPUT "INPUT FORM";T$
25Ø F=Ø
26Ø IF T$="SC" THEN F=1
27Ø IF T$="SCRIPT" THEN F=1.2
28Ø IF T$="RD" THEN F=1.4
29Ø IF T$="STAT" THEN F=1.7
3ØØ IF F>Ø THEN 34Ø
32Ø PRINT "LEGAL VALUES ARE SC, SCRIPT, RD, AND STAT."
33Ø GOTO 24Ø
34Ø INPUT "TIME IN";I$
35Ø INPUT "TIME OUT";O$
36Ø INPUT "MINUTES";M
37Ø IF M>Ø THEN 41Ø
39Ø PRINT "VALUE MUST BE GREATER THAN ZERO"
4ØØ GOTO 36Ø
41Ø INPUT "LINES";L
42Ø IF L>Ø THEN 46Ø
44Ø PRINT "VALUE MUST BE GREATER THAN ZERO"
45Ø GOTO 41Ø
46Ø W=W+F*L
47Ø P=P+M
48Ø GOTO 2ØØ
5ØØ PRINT "REPORT FOR ";N$
51Ø PRINT "   TOTAL WEIGHTED LINES:  ";W
52Ø PRINT "   TOTAL TIME:            ";P
53Ø PRINT "   LINES PER MINUTE:      ";W/P
999 END
```

Lesson 28 — 5 and 9

Line length: 60 spaces
Spacing: single-space (SS)

28a ▶ 6
Conditioning Practice

1. Each line twice SS.
2. A 1′ writing on line 3; find *gwam* (total 5-stroke words completed).

alphabet	1	Gavin made a quick fall trip by jet to Zurich six weeks ago.
figure	2	Today we sold 18 pairs of gloves, 4 coats, and 17 knit caps.
easy	3	The man is to fix the big sign by the field for a city firm.

5-stroke words | 1 | 2 | 3 | 4 | 5 | 6 | 7 | 8 | 9 | 10 | 11 | 12 |

28b ▶ 18
Learn 5 and 9

each line twice SS (slowly, then faster); DS between 2-line groups; if time permits, practice each line again

Follow the Standard Plan for Learning New Keys outlined on page 7.

Reach technique for 5

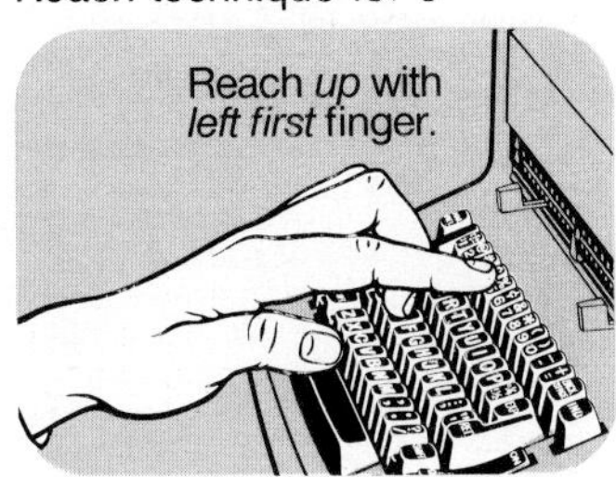

Reach technique for 9

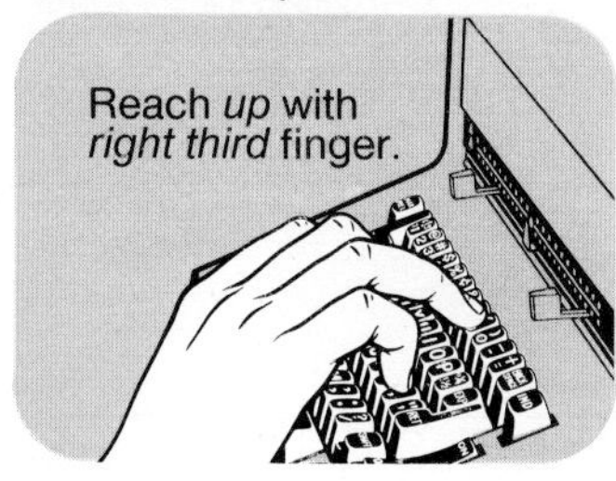

Learn 5

1 f 5 f 5 ff 55 ff 55 f5f f5f 55f Reach up for 5, 55, and 555.
2 Key the figures 5, 55, and 555. Please study pages 5 to 55.

Learn 9

use the letter "l"

3 l 9 l 9 ll 99 ll 99 l9l l9l 99l Reach up for 9, 99, and 999.
4 Add the figures 9, 99, and 999. Have just 9 of 99 finished?

Combine 5 and 9

5 Key 55, 59, 95, and 99. Only 59 of the 99 flags are flying.
6 Reach with the fingers to key 59 and 599 as well as 5 and 9.
7 My goal is to sell 55 tacos, 59 pizzas, and 5 cases of cola.

28c ▶ 12
Improve Keyboarding Technique: Numbers

each line twice SS; DS between 2-line groups

Language skills notes
1. No space is left before or after : when used with figures to express time.
2. Most nouns before numbers are capitalized; exceptions include page and line.

No space

1 She should be on Jetair Flight 1749 at 5:58 p.m. at Gate 48.
2 I used Chapter 18, pages 419 to 457, for my April 19 report.
3 The club meeting will be held in Room 1748 at 59 Park Place.
4 Can you meet me at 1849 Marsh Street at 7:45 a.m. August 11?
5 Of the 79 students, 18 keyed at least 45 w.a.m. on March 19.
6 They had 145 workers in 1987 and expect to have 195 by 1999.

268b-273b (continued)

Document 5
Letters from Boilerplate
(LM pp. 143-147)

Mrs. Witkowski asks you to process letters as requested in the memorandum from Mr. Ngwa. Record the letters as "SC" under storage numbers 6049, 6050, and 6051. Date the letters June 24, 19--.

Electro-Technologies, Ltd.
20 Marietta Street ○ Atlanta, GA 30303-6280

INTEROFFICE COMMUNICATION

June 23, 19--

Word Processing Section

PREPARATION OF LETTERS

Prepare the letter below for my signature to each of the following individuals. In the second paragraph, include the appropriate system name and country as indicated.

Mr. Geoffrey C. Brown, Regional Director
Electro-Technologies, Ltd.
275, Regent Street
LONDON W1R 5HF
ENGLAND

(Fleetwood II System; British office)

Mme. Francoise C. Demarteau, Regional Director
Electro-Technologies, Ltd.
12 Place de la Republique
F-75011 PARIS
FRANCE

(Etoille I System; French office)

Sr. Pasquale T. DiMarco, Regional Director
Electro-Technologies, Ltd.
Via Aurelia Antica 415
I-00165 ROME
ITALY

(Mela Une System; Italian office)

Ms. Capelli has asked me to send you the enclosed computer program, with documentation, for use in the Information Processing Centers to be established at our major headquarters in Europe. The use of this program will permit us to gather standardized information for our work measurement program.

This simple program computes the speed in weighted lines per minute of a word processing operator. It is written in "generic" BASIC which should run on any system which supports BASIC with string-handling capability, including the (system) in our (office).

If you encounter any difficulty with this program or have any questions, contact me without delay.

Thomas Ngwa

Thomas Ngwa
Administrative Assistant

ec

28d ▶ 14
Improve Keyboarding Technique: Response Patterns

1. Each pair of lines twice SS (slowly, then faster); DS between 4-line groups.

2. A 1′ writing on line 2, then on line 4; find *gwam* on each writing.

letter response
1 face jump area only ever upon save milk safe pump vast onion
2 As you are aware, only we look upon him as a great pop star.

word response
3 disk envy alto down hang corn hand body worn lend quay shale
4 He is to pay them for the social work they did for the city.

combination response
5 wish upon|they save|then jump|kept safe|half join|quay trade
6 It was then up to him to pay the duty they set on the ivory.

5-stroke words | 1 | 2 | 3 | 4 | 5 | 6 | 7 | 8 | 9 | 10 | 11 | 12 |

Lesson 29 — 3 and 0

Line length: 60 spaces
Spacing: single-space (SS)

29a ▶ 6
Conditioning Practice

1. Each line twice SS.

2. A 1′ writing on line 3; find *gwam* (total 5-stroke words completed).

alphabet 1 Mazy helped Jared quickly fix the big wood stove in the den.
figure 2 Key 1 and 8 and 4 and 9 and 5 and 7 and 194 and 718 and 584.
easy 3 Alfie is to go to work for the city to fix eighty bus signs.

5-stroke words | 1 | 2 | 3 | 4 | 5 | 6 | 7 | 8 | 9 | 10 | 11 | 12 |

29b ▶ 18
Learn 3 and 0

each line twice SS (slowly, then faster); DS between 2-line groups; if time permits practice each line again

Follow the Standard Plan for Learning New Keys outlined on page 7.

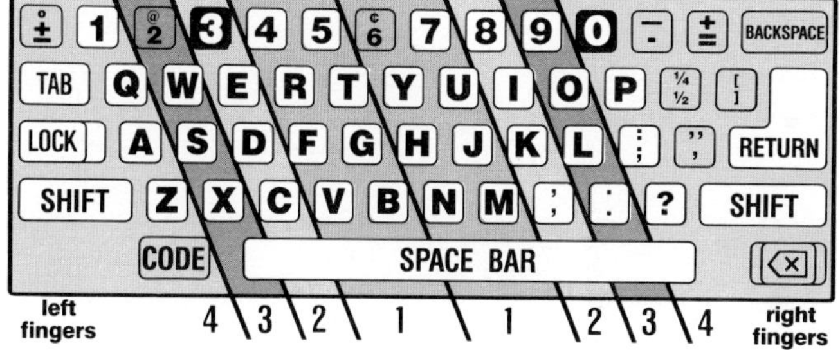

Reach technique for 3

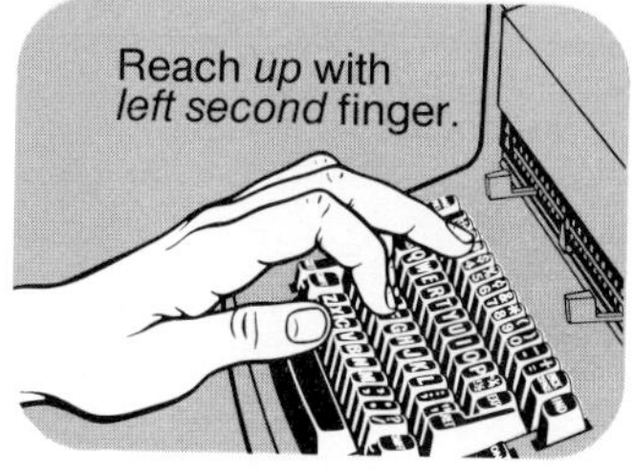

Reach technique for 0

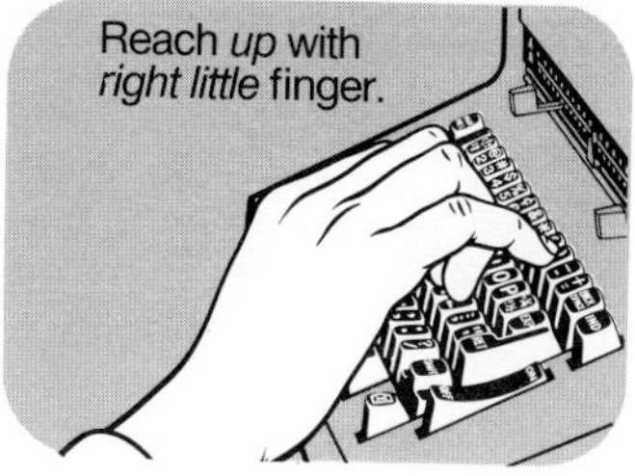

Learn 3

1 d 3 d 3 dd 33 dd 33 d3d d3d 33d Reach up for 3, 33, and 333.
2 Key the figures 3, 33, and 333. Please check Rooms 3 to 33.

Learn 0 (zero)

3 ; 0 ; 0 ;; 00 ;; 00 ;0; ;0; 00; Reach up for 0, 00, and 000.
4 Snap the finger off the 0. Do you want 0, 00, or 000 paper?

Combine 3 and 0

5 Key in the figures 0, 3, and 30; then try 300, 303, and 330.
6 Did they key at the rate of 30, or was it 33 words a minute?
7 Of 33 members, 3 were 30 minutes late for 3 of the meetings.

268b-273b (continued)

Document 4
Magazine Article

Mrs. Witkowski has written a column for a magazine, and she asks you to prepare it in final form as an unbound report DS with the title WORD PROCESSING AND THE FUTURE. Insert "by Joyce T. Witkowski" as a secondary heading. Prepare a reference page.

1. Use proper textual citations. The complete citation for each reference has been included in the text for your convenience in preparing the reference page in proper format.

2. Correct all marked and unmarked errors.

3. Use storage number 6041 for the report; use storage number 6042 for the reference page.

Alvin Toffler (Toffler, Alvin. The Third Wave. New York: William Morrow and Company, Inc., 1980, 202-207) was ~~one of~~ among the first to ~~forsee~~ predict that word processing would revolutionize operations in the "office of the future." Peter McWilliams (McWilliams, Peter The Word Processing Book. Los Angeles: Prelude Press, 1982, 69) forecasted that "By 1990 every Selectric in every office in america will be replaced by a word processing computer." As early as 1976, Konkel and Peck (Konkel, Gilbert j. and Phyllis J. Peck. The Word Processing Explosion. Stamford: Office Publications, Inc., 1976, 139-146) predicted a rapid growth in the use of word processing equipment and ~~finally~~ concluded that "NOW is the time for us to develop our future offices."

The increasing use of automated equipment in the office has not only changed administrative ~~systems~~ methods and procedures but also ~~changed~~ the ~~jobs~~ skills required to ~~produce~~ process documents and communications. Casady (Casady, Mona. Word/Information Processing Concepts. 2d ed. Cincinnati: South-Western Publishing Co., 1984, 169-182) lists career opportunities in positoins with titles such as word processing specialists, which ~~ae~~ are so new that they do not appear in the Dictionery of Occupational Titles. U.S. Government publications include word processing operaters under "secretaries."

What of the future? According to the Bureau of Labor Statistics (U.S. Department of Labor. Employment Projections for 1995. Washington, DC: U.S. Government Printing Office, 1984, 38) there were 2,711,000 secretaries in 1972. By 1995, the Bureau projects this number ~~will~~ may increase to as high as 3,498,000. As Casady (1984, 12) ~~points out~~ concludes, "As a result of advancements in office machines and systems, many challenging and exciting careerdoors are opening."

29c ▶ 12
Improve Keyboarding Technique: Numbers

each line twice SS (slowly, then faster); DS between 2-line groups; if time permits, practice each line again

1/7 1 Kyle will be 17 on Tuesday, October 7; he weighs 177 pounds.
4/8 2 The exam on the 4th is to be over pages 4 to 8 and 48 to 88.
5/9 3 For the answer to Problem 59, see Unit 9, page 595, line 59.
3/0 4 The meeting is to be held June 30 at 3:30 p.m. in Suite 300.
all figures learned 5 Key these figures as units: 30, 40, 50, 91, 85, 73, and 49.
6 Our group sold 850 chili dogs, 497 sandwiches, and 301 pies.

29d ▶ 14
Improve Keyboarding Technique: Service Keys

1. Clear all tab stops; then, starting at left margin, set 2 tab stops 25 spaces apart.
2. Key the drill once as shown.
3. Rekey the drill at a faster speed.

space bar 1 I am|go by|he may|she can|if they|for them|the city|may form
2 They may make their goals if they work with the usual vigor.

shift keys and lock 3 Sachi Kato of Japan won the finals from Lydia Diaz of Spain.
4 Yuan used a quote from FAMILIAR QUOTATIONS by John Bartlett.

tabulator and return
5 she did -------- tab --------→ and the -------- tab --------→ pay for
6 work with they paid make them
7 busy towns worn panel work goals

Lesson 30 — 2 and 6

Line length: 60 spaces
Spacing: single-space (SS)

30a ▶ 6
Conditioning Practice

1. Each line twice SS.
2. A 1′ writing on line 3; find *gwam* (total 5-stroke words completed).

alphabet 1 Gwen asked me to have Buzz cap the six jars of quince jelly.
figure 2 Mandy lives at 1748 Elm Street; Gordy, at 3059 Jayson Drive.
easy 3 Tisha is to go to the lake with us if she is to do the work.

5-stroke words | 1 | 2 | 3 | 4 | 5 | 6 | 7 | 8 | 9 | 10 | 11 | 12 |

30b ▶ 14
Check Keyboarding Technique

1. Key lines 1-10 twice each, SS, as your teacher checks your keyboarding technique.
2. If time permits, take a 1′ writing on line 11, then on line 12. Find *gwam* on each writing.

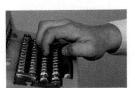

quiet hands and arms 1 Pam wants the quartz box for Belle and a jade ring for Vick.
2 Zip, can you have this quaint jug fixed for Ms. Lock by two?

quick-snap keystrokes 3 Rick paid for both the visual aid and the sign for the firm.
4 Did the bugle corps toot with the usual vigor for the queen?

down-and-in spacing 5 Nan is to go to the city hall to sign the land forms for us.
6 Ty is to pay for the eight pens she laid by the audit forms.

out-and-down shifting 7 Julia and Leon will visit Yang and Chin on their China trip.
8 Are you going in May, or in June? Willa is leaving in July.

finger reaches to top row 9 or 94|if 85|am 17|do 39;|tug 575|lap 910|fork 4948|kept 8305
10 We moved from 3947 Brook Road to 1750 Aspen Place on May 18.

easy sentences 11 Glena kept all the work forms on the shelf by the big chair.
12 Ella may go to the soap firm for title to all the lake land.

5-stroke words | 1 | 2 | 3 | 4 | 5 | 6 | 7 | 8 | 9 | 10 | 11 | 12 |

268b-273b (continued)

Document 3
Statistical Report

Mrs. Witkowski gives you the following instructions for preparing the statistical report for Ms. Cynthia T. Morris.

1. The table will be filed with unbound reports, so be sure it appears within the margins for a 6-inch line.

2. Evenly distribute the intercolumn spaces.

3. Make other placement decisions.

4. Use storage number 6034.

OFFICE OF RESEARCH AND DEVELOPMENT

Projects Under Development as of June 1

Number	Manager	Funds Budgeted	Funds Expended
~~34899~~	~~Davidson~~	~~$2,850,000~~	~~$2,745,000~~
~~34900~~	~~Fredericks~~	~~1,475,000~~	~~1,480,500~~
34901	Matthews	$3,890,000	$2,970,460 ~~2,050,430~~
34902	O'Connor	950,500	685,740 ~~820,635~~
34903	Goldman	1,900,550	1,020,560 ~~874,500~~
34904	Hartley	750,000	592,300 ~~455,000~~
34905	Demalio	2,375,000	1,785,000 ~~1,249,000~~
34906	Parramore	4,500,000	3,691,600 ~~2,980,500~~
~~34907~~	~~Morton~~	~~875,000~~	~~873,500~~
34908	Henderson	1,250,000	1,000,000 ~~970,500~~
~~34909~~	~~Hernandez~~	~~3,850,000~~	~~1,320,000~~
34910	Vasserman	2,000,000	1,460,700 ~~850,500~~
34911	McNeil	900,000	336,700 ~~125,600~~
34912	Allen	5,970,000	4,930,600 ~~3,820,500~~
34913	Wallace	750,600	265,370 ~~300,250~~
34914	Martinez	1,530,500	1,370,500 ~~1,230,000~~
34915	Richardson	4,500,000	260,400
34916	Lee	960,000	50,300
34917	Carpenter	1,870,000	22,600
34918	Sukumo	2,590,500	17,200

30c ▶ 18
Learn 2 and 6

each line twice SS (slowly, then faster); DS between 2-line groups; if time permits, practice each line again

Follow the Standard Plan for Learning New Keys outlined on page 7.

Reach technique for 2

Reach *up* with *left third* finger.

Reach technique for 6

Reach *up* with *right first* finger.

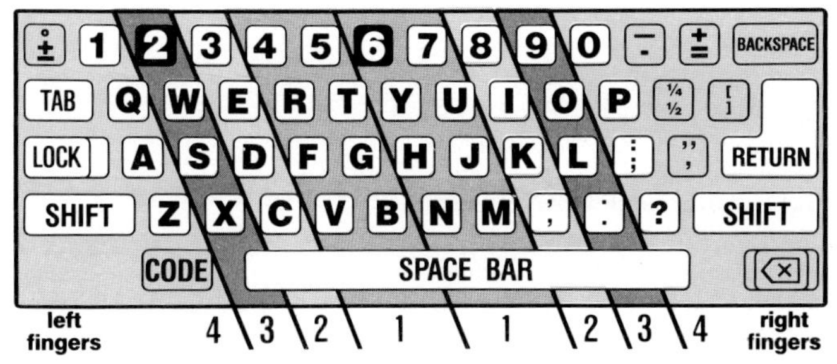
left fingers
4 3 2 1 1 2 3 4
right fingers

Learn 2

1 s 2 s 2 ss 22 ss 22 s2s s2s 22s Reach up for 2, 22, and 222.
2 Key the figures 2, 22, and 222. Review pages 2 to 22 today.

Learn 6

3 j 6 j 6 jj 66 jj 66 j6j j6j 66j Reach up for 6, 66, and 666.
4 Add the figures 6, 66, and 666. Have only 6 of 66 finished?

Combine 2, 6, and other figures

5 Key 22, 26, 62, and 66. Just 22 of the 66 skaters are here.
6 Reach with the fingers to key 26 and 262 as well as 2 and 6.
7 Key the figures as units: 26, 59, 17, 30, 46, 162, and 268.
8 The letter dated June 26, 1987, was vital in Case No. 30564.

30d ▶ 12
Check Keyboarding Speed

1. A 1′ writing on ¶ 1, then on ¶ 2; find *gwam* on each.
2. Two 2′ writings on ¶s 1 and 2 combined; find *gwam* on each writing.
3. A 3′ writing on ¶s 1 and 2 combined (or if your teacher prefers, an additional 1′ writing on each ¶).

1′ *Gwam* Goals

▽ 21 = acceptable
□ 25 = average
○ 29 = good
◇ 33 = excellent

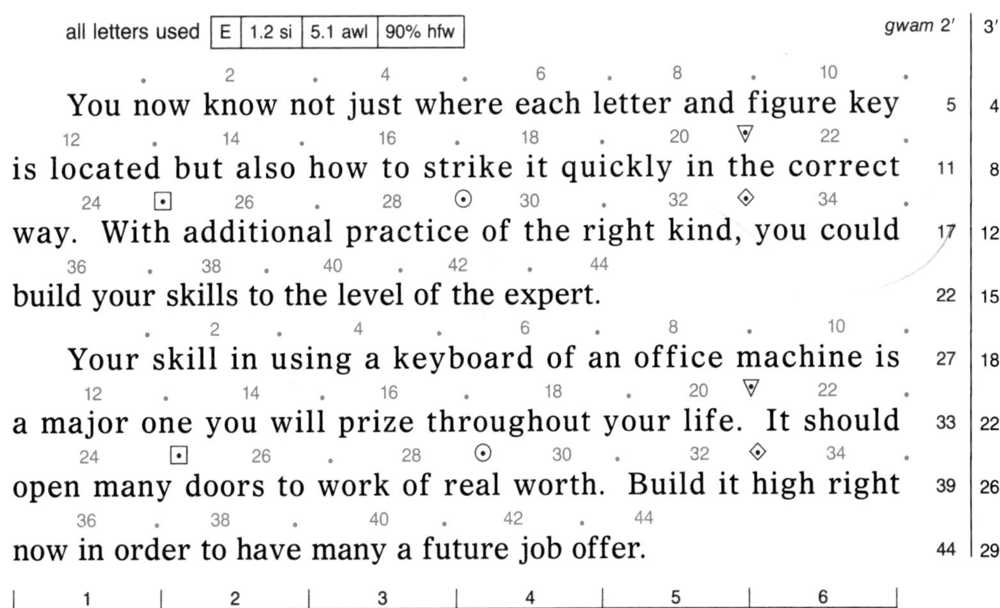

all letters used | E | 1.2 si | 5.1 awl | 90% hfw

	gwam 2′	3′
You now know not just where each letter and figure key	5	4
is located but also how to strike it quickly in the correct	11	8
way. With additional practice of the right kind, you could	17	12
build your skills to the level of the expert.	22	15
Your skill in using a keyboard of an office machine is	27	18
a major one you will prize throughout your life. It should	33	22
open many doors to work of real worth. Build it high right	39	26
now in order to have many a future job offer.	44	29

gwam 2′ | 1 | 2 | 3 | 4 | 5 | 6
gwam 3′ | 1 | 2 | 3 | 4

268b-273b (continued)

Document 2
Progress Report

Your supervisor, Mrs. Witkowski, asks you to process this progress report in final form for Mr. Allen.

1. Log the report under storage number 6023.

2. Correct any marked and unmarked errors.

PROJECT 34912 PROGRESS REPORT

Project {Code Name "SUPER-vision"} was initiated 18 months ago with the goal of applying the latest in electronic improvement to the developement of a new generation of television receivers for pass production. This Project is now in the final stages and a prototype will be available soon.

"SUPER-vision" will be a television receivers with a large screen and a degree of claritety equal to the best moving picture film. Colors are truer and brighter. "Ghosts" and intererference from out side sources will be eliminated. An integral program will monitor the operationsof the set and will make needed adjustments to maintain high-quality performance.

These changes are made possible through the use of chips, similar to those used in computers, which will convert incoming visual and audio signals to numbers. When these dignals are changed, innumerable machinations are possible.

Through the use of digital technology, the vertical and horizontalresolution of waves {currently set by Federal regulations at 250 horizontal lines and 520 vertical lines} change changed to almost double. Impressive improvements in television reception is possible, without changing current

borad cast criteria.

As an "added extra attraction," "SUPER-vision" will be equiped with stereo sound which will provide high-fidelity audeo. Many television stations are all ready broadcasting in stereo and most will do so within a very short time.

Unit 4 Lessons 31-32

Learning Goals

1. To improve alphabetic keyboarding speed and technique.
2. To improve number keyboarding speed and control.
3. To review/improve language skills: number expression.
4. To extend skill on longer paragraph writings.

Machine Adjustments

1. Paper guide at *0*.
2. Ribbon control to use top half of ribbon.
3. Margin sets: left margin (center - 30); right margin (move to right end of scale).
4. Line-space selector set to single-space (SS) drills; to double-space (DS) ¶s.

Lesson 31 Basic/Language Skills

Line length: 60 spaces
Spacing: single-space (SS)

31a ▶ 6 Conditioning Practice

1. Each line twice SS.
2. A 1′ writing on line 3; find *gwam* (total 5-stroke words completed)

alphabet 1 Roz fixed the crisp okra while Jan made a unique beef gravy.
figure 2 I stocked the lake with 628 perch, 759 carp, and 1,340 bass.
easy 3 Six of the big firms may bid for the right to the lake land.
5-stroke words | 1 | 2 | 3 | 4 | 5 | 6 | 7 | 8 | 9 | 10 | 11 | 12 |

31b ▶ 10 Improve Language Skills: Number Expression

1. Read the first rule highlighted in color at the right.
2. Key the *Learn* sentence below it, noting how the rule has been applied. Use the 60-space line for which your machine is set.
3. Key the *Apply* sentence, supplying the appropriate number expression.
4. Practice the other rules in the same way.
5. If time permits, key the three *Apply* sentences again to improve number control.

Spell a number that begins a sentence even when other numbers in the sentence are shown in figures.

Learn 1 Sixteen of the books are now overdue; 37 have been returned.
Apply 2 30 members of the club have signed up; only 12 have not.

Use figures for numbers above ten, and for numbers one to ten when they are used with numbers above ten.

Learn 3 He has ordered 10 computers, 20 disk drives, and 5 printers.
Apply 4 Mrs. Cruz said she will need ten to 12 copies of Z64 and Z98.

Use figures to express dates and times.

Learn 5 I take Wasach Flight 64 at 5:39 p.m. on January 27 to Boise.
Apply 6 At eight ten p.m. on May six, the curtain rises on OUR TOWN.

31c ▶ 18 Improve Keyboarding Technique: Response Patterns

1. Each pair of lines twice SS (slowly, then faster); DS between 4-line groups.
2. Two 1′ writings on line 7, then on line 8; find *gwam* on each writing.

letter response
1 oil case|pop star|you face|pin test|pink area|pump data card
2 As you are on my state tax case, get a few tax rates set up.

word response
3 tie with|big name|key firm|but rush|rich soap|make them risk
4 Sign the work form for the six men to do the city dock work.

combination response
5 you held|raw fish|sat down|oil land|safe auto|they draw maps
6 At the start signal, work with great vigor to make the rate.

easy sentences
7 Did they make the right title forms for the eight big firms?
8 The key social work may end if they turn down the usual aid.

| 1 | 2 | 3 | 4 | 5 | 6 | 7 | 8 | 9 | 10 | 11 | 12 |

268a-273a ▶ 5
Check Equipment

Before you begin work each day, check your machine to see that it is in good working order by keyboarding the paragraph at the right at least twice (first slowly, then faster).

all letters/figures used

Kay questioned my belief that new taxes might jeopardize our venture. If HB #49238-70 is passed, it will cause our net return to drop 16.5% (based on projected earnings). The problem is that the panel may codify provisos to make the firm pay a big penalty.

| 1 | 2 | 3 | 4 | 5 | 6 | 7 | 8 | 9 | 10 | 11 | 12 | 13 |

268b-273b ▶ 45
Document Processing

Now that you have completed your orientation training, you have been assigned as a word processing operator in the Information Processing Center of Electro-Technologies, Ltd.

Under the direction of your supervisor, Mrs. Joyce T. Witkowski, you will process documents submitted in handwritten or rough-draft form by executives throughout the company. You will also process documents from boilerplate (form paragraphs and letters). On occasion, you may be asked to substitute for data processing operators.

Document 1
Formal Interoffice Memorandum
(LM p. 141)

1. Prepare on plain paper at your best speed and in proper format the interoffice memorandum submitted by Mr. Arthur C. Allen, Project Director. Do not correct errors. If you make an error, backspace and strike the appropriate key.*

2. Record the document storage number (5490) on your Document Processing Log Sheet.

3. Proofread and correct, in pencil, the rough draft of the interoffice memorandum. Then, process the memo in final form.

*On electric self-correcting typewriters, errors are corrected by backspacing (which eliminates the incorrect character) and striking the correct key. By backspacing and striking over, you are simulating the use of a self-correcting typewriter.

June 20 Prepare memo to Martha L. Capelli, Executive Vice President, subject, "Status Report, Project 349128~~8~~9."

(¶) ~~Attached~~ Enclosed is a report of the progress we have made in the production of the next generation of television receivers which we have given the development title of "SUPER-vision." If all goes well, we should have a working model of this transceiver in operation by ~~August 21~~ October 1.

(¶) At this point, I suggest that representitives of the Director of Electronics Manufacturing and the Director of Marketing Operations become a part of our project team. I recommend Karen C. McKay, my assistant, who has a complete knowledge of all aspects of this project; Rinji Yukimura, our electronics engineer, who can provide any necessary technical information; and Gloria Rios, who can direct the testing phase of ~~this~~ the project. With their assistance, we can plan for the manufacture and sale of "SUPER-vision" as soon as we have completed our exhaustive ~~trial~~ tests in ~~our~~ the laboratory and in a selected marketing test area.

31d ▶ 16
Improve Keyboarding Skill: Guided Writing

1. Take one 1′ timed writing and two 1′ *guided* writings on ¶ 1 as directed on page 37.
2. Take one 1′ timed writing and two 1′ *guided* writings on ¶ 2 in the same way.
3. Take two 2′ timed writings on ¶s 1 and 2 combined; find *gwam* on each.
4. Take one 3′ writing on ¶s 1 and 2 combined; find *gwam*.

1′ *Gwam* Goals

▽ 23 = acceptable
□ 27 = average
○ 31 = good
◇ 35 = excellent

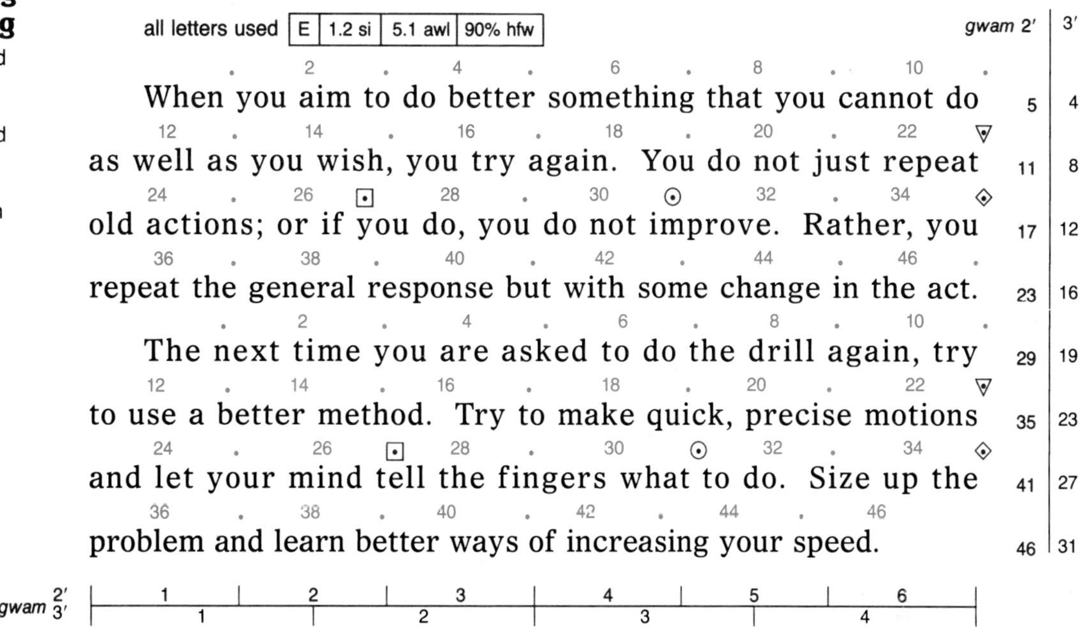

all letters used | E | 1.2 si | 5.1 awl | 90% hfw |

	gwam 2′	3′
When you aim to do better something that you cannot do	5	4
as well as you wish, you try again. You do not just repeat	11	8
old actions; or if you do, you do not improve. Rather, you	17	12
repeat the general response but with some change in the act.	23	16
The next time you are asked to do the drill again, try	29	19
to use a better method. Try to make quick, precise motions	35	23
and let your mind tell the fingers what to do. Size up the	41	27
problem and learn better ways of increasing your speed.	46	31

gwam 2′ | 1 | 2 | 3 | 4 | 5 | 6 |
gwam 3′ | 1 | 2 | 3 | 4 |

Lesson 32 — Basic/Language Skills

Line length: 60 spaces
Spacing: single-space (SS)

32a ▶ 6
Conditioning Practice

1. Each line twice SS.
2. A 1′ writing on line 3; find *gwam*.

alphabet 1 Jacki may have to plan big, unique duets for Zahn next week.
figure 2 Take 485 bags of crab and 630 bags of shrimp to 1792 Market.
easy 3 Nana did sign the usual title forms for the eight box firms.

5-stroke words | 1 | 2 | 3 | 4 | 5 | 6 | 7 | 8 | 9 | 10 | 11 | 12 |

32b ▶ 10
Improve Language Skills: Number Expression

1. Read the first rule highlighted in color at the right.
2. Key the *Learn* sentence below it, noting how the rule has been applied. Use the 60-space line for which your machine is set.
3. Key the *Apply* sentence supplying the appropriate number expression.
4. Practice the other rules in the same way.
5. If time permits, key the three *Apply* sentences again to improve number control.

Use figures for house numbers except house number *One*.

Learn 1 My office is at One Baker Plaza; my home, at 9 Devon Circle.
Apply 2 The Wilsons moved from 3740 Erie Avenue to 1 Beach Place.

Use figures to express measures and weights.

Learn 3 Silvia Vallejo is 5 ft. 6 in. tall and weighs 121 lbs. 8 oz.
Apply 4 The package measures one ft. by six in. and weighs four lbs.

Use figures for numbers following nouns.

Learn 5 Today, review Rules 1 to 12 in Chapter 6, pages 129 and 130.
Apply 6 Case 4657 is reviewed in Volume four, pages seven and eight.

Unit 60 Lessons 268-273

Learning Goals

1. To familiarize you with the field of information processing.
2. To increase your knowledge of keyboarding tasks performed by a word processing operator.
3. To familiarize you with typical procedures in an Information Processing Center.
4. To improve your skill in processing business documents of various kinds.

Documents Processed

1. Interoffice Memorandum
2. Progress Report
3. Statistical Report
4. Magazine Article
5. Letters from Boilerplate
6. Computer Program
7. Documentation for Computer Program

ELECTRO-TECHNOLOGIES, LTD.

STANDARD OPERATING PROCEDURES

Processing Documents

Documents to be processed will be received from the originator in several different forms: script, rough draft, or boilerplate. Keyboard the first draft of a document as rapidly as possible in rough form. If you make an error, backspace and strike the correct key.

When you receive a draft with corrections marked, proofread it carefully for correct grammar, punctuation, spelling, and keyboarding errors before you prepare the document in final form. All documents will be assigned a storage number for quick retrieval. This number will appear a DS below the final line of each document and will follow your initials: st:261.

Standard Formats

If no special instructions are provided, format documents as follows:

Letters. Use block style, open punctuation; a standard 6″ line: 15-87+ (12-pitch) or 12-72+ (10-pitch); date on line 13.

Interoffice Communications. Use block style with a standard 6″ line. Begin heading information two spaces to the right of the colon.

Reports. Use unbound style with 6″ line, DS. Place main heading on line 12 (12-pitch) or line 10 (10-pitch). Leave a bottom margin of at least 1″ on all pages. DS above and below side headings.

Number second and succeeding pages on line 6, at the right margin; continue body on line 8.

Place textual citations in parentheses within the text, including author, date of publication, and page number (Rose, 1987, 57-59). List all references alphabetically on a separate page.

Document Processing Log Sheet

Your teacher will provide you with a document processing log sheet. For each document, record the following information:

Document Originator. Enter the name of the individual who wrote the document.

Storage Number. Enter the storage number given. If no storage number is provided, use the unit number and document number following your initials (st:60-1).

Input Form. Enter SC for boilerplate; SCRIPT for handwritten material; RD for rough draft; and STAT for statistical copy.

Time In. Enter time you begin keyboarding the document.

Time Out. Enter time you finish keyboarding the document.

Total Minutes. Enter the number of minutes required to produce the document.

Lines. Count each line regardless of length (including any titles or subtitles). Count 3 lines for the opening lines of a letter and 3 lines for the closing lines. Count 4 lines for letter envelopes; 1 line for COMPANY MAIL envelopes.

32c ▶ 10
Improve Keyboarding Technique

1. Each pair of lines once SS as shown; DS between pairs.

2. Two 1′ writings on line 6, then on line 8; find *gwam* on each writing.

adjacent reaches
1 a safe|a coin|a tree|to buy|the ads|to stop|is here|the silk
2 Reba has tried various copiers to buy one to suit her needs.

long, direct reaches
3 a peck|a myth|a brim|an ace|to pace|he must|of many|the sums
4 Myra must decide if curved fingers help when keying numbers.

one-hand words
5 at no|we are|no act|my art|set up|saw him|as you see|in case
6 You acted on my tax case only after you saw my estate cards.

balanced-hand words
7 of the|she pays|big risk|but wish|cut work|key city|due them
8 He may profit by good form and a firm wish to make the goal.

5-stroke words | 1 | 2 | 3 | 4 | 5 | 6 | 7 | 8 | 9 | 10 | 11 | 12 |

32d ▶ 12
Check/Improve Keyboarding Speed

1. Two 1′ writings on each ¶; find *gwam* on each writing.

2. A 2′ writing on ¶s 1 and 2 combined; find *gwam*.

3. A 3′ writing on ¶s 1 and 2 combined; find *gwam*.

Goals
1′: At least 24 *gwam*
2′: At least 23 *gwam*
3′: At least 22 *gwam*

all letters used | E | 1.2 si | 5.2 awl | 90% hfw

	gwam 2′	3′
Just how well do you adjust to change? Recognize that	5	4
change is as certain to come as death or taxes. You cannot	11	8
avoid change, but you can adjust to it. How quickly you do	17	12
this is one index of your likely success in the world ahead.	23	16
As well as acts of nature, people cause change to take	29	19
place. Growth in use of computers in homes and business is	35	23
an example of change caused by people. Will you be able to	41	27
handle the many changes the computer may bring to your life?	47	31

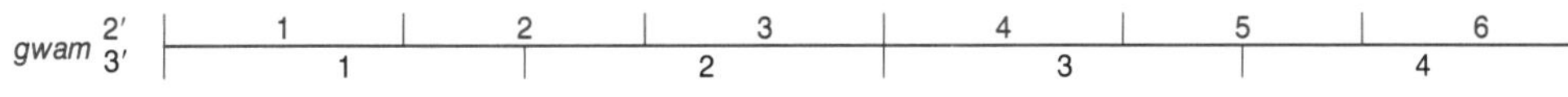

32e ▶ 12
Learn to Proofread Your Copy

1. Note the kinds of errors marked in the typed ¶ at right.

2. Note how the proofreader's marks above the copy are used to mark corrections in the ¶.

3. Using the copy you keyed in the 3′ writing above, proofread and mark for correction each error you made.

Goal: To learn the first step in finding and correcting your errors.

= space ∧ = insert ⁀ = close up ℓ = delete ∿ = transpose (tr)

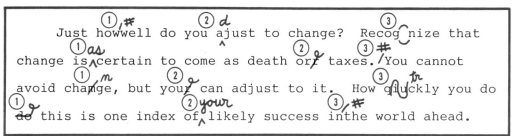

Just howwell do you ajust to change? Recog nize that
change is certain to come as death orf taxes. You cannot
avoid chamge, but your can adjust to it. How qiuckly you do
do this is one index of likely success inthe world ahead.

Line 1	Line 2	Line 3	Line 4
1 Failure to space	1 Omitted word	1 Misstroke	1 Repeated word
2 Omitted letter	2 Added letter	2 Added letter	2 Omitted word
3 Faulty spacing	3 Incorrect spacing	3 Transposition	3 Failure to space

264b-267b (continued)

Document 6
Planning Directive

1. Mr. Ngwa asks you to prepare the document at the right as an unbound manuscript DS.

2. SS the enumerated items with a DS between them. Do not indent the items from both margins.

PLANNING DIRECTIVE *Line 10*
NO. 145-30

REORGANIZATION STUDY

The Planning ~~Committe~~ Committee has directed that a study be conductd to determine the feasability of restructuring the organization of ~~the~~ Electro-Technologies Headquarters in Atlanta to stream line operations and to reduce costs. As a basis for this study, branch and divisoin cheifs will be required to analize there organizations and ~~operatio~~ operations.

The questionnaire which follows will be answered by each branch and division chief. The ~~answered~~ answers will be reviewed at each echelon of the ~~firm~~ company to ensure that they are complete and corect. Completed questionnaires will be submitted to the office of the Executive Vice President no later than September 15. *DS*

QUESTIONNAIRE *DS*

1. What are the ~~organizational~~ major objectives of your organizational element? Be specific.
2. What are the major duties of each ~~employee~~ member of your unit? Provide a currant job discription for each employee.
3. In what way do each employee contribute to the ~~goals~~x acheivement of your organizational objectives? Do employees perform duties which are not directly related to your objectives?
4. Do employees preform duties of a smilier or ~~similar~~ related nature? Is any employee required to perform widely divergent tasks?
5. Is each employee given the authority nessessary to ~~acxxo~~ accomplish the responsibilities he or she have been assigned?
6. How many employees report to each superviser in your unit? List each ~~manager~~ supervisor and ~~indicate~~ show the number of subordinates. Considering factors of distance, time, knowledge, personality, and complexity of work performed, is the number appropriate?
7. In what ways does your employees or subordinate units communicate? Is their a formal process for co-ordination?
8. What is the average cost of each employee in your unit? (Divide the annual budget by the number of employees.)
9. What changes if any have been made in the objectives of your unit during the past year?
10. What changes, if any, have been made in the procedures followed by your unit during the past year?
11. What changes, if any, do you reccomend ~~for~~ in the organizational structure of your unit?
12. What reccommendations can you offer for stream lining the organizational structure of the headquarters?

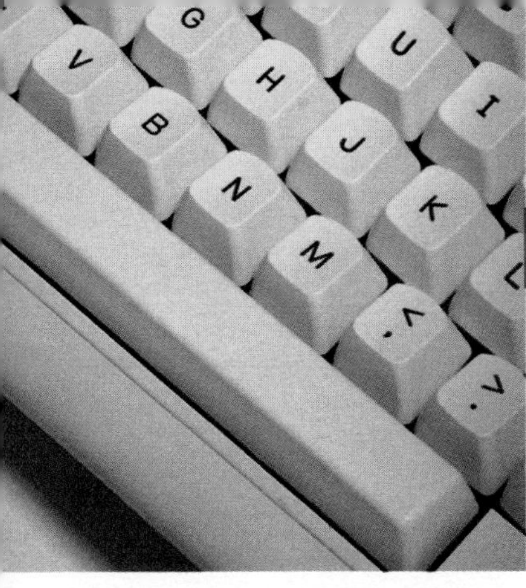

Unit 5 Lessons 33-38

Learning Goals

1. To learn the location of basic symbol keys.
2. To learn how to strike the symbol keys properly with the correct fingers.
3. To improve keyboarding speed/technique on alphabetic and statistical copy.
4. To review/improve language skills.

Machine Adjustments

1. Paper guide at *0*.
2. Ribbon control to use top half of ribbon.
3. Margin sets: left margin (center - 30); right margin (move to right end of scale).
4. Line-space selector set to single-space (SS) drills and to double-space (DS) ¶s.

Lesson 33 / and $

Line length: 60 spaces
Spacing: single-space (SS)

33a ▶ 6 Conditioning Practice

1. Each line twice SS.
2. A 1′ writing on line 3; find *gwam*.

alphabet 1 Quent was just amazed by five great tackles Alex put on him.
figure 2 Our group planted 284 cedar, 375 elm, and 1,690 maple trees.
easy 3 It is their wish to pay for land maps of eight island towns.

| 1 | 2 | 3 | 4 | 5 | 6 | 7 | 8 | 9 | 10 | 11 | 12 |

33b ▶ 18 Learn / and $

each line twice SS (slowly, then faster); DS between 4-line groups; if time permits, practice the lines again

/ = diagonal
$ = dollar(s)

Do not space between a figure and the **/** or the **$** sign.

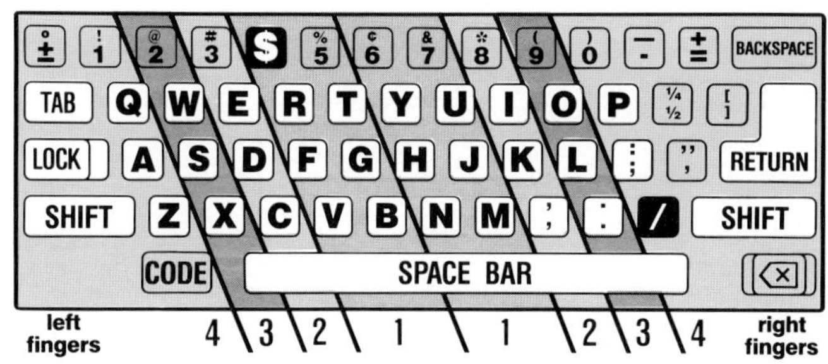

Reach technique for /

Reach *down* to / with *right little* finger.

Reach technique for $

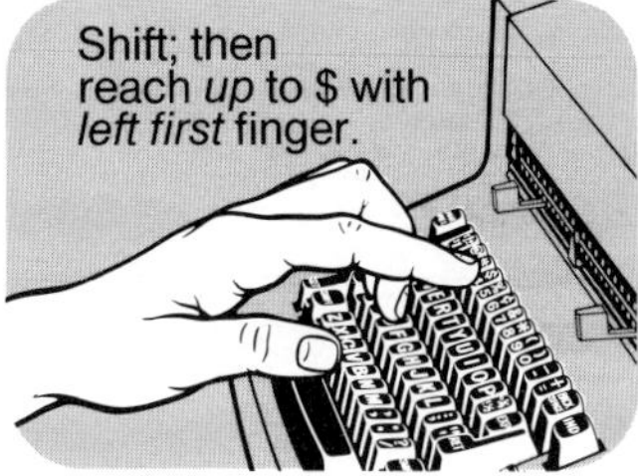

Shift; then reach *up* to $ with *left first* finger.

Learn / (diagonal)

1 ; / ; / /; /; ?/; ?/; 2/3 4/5 and/or Key 1/2, 3/4, and 5/16.
2 Space between a whole number and a fraction: 7 2/3, 18 3/4.

Learn $ (dollar sign)

3 f $ f $ $f $f f$f f$f $4 $4 for $4 Shift for $ then key $44.
4 A period separates dollars and cents: $4.50, $6.25, $19.50.

Combine / and $

5 I must shift for $ but not for /: Order 10 gal. at $16/gal.
6 Do not space on either side of /: 1/6, 3/10, 9 5/8, 4 7/12.
7 We sent 5 boxes of No. 6 3/4 envelopes at $11/box on June 2.
8 We can get 2 sets of disks at $49.85/set, 10 sets at $39.85.

264b-267b (continued)

Document 3
Letter
(LM p. 137)

Ms. Capelli asks you to prepare the letter at the right for her signature dated June 12, 19--. Address the letter to **Mr. Leonard T. Goldman, President of the Atlanta Chapter of the International Information Processing Association, 50 Ivy Street, NE, Atlanta, GA 30303-7193.**

Document 4
Letter
(LM p. 139)

Ms. Capelli has received an invitation to speak at a luncheon meeting from **Miss Ellen C. Emory, Program Chairperson of the Macon Industrial Management Club, 1400 Coleman Avenue, Macon, GA 31207-4126.**

The luncheon will be held at the Macon Towers on July 21 at 1 p.m.

1. Compose a letter to Miss Emory for Ms. Capelli's signature dated June 13, 19--. Ms. Capelli accepts the invitation, and the title of her presentation will be **"Information Processing at the Executive Level."**

2. Use the letter prepared in Document 3 as a model, making necessary changes.

(¶) Thank you for your invitation to address ~~speak to~~ the Atlanta Chapter of the International Information Processing Association ~~at~~ during the dinner meeting at the Peachtree Plaza Hotel on ~~June~~ July 14 at 7:00 p.m. I shall be happy ~~glad~~ to join your group and to share with them some of my ideas ~~thoughts~~ regarding the problems of implementing effective information processing.

(¶) The title of my speech will be "Information Processing at the Cross roads." During this 30-minute presentation, I shall need an overhead projector and screen. At the conclusion, I shall be happy to answer any questions members of your group may have.

(¶) I am looking forward to meeting you and the other members of IIPA on July 14.

Document 5
Schedule

Mr. Ngwa asks you to prepare the schedule at the right in unbound report format in triplicate. SS entries and DS between entries. Add two columnar headings: **Date** and **Goal**.

TIME TABLE FOR COMPLETING STUDY 145-30

Reorganization of Headquarters ~~in~~ Atlanta

August 15	Completion of Planning Directive 145-30.
September 15	Submission of replies to questionaires by branch and division cheifs.
September 16 to November 15	Analysis of data ~~info~~ submited by branch and division chiefs.
November 16 to December 5	Formulation of changes based on analysis of data.
January 6 to January 21	Discussion of changes with branch and division chiefs individually.
January 22 to February 10	Completion of final plans for reorganization.
February 11	Submission of plans for approval.
February 15	Implementation of plans for reorganization ~~.~~ of Atlanta headquarters.

33c ▶ 10
Check Language Skills: Number Expression

1. Read each handwritten (script) line, noting mentally where changes are needed in spacing and number expression.

2. Key each line, making needed changes; then check accuracy of work against rules on pages listed at left of sentences.

3. If time permits, key each line again at a faster speed.

Ref.		
p. 53	1	20 players are in the locker room; twelve are on the field.
p. 53	2	Of the 15 art entries, only two made it to the final judging.
p. 53	3	The tipoff is at eight thirty p.m. on Saturday, December two.
p. 54	4	The wedding is at Four Jay Lane; the reception, at 1 Del Mar.
p. 54	5	Use three oz. steak sauce, 1 bay leaf, and two tsp. mixed herbs.
p. 54	6	You will find it in Volume Two, Section One, pages ten and 11.

33d ▶ 16
Improve Keyboarding Technique

1. Key each 2-line group (lines 1-12) twice SS; DS between 4-line groups. For lines 7-8, set 7 tab stops 8 spaces apart, beginning at left margin.

2. Take a 1′ writing on line 13, then on line 14; find *gwam* on each writing.

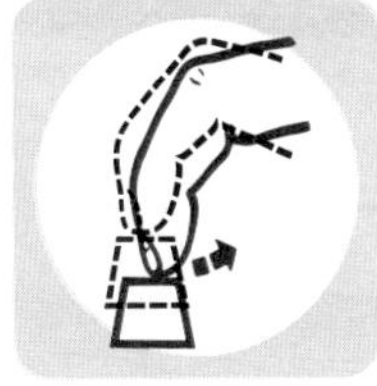

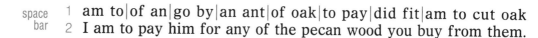

space bar
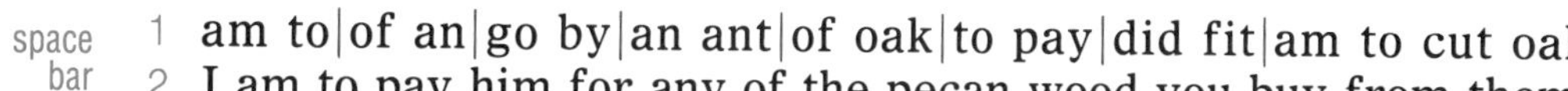
1 am to|of an|go by|an ant|of oak|to pay|did fit|am to cut oak
2 I am to pay him for any of the pecan wood you buy from them.

shift keys
3 Clay Epps is in New Haven; Jan Appel has left for Cole Lake.
4 Mandy Wold works in Towne Hall; Hal Epstein, in Arps Center.

shift lock
5 The musical CATS will be shown live on HBO at 8 p.m., May 3.
6 OLIVER, the play, is based on the classic book OLIVER TWIST.

tab
7 he tab 63 tab or tab 94 tab is tab 82 tab the tab 563
8 as 12 up 70 we 23 opt 905

adjacent keys
9 news quiz|last trip|safe view|same suit|over part|true power
10 Sam Quincy read a short poem about a trip on the Milk River.

long, direct reaches
11 to run|a unit|an echo|so many|an herb|the curb|a bonus check
12 I found that many bonus checks are expected for top service.

alphabet
13 Janet will quickly explain what Dave Gibson made for prizes.
easy
14 I did rush the die to shape the auto panels to the big firm.

| 1 | 2 | 3 | 4 | 5 | 6 | 7 | 8 | 9 | 10 | 11 | 12 |

Lesson 34 — % and -

Line length: 60 spaces
Spacing: single-space (SS)

34a ▶ 6
Conditioning Practice

1. Each line twice SS.

2. A 1′ writing on line 3; find *gwam*.

alphabet 1 Zoe will buy six unique jackets from Davis for a high price.
figure 2 Order 10 boxes of Disk No. 847 and 25 boxes of Disk No. 639.
easy 3 Eight of them did go to the social held by the big box firm.

| 1 | 2 | 3 | 4 | 5 | 6 | 7 | 8 | 9 | 10 | 11 | 12 |

34b ▶ 16
Improve Keyboarding Technique

1. Key lines 1-12 of 33d, above, twice each.

2. Take a 1′ writing on line 13, then on line 14 of 33d.

Goals: To refine technique. To increase speed.

264b-267b (continued)

Document 1, continued

2\. We shall offer competetive wages and salaries together with other benefits which will contribute to the well-being of all employees.

4\. We shall apply all personnel practices in a fair, unbiased, and unprejudiced manner.

5\. We shall promote communications with and between management and employees at all times.

5\. We shall offer opportunities for all employees to develope their skills and abilities to the utmost extent so that they will enjoy the maximum satisfaction form their work.

Our Customers

Satisfied customers from the basis of our success. We must always try to attract number of customers by providing superior products at competetive prices. All actions we take must be conceetrated on satisfying customer's needs. We msut always try to provide prompt, courteous service to insure confidence. In all relations with customers, we msut maintain our integrity.

Our Stockholders

Without the capitol provided by stock holders, the company would not exist. We pledge to achieve a rate of return on our stock which equals or exceeds that of any of our competitors. We further pledge to operate the company on sound financial guidelines and to keep stockholders informed on a quarterly basis.

The Public

Every corporation has social objectives as well as economic objectives. Social objectives include good citizentry and a concern for the areas in which we operate. We encourage employees to engage in civic affairs and will assist in the promoting social and educational causes. Farther, we promise to promote environmental conservation and to conduct all operations in a manner which will provide an ecological balance.

Document 2
Interoffice Memorandum
(LM p. 135)

Attached to the rough-draft policy statement is a note from Mr. Ngwa dated June 11, 19--.

Please prepare a memo today for my signature; send a copy to Aloysius L. Martin, Chief of Personnel; Mrs. Helen C. Lyczak, Director of Marketing Operations; and Mr. John M. Forisaka, Public Relations Officer. Also send them a copy of the Policy Statement on Human Resources.

Tell them in the memo that the attached policy statement on human resources was prepared under the direction of Ms. Martha Capelli, Executive Vice President.

Ask them to review the policy statement carefully and to let me have any recommended changes or additions no later than June 21, 19--.

Note: Prepare the memo in quadruplicate. Leave the heading **To:** blank until you have completed the memo; then place the name of each recipient on a separate copy of the memo. On the final or file copy, indicate at the bottom the names and titles of the executives to whom the memo was sent.

34c ▶ 18
Learn % and -

each line twice SS (slowly, then faster); DS between 4-line groups; if time permits, practice the lines again

% = percent
\- = hyphen

Do not space between a figure and **%**, nor before or after - or -- (dash) used as punctuation.

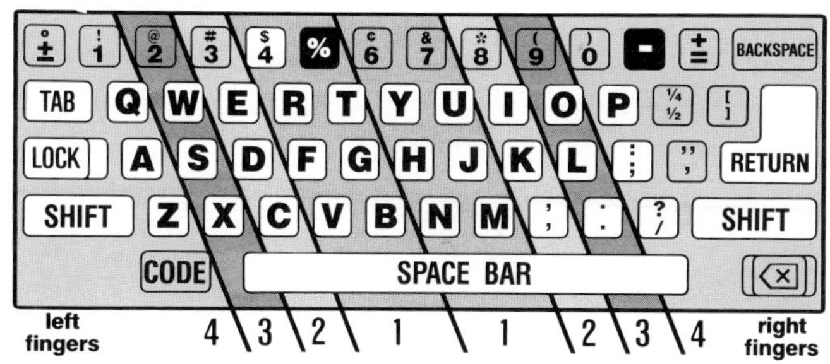

Reach technique for %

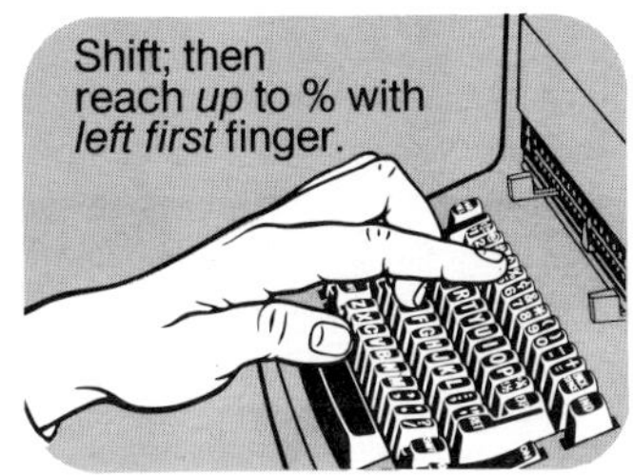

Shift; then reach *up* to % with *left first* finger.

Learn % (percent)

1 f % f % %f %f f%f f%f 5% 5% Shift for % as you key 5% or 4%.
2 Do not space between a number and %: 5%, 75%, 85%, and 95%.

Reach technique for -

Reach *up* to - with *right little* finger.

Learn - (hyphen)

3 ; - ; - -; -; ;-; ;-; 4-ply I use a 4-ply tire on the mower.
4 I gave each film a 1-star, 2-star, 3-star, or 4-star rating.

Combine % and -

5 You can send the parcel by first-class mail at a 50% saving.
6 A dash is two unspaced hyphens--no space before or after it.
7 The new prime rate is 12%--but you have no interest in that.
8 You need 60 signatures--51% of the members--on the petition.

34d ▶ 10
Build Keyboarding Skill Transfer

1. Take a 1′ writing on ¶ 1; find *gwam*.
2. Take a 1′ writing on ¶ 2, then on ¶ 3; find *gwam* on each writing.
3. Compare rates. On which ¶ did you have the highest *gwam*?
4. Take two 1′ writings on each of the slower ¶s, trying to equal your highest *gwam* of the first 3 writings.

Note: Most students key straight copy at the highest *gwam*; script (handwritten) copy at the next highest; and statistical copy at the lowest *gwam*.

E	1.2 si	5.1 awl	90% hfw

Figures and words share a lot in common as far as ease of keying is concerned. A balanced-hand word or number may be keyed more easily than a one-hand one. Through practice you learn to speed up easy ones and to slow down for others.

Two-digit numbers like 16, 37, 49, and 85 that you key with both hands are easy. Longer ones like 142 and 790 are harder since each one is handled by only one of your hands.

Copy that is written by hand, called script, is not as easy to key as copy shown in type. Writing is less easy to read than type is; as a result, the keying speed is reduced.

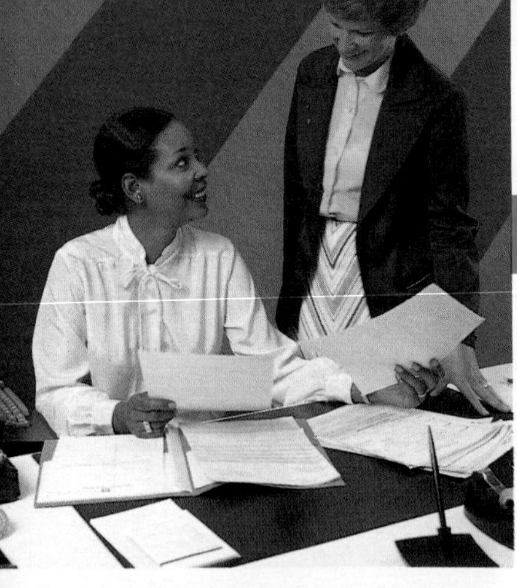

Unit 59 Lessons 264-267

Learning Goals

1. To acquaint you with some of the major functions performed in an executive office.
2. To enlarge your understanding of typical documents and tasks performed in an executive office.
3. To improve your skill in processing business documents.

Documents Processed

1. Statement of Policy
2. Interoffice Memorandums
3. Letters on Executive-Size Stationery
4. Timetable for Study
5. Planning Directive

Lessons 264-267

264a-267a ▶ 5 Check Equipment

65-space line

Before you begin work each day, check your machine to see that it is in good working order by keyboarding the paragraph at the right at least twice (first slowly, then faster).

all letters/figures used

Her unique policy will cover a number of hazards our workers face on the job. Experts say the policy can save us $93,480 (6%) this year and $126,570 (8%) next year. Their goal is to halt the audits, to suspend the penalty, and to risk a formal proxy fight.

| 1 | 2 | 3 | 4 | 5 | 6 | 7 | 8 | 9 | 10 | 11 | 12 | 13 |

264b-267b ▶ 45 Document Processing

You have been assigned to work in the office of Ms. Martha L. Capelli, Executive Vice President of Electro-Technologies, Ltd. You will work closely with Mr. Thomas Ngwa, her Administrative Assistant.

1. All letters will be prepared in block style on executive-size stationery with the date on line 11 and with margins of 1″. All reports will be prepared as unbound manuscripts.
2. Follow directions given for other documents; if no directions are given, use your best judgment.
3. Correct all marked and unmarked errors.

Document 1
Policy Statement

1. Mr. Ngwa asks you to keyboard the policy statement as an unbound report DS.
2. Indent the numbered items 5 spaces from each margin. SS numbered items with a DS between them.

Policy Statements: Human Resources — Center ALL CAPS

There are 4 groups of human resources that are indispensible to the continued success for Electro-Technologies, Ltd. They are, our employees, our coustomers, our stock holders, and the public. It is essential, therefore, that philosophy and attitude toward each of these groups be clearly delineated.

Our Employees

It is our philosophy that the propsperity of the company depends on a qualified group of employees. To that end, our firm's policy toward its employee relations can be told in 6 statements:

1. First and formost, we shall consider each employee as an indicidual irregardless of gender, race, coler, creed, religion, or age.

3. We shall maintain a sfe, suitable work enviroment.

(continued on page 444)

35a ▶ 6 Conditioning Practice

1. Each line twice SS.
2. A 1′ writing on line 3; find *gwam*.

alphabet 1 Grayson was amazed at just how quickly Pavan fixed the bike.
figure 2 Speed up easy pairs of figures: 10, 26, 37, 48, 59, and 61.
easy 3 Diana is to handle all title forms for the eight auto firms.

| 1 | 2 | 3 | 4 | 5 | 6 | 7 | 8 | 9 | 10 | 11 | 12 |

35b ▶ 10 Check Language Skills: Capitalization

1. Read and key each line, making needed changes in capitalization.
2. Check accuracy of work against rules on pages listed; rekey any line that contains errors in capitalization.

Ref.		
39, 40	1	did you read Chapter 3 for monday? i will read it saturday.
39	2	ask if miss alvarez excused anita and keith xica from class.
39	3	jacques said that he will attend mexicana college next year.
39	4	the golden gate bridge connects san francisco and sausalito.
40, 41	5	ayres gives the first monday in september off for labor day.
41	6	citizens bank is located at walnut street and dayton avenue.
39, 42	7	gloria ryan, the club secretary, wrote to president markham.
39, 41, 42	8	dr. h. j. lindon has a ph.d. from brown, an m.d. from emory.

35c ▶ 18 Learn # and &

each set of lines twice SS (slowly, then faster); DS between groups; if time permits, practice the lines again

= number/pounds
& = ampersand (and)

Do not space between # and a figure; space once before and after & used to join names.

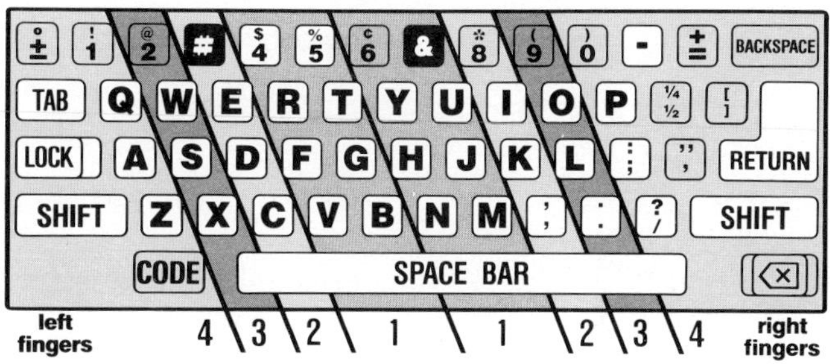

Reach technique for #

Shift; then reach *up* to # with *left second* finger.

Reach technique for &

Shift; then reach *up* to & with *right first* finger.

Learn # (number/pounds)

1 d # d # #d #d d#d d#d 3# 3# Shift for # as you key 3# or #3.
2 Do not space between a number and #: 3# of #33 at $10.35/#.

Learn & (ampersand)

3 j & j & &j &j j&j j&j 7& 7& Have you written to Parks & Lim?
4 Do not space before or after & in initials; as in CG&E, B&O.

Combine # and &

5 Shift for # and &. Recall: # stands for number and pounds.
6 Names joined by & require spaces; a # sign alone does, also.
7 Letters joined by & are keyed solid: List Stock #3 as C&NW.
8 I bought 10# of #830 grass seed from Locke & Uhl on March 3.

263b ▶ 20
Evaluate Language Skills: Proofread/Correct

1. The paragraphs at the right include errors in spelling, punctuation, capitalization, and keystroking.

2. Keyboard the paragraphs as an unbound manuscript, correcting errors as you work.

3. When you have completed the report, study it carefully and correct any errors you may have missed *before* you remove it from the machine.

words

Operational High-Lights 5

Financial. The Balance Sheet for the 3d and 4th quarters of this fisical 22
year are attached. These Quarters were some-what of a disapointment. In 37
the next quarter, how-ever, we shall experiance a 2-fold increase in demand 52
for electronic devises which will prove benificial as out-lined in the attached 68
report. 70

Capitol Improvements. An existant wharehouse at 310 N. 6th Street in 89
Omaha was modifyed to except merchandice transfered from Phoenix. Too 104
improve efficancy, an excellent 9-story comercial facility were built in 119
Los Angelos. It will begin operations on Feburary 1. 130

Earnings. Net income of Common and Preferred stock have been com- 144
puted useing a wieghted average. As of December 31st, stocks taken all 158
together averaged $82 per share--an over-all raise of exactly 6%. 2 prin- 173
ciple firms of attornies has verified our beleif that this figure is consistant 189
with our farther development. Irregardless, a peroid of considerible in- 203
creased income is forcast. 209

Accounting Principals. A new method of accounting for the translation 227
of foriegn currency Financial Statements was addopted as required by fed- 241
eral act 62-31, dated October 20th 1986. 249

263c ▶ 10
Evaluate Figures and Symbols

1. Keyboard each sentence. Correct any errors you make.

2. Proofread each sentence carefully; correct any errors you may have missed.

1. After you revise pages 3, 4, 7, and 9, check pages 18, 20, 35, and 46.
2. For Contract 347, we produced 21,780 pieces; for Contract 629, 36,495.
3. Sue earned commissions of $32.90, $48.75, and $61.35--a total of $143.
4. My son-in-law (from out-of-town) is up-to-date on ready-to-wear items.
5. Item #41 will be increased by 6%; Item #53 by 28%, and Item #70 by 9%.
6. Office size varies from 8′6″×12′9″ (small) to 34′8″×70′5″ (large).
7. K & M Services (now Key & May, Inc.) can be reached at (215) 876-4390.
8. Ship items marked * on 6/15, ** on 7/23, *** on 8/4, and **** on 9/10.

263d ▶ 15
Evaluate Straight-Copy

Take two 5′ writings on the ¶s in 262c, p. 441 as directed.

35d ▶ 16
Improve Keyboarding Skill Transfer

1. Take a 1′ writing on ¶ 1; find *gwam*.

2. Take a 1′ writing on ¶ 2; find *gwam*.

3. Take two more 1′ writings on the slower ¶.

4. Take a 2′ writing on ¶ 1, then on ¶ 2; find *gwam* on each writing; 1′ *gwam* ÷ 2.

5. Take 2 more 2′ writings on the slower ¶.

Goal: To transfer at least 75% of your straight-copy speed to statistical copy.

To determine % of transfer:
¶ 2 *gwam* ÷ ¶ 1 *gwam*

all letters/figures used | LA | 1.4 si | 5.4 awl | 85% hfw

One good way to build speed is called mental practice. When not at a machine, just make believe your hands rest on a keyboard. Next, as you mentally say words like if, also, they, city, and dizzy to yourself, quickly move the fingers through the stroking motions. Doing so can add to speed.

Learn to read and key figures in groups. For example, read 165 as one sixty-five and key it that way. Tackle the longer sequences in like manner. Read 1078 as ten seventy-eight and handle it as 2 units. Try this for 2493, also.

Lesson 36 (and)

Line length: 60 spaces
Spacing: single-space (SS)

36a ▶ 6
Conditioning Practice

1. Each line twice SS.

2. A 1′ writing on line 3; find *gwam*.

alphabet 1 Juan Lopez knew our squad could slip by the next five games.

figure 2 Key these figures with quiet hands: 105, 281, 364, and 947.

easy 3 Dixie may amend the six audit forms if it is right to do so.

| 1 | 2 | 3 | 4 | 5 | 6 | 7 | 8 | 9 | 10 | 11 | 12 |

36b ▶ 12
Recall/Improve Language Skills: Capitalization and Numbers

1. Read the first rule highlighted in color.

2. Key the *Learn* sentence below it, noting how the rule has been applied.

3. Key the *Apply* sentence, supplying the appropriate capitalization (and/or number expression).

4. Practice the other rules in the same way.

5. If time permits, key the four *Apply* lines again to improve decision-making speed.

Capitalize nouns preceding numbers (except page and line).

Learn 1 See Rule 12 in Chapter 3, page 34, lines 24 and 25.
Apply 2 Check volume 10, section 29, page 364, lines 75-82.

Spell (capitalized) names of small-numbered streets and avenues (ten and under).

Learn 3 We walked several blocks along Fifth Avenue to 65th Street.
Apply 4 At 4th Street he took a taxi to his home on 32d Avenue.

Use figures for a series of fractions, but spell isolated fractions and indefinite numbers.

Learn 5 Carl has a 1/4 interest in Parcel A, 1/2 in B, and 2/3 in C.
Learn 6 Nearly twenty-five members voted; that is almost two thirds.

Apply 7 Guide calls: one fourth, 1/2, 3/4, and one -- each 15 seconds.
Apply 8 About 60 students passed the test; that is over 1/2.

262c ▶ 15 Evaluate Straight-Copy Skills

Take two 5′ writings on the ¶s at the right. Record *gwam* and errors on the better writing.

all letters used | A | 1.5 si | 5.7 awl | 80% hfw

	gwam 1′	5′
How well do my employees do their work? This is a question that a	13	3
good supervisor often ponders. Supervisors are always observing the way	28	6
in which their workers do their jobs and, in effect, are evaluating the	42	8
work they do and their value to the organization. In some firms, this	57	11
merit rating is done on a very informal basis, while in other firms there	71	14
are formal procedures. In most large companies today, employees undergo	86	17
periodic ratings of the work they have done.	95	19
How can supervisors rate their employees? The simplest way is for	13	22
the supervisor to list all the workers in order of their merit. Some	27	24
companies develop checklists of appropriate items which the supervisor	42	27
completes for each worker. Forms are also used which include a number of	56	30
items to be rated. After each item is a scale on which the exact degree	71	33
of proficiency can be noted. If the workers are using skills which can	85	36
be measured, a number of tests can be given to measure performance.	99	39
What is the purpose of rating employees? The ratings are used to	13	41
ascertain whether or not employees should be considered for a raise in	27	44
pay, a bonus, a promotion, or if they should be fired. Further, most	41	47
of us like to know how well we are doing. If the ratings are discussed	56	50
with employees, they serve as a basis for employees to strengthen their	70	53
weak points and improve the quality of their performances. If conducted	85	56
properly, a rating system can give employees a feeling of fulfillment.	99	59

gwam 1′ | 1 | 2 | 3 | 4 | 5 | 6 | 7 | 8 | 9 | 10 | 11 | 12 | 13 | 14 |
5′ | 1 | 2 | 3 |

Lesson 263

263a ▶ 5 Check Equipment

Before you begin the evaluations which follow, check your machine to see that it is in good working order by keyboarding the paragraph at the right at least twice (first slowly, then faster).

all letters/figures used

You can sit back, relax, and enjoy the view of those amazing aquatic performers. The shows will commence today at 1:00, 2:30, 4:00, 5:30, 6:00, 7:30, 8:00 and 9:30. A dog, a duck, a snake, a big fish, and a whale work with a pair of girls to make us laugh.

| 1 | 2 | 3 | 4 | 5 | 6 | 7 | 8 | 9 | 10 | 11 | 12 | 13 |

36c ▶ 18
Learn (and)

each set of lines twice SS (slowly, then faster); DS between groups; if time permits, practice the lines again

(= left parenthesis
) = right parenthesis

Do not space between **( )** and the copy they enclose.

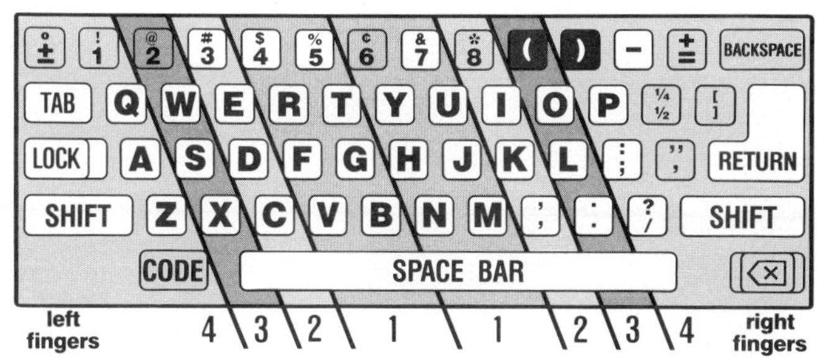

Reach technique for (

Shift; then reach *up* to (with *right third* finger.

Reach technique for)

Shift; then reach *up* to) with *right little* finger

Learn ((left parenthesis)

use the letter "l"

1 l (l ((l (l l(l l(l 9(9(Shift for (as you key (9 or (l.
2 As (is the shift of 9, use the l finger to key 9, (, or (9.

Learn) (right parenthesis)

3 ;) ;));); ;); ;); 0) 0) Shift for) as you key 0) or l).
4 As) is the shift of 0, use the ; finger to key 0,), or 0).

Combine (and)

5 Hints: (1) depress shift; (2) strike key; (3) release both.
6 Tab steps: (1) clear tabs, (2) set stops, and (3) tabulate.
7 Her new account (#495-3078) draws annual interest at 6 1/2%.

36d ▶ 14
Improve Keyboarding Technique

1. Clear all tab stops.
2. Set 5 tab stops 11 spaces apart, beginning at left margin.
3. Key each set of lines once SS as shown.
4. Take two 1′ writings on line 15, then on line 16; find *gwam* on each writing.

fig/sym

1	$44	tab	50%	tab	#39	tab	1/3	tab	(1)	tab	2-day
2	$84	tab	18%	tab	70#	tab	3/4	tab	(9)	tab	6-ply

adjacent-key reaches

3 new are here try dirt say last pot rope buy yule lions coins
4 The trip guide let the pony rest before the last open trail.

long, direct reaches

5 any sync deck once sum mug sun nut nerve debts curbs brought
6 A great many people must make payment at the central branch.

letter response

7 ploy edge join gave pink ever upon save only best pump facts
8 At best, I fear only a few union cases were ever acted upon.

word response

9 their right field world visit chair throw proxy risks eighty
10 The girls did their work then spent their pay for the chair.

combination response

11 maps were hand only sign card pair link also fast paid plump
12 We may amend the rate if the union agrees to the work risks.

alphabetic sentences

13 Jerold quickly coaxed eight avid fans away from Buzz Parker.
14 Having pumped in six quick points, Jaye Wold froze the ball.

easy sentences

15 Do rush the worn panels to the auto firm for them to enamel.
16 The right bid may entitle the girl to the handy ivory forks.

| 1 | 2 | 3 | 4 | 5 | 6 | 7 | 8 | 9 | 10 | 11 | 12 |

Unit 58 Lessons 262-263

Performance Goals

1. To measure your skill in keyboarding straight-copy material.
2. To measure your language skills.
3. To measure your skill in keyboarding figures and symbols.

Machine Adjustments

1. 65-space line for Check Equipment exercises.
2. 75-space line for Language Skills unless otherwise indicated.
3. 70-space line for paragraphs.
4. DS all drills.

Lesson 262

262a ▶ 5 Check Equipment

Before you begin the evaluations which follow, check your machine to see that it is in good working order by keyboarding the paragraph at the right at least twice (first slowly, then faster).

all letters/figures used

The lazy carpenter quit this job six days ago to avoid working for me. He ignored Specifications #69438 for a room 7′10″ by 12′5″ and used Specifications #58347. If all the handiwork is in good shape, I can fix it; if it is a problem, I may dismantle it.

| 1 | 2 | 3 | 4 | 5 | 6 | 7 | 8 | 9 | 10 | 11 | 12 | 13 |

262b ▶ 30 Evaluate Language Skills: Proofread/Correct

1. In each sentence at the right, items have been underlined. The underlines indicate that there *may* be an error in spelling, punctuation, capitalization, grammar, or in the use of words or figures.

2. Study each sentence carefully. Keyboard the line number. If an underlined item is incorrect, correct it as you keyboard the sentence. In addition, correct any typographical errors you may make as you work.

3. When you have completed the sentences and *before* you remove the paper from the machine, study each sentence carefully and correct any errors you may have missed. If necessary, you may keyboard a sentence a second time immediately below your original sentence in order to correct a major error.

4. You may *not* correct any errors once you have removed the paper from the machine.

1. According to the accountent, all of these questions was answered.
2. Every one of the chief's of divisions agreed to impliment the plan.
3. In the abcense of the chairperson, we shall adhear to the agenda.
4. 17 of the attorneys met at 1590 South 4th Avenue on May 11.
5. The principal of the academy is already to reccomend new courses.
6. Fourty of the group paid its dues for the teacher's conference.
7. Between the three of them, he don't know which one is the better.
8. On it's calender, the company showed pictures of their operations.
9. We ordered 275 5-pound boxes of detergent for the laboratory.
10. She asked--"Whose going to take the deposit to the bank?"
11. A large amount of the group voted to sponser the womens' committee.
12. In his speech, he spoke at length about there new word processor.
13. Unfortunately, to many of the employees would not except the plan.
14. The boulevard of the Allies is found in the City of Pittsburgh.
15. The manager and his employees are in an important meeting.
16. The article, "Word Processing," appears in the book, "Computer Mania."
17. The first problem was my lack of pennys, the second, no dollar bills.
18. She listed these items, tools, supplies, equipment, and personnel.
19. Nearly 1/2 of the group will take the plane at 2:00 PM.
20. The shedule for my groups' meeting calls for a lengthy discussion.

Line length: 60 spaces
Spacing: single-space (SS)

37a ▶ 6
Conditioning Practice

1. Each line twice SS.
2. A 1′ writing on line 3; find *gwam*.

alphabet 1 Maria Bow fixed the prized clock seven judges say is unique.
fig/sym 2 I bought the new CMD #940 for $2,385, a TLC #306 for $1,750.
easy 3 The auto firm owns the big signs by the downtown civic hall.

| 1 | 2 | 3 | 4 | 5 | 6 | 7 | 8 | 9 | 10 | 11 | 12 |

37b ▶ 20
Learn ’ and ”

’ = apostrophe
” = quotation mark

Apostrophe (’)

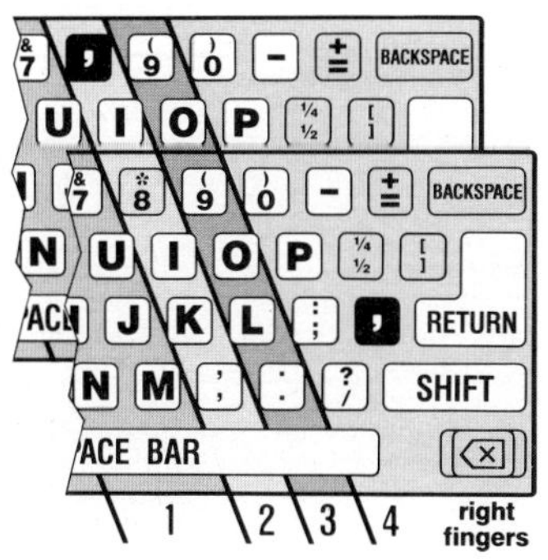

Manual and some computers
Key ’ (shift of **8**) with the *right second finger.* Reach with the controlling finger. Try to hold the other fingers over the home keys.

Electric and most computers
The ’ is to the right of ; and is controlled by the *right little finger.*

Quotation (”)

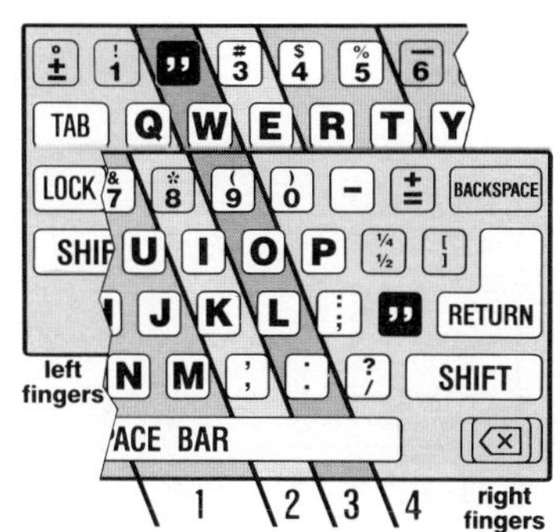

Manual and some computers
Key ” (the shift of **2**) with the *left third finger.* Reach with the controlling finger. Hold other fingers over home keys.

Electric and most computers
Key ” (the shift of ’) with the *right little finger.* Don’t forget to shift *before* striking the ” key.

Learning procedure

1. Locate new key on appropriate chart above (electric or manual); read the reach technique given opposite it.
2. Key twice the appropriate pair of lines given at the right.
3. Repeat steps 1 and 2 for the other new key.
4. Key twice the 4 lines at the bottom of the page.
5. If time permits, key again those lines with which you had difficulty.

Learn ’ (apostrophe)

manual
1 k ’ k ’ ’k ’k k’k k’k 8’ 8’ Is this Rick’s? No, it’s Ike’s.
2 On Lei’s machine the ’ is on 8; on Dick’s, it’s in home row.

electric
3 ; ’ ; ’ ’; ’; ;’; ;’; ’s it’s he’s I’m I’ve It’s his, I see.
4 If it’s his, I’ll return it; but I’m not sure it isn’t Ed’s.

Learn ” (quotation mark)

manual
5 s ” s ” ”s ”s s”s s”s 2” 2” “Go for the goal,” the boy said.
6 I keyed “loss” for “laws” and “sow” for “sew” from the tape.

electric
7 ; ” ; ” ”; ”; ;”; ;”; “Keep going,” he said, but I had quit.
8 Did you use “there” for “their” and Joe use “two” for “too”?

Combine ’ and ”

9 “Its” is an adjective; “it’s” is the contraction of “it is.”
10 Miss Han said, “To make numbers plural, add ’s: 8’s, 10’s.”
11 O’Shea said, “Use ’ (apostrophe) to shorten phrases: I’ll.”
12 “If it’s Jan’s or Al’s,” she said, “I’ll bring it to class.”

259b-261b (continued)

Document 5
Purchase Orders
(LM pp. 121-125)

Three vendors were selected to provide the metric tools. Mr. Matthew Stevens asks you to prepare three purchase orders using information in Documents 2 and 3 and information contained in the low bid register at the right. The register summarizes the low bids for the items identified by stock number.

1. Prepare Purchase Orders MT5893, MT5894, and MT5895 dated June 3. Consolidate the items on the purchase orders by vendor.

2. Compute the total price for each item and for each order.

3. Use the following shipping information.

Booker Tool Co.: **Trans-Am Shipping**
Seaboard Tools, Inc.: **Allied Express**
Long Industries, Inc.: **T & O Express**

Ms. Comer will sign the purchase orders.

LOW BID REGISTER

STOCK NUMBER	LOW BIDDER	VENDOR STOCK NUMBER	TERMS	UNIT PRICE
3249	Booker Tool Co.	6384	Net	21.90/set
5836	Seaboard Tools, Inc.	5-691	2/10, n/30	27.20/set
8965	Long Industries, Inc.	721A	3/30, n/60	3.60/ea.
6590	Long Industries, Inc.	318C	3/30, n/60	31.20/ea.
7401	Long Industries, Inc.	901C	3/30, n/60	1.00/ea.
5420	Booker Tool Co.	7495	Net	5.30/ea.
3604	Seaboard Tools, Inc.	5-702	2/10, n/30	37.00/set
7504	Booker Tool Co.	850	Net	24.10/set
0249	Long Industries, Inc.	347D	3/10, n/60	8.20/ea.
7458	Booker Tool Co.	84	Net	3.20/ea.
4305	Seaboard Tools, Inc.	5-580	2/10, n/30	8.50/set

Document 6
Form Letters from Boilerplate
(LM pp. 127-129)

Miss Krista L. Quinn, Director of Purchasing, requests that the following letters be prepared for her signature. Date the letters June 4, 19--.

Letter to: **Webster Supply Co.**
Item: **electrolytic capacitors**
Quantity: **1,000**
Facility: **Houston, Texas**
Contact: **Mr. James Robinson**

Letter to: **Mr. Joseph Poerio, President, Heritage Industries**
Item: **metal-oxide resistors**
Quantity: **500**
Facility: **San Jose, California**
Contact: **Mrs. Dorothy M. Morton**
Use the alternate final paragraph.

FORM LETTER P 17

Electro-Technologies, Ltd., is interested in entering into a long-term agreement for the supply of {enter item}. Detailed specifications for this item are enclosed.

The agreement will provide for the delivery of {insert quantity} of the item to our facility in {enter location of facility} on a monthly basis for a period of not less than two or more than five years.

If you are interested in negotiating a contract for the delivery of this item, please contact {insert name}, one of our assistant purchasing officers, to arrange for a meeting at a convenient time and place. Your reply within two weeks will be appreciated.

Alternate final paragraph: {Insert name}, one of our assistant purchasing officers, will call you within five days to discuss this proposal with you.

37c ▶ 10
Improve Language Skills: Capitalization

1. Read the first rule highlighted in color.

2. Key the *Learn* sentences below it, noting how the rule has been applied.

3. Key the *Apply* sentences, supplying the appropriate capitalization.

4. Practice the other rule in the same way.

5. If time permits, key the *Apply* lines again at a faster speed.

> Capitalize the first word of a direct quotation unless the quote is built into the structure of the sentence.

Learn 1 Cissy quoted Pope: "To err is human, to forgive is divine."
Learn 2 I said that "making more errors doesn't make us more human."

Apply 3 The message read: "complete Lesson 38 on text pages 63-64."
Apply 4 Ms. York urged all of us to "Dot the i's and cross the t's."

> Capitalize the first word of the first part of an interrupted quotation, but not the first word of the second part.

Learn 5 "To gain speed," she said, "think the word, not the letter."
Apply 6 "curve the fingers," I said, "and make a quick-snap stroke."

37d ▶ 14
Improve Keyboarding Technique

1. Key each pair of lines once SS as shown.

2. Take two 1′ writings on line 11, then on line 12; find *gwam* on each writing.

Technique goals

- curved, upright fingers
- quick-snap keystrokes
- quiet hands and arms

fig/sym sentences
1 I signed a 30-year note--$67,495 (at 12.8%)--with Ott & Jay.
2 Order #26105 reads: "18 sets of Cat. #4716B at $39.25/set."

outside-reach sentences
3 Alex Quails was our prize shortstop for most of last season.
4 Perhaps all will pass a fast quiz on tax laws of past years.

adjacent-key sentences
5 Louisa has opened her radio studio in the new western plaza.
6 Violet reads the meters on the oil heaters in the buildings.

long-reach sentences
7 My group collected a large sum for her musical concert fund.
8 Cecil carved this unique marble lynx for the county exhibit.

alphabetic sentences
9 Marquis has just solved the exciting new puzzle from Byke's.
10 Jack Wilford may have enough cash for six quite big topazes.

easy sentences
11 The signs the six girls wish to hang may handle the problem.
12 He lent the field auditor a hand with the work for the firm.

| 1 | 2 | 3 | 4 | 5 | 6 | 7 | 8 | 9 | 10 | 11 | 12 |

Lesson 38 — _ and *

Line length: 60 spaces
Spacing: single-space (SS)

38a ▶ 6
Conditioning Practice

1. Each line twice SS.

2. A 1′ writing on line 3; find *gwam.*

alphabet 1 Max Pelz has flown the big jet over the quaint, dark canyon.
fig/sym 2 She asked, "Isn't Order #3046 from C&NW dated May 25, 1987?"
easy 3 The auditor is to aid the six antique firms with their work.

| 1 | 2 | 3 | 4 | 5 | 6 | 7 | 8 | 9 | 10 | 11 | 12 |

38b ▶ 14
Improve Keyboarding Technique

1. Key lines 1-12 of 37d, above, once SS as shown.

2. Take two 1′ writings on line 11, then on line 12; find *gwam* on each writing.

Goals: To refine technique. To increase speed.

259b-261b (continued)

Document 3
Mailing List

Ms. Comer asks you to prepare the mailing list at the right. The list contains the names and addresses of vendors who will be sent Request for Quotation forms in Document 4. Prepare the mailing list with the following changes:

1. Add 2 blocked columnar headings: **Company** and **Address**.

2. Arrange the companies in alphabetical order.

3. DS the list.

LIST OF VENDORS

Webster Supply Co.	20 Bay Street, Durham, NC 27701-4193
Star Tool Company	903 Delta Drive, El Paso, TX 79901-8721
Universal Steel	12 Beals Lane, Nashville, TN 37218-6587
Baker & Douglas, Inc.	60 Cherry Street, Macon, GA 31201-2157
~~United Dynamics, Inc.~~	~~213 Blair Road, Richmond, VA 23233-4063~~
Long Industries, Inc.	320 East Street, Monroe, LA 71202-5940
Seaboard Tools, Inc.	1840 Frow Avenue, Miami, FL 33133-2364
Metriconics, Inc.	191 Morton Road, Raleigh, NC 27604-6607
~~Dee & Ess Company~~	~~77 Key Road, Columbia, SC 29201-5398~~
Ace Supply Co.	80 Pryor Street, Memphis, TN 38127-2902
Farley & Jacks, Inc.	986 Avenue M, Birmingham, AL 35214-8611
Hampton Supply Co.	326 Main Street, Sumter, SC 29150-5726
Booker Tool Co.	153 Elk Street, Biloxi, MS 39530-9402
Heritage Industries	78 Iowa Street, Savannah, GA 31404-2475

Document 4
Request for Quotation
(LM p. 119)

Ms. Comer tells you to prepare a Request for Quotation, similar to the one at the right, listing each item that must be reordered in Document 2. This form will be reproduced and sent to each of the 12 vendors on the mailing list. Use May 12, 19-- for the date issued and May 31, 19-- as the last day on which bids will be considered.

Note: No periods follow abbreviations of metric measures.

Request for Quotation - - This is not an order.

Electro-Technologies, Ltd.
20 Marietta Street ○ Atlanta, GA 30303-6280 ○ (404) 555-8100

To: ACE SUPPLY CO
80 PRYOR STREET
MEMPHIS TN 38127-2902

May 12, 19-- May 31, 19--

Quantity	Description
100	Ratchet, Flex-Head, 10 MM, 12 MM Drive
30	Combination Wrench Set, 8-12 MM
50	Rule, Aluminum, 0-1 M
200	Screwdriver Set, 1-5 MM
20	Chisel Set, 7 mm, 8 mm, 12 mm, 14 mm

38c ▶ 18 Learn __ (underline) and * (asterisk)

Underline (__)

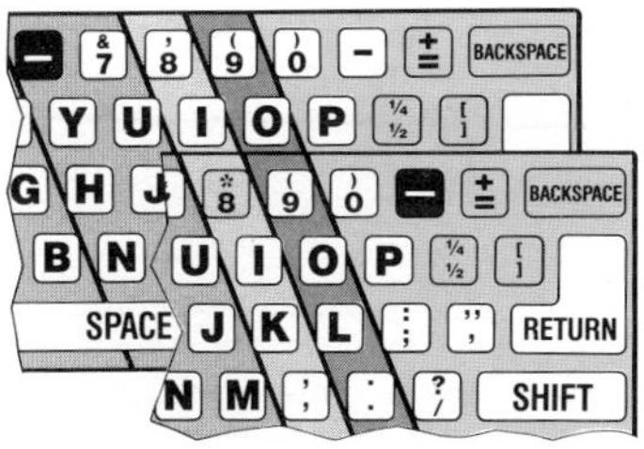

Manual and some computers

Type __ (shift of **6**) with the *right first finger.* Reach with the finger without letting the hand move forward.

Electric and most computers

Type __ (shift of the - key) with the *right little finger.* Reach with the finger without swinging elbow out.

Asterisk (*)

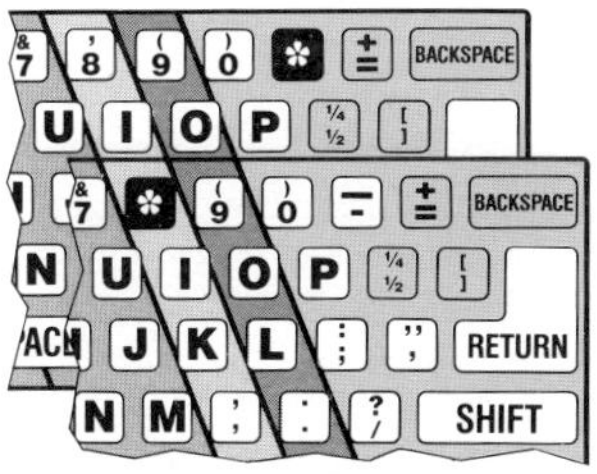

Manual and some computers

Type * (the shift of -) with the *right fourth (little) finger.*

Electric and most computers

Type * (the shift of **8**) with the *right second finger.*

Note: To position the carrier (cursor) to underline a word, strike the backspace key with the right little finger once for each letter in the word.

Learning procedure

1. Locate new key on appropriate chart above (electric or manual); read the reach technique given opposite it.

2. Key twice the appropriate pair of lines given at the right.

3. Repeat steps 1 and 2 for the other new key.

4. Key lines 9-10 three times.

5. If time permits, key again those lines with which you had difficulty.

Learn __ (underline)

manual
1 j _ j _ j_j j_j 6_j 6_j Underline the words fully and daily.
2 Curve your fingers and keep them upright over the home keys.

electric
3 ; _ ; _ ;_; ;_; _; _; They are to underline stop and gallop.
4 To develop, you should plan the work and then work the plan.

Learn * (asterisk)

manual
5 ; * ; * *; *; ;*; ;*; We may use an * for a single footnote.
6 All special gift items are indicated by an *; as 746*, 936*.

electric
7 k * k * *k *k k*k k*k 8*k 8*k Use * for a table source note.
8 All discounted items show an *, thus: 48K*, 588*, and 618*.

Combine __ and *

9 Use an * to mark often confused words such as then and than.
10 An * after a name identifies an understudy for Wizard of Oz.

38d ▶ 12 Check/Improve Keyboarding Skill

1. A 1′ writing on each ¶; find *gwam* on each.

2. A 2′ writing on ¶s 1-2 combined; find *gwam.*

3. An additional 1′ writing on each ¶; find *gwam.*

4. An additional 2′ writing on ¶s 1-2 combined; find *gwam.*

5. If time permits, take a 3′ writing on ¶s 1-2 combined; find *gwam.*

1′ *Gwam* Goals

▽ 25 = acceptable
□ 29 = average
○ 33 = good
◇ 37 = excellent

all letters used | E | 1.2 si | 5.1 awl | 90% hfw

	gwam 2′	3′
You may have noticed that until now the lines you have	5	4
keyed have been even at the right as well as at the left if	11	8
you keyed them properly. They were written that way to aid	17	12
your learning. Next, you will learn to work from materials	23	16
in which the lines vary in length by seven or eight letters.	29	20
When lines vary in length, they are centered on a page	35	23
according to the longest line in the copy. You can quickly	41	27
learn how to center copy, a major concern for a keyboarder.	47	31
You will then not have to puzzle about how to place letters	53	35
and reports on a page so that they will draw the eye.	58	39

gwam 2′ | 1 | 2 | 3 | 4 | 5 | 6
gwam 3′ | 1 | 2 | 3 | 4

259b-261b (continued)

Document 2
Order List for Metric Tools

Electro-Technologies, Ltd. is planning a nationwide promotion of its products during July. In preparation, Ms. Marie T. Comer, Assistant Purchasing Officer, asks you to prepare the order list.

1. Prepare a list of metric tools to be ordered based on the inventory below.

Column Headings:

STOCK NO.
O/Q **Order Quantity**
R/P **Reorder Point**
O/H **Quantity on Hand**

2. Compare quantity on hand with the quantity in the reorder column. If the quantity on hand is equal to or less than the reorder point, the quantity in the order quantity column will be ordered.

3. Include an appropriate main heading. Use (As of May 11, 19--) as the secondary heading. Use column headings of **Stock No.**, **Item**, and **Quantity**. Include the unit (set; ea.) under **Quantity** column.

Note: On most machines, the plus (+) sign is located on the top row and requires the operator to shift and to strike the + with the right little finger. If your machine does not have the + symbol, key a hyphen, backspace, and key the diagonal.

INVENTORY OF METRIC TOOLS

(As of May 11, 19--)

Stock No.		O/Q	R/P	O/H
3249	Chisel Set, 6 mm, 10 mm, 11 mm	100	400	400
4791	Combination Wrench Set, 6-10 mm	50	150	220
5836	Drill Set, 1 mm - 5 mm	200	550	525
7653	Drive Tool Set, 14-17 mm Sockets	50	100	125
8965	Flexible Rule, 185 cm	20	80	72
0531	Flex Key Set, 2-6 mm, 8 mm, 10 mm	25	75	86
6590	Micrometer w/Readings to .01 mm	50	125	123
7401	Rule, Steel, 0 - .9144 m	120	200	192
7402	Rule, Steel, 0 - 1 m	300	220	225
5419	Ratchet, Flex-Head, 12 mm Drive	10	50	54
5420	Ratchet, Flex-Head, 15 mm Drive	10	50	46
3604	Screwdriver Set, 1-3 mm	60	90	85
2190	Socket Set, 5 mm, 5.5 mm, 6-11 mm	20	50	57
7504	Socket Wrench Set, 10-24 mm, 30 mm	100	400	387
0249	Thermometer, -40C to +150C	30	75	71
7458	Universal Box-End Wrench, 9 - 22 mm	100	400	387
4305	Wrench Set, 6 x 8 mm, 10 x 11 mm	20	50	46

Line: 60 spaces
Spacing: single space (SS)

Practice Procedure

1. Key each line of a group 3 times: first, to improve keyboarding technique; next, to improve keyboarding speed; then, to build precise control of finger motions.

2. Take several 1′ writings on the 2 sentences in each set of lines to measure your skill on each kind of copy.

As time permits, repeat the drills. Keep a record of your speed scores to see how your skill grows.

Each of the 120 *different* words used in the drills is among the 500 most-used words in the English language. In a study of over 2 million words in personal and business communications, these 120 words accounted for over 40 percent of all word occurrences. Thus, they are important to you in perfecting your keyboarding skill. Practice them frequently for both speed and accuracy.

Balanced-Hand Words of 2-5 Letters (use word response)

words
1 of to is it he by or an if us so do me am go the and for but
2 a may she did man own end due pay got big air with they when
3 them than also such make then work both down form city their
4 men they when wish name hand paid held half it's world field

phrases
5 of us | to me | she may | and own | but due | pay the | big man | for them
6 is to make | am to work | a big city | by the name | if they wish to

sentences
7 He is to do the work for both of us, and she is to pay half.
8 She paid the big man for the field work he did for the city.

| 1 | 2 | 3 | 4 | 5 | 6 | 7 | 8 | 9 | 10 | 11 | 12 |

One-Hand Words of 2-5 Letters (use letter response)

words
9 a in be we on as at no up my you was are him get see few set
10 tax war act car were only best date case fact area free rate
11 you act him fact only ever card face after state great water

phrases
12 at no | as my | on you | we are | at best | get set | you were | only date
13 get him in | act on my case | you set a date | get a rate on water

sentences
14 We are free only after we get him set up on a tax rate case.
15 A tax rate was set in my area only after we set a case date.

| 1 | 2 | 3 | 4 | 5 | 6 | 7 | 8 | 9 | 10 | 11 | 12 |

Double-Letter Words of 2-5 Letters (speed up double letters)

words
16 all see too off will been well good need feel look less call
17 too free soon week room took keep book bill tell still small
18 off call been less free look need week soon will offer needs

phrases
19 a room | all week | too soon | see less | call off | need all | will see
20 see a need | took a book | need a bill | all will see | a good offer

sentences
21 It is too soon to tell if we will need that small book room.
22 They still feel a need to offer a good book to all who call.

| 1 | 2 | 3 | 4 | 5 | 6 | 7 | 8 | 9 | 10 | 11 | 12 |

Balanced-Hand, One-Hand, and Double-Letter Words of 2-5 Letters

words
23 of we to in or on is be it as by no if at us up an my he was
24 and all him for see you men too are may get off pay him well
25 such will work best then keep were good been only city needs
26 make soon ever wish tell area name bill face paid tell great

phrases
27 is too great | they will be | she will state | the offer was small
28 if at all | may get all | off the case | to tell him | to keep after

sentences
29 If you wish to get to the rate you set, keep the hand still.
30 All of us do the work well, for only good form will pay off.

| 1 | 2 | 3 | 4 | 5 | 6 | 7 | 8 | 9 | 10 | 11 | 12 |

Unit 57 Lessons 259-261

Learning Goals

1. To familiarize you with some of the major functions performed in a purchasing division.
2. To increase your knowledge of typical documents and tasks found in a purchasing division.
3. To improve your skill in processing documents from special sources.

Documents Processed

1. Leftbound Report
2. Order List
3. Mailing List
4. Request for Quotation
5. Purchase Orders
6. Form Letters from Boilerplate

Lessons 259-261

259a-261a ▶ 5 Check Equipment

Before you begin work each day, check your machine to see that it is in good working order by keying the paragraph at the right at least twice (first slowly, then faster).

all letters/figures used

Maybe we can equalize both tax groups if we adjust the rates very quickly. A raise of 50 mills (1/2%) in District 50-498 will equal a raise of 25 mills (1/4%) in District 50-736. If eight of the panel duck the fight with us, they may suspend the amendment.

| 1 | 2 | 3 | 4 | 5 | 6 | 7 | 8 | 9 | 10 | 11 | 12 | 13 |

259b-261b ▶ 45 Document Processing

1. Your next assignment as a word processing trainee will be in the Purchasing Division of Electro-Technologies, Ltd., at the company's main office,

20 Marietta Street
Atlanta, GA 30303-6280.

2. You will be required to prepare documents originated by executives in the Purchasing Division.
3. Follow directions given for each document. If document format is not specified, use your best judgment.
4. Correct all marked and unmarked errors.

Document 1
Leftbound Report

1. Mr. Matthew Stevens, Document Production Manager, asks you to keyboard the report for insertion into the company's procedures manual. Center the heading a DS below the SOP (Standard Operating Procedures) number.
2. List the numbered items SS with a DS between them.
3. In the numbered procedures, change the word **number** to **quantity**.

STANDARD OPERATING — *Begin on line 10 at left margin.*
PROCEDURES P19407

PURCHASE OF TOOLS AND EQUIPMENT

The Engineering Department has *completed* ~~finished~~ the *preparation of* specifications for all tools and equipment used within the company. Each item has been given a *stock* ~~SPEC~~ number *and will be identified by that number.* ~~which will identify it.~~

The ~~following~~ procedures *below* will be followed in the purchase of these items: 1. The Warehouse Supervisor will inventory specific classes of tools and equipment, on a monthly basis, as shown on the attached schedule. The number on hand will be entered into the data bank. 2. The director of Administration will provide the Purchasing Division with a print out showing the number and description of each item, the standard order xxdexx quantity, the reorder point, and number on hand. 3. The Purchasing division will prepare a list of those items which must be re-placed and, for each item, prepare a request for price quotation to solicit bids from reputible vendors. After all bids have been received, a list showing the lowest bidder for each item will be prepared. 4. Based on this list, Purchase Orders will be prepared and a hard copy will be sent to the Warehouse Supervisor and the Finance Department. 5. Upon reciept of the items, the Warehouse Supervisor will notify the Purchasing Department Manager who will then authorize Finance to pay fxxx the invoice. 6. All information in Steps 4 and 5 will be retained in computer memory for reference and follow-up purposes for a period of 6 months.

ENRICHMENT ACTIVITY: Timed Writing

Line: 60 spaces
Spacing: double space (DS)

The two sets of paragraphs are counted internally for 1′ guided and unguided writings; at the side and bottom for 2′ and 3′ measurement writings. They may be used at any time additional timed writing practice is desired.

1. A 1′ writing on ¶ 1; determine *gwam*.
2. Add 4 *gwam* to set a new goal rate.
3. Two 1′ writings on ¶ 1, trying to maintain your goal rate each ¼ minute.
4. Key ¶ 2 in the same way.
5. A 2′ unguided writing on each ¶. If you complete a ¶ before time is called, begin that ¶ again.
6. A 3′ writing on ¶s 1-2 combined; determine *gwam*.

gwam	¼′	½′	¾′	Time
16	4	8	12	16
20	5	10	15	20
24	6	12	18	24
28	7	14	21	28
32	8	16	24	32
36	9	18	27	36
40	10	20	30	40
44	11	22	33	44
48	12	24	36	48

Unit 5 Goals (1′)
▽ 25 = acceptable
□ 29 = average
○ 33 = good
◇ 37 = excellent

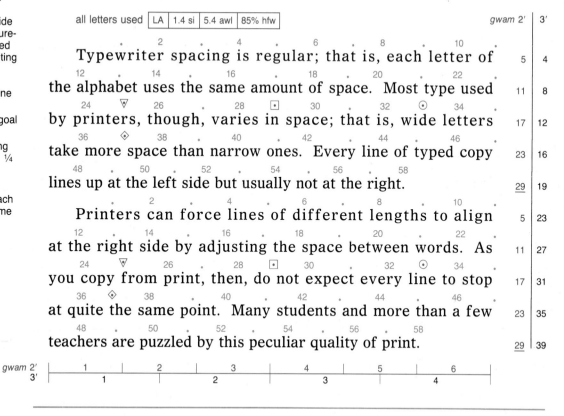

all letters used | LA | 1.4 si | 5.4 awl | 85% hfw

	gwam 2′	3′
2 · 4 · 6 · 8 · 10		
Typewriter spacing is regular; that is, each letter of	5	4
12 · 14 · 16 · 18 · 20 · 22		
the alphabet uses the same amount of space. Most type used	11	8
24 ▽ 26 · 28 □ 30 · 32 ○ 34		
by printers, though, varies in space; that is, wide letters	17	12
36 ◇ 38 · 40 · 42 · 44 · 46		
take more space than narrow ones. Every line of typed copy	23	16
48 · 50 · 52 · 54 · 56 · 58		
lines up at the left side but usually not at the right.	29	19
2 · 4 · 6 · 8 · 10		
Printers can force lines of different lengths to align	5	23
12 · 14 · 16 · 18 · 20 · 22		
at the right side by adjusting the space between words. As	11	27
24 ▽ 26 · 28 □ 30 · 32 ○ 34		
you copy from print, then, do not expect every line to stop	17	31
36 ◇ 38 · 40 · 42 · 44 · 46		
at quite the same point. Many students and more than a few	23	35
48 · 50 · 52 · 54 · 56 · 58		
teachers are puzzled by this peculiar quality of print.	29	39

gwam 2′ | 1 | 2 | 3 | 4 | 5 | 6
3′ | 1 | 2 | 3 | 4

all letters used | LA | 1.4 si | 5.4 awl | 85% hfw

	gwam 2′	3′
2 · 4 · 6 · 8 · 10		
An excellent performance shows the true concern of the	5	4
12 · 14 · 16 · 18 · 20 · 22		
performer for the task. It gives one a feeling of personal	11	8
24 ▽ 26 · 28 □ 30 · 32 ○ 34		
triumph and prompts us as a matter of habit to do our best.	18	12
36 ◇ 38 · 40 · 42 · 44 · 46		
Really successful men and women take great delight in their	24	16
48 · 50 · 52 · 54 · 56		
work and pursue it with a lot of dedication.	28	19
2 · 4 · 6 · 8 · 10		
A factor common to all who succeed is the need to have	5	22
12 · 14 · 16 · 18 · 20 · 22		
a good job recognized by others. If good work goes without	11	26
24 ▽ 26 · 28 □ 30 · 32 ○ 34		
notice, the desire to excel may be reduced. Lucky, indeed,	17	30
36 ◇ 38 · 40 · 42 · 44 · 46		
are those who can study their own performance, evaluate its	23	34
48 · 50 · 52 · 54 · 56		
quality, and do what must be done to improve.	28	37

gwam 2′ | 1 | 2 | 3 | 4 | 5 | 6
3′ | 1 | 2 | 3 | 4

256b-258b (continued)

Document 5
Unbound Report

Helen Lyczaks, Director of Marketing Operations, asks you to prepare this copy as an unbound report DS with items indented 5 spaces.

Indent enumerated items 5 spaces

ELEC-TECH SUPPLY CENTERS — Center

Standard Operating Procedures for Processing Orders — Center

1. Record the time and date received on each order, and number it serially by calendar year. All terms are Net unless Atlanta has given a volume discount.

2. Process all orders within 48 hours of receipt, if possible. Notify Atlanta if any item cannot be shipped within 4 working days.

3. Invoices will be prepared in Atlanta to facilitate accounting and centralize^d inventory control. Upon shipment of an order, send Atlanta through the telecommunications network: date of shipment; customer's name, address, and order number; our order ~~num~~ number; method of shipment; quantity; ~~description and unit price~~ and catalog number.

4. Marketing Operations ^in Atlanta will process each invoice, send two hard copies to the customer, enter information into data base for accounting, make inventory adjustment, and retain the invoice in computer storage for ^the marketing Department's reference and follow-ups.

Document 6
Invoices
(LM pp. 115-117)

Mr. Clark asks you to prepare invoices from information received by telecommunications from Electro-Technologies Supply Centers in Dallas and Newark.

1. Using the price list on p. 434, extend each item and find the total of each invoice.

2. Identify items by major headings and stock number **(ET Floppy Disks, 5¼″, 8775).**

ET, ATLANTA. SHIPPED 5/8 TO GOTHAM COMPUTER CENTER 41 MADISON AVENUE, NEW YORK, NY 10010-4529 ORDER C6518, OUR ORDER 203, TERMS NET, BY CITY EXPRESS 100 #8775; 100 #8776; 10 #5373; 1000 S241. ETSC NEWARK

ET, ATLANTA. SHIPPED 5/8 TO INTERNATIONAL COMPUTERS, INC. 1212 MAIN STREET, HOUSTON, TX 77002-4376 ORDER 5490, OUR ORDER 106, TERMS NET, BY S & W TRANSIT 100 #8777; 100 #8779; 10 #5370; 10 #5371. ETSC DALLAS

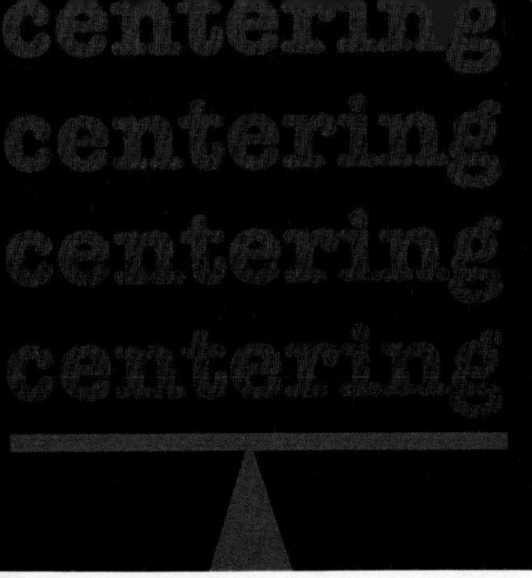

Unit 6 Lessons 39-42

Learning Goals

1. To learn how to center lines horizontally (side to side).
2. To learn how to format a numbered list with a centered heading.
3. To learn how to format short personal notes.
4. To learn how to format short simplified memos.

Machine Adjustments

1. Paper guide at *0*.
2. Ribbon control to use top half of ribbon.
3. Margin sets: left margin (center - 30); right margin (move to right end of scale).
4. Line-space selector set to single-space (SS) drills and to double-space (DS) ¶s.

Lesson 39 Centering Lines

Line length: 60 spaces
Spacing: single-space (SS)

39a ▶ 6 Conditioning Practice

1. Each line twice SS.
2. A 1′ writing on line 3; find *gwam*.

alphabet 1 Flo Gomez may have a jinx on our squad, but we kept the cup.

fig/sym 2 Key these data: $40, $84, 95%, #30, 6-point, 1/5, J&W 27's.

speed 3 They risk a big penalty if they throw a fight for the title.

| 1 | 2 | 3 | 4 | 5 | 6 | 7 | 8 | 9 | 10 | 11 | 12 |

39b ▶ 9 Correct Errors as You Keyboard

Errors in the paragraph at the right have been circled.

1. Key the ¶ once DS, correcting the circled errors.
2. Proofread your completed work and mark any errors for correction. (Use proofreader's marks.)
3. Key the ¶ again from your marked copy.

Change letter — Delete space — Insert space — Delete

Close up — Insert letter — Transpose

Standerd-size paper is 81/2 inches wide by 11 inches long. The maximun line length for such papre is 102 elite spaces or 85 pica spaces . The horizontal (side toside) center point fir such pa per is 51 for elite tyep or 42 for pica. A full sheet has a total of 6 6 vertical line spaces; a half shet used longg edge up, 33 line spazes .

39c ▶ 5 Learn to Use the Backspace Key

1. Read the copy in the block at the right to learn one use of the backspace key.
2. Key each word of each line *exactly* as shown. After you complete a word with a missing letter, backspace and fill in the missing letter **e**.

Backspacer
To position the printing point (or cursor) to fill in an omitted letter, depress the backspace key. Locate the key on your machine.

Electric/Electronic
Make a light, quick stroke with the little finger. Release the key quickly to avoid a double backspace. Hold the key down when you want repeat backspacing.

Manual
Straighten the little finger slightly and reach it to the backspace key with minimum hand motion. Depress the backspace key firmly; release it quickly.

1 Do try to ke p your ey s on th copy as you key th se lin s.

2 Backspace to th point of an omitt d lett r; k y the l tter.

256b-258b (continued)

Document 4
Price List

You are asked to prepare a price list which will be used when preparing invoices for Electro-Technologies, Ltd. Leave an approximate 2" top margin; SS items under major headings.

ELEC-TECH SPECIAL ^SALE PRICE LIST

ET FLOPPY DISKS, 5¼"

No.	Type	Price Per 100
8775	Single Side, Single Density, Soft Sectored . . . (Insert leaders)	275.00
8776	Single Side, Double Density, 16 Hard Sectors . .	~~290.00~~ 285.00
8777	Dual Side, Double Density, Soft Sectored	~~385.00~~ 360.00
8778	Dual Side, Double Density, 16 Hard Secøtors . . .	520.00
8779	Single Side, Quad Density, Soft Sectored	425.00
8780	Dual " " " " "	520.00

ET PLASTIC DAISY WHEELS

No.	Type Style	Price Per 10
5370	Courier 10-pitch	105.00
5371	Pica 10-pitch	~~100.00~~ 105.00
5372	Prestige Elite 12-pitch	~~110.00~~ 105.00
5373	Orator 10-pitch	~~115.00~~ 105.00
5374	Gothic 12-pitch	~~125.00~~ 105.00
5375	Quadro 15-pitch	105.00

ET LETTERHEADS, Continuous Feed (including ^printing ~~letterhead~~)

No.	Weight/Ink	Price Per 1,000
S240	20# White, Black Ink Impression	79.80
S241	20# Blue, Black Ink Impression	79.80
S24~~1~~2	20# 2-ply White (14# carbonless copy), Black	89.50

EQUIPMENT SPECIALS

No.	Item	Price
8840	SUPERWRITER Printer, Standard Centronics Parallel 36-pin ASCII	1,495.00
9375	Universal Connector Cable, 10', 36-pin Centronics	3~~1~~4.00

39d ▶ 30
Learn to Center Lines Horizontally (Side to Side)

3 half sheets (long edge at top)

1. Insert a half sheet with the long edge at top (short edge against the paper guide).
2. Set line space selector to double-space (DS) the lines.
3. Read the copy in the block at the right.
4. Center horizontally (side to side) each line of Drill 1. Begin the drill on line 14 from the top edge of the half sheet.
5. Key Drills 2 and 3 in the same way.
6. If time permits, key Drill 3 again, substituting your name, *gwam*, and *eam* (errors a minute).

Enrichment problems appear on page 73.

Get ready to center

1. Insert paper with left edge at *0*.
2. Move left margin stop to *0*; move right margin stop to right end of scale.
3. Clear all tab stops; set a new stop at horizontal center of paper; elite, 51; pica, 42.

How to center

1. Tabulate to center of paper.
2. From center, backspace *once* for each 2 letters, spaces, figures, or punctuation marks in the line.
3. Do not backspace for an odd or leftover stroke at the end of the line.
4. Begin the line where backspacing ends.

Example

• center point

backspace ◀ 1 | 1 | 1 | 1 | 1 | 1 | 1 | 1 | 1

LE | AR | NI | NG | space T | O space | CE | NT | ER

Drill 1

WORDS I MISSPELLED
DS
judgment

experience

accommodates

Drill 2

GOALS
DS
Good Technique

High Speed

Low Error Rate

Drill 3

LEE W. TIBBS
DS
Speed: 25 gwam

Error Rate: 2 eam

Time: 3 minutes

Lesson 40 Formatting Numbered Lists

Line length: 60 spaces
Spacing: single-space (SS)

40a ▶ 6
Conditioning Practice

1. Each line twice SS.
2. A 1′ writing on line 3; find *gwam*.

alphabet 1 David Jakes may win the next big prize for our racquet club.

fig/sym 2 Roe & Hahn's note (#8927) for $6,490 at 13% is due August 5.

speed 3 A neighbor paid the girl to fix the turn signal of the auto.

| 1 | 2 | 3 | 4 | 5 | 6 | 7 | 8 | 9 | 10 | 11 | 12 |

40b ▶ 12
Improve Keyboarding Speed: Skill Comparison

1. A 1′ writing on each line; find *gwam* on each writing.
2. Compare rates and identify your 3 slowest writings.
3. A 1′ writing on each of the 3 slowest lines.
4. As time permits in later lessons, do this drill again to improve speed and control.

balanced-hand 1 When did the field auditor sign the audit form for the city?

combination 2 You may chair my panel if you work on the tax audit for him.

double-letter 3 I need to use a little more effort to boost my keying skill.

outside-reach 4 Sal amazed us all as she won two prizes for six old plaques.

adjacent-key 5 Three bands played as he walked cheerfully up to the podium.

one-hand 6 You deferred my tax case after my union traced my wage card.

figure 7 The number of votes cast was 29,571 in 1980; 35,640 in 1988.

fig/sym 8 Tina asked, "Can't you touch-key 65, 73, $840, and 19 1/2%?"

| 1 | 2 | 3 | 4 | 5 | 6 | 7 | 8 | 9 | 10 | 11 | 12 |

256b-258b (continued)

Document 2
Directory

Mr. Clark would like a directory prepared in the form of a table with these headings: **District, Manager,** and **Location**. Include the telephone number as the final line under Location. Leave an approximate 2″ top margin.

ELEC-TECH SUPPLY CENTERS

North east District

Miss Terry L. McGuire, Manager
1010 Brunswick Avenue
Newark, NJ 07114-6318
(20~~2~~1) 630-4500

North Central District

Mr. ~~A. James Seneca~~ Edward C. Polk, Manager
6710 Washington Avenue
Des Moines, IA 50322-5988
(515) 365-4300

Southeast District

Mr. Ashley M. Jefferson, Manager
4809 Buford Highway, NE
Atlanta, GA 30341-2197
(404) 567-3100

North west District

Mrs. Mary C. Kaiser, Manager
12201 Hoyt Street, NE
Portland, OR 97230-3749
(503) 246-5720

South Central District

Ms. Kim S. Divo, Manager
7107 Douglas Avenue
Dallas, TX 75225-4163
(214) 567-4210

Southwest District

Mr. ~~John C. Robert~~ Carlos J. Melendez, Manager
3410 Ming Avenue
Bakersfield, CA 93309-7474
(805) 698-5300

Document 3
Form Letters from Boilerplate
(LM p. 107-113)

Prepare a letter to each of the people listed below. Date the letters May 7 a DS below the last line of the letterhead, and prepare the letters for the signature of Mrs. Helen C. Lyczak, Director of Marketing Operations. Insert into each letter the appropriate name, address, and phone number of the manager of the district in which the addressee is located. This information is included in the directory of Elec-Tech Supply Centers.

Mr. Richard D. Joslin
American Electronics, Inc.
200 E. 7th Avenue
Eugene, OR 97401-2379

Mr. Kenneth E. Shinoda
Marketing Director
Gotham Computer Center
41 Madison Avenue
New York, NY 10010-5173

Miss LeeAnna Hilty, President
International Computers, Inc.
1212 Main Street
Houston, TX 77002-6326

Ms. Sheila Ralston
Dynatronics Corporation
21330 Hawthorne Boulevard
Torrance, CA 90530-2716

Looking for quality, service, and economy when you purchase computer peripherals and supplies? Look no further. Six new ELEC-TECH Supply Centers are prepared to serve you in six ways:

QUALITY. Electro-Technologies has earned an international reputation for providing high-quality products. We guarantee you will be satisfied or we shall refund the purchase price.

VALUE. Our competitive prices, as shown on the special sale price list enclosed, give you the best value for your dollar.

SELECTION. Our expanded facilities ensure that we shall have in stock almost every standard item you need.

SPEED. Our streamlined, computerized order procedures are geared to process and ship your order without delay--in many cases, just 48 hours after we receive it.

SERVICE. At each ELEC-TECH Supply Center, experts stand ready to assist you with any problems you may have.

QUANTITY. We offer discounts for volume purchases. Just ask for a price quotation on any order of 100 items or more.

Need anything more? If so, contact (insert name), Manager of our ELEC-TECH Supply Center at (insert appropriate address) or phone him or her collect, of course, at (insert telephone number).

Space down 6 times, then center the heading

STEPS IN HORIZONTAL CENTERING

QS (quadruple-space); space down 4 times

2 spaces

1. Check to see that paper is inserted with left edge at 0 on the line-of-writing scale.
DS
2. Move left margin set to extreme left and right margin set to extreme right of line-of-writing scale.
DS
3. Clear all tabulator (tab) stops.
DS
4. Set a tabulator stop at horizontal center point of paper.
DS
5. For each line to be centered, tabulate to center point.
DS
6. From center point, backspace once for each two characters and spaces in the line as you spell-say them in pairs. If an odd or leftover stroke remains at the end of a line, do not backspace for it.
DS
7. Begin each line where the backspacing for it ends.

Numbered List with Centered Heading

40c ▶ 32
Learn to Format Numbered Lists

2 half sheets, long edge at top; 60-space line; tabs: one 4 spaces from left margin, one at center point

Problem 1

Format and key the list shown above. Use the spacing directions given in color on the model. (SS each numbered item.) When an item has more than 1 line, tab over 4 spaces to begin each line after the first (to align it with first line).

Problem 2

Format and key in the same way the list at the right.

An enrichment problem appears on page 73.

SPACING WITH SYMBOLS

1. Do not space between a figure and $, %, #, and /.
2. Do not space before or after - used to join words or a figure and a word -- nor before or after a dash (2 hyphens).
3. Do not space between ( ) and the copy they enclose. Space once before the opening (and once after the closing) except when) is followed by a quotation or punctuation mark.
4. Do not space between ' and a preceding or following letter.
5. Do not space between opening " and the copy it precedes, nor between closing " and the copy it follows.
6. Do not space between & and the letters it joins; space once before and after & used to join words.
7. Do not space between * and the copy it precedes or follows.

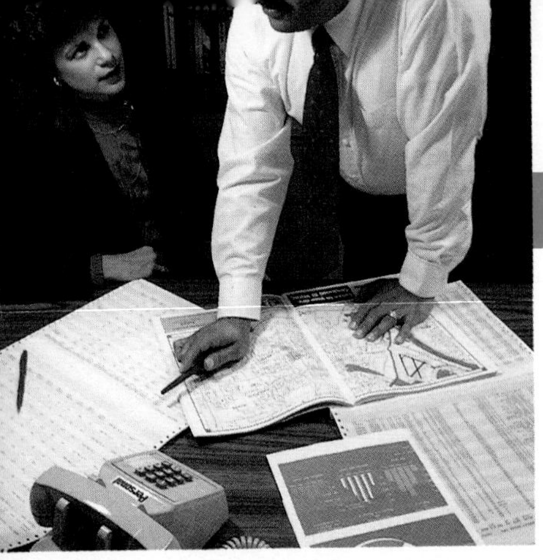

Unit 56 Lessons 256-258

Learning Goals

1. To familiarize you with some of the major functions performed in a marketing division.
2. To increase your knowledge of typical documents processed and tasks performed in marketing operations.
3. To improve your skill in processing special documents.

Documents Processed

1. Interoffice Memorandum
2. Directory
3. Form Letters from Boilerplate
4. Price List
5. Unbound Report
6. Invoices

Lessons 256-258

256a-258a ▶ 5 Check Equipment

Before you begin work each day, check your machine to see that it is in good working order by keying the paragraph at the right at least twice (first slowly, then faster).

all letters/figures used

Moya moved the complex equipment into place to begin the job of making highway repairs -- Route 9 (6 miles), Route 45 (8 miles), and Route 30 (17 miles). Since costs may rise close to 25%, this problem may signal the end to a fight to augment the civic panel.

| 1 | 2 | 3 | 4 | 5 | 6 | 7 | 8 | 9 | 10 | 11 | 12 | 13 |

256b-258b ▶ 45 Document Processing

1. As a word processing trainee with Electro-Technologies, Ltd., your next work experience will be in the Marketing Division.
2. As a part of your orientation, you will be asked to process a variety of documents originated by executives in the Marketing Division.
3. Follow directions given for each document. If the format of a document is not specified, use your best judgment and arrange it neatly on the page.
4. Correct errors as marked and correct any additional errors you may find.

Document 1

Interoffice Memorandum
(LM p. 105)

Prepare in final form the interoffice memo originated by Henry C. Clark, Marketing Service Manager.

Staff and Operating

Send memo dated May 6 to all executives in regard to the establishment of regional ~~distribution~~ Supply centers.

¶1 In complience with directive 87302, ~~written~~ issued by the Vice President of Marketing on April 20, Distribution Centers for peripheral computer equipment and suplies will be ~~established~~ stet on September 1.

¶2 These Service ~~Centers~~ facilities, to be ~~called~~ known as ELEC-TECH supply centers, will serve the geographical ~~areas~~ districts shown:

Reverse columns

DS

DISTRICT	SUPPLY CENTER
Northeast	Newark, ~~NJ~~ New Jersey
Southeast	Atlanta, ~~GA~~ Georgia
South Central	Dallas, Texas
North Central	~~Denver, CO~~ Des Moines, Iowa
Northwest	Protland, Oregon
Southwest	~~Long Beach~~ Bakersfield, California

¶3 A complete directory of these distribution facilities is attached.

Lesson 41 Formatting Personal Notes

Line length: 60 spaces
Spacing: single-space (SS)

41a ▶ 6 Conditioning Practice

1. Each line twice SS.
2. A 1′ writing on line 3; find *gwam*.

alphabet 1 Gwen Jackson placed the next bid for my prized antique vase.
fig/sym 2 Items marked * are out of stock: #391*, #674A*, and #2850*.
speed 3 The audit by the city signals the end of their profit cycle.

| 1 | 2 | 3 | 4 | 5 | 6 | 7 | 8 | 9 | 10 | 11 | 12 |

41b ▶ 44 Learn to Format Personal Notes

3 half sheets, long edge at top; 60-space line; block format

Problem 1

Format and key the model note shown below. Use the spacing instructions given in color on the model. (Problems 2 and 3 are on page 71.)

Personal notes
Personal notes are messages between two people on topics of mutual interest. Notes consist of a dateline, salutation (greeting), message (body), complimentary close (farewell), and typed or printed name of the writer. They are often prepared on half sheets.

Block format and placement
Because it is easy to arrange, block format is often used for personal notes. In block style all lines begin at the left margin. The dateline is placed on line 6 of a half sheet (long edge at top). Because such notes are short, a 60-space line is commonly used for both 10-pitch (pica) and 12-pitch (elite) machines.

Spacing of parts
A quadruple space (4 line spaces) separates the dateline and the salutation as well as the complimentary close and the typed or printed name. A double space is left between salutation and body, between the paragraphs, and between body and complimentary close. The body of the note is single-spaced.

Space down 6 times to place the date

Date November 6, 19--

QS (quadruple-space); space down 4 times

Salutation Dear Ralph

DS

There is a book that you just must read since you are "into" computers. It is MEGATRENDS by John Naisbitt.

DS

Body

The author traces the impact on people of the high-tech society brought about by the growing use of computers. He also describes the trend toward the offsetting high-touch society that is developing to help us cope with the many changes (not all positive) the computer has brought into our lives.

DS

The book is at the same time frightening and reassuring. Do read it; then let's compare notes.

DS

Complimentary close Cordially

QS (quadruple-space); space down 4 times

Dee

Typed (printed) name Dolores

Personal Note on a Half Sheet

251b-255b (continued)

Document 6

Mr. Fuentes asks you to center the table DS for Mrs. Engles, who is preparing a budget report.

ADMINISTRATIVE SUPPORT DIVISION

Actual vs. ^Budgeted Costs for First Fiscal Quarter

Item	Budget	Actual	Difference
Executive Salaries	$ 1,245,000	$ 1,140,000	-105,000 (1)
Administrative and Secretarial Salaries	290,500	360,700	+ 70,200
Postage	150,000	163,500	+ 13,500
Telecommunications	175,000	104,000	- 71,000 (2)
Supplies	100,000	113,600	+ 13,600 (3)
Maintenance	75,000	74,800	- 200
Overhead	125,000	125,000	0
Equipment	900,000	720,500	-179,500 (4)
Depreciation	85,000	85,000	0
Reserves for Insurance and Taxes	140,000	140,000	0
Miscellaneous	65,000	57,000	- 8,000

---

(1) Two vacancies: Assistant Chief of Telecommunications and Chief Supply Clerk.

(2) Telecommunications system not complete.

(3) Additional supplies required for microfilm equipment.

(4) Conversion from electric to electronic equipment not completed on schedule.

41b (continued)

Problem 2

Format and key the note given at the right. Use the same directions as you used for Problem 1.

Problem 3

Proofread the note you prepared in Problem 2. Using proofreader's marks, mark any errors for correction. Prepare another copy of the note from your marked copy.

An enrichment problem appears on page 74.

November 8, 19--

Dear Della

The TV people are very unhappy with you. Since I received the trivia game you sent for my birthday, the "pursuit" begins as soon as dinner is over and the TV is OFF. My entire family sends its thanks.

I need one of those "trivia facts" books, though. I play so poorly that I have been nicknamed N. T. for "No Trivia."

Thanks, Della, for helping us learn to play together again. I didn't know mom and dad were so smart.

Cordially

Nelson

Lesson 42 Formatting Simplified Memos

Line length: 60 spaces
Spacing: single-space (SS)

42a ▶ 6 Conditioning Practice

1. Each line twice SS.
2. A 1′ writing on line 3; find *gwam*.

alphabet 1 Jack Todd will have a quiet nap before his big zoology exam.
fig/sym 2 Our 1987 profit was $53,649 (up 20% from the previous year).
speed 3 The firms may make a profit if they handle their work right.

| 1 | 2 | 3 | 4 | 5 | 6 | 7 | 8 | 9 | 10 | 11 | 12 |

42b ▶ 14 Check/Improve Keyboarding Skill

1. A 1′ writing on each ¶; find *gwam* on each writing.
2. A 2′ writing on each ¶. If you finish a ¶ before time is called, start over. Find *gwam*; your 2′ *gwam* is your 1′ *gwam* ÷ 2.
3. A 3′ writing on ¶s 1-2 combined; find *gwam*.
4. Proofread your copy and mark it for correction. If time permits, key the ¶s again from your marked copy.

1′ Gwam Goals
▽ 25 = acceptable
□ 29 = average
○ 33 = good
◇ 37 = excellent

all letters used | LA | 1.4 si | 5.4 awl | 85% hfw |

gwam 3′

2 . 4 . 6 . 8 . 10 .
All of you make an error now and then in performing an 4
12 . 14 . 16 . 18 . 20 . 22 .
act like driving a car, doing the high jump, or playing the 8
24 ▽ 26 . 28 □ 30 . 32 ○ 34 .
piano. Keying is no different. To err is human. The more 12
36 ◇ 38 . 40 . 42 . 44 . 46 .
difficult the activity, the greater the opportunity to make 16
48 . 50 . 52 . 54 . 56 . 58
errors. Do not expect all your work to be perfect now. 19
. 2 . 4 . 6 . 8 . 10 .
Do not infer from this, though, that the more mistakes 23
12 . 14 . 16 . 18 . 20 . 22 .
you make, the more human you are. A lot of your errors are 27
24 ▽ 26 . 28 □ 30 . 32 ○ 34 .
merely chance; why you make them is a real puzzle. Others, 31
36 ◇ 38 . 40 . 42 . 44 . 46 .
however, are known to be due to lack of attention, improper 35
48 . 50 . 52 . 54 . 56 . 58
reading, and bad techniques. Try to reduce the latter. 39

gwam 3′ | 1 | 2 | 3 | 4 |

251b-255b (continued)

Document 5

Form Letters from Boilerplate
(LM pp. 97-103)

1. Boilerplate consists of standardized text, similar to the form paragraphs at the right, which can be used to customize documents. These paragraphs can be combined to form replies to individuals who have applied for jobs with Electro-Technologies, Inc.

2. Mr. Fuentes asks you to prepare letters dated April 10 to the following job applicants using the paragraphs indicated. The letters will be signed by Kenneth T. Wolfe, Assistant Personnel Director.

Applicant 1:

Mr. Lu Huang
513 Fair Street
Atlanta, GA 33014-2685

Position: **WP Specialist**
¶s: 1b, 2a, 2d

Applicant 2:

Ms. Tracy R. Parkes
Box 33800 North
Decatur, GA 30031-4620

Position: **WP Trainee**
¶s: 1c, 3a, 3b

Applicant 3:

Miss Juanita L. Marietta
62 Orchard Street
Forest Park, GA 30050-6978

Position: **Secretary**
¶s: 2c, 3c, 3b

Applicant 4:

Mr. Patrick K. Ridgewood
809 Milner Avenue
Riverdale, GA 30274-3811

Position: **WP Supervisor**
¶s: 1e, 2b, 3d

1a Thank you for your recent telephone inquiry regarding vacancies for office personnel in Electro-Technologies, Ltd.

1b Thank you for your recent letter in which you applied for a position as a/an (insert title of position). We appreciate your interest in Electro-Technologies, Ltd.

1c Thank you for applying for the position of (insert title of position).

1d We acknowledge, with thanks, your application for a position as a/an (insert title). We may have a position for which you are qualified.

1e Several months ago, you applied for a position as a/an (insert title of position). At that time, we did not have a vacancy for which you were qualified. It is possible, however, that we shall have an opening in the very near future.

2a Will you please complete the enclosed application blank and return it to us promptly. After we have had an opportunity to review your background, we shall be able to determine whether you have the necessary qualifications to fill the position.

2b Will you please call our office at 555-8100, Ext. 410, and arrange for a personal interview so that we can discuss the position.

2c Recently, you were interviewed by a member of our staff for a position in the office of Electro-Technologies, Ltd. The competition for this job was very keen, and it was quite difficult to select the person to fill the position.

2d Within ten days after we receive your application blank, we shall let you know whether we have a position for which you are qualified.

3a At this time we do not have a position for which you are qualified. We shall keep your application on file for six months and if the need arises for someone with your skills, we shall contact you.

3b Your interest in becoming an employee of our company is appreciated.

3c We regret that you were not selected for the position. We shall keep your application on file for six months and will call you if another vacancy occurs.

3d If you are no longer interested in a position with our company, will you please call and let us know.

Space down 6 times
to place the date

Date November 9, 19--

QS (quadruple-space);
space down 4 times

Addressee All Students

DS

Subject STUDENT ASSEMBLY

DS

Next week's student assembly will be held in the auditorium on Friday, November 16, at 12:45 p.m. All students are expected to attend.

DS

Body Ms. Janet Quinlan of Future Training & Placement Service will speak on the topic

DS

COMPUTERS: INVADERS OF FUTURE CAREERS

DS

You will want to bring a notebook and pen so that you can take notes on this highly informative slide presentation.

QS

Name of writer Eleanor Sanchez, Assistant Principal

Simplified Memo on a Half Sheet

42c ▶ 30

Learn to Format Simplified Memos

3 half sheets, long side at top; 60-space line; block format

Study the model memo above. Its format and spacing are *similar* to those of a personal note.

Problem 1

Format and key the model; center the talk topic on a separate line. Use spacing directions shown in color.

Problem 2

Format and key the memo given at the right. Make placement and spacing decisions.

Problem 3

Format and key Problem 2 again, but address it to **Willis Jones** and change the appointment time to **1:45 p.m.**

An enrichment problem appears on page 74.

November 10, 19--

Jeanne Budka

FOREIGN EXCHANGE STUDY

On Tuesday, December 4, Mr. Adam Doza of Rotary, International, will be here to discuss foreign study with prospective exchange students.

The meeting will be in Conference Room C of Hutchins Library at 11:15 a.m. After the general session, Mr. Doza will visit with each applicant separately. Your appointment is at 2:30 p.m.

Please be prompt for these meetings and bring all your application materials with you.

Joseph M. Quade, Principal

251b-255b (continued)
Document 4
Report (continued)

① Other employees depend upon the work you do in order to complete their jobs. You will gain their respect and enhance your reputation as a responsible, cooperative employee if you are on the job regularly. Keep in mind that attendance is a major factor when an individual is considered for promotion or a bonus.

② If your supervisor decides that the absence is unexcused, you have the right to appeal the decision to your next higher supervisor and to the Human Relations Board, if you so desire.

③ These actions are to insure that you do not return to work before you are entirely well and to protect the well-being of your fellow workers.

④ counseled by your supervisor in an effort to discover the cause of your absence and to determine if problems exist which can be corrected. A record of the discussion will be placed in your employee file.

⑤ Any employee who maintains a perfect attendance record for a period of three consecutive months will be awarded an additional day of vacation with pay; for six consecutive months, two additional days; for one year of perfect attendance, four additional days.

ENRICHMENT ACTIVITY: Supplementary Problems for Unit 6

Problem 1a
Centered Announcement

Beginning on line 10 of a half sheet (long edge at top), center each line of the announcement horizontally.

Problem 1b
Centered Poem

Beginning on line 10 of a half sheet (long edge at top), center the poem according to the longest line. DS below the title and the author's name; SS the body of the poem.

Problem 1a

SCHOOL OF PERFORMING ARTS

presents

"The Mouse That Roared"

January 21, 22, 23

Marx Theater

All seats: $3.50

Problem 1b

OUTWITTED
DS
by
DS
Edwin Markham
DS

He drew a circle that shut me out—
Heretic, rebel, a thing to flout.
But Love and I had the wit to win:
We drew a circle that took him in!

Reprinted by permission of Virgil Markham

> **Learn to "make" an exclamation mark (!)**
>
> If your machine has an exclamation mark key, the left little finger is used to strike it. To "make" the !:
>
> Strike ' (apostrophe); backspace and strike . (period).

Problem 2
Numbered List

full sheet; begin on line 10; 60-space line; SS numbered items, leaving a DS between items

words

SOME POINTS TO REMEMBER ABOUT SPACING 8

1. Space once after , and ; used as marks of punctuation. 20

2. Space twice after . ending a sentence. Space once after . 32
following an initial (J. W. Mills) or an abbreviation, but 44
not after . within an abbreviation. (The candidate has a 55
Ph.D. in English.) 59

3. Space twice after ? at the end of a sentence. (Is the meet- 72
ing at ten o'clock? If so, please have coffee set up.) 83

4. Space twice after : used to introduce a list, an example, 96
or a quotation. (He said: "Return my call at 3 p.m.") 107
Do not space after : used to express time (3:15 p.m.). 118

5. Do not space between a figure and a symbol used with it 130
($45, 18%, #75). 134

6. One space should precede (and one should follow), but 146
no space should follow (nor should one precede). If 157
) is followed by a punctuation mark, no space is left 167
between them. (See examples in Items 4 and 5.) 177

7. Between a two-letter state name abbreviation and the ZIP 189
Code, space twice (Dallas, TX 75205-3382). This rule 200
applies in textual copy as well as in addresses. 210

251b-255b (continued)

Document 4

Report

After reviewing the information presented by Mrs. Engles, Mr. Martin has revised the firm's policies on absenteeism.

Prepare the manuscript as a leftbound report DS for insertion into the OFFICE EMPLOYEE HANDBOOK. Additions to the policy found on the next page should be inserted as indicated.

POLICY ON ABSENTEEISM

3 blank spaces

The absence of an employee from work has a serious effect upon the operations of *your* ~~any~~ work group. *(Insert material numbered ① on the next page.)* ~~The absence of a worker reflects a lack of dependability and respect for other employees.~~ ~~Furthermore,~~ absenteeism can also result in lower productivity which, in turn, may *affect the company's ability to increase pay and benefits.* ~~cause a great financial loss to the firm.~~

Absence from work is excusable only in the case of serious illness, death in the immediate family, or *an* ~~serious~~ emergency. In such cases, *please* ~~you will be expected to~~ notify your immediate supervisor at the earliest possible *time* ~~moment~~. Upon your return to work, you will *be asked to* complete a~~n~~ ~~absentee~~ form giving the reason for your absence. Your supervisor has the *authority* ~~right~~ to determine whether the absence is excused or unexcused. *(Insert material numbered ② on the next page.)*

If you are absent because of illness, you will be expected to report to the company doctor *for a brief examination* prior to returning to your ~~desk~~ workstation. For an absence of three or more days, *please obtain* a certificate from your physician. ~~will be needed.~~ *(Insert material numbered ③ on the next page.)* ¶ If you are absent for three days with no acceptable excuse, you will be ~~given a verbal and written reprimand that will be placed in your personnel file~~. *(Insert material numbered ④ on next page.)* If you are absent for five days with no acceptable excuse, you will be suspended for twenty-one days. *An* unexcused absence of six days will lead to immediate dismissal.

In the event of a death in your immediate family (parents, siblings, spouse, or children), you will be permitted an absence of three days with pay. For the death of grandparents, aunts, *and* uncles, you will be *permitted an absence of one day with pay.* ~~allowed time off for the funeral only.~~ *(Insert paragraph numbered ⑤ on next page.)*

(continued on page 429)

Problem 3
Personal Note in Script

half sheet (long edge at top); line: 60; spacing: SS

Format the note in block style, line for line as shown. Read carefully to avoid reading errors.

words

November 10, 19-- 4

Dear Marianne 6
On December 18, our Music/Drama Club is sponsoring a special 19
event, "Holiday Sounds," at the Village Center. Instrumental, 31
vocal, and dramatic selections are to be featured. 42

Even though I have only a minor role, I'd like to know that you 54
are in the audience applauding our performance. I really hope 67
that you can be here for the holidays and that you will come to 80
see our show. 83

I have a super ticket for you. You will be seated among people 96
you know and like. We hope to see you on the 18th and through- 108
out the holiday season. 113

Cordially 115

Douglas Mason 117

Problem 4
Simplified Memo in Rough Draft

half sheet (long edge at top); line: 60; spacing: SS

Format the memo in block style, line for line as shown. Read carefully to avoid reading errors.

- ^ insert comma
- # insert space
- ∿ transpose
- sp. spell out
- ⁀ close up space
- ≡ capitalize

Note: **xx** at the end of a document indicates the keyboard operator's initials. Substitute your own initials.

```
November 10 19--                                             4

Junior AchievementMembers                                    9

ORIENTATION MEETING WITH SPONSORS                           16

On Thrusday evening, November 29, at 7 o'clock, JA members  28
and their sponsors will meet in Emory Auditorium.           39

The purpose of the meeting is to intorduce the officers and the  51
sponsor from each company.  In addition, a representative of     64
each company will describe its purpose, organization and plan    76
of operation.                                                    79

The president of each JA com pany is responsible for planning   91
and conducting her/his company's part of the program.          102

Elliott Richards, ja sponsor                                   108

xx                                                             109
```

251b-255b (continued)

Document 2

Table

Mrs. Susan Engles, Director of the Administrative Support Division, is compiling information about employee absenteeism. For your next assignment, Mr. Fuentes asks you to prepare the table at the right. In the final column, indicate the increase (+) or decrease (−) in %.

Note: If your machine does not have the + symbol, key the hyphen, backspace and key the diagonal (/). To make a minus (−) symbol, key a hyphen.

ADMINISTRATIVE SUPPORT DIVISION

Employee Absenteeism for 2d and 3d Quarters of Year*

Department	2d	3d	+ or −
Mail	14%	16 %	+2%
Telecommunications	8%	11 %	
Reprographics	10%	14 %	
Records	12%	17 %	
Personnel	9%	9 %	
Training	10%	8 %	
Industrial Relations	9%	10 %	
Pay and Benefits	7%	12 %	
Forms Control	15%	16 %	
Office Supplies	11%	15 %	

*Time lost as a percentage of total work time.

Document 3

Interoffice Memorandum

(LM p. 95)

Ms. Gail Turner, Administrative Assistant to Mrs. Susan Engles, asks you to prepare the memo at the right to Aloysius Martin, Chief of Personnel. Ms. Turner would like an original and one carbon copy of the memo.

TO: Aloysius L. Martin

FROM: Gail M. Turner

DATE: April 3, 19--

SUBJECT: Employee Absenteeism

(¶) Mrs. Engles notes with some concern the increase in employee absenteeism during the past quarter. She plans an all-out campaign to reverse this trend. The enclosed table outlines the time lost in each department for the second and third quarters of this fiscal year.

(¶) As a part of the campaign, Mrs. Engles wishes you to review and revise our current absentee policies. She would like the policy to reflect a more positive approach.

(¶) Please let us have a suggested revision within the next two weeks.

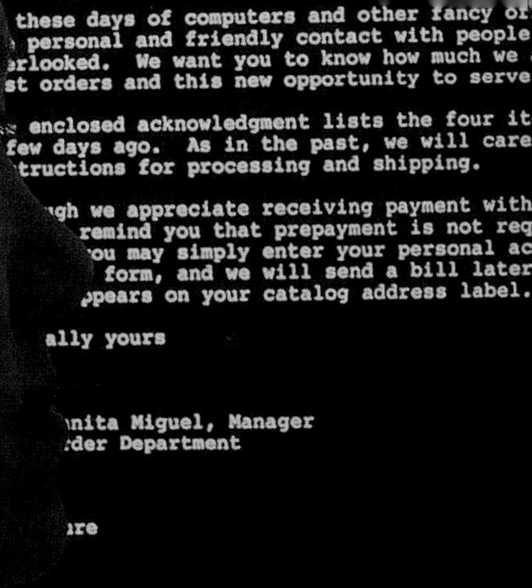

these days of computers and other fancy of
personal and friendly contact with people
rlooked. We want you to know how much we a
st orders and this new opportunity to serve

enclosed acknowledgment lists the four ite
few days ago. As in the past, we will caref
tructions for processing and shipping.

gh we appreciate receiving payment with
remind you that prepayment is not requ
ou may simply enter your personal acc
form, and we will send a bill later.
ppears on your catalog address label.

ally yours

nita Miguel, Manager
der Department

re

Unit 7 Lessons 43-48

Learning Goals

1. To learn how to format business and personal business letters in block style.
2. To learn how to listen for the warning bell and divide words at line endings.
3. To learn how to address large and small envelopes.

Machine Adjustments

1. Paper guide at *0*.
2. Ribbon control to use top half of ribbon.
3. Margin sets: left margin (center - 30); right margin (move to right end of scale).
4. Line-space selector set to SS drills and DS ¶s; set as directed for problems.

FORMATTING GUIDES: LETTERS IN BLOCK STYLE

Modern Office Systems, Inc.

November 11, 19--

Mrs. Dorinda O'Neil, Director
Sooner Office Temporaries, Inc.
One Williams Center
Tulsa, OK 74172-4280

Dear Mrs. O'Neil

The block format in which this letter is arranged has grown rapidly in popularity for business and personal letters.

Users of personal computers, word processors, and typewriters prefer block format because no tab stop settings or indenting motions are required. The result is greater efficiency. In addition, block style avoids the errors that occur in other formats when operators forget to indent certain letter parts.

Changes are being made in document formats and placement to simplify the use of modern office machines and to make people more productive. The growing use of block format is just one of many such changes. Some of the other changes are described in the enclosed pamphlet.

Sincerely yours

J. T. Bellamah

Jeffrey T. Bellamah, Head
Work Simpification Unit

ke

Enclosure

Block Format

When *all* lines of a letter begin at the left margin, as illustrated in the model, the letter is arranged in *block format* (style). Block format is easy to learn and easy to arrange. It is widely used for both business and personal letters.

Open Punctuation

When no punctuation follows any of the opening or closing lines (except one that may end in an abbreviation), *open* punctuation has been used. Open punctuation is compatible with block format because both save time and reduce errors. All letters in this unit will be formatted with open punctuation.

Model Description

The basic parts of letters written by individuals and businesses to solve business problems are described below in order of their occurrence in a letter.

Heading. On letterhead paper, the printed top portion is the heading or letterhead. It gives the company name, address, and telephone number. On plain paper, often used for personal-business letters, the writer's address appears on the two lines immediately above the date.

Date. When standard letter placement is used -- a practice that is becoming more and more common -- the date is entered or typed on a specified line (line 15 being a common placement) for all letters.

Letter Address. The letter address is begun on the fourth line space below the date. If the letter is addressed to a company, the address *may* include an attention line (the second line of the address) to call the letter to the attention of a specific person, department, or job title.

Salutation. The salutation (greeting) is placed a double space (DS) below the letter address.

Body. The letter body (message) is begun a double space (DS) below the salutation. The paragraphs of the body are blocked and single-spaced (SS) with a double space left between paragraphs.

Complimentary Close. The complimentary close (farewell) appears a double space below the body.

Name of Writer. The name of the writer (the originator of the message) is placed on the fourth line space below the complimentary close. It may be followed on the same line or on the next line by a business or professional title such as Manager, Vice President, Ph.D., or a department name.

Reference Initials. The initials of the typist or machine operator are placed a double space below the writer's name (or the writer's title or department if placed on a separate line).

Enclosure Notation. The enclosure notation, which indicates that something in addition to the letter is included in the envelope, is placed a double space below the reference initials.

Special Letter Parts

A letter may include one or more of the following special parts:

- mailing notation (a DS below date)
- subject line (a DS below the salutation; a DS above the letter message)
- copy notation (*cc* or *pc* a DS below the enclosure notation or the reference initials if there is no enclosure)
- postscript (a DS below the last item in the letter)

Because such parts are used sparingly, they will be practiced later in the book.

Letter Spacing Summary

Three blank line spaces (a *quadruple space*) separate date from address and complimentary close from typed name of writer. A *double space* separates *all* other letter parts.

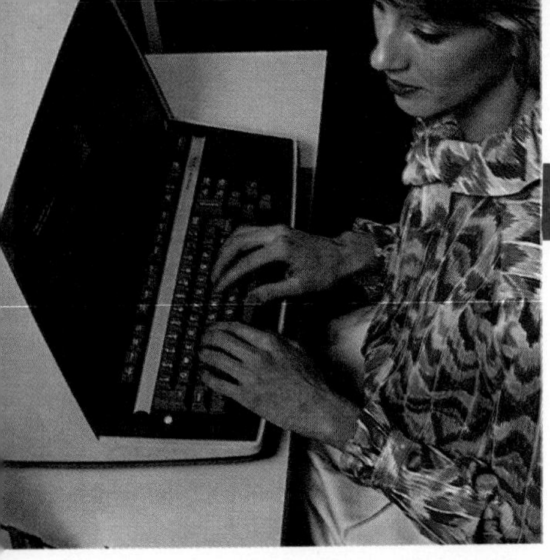

Unit 55 Lessons 251-255

Learning Goals
1. To increase your skill in planning and organizing a variety of production jobs.
2. To prepare in an acceptable form with all errors corrected a series of typical documents processed in an administrative office.
3. To improve your basic keyboarding and language skills.

Documents Processed
1. Letters
2. Tables
3. Interoffice Memorandum
4. Leftbound Manuscript
5. Letters from Boilerplate

Lessons 251-255

251a-255a ▶ 5
Check Equipment

Before you begin work each day, check your machine to see that it is in good working order by keying the paragraph at the right at least twice (first slowly, then faster).

all letters/figures used

Texley quietly criticized the vague remarks published in the news journals (see pages 8, 827, and 1045 of Vol. #167 as well as pages 5 and 19 of Vol. #173). Did the author augment the body of the work and form an authentic theory with the usual proficiency?

| 1 | 2 | 3 | 4 | 5 | 6 | 7 | 8 | 9 | 10 | 11 | 12 | 13 |

251b-255b ▶ 45
Document Processing

Your first experience as a word processing trainee will be in the Administrative Support Division of Electro-Technologies, Ltd., at the company's main office.

20 Marietta Street
Atlanta, GA 30303-6280.

As a trainee, you will parpare a variety of documents originated by a number of executives.

Follow directions given for each document. If the format of a document is not specified, use your best judgment and place it neatly on the page. Correct all marked and unmarked errors.

Document 1

Block Style Letter; Open
(LM p. 93)

Mr. Arturo Fuentes, Word Processing Supervisor, asks you to compose a letter using the information at the right. Miss Helen T. Murray, Assistant Personnel Officer, will sign the letter.

April 2 - Prepare letter to attention of Classified Ad Department of Atlanta Tribune, 34 Broad Street, NW, Atlanta, GA 30303-7142 requesting that the advertisements below be published for five days beginning April 9. Tell them to send the bill to Mr. Frank Wilson in our Accounting Department. Helen T. Murray

SECRETARY - Minimum typing speed of ~~60~~ 55 WPM (lc); short~~ ~~hand skills of 80 wpm or ~~voice~~ machine transcription skills; superior ~~word~~ language skills. Excellent pay and benifits. Send resume to box 237a, Atlanta Tribune.

TYPIST - Good typing, ~~verbal~~ language, and ~~arithmetic~~ figure skills. Excellent starting pay. Send resume to Box 237a, Atlanta Tribune.

WORD PROCESSING SUPERVISOR - Experience in W~~O~~P ~~S~~ystems (lc), general office ~~procedures~~ operations, and train~~g~~ing ~~Word Processing~~ WP ~~O~~perators (lc). Exceptional opportunity for ~~promotion~~ advancement. Send resume to Box 237a, Alanta Tribune.

Lesson 43 Letters

Line: 60 spaces
Spacing: SS (or as directed)

43a ▶ 6
Conditioning Practice

1. Each line twice SS.
2. A 1′ writing on line 3; find *gwam*.

alphabet 1 Vicki Jewel can make six quaint prizes for the bridge party.
fig/sym 2 Gene's telephone number in 1986 was (917) 627-4039, Ext. 25.
speed 3 Good form is the key if all of us wish to make the big goal.

| 1 | 2 | 3 | 4 | 5 | 6 | 7 | 8 | 9 | 10 | 11 | 12 |

43b ▶ 14
Learn to Place and Space Letter Parts

2 plain full sheets; line: 60 spaces; date: line 15

1. Study the material on page 75; check each placement point with the model letter on page 77.

2. On a full sheet, arrange and key the opening lines of Drill 1, beginning on line 15 from top edge.

3. After keying the salutation, return 14 times to key the closing lines.

4. Do Drill 2 in the same way, but start the return address on line 13.

Note: Reference initials are not used in personal-business letters.

Language Skills Notes:

1. Note that months, titles, names, abbreviations, and initials (except reference initials) are capitalized.

2. Note that 2 spaces are left between the 2-letter state name abbreviation and the ZIP Code.

Drill 1

November 21, 19--

Miss Rhonda McMahon
2000 Columbus Avenue
Springfield, MA 01103-2748

Dear Miss McMahon

Space down 14 times (using INDEX or RETURN) to allow for body of letter.

Sincerely yours

George C. Ogden
Sales Manager

jr

Enclosure

Drill 2

3899 Norton Avenue
Kansas City, MO 64128-3357
November 21, 19--

Mr. Alan Ditka
Simon & Lowe, Inc.
215 Madison Street, E
Tampa, FL 33602-2936

Dear Mr. Ditka

Space down 14 times (using INDEX or RETURN) to allow for body of letter.

Sincerely yours

Ms. Leona Watkins

Enclosure

43c ▶ 30
Learn to Format Business Letters

1 letterhead (LM p. 29); 2 plain sheets; line: 60; date: line 15

1. Study the letter on page 77 illustrating *block style, open punctuation.* Note the vertical and horizontal placement of letter parts.

2. On a letterhead (or plain paper) type line for line a copy of the letter on page 77.

3. Proofread your copy and mark it for correction.

4. If time permits, take a 2′ writing on opening lines (date through salutation); then a 2′ writing on closing lines (complimentary close through enclosure notation). If you complete the copy before time is called, start over.

ELECTRO-TECHNOLOGIES, LTD.

Before you begin your first assignment, Ms. Gail M. Turner, an administrative assistant to Mrs. Susan Engles, Director of Administrative Support Division, asks you to read the information in the OFFICE EMPLOYEE HANDBOOK.

Excerpts from OFFICE EMPLOYEE HANDBOOK
Word Processing Trainee/Operator

Qualifications. To be successful as a Word Processing Trainee/Operator, you must possess the following minimum qualifications:

1. Excellent keyboarding skills.
2. A good knowledge of grammar, punctuation, spelling, and formatting.
3. The ability to use reference materials such as dictionaries, directories, and manuals.
4. Good proofreading skills.
5. The ability to listen, understand, and follow directions.
6. A knack for working well with others.

Major Duties. Under the general direction of a Word Processing Supervisor, you will:

1. Compile information as the basis for preparing business documents.
2. Keyboard documents such as correspondence, reports, forms, and tables.
3. Prepare business documents from dictation, handwritten or rough-draft copy, and from source materials.
4. Compose short documents based on data and instructions provided.
5. Compute amounts in pencil or by using a calculator.

Special Instructions. As a Word Processing Trainee/Operator, you will be expected to:

1. Determine the format for a document.
2. Provide the date for correspondence (use the current date if a date is not given).
3. Provide an appropriate salutation, complimentary close, typed signature and title of the originator of correspondence as well as your initials.
4. Include the proper notation if the content of the document indicates there are enclosures or attachments.
5. Correct errors you make as you prepare a document in final form.
6. Correct any errors made by the originator of the document -- check spelling, punctuation, grammar, and word usage.
7. Proofread all documents and correct any errors you may have missed *before* submitting them to your supervisor.
8. Produce neat, error-free, usable business documents.

Formatting. The Information Processing Center is expected to begin operations in the next few weeks. Until it becomes operational, each division of the company is free to adopt any document format it chooses. Follow directions given by the document originator. If no format is specified, use your best judgment in placing the material neatly on the page.

Major Organizational Functions

The following are a few of the major organizational functions performed by the divisions in which you will work.

Administrative Support Division

1. Provides central records management.
2. Directs programs for human resources and industrial relations.
3. Administers employee remuneration and benefit programs.
4. Supplies telecommunications services.
5. Conducts training programs as required.

Marketing Division

1. Conducts economic and market research.
2. Merchandises goods.
3. Distributes goods to customers.
4. Provides customer services.
5. Conducts advertising and other sales campaigns.

Purchasing Division

1. Determines sources of supply.
2. Obtains necessary machinery, tools, and facilities.
3. Buys the proper materials, components, and products at the best possible price.
4. Stores materials necessary so that they will be available when needed.

Executive Office

1. Determines broad objectives, policies, and procedures.
2. Makes timely decisions.
3. Develops current and future plans and procedures.
4. Provides inspirational leadership.

Information Processing Center

1. Provides word and data processing services.
2. Provides graphic, reprographic, printing, and phototypesetting services.
3. Maintains data bases.
4. Maintains a micrographics storage systems.
5. Established, maintains, and operates local and worldwide communications networks.

		words in parts	total words
Dateline	November 11, 19-- Line 15	4	4
	QS: operate return 4 times to quadruple-space (3 blank lines)		
Letter address	Mrs. Dorinda O'Neil, Director	10	10
	Sooner Office Temporaries, Inc.	16	16
	One Williams Center	20	20
	Tulsa, OK 74172-4280	24	24
	DS		
Salutation	Dear Mrs. O'Neil	28	28
	DS		
Body of letter	The block format in which this letter is arranged has grown	12	40
	rapidly in popularity for business and personal letters.	24	51
	DS		
	Users of personal computers, word processors, and typewriters	36	64
	prefer block format because no tab stop settings or indenting	48	76
	motions are required. The result is greater efficiency. In	61	88
	addition, block style avoids the errors that occur in other	73	100
	formats when operators forget to indent certain letter parts.	85	113
	DS		
	Changes are being made in document formats and placement to	97	125
	simplify the use of modern office machines and to make people	110	137
	more productive. The growing use of block format is just one	122	150
	of many such changes. Some of the other changes are described	135	162
	in the enclosed pamphlet.	140	167
	DS		
Complimentary close	Sincerely yours	3	170
	QS: operate return 4 times to quadruple-space (3 blank lines)		
	J. T. Bellamah		
Name/title	Jeffrey T. Bellamah, Head	8	176
Department	Work Simplification Unit	13	181
	DS		
Initials of operator	ke	14	181
	DS		
Enclosure notation	Enclosure	16	183

Shown in pica type on a 60-space line (camera-reduced)

Block Format, Open Punctuation

Lessons 251-275

PHASE 11

Electro-Technologies, Ltd.: Internship Training

You have been hired as a word processing trainee by **Electro-Technologies, Ltd.**, a multinational company that manufactures and markets electronic parts, components, and equipment. The firm's main office is located at **20 Marietta Street, Atlanta, GA 30303-6280**. Electro-Technologies, Ltd. has numerous facilities throughout the United States and branch offices in London, Paris, Rome, and Yokohama.

To gain first-hand experience of the company's operations, you will work in several offices. Upon completion of your training, you will become a word processing operator in the company's newly organized Information Processing Center.

Your objectives at Electro-Technologies, Ltd., are to:

1. Become familiar with the functions of some of the major divisions of a large company: Administrative Support, Marketing, Purchasing, Executive, and Information Processing.
2. Increase your knowledge of typical office procedures.
3. Accept responsibility for producing acceptable documents.
4. Learn how to plan and organize work.
5. Improve speed and accuracy in producing business documents.
6. Improve basic keyboarding skills.

Line: 60 spaces
Spacing: SS (or as directed)

44a ▶ 6
Conditioning Practice

1. Each line twice SS.

2. A 1′ writing on line 3; find *gwam*.

alphabet 1 Joey Knox led a big blitz which saved the play for my squad.
fig/sym 2 Martha ordered 26 5/8 yards of #371 percale at $4.09 a yard.
speed 3 Dorian may lend them a hand with the audit of the soap firm.

| 1 | 2 | 3 | 4 | 5 | 6 | 7 | 8 | 9 | 10 | 11 | 12 |

44b ▶ 9
Improve Language Skills: Word Division

1. Read each rule and type (key) the Learn and Apply lines beneath it.

Note: As you key the Apply lines, insert a hyphen at the point where the word can be divided.

2. Check with your teacher the accuracy of your Apply lines; and if time permits, key again the Apply lines in which you made errors in dividing words.

Divide a word only between syllables; words of one syllable, therefore, should not be divided.

Learn 1 pro-gram, through, in-deed, straight, pur-pose, con-tracts
Apply 2 decides, brought, control, wonders, thoughts, practice

Do not separate a one-letter syllable at the beginning of a word or a one- or two-letter syllable at the end of a word.

Learn 3 ideal, prior, ready, enough, ahead, en-try, de-lay, aw-ful
Apply 4 agent, early, party, under, quickly, about, items, fully

Divide a word between double consonants except when adding a syllable to a word that ends in double letters.

Learn 5 writ-ten, sum-mer, run-ning, sud-den, add-ing, will-ing
Apply 6 gotten, dinner, guessing, thinner, agreeing, dressing

44c ▶ 10
Learn to Use the Line-Ending Bell

1. Set margin stops for exact 60-space line: center − 30; center + 30.

2. Key sentence given at right at a slow pace; stop as soon as bell on machine rings. Instead of keying remainder of sentence, key figures **1234**, etc., until the machine locks. Subtract 5 (the desired warning) from final figure; move right stop one space to the right for each remaining figure (usually 3 to 10 spaces). See the illustrative example under the sentence at the right.

3. Key sentence again to check accuracy of your setting of the right margin stop.

4. Using same margin settings, key the ¶ given at the right. Be guided by bell as cue to complete a word, divide it, key another word, or return.

```
Copy:    Move stop so bell rings 5 spaces before desired line ending.
                                                           ↓ bell
Example: Move stop so bell rings 5 spaces before desired liB123456789
         Move stop so bell rings 5 spaces before desired line en////.
                                                                ↑
                                                               bell
                                                                ↓
```

Set the right margin stop at a point that will cause the warning bell on your machine to ring exactly 5 spaces before the line ending desired by moving the right margin stop 3 to 10 spaces to the right of the exact setting for a specified line length (a 60-space line, for example). You can then key 1 to 7 spaces after the warning bell before the machine locks. By adjusting the number of spaces in the buffer zone (from the bell to the desired line ending), you can complete a word or divide it to maintain a fairly even right margin.

250b (continued)

Document 3, continued

Document 4

Reference Page

Prepare a reference page for the report completed in Document 3.

Total: 110 words on reference page.

words

What do employers look for during ~~an~~ a job interview? 111
According to Ristau and Baggett (Ristau, Robert A. and 117
Harry Baggett. <u>Business Careers</u>. 2d ed. Cincinnati: 117
South-Western Publishing Co., 1984, 112.), careful ~~at-~~ 121
~~tention will be given to~~ note is made of your 125

center

1. General Appearance 130
2. Personal Manners 134
3. Speech and Grammar 139
4. Questions Asked 143
5. Attitude Toward Work 148
6. Interest in Job 152

Make a ~~concerted~~ special effort, therefore, to "put your best 162
foot forward" in these areas. 168

Willard daggett Suggests that you prepare for a 178
job interview by knowing something about the company, 189
being prompt, and dressing appropriately. (Daggett, 197
Willard R. <u>The Dynamica of Work</u>. Cincinnati: South- 197
Western Publishing Co., 1984, 75.) In a special pam- 203
phlet, the U. S. Dept. of Labor ~~also~~ suggests that you 214
"be pleasant and friendly but business like." (U.S. 222
Department of Labor, Employment and Training Informa- 222
tion. "Merchandising Your Job Talents." Washington, 222
DC: U.S. Government Printing Office, 1983, 19.) This 226
agency also recommends that you be candid, complete, 237
and brief in your responses. 242

44d ▶ 25
Format Letters in Block Style

2 letterheads (LM pp. 31-34);
1 plain sheet;
line: 60; date: line 15

Problem 1
Business Letter

Format in block style the letter given at the right. Return at the color bars in the opening and closing lines. Key the body of the letter line for line as shown. Listen for the warning bell as you approach the line endings.

words (parts | total)

November 12, 19-- | Mr. Julio M. Perez | 3849 Canterbury Road | 12 12
Baltimore, MD 21218-3365 | Dear Mr. Perez | 20 20

Congratulations! You are now the sole owner of the car you 12 32
financed through our bank. We also want to say thank you for 24 44
choosing us to serve your credit needs. 33 52

The original Certificate of Title and your Installment Loan 45 64
Contract marked "Paid in Full" are enclosed. These papers are 57 77
evidence that you have fulfilled all the obligations of your 69 89
automobile loan. File the papers in a safe place with your 81 101
other important records. 87 106

The promptness with which you made all monthly payments gives 99 119
you a preferred credit rating at our bank. Please let us know 112 131
when we may be of service to you again. 119 139

Cordially yours | Ms. Jennifer Lindgren | Automobile Loan 11 149
Department | hq | Enclosures 16 155

Problem 2
Business Letter

Format the letter given at the right using the directions for Problem 1.

words (parts | total)

November 12, 19-- | Mrs. Gwendolyn Quade | 7257 Charles Plaza | 12 12
Omaha, NE 68114-3219 | Dear Mrs. Quade | 19 19

In these days of computers and other fancy office equipment, 12 31
the personal and friendly contact with people is sometimes 24 43
overlooked. We want you to know how much we appreciate your 36 55
past orders and this new opportunity to serve you. 47 66

The enclosed acknowledgment lists the four items you ordered 59 78
a few days ago. As in the past, we will carefully follow your 71 90
instructions for processing and shipping. 80 99

Although we appreciate receiving payment with an order, we 92 111
want to remind you that prepayment is not required. If you 104 123
prefer, you may simply enter your personal account number on 116 135
the order form, and we will send a bill later. Your account 128 147
number appears on your catalog address label. 137 156

Cordially yours | Ms. Juanita Miguel, Manager | Mail Order 11 167
Department | jb | Enclosure 15 172

Problem 3

As time permits, take two 1′ writings on the opening lines and then on the closing lines of Problem 2 to increase your speed.

250b (continued)

Document 2

(LM p. 91)

Prepare the memo to Gregory C. Torres, Director of Research, from Nancy L. Duval, Administrative Assistant to OOU's President, Christine May.

words

Office Opportunities UNLIMITED

INTEROFFICE COMMUNICATION

TO: Gregory C. Torres 4

FROM: Nancy L. Duval 7

DATE: August 24, 19-- 10

SUBJECT: Development of Seminars 15

¶ Dr. May requests that you investigate the feasibility of 26
developing a series of one-day, in-house seminars for 37
large business firms. The seminars, complete with appropriate 50
multimedia teaching aids, should be aimed at one of three 61
levels: secretarial, managerial, or executive. 71

¶ Suggested topics for seminars include: Communication 82
Skills, Supervisory Techniques, and Time Management. 92

¶ Please let Dr. May have your initial thoughts on this 103
suggestion by September 15. 108/119

Document 3

Unbound Report with Textual Citations

1. Use the title, THE EMPLOYMENT INTERVIEW -- AN OPPORTUNITY TO SELL YOURSELF.

2. Center and list, DS, the numbered items in ¶ 2 (p. 423).

Special Instructions

For each citation, the complete reference information has been included in the text of the report for your convenience in preparing the reference page (Document 4, p. 423). As you prepare the report, insert the proper textual citation and make a note of the complete reference for the reference page.

title 12

In the selection of employees, most ~~firms~~ companies use 22
a ~~number~~ variety of devices, including the application blank, 33
numerous ~~kinds~~ types of tests, and interviews. "It is quite 44
~~possible~~ probable that if companies were restricted to 53
the use of a single method of evaluation in a hiring 63
proc~~u~~edure, they would choose interviewing most fre- 73
quently." (Flippo, Edwin B. Principles of Personnel 75
Management. 4th ed. New York: McGraw-Hill Book Co., 75
1976, 146.) Since this is the case, ~~you should so so~~ 83
~~all you can~~ it is important that you make every effort to sell yourself during the job interview. 100

(continued on page 423)

Lesson 45 — Letters/Word Division

Line: 60 spaces
Spacing: SS (or as directed)

45a ▶ 6

Conditioning Practice

1. Each line twice SS.

2. A 1′ writing on line 3; find *gwam*.

alphabet 1 Jack Hud won first prize by solving a tax quiz in less time.

fig/sym 2 We received Marx & Abel's $729.48 check (#1659) on April 30.

speed 3 Suella may row to the small island to dig for the big clams.

| 1 | 2 | 3 | 4 | 5 | 6 | 7 | 8 | 9 | 10 | 11 | 12 |

45b ▶ 9

Improve Language Skills: Word Division

1. Read each rule and type (key) the Learn and Apply lines beneath it.

Note: As you key the words in the Apply lines, insert a hyphen at the point where the word can be divided.

2. Check with your teacher the accuracy of your Apply lines; and if time permits, key again the Apply lines in which you made errors in dividing words.

> Divide a word after a single-letter vowel syllable that is not a part of a word ending.

Learn 1 vari-ous, sepa-rate, usu-ally, ori-ent, situ-ate, edi-fice

Apply 2 holiday, evaluate, gradually, saturate, granulate

> Divide a word before the word endings -able, -ible, -acle, -ical, and -ily when the vowel **a** or **i** is a separate syllable.

Learn 3 prob-able, convert-ible, mir-acle, op-ti-cal, heart-ily

Apply 4 variable, edible, lyrical, handily, manacle, tropical

> Do not divide a word that contains a contraction (a word in which one or more omitted letters have been replaced by an apostrophe).

Learn 5 didn't, haven't, they'll, couldn't, you're, we've, hadn't

Apply 6 aren't, shouldn't, doesn't, you've, you'll, we'll, hasn't

> Divide only between the two words that make up a hyphenated (compound) word.

Learn 7 ill-advised, self-satisfied, well-groomed, self-concerned

Apply 8 ill-mannered, self-contained, well-meaning, self-centered

45c ▶ 10

Identify Word-Division Points

60-space line; DS

1. Clear all tab stops; then starting at left margin, set 3 new tab stops 17 spaces apart.

2. On a full sheet, center **WORD-DIVISION POINTS** on line 12; then DS.

3. Key the first line as shown.

4. In line 2 and following lines, key the words as shown in Columns 1 and 3; in Columns 2 and 4, rekey each word with a hyphen showing the correct division point.

WORD-DIVISION POINTS
DS

strangely	Tab	strangely	Tab	self-help	Tab	self-help
wouldn't				doubtful		
daily				support		
gasoline				physical		
changes				laudable		
getting				policies		
key 9	8	9	8	9	8	9

Lesson 250

250a ▶ 5
Check Equipment

Before you begin the employment test below, check your machine to see that it is in good working order by keying the paragraph at the right at least twice (first slowly, then faster).

all letters/figures used

Vicky will quiz the group about the rate of their latest tax adjustment. Taxes were raised 2 mills in 1986 (7.03%); if an increase of 1.5 mills (4%) is added, it will equal 11.03%. A panel may also amend the proviso to suspend their audit of the problem.

| 1 | 2 | 3 | 4 | 5 | 6 | 7 | 8 | 9 | 10 | 11 | 12 | 13 |

250b ▶ 45
Document Production Test

Time Schedule

Plan and Prepare .... 5′
Timed Production .... 30′
Proofread; compute *n-pram* .... 10′

Note: To find *n-pram* (net production rate per minute), deduct 15 words for each uncorrected error; divide remainder by 30 (time).

1. Prepare the documents beginning at the right and continuing on pages 422 and 423 in the order given for 30 minutes. Correct any errors that may have been overlooked.

2. At the end of 30 minutes, proofread the documents that you prepared and correct any errors you may have missed, but do not redo any problems. After you have made corrections, compute *n-pram*.

Document 1

Block Style Letter, Open
(LM p. 89)

Send the letter at the right by Certified Mail to

Mr. Dennis K. Stone
18 Elm Street
Lansdowne, PA 19050-8761

Date the letter August 24. The letter will be signed by Ralph T. Zimmerman, Director of Finance.

words

opening lines 21

Under the provisions of your contraact 29
No. 14139 with OOU, you agreed to pay the tuition 39
for your individualized Course of Instruction in 48
data processing skills in two installments of $475 59
each; the first installment *was to be paid* on July 5 and the sec 71
second installment at the mid point of your course, 81
August 16. 83

On August 7, we *notified* sent you *by* a letter *(copy enclosed)* that your next 96
second installment was due on August 16 and re- 106
quested you to send a check or money order for the 116
amount due or to pay *the amount due* at Student Accounts in room 129
110. *To date, however, we have not received payment.* 140

Will you please take immediate action to fulfil 149
your financail obligations. If you are having fi- 159
nancial or other difficulties, please contact 168
Ms. Kathy Bernstein, our Director of Student affairs 178
on (Ext. 493) for an appointment. It is possible 189
that she may be able to work out a mutually agree- 199
able *solution* answer to *your* the problem. 205

Yours very truly 208

closing lines 219/**233**

45d ▶ 25
Format Letters in Block Style

1 letterhead (LM p. 35); 2 plain sheets;
line: 60; date: line 15

Problem 1
Business Letter

Format the letter in block style on the letterhead sheet. Be guided by the color bars to end lines throughout the letter. Although you will not have to divide words, listen for the bell toward the ends of the lines of the letter body.

	words parts	words total
November 13, 19-- | Mr. Evan K. Fletcher | 910 South Avenue |	11	11
Niagara Falls, NY 14305-2267 | Dear Mr. Fletcher |	21	21
Did you forget? |	3	24
As indicated on the statement you just received, your credit | card	17	37
account with us is overdue. More than half the balance | is past due	30	51
by over 30 days. |	34	55
Because we do not maintain revolving accounts in which partial |	46	67
payments can be made, full payment is due each month when you |	59	80
receive your statement. Accounts that habitually exceed 30 | days	72	93
before payment are subject to cancellation. |	81	102
If your overdue and current payments are in the mail, accept | our	94	115
thanks. If not, please send us your check for the full | amount today	108	128
to assure continued use of your card. |	116	136
Sincerely yours | Kyle C. Hoggatt, Manager | Credit Card Center | cp	12	149

Problem 2
Personal-Business Letter

Format the letter in block style on a plain sheet, using the directions for Problem 1. Begin the return address on line 13 so that the date will be on line 15.

line 13

```
2905 College Drive
Columbus, GA  39106-3628
November 13, 19--
```

	parts	total
2905 College Drive | Columbus, GA 31906-3628 | November 13, 19-- |	12	12
Mr. Hans Schmidt | Bucherer Watch Company | 730 Fifth Avenue |	24	24
New York, NY 10019-2046 | Dear Mr. Schmidt |	32	32
If anyone can repair a thinline Bucherer watch, you are that | per-	13	45
son. So said Olga Melchior, manager of the jewelry repair | depart-	26	58
ment of Lorings here in Columbus. |	33	65
Ms. Melchior has fixed my watch twice before, but she thinks | it	46	78
now needs attention that only a licensed Bucherer shop can | give.	59	91
In fact, she believes the entire works may need to be | replaced.	72	104
The case and band are of such value that I want to | do whatever	85	117
must be done to make the watch useful again. |	94	126
Please use the enclosed envelope to send me a rough estimate | of	107	139
the cost of repair and to tell me what I should do next. | The watch	120	153
case number is 904618 in the event the number may | be of use. The	134	166
watch was purchased in Geneva. |	140	172
Sincerely yours | David C. Copeland | Enclosure |	9	181

Problem 3
Skill Building

As time permits, take a 2′ writing on the opening lines and a 1′ writing on the closing lines of Problem 2 to increase speed.

246b-249b ▶ 45 Prepare Employment Documents

(plain sheets; Application Form)

Ms. Dorothy C. Bates, Placement Officer for Office Opportunities Unlimited, has told you about a job as a word processing trainee that is available. You decide to apply for the position.

1. Data Sheet. Compose at the keyboard a data sheet similar to the one at the right. Use your own personal data. Arrange the material attractively. When finished, make corrections in pencil and redo the data sheet in final form.

2. Letter of Application. Compose at the keyboard a letter of application similar to the one below. Address the letter to **Mr. Bryan Hunter/Director of Human Resources/Columbia Industries/1070 State Street/ your city, state, and ZIP Code.** When you have finished, make corrections in pencil and redo the letter in final form.

3. Application Blank (LM p. 87). Read carefully the headings and questions on the application blank. Before completing the form, keyboard on a lined sheet of paper the data to be placed on each line. Edit the material as necessary so that it will fit in the space provided. Then keyboard it onto the form.

CHERYL M. WASHINGTON
101 N. Olive Street
Media, PA 19063-6452
(215) 547-6382

PERSONAL INFORMATION

Age:	19
Place of Birth:	Chester, Pennsylvania
Health:	Good

EDUCATION

High School:	Booker T. Washington High School (received diploma in June, 1986)
Major:	Office Education
Business School:	Office Opportunities Unlimited (will receive my certificate of completion on August 30)
Skills Attained:	Keyboarding straight-copy rate: 60 words a minute; transcribing machine rate: 45 words a minute
Office Machines:	Ten-key electronic calculator; electronic typewriter; word processor; copier

HIGH SCHOOL ACTIVITIES

Chairperson of the Spring Festival
Secretary of the Student Government Association (two years)
President of the Future Business Leaders of America (one year)
Inducted into the National Honor Society in senior year

WORK EXPERIENCE

Keyboard operator in the office of Continental Oil Company for two summers. Prepared correspondence, answered telephone calls, and performed other general office duties.
Word Processing Trainee, Office Opportunities Unlimited, part-time for six months. Prepared documents from script, rough-draft, and boilerplate copy, including editing, revising, and making necessary changes.

REFERENCES (by permission)

Mr. Dale Marshall, Document Production Manager, Office Opportunities Unlimited, Route 252 & Media Line Road, Media, PA 19063-4639

Mrs. Pat Chung, Chief of Administrative Branch, Continental Oil Company, One Wayne Road, Radnor, PA 19087-6325

Miss Sylvia Hilty, Chairman, Office Education Department, Booker T. Washington High School, 9 Elm Street, Media, PA 19063-7450

---

101 N. Olive Street
Media, PA 19063-6452
August 20, 1987

Mr. Bryan Hunter
Director of Human Resources
Columbia Industries
1070 State Street
Media, PA 19063-6379

Dear Mr. Hunter

Ms. Dorothy C. Bates, Placement Officer for Office Opportunities Unlimited, has told me that you have a vacancy for a word processing trainee. If you are looking for someone who is industrious and who is well prepared to assume the responsibilities of a word processing operator, your search is over.

I can keyboard 60 words a minute in a five-minute timed writing and produce documents from machine transcription at a rate of 45 words a minute. My activities while a student at the Booker T. Washington High School show that I can fill positions of responsibility. In addition, I have held several part-time jobs in the secretarial field. Specific details of my activities in high school and my experience are listed on the enclosed personal data sheet.

I enrolled at OOU to improve my formatting, document production, language, and basic keyboarding skills. Among the courses I have completed are keyboarding, communications, word processing, and general office practice which included machine transcription.

I shall complete my refresher course at OOU on August 30 and shall be available for work any time after that date. May I have an interview at your convenience? I can be reached by mail at the address at the top of this letter or by telephone at 547-6382.

Sincerely yours

Ms. Cheryl M. Washington

Enclosure

APPLICATION FOR EMPLOYMENT

PLEASE PRINT WITH BLACK INK OR USE TYPEWRITER — AN EQUAL OPPORTUNITY EMPLOYER

Name (last, first, middle initial): Washington, Cheryl M. — Social Security Number: 309-02-4402 — Current Date: August 20, 1987
Address: 101 N. Olive Street, Media, PA 19063-6452 — Phone No.: 547-6382
U.S. Citizen? Yes X — Date You Can Start: September 1, 1987
Are you employed now? No
Type of work desired: Word Processing Trainee — Referred by: Office Opportunities Unlimited — Salary desired: open
If related to anyone in our employ, state name and position: No one
Do you have any physical condition that may prevent you from performing certain kinds of work? No X
Have you ever been convicted of a felony? No X

Education	Educational Institution	Location (City, State)	From Mo	From Yr	To Mo	To Yr	Diploma, Degree, or Credits Earned	Class Standing 1	2	3	4	Major Subjects Studied
College												
High School	Booker T. Washington	Media, PA	9	83	6	86		X				Office Education
Grade School												
Other	Business School	Media, PA	3	87	8	87						

LIST BELOW THE POSITIONS THAT YOU HAVE HELD (LAST POSITION FIRST)

1. Name and address of firm: Office Opportunities Unlimited, Route 252 & Media Line Road, Media, PA 19063-4639
Name of supervisor: Mr. Dale Marshall
Employed (mo-yr) from 3/1/87 to 8/30/87
Describe position responsibilities: Prepared documents from script, rough-draft, and boilerplate; edited and revised documents when necessary
Reason for leaving: Completed course of instruction

2. Name and address of firm: Continental Oil Company, One Wayne Road, Radnor, PA 19087-6325
Name of supervisor: Mrs. Pat Chung
Employed (mo-yr) from Summer (July-August) 1985 and 1986
Describe position responsibilities: Prepared correspondence; answered telephone; performed other general office duties
Reason for leaving: Part-time job

3. Name and address of firm:
Name of supervisor:
Employed (mo-yr) from to
Describe position responsibilities:
Reason for leaving:

Cheryl M. Washington
Signature of Applicant

Lesson 46 Letters/Error Correction

Line: 60 spaces
Spacing: SS (or as directed)

46a ▶ 6 Conditioning Practice

1. Each line twice SS.

2. A 1′ writing on line 3; find *gwam*.

alphabet 1 Five boys quickly mixed the prizes, baffling one wise judge.

fig/sym 2 My income tax for 1987 was $5,320.46 -- up 3% over 1986's tax.

speed 3 Dodi is to handle all the pay forms for the small lake town.

| 1 | 2 | 3 | 4 | 5 | 6 | 7 | 8 | 9 | 10 | 11 | 12 |

46b ▶ 14 Learn to Correct Errors

60-space line; DS

1. Read the ¶ at the right; then watch your teacher demonstrate one or more of the correction methods.

2. As you key the ¶, correct any errors you make and listen for the warning bell as a signal to complete a word or divide it at the end of the line.

3. If time permits, rekey the ¶ to improve skill.

The abrasive typing eraser has "bitten the dust" in thousands of business offices in the country. Other error correcting devices are now replacing it even in schools. These tools include cover-up tape, liquid paper, lift-off tape, and electronic correcting keys. Ask your teacher to demonstrate how to use one or more of these, then use whatever correcting device he or she directs you to use in correcting your work.

46c ▶ 15 Format a Letter from Script

1 letterhead (LM p. 37); line: 60 spaces; format: block style

1. Use **November 14** of the current year as the date.

2. Address the letter to:

Mr. James Sipes, Manager
Huckleberry Square
315 Seneca Street
Seattle, WA 98101-4462

3. Use **Dear Jim** as the salutation.

4. As you key the body of the letter, listen for the bell as a signal to complete a word or divide it at the end of the line.

5. The letter will be signed by **Georgeann Blair** who is **President** of her company. She prefers to use **Cordially** as a complimentary close. Use your own reference initials.

6. Before you remove the letter from your machine (or print out a copy on a computer), proofread it and correct any errors you find.

Your velvety cream-of-peanut soup brought me back to Huckleberry Square yesterday. We were taken to our table promptly, but we waited over ten minutes before menus were presented.

Several times I provided clues to the server that I was hosting the luncheon. Without noting these clues or asking who should receive the check, the server gave it to the man across from me. Had the check been placed upside down in the middle of the table, my client wouldn't have been "put on the spot."

Almost every day of the week someone from Seacom will entertain clients at Huckleberry Square. Will you talk with your staff about greeting diners promptly and about handling checks. But please, Jim, don't disturb the chef!

245c ▶ 30
Measure Language Skills: Proofread/ Correct

75-space line

1. In each sentence at the right, items have been underlined. The underlines indicate that there *may* be an error in spelling, punctuation, capitalization, grammar, or in the use of words or figures.

2. Study each sentence carefully. Keyboard the line number. If an underlined item is incorrect, correct it as you keyboard the sentence. In addition, correct any typographical errors you may make.

1. Do they beleive that this years' profits will be down?
2. It has been my experience that there judgment is sound.
3. Our foriegn representative, with his staff, was on the plane.
4. We received 6 fifty pound packages in the mail.
5. In a seperate letter, he asked, "When will the item be shipped"?
6. Did he say who's recommendations will be accepted?
7. It maybe that we will develope the new product next year.
8. The Hotel is located at the corner of 13th and broad.
9. When the letters are already to go, you're job will be finished.
10. Please send the article MICROCOMPUTERS to the principal's office.
11. I shall be happy to send you a copy of there article.
12. How much further must we go befor we make the left turn?
13. Is it to late for us to sign up for the six lessons?
14. The accomodations in the resturant were excellent.
15. After reading the results of the questionaire, I summarized it.
16. She asked; "Is it permisable for us to tour the plant this Saturday?"
17. His acknowledgement of the amount of letters received came today.
18. We depart on flight 907 at 8 p.m. on March 5.
19. It ocurred to me that we should altar the proposal.
20. More than 1/2 the employees would not except the contract.
21. She ordered, letterheads, envelopes, stamps, and bond paper.
22. The forth item on the invoice was recieved.
23. Will the book "Office Procedures" be available in the spring?
24. Apparantly, the bank guard was very observent
25. The womens' fashions were featured in today's newspapers.

46d ▶ 15 Learn to Address Envelopes

1. Study the guides at the right and the illustrations below.

Envelope address
Set a tab stop 10 spaces left of center of small envelope, 5 spaces left of center for a large envelope. Space down 12 lines from top edge of small envelope, 14 spaces for a large envelope. Begin the address at the tab stop position.

Style
Use *block style*, SS. Use all capitals; omit punctuation. Place city name, 2-letter state name abbreviation, and ZIP Code on last address line. Two spaces precede the ZIP Code.

Return address
Use *block style*, SS, cap and lowercase. Begin on line 2 from top of envelope, 3 spaces from left edge.

Special notations
Place *mailing notations* such as REGISTERED and SPECIAL DELIVERY below the stamp position on line 8 or 9.

Place *addressee notations* such as PERSONAL and HOLD FOR ARRIVAL a TS below return address and 3 spaces from left edge of envelope.

Formatting personal and business envelopes as recommended by U.S. Postal Service

small, number 6¾ (6½″ × 3⅝″)

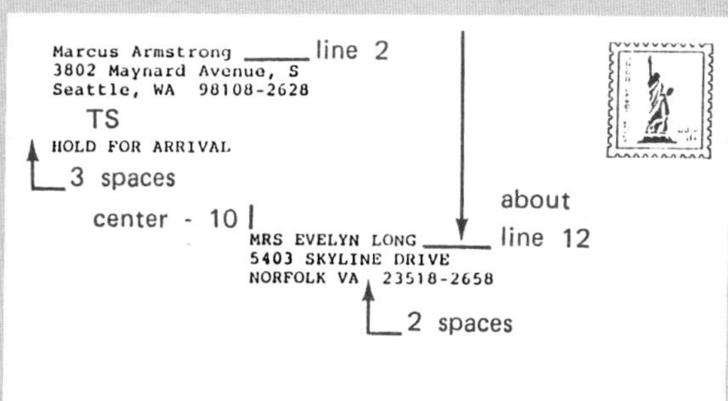

large, number 10 (9½″ × 4⅛″)

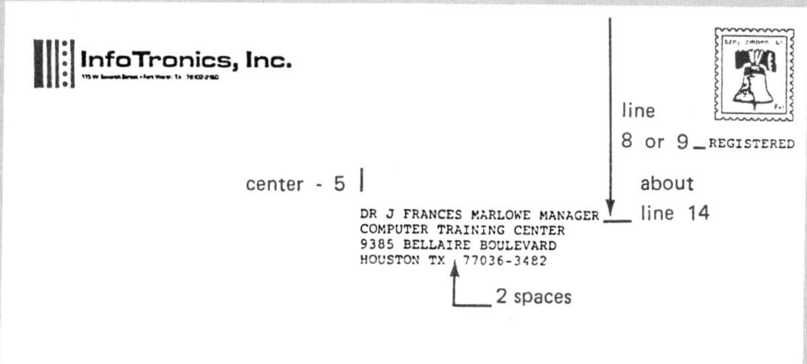

2. Format a small (No. 6 3/4) and a large (No. 10) envelope for each of the addresses given at the right (LM pp. 39-48). Use your own return address on the small envelope.

3. If time permits, practice folding standard-size sheets of paper for both large and small envelopes. (See Reference Guide page RG 7.)

DR LATOYA J HAUSMANN
ROUTE 6 BOX 32
GRAND JUNCTION CO 81501-1177

MS ARVELLA BLACKSTONE
8275 DORCHESTER ROAD APT H
CHARLESTON SC 29418-3926

MISS AIDA HERNANDEZ
BAY CITY OFFICE PRODUCTS INC
ONE POST STREET
SAN FRANCISCO CA 94104-3572

MR HAN SONG KI ASST VP
SATURN ELECTRONICS CORP
110 LOCKWOOD STREET
PROVIDENCE RI 02903-4848

Lesson 47 — Letters/Word Division

Line: 60 spaces
Spacing: SS (or as directed)

47a ▶ 6 Conditioning Practice

1. Each line twice SS.

2. A 1′ writing on line 3; find *gwam*.

alphabet 1 Jody Fox left my quiz show and gave back a prize he had won.

fig/sym 2 Installment loan #47293 at 13% is for $5,800 over 36 months.

speed 3 Robby may sign the six forms and work with the city auditor.

| 1 | 2 | 3 | 4 | 5 | 6 | 7 | 8 | 9 | 10 | 11 | 12 |

245a-249a ▶ 5 Check Equipment

Before you begin work each day, check your machine to see that it is in good working order by keying the paragraph at the right at least twice (first slowly, then faster).

all letters/figures used

Weingate quickly emphasized the value of expert analysis for ranking jobs. Of the 1,380 jobs, 207 (15%) have been analyzed as of May 4 and 828 (60%) may be done by June 9. If the auditors do their work with usual vigor, they may make the goals of the firm.

| 1 | 2 | 3 | 4 | 5 | 6 | 7 | 8 | 9 | 10 | 11 | 12 | 13 |

245b ▶ 15 Measure Basic Skill: Straight Copy

1. Take two 5′ writings on ¶s 1-3 combined.

2. Determine *gwam* and errors on better writing. Compare with scores achieved on 243b, page 413.

all letters used | A | 1.5 si | 5.7 awl | 80% hfw |

	gwam 1′	5′	
Once you have found a job, it may be more difficult to keep it	13	3	59
than it was to find it. The criteria for selecting office workers are	27	5	62
chiefly objective in nature. Workers are chosen on the basis of their	41	8	64
ability to keyboard quickly and accurately, to prepare business docu-	55	11	67
ments, to use standard office machines, and to pass a standardized test	69	14	70
on language skills. Based on these tests, the persons with the best	83	17	73
skills are selected.	87	17	74
Only a small number of those who lose their jobs do so because they	14	20	76
lack the proper skills to do a good job. A number of studies have been	28	23	79
made which indicate that poor work patterns and bad personality traits	42	26	82
are two of the major reasons given by employers for the firing of office	57	29	85
workers. These include the failure to adapt to the work situation, a	71	32	88
lack of cooperation, the inability to get along with other employees,	85	34	91
and frequent absences for reasons other than illness.	95	36	93
Employers today expect a great deal more from their office workers	13	39	95
than secretarial skills. They seek employees who will display sincere	28	42	98
interest in their jobs, who will take pride in their work, and who will	42	45	101
persevere until all the tasks they have been requested to do have been	56	46	104
completed. They also seek employees who can follow directions exactly	70	51	107
and use their time to the best advantage, who are on the job unless they	85	53	110
are ill, and who possess the ability to get along well with others.	98	56	112

gwam 1′ | 1 | 2 | 3 | 4 | 5 | 6 | 7 | 8 | 9 | 10 | 11 | 12 | 13 | 14 |
gwam 5′ | 1 | 2 | 3 |

47b ▶ 9
Identify Word-Division Points
60-space line; DS

1. Clear all tab stops; then starting at left margin, set 3 new tab stops 17 spaces apart.

2. On a full sheet, center WORD-DIVISION POINTS on line 12; then DS.

3. Key the first line as shown.

4. In line 2 and following lines, key each word as shown in Columns 1 and 3; in Columns 2 and 4, rekey each word with a hyphen showing the correct division point.

WORD-DIVISION POINTS
DS

hand-feed	hand-feed	self-made	self-made
increase		greatest	
teletype		tabulate	
agreeing		musical	
plotting		provided	
defend		sharpen	
key 9	8	9	8	9	8	9

47c ▶ 35
Format Letters in Block Style
2 letterheads (LM pp. 49-52); 1 plain full sheet; line: 60; date: line 15; address envelopes

Problem 1
Business Letter

Format the letter in block style. As you key the body of the letter, listen for the warning bell as a signal to prepare for the return at line endings. Correct any errors you make as you key.

The final figure in the word count column includes the count for the envelope address.

	words parts	total
November 15, 19-- | Ms. Phyllis Feldman | Camelback Vocational	12	12
School | 6200 Mariposa, W | Phoenix, AZ 85033-2266 | Dear Ms.	23	23
Feldman	25	25
If I were to name just two reasons why you should choose the	12	37
Saturn personal computer for use in your school, I would say its	25	50
standard keyboard and user-friendly controls.	35	59
A standard keyboard is vital for keyboarding skill to transfer	47	72
readily from the keyboard used in school to the one most likely	60	85
to be used on the job. A keyboard on which familiar keys are	72	97
located in nonstandard places should be avoided.	82	107
A key used to make a computer perform a special function	94	119
should be labeled to suggest the function it generates. Keys	106	131
labeled with letters or combinations of letters that identify their	120	145
functions are easier for a user to remember than keys labeled	132	157
F1, F2, etc. Thus, they are user-friendly.	141	166
These features, along with a large selection of classroom-tested	154	179
software, are critical in computer selection.	163	188
Cordially yours | Ellis D. Strong, Ph.D. | Educational Services	12	200
Staff | xx*	14	202
		220

*When you see xx, use your own initials for reference.

Problem 2
Business Letter

Prepare a second letter from Problem 1 copy but substitute for ¶ 3 the handwritten ¶ beneath the letter.

Address the letter to:

Mr. George C. Sato, Principal
Seven Hills Community College
15000 New Halls Ferry Road
Florissant, MO 63031-4827

Supply an appropriate salutation.

Function keys should be user-friendly; that is, the labels on the keys should suggest the functions they cause the computer to perform. Words or abbreviations rather than figures should be used because they are easier for the user to remember.

Problem 3
Skill Building

As time permits, take two 1′ writings on the opening lines and then on the closing lines of the letter in Problem 1 to increase your speed.

Unit 54 Lessons 245-250

Learning Goals

1. To prepare application documents in usable form.

2. To demonstrate in an employment test: (1) speed and accuracy on a 5-minute timed writing; (2) proficiency in language skills; and (3) ability to produce business documents.

Documents Produced

1. Personal Data Sheet
2. Letter of Application
3. Application Blank
4. Correspondence
5. Report Manuscripts

OFFICE OPPORTUNITIES UNLIMITED

Training Manual Excerpts: Applying for a Job

After you have successfully completed your training at OOU, you are ready to find a job. You are not seeking just *any* job, but one which will utilize your knowledge, abilities, and skills. You want a job that will offer a challenge and opportunities for advancement.

Although application procedures differ, three documents are used almost universally: (1) a personal data sheet or resume, (2) a letter of application, and (3) an application form. Through these documents, you present your qualifications in a manner that will convince an employer that you will be an asset to the firm.

Personal Data Sheet

The personal data sheet is a one-page summary of your personal traits, skills, and abilities. It is often divided into five major sections: personal data, education, school activities, work experience, and references.

The personal information includes your name, address, telephone number, date of birth (optional), your marital status, and number of dependents. A general statement regarding your health is sometimes included.

Under education, list schools you have attended, your major, courses related to the job you seek, and any special skills. Extracurricular activities, scholarships, awards, and honors are included under school activities with special emphasis on any leadership positions you have held.

List your work experience, including summer and part-time jobs, starting with the most recent one. Show the dates of employment, the name and address of your employer, the position you held, and your responsibilities. Finally, give as references the names, positions, and addresses of people who have knowledge of your competence.

Letter of Application

Include a letter of application whenever you send your personal data sheet to a prospective employer. In the first paragraph, indicate the position for which you are applying and how you learned the position was available. In succeeding paragraphs, tell *why* you want to work for the firm and *why* you feel you are qualified for the job. In the closing paragraph, make a specific request for an interview at a mutually convenient time. You will impress the prospective employer if your letter is clear, brief, and businesslike.

Since the letter of application represents you on paper, be sure that it is typed neatly and is free of errors. Take particular care in structuring the letter, and pay close attention to grammar, spelling, and punctuation.

Application Blank

Most organizations require job applicants to complete an application form. When you do so, be neat and thorough. Some employers check with former teachers, employers, and personal references to verify the information on an application. It is essential, therefore, that the information you give is accurate in all respects.

How you complete an application form might reveal more about you than you realize. If you are required to print or complete the form in longhand, it may be a test of your ability to produce documents neatly and legibly. If you are asked to type the form, it may be a check of your ability to produce neat and error-free copy. Further, it might be a test of your ability to understand and follow directions as well as a test of your ability to express yourself clearly and concisely.

You may be compared with other applicants through your application form. The way you fill out the form may well determine whether you will be considered for the job.

48a ▶ 6 Conditioning Practice

1. Each line twice SS.
2. A 1′ writing on line 3; find *gwam*.

alphabet 1 Kovina will prize six jade chips sent by Marquis for a gift.
fig/sym 2 Order #5647-1839 was shipped August 20 by J&P Freight Lines.
speed 3 Dirk may lend an antique box to the man for the town social.

| 1 | 2 | 3 | 4 | 5 | 6 | 7 | 8 | 9 | 10 | 11 | 12 |

48b ▶ 9 Improve Keyboarding Skill

1. A 1′ speed writing on ¶ 1, then on ¶ 2; find *gwam* on each.
2. A 3′ writing on ¶s 1 and 2 combined; find *gwam*, circle errors.

1′ Goal: At least 24 *gwam*
3′ Goal: At least 21 *gwam*

all letters used | A | 1.5 si | 5.7 awl | 80% hfw |

gwam 1′ | 3′

A letter message, like any other message, ought to have a 12 4
major purpose. This purpose is usually stated in the opening 24 8
paragraph. A useful way to focus on the primary objective is 36 12
to pose the question: Just why am I writing this letter? Until 49 16
you have answered this question, you are not prepared to write. 62 21

Like any other message, a letter ought to begin with a 11 24
brief statement of its objective. The next paragraph or two 23 28
should convey in a clear, direct manner the ideas, facts, and 36 32
details required to realize the purpose. The final paragraph 48 37
should end the message in a positive, friendly way. 58 40

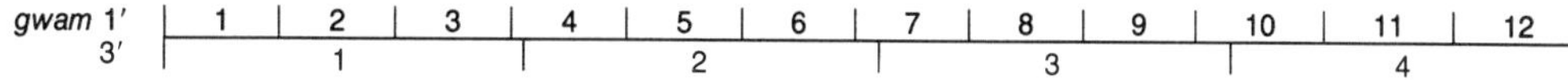

48c ▶ 35 Format Letters in Block Style

1 plain full sheet;
2 letterheads (LM pp. 53-56)
additional plain sheets;
line: 60 spaces;
date: line 15

Problem 1
Personal-Business Letter

Format the letter (shown at the right) in block style with open punctuation on a plain sheet. Correct any errors you make as you key. Before you remove the letter from your machine (or print it out on a computer), proofread the copy and correct any additional errors you find.

Problems 2 and 3 are on p. 86.

words

4026 Eastway Drive | Charlotte, NC 28205-2736 | November 16, 12
19-- | Sentinel Electronics Company | 401 Euclid Avenue | Cleve- 23
land, OH 44144-3561 | Ladies and Gentlemen | 32

When I bought a Sentinel clock radio several weeks ago, I 43
was assured of trouble-free service. Further, I was told that 56
repairs could be made locally in the unlikely event something 68
went wrong. 71

About a week ago, severe static developed in the radio, and a 83
recurring click began in the digital clock. I returned the radio 96
to the store where I bought it only to be told that I would have 109
to return it to you for repair. 116

Before being further inconvenienced, I want to be sure that re- 127
turning the radio to you is the proper course of action. I am 141
certain you want to stand behind your products and to be sure 154
that your outlet stores properly represent your products and 166
service. You should have my warranty card on file. 177

Sincerely yours | Miss Gloria Prentice 184

244b (continued)

Document 2

Unbound Report
(from uncorrected manuscript)

Prepare the report for Gregory C. Torres, who will present this information at an OOU faculty meeting.

1. Use unbound report style, DS. Watch carefully for uncorrected errors and correct them as you keyboard.

2. Although the entire reference has been included in the text, use only textual citations.

3. Prepare a reference page.

Goal: To complete the report and reference page in 25′ or less with all errors corrected.

Watch Your Language!

"Language, like all other aspects of human culture, is constantly changing." (Francis, W. Nelson. "The History of English." Webster's New Collegiate Dictionary. Springfield, MA: G. & C. Merriam Company, 1980, p. 25a) As our environment and our way of life changes, some words are lost. How long has it been since any one stepped on the "running board" of an automobile or replaced a "tube" in a radio? Other words are lost simply through dis use. The word "beseem," for example was once used to discribe something or some one who was "fitting" or "becoming"; the word "shend" meant to ruin or destroy."

As new machines, new materials, and new processes are developed, new words are added to our language. "Nylon," "plastic", "jet planes," and "television" are prime exampels. Civilization's greatest progress in technology has taken place in this centery. As a result, a multitude of new words have been added to our language.

The development and proliferation of the computer throughout all aspects of our lifes has added many new words to our vocabularies and has given new meaning to some old words. The following are just a few examples.

McWilliams (McWilliams, Peter A. The Word Processing Book. Los Angeles: Prelude Free Press, 1982, p. 29) explains that "The computer has two main components. The first is the CPU or central processing unit." The second part consists of two types of memory: Random Access Memory (RAM) and Read Only Memory (ROM). McWilliams says that "RAM means that the CPU can add to or take away from this memory at any time it wants; it has random access to the memory. . . . ROM stands for read only memory. The information in the ROM memory was placed there by the manufacturer, and although the CPU has access to it, a ROM cannot be changed."

According to Casady (Casady, Mona J. Word Information Processing Concepts. 2d ed. Cincinnati: South-Western Publishing Co., 1984, pp. 209-210), a floppy disk is "a magnetic recording medium about the size and shape of a flexible 45 rpm record; it holds about 100 pages of text." She also defines a disk drive as "the mechanism of a word processor that houses the disk/diskette and controls its movement for recording, editing, and printing functions."

Waterhouse (Waterhouse, Shirley A. Word Processing Fundamentals. San Francisco: Canfield Press, 1979, p. 213) defines a terminal as "any device capable of sending and recieving information over a communications line to and from a computer." She identifies a video display terminal as "a CRT display screen terminal (similer to a TV) or keyboard console that allows keyed or stored text to be reviewed."

48c (continued)

Problem 2
Business Letter

Format the letter in block style on a letterhead sheet. Correct any errors you make as you key. Use your own initials for reference in the closing lines. When you complete the letter, proofread it and make any needed corrections before you remove it from the typewriter or print out a copy on a computer. Address an envelope.

words

November 20, 19-- Miss Gloria Prentice 4026 Eastway Drive 12
Charlotte, NC 28205-2736 Dear Miss Prentice 21

¶ We apologize for the inconvenience you were caused 31
by one of our Sentinel products and for the incorrect 42
information given you by one of our dealers. 51
¶ Only on rare occasions does one of our products 61
malfunction. We regret that you were the victim 70
of one of these events. I am pleased to tell you, 81
though, that your Sentinel clock radio will be 90
repaired free of charge. Just take it and this 100
letter to Quik Repair Center, our authorized repair 110
service in your city, and your radio will be put 120
in like-new condition. 125
¶ Please accept the enclosed $10 credit coupon 134
toward your next Sentinel purchase as a token of 143
our appreciation for your patience and understanding. 154

Cordially yours Anthony M. Oliver Assistant Vice 164
President xx Enclosure 169/**182**

Problem 3
Business Letter

Format the letter in block style on a letterhead sheet, using the directions for Problem 2. Correct all marked errors and any you make as you key.

Computer printers often print copy with distinctive punctuation marks. Study the chart below before you key the letter at the right.

	typewriter	computer
comma	,	˺

Proofreader's Marks

- delete
- close up
- ^ insert
- ¶ paragraph
- transpose
- lc lowercase
- sp. spell out
- ≡ capitalize
- ⊙ insert period

Novembeer 20˺ 19-- ~~Miss~~ Ms. Lorraine Helmsley 2398 Hemlock 11
Way Santa Ana˺ CA 92704-4628 Dear Ms. Helmsley 20
¶ I beleive you will like the ~~changes~~ improvements we've made in packaging 33
materials for our Entree royale line of boil-in-the-bag 44
meals. Please accept our apologies for the dinner that was ruined. 58
¶ Since we introduced Entree Royale˺ the factory has had a 70
problem making bags that protect food from freezer burn and 82
boiling water and that still permit a Variety of foods to 93
cook within (15) minutes. Three times we have reported com- 106
plaints about bags that ~~let in~~ admit water as the food is cooked. 118
The factory has assured us that the problem has been solvd. 130
¶ Help us prove them right. use the enclosed coupons to get 142
another bag of Shrimp Primavera and to receive a 25 percent 154
discount on ~~a~~ an Entree Royale of your choice. enjoy! 165

Sincerely yours Brown Co Mills˺ manager Customer Ser- 176
vice xx Enclosures 179/**192**

Document 3
Block Style Letter, Open
(LM p. 85)

Prepare the letter at the right to Mr. Harry Schwartz of American Office Institute. Date the letter August 17, 19--. Correct errors as marked and correct any additional errors you may find. Miss Barnes will sign the letter.

Goal: Complete letter in 10′ or less with all errors corrected.

Thank you for your order #32901 of August 24 for a number of our Video Cassettes. We asre sure you will find these computer instructional materials of invaluable help. The enclosed booklet provides detailed instructions for using these cassettes to attain best results.

As we agreed in our conversation, weshall provide a discount of 10% on each order of 100 or more videocassettes. The terms will remain as "net," but we shall reduce the price of each cassettes by 10%. The invoice for you order reflects this dic count.

If we can be of any assistance to you, please call me personaly.

244b ▶ 45
Document Review

Document 1
Table

Mrs. Carpenter, Director of Instruction, needs a copy of the table at the right.

Main Heading: OFFICE OPPORTUNITIES UNLIMITED

Secondary Heading: Course Sections Added as of September 9

Goal: Complete the table in 15′ or less with all errors corrected.

Course	Title	Section	Time
BU 101	Introduction to Business	4	MF 2:10-3:00
		5	M 3:30-5:10
BU 120	Accounting Principles	3	T 6:30-8:10
		4	TTh 3:30-4:20
BU 205	Business Correspondence	6	M 6:30-8:10
CS 100	Introduction to Computers	8	T 6:30-8:10
		9	W 3:30-5:10
CS 101	Word Processing I	5	MW 2:10-3:00
		6	TTh 8:30-9:20
CS 102	Word Processing II	3	M 4:30-6:10
CP 101	Computer Programming I	4	TTh 8:30-9:20
		5	MW 6:30-7:20
CP 102	Computer Programming II	3	M 2:10-3:50

Unit 8 Lessons 49-50

Measurement Goals

1. To demonstrate that you can key straight-copy ¶s for 3 minutes at the speed and control level specified by your teacher.
2. To demonstrate that you can format and key letters, personal notes, and memos in block style.
3. To demonstrate that you can format numbered lists with centered headings.

Machine Adjustments

1. Paper guide at *0*.
2. Ribbon control to use top half of ribbon.
3. Margin sets: left margin (center − 30); right margin (center + 30 + bell adjustment).
4. Line-space selector set to SS drills and problems; to DS ¶ timed writings.

Lesson 49 Letters

Line: 60 spaces
Spacing: SS (or as directed)

49a ▶ 6 Conditioning Practice

1. Each line twice SS.
2. A 1′ writing on line 3; find *gwam*.

alphabet 1 Jack Waven dozed off as he quietly prepped for his big exam.

fig/sym 2 I moved from 135 Este Lane to 937-24th Street on 6/10/86.

speed 3 Of the eighty small robot firms, half may make a big profit.

| 1 | 2 | 3 | 4 | 5 | 6 | 7 | 8 | 9 | 10 | 11 | 12 |

49b ▶ 12 Check Keyboarding Skill

1. A 1′ writing on ¶ 1; find *gwam*, circle errors.
2. A 1′ writing on ¶ 2; find *gwam*, circle errors.
3. A 2′ writing on ¶s 1 and 2 combined; find *gwam*, circle errors.
4. A 3′ writing on ¶s 1 and 2 combined; find *gwam*, circle errors.

Skill-Building Practice

As time permits, take a series of 1′ *guided* writings on each ¶ with the call of the guide each 15 seconds. Use the better 1′ writing rate in Steps 1 and 2 as your base rate.

gwam	1/4′	1/2′	3/4′	Time
20	5	10	15	20
24	6	12	18	24
28	7	14	21	28
32	8	16	24	32
36	9	18	27	36
40	10	20	30	40
44	11	22	33	44
48	12	24	36	48
52	13	26	39	52

all letters used | A | 1.5 si | 5.7 awl | 80% hfw |

	gwam 2′	3′
It is a satisfying feeling to be a winner. Every person	6	4
prefers to serve on a winning team. Although the prize might	12	8
not be worth either the time or effort involved, the desire to	18	12
excel may justify both. Realize that team members must meet	24	16
the requirements for a winning exhibition each time they play.	31	20
An office work force is a team, also; and the same basic	36	24
principles apply there as apply on an athletic field. A major	43	28
difference, however, is that in the office the rewards are in-	49	32
creased pay and promotions instead of trophies and letters.	55	37
Winning is fun on any team, but winning takes effort from all.	61	41

gwam 2′ | 1 | 2 | 3 | 4 | 5 | 6 |
3′ | 1 | 2 | 3 | 4 |

243c ▶ 30
Document Review

Document 1

Interoffice Memorandum

(LM p. 81)

Mr. Marshall asks you to prepare the memo at the right for Miss Joyce T. Barnes, Sales Manager.

Goal: Complete memo in 10′ or less with all errors corrected.

Office Opportunities UNLIMITED

INTEROFFICE COMMUNICATION

TO: Ralph T. Zimmerman

FROM: Joyce T. Barnes

DATE: August 17, 19--

SUBJECT: Discount for American Office Institute

¶ We have received an order from ~~the~~ American Office Institute, Chicago, Illinois. A.O.I. is a national chain with 26 branch institutes in the U.S. and Canada.

¶ In a seperate letter, A.O.I. requested a discount of 10% on all purchases of 100 or more ~~of our~~ individual video-cassettes. To encourage future business from them, I have agreed. Terms will remain as "Net," but the price of each cassette will be reduced 10%.

Document 2

Invoice

(LM p. 83)

Mr. Marshall directs you to make the necessary changes in the invoice as indicated by Miss Barnes in the memo above.

Goal: Complete invoice in 10′ or less with all errors corrected.

AMERICAN OFFICE INSTITUTE

501 N. Michigan Avenue • Chicago, IL 60611-4987 (312) 451-8700

PURCHASE ORDER

OFFICE OPPORTUNITIES UNLIMITED
ROUTE 252 & MEDIA LINE ROAD
MEDIA PA 19063-4639

Purchase Order No.: E32901

Date: August 14, 19--

Terms: net

Shipped Via: C & C Express

Quantity	Description/Stock Number	Price	Per	Total
100	Correspondence Cues (C159)	~~14 80~~ 13.32	~~ea~~	~~1,480 00~~
100	Advanced Word Processing (C177)	~~15 20~~ 13.68	~~ea~~	~~1,520 00~~
20	Data Base Management (C188)	14 30	ea	286 00
50	Principles of Office Automation (C195)	21 40	ea	1,070 00
8/17	Prepare Invoice 6435C. Extend price totals of changes and determine total price. Shipped 8/16. J.T.B.			~~4,356 00~~

By Harry L. Schwartz

49c ▶ 32
Check Formatting Skills: Letters

1 plain sheet;
2 letterheads (LM pp. 65-68) or additional plain sheets;
line: 60; date: line 15;
listen for bell to return; correct errors; address envelopes

Problem 1
Personal-Business Letter from Script
plain sheet

words

4450 Markham, W Little Rock, AR 72205-3674 November 21, 19-- 12
Unique Gardens, Inc. 4199 - 57th Street Des Moines, IA 23
50310-4729 Ladies and Gentlemen 30

Here is my bulb and plant order for the coming spring 41
planting season. A check is attached to the order form. 52

This is the fourth year I have ordered from you. The 63
quality of your plants is excellent, and your service is 75
unequalled. Your location suggestions for annuals and 86
your zone ratings for perennials are quite helpful. 96

If I may offer just one suggestion, a list of soil prepa- 108
ration and planting instructions for each type of plant 119
ordered would be welcomed by those of us who do not 129
have a "green thumb." 134

Cordially Alexander Wormwood Enclosures 142/**167**

Problem 2
Business Letter
letterhead sheet

words

November 26, 19-- | Mr. Alexander Wormwood | 4450 Markham, 11
W | Little Rock, AR 72205-3674 | Dear Mr. Wormwood 21

Thank you for the letter which accompanied your recent order. 33
We humbly accept the praise and welcome the suggestions of 45
one of our valued customers. 51

Instructions for preparing the soil and planting should be in- 63
cluded with each type of bulb and plant we ship. If any of these 77
instructions has been missing from your orders, someone has 89
slipped up. We shall make every effort to see that this omission 101
does not occur again. 106

Would you be willing to let us quote a portion of your letter in 119
our next catalog? If so, will you please sign and return the 131
enclosed Permission to Quote form. We like to let those who 143
receive our catalogs know that our services as well as our prod- 156
ucts bring satisfaction to our customers. 165

As usual, each item you recently ordered will be sent at just the 178
right planting time so you won't have a storage problem. 190

Cordially yours | Miss Elaine Rodriguez | Manager, Customer 201
Service | xx | Enclosure 205/**217**

Problem 3 (Extra Credit)
Prepare on a letterhead sheet another copy of the letter formatted in Problem 2. Address it to yourself at your home address; supply an appropriate salutation.

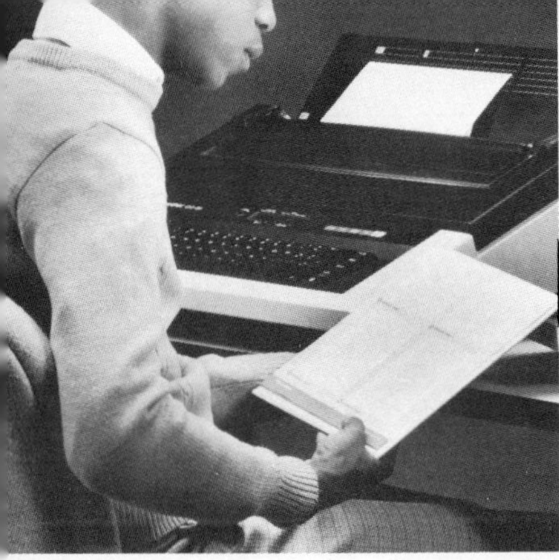

Unit 53 Lessons 243-244

Learning Goals

1. To improve speed and accuracy on straight-copy material of average difficulty.
2. To practice producing documents under timed conditions prior to formal measurement.

Documents Reviewed

1. Correspondence
2. Reports
3. Forms
4. Tables

Lessons 243-244

243a-244a ▶ 5 Check Equipment

65-space line

Before you begin 243b or 244b, keyboard the drill which follows to see that your machine is in good working order. Keyboard the paragraph at least twice (first slowly, then faster).

all letters/figures used

The board will fight the complex request to raze or move the junkyard. Section 546-9 of Ordinance #21037 (passed May 8, 1986) established a 30-day notice for any action. The key to the problem is to codify the amendment to make the men pay a big penalty.

| 1 | 2 | 3 | 4 | 5 | 6 | 7 | 8 | 9 | 10 | 11 | 12 | 13 |

243b ▶ 15 Improve Basic Keyboarding Skill

Take two 5′ writings; determine *gwam* and errors.

all letters used | A | 1.5 si | 5.7 awl | 80% hfw |

	gwam 1′	5′	
What is an office? Thousands of years ago, the office was the	12	3	60
site of the secrets of an organization. A secretary, in fact, was known	27	5	63
as the one who kept the secrets because he wrote in a secret language.	42	8	66
In the minds of many people, an office is just a place where you will	56	11	69
find furniture, equipment, people, and papers of all kinds. The office	70	14	72
is also said to be a place where administrative functions are performed,	85	17	75
such as preparing, storing, and distributing documents.	96	19	77
In the world of business today, information is not only essential	13	22	79
but critical to the success of any company. Executives spend most of	27	25	82
their time making decisions which lead to the sale of goods and services	42	27	85
to the public. If the goals of the company are to be accomplished, the	56	30	88
decisions made must be based on current, precise information. Today,	70	33	91
business thrives on data; and the lack of the facts and figures upon	84	36	94
which to base decisions may well spell the failure of the company.	97	39	96
An office is something more than just a place occupied by people,	13	41	99
equipment, furniture, and documents. The people in an office assemble	27	44	12
and analyze data in great amounts; they process, revise, store, print,	42	47	105
and transmit a large volume of data. The office is the nerve center of	56	50	107
any company; it runs a communication network through which vital data	70	53	110
flow. This information makes it possible for all of the other parts of	84	55	113
the firm to reach their goals so that success can be won.	96	58	115

gwam 1′ | 1 | 2 | 3 | 4 | 5 | 6 | 7 | 8 | 9 | 10 | 11 | 12 | 13 | 14 |
5′ | 1 | 2 | 3 |

50a ▶ 6
Conditioning Practice

1. Each line twice SS.
2. A 1′ writing on line 3; find *gwam*.

alphabet 1 Mickie gave Quincy six jigsaw puzzles for his last birthday.
fig/sym 2 Ike asked, "Is the ZIP Code 45208-3164 or is it 45209-2748?"
speed 3 Shana may make a bid for the antique bottle for the auditor.

| 1 | 2 | 3 | 4 | 5 | 6 | 7 | 8 | 9 | 10 | 11 | 12 |

50b ▶ 12
Check Language Skills

full sheet; DS; line: 60 spaces; begin on line 12

1. Read line 1, noting the words that should be capitalized; then key the line, supplying needed capitals.
2. Complete the other lines in the same way. If numbers appear in the lines, express them correctly.

1 you may have the blue sweater. i'll take the brown one.
2 did mr. watts tell us to report to miss knight, the coach?
3 yellowstone national park is located in the state of montana.
4 the local chapter of ams meets on tuesday, december fifth.
5 the civil war is also known as the war between the states.
6 american electric company gives generously to united appeal.
7 she said that ph.d. means doctor of philosophy.
8 when does the president give the state of the union address?
9 does ups deliver on saturday or only monday through friday?
10 the play begins at seven fifteen p.m. on sunday, june two.
11 the kendrick building is located at one madison avenue.
12 14 applicants took the test, but only 3 were hired.

50c ▶ 32
Check Formatting Skills

60-space line; listen for bell as signal to return

Problem 1 (half sheet)
Personal Note in Block Style

Format the note using **November 27** and the current year as the date. Use your first name in the closing lines. Correct any errors you make as you key the note.

	words
date	4
Dear Doug	6
Thank you for inviting me to "Holiday Sounds" on	15
December 18. Having been a member of your group	25
for two years, I wouldn't miss it.	32
Our holiday break begins December 13. I have a	42
term paper to complete here before I leave, but I	52
should be home no later than the 16th.	60
It will be great to see all of you do your theatrics.	71
Perhaps there will be time for some skiing, too.	81
Sincerely	83
name	84

238b-242b (continued)

Job 7

Table

Ralph T. Zimmerman, Director of Finance, asks you to prepare the table at the right.

Special Instructions:

Leaders (. . . .)

1. Space once after entering "Secretarial." Note whether the point indicator is on an even or odd number.

2. Key a period, then a space alternately across the line; stop 2 or 3 spaces before the beginning of Column 2.

3. On the following lines, align periods with those above, keying the periods on an odd or even number.

Job 8

Table

Mr. Zimmerman requests that you redo the table on gross receipts with a fourth column labeled Change. Under this column, indicate for each item whether this year's amount is an increase (indicated by a plus sign +) or a decrease (indicated by a minus sign −).

Note: If your machine does not have the + symbol, key a hyphen, backspace, and key the diagonal. Use a hyphen to represent a minus sign.

Job 9

Ruled Table

Ms. Colby, Director of Admissions, needs a list of the students who are enrolled in OOU. Mr. Marshall asks you to prepare a copy of the table at the right.

Special Instructions:

1. When you have determined the end of the longest item in the final column, note the location on the scale. This marks the end of the typed lines.

2. After entering the main and secondary headings, SS and enter the first rule. DS and begin columnar headings. SS and enter the second rule. DS and begin the body of the table.

3. After entering the final item in the table, SS and enter the rule.

OFFICE OPPORTUNITIES UNLIMITED

Gross Receipts for Past Two Years

Category	Last Year ~~Amount~~	This Year
Instruction (by curriculum):		
Secretarial	$ 65,930	$ 70,095
Word Processing	87,415	91,634
Data Processing	108,753	106,928
Records Management	63,548	59,873
Office Management	58,462	61,342
Textbooks and Supplies	78,956	81,720
Instructional Tapes and Cassettes . .	84,931	83,619
Job Placement Fees	480,000	520,000
Total	$1,027,995	$1,075,211

(DS between instruction items)

OFFICE OPPORTUNITIES UNLIMITED

Enrollment as of ~~June~~ May 30 and July 30, 19--*

Curriculum	May 30 ~~Number~~	July 30
Full-time Students	844	868
Secretarial	(165)	(181)
Word Processing	(249)	(280)
Data Processing	(250)	(276)
Records Management	(81)	(72)
Office Management	(99)	(59)
Part-time Students	772	887
Secretarial	(110)	(121)
Word Processing	(124)	(138)
Data Processing	(204)	(225)
Records Management	(190)	(168)
Office Management	(144)	(235)
Total Enrollment	1,616	1,755

*Not including those students who have enrolled but who have not yet begun their programs.

50c (continued)

words

Problem 2 (half sheet)
Simplified Memo in Block Style

Format the memo using **November 27** and the current year as the date. Use your full name as the writer of the memo. Make the corrections indicated in the memo, and correct any errors you make as you key the copy.

date 4

Keyboard Operat~~e~~ors (o) 7

Keyboarding Efficiency) ALL CAP 12

You can increase your input speed (and accuracy) by reaching to each ser- 26
vice and function key with the proper finger while ke(e)ping 38
the other fingers on (or very near) their home positions. 49
~~If~~ (When) you move the entire hand to the service (or function) key(s), you use 63
more time and increase your chances of making errors. (¶ #) You 75
can increase your productivity with less effort (if) you (will) 87
reach with the fingers, (not the hands). 95

name 98

Problem 3 (full sheet)
Numbered List

Format and key the list. Correct any errors you make as you key. If you do not complete the list before time is called, finish it at a later time and keep it as a convenient reference.

SOME FACTS TO REMEMBER 5

1. Standard-size paper is 8 1/2" wide by 11" long. 15
2. A full sheet has 66 vertical line spaces; a half 26
sheet, 33 line spaces. 31
3. On a sheet of paper 8 1/2" wide, you can enter 41
102 elite (12-pitch) or 85 pica (10-pitch) char- 50
acters and spaces. 54
4. The horizontal center point of an 8 1/2" sheet 65
is 51 on a 12-pitch machine, 42 on a 10-pitch 74
machine. 76
5. Many keyboarding machines today have dual 85
pitch; that is, they can print in either 10- or 95
12-pitch type. 98
6. To center a heading: From the horizontal center 108
point of the paper, backspace once for each 2 117
characters and spaces in the heading; begin 126
the heading where backspacing ends. 133

238b-242b
(continued)

Job 6

(LM pp. 69-71)

1. Prepare invoices, which will be processed on computer-ruled forms, as requested by Joyce T. Barnes, Sales Manager. Follow the directions she has given at the bottom of each purchase order.

2. The purchase orders do not reflect the current prices for the cassettes. Use the price list that you prepared in Job 5, p. 410. Check your arithmetic for each item and total price.

Note: Computer-ruled forms use each ruled line of the form; therefore, SS to first columnar entry. Commas are omitted in figure columns.

COLONIAL TELECOMMUNICATIONS, INC
1100 East Main Street • Richmond, VA 23219-6631 (804) 231-8900

PURCHASE ORDER

OFFICE OPPORTUNITIES UNLIMITED
ROUTE 252 & MEDIA LINE ROAD
MEDIA PA 19063-4639

Purchase Order No.: A593-87
Date: August 3, 19--
Terms: Net
Shipped Via: Star Express

Quantity	Description/Stock Number	Price		Per	Total	
20	WP Fundamentals (C173)	16	20	ea	324	00
~~20~~	~~Introduction to Word Processing (C172)~~	~~14~~	~~80~~	~~ea~~	~~296~~	~~00~~
20	Advanced Word Processing (C177)	14	80	ea	296	00
10	Automating the Office (C192)	17	10	ea	171	00
5	Records Management (C193)	16	25	ea	81	25
5	Managing the Modern Office (197)	24	90	ea	124	50
8/11	Bill Colonial at current prices. Changes approved by J. T. Monroe of Colonial. Invoice # 6341C Shipped 8/9. J.T.B.				~~960~~ 996	~~75~~ 75

By J. T. Monroe

Bryan & Dickinson, Inc.
1400 Berlin Road • Cherry Hill, NJ 08003-4321 (609) 691-5100

PURCHASE ORDER

OFFICE OPPORTUNITIES UNLIMITED
ROUTE 252 & MEDIA LINE ROAD
MEDIA PA 19063-4639

Purchase Order No.: 14098
Date: August 4, 19--
Terms: Net
Shipped Via: Allied Express

Quantity	Description/Stock Number	Price		Per	Total	
10	Introducing Computers (C168)	14	00	ea	140	00
10	Advanced Word Processing (C177)	14	80	ea	148	00
5	Data Base Management (C188)	13	90	ea	69	50
1	Measuring WP Productivity (C183)	15	60	ea	15	60
1	Local Area Networks (C191)	16	75	ea	16	75
1	Successful Supervisory Practices (C196)	20	00	ea	20	00
	8/11 Prepare Invoice #3687C. Bill Bryan & Dickinson at current prices. Changes approved by Alan Hudock. Shipped 8/10 J.T.B.				409	85

By Alan Hudock

ENRICHMENT ACTIVITY: Timed Writing

Line: 70 spaces
Spacing: double-space (DS)

As time permits during Units 9 and 10, use the ¶s at the right to improve keyboarding skill.

1. A 1′ writing on ¶ 1; find *gwam*. Add 2-4 words to set a new goal.

2. Two 1′ writings on ¶ 1 at your new goal rate, guided by ¼′ guide call.

3. Key ¶ 2 in the same way.

4. A 2′ writing on ¶ 1, then on ¶ 2. If you finish a ¶ before time is called, start over.

5. A 3′ writing on ¶s 1-2 combined; find *gwam*.

gwam	¼′	½′	¾′	1′
20	5	10	15	20
24	6	12	18	24
28	7	14	21	28
32	8	16	24	32
36	9	18	27	36
40	10	20	30	40
44	11	22	33	44
48	12	24	36	48
52	13	26	39	52
56	14	28	42	56

all letters used | A | 1.5 si | 5.7 awl | 80% hfw

	gwam 2′	3′
We live in a society of numbers. From the number of a birth cer-	7	4
tificate to the number of a death certificate, numbers play a very vital	14	9
role in the daily life of each of us. Virtually all typed business and	21	14
personal papers contain figures. Quite often these documents contain	28	19
some commonly used symbols, also. Therefore, skill in keying on the top	35	24
row is critical to your future use of the machine.	40	27
Data arranged in table form shows a common use of figures and sym-	7	31
bols. Although some tables include no figures, the greatest percentage	14	36
of them do. Just as top skill on a letter keyboard may pay well, expert	21	41
skill on figure copy may land you a prized job as a data-entry worker	28	46
that will pay even better. Workers in accounting and data processing	35	50
offices must know how to operate the number row with efficiency.	42	55

gwam 2′ | 1 | 2 | 3 | 4 | 5 | 6 | 7
3′ | 1 | 2 | 3 | 4 | 5

ENRICHMENT ACTIVITY: Composing at the Keyboard

Line: 65 spaces, pica; 78, elite
Spacing: double-space (DS)

As time permits during the completion of Phase 3, choose a "Thought Starter" from those listed below. Develop the idea into a 2- or 3-paragraph theme, giving reasons for what you would do.

1 If I had a lot of money, I would...

2 I chose to take a keyboarding course because...

3 During next summer vacation, I plan to...

4 If I had it to do over, I would...

5 I plan to (or do not plan to) go to college because...

6 If I could be the person I want to be, I would...

7 I admire (your mother, father, or someone else of your choice) because...

8 If I could talk with the President of the United States, I would ask...

9 Of my hobbies, I prefer (reading, computer games, swimming, or other hobby choice) because...

10 I want to become a (teacher, data/word processor, salesperson, or other career choice) because...

11 If I could choose my "boss" when I go to work, I would choose one who...

12 Of my personality traits, the three that seem most to attract others are...

13 When I choose my friends, the three most important qualities I look for are...

14 Of all the subjects I have studied in school, the one I have found most useful is (keyboarding, English, mathematics, etc.) because...

15 When I finish this keyboarding course, I want to be able to use my skill to...

238b-242b (continued)

Job 5

Table

In addition to providing courses of instruction, OOU prepares special seminars on cassettes for secretaries, administrators, and executives in business and other organizations.

1. Mr. Marshall requests that you prepare the latest cassette price list at the right.

2. Place additions in proper numeric order by stock number.

PROFESSIONAL IMPROVEMENT CASSETTES FOR OFFICE PERSONNEL

Prices as of August 1, 19--

Stock Number	Title	Price
C156	Communication Skills	$~~12.95~~ 14.10
C159	Correspondence Cues	~~13.50~~ 14.80
C160	Grammar Update	~~10.75~~ 11.60
C164	Report Writing Made Easy	~~11.25~~ 12.50
~~C165~~	~~Modern Typewriting~~	~~16.00~~
C168	Introducing Computers	~~14.00~~ 15.40
C170	How to Use WORDPRO	~~15.20~~ 16.70
~~C172~~	~~Introduction to Word Processing~~	~~14.00~~
C177	Advanced Word Processing	~~14.80~~ 15.20
C178	Word Processing Software	~~14.80~~ 15.20
C179	Introduction to Data Processing	~~14.80~~ 15.20
C180	Advanced Data Processing	~~14.80~~ 15.20
C183	Measuring WP Productivity	~~15.60~~ 17.10
C188	Data Base Management	~~13.90~~ 14.30
C191	Local Area Networks	~~16.75~~ 17.45
C192	Automating the Office	~~17.10~~ 18.80
C193	Records Management	~~16.25~~ 17.85
C195	Principles of Office Automation	~~19.50~~ 21.40
C197	Managing the Modern Office	~~24.90~~ 26.50
C199	Problem Solving With (lc.) Computers	~~28.00~~ 30.80
C166	Modern Keyboarding	17.60
C173	W P Fundamentals	16.20
C196	Successful Supervisory Practices	20.00

Lessons 51-75

PHASE 3

Learn to Format Reports and Tables

In the 25 lessons of Phase 3, you will:

1. Learn to format and process report manuscripts, reference lists, and title or cover pages.

2. Learn to format and process data in columnar or table form.

3. Improve basic keyboarding and language skills.

4. Apply your formatting skills to process a series of documents typical of those prepared in the office of a summer camp.

5. Measure and evaluate your basic/document processing skills.

Drills and timed writings in this phase are to be keyed on a 70-space line. Line length for problems varies according to the format required.

You will work part of the time from model typescript, part of the time from print, and some of the time from handwritten (script) and rough-draft (corrected) copy. Keyboarding for personal and business use is often done from script and rough draft.

238b-242b (continued)

Job 3

Purchase Requisition

(LM p. 65)

Mr. Marshall asks you to prepare in duplicate the purchase requisition submitted by Avery T. Alexander.

PURCHASE REQUISITION

Deliver to: Supply Shop
Location: Room 302
Job No. None

Requisition No. 926-1
Date August 1, 19--
Date Required September 15, 19--

Quantity	Description
100	Practical Keyboarding (K70)
100	Wbks. for Practical Keyboarding (K701)
100	Word Processing Principles (W42)
100	Introduction to Computers (C30)
50	Basic Communications (L19)

Requisitioned by: Avery T. Alexander

Job 4

Purchase Order

(LM p. 67)

Mr. Marshall asks you to prepare a purchase order as directed in the memo at the right.

Office Opportunities
UNLIMITED

INTEROFFICE COMMUNICATION

TO: Document Production Center

FROM: T. Frank Mills, Student Store Manager

DATE: August 3, 19--

SUBJECT: Preparation of Purchase Order No. 58390

Prepare, in duplicate, Purchase Order No. 58390 with today's date to Baker Publishing Co., 140 N. Main Street, Dayton, OH 45402-3678 for the books requested by Mr. Alexander on Requisition No. 926-1. The terms will be net, and the books will be shipped via Ace Van Lines. Prices are as follows:

K70	$16.00	each
K701	3.50	each
W42	24.00	each
C30	28.75	each
L19	18.50	each

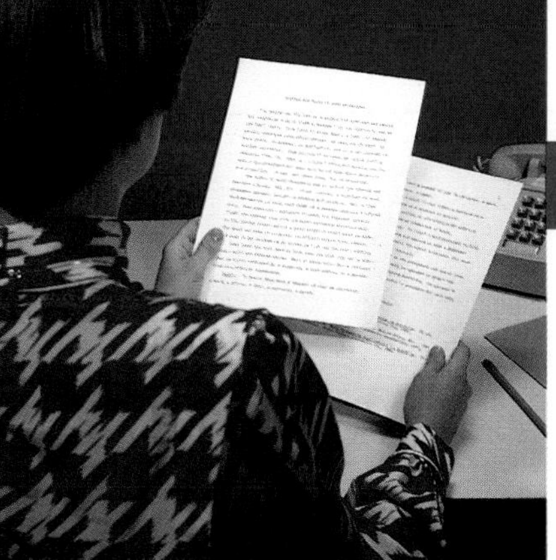

Unit 9 Lessons 51-57

Learning Goals

1. To learn to format, space, and key topic outlines.

2. To learn to format, space, and key unbound reports, reference lists, and title pages.

3. To learn to align copy vertically and horizontally.

4. To improve basic keystroking skills.

Machine Adjustments

1. Paper guide at *0*.

2. Ribbon control to use top half of ribbon.

3. Margin sets: left margin (center − 35); right margin (center + 35 + 5).

4. Line-space selector set to SS drills; DS ¶s; as directed for problems.

FORMATTING GUIDES: UNBOUND REPORTS

Unbound Report Format

Some reports are placed in protective covers (ring binders or heavy paper covers with clasps or clamps). When reports are to be bound, an extra half inch of space is left in the margin of the binding edge.

Many short, less formal reports are left unbound. If such reports consist of more than one page, the pages are fastened together in the upper left corner by a staple or other fastening device. No extra margin space is left for stapling.

Standard Margins. In unbound reports, as shown in the model, 1-inch (1″) *side margins* are used (10 pica spaces, 12 elite spaces). With the paper guide set at 0 (zero) on the line-of-writing scale, this means that the left margin is set at 10 on 10-pitch machines or at 12 on 12-pitch ones.

A *top margin* of about 2 inches (2″) is customarily used in unbound reports; so place the title on line 12. (In school settings where the same report is done on both pica and elite machines, a 1½″ [line 10] top margin for pica machines may be used so that all students have similar end-of-page decisions to make.)

A 1-inch (1″) *bottom margin* is recommended. Because of variable internal spacing of report items, however, a bottom margin of exactly 1 inch is often not possible. For that reason, a bottom margin of *at least* 1 inch is acceptable.

Internal spacing. A quadruple space (QS) is left between the report title and the first line of the body. A double space (DS) is left above and below side headings and between paragraphs. Paragraphs are usually double-spaced.

Page numbering. The first page of an unbound report is not numbered. On the second page and following ones, the page number is placed on line 6 at the right margin. A double space is left below the page number. This means that the first line of the report body appears on line 8.

CORRECTION DEVICES

"To err is human, to forgive divine." So said Alexander Pope more than two centuries ago (Bartlett, 1968, 403). To err in the keyboarding process is human, but failure to correct errors is hardly forgiveable. That is why a variety of correcting devices have been invented to remove or cover up inevitable errors made at the input stage of typewriter or computer keyboarding. These devices are of two types: manual devices and electronic devices.

Manual Devices

Manual correcting devices include the typing eraser, cover-up tape, cover-up liquid, lift-off film, and lift-off tape. The most time-consuming and least satisfactory of these devices is the abrasive rubber typing eraser which was used for many years before more effective devices were invented. Of the manual devices available, the quickest and most satisfactory is lift-off tape which literally lifts the error off the paper when a special backspace (correction) key is used to position the printing point over the error and the key struck in error is restruck.

Electronic Devices

The use of special correction keys on electronic typewriters, computers, and word processors permits the automatic removal of individual letters, words, word groups, lines, and paragraphs so that all corrections can be made before paper copy printout occurs. Electronic error correction is the most efficient method for producing error-free documents and is being used increasingly to prepare

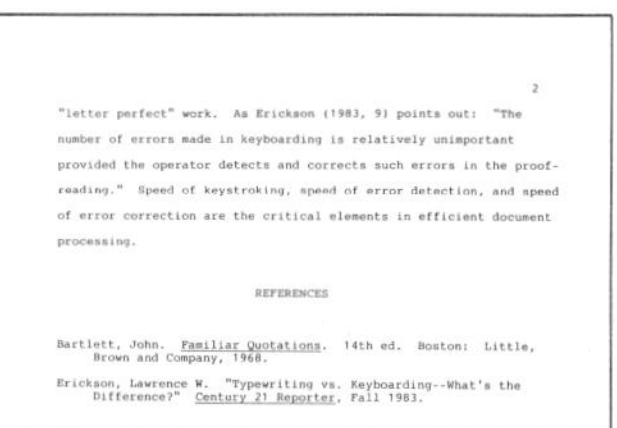

2

"letter perfect" work. As Erickson (1983, 9) points out: "The number of errors made in keyboarding is relatively unimportant provided the operator detects and corrects such errors in the proofreading." Speed of keystroking, speed of error detection, and speed of error correction are the critical elements in efficient document processing.

REFERENCES

Bartlett, John. Familiar Quotations. 14th ed. Boston: Little, Brown and Company, 1968.

Erickson, Lawrence W. "Typewriting vs. Keyboarding--What's the Difference?" Century 21 Reporter, Fall 1983.

Reference citations. References used to give credit for quoted or paraphrased material are cited in parentheses in the report body. This internal citation method of documentation is rapidly replacing the footnote method because it is easier and quicker. Internal citations should include the name(s) of the author(s), the date of the referenced publication, and the page number(s) of the material cited.

All references cited are listed alphabetically by author surnames at the end of the report (usually on a separate page) under the heading REFERENCES. The reference page uses the same top margin and side margins as the first page of the report. Each reference is single-spaced; a DS is left between references. The first line of each reference begins at the left margin; other lines are indented 5 spaces.

238b-242b ▶ 45

Improve Forms and Tables Skills

Job 1

File Cards, Mailing Labels, and File Labels

(LM pp. 47-63)

1. Ms. Colby, Director of Admissions, has requested a file card, a mailing label, and a file folder label for each of the students on the computer printout below. (The printout is arranged according to ZIP Code -- lowest to highest.)

2. Assign each student an ID number beginning with 14582 for Mr. Sykes and continuing in numeric order down the list. Place the number on the file card in the upper right corner on the second line.

Special Note:

Computer printers often print copy with distinctive punctuation marks. The comma in this printout appears as ¬ .

STUDENTS ADMITTED DURING THE WEEK BEGINNING AUGUST 3¬ 19--

Name	Address	Telephone
Mr. William T. Sykes	2908 Sproul Road¬ Ardmore¬ PA 19003-6856	480-2601
Mrs. Martha D. Crosby	2101 Concord Road¬ Chester¬ PA 19013-7988	458-5574
Mr. Joseph M. Conte	101 School Lane¬ Chester¬ PA 19015-4606	458-6593
Mrs. Teresa K. Diaz	6 Penn Street¬ Primos¬ PA 19018-7121	549-3402
Miss Bernice O. Chou	7921 First Street¬ Darby¬ PA 19023-5213	876-4425
Ms. Brenda C. James	142 25th Street¬ Darby¬ PA 19023-8234	479-3210
Mr. Andrew Q. Lee	956 Clay Drive¬ Glenolden¬ PA 19036-6856	548-2391
Mrs. Rachel R. Stein	296 Dupont Avenue¬ Yeadon¬ PA 19050-6542	481-3652
Mr. Dennis K. Stone	18 Elm Street¬ Lansdowne¬ PA 19050-8761	478-2109
Mr. George L. Palmer	14 Green Street¬ Elwyn¬ PA 19063-2184	349-8510
Ms. Wanda T. Jeffries	28 Colt Road¬ Media¬ PA 19063-4211	349-9621
Miss Betty A. Sillas	381 Beatty Road¬ Media¬ PA 19063-9123	564-6790
Miss Alice E. Shank	231 Main Street¬ Linwood¬ PA 19064-6121	458-9557
Mr. Chad L. Franklin	38 Fox Lane¬ Media¬ PA 19064-6554	564-0238
Mr. Ralph M. Stoner	6 Fox Lane¬ Media¬ PA 19064-7138	564-4938
Ms. Penny L. Delancey	25 Grove Avenue¬ Morton¬ PA 19070-3811	480-4563
Mr. M. Gareth Mayes	P.O. Box 145¬ Ridley Park¬ PA 19078-2111	486-3005
Mr. Mark L. Verdon	1021 Newton Road¬ Wayne¬ PA 19087-3712	785-2658
Miss Debra T. McBride	460 Drexel Lane¬ Devon¬ PA 19333-9403	784-1547
Miss Clara P. O'Brien	1340 Third Street¬ Exton¬ PA 19341-7656	785-9436
Ms. Jenny J. Parker	49 Olive Street¬ Malvern¬ PA 19355-5787	483-5731
Mrs. Helen A. Simpson	27 Ivy Street¬ Thornton¬ PA 19373-4279	793-4620

Job 2

Table of Students

1. Mrs. Carpenter, Director of Instruction, would like an alphabetic list DS of the students admitted during the week of August 3, including name (without title), address, and ID Number but not the telephone number.

2. Arrange the file cards from Job 1 in alphabetic order and prepare the list. Provide an appropriate title.

3. Arrange the information in three columns: (1) Name; (2) Address; and (3) ID Number.

51a ▶ 7
Conditioning Practice

each line twice SS (slowly, then faster); if time permits, rekey selected lines

alphabet 1 Pat became very quiet just as an extra golf cart zoomed down the walk.

figures 2 They washed 59 cars, 28 vans, 47 campers, and 30 bikes on November 16.

s/es/ies 3 aid aids job jobs car cars do does class classes try tries copy copies

speed 4 Dory may make a fuchsia gown for the civic social to be held downtown.

| 1 | 2 | 3 | 4 | 5 | 6 | 7 | 8 | 9 | 10 | 11 | 12 | 13 | 14 |

51b ▶ 8
Learn to Align Roman Numerals

half sheet (long edge at top)

1. Set left margin stop for a 40-space line.

2. Clear all tab stops; from left margin, space forward to set new tab stops as indicated by the KEY below and the guides above the columns.

3. Center the heading on line 14.

4. As you key the Roman numerals, tabbing from column to column, align them at the right. To do this, space forward or backward from the tab stop as needed.

> **Margin Release**
> To begin the numeral III in Column 1, depress the **margin release (6)** with the nearer little finger and backspace once into the left margin.
> To key outside the right margin, depress the margin release when the right margin locks and continue to key.

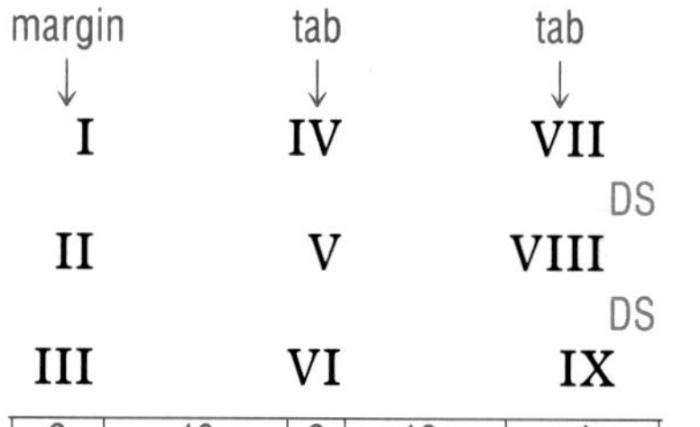

51c ▶ 20
Learn to Format a Topic Outline

Study the information and outline shown at the right; then format the outline as directed.

full sheet; 1" side margins (elite, 12 spaces; pica, 10); start on line 12 for elite, on line 10 for pica

- Major headings are preceded by I. and II.
- First-order subheadings are preceded by A., B., etc.
- Second-order subheadings are preceded by 1., 2., etc.

```
                    SPACING TOPIC OUTLINES
                                          QS (quadruple-space)--
                                          to leave 3 blank line spaces
Space forward once from margin   I.  VERTICAL SPACING   (2 spaces)
                                                 DS
Reset margin ──►   A.  Title of Outline
1st tab ──►            1.  Line 12, elite (12-pitch); line 10, pica (10-pitch)
Set 2 tab stops        2.  Followed by 3 blank line spaces (QS)
4 spaces apart.    B.  Major Headings
                       1.  First major heading preceded by a quadruple space;
2d tab ──►                 all others preceded by 1 blank line space (DS)
                       2.  All followed by 1 blank line space
                       3.  All subheadings single-spaced
                                                 DS
Use margin release;
backspace 5 times  II.  HORIZONTAL SPACING
                                                 DS
                   A.  Title of Outline Centered over the Line of Writing
                   B.  Major Headings and Subheadings
                       1.  Identifying numerals at left margin (periods aligned)
                           followed by 2 spaces
                       2.  Identifying letters and numbers for each subsequent
                           level of subheading aligned below the first word of
                           the preceding heading, followed by 2 spaces
```

> **Language Skills Notes**
> **1.** Title in ALL CAPS (*may be underlined*)
> **2.** Major headings in ALL CAPS (not underlined)
> **3.** Important words of first-order subheadings capped
> **4.** Only first word of second-order subheadings capped

(continued)
OFFICE OPPORTUNITIES UNLIMITED

Centering Columnar Headings

1. Add the beginning and ending points for the column (found above). Divide by 2. Move to this point and backspace from center once for each 2 strokes in the heading. Begin the heading at this point.

2. If the columnar heading is the longest item, key it at the beginning point. Then, backspace from the center of the column for the next longest item in the column and reset the tab stop.

Many secretaries, even those in automated offices, keep informal files of many kinds. Among the most popular are alphabetic or numeric indexes which are usually kept on 5″ × 3″ cards and in folders for filing information of all sorts. Many secretaries also prepare mailing labels from address lists. The following are guides for your use in preparing (1) file cards; (2) file-folder labels; and (3) mailing labels.

Standard Format for File Cards

1. Place the name of the individual or company on the second line from the top edge of the card beginning three spaces from the left edge.

2. Key the name of an individual in inverse order -- family name first, given name second, and middle name or initial last. Place a title, such as *Ms.* or *Dr.*, in parentheses immediately following the given name.

3. Double-space below the name of the individual or company. SS the name and address in postal order -- name, address, city, state, and ZIP Code.

4. DS and include any additional information desired, such as telephone numbers, previous orders, or important dates.

```
Crosby, Martha D. (Mrs.)

Mrs. Martha D. Crosby
2101 Concord Road
Chester, PA  19013-7988

(215) 458-5574
```

Standard Format for File Folder Labels

1. Using no punctuation marks (except a hyphen), key the name of the company or the individual on the second line from the top edge of the label. Begin three spaces from the left edge. The name of the individual is shown in inverse order -- last name, first name, and middle initial followed by the title.

2. Key the city, state, and ZIP Code on the next line, followed by the local address, if necessary, on the following line. *Note that the second and third lines of a file folder label are the reverse of those on a mailing label.*

```
Crosby Martha D Mrs
Chester PA  19013-7988
2101 Concord Road
```

Standard Format for Mailing Labels

1. Place the name of the individual or company in ALL CAPS with no punctuation on the second line from the top edge of the label beginning three spaces from the left edge. Give the name of an individual in mailing order -- title, first name, middle initial, and family name.

2. Place the local address on the next line followed by the city and ZIP Code on the following line in ALL CAPS.

```
MRS MARTHA D CROSBY
2101 CONCORD ROAD
CHESTER PA  19013-7988
```

Lessons 238-242

238a-242a ▶ 5
Check Equipment

Before you begin work each day, check your machine to see that it is in good working order by keying the paragraph at the right at least twice (first slowly, then faster).

all letters/figures used

The blaze badly damaged large quantities of expensive winter jackets. Included were 240 jackets valued at $1,596 each and 380 jackets at $1,740 -- a total of $1,044,240. They may fix the burns in the eight formal gowns and also mend all of the ivory flannel.

| 1 | 2 | 3 | 4 | 5 | 6 | 7 | 8 | 9 | 10 | 11 | 12 | 13 |

51d ▶ 15
Format an Outline

full sheet; 1″ side margins; start on line 12 for elite, on line 10 for pica; format the outline; correct errors

BASIC TEXT-EDITING FUNCTIONS

I. DELETE FUNCTION
   A. Using Cursor Movement Keys, Locate on Screen Point of Deletion
   B. Delete Character, Word, or Line Using Proper Keys

II. INSERT FUNCTION
   A. Using Cursor Movement Keys, Locate on Screen Point of Insertion
   B. Insert Character, Word, or Line into Existing Text
   C. Replace Existing Text
      1. Delete existing text
      2. Insert new text (character, word, or line)

III. AUTOMATIC CENTERING FUNCTION
   A. Strike Proper Key for Automatic Centering
   B. Enter Copy to Be Centered (Machine Will Center It)

Lesson 52 Unbound Reports

52a ▶ 7
Conditioning Practice

each line twice SS (slowly, then faster); if time permits, rekey selected lines

alphabet	1	Joyce paid the exotic woman a quarter for the three black gauze veils.
figures	2	Can 58 students answer the 37 questions about the dates 1492 and 1066?
d/ed/ied	3	use used form formed work worked reach reached fry fried apply applied
speed	4	The girls cut and curl their hair when they visit their rich neighbor.

| 1 | 2 | 3 | 4 | 5 | 6 | 7 | 8 | 9 | 10 | 11 | 12 | 13 | 14 |

52b ▶ 43
Learn to Format an Unbound Report and Reference List

1. Study the report formatting information on page 93.

2. On two full sheets of plain paper, format the model report shown on pages 96 and 97. Do not correct your errors as you keyboard.

3. When you have finished, proofread your copy, mark it for correction, and prepare a final copy with all errors corrected. (Line endings of elite/pica solutions differ.)

CORRECTION DEVICES

"To err is human, to forgive divine." So said Alexander Pope more than two centuries ago (Bartlett, 1968, 403). To err in the keyboarding process is human, but failure to correct errors is hardly forgiveable. That is why a variety of correcting devices have been invented to remove or cover up inevitable errors made at the input stage of typewriter or computer keyboarding. These devices are of two types: manual devices and electronic devices.

Manual Devices

Manual correcting devices include the typing eraser, cover-up tape, cover-up liquid, lift-off film, and lift-off tape. The most time-consuming and least satisfactory of these devices is the abrasive rubber typing eraser which was used for many years before more effective devices were invented. Of the manual devices available, the quickest and most satisfactory is lift-off tape which literally lifts the error off the paper when a special backspace (correction) key is used to position the printing point over the error and the key struck in error is restruck.

Electronic Devices

The use of special correction keys on electronic typewriters, computers, and word processors permits the automatic removal of individual letters, words, word groups, lines, and paragraphs so that all corrections can be made before paper copy printout occurs. Electronic error correction is the most efficient method for producing error-free documents and is being used increasingly to prepare "letter perfect" work. As Erickson (1983, 9) points out: "The number of errors made in keyboarding is relatively unimportant provided the operator

2

detects and corrects such errors in the proofreading." Speed of keystroking, speed of error detection, and speed of error correction are the critical elements in efficient document processing.

REFERENCES

Bartlett, John. Familiar Quotations. 14th ed. Boston: Little, Brown and Company, 1968.

Erickson, Lawrence W. "Typewriting vs. Keyboarding--What's the Difference?" Century 21 Reporter, Fall 1983.

Elite (12-pitch) Layout

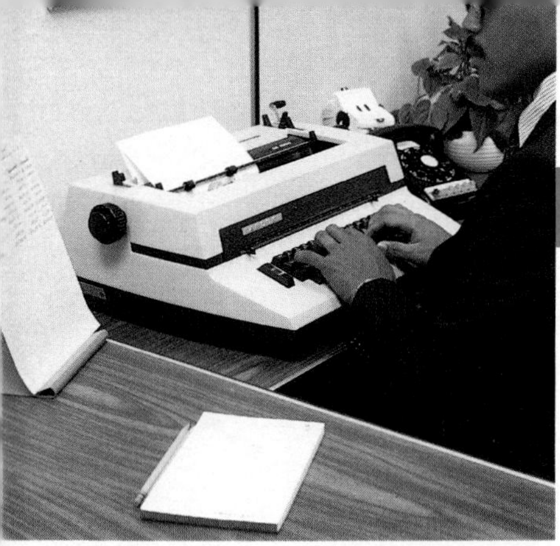

Unit 52 Lessons 238-242

Training Goals

1. To review the format of tables and typical forms prepared in the office.

2. To improve your ability to plan, organize, and produce tables and forms quickly and correctly.

Documents/Forms Reviewed

1. File Card
2. File and Mailing Labels
3. Table
4. Purchase Requisition
5. Purchase Order
6. Invoice

OFFICE OPPORTUNITIES UNLIMITED

Mr. Dale Marshall, Document Production Manager, asks you to review the formats for common forms in the OOU training manual.

Training Manual Excerpts: Standard Formats for Common Forms

Many different kinds of forms are found in the business office. Among the most common forms are the (1) purchase requisition which is used to order goods and services *within* an organization; (2) a purchase order which is used to order goods and services from *another* company; and (3) an invoice which is used to bill a customer for goods and services provided. Such forms are usually single-spaced.

When preparing these documents, follow these general guidelines:

1. Place the address 1 or 2 spaces to the right and a DS below the top line in the address area. Some forms indicate the starting point with a dot.
2. Place date and shipping information 1 or 2 spaces to the right of printed headings.
3. Set left margin to place items in Quantity column in approximate center. Key first entry on the first or second line below the horizontal rule under the heading.
4. Begin items in the Description column 1 or 2 spaces to the right of the vertical rule.
5. If forms list prices and totals, position amounts so that cent figures fall to the right of the vertical rules. Use of a comma to indicate thousands is optional.
6. Underline the amount of the final item in the Total column; DS and key total.

Standard Format for Tables

Vertical Centering

1. Count all lines needed for the table.
2. Subtract lines needed from lines available (66 full sheet, 33 half sheet -- long side up).
3. Divide by 2 to determine the number of the line on which to key the main heading.

Disregard any fraction. If the number that results is **even**, space down that number from the top of the paper and key the heading. If the number is **odd**, use the next lower number. Using this method, the main heading of a table will always begin on an even number.

Horizontal Centering -- Headings

1. Move left and right margin stops to the extreme ends of the scale.
2. Clear all tab stops; set a tab stop at the center of the paper.
3. Backspace from center once for each 2 strokes in the heading. Do not backspace for an odd or leftover character at the end of a line. Key the main heading. DS and key the secondary heading in the same manner.

Horizontal Centering -- Columns

1. Select an even number of intercolumn spaces.
2. Find the longest item in each column. The columnar heading may be the longest item.
3. Backspace from center once for each 2 strokes in the longest item in each column and once for each 2 strokes in the spaces between columns.
4. Set the left margin stop at this point. Note the location of the margin stop on the horizontal scale.
5. Space forward once for each stroke in the longest item in Column 1. At the end, note the number on the scale. You now have the beginning and ending numbers in Column 1.
6. Space forward once for each space between Columns 1 and 2. Set a tab stop and note the location on the scale.
7. Space forward once for each stroke in the longest item in Column 2. At the end, note the number on the scale. You now have the beginning and ending numbers of Column 2.
8. Repeat Steps 6 and 7 for each additional column.

Line 10, pica
Line 12, elite

Title

CORRECTION DEVICES

QS (space down 2 DS)

"To err is human, to forgive divine." So said Alexander Pope more than two centuries ago (Bartlett, 1968, 403). To err in the keyboarding process is human, but failure to correct errors is hardly forgiveable. That is why a variety of correcting devices have been invented to remove or cover up inevitable errors made at the input stage of typewriter or computer keyboarding. These devices are of two types: manual devices and electronic devices.

Internal citation

Report body or text

DS

Side heading

Manual Devices

DS

Manual correcting devices include the typing eraser, cover-up tape, cover-up liquid, lift-off film, and lift-off tape. The most time-consuming and least satisfactory of these devices is the abrasive rubber typing eraser which was used for many years before more effective devices were invented. Of the manual devices available, the quickest and most satisfactory is lift-off tape which literally lifts the error off the paper when a special backspace (correction) key is used to position the printing point over the error and the key struck in error is restruck.

1"

1"

DS

Side heading

Electronic Devices

DS

The use of special correction keys on electronic typewriters, computers, and word processors permits the automatic removal of individual letters, words, word groups, lines, and paragraphs so that all corrections can be made before paper copy printout occurs. Electronic error correction is the most efficient method for producing error-free documents and is being used increasingly to prepare

At least 1"

Shown in pica type (10 pitch)

Unbound Report

Lesson 237

237a ▶ 5
Check Equipment

Before you begin the drills which follow, check your machine to see that it is in good working order by keyboarding the paragraph at the right at least twice (first slowly, then faster).

all letters/figures used

I will be expected to provide quality flight jackets in many sizes at low prices. Item #438 will sell for $175 and Item #926A for only $109 with terms of 2/10, net 30. If we wish emblems for both of their lapels, they may pay me or the airmen for the work.

| 1 | 2 | 3 | 4 | 5 | 6 | 7 | 8 | 9 | 10 | 11 | 12 | 13 |

237b ▶ 18
Improve Language Skills: Proofread/ Correct

1. In each sentence at the right, items have been underlined. The underlines indicate that there **may** be an error in spelling, punctuation, capitalization, grammar, or in the use of words or figures.

2. Study each sentence carefully. Keyboard the line number. If an underlined item is incorrect, correct it as you keyboard the sentence. In addition, correct any typographical errors you may make.

1. My mechanical devise is interesting; but it's function is questionible.
2. All most all prices on the New York stock exchange rose considerable.
3. It is to difficulty to chose a winner from between the four girls.
4. The questionaire was a devise to illicit locale beliefs.
5. She said he was greatful to recieve the comittees' vote of "thanks."
6. Velda asked; "was she studying grammer in the librery"?
7. The sallutation is "Dear Sir," the complementary close "yours truely.
8. According to the pole, most voted to cancell the bizaarre.
9. Jun exclaimed, "Speek the quote from 'Macbeth'!"
10. He usually payed the bill by seperate check on the nineth of the month.
11. In Aurelia's speach she quoted from "Time" and "The New York Times."
12. Irregardless, the cheif's secretary don't use the copyer.

237c ▶ 12
Improve Keystroking Skills — Figures and Symbols

1. Take four 1′ writings on each ¶.

2. Strive for accuracy, particularly when keyboarding the figures and symbols.

237d ▶ 15
Improve Basic Keyboarding Skills

1. Take two 1′ writings on each ¶ of 236c, p. 404.

2. Take one 5′ writing on the three ¶s combined.

Goal: Improved speed and accuracy.

gwam 1′

Ray receives $3.80 for each of the first 50 pieces he makes. For 13
10 more pieces, he gets $4.10 each, and for more than 60 pieces, he gets 28
$4.50 each. If Ray produces 68 pieces, he earns $190 ($3.80 × 50), plus 42
$41 ($4.10 × 10), plus $36 ($4.50 × 8) for a total of $267 for the week. 57

From his gross pay, $39.10 is withheld for federal taxes, $4.15 for 14
state taxes, $19.66 for Social Security, and $3.55 for his company's re- 28
tirement plan. His total deductions are $66.46 for a net pay of $200.54 43
($267 × $66.46). Ray's take-home pay is less than 76% of his gross pay. 57

| 1 | 2 | 3 | 4 | 5 | 6 | 7 | 8 | 9 | 10 | 11 | 12 | 13 | 14 |

Page number Line 6 2

DS

Internal citation "letter perfect" work. As Erickson (1983, 9) points out: "The number of errors made in keyboarding is relatively unimportant provided the operator detects and corrects such errors in the proof-

1" reading." Speed of keystroking, speed of error detection, and speed 1"

of error correction are the critical elements in efficient document processing.

QS (space down 2 DS)

REFERENCES

QS (space down 2 DS); then change to SS

List of references

Bartlett, John. Familiar Quotations. 14th ed. Boston: Little, Brown and Company, 1968.

DS

Erickson, Lawrence W. "Typewriting vs. Keyboarding--What's the Difference?" Century 21 Reporter, Fall 1983.

Lesson 53 Unbound Reports

53a ▶ 7 Conditioning Practice

each line twice SS (slowly, then faster); if time permits, rekey selected lines

alphabet 1 The prize for the eleven-kilometer race was a square gold jewelry box.

figures 2 On June 23 she served 461 hamburgers, 597 sodas, and 80 bags of chips.

ing 3 do doing go going get getting run running shave shaving build building

speed 4 They may visit their pen pal in the small island town by the big lake.

| 1 | 2 | 3 | 4 | 5 | 6 | 7 | 8 | 9 | 10 | 11 | 12 | 13 | 14 |

53b ▶ 8 Learn to Format a Title Page

A title or cover page is prepared for many reports. Using the following guides, format a title page for the report you prepared in Lesson 52.

1. Center the title in ALL CAPS on line 16 of a full sheet (from top edge space down 8 double spaces).

2. Center your name in capital and lowercase letters on the 16th line below the title.

3. Center the school name a DS below your name.

4. Center the date on the 16th line below the school name.

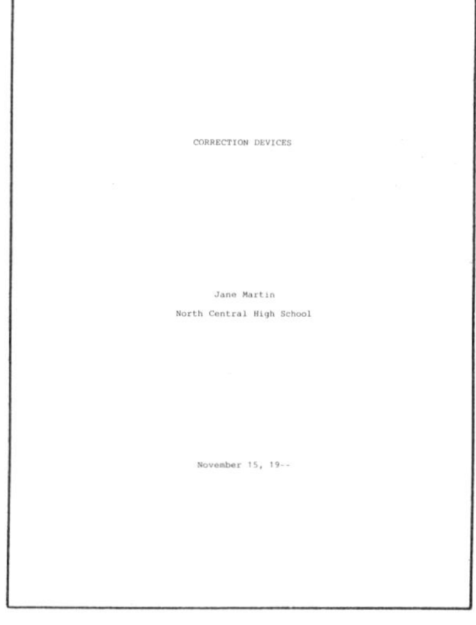

CORRECTION DEVICES

Jane Martin

North Central High School

November 15, 19--

Title Page

236c ▶ 15
Improve Basic Keyboarding Skills

Take two 5′ writings on the ¶s at the right. Record *gwam* and errors.

all letters used | A | 1.5 si | 5.7 awl | 80% hfw |

	gwam 1′	5′	
One of the most essential documents found in an office today is the	14	3	61
report. Reports are so vital because they have many uses. They are one	28	6	64
of the prime means by which an executive at any level of an organization	43	9	66
can keep informed. Reports can also establish a two-way channel of com-	57	11	69
munication through which data essential to the efficient conduct of the	72	14	72
firm can flow. Information today is vital to the dynamic growth of any	86	17	75
enterprise. Without up-to-date data, no firm can survive.	98	20	77
To be effective, a report must be complete, correct, clear, and	13	22	80
concise. It must contain all the pertinent information an executive	26	25	83
needs to analyze the situation and reach a valid conclusion. It must	40	28	85
be written in a fashion that leaves no doubt in the reader's mind about	55	30	88
the cogent facts. Essentially, it should be written in as few words as	69	33	91
possible, not only for the sake of clarity, but to save the executive's	84	36	94
time. The most useful report is almost always the shortest one.	96	39	97
The overall appearance of a report is an important factor. The	13	41	99
person who receives the report views it initially as a whole. A report	27	44	102
that is not attractive may be just set aside and ignored. On the other	42	47	105
hand, a report that is attractively placed on the page with clean, even	56	50	108
type and no untidy erasures will certainly attract attention. A report	71	53	111
of quality that is well written and well typed reflects favorably on	84	56	114
the secretary as well as the executive who prepared it.	95	58	116

gwam 1′ | 1 | 2 | 3 | 4 | 5 | 6 | 7 | 8 | 9 | 10 | 11 | 12 | 13 | 14 |
gwam 5′ | 1 | 2 | 3 |

236d ▶ 12
Improve Keystroking Skills — Figures

Practice each sentence twice; keyboard *by touch.* Repeat sentences that contain errors in figures if time permits.

1 Team 3 will meet in Room 64; Team 5, in Room 82; Team 17, in Room 190.

2 On October 9, 16, 23, and 30, Room 84 will be open from 5 to 7:30 p.m.

3 Volume 114 includes notes on pages 248, 390, 571, 642, 1007, and 1264.

4 Items 96, 328, and 709 will be replaced by Items 5634, 9723, and 1042.

5 Phone me at 465-9320 or 598-4321 as soon as Project 79301 is approved.

6 Repair the machines with serial numbers 5834107, 6897065, and 7941231.

| 1 | 2 | 3 | 4 | 5 | 6 | 7 | 8 | 9 | 10 | 11 | 12 | 13 | 14 |

53c ▶ 35
Format a Book Report in Unbound Style

1. Review the formatting guides for unbound reports (page 93).

2. Format the material given at the right as an unbound report. Substitute your name for the one given. Correct any errors you make as you key.

3. Place the reference below the last line of the report.

4. Staple the pages together across the upper left corner or fasten them with a paper clip.

Title of books or magazines may be shown in all-caps or underlined with only the first letter of important words capitalized (for example, LINCOLN or <u>Lincoln</u>).

words

BOOK REVIEW 2
DS
by 3
DS
Kevin Raintree 6
QS

LINCOLN, a historical novel by Gore Vidal, begins as Abraham Lincoln 20
arrives in Washington, D.C., to be inaugurated as the sixteenth President of 35
a disintegrating United States. He arrives in disguise because there has al- 50
ready been talk of a plot to kill him before the swearing-in ceremony to be 66
held in a few weeks. During the next four years there would be many plots 81
to murder this man who had sworn to unite a nation split apart over the con- 96
troversial issue of slavery. 101

Isolated in the White House in a pro-slavery city, Lincoln tries to preside 117
over a divided government. Even some of the members of his own Republi- 131
can Party view him with contempt, call him "Honest Ape," and accuse him in 146
turn of weakness and vacillation and of high-handedness and dictatorship. 161

In this moving historical novel, Lincoln is observed by his loved ones, his 176
rivals, and his future assassins. The result is a view of the man that is at the 193
same time stark and complex as well as intimate and monumental. It is a 207
portrait of the living Lincoln during the war years. 218

Lincoln emerges as seen by his abolitionist spendthrift wife, Mary, who 232
is going mad; by Seward, his Secretary of State, who first scorns and then 247
worships him; by his intense rival, Salmon P. Chase, who would like to be 262
President; by the druggist's clerk who was central to the plot that would 277
eventually take Lincoln's life; and by his young presidential secretary, John 293
Hay, who realizes as the reader will that there would be no nation had there 308
been no Lincoln. 312

Vidal's LINCOLN deals not so much with the Civil War itself as with the 326
people (politicians, influential businessmen, and generals) whose decisions 341
determine the purpose, scope, and execution of war. Viewed from this 355
perspective, Lincoln is seen as a person of both great conviction and indeci- 371
siveness, of both strength and weakness, of both deep sadness and high 385
humor. Thus, the reader comes to know the legendary Lincoln as a fellow 399
human being. 402

REFERENCE 404

Vidal, Gore. <u>Lincoln</u>. New York: Random House, 1984. 416

Unit 51 Lessons 236-237

Learning Goals

1. To improve your basic keyboarding skills with emphasis on figures and symbols.
2. To increase your keystroking speed and to improve your accuracy on straight copy.
3. To improve your communication skills.

Machine Adjustments

1. 65-space line for Check Equipment exercises.
2. 75-space line for Language Skills.
3. 70-space line for drills and paragraphs.
4. SS sentence drills with a DS between groups; DS paragraph writings; DS Language Skills sentences.

Lesson 236

236a ▶ 5 Check Equipment

Before you begin the drills which follow, check your machine to see that it is in good working order by keyboarding the paragraph at the right at least twice (first slowly, then faster).

all letters/figures used

David quietly examined some broken Aztec water jugs and pots he found. On June 27 and 30, he found only 15 items of interest; on July 4, 9 items; and on July 18, 6 items. The problems of the quantity, title, and authenticity of the items may halt the work.

| 1 | 2 | 3 | 4 | 5 | 6 | 7 | 8 | 9 | 10 | 11 | 12 | 13 |

236b ▶ 18 Improve Language Skills: Proofread/Correct

1. In each sentence at the right, items have been underlined. The underlines indicate that there **may** be an error in spelling, punctuation, capitalization, grammar, or in the use of words or figures.

2. Study each sentence carefully. Key the line number. If an underlined item is incorrect, correct it as you keyboard the sentence. In addition, correct any typographical errors you may make.

1. The employe said his abcense was caused by an automobile acident.
2. The accomodations at the Hotel were all ready filled when I called.
3. Dispite the bad news, we shall take farther steps to excede our quota.
4. Will he ascent to the changes in the marketting of the bloc of stock?
5. Jo canvased the crew in the hangar to find some one to fix the plane.
6. The caste of the new play will read and discus the scrip.
7. Executives who cant key board will have difficulty using computers.
8. She said "my friends please listen, and consider these points".
9. Niether he or she have the necessary knowlege.
10. After studying his figures on the enviroment, I questioned it.
11. She emphasised these points, "Appearance, Attendence, and Attention."
12. Ben is a secretary who's appearence and work are outstanding.

54a ▶ 7 Conditioning Practice

each line twice SS (slowly, then faster); if time permits, rekey selected lines

alphabet 1 Tex Quinn just received a sizable rebate check from the wagon company.
figures 2 Order 196 was for 38 vests, 72 jackets, 40 skirts, and 25 plaid suits.
ly/ily 3 apt aptly near nearly great greatly true truly busy busily easy easily
speed 4 They shall amend the form to entitle their heir to half of the profit.

| 1 | 2 | 3 | 4 | 5 | 6 | 7 | 8 | 9 | 10 | 11 | 12 | 13 | 14 |

54b ▶ 43 Format an Unbound Report

1. Format the copy shown here and on page 100 as an unbound report. Do not correct your errors.
2. Place the reference list on a separate sheet.
3. Prepare a title page.
4. Proofread all pages and mark errors for correction; then prepare a final copy with all errors corrected.
5. Fasten the pages together across the upper left corner.

words

EDITING FUNCTIONS OF WORD PROCESSORS 7

Few people can sit down at a keyboard or with pen and paper and com- 21
pose as a first draft a message they are willing to use as the final draft. 36
From first to final draft, a letter or report usually undergoes substantial 52
change: in sequence of ideas, in word choice, in grammar, in punctuation, 67
and in other elements of written expression. This process of revision is 82
called editing (Meroney, 1984, 5). Editing includes finding and marking 96
routine errors (proofreading) but goes much beyond mere error detection 111
and correction. It may, and often does, involve rewriting. 123

The author or word originator may do much of the editing and revising 137
(Casady, 1984, 25). Often, however, a secretary or word processor operator 152
assists in editing and revision. When a standard typewriter is used, each 167
draft of a message requires a retyped copy. When electronic equipment is 182
used, the keyboard operator inputs the message only once and makes revi- 196
sions electronically on the display screen before a paper printout (hard 211
copy) is made. The speed and ease of on-screen corrections reduce time, 225
effort, and cost in the processing of documents that require heavy editing. 241

Some terms you will need to know when you edit copy using elec- 253
tronic media are defined below. Each of these describes a function that is 269
easily performed by a computer, a text-editor, or a sophisticated electronic 284
typewriter. 287

Delete. To remove from text a segment of copy (a character, a word, a 302
phrase, a line, a sentence, a page). 310

Insert. To add to text a segment of copy (a character, a word, a phrase, a 326
line, a sentence, a page). 332

Block move. To move a block of copy (often a sentence or a paragraph) 348
from one location in a document to another. 357

Search. To locate an editing or correcting point within a document by 372
matching a series of characters or words. 381

Global search and replace. To direct a word processor to find a repeated 401
series of characters and replace it with a different series of characters auto- 416
matically throughout a document (for example, find and replace Co. with 431
Company). 433

(continued on next page)

232b-235b (continued)

Document 3, continued

Aside from the fact that there is no standard unit of measure in word processing, other factors have a big impact upon the amount of work operators can produce. Input, for instance, can range from garbled voice recordings and barely legible handwriting to easily understood dic tation or well-printed pages. The material to be produced also can affect production. The difficulty of the material can range from easy straight copy to statistical formulas or from easy letters and repots to complex forms.

To overcome these circumstances, firms have set up work measurement programs under which records are kept of the time needed to produce documents of various difficulty. "After collecting production records for a period of six months or a year, the supervisor can set standards." (Casady, Mona J. Word/Information Processing Concepts. 2d ed. Cincinnati: South-Western Publishing Co., 1984, 171.) Keep in mind that these "standards" are solely for the one company. "No national standard has been set because there are many variables. . . . It is impossible for one set of standards to be appropriate for all word procesing systems. Therefore, each company has to keep production records upon which to base its own standard." (Casady, Mona J. Word/Information Processing Concepts. 2d ed. Cincinnati: South-Western Publishing Co., 1984, 132.)

Document 4

Unbound Report with Textual Citations

The Document Production Center will prepare materials to be used at the next in-service meeting of the OOU faculty. Emily Carpenter, who directs teacher-training activities at OOU, asks Mr. Marshall to have the previous three documents prepared as an unbound report with textual citations.

1. SS the report.
2. Title the report: STANDARDS AND MEASURES OF PRODUCTIVITY.
3. Use the title of each document as a side heading at the beginning of that part of the report.
4. Prepare a reference page.

54b (continued)

words

Electronic machines differ in the assignment and use of code, command, and function keys that must be operated to direct the machine to perform the various editing functions. An operator's manual which gives step-by-step guides is available for each make and model of equipment. 447 461 476 489

REFERENCES 491

Remember to DS between references.

Casady, Mona J. Word/Information Processing Concepts. 2d ed. Cincinnati: South-Western Publishing Co., 1984. 512 521

Information/Word Processing Glossary. Willow Grove, PA: International Information/Word Processing Association, 1982. 543 552

Meroney, John W. Word Processing Applications in Practice. Cincinnati: South-Western Publishing Co., 1984. 575 582

Lesson 55 Report from Rough Draft

55a ▶ 7 Conditioning Practice

each line twice SS (slowly, then faster); if time permits, rekey selected lines

alphabet 1 The jazz performer quickly ate six large bologna sandwiches every day.

figures 2 Of 1,302 persons who took the test in 1987, 856 passed and 446 failed.

r/er 3 use user give giver drive driver help helper sing singer great greater

speed 4 Cy may be the right man to blame for the big fight in the penalty box.

| 1 | 2 | 3 | 4 | 5 | 6 | 7 | 8 | 9 | 10 | 11 | 12 | 13 | 14 |

55b ▶ 43 Format an Unbound Report from Rough Draft

1. Format the copy shown here and on page 101 as an unbound report, making all corrections marked in the copy and correcting any errors you make as you key.
2. Place the reference list on a separate sheet.
3. Prepare a title page.
4. When the work is completed, proofread again, correct any remaining errors, and fasten the pages together across the upper left corner.

Proofreader's Marks

- ^ insert
- ^, insert comma
- # space
- ∾ transpose
- ⊐ move right
- ⁀ close up
- ≡ capitalize

words

Planing and Preparing Reports ALL CAPS QS 6

Whether written for personal or business use,

A report should present a message that is well organized, 27

stated simply and clear in meaning (Burtness, 1985, 392). A 42

report that does not meet these criterion shows lack of care 55

in planning and preparation. The following suggestions will 67

help you plan and prepare reports that are clear that the 82

reader will not have ot puzzle over them. 94

Planning a Report 101

Three steps should be used in planning a report. Selecting 114

the topic isnot merely the first step but also the most vital 127

one. It is vital that you chose a subject in which you have 139

suficient interest to do the necessary reading and research. 153

Next, it is essential that you limit the topic so that you 165

can handle the subject adequately with in the space and time 177

(continued on next page)

Note: The ellipsis, indicating omission of words from a quotation, is keyed by alternating 3 periods and spaces (. . .) or 4 (. . . .) if the end of a sentence is included in the quotation.

logs; (5) number of documents a day; and (6) quantity and quality of work." (Robinson, Jane R. and Judy R. West. "Word Processing Curriculum: Attitudes/Skills Business Educators Should Update." Journal of Byusiness Education, vol. 59, (January 1984), 163-167.) It is obvious form these answers that there is no standard way of measuring out put in word processing.

Efforts have been made to establish the line as a standard unit of measure in word processing. Exactly what consitutes a "line"? According to the Valdocs User's Guide, "When you first bring up the Valdocs system, the left margin is set at 10 and the right margin at 70. This gives you a standard (10-pitch) 60-character line . . ." (valdocs User's Guide. Torrance, CA: Epson America, Inc., 1983, 3-19.) J. R. Little, founder and first President of the International Word Processing Association, states: "Almost the entire word processing industry has moved to weighted-line count as a means of production measurement. For this purpose, we define a line as 72 characters of typed material on a single-line line (the number of 12-pitch characters on a six-inch line)." (Little, J. R. "Measured Typing Output: Does it Help or Hinder?" The Office, Vol. 91, (February 1980), 24-32.) Konkel and Beck Peck state that "a 6 1/2" line is counted as one standad . . ." (Konkel, Gilbert J. and Phyllis J. Peck. The Word Processing Explosion. Stamford: Office Publications, Inc., 1976, 117.) They do not indacate whether the line is 10- or 12-pitch.

(continued on page 402)

words

limitations ^that have been set^. Finally, you should decide ^upon^ and list in logical 194

^outline^ form the major ideas and the subordinate ~~ideas~~ ^points^ for each idea 208

that you want to use as support (Gonzalez et al., 1981, 499- 220

518). 221

Preparing the report 229

Three steps should be followed in preparing the report ^also^. 242

The first of these is to look for ~~information~~ ^data and authoritative statements^ to support your 259

ideas. ~~you want to express.~~ The next step is to ~~write~~ ^prepare^ a rough 268

draft ^of the report^, organizing the data in ^to^ a series of related paragraphs, 283

each with a topic sentence to announce its major theme. The 295

last step is to read the rough draft ^carefully^ for sequence of ideas, 309

clarity^,^ and accuracy and to prepa~~ir~~^re^ the final draft in correct 322

form with all errors corrected. In checking for ac^c^uracy, be 335

certain that 337

DS

1. all words are spel^l^ed correctly; 345
2. punctuation rules have been correctly applied; 355
3. proper spacing follows each punctuation mark; 365
4. capitalization rules have been correctly ~~used~~ ^applied^; 376
5. all numbers are accurate; and 382
6. number expression rules have been correctly applied. 394

Whether the report is typed or printed^,^ it should be neat 406

and arranged in proper ~~style~~ ^format^. A neat report presented in an 418

orderly style makes an im^m^ediate ^positive^ impression on the reader. 431

REFERENCES 2

Burtness, Paul S., and Jack E. Hulbert. Effective 14
Business Communication. 8th ed. Cincinnati: 28
South-Western Publishing Co., 1985. 35

Gonzalez, Roseann, Ruby Herlong, Mary Hynes-Berry, 45
and Paul Pesce. Language: Structure and Use. 61
Glenview, IL: Scott, Foresman and Company, 69
1981. 70

232b-235b (continued)

Document 3

Topbound Report with Textual Citations

For your next assignment, Mr. Marshall directs you to prepare the report at the right using textual citations.

Special Instructions:

For each citation, the complete reference information has been included in the text of the report. As you prepare the report, insert the proper textual citation and make a note of the complete reference for the reference page.

Textual Citations

1. If the reference is identified by name or author within the text, merely give the date of the publication and the page number following the reference, for example: **(1977, 153).**

2. If the source of the reference or quotation is not identified in the body of the report, give the source, the date, and page number following the reference, for example: (**Casady, 1984, 132).**

MEASURING PRODUCTIVITY OF OFFICE EMPLOYEES

3 blank lines

How much work should an office employee be expected to do in a given time frame? On what bases should an office worker be reimbursed? These probing questions are all most impossible to answer for a number of reasons. The classification "office employee" incldes innumerable jobs. One of the major occupational categories listed in the Dictionary of Occupational Titles is the "Clerical and Saleds Occupations." "Clerical occupations, which are classified in Division 20 through 24, include those activities with preparing, transcribing, systematizing, and preserving written communications and records; distribution information; and collecting accounts." (U.S. Department of Labor, Employment Service. Dictionary of occupational Titles. Washingotn, U.S. Government Printing Office, 1977, 153.) Innumerable jobs are listed in this divisions ranging from Social Secretary to Library Page. Because of the diversity of work preformed by office employees these workers traditionally have be paid on a time basis--by the hour, day, week, month, or year.

With the adoption of Word Processing, attempts have been made to establish standards for those who key board materials. In a study conducted with word processing originaters and supervisors in Tennessee, 41.3% indicated that they measured word processing production whiled 53.8% did not. "Typical responses regarding how production was measured included: (1) keystrokes; (2) line count; (3) number of pages; (4) weekly

(continued on page 401)

Lesson 56 Prepare for Measurement

56a ▶ 7 Conditioning Practice

each line twice SS (slowly, then faster); if time permits, rekey selected lines

alphabet 1 Jacintha expects my crazy quilt to fit nicely on Geneva's new oak bed.

figures 2 The data are given in Figures 26 and 27 of Part 14, Unit 39, page 508.

n/en 3 ox oxen take taken drive driven prove proven less lessen sharp sharpen

speed 4 Did the eight sorority girls clap with vigor for the city bugle corps?

| 1 | 2 | 3 | 4 | 5 | 6 | 7 | 8 | 9 | 10 | 11 | 12 | 13 | 14 |

56b ▶ 8 Check Keyboarding Skill: Straight Copy

1. A 1′ writing on ¶ 1, then on ¶ 2; find *gwam* on each writing.

2. A 2′ writing on ¶s 1-2 combined; find *gwam*.

3. A 3′ writing on ¶s 1-2 combined; find *gwam*.

all letters used | A | 1.5 si | 5.7 awl | 80% hfw |

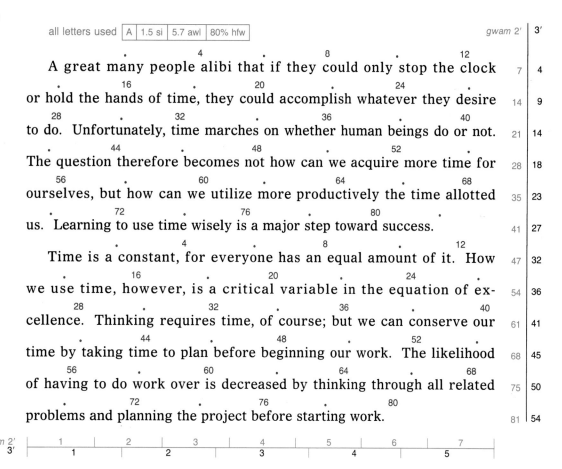

Text	gwam 2′	3′
A great many people alibi that if they could only stop the clock	7	4
or hold the hands of time, they could accomplish whatever they desire	14	9
to do. Unfortunately, time marches on whether human beings do or not.	21	14
The question therefore becomes not how can we acquire more time for	28	18
ourselves, but how can we utilize more productively the time allotted	35	23
us. Learning to use time wisely is a major step toward success.	41	27
Time is a constant, for everyone has an equal amount of it. How	47	32
we use time, however, is a critical variable in the equation of ex-	54	36
cellence. Thinking requires time, of course; but we can conserve our	61	41
time by taking time to plan before beginning our work. The likelihood	68	45
of having to do work over is decreased by thinking through all related	75	50
problems and planning the project before starting work.	81	54

gwam 2′ | 1 | 2 | 3 | 4 | 5 | 6 | 7 |
3′ | 1 | 2 | 3 | 4 | 5 |

56c ▶ 35 Prepare for Measurement

3 plain full sheets; correction supplies

List on a slip of paper the page numbers and lesson parts given below:

p. 95, 51d
pp. 95-97, 52b

1. Format the outline of 51d as directed there. Correct any errors you make as you key the copy. (See the model in 51c if you need help.)

2. Format and key the report shown as a model on pages 96 and 97. Correct any errors you make as you key. If time permits, format a title page for the report.

232b-235b (continued)

Document 2, continued

When, under standardized conditions, ~~workers finish~~ employees produce "pieces" which can be counted, their efforts can be measured and compensated on the basis of the number of pieces produced in a given time. ". . . <u>piece</u> <u>rate</u> is one of the oldest means of tying productivity and effort together."[1] The piece rate is simple and easy to understand. "It is eminently fair in its rewards since earnings are directly proportional to all output levels. . . ."[2] The piecework system has its disadvantages, however. Human effort is only one part of production. Materials, equipment, ~~equipment~~ and environment, among other factors, have a direct bearing upon production. The problem lies in determining the contribution the employee makes, taking into consideration the effects of other essential factors.

"The payment of salaries or wages on the basis of a specific period ~~time~~ of time (a year, a month, a week, a day, or an hour) is probably the most common method of compensation."[3] Hourly, weekly, monthly, or yearly, rates are established, on the basis of the difficulty of the various tasks performed rather than upon the production of a physical unit. Once the time rate has been established, this is a simple system to administer. Unfortunately, the rate must be ~~alter each time~~ changed every time there is a change in the job tasks. The greatest disadvantage of paying wages or salaries based on time is that there is no incentive for an employee to work harder.

"The compensation ~~plan~~ program, therefore, must be tailored to the needs of the organization and of its employees."[4] Some of the plans are ~~very~~ similar, but none could be classified as "standard." To be successful, ~~the wage~~ any wage and salery plan must be carried out effectively, consistently, and fairly. "No employee--minority or majority, executive or operator, man or woman--is willing to tolerate poorly administered compensation plans for long."[5]

---

[1] Robert L. Mathis and John H. Jackson, <u>Personnel</u> (New York: West Publishing Company, 1976), p. 160.

[2] Dale S. Beach, <u>Personnel, the Management of People at Work</u> (New York: MacMillan Publishing Co., Inc., 1976), p. 690.

[3] Kenneth E. Everard and Jim Burrow, <u>Business Principles and Management</u> (Cincinnati: South-Western Publishing Co., 1984), p. 430.

[4] Herbert J. Chruden and Arthur W. Sherman, Jr., <u>Managing Human Resources</u> (Cincinnati: South-Western Publishing Co., 1984), p. 405.

[5] Raymond E. Gloss, Richard D. Steade, and James R. Lowry, <u>Business: Its Nature and Environment</u> (Cincinnati: South-Western Publishing Co., 1984), p. 140

57a ▶ 7 Conditioning Practice

each line twice SS (slowly, then faster), if time permits, rekey selected lines

alphabet 1 Quin just got a dark pink vase from his uncle for my next lawn bazaar.
figures 2 Our group read 45 plays, 178 books, and 203 articles during 1986-1987.
ion 3 act action opt option except exception digest digestion elect election
speed 4 Guthrie may wish to dismantle the antique chair for the busy neighbor.

| 1 | 2 | 3 | 4 | 5 | 6 | 7 | 8 | 9 | 10 | 11 | 12 | 13 | 14 |

57b ▶ 33 Check Formatting Skill: Report

2 plain full sheets; correction supplies

Format and key the report in unbound style. SS the listed items and indent them 5 spaces from the left margin only; DS between items. Format the reference list on a separate sheet. Correct any errors you make as you key.

words

WORD PROCESSING TRAINING 5

Office support personnel must have superior keyboarding skill in order 19
to work with confidence and efficiency. They must use that skill with profi- 35
ciency in processing a wide assortment of business papers and technical 49
documents. These abilities are required of employees who work in face-to- 64
face settings with executives or with supervisors in word processing centers 79
(Beaumont, 1981, 7). 84

In addition to keyboarding skill and formatting knowledge, good work 97
habits are essential. Office support personnel must organize, plan, and 112
complete their job tasks efficiently. They must edit source documents from 127
which they work as well as proofread and correct the copy (output) they 142
produce. They must perform all these tasks with minimal direction and 156
supervision. 159

A keyboarding, formatting, and document processing course, therefore, 172
has several purposes. Those listed below are among the most important. 187

1. Help students reach the keyboarding speeds most often required for 201
employment: 40, 50, 60, and 70 words a minute (Occupational Outlook 219
Handbook, 1980-81, 95). 226

2. Help students learn and apply the formatting guides and procedures 240
for processing a variety of documents. 248

3. Familiarize students with word processing functions and procedures 262
that are performed on electronic equipment in the modern office 275
(Occupational Projections and Training Data, 1984, 46-48). 295

4. Ease the transition from school to office by providing students with 310
sets of simulated office job tasks that closely reflect the real world 324
of work. 326

REFERENCES 328

Beaumont, L. R. "Typing vs. Keyboarding -- Is There a Difference?" 341
Century 21 Reporter, Spring 1981. 352

Occupational Outlook Handbook. 1980-81 ed. Washington, DC: Bureau of 372
Labor Statistics. 376

Occupational Projections and Training Data. 1984 ed. Washington, DC: 398
Bureau of Labor Statistics. 404

232b-235b (continued)

Document 1, continued

During the days of the Holy Roman empire, an attempt was made to set up an arbitrary set of measures which would the be same throughout the empire. This standard disappeared after the fall of the empire, and it was not until the latter part of the Nineteenth Century that steps were once again taken--this time by a group of French scientists--to establish a system of standard international weights and measures. As a result of their efforts, an international treaty was signed in 1875 which provided for an international Bureau of Weights and Measures.

The metric sysem is now used by all the nations of the world with the exception of the United States and a few small natoins. In 1975, Congress voted for a gradual and voluntary changeover to the metric system. At that time, it was expected that the switch would be completed by 1985. Now, however, proponents of the metric system "do not expect metric to prevail (in the United States) before the year 2000."[3] Until that time, a truly international system of weights and measures will not be in use.

---

[3]"Getting the U.S. to Meausre Up," Time, May 9, 1983, p. 70.

Document 2
Leftbound Report with Endnotes

Mr. Marshall asks you to prepare the report at the right for Mrs. Emily M. Carpenter, who wants a letter-perfect copy of the report prepared in leftbound manuscript style DS with endnotes for references. The endnotes are listed at the end of the document. Be sure to place them on a separate sheet as directed in the "Standard Formats for Report Manuscripts," on page 396.

MEASURING EMPLOYEE PRODUCTIVITY

How much work should an ~~office~~ employee produce in a given period of time? How much should an employee be paid for the work he or she ~~does~~ produces? These questions were first asked when people gave up their self-sufficient status and began to work for others. Through the years, these questions have been examined, studied, and pondered by managers, engineers, psychologists, ploiticians, and philosophers. Thousands of years after they were first asked, the questions ~~has~~ have not yet been answered to the satisfaction of everyone.

The basic problem, of course, *stet* is one of measurement. How do you measure work ~~completed~~ produced? How do you measure the value of the effort employees contribute to the end product? Numerous plans have been developed over the years to solve these problems. Most of these plans use one or a combonation of two factors that can be measured easily: (1) the number of units an employee produces and (2) the amount of time an employee spends at work.

(continued on page 399)

57c ▶ 10
Check Formatting Skill: Outline

1 plain full sheet; correction supplies

Using the same top and side margins as for an unbound report, format and key the outline shown in rough draft at the right. Correct any errors you make as you key.

Computer printers often print copy with distinctive punctuation marks. Study the charts of computer punctuation marks below before you key the copy.

	typewriter	computer
ampersand	&	&
comma	,	،
parentheses	( )	{ }
question mark	?	?
quotation marks	"	"
semicolon	;	;

If time permits at the end of the class period, take another 3′ timed writing on the ¶s of 56b, p. 102; find *gwam*, circle errors.

COMPOSING
WRITING EFFECTIVE MESSAGES

I. PLAN THE MESSAGE

A. Determine the Main Purpose and Gist of the Message

B. Select All the Pertinent Ideas and Data to Be Used Presented

C. Keep the Reader (the Audience) in Mind as You Plan

II. ORGANIZE THE MESSAGE

A. Decide on the Order of Ideas and Data to Be Presented

1. List in logical order the major points to make

2. Jot down pertinent facts under each point

3. Develop each major idea into a paragraph

B. Give Present each Main Point Clearly and Precisely Concisely

1. Use simple language; avoid "jargon" words

2. Use short sentences for simplicity and clarity

3. Avoid long and involved paragraphs

III. REVISE, REFINE, AND PREPARE A AN ERROR-FREE COPY OF THE MESSAGE

ENRICHMENT ACTIVITY: Language Skills

Divide Words at Acceptable Points

full sheet; 70-space line; begin on line 10; DS

1. Clear all tab stops.
2. From left margin, set 3 new tab stops as indicated by the key beneath the copy.
3. Key the first word in Column 1; tab to Column 2 and rekey the word, showing by a hyphen where it may be acceptably divided.
4. Key the first word in Column 3; tab to Column 4 and rekey the word, showing by a hyphen where it may be acceptably divided.
5. Key all other words in the same manner.

ACCEPTABLE WORD DIVISION POINTS

specialist		wraparound	
technique		acceptable	
readily		condition	
computer		printout	
processor		automated	
electronic		delete	
insert		text-editor	
ergonomic		processing	
formatting	for-mat-ting	keyboarding	key-board-ing

KEY | 10 | 8 | 12 | 8 | 11 | 8 | 13 |

232a-235a ▶5
Check Equipment

65-space line

Before you begin work each day, check your machine to see that it is in good working order by keyboarding the paragraph at the right at least twice (first slowly, then faster).

all letters/figures used

David found that making beautiful topaz jewelry was quite an experience. He made 20 pins and 36 rings. He sold 8 pins at $39 each and 9 rings at $45 each -- a total of $717! Pamela and he may also make the big enamel emblem and bowls for the sorority girls.

| 1 | 2 | 3 | 4 | 5 | 6 | 7 | 8 | 9 | 10 | 11 | 12 | 13 |

232b-235b ▶ 45
Improve Report Manuscript Skills

Special Instructions:

When you prepare a report you will be expected to:

1. Follow the format requested.

2. Prepare a reference page for each report.

3. Correct any marked or unmarked errors made by the originator of the document (spelling, punctuation, and grammar).

4. Correct errors you make as you prepare a document in final form.

5. Proofread all documents and correct any errors you may have missed.

Special Note:

If the equipment you are using does not have the capability of printing superior (raised) figures, an alternative method is to enclose the figures in parentheses on the line of writing.

Document 1
Unbound Report with Footnotes

Mr. Marshall asks you to prepare the report at the right in unbound style DS with references shown as footnotes.

STANDARDS OF MEASUREMENT

What is the size of a a sheet of letter stationary? How much does this package wiegh? How much fluid will the liquid cipier hold? How much floorspace will this computer furniture ocupy? These are qxxk quite simple questions, but none of them could be answered without a standard system of weights and measures.

For many years, it has been redognized that a standard syustem of weights and measures is one of the cornerstones of civilization. "Weights and measures are fundamental necessities of commerce, industry, and science."[1] With out a standard system of measurement, we would not have progressed beyond the Stone age.

The key to weights and measures lies in the word "stanard." According to Webster's Ninth New Collegiate dictionary, a standard is "something set up and established by authority as a rule for the measure of quantity, weight, extent, value, or quality."[2] In other words, standards result in measurements that are acepted by all and that are all ways the same regardless of who does the mxxxxxxxxx measuring.

All standards of measurement are established arbitrarily. The foot was originally the length of some one's foot. In primitive tribes, it was the length of the ruler's foot, thus, the measuring instrument was called a "ruler." According to tradition, the yard was established by royal decree as the distance form the nose to the end of the thumb of Henry IV I of England. Shoe sizes were measured by "barleycorns," an archaic measure which is actually one third of an inch. A size 10 shoe, for example, is txxxx 3 barleycorns or an inch longer than a size 7.

---

[1]Lewis V. Judson, "Weights and Measures," Encyclopedia Americana (1979), Vol. 28, p. 579.

[2]Webster's Ninth New Collegiate Dictionary (Springfield, MA: Merriam-Webster, Inc., 1984), p. 1148.

(continued on page 398)

Unit 10 Lessons 58-64

Learning Goals

1. To learn to format and center 2- and 3-column tables.
2. To improve keyboarding skill on copy containing figures and symbols.
3. To learn to align figures at the right.
4. To improve keyboarding skill on straight copy.

Machine Adjustments

1. Paper guide at *0*.
2. Ribbon control set to use top half of ribbon.
3. Margin sets: 70-space line (center − 35; center + 35 + 5) unless otherwise directed.
4. Line-space selector to SS drills, DS ¶s; as directed for problems.

FORMATTING GUIDES: TABLES

Parts of a Simple Table

Table information is arranged in rows and columns for convenience of reader reference. Tables range in complexity from those with only two columns and a main heading to those of several columns with main, secondary, and column headings; totals; source notes; leaders; and rulings. The tables in this unit are limited to the following parts:

1. main heading (title) in ALL CAPS
2. secondary heading in capital and lowercase letters
3. blocked column headings
4. body (column entries)
5. source note

The first tables you will format consist of only a main heading and two columns of data. The tables progress gradually in complexity so that, finally, they will include three columns and all five of the listed parts.

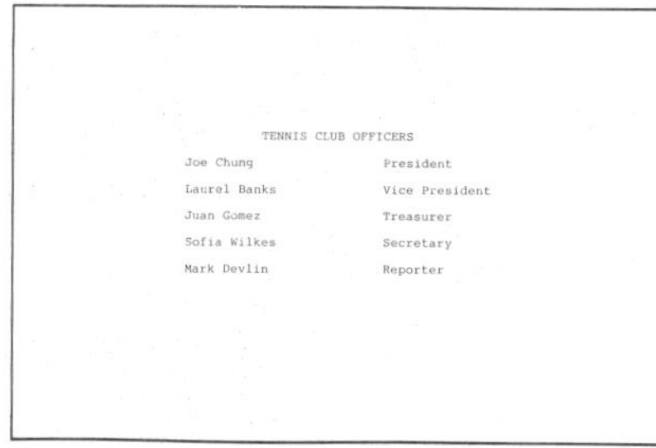

TENNIS CLUB OFFICERS

Joe Chung	President
Laurel Banks	Vice President
Juan Gomez	Treasurer
Sofia Wilkes	Secretary
Mark Devlin	Reporter

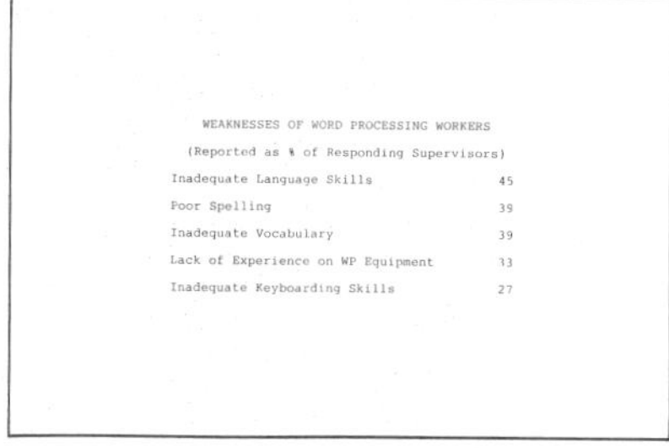

WEAKNESSES OF WORD PROCESSING WORKERS

(Reported as % of Responding Supervisors)

Inadequate Language Skills	45
Poor Spelling	39
Inadequate Vocabulary	39
Lack of Experience on WP Equipment	33
Inadequate Keyboarding Skills	27

Spacing Table Parts

Short, simple tables are usually double-spaced (DS) throughout. Double spacing between all parts of a table simplifies the processing of tables on typewriters and, especially, on microcomputers which require the use of special commands to change the spacing within a document.

Horizontal/Vertical Placement of Tables

Tables are placed on the page so that the left and right margins are approximately equal (about half the characters in each line at the left of horizontal center; about half, at the right).

When prepared on separate sheets, tables are placed so that the top and bottom margins are approximately equal (about half the lines above center; about half below). Tables that are placed slightly above exact center (sometimes called "reading position") are considered to look more appealing than those placed at or below exact center.

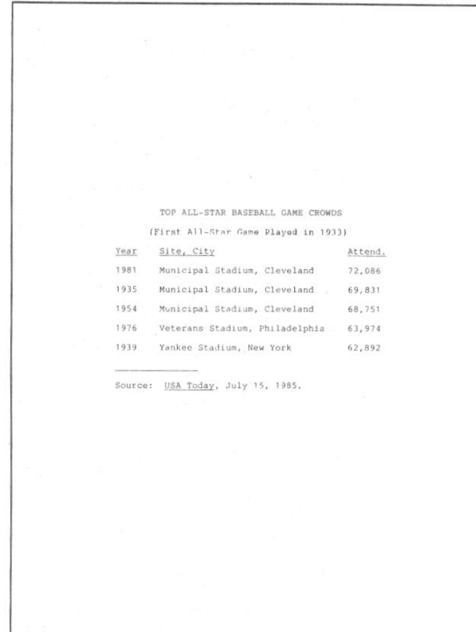

TOP ALL-STAR BASEBALL GAME CROWDS

(First All-Star Game Played in 1933)

Year	Site, City	Attend.
1981	Municipal Stadium, Cleveland	72,086
1935	Municipal Stadium, Cleveland	69,831
1954	Municipal Stadium, Cleveland	68,751
1976	Veterans Stadium, Philadelphia	63,974
1939	Yankee Stadium, New York	62,892

Source: USA Today, July 15, 1985.

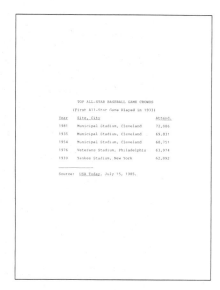

Unit 50 Lessons 232-235

Learning Goals

1. To review basic formats for report manuscripts.
2. To improve your ability to plan, organize, and produce business reports quickly and correctly.

Formats Reviewed

1. Unbound Manuscript
2. Leftbound Manuscript
3. Topbound Manuscript
4. Documentation Systems

OFFICE OPPORTUNITIES UNLIMITED

Mr. Dale Marshall, Document Production Manager, asks you to review the formats for report manuscripts in the OOU training manual.

Training Manual Excerpts: Standard Formats for Report Manuscripts

There are many different formats for manuscripts depending upon the type and purpose of the report. Three standard formats -- unbound, leftbound, and topbound -- are in frequent use in business and education. These formats are included in the following guides. Consult them whenever you have a question.

Unbound margins

Left margin .... 1″
Right margin .... 1″
Top margin, page 1, 10-pitch, main heading .... line 10
Top margin, page 1, 12-pitch, main heading .... line 12
Bottom margin (minimum) .... 1″

Pagination: number second and succeeding pages on line 6, 1″ from right edge; begin body on line 8.

Leftbound margins

Same as unbound report, except that left margin is 1½″.

Topbound margins

Same as unbound report, except:

Top margin, page 1, 10-pitch, main heading .... line 12
Top margin, page 1, 12-pitch, main heading .... line 14
Top margin, succeeding pages .... line 10

Pagination: center page numbers of the second and succeeding pages .... line 62

Headings

Main heading: Center in all caps over the line of writing; quadruple-space (two double spaces) below it unless followed by a secondary heading.

Secondary heading: Center over line of writing; DS below main heading, with the first letter of major words capitalized; quadruple-space before beginning body.

Side headings: Place even with left margin; underline with the first letter of major words capitalized. DS above and below heading.

Paragraph headings: Indent and underline with first word capitalized and a period at the end.

Body

Begin a quadruple-space below main or secondary headings. Indent paragraphs 5 spaces; SS or DS as directed. SS quoted material of 4 or more lines *within* the body; indent 5 spaces from side margins.

Documentation

Footnotes: Identify references within the body by a superior figure and repeat it at the bottom of the page followed by the footnote. Place a 1½″ divider line a DS beneath the last line of the body and a DS above the first footnote. SS each footnote; DS between them.

Endnotes: Use superior figures to identify material cited. On a separate sheet, center ENDNOTES on line 10 (10-pitch) or line 12 (12-pitch). List each reference in footnote form beginning on the fourth line below the title.

Textual citations: Place the last name of the author, date of publication, and page number in parentheses. Example: (Pasewark, 1985, 64-66). If the reference is identified by name or author within the text, give the date of the publication and the page number following the reference. Example: (1977, 153). List all references alphabetically on the reference page.

Reference page: Center the title REFERENCES or BIBLIOGRAPHY (if footnotes are used) over the line of writing on line 10 (10-pitch) or line 12 (12-pitch). Begin the first reference on the fourth line below the title. Begin each reference at the left margin; indent second and succeeding lines 5 spaces. SS each reference; DS between them.

Lesson 58 Simple Two-Column Tables

58a ▶ 7 Conditioning Practice

each line twice SS (slowly, then faster); if time permits, rekey lines 2 and 4

alphabet 1 Mack just questioned the five zoologists about the extra fawn display.

figures 2 We have stores at 396 Hogan Lane, 802 Petri Court, and 4175 Taft Road.

fig/sym 3 There was a credit on 8/19 for $487.23 and a debit on 9/5 for $360.82.

speed 4 Audit the work forms and then pay the six girls for the work they did.

| 1 | 2 | 3 | 4 | 5 | 6 | 7 | 8 | 9 | 10 | 11 | 12 | 13 | 14 |

58b ▶ 8 Review/Improve Use of Backspacer and Tabulator

1. On a plain sheet, center each of lines 1-3 horizontally.

2. For lines 4-6, beginning at the left margin set 3 tab stops according to the key beneath the lines. Key the lines, tabbing from column to column.

Backspacer

1 Find center point of paper;

2 backspace once for each two strokes in line;

3 begin keyboarding where backspacing ends.

Tabulator

4	to do so	Tab	work with us	Tab	all the firms	Tab	make them pay
5	to go to		she may sign		sign the form		kept the form
6	if he is		go with them		they work for		they may lend
KEY	8	8	12	8	13	8	13

58c ▶ 35 Learn to Format a Simple Two-Column Table

half sheet (long edge at top)
horizontal center points:
elite, 51; pica, 42

1. Study the guides for vertical and horizontal centering given at the right.

2. Using the model table on page 107, set left margin to begin Column 1; set a tab stop for Column 2, leaving 14 spaces between columns.

3. Determine the line on which to place the heading of the double-spaced table. If an odd number results, use next lower even number to raise the table to visual center.

4. Format and key the model table.

5. Proofread and check your completed table, mark it for correction, and prepare a final copy with all errors corrected.

Vertical Centering Steps

1. Count the lines to be keyed and the blank line spaces to be left between them (1 blank line space between double-spaced lines).

2. Subtract *lines needed* from *total lines available* (33 on a half sheet; 66 on a full sheet).

3. Divide remainder by 2 to determine top margin. If the number that results ends in a fraction, drop the fraction. *If an odd number results, use the next lower even number.*

4. From top edge of paper, space down once for each line determined in Step 3 and key the main heading.

Example: lines available = 33
total lines needed = 12
21 ÷ 2 = 10½
place heading on line 10

Horizontal Centering of Columns

1. Move margin stops to ends of scale.

2. Clear all tabulator stops.

3. Move printing point to horizontal center point of paper.

4. Decide spacing between columns (if spacing is not specified) -- preferably an even number of spaces (4, 6, 8, 10, 12, 14, etc.).

5. Set left margin stop:

a. From center of paper, backspace once for each 2 characters and spaces in longest line of each column, then once for each 2 spaces to be left between columns. If the longest line in one column has an extra letter or number, combine that letter or number with the first letter or number in the next column when backspacing by 2s, as in **check####proofread.**

◀ 1 1 1 1 1 1 1 1 1
ch|ec|kp|ro|of|re|ad|##|##

If you have 1 stroke left over after backspacing for all columnar items, disregard it.

b. Set the left margin at the point where all backspacing ends.

6. Set tabulator stops:

a. From the left margin, space forward once for each character and space in longest line in the first column and once for each space to be left between first and second columns.

b. Set tab stop at this point for second column.

c. When there is a third column, continue spacing forward in the same way to set a tab stop for it.

Lesson 231

231a ▶ 5
Check Equipment

Before you begin the drills which follow, check your machine to see that it is in good working order by keyboarding the paragraph at the right at least twice (first slowly, then faster).

all letters/figures used

The objective of the odd exercise was to analyze quickly the small graph. Only 2.5″ × 3″, the graph showed 1,798 bits of data (40.6% more than previous displays). With this aid, the panel of eight might fix the problem of the chaotic signal light downtown.

| 1 | 2 | 3 | 4 | 5 | 6 | 7 | 8 | 9 | 10 | 11 | 12 | 13 |

231b ▶ 18
Improve Language Skills: Proofread/Correct

1. In each sentence at the right, items have been underlined. The underlines indicate that there **may** be an error in spelling, punctuation, capitalization, grammar, or in the use of words or figures.

2. Study each sentence carefully. Keyboard the line number. If an underlined item is incorrect, correct it as you keyboard the sentence. In addition, correct any typographical errors you may make.

1. He will make his forth attempt to lesson the tension in the shop.
2. While living in the west I wrote the book: "Where To Go On Vacation."
3. Under the terms of the sail, she is libel to pay for the buildig.
4. You will find model 462 on Line 12, Page 38, of catalog 571.
5. Did his atorney counsel him to co-operate with the group?
6. We shipped 10 one hundred pound crates to 1025 1st avenue.
7. The office personel will take a thorough inventory of the equipment.
8. At three o'clock on the third of July, we leave for the Texas rodeo.
9. She mentioned the success of the companies activitys over seas.
10. My boss's question was: "when was the board of directors' meeting"?
11. Do you think he will chose our products rather then the foriegn ones?
12. Last weeks' conferance, which included all top executives, was long.

231c ▶ 12
Improve Keystroking Skills

65-space line

each sentence twice: once for speed, then slower for accuracy

direct reaches 1 I doubt that my breif ^annual speech will ~~e~~ffect (a) ^my ~~the~~ large company.

double letters 2 The inn keeper says she ^will ~~may~~ add a pool and ^better accommodations ~~up-to-date lodgings~~.

adjacent keys 3 The treasurer's ^report ~~plan~~ proposed ^action to buy ^us safer equipment ~~for us~~.

one hand 4 As ^Yuki feared ~~Uri said~~, minimum union ~~oil~~ wages ^in oil were ~~e~~ffected (a) ^in ~~last~~ July.

balanced hand 5 Thier neighbor ^may lend ~~will loan~~ them an ^ancient map ~~old atlas~~ of the ^land downtown.

231d ▶ 15
Improve Basic Keyboarding Skills

1. Take two 1′ writings on each ¶ of 230d, p. 394.

2. Take one 5′ writing on the three ¶s combined.

Goal: Improved speed and accuracy.

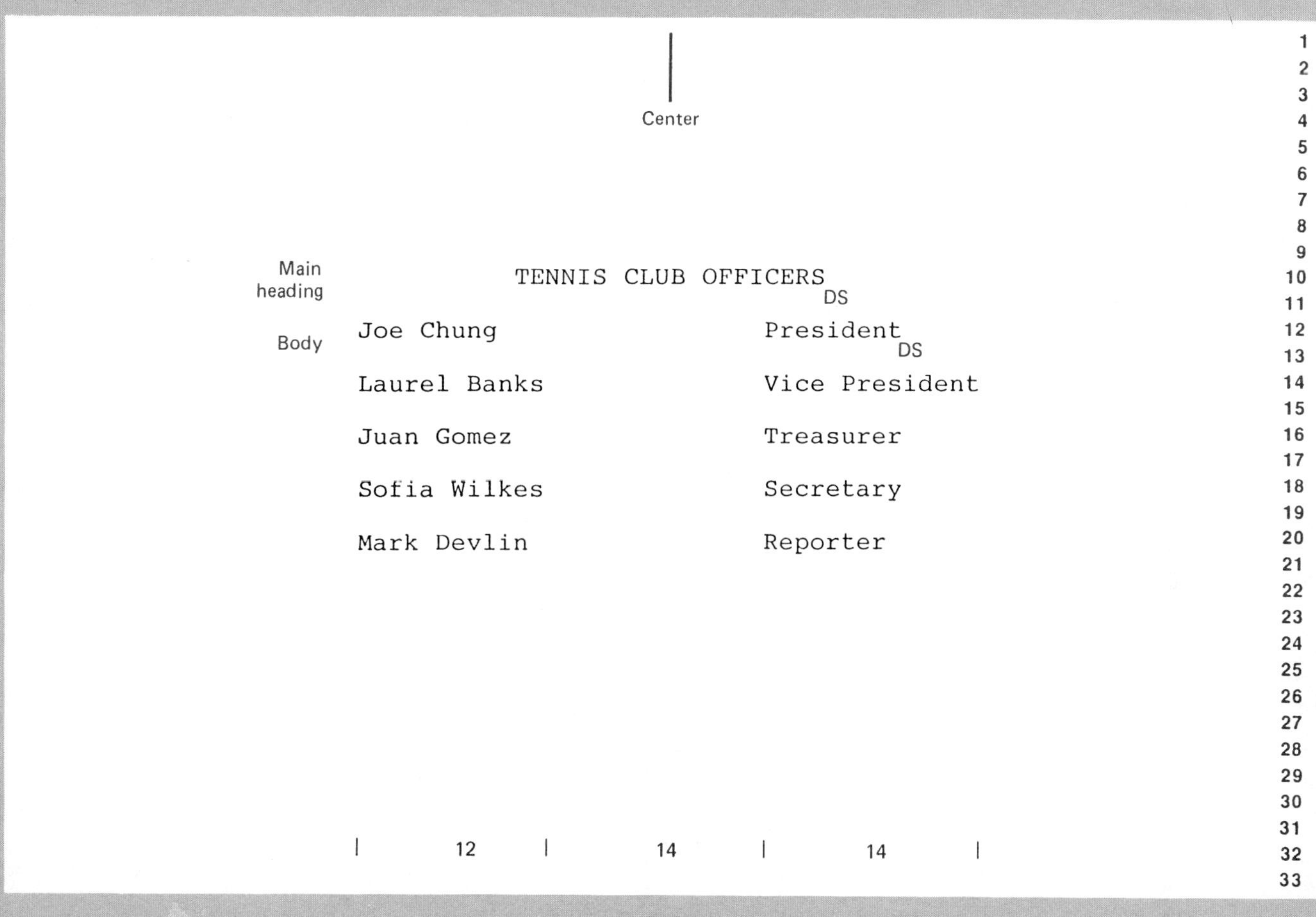

TENNIS CLUB OFFICERS

Joe Chung	President
Laurel Banks	Vice President
Juan Gomez	Treasurer
Sofia Wilkes	Secretary
Mark Devlin	Reporter

Two-Column Table Centered Vertically and Horizontally

Lesson 59 Simple Two-Column Tables

59a ▶ 7 Conditioning Practice

each line twice SS (slowly, then faster); if time permits, rekey lines 2 and 4

alphabet	1	Ray expected a quick quiz on the five women's boring journal articles.
figures	2	On April 6 you ordered 5 TABCO filing cabinets: 2 HC-7850; 3 VC-9146.
s/es/ies	3	age ages win wins run runs go goes reach reaches cry cries rely relies
speed	4	The duty of the auditor is to sign the usual audit forms for the city.

| 1 | 2 | 3 | 4 | 5 | 6 | 7 | 8 | 9 | 10 | 11 | 12 | 13 | 14 |

59b ▶ 8 Review Procedures for Vertical/Horizontal Centering

half sheet; DS

Using the model table above, see how quickly you can make needed machine adjustments and key the copy.

1. Review formatting guides on page 106 if necessary.

2. Double-space all lines.

3. Leave 12 spaces between columns.

4. Check your work for proper placement. Did you place the main heading on line 10? Are left and right margins approximately equal?

230c ▶ 18 Improve Language Skills: Proofread/Correct

1. In each sentence at the right, items have been underlined. The underlines indicate that there **may** be an error in spelling, punctuation, capitalization, grammar, or in the use of words or figures.

2. Study each sentence carefully. Keyboard the line number. If an underlined item is incorrect, correct it as you keyboard the sentence. In addition, correct any typographical errors you may make.

1. The bank will credit thier account with the principle of the note.
2. The Company President and the treasurer, signs all checks.
3. The lawyer didnt advice them to pay the capitol of the loan.
4. She bought, Canadian Bacon, Italian bread, and French wine.
5. Will the inclement weather effect the spirit and moral of the troupe?
6. The School is on the avenue of the Americas, in New York city.
7. My two assistance tells me the merchandice is already to be shipped.
8. The Sand's boutique ordered 12 gross of mens' shirts, model 3204.
9. It is definetely time to order more stationary for the office.
10. About 1/3 of the group voted "yes" on proposition 16.
11. They beleive that the second Model is the better of the too.
12. Each of us are going to the theater on Arch street.

230d ▶ 15 Improve Basic Keyboarding Skills

Take two 5′ writings on the ¶s shown at the right. Record *gwam* and errors.

all letters used | A | 1.5 si | 5.7 awl | 80% hfw

gwam 1′ | 5′

As a result of technological advances in equipment and methods, 13 3
many changes are being made in the modern office. The use of the com- 27 5
puter continues to grow by leaps and bounds because of its ability to 41 8
process figures with amazing speed and accuracy. In a matter of sec- 55 11
onds or minutes the computer can process numerical data which, in the 69 14
past, took hours or days. These data, in turn, help people to make 82 16
judgments or decisions which a computer is unable to do. 93 19

New equipment is now available that will improve the processing of 13 21
words. Included are machines which permit a person to make changes at 28 24
the keyboard. Errors can be corrected merely by backspacing and enter- 42 27
ing the correct information. As it is entered, the material is recorded 56 30
in memory. After the text has been entered and edited, the operator can 70 33
put a sheet of paper in the machine or printer, press a key, and the copy 84 35
will be printed at a high rate of speed. 94 37

Most of the new equipment for processing figures and words have one 14 40
thing in common -- they are operated through the use of a typewriter key- 28 43
board. Although these keyboards may not be identical, the location of 42 46
the letter keys is almost always the same. As a result, an operator can 57 49
learn to run one of the new machines with little or no difficulty. For 71 52
the speedy and accurate operator, these machines open new horizons. 85 55

gwam 1′ | 1 | 2 | 3 | 4 | 5 | 6 | 7 | 8 | 9 | 10 | 11 | 12 | 13 | 14
gwam 5′ | 1 | 2 | 3

59c ▶ 35 Format Two-Column Tables with Main Headings

3 half sheets (long edge at top)

Problem 1

Center table vertically DS; center table horizontally leaving 12 spaces between columns.

MEN'S TEAM CAPTAINS		words
		4
Baseball	Ken Morrison	8
Basketball	Cy Briggs	13
Football	Joe Hererra	17
Gymnastics	Kevin Kwan	21
Soccer	Bo Simpson	25
Volleyball	Greg Diablo	29

Problem 2

Center table according to Problem 1 directions, but leave 10 spaces between columns.

Problem 3

Proofread Problem 2, mark it for correction, and prepare a final copy with all errors corrected.

WOMEN'S TEAM CAPTAINS		4
Basketball	Diana Lindsay	9
Gymnastics	Lili Wong	14
Soccer	Aida Lopez	17
Softball	Fran Hildebrand	22
Volleyball	Glenda Washington	28

Lesson 60 Simple Two-Column Tables

60a ▶ 7 Conditioning Practice

each line twice SS (slowly, then faster); if time permits, two 1′ writings on line 4

alphabet 1 Jack pleased the mayor by awarding the prized onyx plaque for service.

figures 2 The shop is 278.4 meters long, 90.6 meters wide, and 13.5 meters high.

fig/sym 3 Both start today (2/14): Sam Hahn at $98.75/wk.; Tia Dun at $3.60/hr.

speed 4 Both of them may also wish to make a formal bid for the big auto firm.

| 1 | 2 | 3 | 4 | 5 | 6 | 7 | 8 | 9 | 10 | 11 | 12 | 13 | 14 |

60b ▶ 13 Learn to Align Figures

key twice DS; center horizontally according to KEY, 12 spaces between columns

To align whole numbers at right: Set a tab stop for the digit in each column (after Column 1) that requires the least forward and backward spacing. To align the figures, space forward ▶ or backward ◀ as necessary.

margin ↓		tab ↓		tab ↓		tab ↓
294		1827		10		2619
▶36		▶750		◀305		▶475
110		3046		61		1950
KEY 3	12	4	12	3	12	4

SOUTH-WESTERN
PUBLISHING CO.

Unit 49 Lessons 230-231

Learning Goals

1. To improve basic keyboarding techniques.
2. To increase keystroking speed and to improve accuracy on straight copy.
3. To improve language skills.

Machine Adjustments

1. 65-space line for Check Equipment exercises.
2. 75-space line for Language Skills.
3. 70-space line for drills and paragraphs.
4. SS sentence drills with a DS between groups; DS paragraph writings; DS Language Skills sentences.

Lesson 230

230a ▶ 5 Check Equipment

Before you begin the drills which follow, check your machine to see that it is in good working order by keyboarding the paragraph at the right at least twice (first slowly, then faster).

all letters/figures used

Juan Vasquez worked very hard to pass the big exam with flying colors. (In earlier tests, he received scores of 83.5%, 92%, 71%, 65%, 84%, and 90% -- an average of 80.9%). If he did eight of the theory problems and the theme with proficiency, he may do so.

| 1 | 2 | 3 | 4 | 5 | 6 | 7 | 8 | 9 | 10 | 11 | 12 | 13 |

230b ▶ 12 Skill-Comparison Keyboarding

1. Take three 1′ writings on ¶ 1. Note highest *gwam*.
2. Take three 1′ writings on ¶ 2. Note highest *gwam*.
3. Take three 1′ writings on slower ¶ to increase speed.

all letters used ¶ 1 | E | 1.2 si | 5.1 awl | 90% hfw | ¶ 2 | D | 1.8 si | 6.3 awl | 70% hfw |

Do you ever think about how much we depend on words? When we are young, we learn to speak quite early. As we grow older, we learn to read and express our ideas in writing. Rarely, though, do many of us consider that words are vital tools. Without words, our ideas would be of little value and we would make little or no progress in life.

Businesses place a premium on employees who can utilize language skillfully. Individuals who are adept in keyboarding skills can obtain excellent jobs, but employees who have also developed an ability to express ideas vividly and concisely advance more rapidly. If you excel in language skills, you will be rewarded in terms of a better job.

60c ▶ 30 Learn to Format Two-Column Tables with Secondary Headings

3 half sheets
(long edge at top)

Problem 1

Center the table vertically DS and horizontally with 8 spaces between columns. DS all headings and entries.

		words
WEAKNESSES OF WORD PROCESSING WORKERS		8
(Reported as % of Responding Supervisors)		16
Inadequate Language Skills	45	22
Poor Spelling	39	25
Inadequate Vocabulary	39	30
Lack of Experience on WP Equipment	33	38
Inadequate Keyboarding Skills	27	44

Problem 2

Center the table as in Problem 1, but leave 10 spaces between columns. Align figures at decimal.

Problem 3

Proofread Problem 2, mark it for correction, and prepare a final copy with all errors corrected.

WHERE ACCIDENTS HAPPEN		5
(Percent at Each Location)		10
At home	38.7	13
At industrial sites	13.0	18
On roads	10.8	20
At recreational sites	8.9	26
In schools	8.9	29
On farms	1.4	31
Other locations	18.3	35

Lesson 61 Three-Column Tables

61a ▶ 7 Conditioning Practice

each line twice SS (slowly, then faster); if time permits, rekey lines 2 and 4

alphabet 1 Luci Kwan said the boutique might have jade, onyx, and topaz for sale.

figures 2 The 405 members voted 267 to 138 to delay the tax increase until 1992.

d/ed/ied 3 tie tied list listed walk walked check checked dry dried reply replied

speed 4 The city auditor is due by eight and she may lend a hand to the panel.

| 1 | 2 | 3 | 4 | 5 | 6 | 7 | 8 | 9 | 10 | 11 | 12 | 13 | 14 |

61b ▶ 8 Build Skill in Formatting and Keying Table Headings

Using the copy of Problem 1 above, see how quickly you can make machine adjustments and key the headings and the first 2 or 3 entries.

1. Review centering guides on page 106 if necessary.

2. Double-space all lines.

3. Leave 8 spaces between columns.

4. Check your work for proper placement. Did you place the main heading on line 10? Are left and right margins about equal?

226b-229b (continued)

Document 8

Interoffice Memorandum Form
(LM p. 29)

Prepare the memorandum written by Christine L. May, President, and send it to all members of the faculty. Center and list committee members at the end of ¶ 2; center and list courses at the end of ¶ 3.

According to the National Survey ~~conducted~~ completed by our Research Staff last month, the use of electronic ~~machines~~ equipment is growing rapidly in the business office. ~~The~~ Shipments of electronic typewriters ~~annually~~ each year have now ~~reached~~ topped the ~~two~~ 2 million mark and the number of micro computers installed annualy has ~~gone~~ grown to more than 30 million. During the past ~~five~~ 5 years, american bsinesses have spent ~~almost~~ about 1 trillion dollars on informatoin processing, which includes word processing, data processing, and electronic comunications (both voice and written).

This ~~growing~~ increasing use of electronic ~~machines~~ equipment in ~~our~~ the business office ~~means~~ indicates that we must ~~study~~ continually monitor our courses of instruction to ensure that we are ~~providing~~ giving our students ~~with~~ the best training possible. To attain this ~~aim~~ objective, I am appointing a standing curriculum committee to study the purpose and contnet of our entire curriculum. This committtee will ~~be made up~~ consist of the following people: Ruth T. Shih, Chairperson; William L. Parks, Mary T. Imburgio, Mark K. Foster, and Helen W. Mason.

The curriculum commitee will ~~study~~ review our over all curriculum and all courses of instruction during the next 6 months. ~~At first~~ Initially, the following courses should be ~~previewed~~ studied on a priority basis: Keyboarding 1, Keyboading, 2, Introduction to Information Processing, Advanced Information Processing, and Micro computer Applications.

All members of the faculty are ~~asked~~ requested to cooperate with the committee in ~~their~~ its efforts to ~~analyze~~ study and improve our curriculum. At ~~six~~ 6-week intervals, the committee will submit to me reports of the progress it si making.

61c ▶ 35 Learn to Format Three-Column Tables

3 half sheets
(long edge at top)

Problem 1
Table with Blocked Column Headings

Center vertically DS and horizontally with 6 spaces between columns. Block the column headings at left edge of columns; DS above and below them.

			words
TICKET SALE WINNERS			4
Event	Winner	No.	10
Winter Wonderland	Janelle Lindstrom	408	18
Octoberfest	Sally Williams	372	24
Holiday Sounds	Michel Durate	250	31
Football Festival	Helmud Franks	169	38

Problem 2
Table with Main, Secondary, and Column Headings

Center vertically DS and horizontally with 8 spaces between columns. DS all headings and entries.

Problem 3

Reformat Problem 1 with 8 spaces between columns. Correct all errors you make as you key.

			words
JANUARY SALES REPORT			4
(In Thousands of $)			8
Salesperson	Goal	Final	17
Amorini, Joseph	23.5	23.75	22
Cartwright, Susan	28.0	28.50	28
Ellington, Maxine	30.2	30.10	34
Hernandez, Eduardo	26.7	26.80	40
Jackson, Della	29.5	30.20	45
McKay, Eldon	31.9	32.00	50
Wang, Howard	34.6	33.90	54

Lesson 62 Tables on Full Sheets

62a ▶ 7 Conditioning Practice

each line twice SS (slowly, then faster); if time permits, two 1′ writings on line 4

alphabet 1 Barth was given a big prize for completing six quick high jumps today.
figures 2 Ozark has a flight at 8:26; Delta, at 9:37; and Continental, at 10:54.
fig/sym 3 Strikes in 1986 delayed delivery of 524,350# (or 7% of all shipments).
speed 4 The firm may wish to bid by proxy for title to the lake and the docks.

| 1 | 2 | 3 | 4 | 5 | 6 | 7 | 8 | 9 | 10 | 11 | 12 | 13 | 14 |

62b ▶ 8 Build Skill in Formatting and Keying Table Headings

Using the copy of Problem 2 above, see how quickly you can make machine adjustments and key the headings and the first 2 or 3 entries.

1. Review centering guides on page 106 if necessary.
2. Double-space all lines.
3. Leave 8 spaces between columns.
4. Check your work for proper placement and spacing. Did you place the main heading on line 6? Are left and right margins about equal?

226b-229b (continued)

Document 6

(LM p. 25)

Modified Block Style, Indented ¶s, Mixed Punctuation

Prepare the letter at the right and direct it to the attention of the Marketing Division of the **McDade Publishing Company, 2054 Broadway, New York, NY 10023-4217**. Date the letter July 17, 19--. The letter will be signed by T. Frank Mills, Student Store Manager. Make one carbon copy for Emily M. Carpenter.

On June 25, by our Purchase Order No. ~~#~~ 25670, we ordered 250 copies of Professional Keyboarding, Third Edition (Stock No. P90) and 250 copies of the ~~S~~tudent workbook (Stock No. 90A) to accompany the te~~s~~xt.

Yesterday, ~~W~~we recieved a shipment from you that included ~~contained~~ the 250 copies of Professional Keyboarding, Third Edition. ~~The~~ The student workbooks you shipped, ~~sent~~ however, are for the Second ~~previous~~ edition of the book.

Will you please send us 250 copies of the correct ~~right~~ edition of the ~~W~~orkbook by the fastest means ~~way~~ possible. We shall keep the workbooks you shipped until we recieve disposition instructions ~~word~~ from you.

If you cannot ship the correct workbooks within two weeks, will you please call my office so that we can decide what course of action to take.

Document 7

Interoffice Memorandum Form

(LM p. 27)

Prepare the memorandum to Emily M. Carpenter, Director of Instruction, from T. Frank Mills, Student Store Manager. Date the memo August 1, 19--.

As you requested in your Purchase Requisition No. ~~order #~~117, we ordered from ~~the~~ McDade Publishing Co. (sp.), 250 copies of Professional Keyboarding, third edition, and 250 copies of the ~~S~~tudent workbook~~s~~ which acompanies the text ~~book~~.

On July 1~~7~~6, we recieved a ship ment from the publisher ~~company~~ that included ~~contained~~ the 250 copies of the third edition of the text book and 250 copies of the work book~~s~~ for the second edition. We immediately wrote to McDade ~~the comapny~~ and asked them ~~requested it~~ to ship the correct work books by the fastest means possible. ~~in two weeks.~~

The publisher ~~company~~ has notified my office that the workbooks are not yet ready for distribution and will not be available until Sept. (sp.) 10. Under these circumstances ~~conditions~~, will you please let me know what action ~~steps~~ you wish ~~want~~ me to take.

62c ▶ 35 Format Tables on Full Sheets

full sheets; DS

Problem 1
Two-Column Table with Source Note

Center vertically and horizontally, leaving 12 spaces between columns. DS above and below the 1½-inch rule (15 underline spaces, pica; 18 underline spaces, elite).

Note: Do not count $ as part of a column.

		words
head in ALL CAPS–Annual Cost of Eating Out DS		5
(Per Person by Region) Tab ↓		10
Pacfiic	$673	13
New England	659	16
Mountain	563	18
Mid Atlantic	501	22
South	478	24
East north Central	473	28
West North Central	441	33
DS ______________		36
Source: The Food Institute.		42

Problem 2
Three-Column Table with Blocked Column Headings

Center vertically and horizontally, leaving 4 spaces between columns. DS above and below column headings; begin column headings at left edge of columns.

Problem 3

Reformat Problem 2. Add as a secondary heading: (First All-Star Game Played in 1933).

TOP ALL-STAR BASEBALL GAME CROWDS 7

Year	Site, City	Attend.	
			16
1981	Municipal Stadium, Cleveland	72,086	24
1935	Municipal Stadium, Cleveland	69,831	32
1954	Municipal Stadium, Cleveland	68,751	40
1976	Veterans Stadium, Philadelphia	63,974	49
1939	Yankee Stadium, New York	62,892	56

______________ 60

Source: USA Today, July 15, 1985. 69

Lesson 63 Prepare for Measurement

63a ▶ 7 Conditioning Practice

each line twice SS (slowly, then faster); if time permits, rekey lines 2 and 4

alphabet 1 Marvin, the tax clerk, was puzzled by the quaint antics of the judges.
figures 2 I ordered 36 desks, 49 chairs, 15 tables, 80 lamps, and 72 file trays.
ing 3 be being row rowing hum humming read reading pave paving carve carving
speed 4 The panel may then work with the problems of the eight downtown firms.

| 1 | 2 | 3 | 4 | 5 | 6 | 7 | 8 | 9 | 10 | 11 | 12 | 13 | 14 |

63b ▶ 43 Prepare for Measurement

3 half sheets; 1 full sheet

Make a list of the problems and page numbers given below:
page 108, 59c, Problem 1
page 109, 60c, Problem 1
page 110, 61c, Problem 2
page 111, 62c, Problem 1

To prepare for measurement in Lesson 64, format and key each of the tables according to the directions given with the problems.

Refer to the centering guides on page 106 as needed. Correct any errors you make as you key the tables.

226b-229b (continued)

Document 4

(LM p. 21)

Modified Block Style, Open Punctuation

At the right is a copy of a form letter used by OOU to get contracts signed and to bill students for courses of instruction. Send a copy of the letter by CERTIFIED MAIL to each of the people listed below. Insert the pertinent information for each person in the spaces indicated. The letter will be signed by Ralph T. Zimmerman, Director of Finance.

Miss Marie D. Alverez
29588 Market Street
Darby, PA 19023-4832

Contract No. 14016
$380
Student No. 88-190-23

Ms. Myrtle H. Washington
902 Haddon Avenue
Camden, NJ 08108-7132

Contract No. 14017
$220
Student No. 88-08-108

Mr. Sydney A. Green
1421 Arch Street
Philadelphia, PA 19102-6124

Contract No. 14018
$460
Student No. 88-19-102

Enclosed is Contract No. ______, in duplicate, for your individualized course of instruction which was designed to refresh and improve your secretarial skills. Will you please sign both copies in the space indicated and return one copy to us as soon as possible.

With the contract, please include a check or money order for $______. This represents the tuition for the first half of your course. The second payment will be due at the midpoint of your course. You will receive a reminder about one week before that payment is due.

Your student number is ______. Please be sure to place this number on your checks and also on any correspondence you may write to us. This will ensure that your payments and correspondence will be properly recorded and acknowledged.

On behalf of our staff and faculty, I would like to welcome you to OFFICE OPPORTUNITIES UNLIMITED. I am sure you will find the time you spend with us both pleasant and profitable.

Document 5

(LM p. 23)

Modified Block Style, Mixed Punctuation

Prepare the letter at the right to **Mr. Akeo Yoshino, 12040 Roosevelt Boulevard, Philadelphia, PA 19116-4537**. Mrs. Emily M. Carpenter, Director of Instruction, will sign the letter.

Your *special* ~~individualized~~ course of instructoin in office operations will *start* ~~commence~~ on Monday of next week. Enclosed is your schedule for the ~~next~~ week. Please *note* ~~be aware~~ that there will be an orientation meeting beginning at 9:00 a. m. on Monday in Room 302. ~~It is very important that you~~ *Please* be prompt. ~~for this meeting.~~

Also enclosed is a ~~sheet~~ list~~ing~~ *of* the supplies that you will need during your ~~entire~~ course of instruction. You can *buy* ~~obtain~~ these supplies from our *Student Store* ~~Supply Shop~~ on the third floor, next to the Snack Bar, or from your local stationary store. Be *sure* ~~certain~~ you get the supplies in the quantit*ies*, quality, and sizes *indicated.* ~~that we have specified on the sheet.~~

All ~~of the~~ members of our staff and faculty ~~are~~ look~~ing~~ forward to preparing you for *a rewarding career* ~~an excellent job~~ in the ~~modern~~ office of today *and* ~~as well as in~~ the of*f*ice of the future.

Lesson 64 Measurement and Evaluation

64a ▶ 7 Conditioning Practice

each line twice SS (slowly, then faster); if time permits, two 1′ writings on line 4

alphabet 1 Suzi can equal a track record by jumping twelve feet at the next meet.

figures 2 Their team took some close games: 97 to 96, 84 to 83, and 105 to 102.

fig/sym 3 My statement read: "Payment #36 will be $590.78 plus 12.4% interest."

speed 4 The eighty girls did rush down the field with usual and visible vigor.

| 1 | 2 | 3 | 4 | 5 | 6 | 7 | 8 | 9 | 10 | 11 | 12 | 13 | 14 |

64b ▶ 8 Check Keyboarding Skill: Straight Copy

1. A 1′ writing on each ¶; find *gwam*; circle errors.

2. A 3′ writing on the 2 ¶s combined; find *gwam*; circle errors.

3. If time permits, take an additional 1′ writing on each ¶ to build skill.

all letters used | A | 1.5 si | 5.7 awl | 80% hfw |

	gwam 3′	5′
If success is vital to you, you have a distinct advantage over many	5	3
people who have no particular feeling one way or the other. The desire	9	6
to succeed is helpful, for it causes us to establish goals without which	14	9
our actions have little or no meaning. Success may not necessarily mean	19	11
winning the big prize, but it does mean approaching a goal.	23	14
It is foolish, of course, to believe that we can all be whatever	27	16
we wish to become. It is just as foolish, though, to wait around hop-	32	19
ing for success to overtake us. We should analyze our aspirations, our	37	22
abilities, and our limitations. We can next decide from various choices	42	25
what we are best equipped with effort to become.	45	27

gwam 3′ | 1 | 2 | 3 | 4 | 5 |
5′ | 1 | 2 | 3 |

64c ▶ 35 Check Formatting Skill: Tables

2 half sheets; 1 full sheet; DS all lines; format the table at the right and those on page 113; correct errors

Problem 1
Table with Main and Secondary Headings

half sheet; 8 spaces between columns

		words
DEFICIENCIES OF HIGH SCHOOL GRADUATES		8
(Reported as a % of Responding Companies)		16
Do not find and correct errors	77.3	23
Lack of pride in work done	47.7	30
Lack of telephone courtesy	46.6	36
Lack of initiative, drive, and ambition	45.1	45
Lack of respect for work	39.4	51
Poor personal appearance, grooming	28.0	59
Do not accept responsibility	25.0	66

226b-229b (continued)

Document 2

(LM p. 17)

Block Style, Open Punctuation

Prepare the letter to **Miss Tara C. O'Connor, 316 Furness Lane, Ardmore, PA 19003-2711**. Ms. Anne M. Colby, Director of Admissions, will sign the letter.

"What skills msut I have to get an office job today?" This question which you raised in your recent letter is one we here often. Though hiring practices differ from office to office, and their are no standards. Based on our years of experience and up-to-date research, however, we can give your a good idea of the skills you need.

The ability to key board with accuracy is a most imprtant skill. Most comapnies demand a minimum of 50 words a minute. Langauge skills--the talent to spell, punctuate, and capitalize--are laso needed. Some jobs require the use of dictation equipment, and a knowlege of filing systems. Another important skill often mentioned by employers is "the ability to get along with others."

The inclosed pamphlet discribes our flexible programs that will help you develop your skills, not only for a first job but for better jobs in the future. Someone in my office will call you in a few daus to arrange a meeting so that we can determine your future at length

Document 3

(LM p. 19)

Block Style, Open Punctuation

Prepare the letter in Document 2 to **Mr. John L. Conte, 1406 State Street, Media, PA 19063-7192**. Substitute the paragraph at the right for the first paragraph of the letter. Ms. Colby will sign the letter.

Note: If you are working at a word processor or microcomputer, the body of the form letter can be entered into memory and only variables need to be changed on each copy.

This letter is in response to your telephone questions about the the qualifications needed for a secretrial job today. Since hiring practices differ from office to office, their are no universal standard. We can, however, give you a general idea the skills you must have based on our many years of training people for placing individuals in office jobs.

64c (continued)

Problem 2
Table with Main and Column Headings and Source Note

half sheet; 12 spaces between columns

U.S. DOLLARS SPENT IN SPACE		words
		6
Program	Cost to Date	14
Apollo	21.3 billion	18
Space Shuttle	18.8 billion	23
Skylab	2.5 billion	27
Gemini	1.3 billion	31
Mercury	392.6 million	35

____________________ 38

Source: NASA, 1985. 42

Problem 3
Table with Main, Secondary, and Column Headings

full sheet; 8 spaces between columns

Punctuation Marks

	typewriter	computer
ampersand	&	&
comma	,	,
parentheses	( )	{ }
question mark	?	?
quotation marks	"	"
semicolon	;	;

LONGEST RUN BROADWAY PLAYS 5

(As of August 5, 1984) 10

Play	Open.	Perf.	words
			16
A Chorus Line	1974	3,744	21
Grease	1972	3,388	25
Oh! Calcutta! (revival)	1976	3,359	32
Fidler on the Roof	1964	3,242	38
Life with father	1993	3,224	44

________________ 47

DS Source: Information Please Almanac, 1985, p. 798. 62

ENRICHMENT ACTIVITY: Language Skills

Capitalization and Number Expression

60-space line; DS

1. Read and key each line, making needed changes in capitalization and number expression.

2. Check accuracy of work with your teacher; rekey any line that contains errors in rule applications.

1 the fourteen boys left on may third to hike in lone star park.

2 she bought twelve place settings of oneida flatware.

3 the new marx theater is located at 1 east 10th avenue.

4 ms. jeanne hanna, the manager of edit, inc., has arrived.

5 he told us to study chapter four and to review chapter three.

6 about 20 voted; that's nearly two thirds of the members.

7 jill gave one third to ken, one third to jo, and one third to me.

8 "keep up the good work," he said, "and you'll make the goal."

9 my flight for new york leaves at four ten p.m. on january three.

10 dodi read Pages 1-150 of vidal's lincoln sunday afternoon.

Lessons 226-229

226a-229a ▶ 5 Check Equipment

65-space line

Before you start work each day, check your machine to see that it is in good working order by keying the paragraph at least twice (first slowly, then faster).

all letters/figures used

The objective of the experiment was to analyze quickly their new Model #28546 which has 15 digits, 30 memories, and 97 program steps. This model sells for $397 (less discounts of 10% and 5%). If they wish me to do so, I shall rush the panels to them by air.

| 1 | 2 | 3 | 4 | 5 | 6 | 7 | 8 | 9 | 10 | 11 | 12 | 13 |

226b-229b ▶ 45 Improve Formatting Skills: Correspondence

Special Instructions

As a secretary in an office, you will be expected to:

1. Supply the date for correspondence (the current date if a date is not specified).
2. In a letter, include an appropriate salutation, complimentary close, signature block (name and title of the person who originated the letter), and your initials as reference.
3. If the content of the document indicates an enclosure or attachment, supply a proper notation.
4. Use proper document format.
5. Correct any marked or unmarked errors made by the originator of a document (spelling, punctuation, grammar, and the like).
6. Correct any errors you make as you prepare a document in final form.
7. Proofread all documents and correct any errors you may have missed.

Mr. Dale Marshall, Document Production Manager, asks you to prepare the following pieces of correspondence and to submit each document to the appropriate originator for approval or signature.

Document 1

(LM p. 15)

Block Style, Open Punctuation

Prepare the letter to **Mrs. Judith M. Krastell, 1450 Chester Pike, Ridley Park, PA 19078-0358**. Mr. Gregory C. Torres, Director of Research, will sign the letter.

Some of the questions you *raised* ~~asked~~ in your recent letter are *difficult* ~~very hard~~ to answer because of the rapid changes which are now ocurring in the office. The introduction of electronic equipment *such as word processors and microcomputers,* has had a great impact on office procedures and practices. ¶ The use of electronic equipment, *however,* ~~though~~ has not changed the *work* ~~tasks~~ done by secretareis. *Several* ~~A number of~~ surveys, including the one we *concluded* ~~finished~~ last month, reveal that secretaries spend more than 90 percent of thier time preparing correspondence *(letters and memorandums),* reports, manuscripts, forms, and tables. Correspondance accounts for *almost* ~~about~~ 50 percent of *all* ~~the~~ documents produced.

Despite ~~In spite of~~ the growing use of electronic equipment, ~~several~~ studies reveal that *almost half* ~~about 50 percent of~~ the *original* documents received by secretaries are in hand written form. Reports are often handwritten, but many are produced *in final form* ~~a second time~~ from rough-draft*s* ~~copy~~. There are some *indications* ~~signs~~, thuogh, that the use of dictation machines are growing in popularity.

More detailed *information about office practices* ~~data~~ can be obtained from the report of our *national* ~~nation wide~~ survey. If you would like ~~to have~~ a copy, please complete the inclosed form and return it to us.

Unit 11 Lessons 65-67

Learning Goals
1. To refine your keyboarding techniques.
2. To increase your keyboarding speed.
3. To improve your keyboarding control.
4. To improve your language skills.

Machine Adjustments
1. Paper guide at *0*.
2. Ribbon control set to use top half of ribbon.
3. Margin sets: 70-space line (center − 35; center + 35 + 5) unless otherwise directed.
4. Line space selector to SS drills, DS ¶s; as directed for problems.

Lesson 65 Improve Keyboarding/Language Skills

65a ▶ 7 Conditioning Practice

each line twice SS (slowly, then faster); if time permits, two 1′ writings on line 4

alphabet 1 Zig will do extra jobs for the antique clock firm if it pays overtime.
figures 2 Our ZIP Code was expanded from 45236 to 45236-1057 on August 18, 1981.
ly/ily 3 low lowly full fully lazy lazily noisy noisily dear dearly glad gladly
speed 4 Both of the girls may go with the busy auditor to visit the auto firm.

| 1 | 2 | 3 | 4 | 5 | 6 | 7 | 8 | 9 | 10 | 11 | 12 | 13 | 14 |

65b ▶ 13 Improve Language Skills: Capitalization

70-space line; DS

1. Read the ¶ at the right, noting words that need to be capitalized.
2. Key the ¶, capitalizing words where appropriate.
3. Check your work, marking all errors for correction.
4. Prepare a final copy with all errors corrected.

in her book, human relations in the workplace, ms. kimberly said: "it is not sufficient to have good office skills." writing on the basis of twenty years' experience with Pro-Tech temporary employee services, inc., she said that "more office workers lose their jobs because of personal and human relations factors than because of inadequate skills." among the factors she mentioned are: lack of dependability, lack of responsibility for the accuracy of work produced, and poor concept of the value of one's job effort.

65c ▶ 13 Improve Keyboarding Technique: Response Patterns

each line twice SS (slowly, then faster); as time permits, a 1′ writing on lines 3, 6, and 9; find *gwam* and compare rates

letter response
1 as you are him was ill get oil few ink tax pop set kin ads hip raw pin
2 as you | you set | as you set | set up | you set up | as you set up | set up rates
3 Lonny created a great dessert treat: stewed plum in a sweet egg tart.

word response
4 of dot pen lay eye tie bus rug bit key oak map bid via aid got fit air
5 of the | the world | of the world | to the | the problem | to handle the problem
6 Did the chair signal the man to name the auditor of the downtown firm?

combination response
7 we the you and are for was may get but tax pay few due him own set men
8 is up | up to | is up to | he was | was to | he was to | if you | you did | if you did
9 Di is as aware as they are that the state tree of Ohio is the buckeye.

| 1 | 2 | 3 | 4 | 5 | 6 | 7 | 8 | 9 | 10 | 11 | 12 | 13 | 14 |

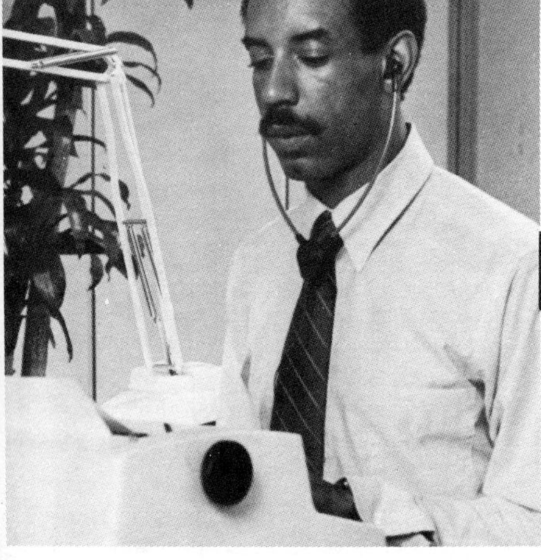

Unit 48 Lessons 226-229

Learning Goals

1. To review basic formats for business correspondence.

2. To improve your ability to plan, organize, and produce business correspondence quickly and correctly.

Formats Reviewed

1. Block style letter

2. Modified block style letter (with indented as well as blocked paragraphs)

3. Interoffice memorandum

OFFICE OPPORTUNITIES UNLIMITED

After a tour of the facilities of Office Opportunities Unlimited (OOU), Mr. Dale Marshall, Document Production Manager, shows you to your workstation in the Document Production Center. He gives you a copy of OOU's training manual and asks you to review the section on correspondence.

A&J LEARNING SYSTEMS
488 West Forsyth Street Jacksonville, FL 32202-1529 (904) 381-2789

September 25, 19--

Mr. Robert M. Pickens
Director of Human Resources
Community National Bank
P.O. Box One
Gainesville, FL 32602-8621

Dear Mr. Pickens

Your participation in our seminar on Understanding Leadership Styles will result, we believe, in some positive changes for you and your company. This is the feedback that we get over and over again from those who have attended the program.

So that your Leadership Style Profile can be processed before the seminar, would you please ask five business associates to complete the enclosed instruments and mail them to us in the envelopes that are also enclosed. We need to receive them by October 8, 19--.

We look forward to seeing you on October 12 at 8:30 a.m.

Sincerely yours

Ms. Sheila K. Weigand
Vice President

xx

Enclosures

Block Style; Open Punctuation

A&J LEARNING SYSTEMS
488 West Forsyth Street Jacksonville, FL 32202-1529 (904) 381-2789

September 25, 19--

Mr. Robert M. Pickens
Director of Human Resources
Community National Bank
P.O. Box One
Gainesville, FL 32602-8621

Dear Mr. Pickens:

Your participation in our seminar on Understanding Leadership Styles will result, we believe, in some positive changes for you and your company. This is the feedback that we get over and over again from those who have attended the program.

So that your Leadership Style Profile can be processed before the seminar, would you please ask five business associates to complete the enclosed instruments and mail them to us in the envelopes that are also enclosed. We need to receive them by October 8, 19--.

We look forward to seeing you on October 12 at 8:30 a.m.

Sincerely yours,

Ms. Sheila K. Weigand
Vice President

xx

Enclosures

Modified Block Style; Indented ¶s; Mixed Punctuation

Training Manual Excerpts: Standard Formats for Correspondence

Few offices format documents in the same way. There are standard formats, however, that are used in many offices including the Document Production Center. These formats are explained in the following guides. Please consult them whenever you have any questions about format.

Letter Styles

Block: All lines begin at left margin.

Modified block: Date and closing lines begin at center of page; all other lines begin at left margin. Paragraphs, however, may be indented 5 spaces or blocked at the left margin.

Letter Placement Table

Length	Margins	Date (line #)
Short	2″	19
Average	1½″	16
Long	1″	13

Letter Parts

Date: Use Letter Placement Table to place the current date.

Mailing notation (if used): DS below the date in ALL CAPS.

Letter address: Space down 4 times (QS) below dateline (or DS below mailing notation).

Attention line (if used): Place on the second line of the letter address.

Salutation: DS below letter address.

Subject or reference line (if used): DS below the salutation in ALL CAPS.

Body: SS with a DS between ¶s.

Complimentary close: DS below body.

Company name (if used): DS below the complimentary close in ALL CAPS.

Signature block: Begin on fourth line (QS) below the complimentary close or the company name.

Operator's initials: DS below last line of signature block.

Enclosure notation: DS below initials.

Copy notation: DS below operator's initials or enclosure notation (cc = carbon copy; pc = photocopy).

Punctuation Styles

Open: No punctuation after salutation or complimentary close.

Mixed: Colon after salutation; comma after complimentary close.

Interoffice Memorandum

Style: Block

Side margins: 1″

Headings: Begin the information in the heading 2 spaces to the right of the printed items.

TO: Insert name. Do not use personal titles such as Ms. or Mr.

FROM: Insert name without personal titles.

DATE: If no date is specified, use the current date.

SUBJECT: If no subject is specified, provide an appropriate one.

Body: Begin a DS below the printed heading. SS ¶s with a DS between them.

Operator's initials: DS below last line of the body.

Enclosures or attachments: DS below the operator's initials.

65d ▶ 17
Improve/Check Keyboarding Skill

1. A 1′ writing on ¶ 1; find *gwam*.

2. Add 2-4 *gwam* to the rate attained in Step 1, and note quarter-minute check points from table below.

3. Take two 1′ guided writings on ¶ 1 to increase speed.

4. Practice ¶s 2 and 3 in the same way.

5. A 3′ writing on ¶s 1-3 combined; find *gwam* and circle errors.

6. If time permits, take another 3′ writing.

gwam	¼′	½′	¾′	1′
24	6	12	18	24
28	7	14	21	28
32	8	16	24	32
36	9	18	27	36
40	10	20	30	40
44	11	22	33	44
48	12	24	36	48
52	13	26	39	52
56	14	28	42	56

all letters used | LA | 1.4 si | 5.4 awl | 85% hfw | *gwam 3′*

Few people know which direction their lives may take or by what 4
road they may travel to their final destination. When they come to a 9
crossroad, many stop to decide which road to take. Many take the easy 14
road and puzzle over what might have happened on the road not taken. 18

Who of us knows exactly what we shall want tomorrow? None of us, 23
hopefully, makes a choice that cannot at some point in the future be 27
changed. All should ask questions of the future for which we have no 32
answers. By always seeking to learn, however, we improve our choices. 37

All of us should pause from time to time and ask ourselves what 41
we desire from life and, if necessary, choose a new road to follow to 45
obtain our goals. Unfortunate, indeed, are those with no purpose in 50
life, people who have set no major goals to investigate or to pursue. 55

gwam 3′ | 1 | 2 | 3 | 4 | 5 |

Lesson 66 Improve Keyboarding/Language Skills

66a ▶ 7
Conditioning Practice

each line twice SS (slowly, then faster); if time permits, two 1′ writings on line 4

alphabet 1 Joe very quickly seized the wheel as big cars pulled out from an exit.
figures 2 The 17 jobs will be done by May 30, 1992, at a cost of $465.8 million.
r/er 3 make maker late later dive diver play player deal dealer train trainer
speed 4 She did signal the chair to hand the proxy to the auditor of the firm.

| 1 | 2 | 3 | 4 | 5 | 6 | 7 | 8 | 9 | 10 | 11 | 12 | 13 | 14 |

66b ▶ 13 Improve Language Skills: Number Expression

70-space line; DS

1. Read the ¶ at the right, noting the numbers that should be expressed as words and those that should be expressed as figures.

2. Key the ¶, expressing the numbers correctly.

3. Check your work and mark all errors for correction.

4. Prepare a final copy with all errors corrected.

The fifty most-used words account for 46% of the total of all words used in a study of four thousand one hundred letters, memos, and reports. The first hundred account for 53%; the first 500, 71%; the first thousand, 80%; and the first 2,000, 88%. Of the first 7,027 most-used words, 209 are balanced-hand words and 284 are one-hand words. Balanced-hand words account for 26% of all word uses; one-hand words account for 14%.

Lessons 226-250

PHASE 10

Office Opportunities Unlimited: Intensive Word Processing Training

Welcome to **Office Opportunities Unlimited**, a training center for people who are preparing to apply for an office job. We are located on **Route 252 & Media Line Road** in **Media, PA 19063-4639**.

As a student at OOU, you will take short courses designed to improve your formatting, document production, language application, and basic keyboarding skills.

To gain practical experience, you will work in OOU's Document Production Center under the Document Production Manager, Mr. Dale Marshall. In the Center, you will produce documents most commonly prepared in a business office: letters, memorandums, reports, tables, and forms. As you prepare these documents from script, rough-draft, or boilerplate copy, you will be expected to edit, revise, and make any necessary changes. Special language skills activities are provided to sharpen your editing and correcting skills.

OOU will also teach you how to apply for a job. You will learn to prepare employment documents, such as a data sheet, a letter of application, and a formal employment application form. As a final activity, you will take a typical employment test.

66c ▶ 13
Improve Keyboarding Technique

1. Key each line twice.
2. Take a 1′ writing on each of lines 2, 4, 6, 8, and 10.

Shift keys

1 Robert and Mandy left with Spence and Jacki on a South Pacific cruise.
2 Nan visited Rockland, Maine, and Springfield, Massachusetts, in April.

Space bar

3 Did all the men on the dock go to bid on an oak chair and a clay bowl?
4 The dog is too big to sit on my lap, but he may sit on a cozy fur rug.

Adjacent keys

5 Louisa was aware that the three ponds were polluted with oily residue.
6 The top stagehands were eager to join the powerful new worker's union.

Long direct reaches

7 The recent survey is summarized in a brochure she found in my library.
8 Margaret's unusual gift for the bride was a bright green nylon caftan.

Balanced-hand sentences

9 Dirk may hang the bugle by the antique ornament or by the oak workbox.
10 Eighty firms may bid for the right to make the big signs for the city.

| 1 | 2 | 3 | 4 | 5 | 6 | 7 | 8 | 9 | 10 | 11 | 12 | 13 | 14 |

66d ▶ 17
Improve/Check Keyboarding Skill

1. A 1′ writing on ¶ 1; find *gwam*.
2. Add 2-4 *gwam* to the rate attained in Step 1, and note quarter-minute check points from table below.
3. Take two 1′ guided writings on ¶ 1 to increase speed.
4. Practice ¶s 2 and 3 in the same way.
5. A 3′ writing on ¶s 1-3 combined; find *gwam* and circle errors.
6. If time permits, take another 3′ writing.

gwam	1/4′	1/2′	3/4′	1′
24	6	12	18	24
28	7	14	21	28
32	8	16	24	32
36	9	18	27	36
40	10	20	30	40
44	11	22	33	44
48	12	24	36	48
52	13	26	39	52
56	14	28	42	56

all letters used | A | 1.5 si | 5.7 awl | 80% hfw | *gwam 3′*

Words are the major building blocks of written communication, and 4
the keyboard is a very vital tool we use to put those words on paper 9
with speed and ease. To develop an effective message, we must choose 14
our words precisely and arrange them into clear paragraphs. 18

Some communication experts say we think in words; others insist 22
that words follow our thoughts. Quite simply, however, we do not draft 27
really good messages unless we make at least a mental plan first and 31
then select carefully each of the words to execute our plan. 35

All who keyboard with skill can record their ideas at a machine 39
more quickly than in longhand. Therefore, jotting down the main ideas 44
of a message before starting to compose is critical. The prize for a 49
good letter or report depends on planning as well as actual writing. 53

gwam 3′ | 1 | 2 | 3 | 4 | 5 |

225b (continued)

Problem 3
(LM p. 233)
Purchase Order

Marketing Research & Developers, Inc.

200 Bordon Street • Houston, TX 77029-1934 • (713) 921-7685

PURCHASE ORDER

words

ERGONOMIC BUSINESS INTERIORS — Purchase Order No.: D198-241 — 8
472 SOUTH MICHIGAN AVENUE — Date: June 27, 19-- — 16
CHICAGO IL 60605-7904 — Terms: 2/10, n/30 — 22
Shipped Via: Midway Freight — 25

Quantity	Description/Stock Number	Price		Per	Total		words
10 rolls	Magic Mending Tape (34181)	1	44	ea	14	40	35
5 reams	Duplicating Paper, 20# (33486)	4	98	rm	24	90	45
5 reams	Duplicating Paper, 20# (33517)	4	44	rm	22	20	55
8 boxes	Typewriter Ribbons, Selectric (33956)	7	83	bx	62	64	67
2 pads	Mailing Labels, 100 count (33285)	1	04	pd	2	08	78
					126	22	80

By Eric Logan — 82

Problem 4 (LM p. 235)
Invoice

Centek Office Systems, Inc.

400 Garfield Avenue
Aurora, IL 60506-9250
(312) 797-8822

INVOICE

A M MATTHEWS ASSOCIATES — Date: January 13, 19-- — 8
845 CROSS CREEK COURT — 13
ROSELLE IL 60172-2755 — Customer Order No.: 2009-A — 19

Terms	Shipped Via	Our Order No.	Date Shipped	words
2/10, n/30	Southside Transport	B699-1588	12/18/--	29

Quantity	Description/Stock No.	(Unit Price)		(Amount)		words
2	Pedestal Desk, Left-Hand Return (30B64)	279	95	559	90	39
2	Executive Swivel Chair (80613-B)	114	95	229	90	49
1	Three-Drawer File Cabinet (B4529-AL)	159	95	159	95	59
2	All-Steel Bookcase (B5864-AL)	99	95	199	90	69
				1,149	65	70
	Tax			68	98	73
				1,218	63	75

Lesson 67 Improve Keyboarding/Language Skills

67a ▶ 7 Conditioning Practice

each line twice SS (slowly, then faster); if time permits, two 1′ writings on line 4

alphabet 1 Xavier quit pouring cement when jet black clouds filled the azure sky.

figures 2 Joe must sell 27 to 28 tickets for the 19th and 35 to 40 for the 26th.

ion 3 tense tension express expression suggest suggestion protect protection

speed 4 I wish to do the work so the girls may go with them to make the signs.

| 1 | 2 | 3 | 4 | 5 | 6 | 7 | 8 | 9 | 10 | 11 | 12 | 13 | 14 |

67b ▶ 13 Improve Language Skills

1. Read the ¶ at the right, mentally noting words that should be capitalized and numbers that should be shown in figures.

2. Key the ¶, making the needed changes.

3. Check your work and mark all errors for correction.

4. Prepare a final copy with all errors corrected.

of the forty-five members of the footlight club, 36 were present at the meeting on friday, february 7. the club president, sybil harshman, called the meeting to order at three thirty p.m. the meeting involved a discussion of plans for the big spring show, "footlight serenade." at the suggestion of the vice president, john sparkman, it was decided to stage the show on april thirtieth and may first and second to celebrate may day.

67c ▶ 13 Improve Keyboarding Speed: Skill Transfer

1. A 1′ writing on each ¶; find *gwam* on each.

2. Compare *gwam* on the 3 writings.

3. Another 1′ writing on the slowest ¶.

4. A 2′ writing on each ¶; find *gwam* on each. If you finish a ¶ before time is called, start over.

5. Compare *gwam* on the 3 writings.

6. As time permits, take another 2′ writing on the slowest ¶.

Recall

^ insert

ℓ delete

⁀‿ close up

all letters used | A | 1.5 si | 5.7 awl | 80% hfw |

	gwam 1′	2′
It has frequently been said that talk is cheap, but this	11	6
is not true in a business office. Whether workers are engaged	24	12
in a work-related conversation or in idle chatter, the cost	36	18
per minute to the company is the same. In business, time is	48	24
money. That is why workers who waste time in social conversa-	61	30
tion are often criticized by office supervisors and managers.	73	36
Another work^er habit that often costs a company ^needless ~~a lot of~~	11	6
money is the failure to find and correct er^r^ors before work is	24	12
~~given~~ presented to the supervisor for approval. A manager is quite	36	18
critical of those who expect others to proof read and mark	48	24
errors ^for them. Using highly paid people to find ~~the~~ errors made	61	30
by those at a lower level can't be ^justified ~~tolerated~~.	70	35
Finally, workers who are frequently late getting to work	11	6
and are often absent multiply the cost of getting work done.	24	12
Such employees come in for criticism when an executive is	35	18
asked to identify the prime weaknesses of office workers be-	47	24
cause they are not giving a fair day's work for a fair day's	60	30
pay. Time is money whether a worker uses it wisely or not.	71	36

225b ▶ 45
Measure Production Skill: Business Forms

Time Schedule

Plan and prepare .... 5′
Timed production .... 30′
Proofread; compute *n-pram* .... 10′

1. Arrange materials for ease of handling (LM pp. 229-235).

2. Format and key Problems 1-4 for 30′. Proofread and correct errors before removing forms from machine.

3. After time is called (30′), proofread again and circle any uncorrected errors. Compute *n-pram*.

Problem 1 (LM p. 229)
Message/Reply Memorandum

words

(Message) TO: Eric Logan Purchasing Department DATE: January 5, 19-- 10
SUBJECT: Office Furniture (¶) Last week at the board meeting, our depart- 22
ment was allocated two additional accounting positions. We will try to fill 37
these positions by the first of February. We will need two desks, two chairs, 53
two bookcases, and one filing cabinet to complete the office furnishings in 68
Rooms 216 and 218. Please check with several area office furniture dealers 83
to see where we can receive the best prices and the quickest delivery so 98
that we will have offices ready for the new accountants. SIGNED: Jana Car- 111
ling, Accountant 114

(Reply) DATE: January 13, 19-- (¶) I have ordered the office furniture you 125
requested through Ergonomic Business Interiors. They offered the quick- 140
est delivery and the best prices. They will be able to deliver all the furni- 155
ture with the exception of the bookcases before the end of January. They 170
are expecting a shipment of bookcases during the first week of February 184
and have promised next-day delivery. SIGNED: Eric Logan, Purchasing 196
Department 198

Problem 2 (LM p. 231)
Purchase Requisition

Marketing Research & Developers, Inc.
200 Bordon Street • Houston, TX 77029-1934 • (713) 921-7685

PURCHASE REQUISITION

Deliver to: Bob Johnson Requisition No. B-14 3
Location: Word Processing Center Date June 23, 19-- 11
Job No. 10-401 Date Required August 15, 19-- 15

Quantity	Description	
10 rolls	Magic Mending Tape, 3/4" width	23
5 reams	Duplicating Paper, blue, 11", 20#	32
5 reams	Duplicating Paper, white, 11", 20#	40
8 boxes	Typewriter Ribbons, #113610, selectric	50
2 pads	Mailing Labels, 100 pad count	57

Requisitioned by: Brent Snell 59

67d ▶ 17 Improve/Check Keyboarding Skill

1. A 1′ writing on ¶ 1; find *gwam*.

2. Add 2-4 *gwam* to the rate attained in Step 1, and note quarter-minute check points from table below.

3. Take two 1′ guided writings on ¶ 1 to increase speed.

4. Practice ¶s 2 and 3 in the same way.

5. A 3′ writing on ¶s 1-3 combined; find *gwam* and circle errors.

6. If time permits, take another 3′ writing.

gwam	1/4′	1/2′	3/4′	1′
24	6	12	18	24
28	7	14	21	28
32	8	16	24	32
36	9	18	27	36
40	10	20	30	40
44	11	22	33	44
48	12	24	36	48
52	13	26	39	52
56	14	28	42	56

all letters used | A | 1.5 si | 5.7 awl | 80% hfw | — gwam 3′

To hear is to perceive or to sense by the ear. To listen means to 4
hear with quite careful attention. Except for those with impaired hear- 9
ing, hearing is easy. Listening, on the contrary, is a difficult and 14
an often undeveloped skill which one can perfect only by practice. 18

To listen effectively, one must intend to hear and understand and 23
must concentrate on what is being said. Do not permit your mind to 27
drift to anything else. As you attempt to listen, think about and em- 32
phasize the idea being presented. Think along with the speaker. 36

Don't let your mind get distracted by the looks or gestures of the 40
speaker or by some noise or activity in the immediate area. Just con- 45
centrate on the message. Don't allow yourself to react too quickly to 50
what is being said. Instead, hear the whole message before you react. 55

gwam 3′ | 1 | 2 | 3 | 4 | 5 |

ENRICHMENT ACTIVITY: Aligning Copy

Learn to Align and Type over Words

1. Key the sentence as shown below.

```
I can align this copy.
```

2. Study and follow the numbered steps given at the right.

Your typed line should look like this:

```
I can align this copy.
```

Not like this:

```
I can align this copy.
I can align this copy.
```

3. If time permits, repeat the drill to develop skill in aligning and typing over to make corrections in copy.

Aligning and Typing over Words

It is sometimes necessary to reinsert the paper to correct an error. Follow these steps to do so correctly.

1. Key a line of copy in which one or more *i's* appear (such as *I can align this copy*, which you have just keyed). Leave the paper in your machine.

2. Locate **aligning scale (26)** and **variable line spacer (9)** on your machine.

3. Move element (carriage) so that a word containing an *i* (such as *align*) is above the aligning scale. Be sure that a vertical line points to the center of *i*.

4. Study the relation between top of the aligning scale and bottoms of letters with downstems (*g, p, y*). Get an exact eye picture of the relation of typed line to top of scale so you will be able to adjust the paper correctly to type over a word with exactness.

5. Remove the paper; reinsert it. Gauge the line so bottoms of letters are in correct relation to top of the aligning scale. Operate the *variable line spacer*, if necessary, to move the paper up or down. Operate the *paper release lever* to move paper left or right, if necessary, when centering the letter *i* over one of the lines on the aligning scale.

6. Check accuracy of alignment by setting the *ribbon control* in stencil position and typing over one of the letters. If necessary, adjust paper again.

7. Return ribbon control to use top half of ribbon.

8. Type over the words in the sentence.

224b (continued)

Problem 3 (full sheet)
Four-Column Table

Prepare the table at the right; DS body of table; leave 4 spaces between Cols. 1 & 2; leave 8 spaces between Cols. 2 & 3; leave 4 spaces between Cols. 3 & 4.

				words
MEN'S AND WOMEN'S GYMNASTICS TEAM MEMBERS				8
1984 Olympics				11
Men's Team	Home State	Women's Team	Home State	29
Bart Conner	Oklahoma	Pamela Bileck	California	38
Tim Daggett	Massachusetts	Michelle Dusserre	California	49
Mitch Gaylord	California	Kathy Johnson	California	59
Jim Hartung	Nebraska	Julianne McNamara	California	69
Scott Johnson	Colorado	Mary Lou Retton	West Virginia	79
Peter Vidmar	California	Tracee Talavera	California	89

Problem 4 (full sheet)
Three-Column Table with Source Note

Prepare the table at the right; DS body of table; leave 6 spaces between columns.

			words
TEN MOST SUCCESSFUL MOVIES			5
Determined by Gross Revenues			11
Rank	Movie	Studio	18
1	E. T. The Extra-Terrestrial	Universal	26
2	Star Wars	20th Century Fox	32
3	Return of the Jedi	20th Century Fox	39
4	The Empire Strikes Back	20th Century Fox	48
5	Jaws	Universal	51
6	Raiders of the Lost Ark	Paramount	58
7	Grease	Paramount	62
8	Tootsie	Columbia	66
9	The Exorcist	Warner Bros.	72
10	The Godfather	Paramount	77
______________			81
Source: Information Please Almanac, 1985.			89

Lesson 225 Evaluation: Business Forms

225a ▶ 5 Conditioning Practice

each line twice SS (slowly, then faster); repeat if time permits

alphabet 1 Dix Zoz broke his wrist when he quickly jumped from the burning eaves.

figures 2 An increase of 320 people changed the 1987 population total to 64,725.

fig/sym 3 He dialed 1-801-756-9473 (a UT number) instead of 1-802 (a VT number).

speed 4 Jane kept antique gowns for the eight girls to aid them in their work.

| 1 | 2 | 3 | 4 | 5 | 6 | 7 | 8 | 9 | 10 | 11 | 12 | 13 | 14 |

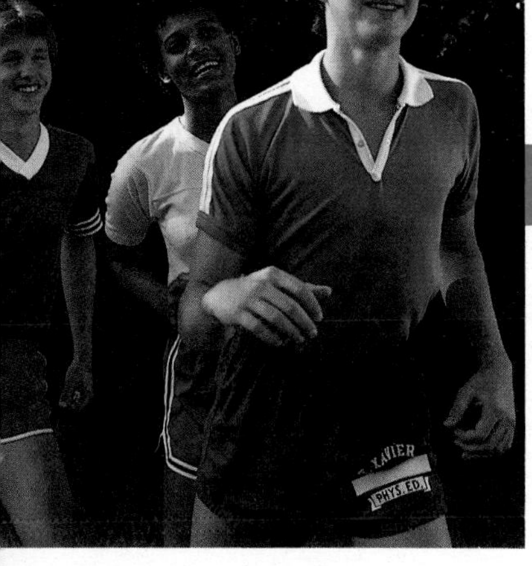

Unit 12 Lessons 68-70

Learning Goals

1. To learn to apply your keyboarding and formatting skills in an office setting.

2. To learn to process a variety of keyboarding jobs in an orderly, efficient manner.

3. To learn to prepare usable business documents with all errors corrected and with only minimum assistance.

Machine Adjustments

1. Paper guide at *0*.

2. Ribbon control set to use top half of ribbon.

3. Margin sets: 70-space line for warm-up practice; as required by formatting guides for various documents.

4. Line space selector as required by formatting guides for various documents.

KILMER YOUTH CAMP (AN OFFICE JOB SIMULATION)

Before beginning the jobs on pages 120-122, read the copy at the right. When planning the assigned jobs, refer to the excerpts from the Kilmer Document Processing Manual to refresh your memory about proper formatting and spacing of documents.

Work Assignment

You have been hired for part-time office work at Kilmer Youth Camp where you are to spend part of the summer.

Kilmer Youth Camp is located near Tapoco, North Carolina, on Lake Santeetlah at the edge of Joyce Kilmer Memorial Forest in the foothills of the Great Smoky Mountains. It is a coeducational camp for youths between the ages of 10 and 16. The camp consists of two villages: the Girls' Village and the Boys' Village. Each village is subdivided by age into Junior Campers (ages 10-13) and Senior Campers (ages 14-16) for housing, training classes, and recreational activities.

The camp is organized and operated by the following people:

Mrs. Alice Lindsay, Camp Director
Mr. James S. Lindsay, Assistant Camp Director
Mr. Neal Adams, Boys' Village Director
Ms. Debra Rountree, Girls' Village Director

The directors are assisted by five boys' counselors and five girls' counselors. Each counselor is assisted by a counselor-in-training (CIT).

As an office assistant, you will work in the office of Mrs. Alice Lindsay. In addition to answering the telephone, filing correspondence and other records, and entering data into the office computer, you will also process letters, memos, and other documents. Because the camp does not yet have a word processor, you will process the documents on a typewriter.

Your keyboarding teacher has verified that you know how to format documents in the basic styles used by Kilmer Youth Camp: letters in block format; reports in unbound format; simplified memos; announcements centered on half sheets; tables centered on full sheets.

To assist you in formatting documents, Mrs. Lindsay gives you the following excerpts from the Kilmer Document Processing Manual.

Letters

1. Letters are prepared on camp letterheads; block format with open punctuation is used.
2. A standard 60-space line is used.
3. The date is placed on line 15.
4. Three blank line spaces (a quadruple space) are left between date and letter address and between complimentary close and typed name of writer. All other letter parts are separated by a double space.

Memos

1. Memos are prepared on camp letterheads; simplified format is used.
2. Side margins of 1″ are used.
3. The date is placed on line 12.
4. Three blank line spaces (a quadruple space) are left between date and addressee lines and between last line of message and name of writer. A double space separates all other memo parts.

Announcements and Tables

1. Announcements are prepared on half sheets; tables, on full sheets.
2. Double spacing is used for announcements and tables. Both are centered vertically and horizontally.

Reports

1. Unbound format is used for all reports: side margins, 1″; top margin, line 10 (pica), line 12 (elite); bottom margin, at least 1″.
2. Three blank line spaces (a quadruple space) separate the title from the body; a double space separates all other lines of reports, including side headings.
3. Page numbers are placed on line 6 at the right-hand margin of all pages except the first, which is not numbered; the report body continues on line 8.

Lesson 224 Evaluation: Tables

224a ▶ 5 Conditioning Practice

each line twice SS (slowly, then faster); repeat if time permits

alphabet 1 Kim Grabowski just quizzed the police officer extensively on the case.

figure 2 Over 109,860 students from 354 cities attended the concert on June 27.

fig/sym 3 Total cost for the September 15 invoices (#863 and #2045) was $17,914.

speed 4 The key to the eight maps was right in the rich neighbor's corn field.

| 1 | 2 | 3 | 4 | 5 | 6 | 7 | 8 | 9 | 10 | 11 | 12 | 13 | 14 |

224b ▶ 45 Measure Production Skill: Tables

Time Schedule

Plan and prepare .... 5′
Timed production .... 30′
Proofread; compute *n-pram* .... 10′

1. Arrange 4 full sheets for ease of handling.

2. Format and key Problems 1-4 for 30′. Proofread and correct errors before removing tables from machine.

3. After time is called (30′), proofread again and circle any uncorrected errors. Compute *n-pram*.

Problem 1 (full sheet)
Three-Column Table

Prepare the table at the right; DS body of table; leave 10 spaces between columns.

words

AMERICAN LEAGUE 3

MVP* for 1975-85 7

Year	Player	Team	words
1985	Don Mattingly	New York	18
1984	Willie Hernandez	Detroit	24
1983	Cal Ripkin, Jr.	Baltimore	30
1982	Robin Yount	Milwaukee	36
1981	Rollie Fingers	Milwaukee	42
1980	George Brett	Kansas City	48
1979	Don Baylor	California	53
1978	Jim Rice	Boston	57
1977	Rod Carew	Minnesota	62
1976	Thurman Munson	New York	68
1975	Fred Lynn	Boston	72

(column headings: 13)

________ 76

*Most Valuable Player 80

Problem 2 (full sheet)
Four Column Ruled Table

Prepare the table at the right; DS body of table; leave 6 spaces between columns.

JOHNSON COMPANY 3

1987-88 Salary Structure 8

(rule: 22)

Name	Position	1987 Salary	1988 Salary	words
				29
(rule)				43
Carmen Martinez	President	$73,700	$76,900	51
Brett Etheridge	Vice President	58,500	60,100	60
Reed Van Noy	Marketing Manager	42,800	44,200	69
Oki Yukimura	Financial Manager	40,600	42,400	78
Rebecca Bryant	Production Manager	36,400	39,600	88
Darby Kintz	Personnel Manager	34,200	36,300	97
Dennis Murphy	Purchasing Manager	32,600	34,400	106

(rule: 120)

Unit 12 Lessons 68-70

Learning Goals

1. To learn to apply your keyboarding and formatting skills in an office setting.
2. To learn to process a variety of keyboarding jobs in an orderly, efficient manner.
3. To learn to prepare usable business documents with all errors corrected and with only minimum assistance.

Machine Adjustments

1. Paper guide at *0*.
2. Ribbon control set to use top half of ribbon.
3. Margin sets: 70-space line for warm-up practice; as required by formatting guides for various documents.
4. Line space selector as required by formatting guides for various documents.

KILMER YOUTH CAMP (AN OFFICE JOB SIMULATION)

Before beginning the jobs on pages 120-122, read the copy at the right. When planning the assigned jobs, refer to the excerpts from the Kilmer Document Processing Manual to refresh your memory about proper formatting and spacing of documents.

Work Assignment

You have been hired for part-time office work at Kilmer Youth Camp where you are to spend part of the summer.

Kilmer Youth Camp is located near Tapoco, North Carolina, on Lake Santeetlah at the edge of Joyce Kilmer Memorial Forest in the foothills of the Great Smoky Mountains. It is a coeducational camp for youths between the ages of 10 and 16. The camp consists of two villages: the Girls' Village and the Boys' Village. Each village is subdivided by age into Junior Campers (ages 10-13) and Senior Campers (ages 14-16) for housing, training classes, and recreational activities.

The camp is organized and operated by the following people:

Mrs. Alice Lindsay, Camp Director
Mr. James S. Lindsay, Assistant Camp Director
Mr. Neal Adams, Boys' Village Director
Ms. Debra Rountree, Girls' Village Director

The directors are assisted by five boys' counselors and five girls' counselors. Each counselor is assisted by a counselor-in-training (CIT).

As an office assistant, you will work in the office of Mrs. Alice Lindsay. In addition to answering the telephone, filing correspondence and other records, and entering data into the office computer, you will also process letters, memos, and other documents. Because the camp does not yet have a word processor, you will process the documents on a typewriter.

Your keyboarding teacher has verified that you know how to format documents in the basic styles used by Kilmer Youth Camp: letters in block format; reports in unbound format; simplified memos; announcements centered on half sheets; tables centered on full sheets.

To assist you in formatting documents, Mrs. Lindsay gives you the following excerpts from the Kilmer Document Processing Manual.

Letters

1. Letters are prepared on camp letterheads; block format with open punctuation is used.
2. A standard 60-space line is used.
3. The date is placed on line 15.
4. Three blank line spaces (a quadruple space) are left between date and letter address and between complimentary close and typed name of writer. All other letter parts are separated by a double space.

Memos

1. Memos are prepared on camp letterheads; simplified format is used.
2. Side margins of 1" are used.
3. The date is placed on line 12.
4. Three blank line spaces (a quadruple space) are left between date and addressee lines and between last line of message and name of writer. A double space separates all other memo parts.

Announcements and Tables

1. Announcements are prepared on half sheets; tables, on full sheets.
2. Double spacing is used for announcements and tables. Both are centered vertically and horizontally.

Reports

1. Unbound format is used for all reports: side margins, 1"; top margin, line 10 (pica), line 12 (elite); bottom margin, at least 1".
2. Three blank line spaces (a quadruple space) separate the title from the body; a double space separates all other lines of reports, including side headings.
3. Page numbers are placed on line 6 at the right-hand margin of all pages except the first, which is not numbered; the report body continues on line 8.

224a ▶ 5
Conditioning Practice

each line twice SS (slowly, then faster); repeat if time permits

alphabet	1	Kim Grabowski just quizzed the police officer extensively on the case.
figure	2	Over 109,860 students from 354 cities attended the concert on June 27.
fig/sym	3	Total cost for the September 15 invoices (#863 and #2045) was $17,914.
speed	4	The key to the eight maps was right in the rich neighbor's corn field.

| 1 | 2 | 3 | 4 | 5 | 6 | 7 | 8 | 9 | 10 | 11 | 12 | 13 | 14 |

224b ▶ 45
Measure Production Skill: Tables

Time Schedule

Plan and prepare .... 5′
Timed production .... 30′
Proofread; compute *n-pram* .... 10′

1. Arrange 4 full sheets for ease of handling.

2. Format and key Problems 1-4 for 30′. Proofread and correct errors before removing tables from machine.

3. After time is called (30′), proofread again and circle any uncorrected errors. Compute *n-pram*.

Problem 1 (full sheet)
Three-Column Table

Prepare the table at the right; DS body of table; leave 10 spaces between columns.

words

AMERICAN LEAGUE 3

MVP* for 1975-85 7

Year	Player	Team	words
1985	Don Mattingly	New York	18
1984	Willie Hernandez	Detroit	24
1983	Cal Ripkin, Jr.	Baltimore	30
1982	Robin Yount	Milwaukee	36
1981	Rollie Fingers	Milwaukee	42
1980	George Brett	Kansas City	48
1979	Don Baylor	California	53
1978	Jim Rice	Boston	57
1977	Rod Carew	Minnesota	62
1976	Thurman Munson	New York	68
1975	Fred Lynn	Boston	72

(header line: 13)

______________ 76

*Most Valuable Player 80

Problem 2 (full sheet)
Four Column Ruled Table

Prepare the table at the right; DS body of table; leave 6 spaces between columns.

JOHNSON COMPANY 3

1987-88 Salary Structure 8

(rule: 22)

Name	Position	1987 Salary	1988 Salary	words
				29
(rule)				43
Carmen Martinez	President	$73,700	$76,900	51
Brett Etheridge	Vice President	58,500	60,100	60
Reed Van Noy	Marketing Manager	42,800	44,200	69
Oki Yukimura	Financial Manager	40,600	42,400	78
Rebecca Bryant	Production Manager	36,400	39,600	88
Darby Kintz	Personnel Manager	34,200	36,300	97
Dennis Murphy	Purchasing Manager	32,600	34,400	106
(rule)				120

Lessons 68-70 A Part-Time Work Simulation

68a-70a ▶ 5 (daily) Prepare for Keyboarding Tasks

Warm up daily before starting job tasks by keying each line twice (slowly, then faster).

alphabet 1 Max Jevon saw a gray squirrel lift up his tail, bark once, and freeze.

figure 2 Ms. Coe bought 976 of the 2,385 new library books; 1,409 were donated.

fig/sym 3 Does Mrs. Ludlow's Policy #304156 for $58,500 expire on June 27, 1992?

speed 4 He may visit the firm to work with the title forms they handle for me.

| 1 | 2 | 3 | 4 | 5 | 6 | 7 | 8 | 9 | 10 | 11 | 12 | 13 | 14 |

68b-70b ▶ 45 (daily) Office Work Assignments

Job 1
Bulletin Board Announcement

Mrs. Lindsay asks you to prepare an error-free copy of an announcement for square dance night. She wants it centered on a half sheet. Miss Renfro will make photocopies to be posted on the bulletin board in each village.

SQUARE DANCE NIGHT
For Junior and Senior Campers
Kilmer Youth Camp Pavilion
8:00 p.m., July 20
Refreshments and Prizes
Sponsor: Miss Julie Renfro

Job 2
Simplified Memo
(LM p. 73)

Mrs. Lindsay hands you handwritten copy for a memo that she wants prepared in final form. She lists these instructions:

1. Use **June 27** of the current year as the date.
2. It is to go to **All Camp Counselors and Directors.**
3. As a subject, use **SPECIAL EVENTS PLANNING MEETING.**
4. Use my name as the writer.
5. Use your initials for reference.
6. Don't forget to indicate the enclosure.

Enclosed is a schedule of special events planned for this summer's group of campers. As you can see, it is a busy schedule that will require careful planning if everything is to run smoothly.

As in the past, each event will be planned and supervised by one of the camp or village directors, two counselors, and two CITs. A general planning meeting will be held at 7 p.m. on July 1 in the guest dining room of the pavilion. All camp directors and counselors should be there. Counselors should leave their CITs in charge of the campers.

Please study the schedule of events, identify the events on which you would most like to work, and come with ideas for organizing and directing the events of your choice. Insofar as we are able, we'll try to honor your choices.

Word Processing Personnel 80

Word processing personnel usually have titles such as word 92

word
processing specialist, correspondence secretary, or processing 105

s
operator. Word processing personnel are expert ~~typists who~~ 115

in keyboarding information
~~produce printed copy~~ from machine dictation, handwritten copy, 129

direct
typewritten copy, rough-draft copy, or from dictation. 141

Word processing personnel should have keyboarding skills 153

65
(minimum typing speeds of 45 to ~~55~~ words per minute are usually 166

required for entry level), transcription skills, language arts 178

skills, decision-making skills, formatting skills, proofreading 191

s
skills, and reference useage skills. Additionally, word pro- 203

e *to be*
cissing personnel need to have a positive attitude, ~~take pride~~ 215

quality conscious,
~~in their work~~ to be flexible, and to be willing to take on 227

additional responsibilities. 233

Administrative Support Personnel 247

r
The administrative suppott personnel are known by various 258

titles, depending on the particular organization. Some of the 271

more common titles used today are administrative secretary, 283

and
administrative support secretary, administrative assistant. 296

responsibilities
The ~~duties~~ of the administrative support personnel ~~will~~ vary 309

from organization to organization
~~depending again on the particular organization~~, but will gen- 319

erally include telephone handling, greeting office callers, 331

s
processing mail, fileing, and routine clerical duties. Other 342

responsibilities may include assisting with meetings and con- 355

c
ferences, maintaining resords, preparing itineraries and making 368

the arrangements necessary for travel, and requisitioning 380

supplies. Administrative support personnel ~~will~~ also have 390

set priorities and *s*
the opportunity to make decisions, use good oraganizational 406

p
skills, and utilize good human relation skills. 416

Problem 3 (2 full sheets)
Leftbound Report with Side Headings
Repeat Problem 2 as a leftbound report.

68b-70b (continued)

Job 3
Schedule in Table Form

Mr. Lindsay gives you a rough-draft copy of the schedule of special events for the summer. He asks you to prepare the table in final form on a full sheet, all errors corrected. He suggests that you leave 6 spaces between columns. It will be photocopied to be enclosed with copies of the memo you have just processed.

SCHEDULE of SPECIAL EVENTS

Event	Date	Time
Nature trail Campout	July 10-12	10:30 a.m.
Square Dance Night	July 20	8:00 p.m.
Swimming/Diving Conpetition	July 27	9:30 a.m.
Tennis Tournament	July 31	10:30 a.m.
Soft ball Playoffs	August 1-3	1:30 p.m.
Hot Dog/Marshmallow Roast	August 6	7:30 p.m.
Volleyball Playoffs	August 10-11	1:30 P.M.
Arts and Crafts Exhibit	August 12-15	All Day
Atheletics Exhibition	August 14	9:30 a.m.
Sailboat Regata	August 14	3:00 p.m.
Parents/Awards Banquet	August 14	7:00 p.m.
Bon Voyage Brunch	August 15	11:00 a.m.

Job 4
Form Letter in Block Style
(LM pp. 75-82)

Mrs. Lindsay hands you the body copy for a letter she wants sent to each of the addresses she gives you. She asks you to prepare an original copy for each addressee. She tells you to date each letter **July 14** of the current year and supply an appropriate salutation, complimentary close, and enclosure notation. As the **Camp Director**, she will sign each letter. She asks you to use large business envelopes.

The Kilmer Youth Camp ends its summer activities on Sunday, August 15. Starting at 9:30 Saturday morning, a fun-filled weekend of camper/parent activities is planned.

The directors and counselors at Kilmer cordially invite you to attend the Athletics Exhibition which begins at 9:30 on Saturday morning, the Sailboat Regatta which begins at 2:00 that afternoon, and the Parents/Awards Banquet which starts at 7:00 Saturday evening. And be sure to join us for the Bon Voyage Brunch at 11:00 Sunday morning. All these events are provided with the compliments of Kilmer Youth Camp.

Please check on the enclosed card those events you plan to attend and return the card to me by July 31. I am also enclosing a list of motels and hotels in the Tapoco and Robbinsville area where you may obtain weekend accommodations.

Please join in the final festivities of a successful summer camp experience for your youngsters.

Addresses

Mr. and Mrs. Eduardo Basanez
3100 Wilson Road
Bakersfield, CA 93304-4903

Mrs. Belinda Jamieson
4384 W. Prien Lake Road
Lake Charles, LA 70605-7281

Dr. and Mrs. Lee Chang
One Sage Court
White Plains, NY 10605-2256

Mr. Kermit J. Hendricks
8205 Wasco Street, NE
Portland, OR 97220-8101

223a ▶ 5
Conditioning Practice

each line twice SS (slowly, then faster); repeat if time permits

alphabet 1 Jacob Klugman awarded Ashley sixth place for her very high quiz score.

figures 2 In 1987, 253 contestants won 6 gold and 40 silver medals in the races.

fig/sym 3 Store sales increased $34,871 (5%) for May and $69,742 (10%) for June.

speed 4 The man is by the sign to the city lake and a big dog is in the field.

| 1 | 2 | 3 | 4 | 5 | 6 | 7 | 8 | 9 | 10 | 11 | 12 | 13 | 14 |

223b ▶ 45
Measure Production Skill: Memos/Reports

Time Schedule

Plan and prepare .... 5′
Timed production .... 30′
Proofread; compute *n-pram* .... 10′

1. Arrange materials for ease of handling (LM p. 227 and 4 full sheets).

2. Format and key Problems 1-3 for 30′. Proofread and correct errors before removing paper from machine.

3. After time is called (30′), proofread again and circle any uncorrected errors. Compute *n-pram*.

Problem 1 (LM p. 227)
Interoffice Memorandum
address a company mail envelope

words

TO: Mike Johnson, Administrative Support Supervisor FROM: 10
Tina McMichaels, Personnel Director DATE: April 15, 19-- 20
SUBJECT: Employment Opportunities in the Office 28

¶ The business education teacher at North High School 38
has asked me to give a presentation on employment 48
opportunities to her secretarial procedures class on 59
May 15. She would like me to stress the job skills and 70
personal qualities that are desirable for individuals 81
to possess to be successful in office employment. 91
¶ Would you have any material that would be beneficial 101
to me in preparing for this presentation? I will stop 112
by sometime next week to talk with you. XX 122

Problem 2 (2 full sheets)
Unbound Report with Side Headings

EMPLOYMENT OPPORTUNITIES IN THE OFFICE 8

~~With~~ Since the beginning of word processing, many changes 18
have ~~taken place~~ occurred in the types of ~~jobs~~ tasks now ~~available~~ being performed in the 31
office. In many organizations, office workers are ~~now~~ clas- 42
sified by keyboarding-related tasks (word processing personnel) or 56
by nonkeyboarding-related tasks (administrative support personnel). 70

continued on next page

68b-70b (continued)

Job 5
Report from Rough Draft

Mr. Adams and Ms. Rountree, directors of the boys' and girls' villages, have prepared rough copy for a page of the brochure that will be used to promote attendance at Kilmer next summer.

Mr. Adams asks you to prepare a final copy in unbound report form. The copy will be sent to a phototypesetter, so he wants letter-perfect copy. Because this copy will be part of the final printed brochure, page numbers will be added when the brochure is typeset.

EXCITING NEW PROGRAMS — center main heading

The Directors of Kilmer Youth Camp have underway some brand new facilities and programs that we expect will be in operation for next summers campers.

New Aquatics Facility

Nearing completion is a new facility that permits under-cover swimming activities. The Olympic-size pool will also be used for sports like water polo and water volleyball.

New Gymnastics Facility

A new gym is being built housing raquetball courts, weight-training rooms, indoor Volleyball, basketball, and some gymnastic equipment such as trampoline, balance beam, paralel bars, and side horse.

New Computer-Literacy Center

As part of our "Learning Is Fun" program, we are installing a computer area where formal instruction and supervised informal practice on computers will be provided. In addition to group and tutorial instruction, learning packages will be available to motivate additional pratcice through electronic games.

New Soccer Field and Archery Range

Contributions from several alumni have made possible the adition of a soccer field. Both soccer and archery will be added to the program of events next summer.

¶ Thanks to the fund raising drive spear headed by parents of many of our ucrrent and former Campers, we have been able to expand our facilitys and improve our programs. This kind of support speaks well for the educational and recreational programs we have provided our alumni campers in the 27 years since our camp was founded.

222b (continued)

words

Problem 2 (LM p. 223)
Block-Style Letter
open punctuation; address envelope

December 15, 19-- Mr. Eric Hudson 371 Curtis Street 10
Evansville, WY 82636-8981 Dear Mr. Hudson 19
(¶) Thank you for your interest in working for our company. We 31
do have two positions that will be opening next month which 43
seem to be similar to your qualifications and may be of 54
interest to you. (¶) The first position will be in our word 66
processing center as a word processing operator. The other 78
position will be in our marketing department as an admin- 89
istrative secretary to the marketing manager. (¶) To apply 100
for either position, you will need to submit your resume 112
and letter of application to Mary Vermillion, who is our 123
personnel director. If you have additional questions about 135
either of the positions or our company, feel free to contact 147
Ms. Vermillion or me. 151
Sincerely Chad Bryant Personnel Department xx 160
pc Ms. Mary Vermillion 165/**177**

Problem 3 (LM p. 225)
Modified Block Style Letter
indented paragraphs; mixed punctuation; address envelope

Problem 4 (plain full sheet)
AMS Style Letter
Format the letter in Problem 3 in AMS style and address it to:
Ms. Linda Mathis
The Word Power Center
810 Amanda Avenue
Salt Lake City, UT 84105-1993
Use **PROPOSAL FOR WORD PROCESSING EQUIPMENT** as the subject line.
Total words: 156

```
June 1, 19--  Mr. Paul Jones, Manager  The Word Processing       11
Center  1320 Lorl Lane  Ogden, UT  84404-2634  Dear Mr. Jones:   23
                                          July 1
Our company will have funds available ~~next fiscal year~~ for the           34
                              word processing
purchase of additional ^ ~~wp~~ equipment. We are ~~currently~~ inviting      47
several ~~leading~~ companies to submit proposals for improving our          58
word processing facilities. ¶ Would your company be interested in            71
                                              or one of your representatives
submitting a propoasl? We would like to have you ^ visit our com-            90
                                                      #
pany as soon as pos sible to discuss our specific needs^with Mrs.           103
Valerie                     word processing.
^Martinez, our supervisor of ^ ~~wp~~.                                       114
                                                  #
    ¶ If your company is interested in submitting a^proposal, ~~let~~        125
                  lc                       to set up
~~me know,~~ Call me next week at 801-836-4877 ^ ~~for~~ an appointment.     137
Sincerely yours, Ms. Judy Goodwin  Acquisitions Manager xx                  149
pc Mrs. Valerie Martinez                                                154/171
```

Unit 13 Lessons 71-72

Learning Goals

1. To improve basic keyboarding skill.

2. To review formatting guides and procedures for letters, reports, and tables.

3. To demonstrate the application of formatting guides and procedures in preparing letters, reports, and tables.

Machine Adjustments

1. Paper guide at *0*.

2. Ribbon control set to use top half of ribbon.

3. Margin sets: 70-space line for drills and ¶s; as required for problems.

4. Line space selector to SS drills, DS ¶s; as required for problems.

Lesson 71 Prepare for Measurement

71a ▶ 5 Conditioning Practice

each line twice SS (slowly, then faster); if time permits, rekey line 4

alphabet	1	Jen can get five quiet days off, for she works extra at my plaza club.
figures	2	They replaced at cost 50 plates, 78 knives, 194 forks, and 362 spoons.
fig/sym	3	Boyd & Co. is #307 of 1,648 top firms rated in <u>Fortune</u>, June 25, 1987.
speed	4	Both of us may wish to bid for the antique bicycle or the ivory whale.

| 1 | 2 | 3 | 4 | 5 | 6 | 7 | 8 | 9 | 10 | 11 | 12 | 13 | 14 |

71b ▶ 15 Improve Keyboarding Skill: Skill Comparison

1. A 30″ writing on each line; find *gwam* on each writing:

1′ *gwam* × 2

2. Compare *gwam* rates; identify 4 slowest lines.

3. Take a 30″ and a 1′ writing on each of those lines to improve speed.

balanced-hand	1	The goal of the panel is to handle the big fuel problem for the towns.
double letters	2	Ann will assess the food served at the inn to see if it is acceptable.
combination	3	An audit crew is due at noon; we shall look into the tax problem then.
3d row	4	Terry tried to type the two weather reports with the quiet typewriter.
1st/3d rows	5	Bix quit my new committee on community power to rezone river property.
adjacent-key	6	We built a radio forum on the premise that expert opinion was popular.
outside-reach	7	Alex lost a list of top wallpaper sizes so he will not sell his quota.
direct-reach	8	Brenda checked both number columns twice before she plotted the curve.
one-hand	9	You saw him test a rated water pump on my extra car at a union garage.
shift keys	10	Sumio and Luisa beat Drucilla and Michi in the tournament in San Juan.
figures	11	Of 1,089 pages, 764 were textual pages and 325 were appendix material.
balanced-hand	12	Eighty of the city firms may form a panel to handle the fuel problems.

| 1 | 2 | 3 | 4 | 5 | 6 | 7 | 8 | 9 | 10 | 11 | 12 | 13 | 14 |

71c ▶ 30 Prepare for Measurement

3 full sheets
1 half sheet

Make a list of the problems and page numbers given below:

page 76, 43b, Drills 1 and 2
page 79, 44d, Problem 1
page 110, 61c, Problem 1

Review the formatting guides for letters on page 75 and for tables on pages 105-106.

Format and key the problems on your list according to the directions given with the problems. Correct any errors you make as you key.

SOUTH-WESTERN PUBLISHING CO.

Unit 47 Lessons 222-225

Measurement Goals

To demonstrate skill in preparing acceptably:

1. Letters.
2. Memos and reports.
3. Tables.
4. Business forms.

Machine Adjustments

1. Margin sets: 70-space line for drills; as directed for problems.
2. Spacing: SS sentence drills; space problems as directed.

Lesson 222 Evaluation: Letters in Various Formats

222a ▶ 5 Conditioning Practice

each line twice SS (slowly, then faster); repeat if time permits

alphabet 1 Being extra cautious kept Hector Vasquez from broad jumping very well.

figures 2 Of 1,089 members in attendance, 637 were juniors and 452 were seniors.

fig/sym 3 Invoice #796 must be paid by 12/3/89 to receive a 5% discount ($684).

speed 4 The six girls may go by bus to visit the chapel and docks at the lake.

| 1 | 2 | 3 | 4 | 5 | 6 | 7 | 8 | 9 | 10 | 11 | 12 | 13 | 14 |

222b ▶ 45 Measure Production Skill: Letters

Time Schedule

Plan and prepare .... 5′
Timed production .... 30′
Proofread; compute *n-pram* .... 10′

1. Arrange materials for ease of handling (LM pp. 221-225 and plain full sheet).
2. Format and key problems 1-4 for 30′. Proofread and correct errors before removing letters from machine.
3. After time is called (30′), proofread again and circle any uncorrected errors. Compute *n-pram*.

Problem 1 (LM p. 221)
Executive-Size Letter

modified block style, mixed punctuation; address envelope

words

March 28, 19-- Mr. Charles Walstrom Washington High School 2525 North 14
Sherman Boulevard Milwaukee, WI 53210-6428 Dear Mr. Walstrom 27

It is a real pleasure to accept your invitation to speak at your leadership con- 42
ference on June 23. To see students from three outstanding organizations 57
combine their efforts to sponsor this worthwhile conference is just fantastic. 73

I am well aware of the contributions being made by these organizations to 88
the development of today's youth. As a student, I was a member of both FBLA 103
and DECA. For the past three years, I have been an advisory board member 118
for Lincoln High School's OEA chapter. 126

"Take a Chance -- Be a Leader" will be the title of my presentation. I will try 142
to make the presentation such that members in each of the three groups will 157
feel that it was designed especially for their group. 168

I am looking forward to being a part of your program. If there is any other 183
information that you feel would be helpful to me in preparing my talk, please 199
let me know. Best of luck with final preparations for your conference. 213

Sincerely, Miss Lorraine Ling xx 220

Lesson 72 Prepare for Measurement

72a ▶ 5 Conditioning Practice

each line twice SS (slowly, then faster); if time permits, rekey line 4

alphabet 1 Jacki Veloz hung exquisite paintings on a wall of the academy library.

figures 2 I shall print 850 cards, 173 calendars, 96 leaflets, and 24 circulars.

fig/sym 3 Check #84 (dated 6/5) for $93 covers Invoice #275 less a 10% discount.

speed 4 Is she to pay the six firms for all the bodywork they do on the autos?

| 1 | 2 | 3 | 4 | 5 | 6 | 7 | 8 | 9 | 10 | 11 | 12 | 13 | 14 |

72b ▶ 10 Check Keyboarding Skill: Straight Copy

1. A 3′ writing on ¶s 1-3 combined; find *gwam*, circle errors.

2. A 1′ writing on each ¶; find *gwam* on each.

3. Another 3′ writing on ¶s 1-3 combined; find *gwam*, circle errors.

all letters used | A | 1.5 si | 5.7 awl | 80% hfw

	gwam 3′	5′
Human relations skills on the job are very critical in terms of	4	3
how you will be perceived by peers as well as by superiors. During	9	5
your early weeks at work, you will be sized up quickly by co-workers.	14	8
How they observe and evaluate you will help to determine whether your	18	11
work experience will be pleasant, successful, and valuable.	22	13
Be cautious at first and do not align yourself closely with any	26	16
of the cliques that often develop in the workplace. Show understand-	31	19
ing and be courteous to everybody, but don't take sides in a dispute	36	21
that may occur between members of any group of workers. Show that you	40	24
can think for yourself, but don't convey your ideas too freely.	45	27
Look, listen, and learn before you take an active part in the poli-	49	29
tics of the workplace. Let the older, experienced workers be the agents	54	32
of change. Study and learn from them and carefully notice what seems	59	35
to cause their successes or failures. As you develop on a job, all	63	38
positive human relations skills will be rewarded.	66	40

gwam 3′ | 1 | 2 | 3 | 4 | 5 |
5′ | 1 | 2 | 3 |

72c ▶ 35 Prepare for Measurement

3 full sheets

Make a list of the problems and page numbers given below:
pages 95-96, 52b
page 97, 53b

Review the formatting guides for preparing reports, reference lists, and title pages on pages 93 and 97.

Format and key the problems on your list according to the directions given with the problems. Correct any errors you make as you key.

221c ▶ 12 Measure Keyboarding Skill

1. A 3′ writing on both ¶s; find *gwam*; circle errors.

2. A 5′ writing on both ¶s; find *gwam*; circle errors.

all letters used | A | 1.5 si | 5.7 awl | 80% hfw |

	gwam 3′	5′	
Economic development planning in our country has become big busi-	5	3	49
ness in recent years. This is due to the problem of high unemployment	10	6	52
in nearly every area of our nation. Government agencies at national,	14	9	55
state, and local levels are quite involved in studying the vast problems	19	12	58
linked to our growing economy. They, along with groups in industry,	24	15	61
find it useful and necessary to forecast where jobs in the future likely	29	17	64
will be. Predicting new jobs is not easy to do, but the data is needed	34	20	66
to seek out stable ways and means to foster a good healthy economy.	38	23	69
While it is good to have many agencies and organizations researching	43	26	72
economic issues, some of the reports generated from these groups are in	48	29	75
conflict. Many of these reports are confusing to the reader. It is not	53	32	78
that the data are inaccurate. Diverse groups tend not to stress the same	58	35	80
facts when compiling study data. On the other hand, there is agreement	62	37	83
on the major ways a trend is predicted and how it will affect our nation.	67	40	86
Experts realize that our efforts must be centered on more than a single	72	43	89
industry and that new jobs must be created in traditional fields.	77	46	92

gwam 3′ | 1 | 2 | 3 | 4 | 5
5′ | 1 | 2 | 3

221d ▶ 25 Prepare for Measurement

forms (LM pp. 215-219)

Problem 1
Message-Reply Memo
Key the message-reply memo shown at the right.

Problem 2
Purchase Order
Key the purchase order shown at the right.

Problem 3
Invoice
Prepare an invoice from the purchase order at the right. Address it to:

THE GEORGIAN INN
4025 AVENUE Q
DAVENPORT IA 52805-4721

Date it **December 15, 19--**
Date shipped: **12/8/--**
Add 6% sales tax
Use our order no. 113-9618
Total words: 86

words

(Message) TO: Kirsten Reed, Marketing Manager Suite 413 Crowne Center 10
#4 DATE: November 16, 19-- SUBJECT: Trade Show Display 20
(¶) The Symington Convention Center informed me today of four additional 33
corner booths available for exhibits at the Portland Electronics Trade Show. 48
Should we take a left front aisle or back center main aisle booth? They are 62
both 12′ × 12′. SIGNED: Jerry Alden, Vice President 73

(Reply) DATE: November 17, 19-- (¶) I think the left front aisle booth is best 84
for our exhibit. Because the booth is 10 sq. ft. larger than originally planned, 98
we can also display the PowerTechMate III. I will get a revised display lay- 112
out to you Wednesday of next week. 124
SIGNED: Kirsten Reed, Marketing Manager 130

To: DUNFY RESTAURANT SUPPLY — Purchase Order No.: 7R-795436 7
5871 SOUTH ARBOR WAY — Date: November 21, 19-- 15
WILMINGTON NY 12997-3004 — Terms: 2/10, n/60 22
Shipped Via: REA Express 24

Quantity	Description/Stock Number	Price	Per	Total	words
16 doz	Dessert Plate, Fluted (B-3484)	72.00	dz	1152.00	36
16 doz	Cordial, Cranberry Swirl (B-6195)	132.00	dz	2112.00	48
25	Bradford Decanter, 750 ml (F-4111)	21.95	ea	548.75	59
18	Serving Tray, 15″ Silverplate (I-862)	19.25	ea	346.50	71
7	Crystal Flower Bowl, Lead Cut (S-2753)	58.00	ea	406.00	84
				4565.25	85

Francine Quintella, Purchasing Agent 92

SOUTH-WESTERN PUBLISHING CO.

Unit 14 Lessons 73-75

Measurement Goals

1. To demonstrate that you can keyboard for 3′ on straight copy material at an acceptable speed within an error limit specified by your teacher.

2. To demonstrate that you can format and key (with errors corrected) letters, reports, and tables according to standard formatting guides.

Machine Adjustments

1. Paper guide at *0*.

2. Ribbon control set to use top half of ribbon.

3. Margin sets: 70-space line for drills and ¶s; as required by formatting guides for letters, reports, and tables.

4. Line-space selector to SS drills, DS ¶s; as required for problems.

Lesson 73 Measure Straight Copy and Letter Skills

73a ▶ 5 Conditioning Practice

each line twice SS (slowly, then faster); if time permits, a 1′ writing on line 4

alphabet 1 Quite a few men like to do juggling exercises on the very big trapeze.
figures 2 Add 14 meters 25 centimeters, 89 meters 36 centimeters, and 70 meters.
fig/sym 3 The amount of $3,469 I quoted on Order #82071 included a 5% sales tax.
speed 4 Key firms of both towns may risk a penalty if the fuel profit is down.

| 1 | 2 | 3 | 4 | 5 | 6 | 7 | 8 | 9 | 10 | 11 | 12 | 13 | 14 |

73b ▶ 10 Check Keyboarding Skill: Straight Copy

1. A 3′ writing on ¶s 1-3 combined; find *gwam*; circle errors.

2. A 1′ writing on ¶ 1; find *gwam*; circle errors.

3. A 1′ writing on ¶ 2 and on ¶ 3 in the same way.

4. Another 3′ writing on ¶s 1-3 combined; find *gwam*, circle errors.

all letters used | A | 1.5 si | 5.7 awl | 80% hfw |

gwam 3′ | 5′

You have learned a great many things since you began a keyboard- 4 3
ing course. Not only have you built good operational technique with 9 5
speed, you have also grown confident in using a machine with ease and 14 8
control as you key a letter, report, table, or other document. 18 11

Although you have learned a lot, there is much yet for you to mas- 22 13
ter. For example, you should learn to format additional letter and 27 16
report styles because they are widely used in business. You can format 31 19
simple tables; however, you have not attempted a complex one. 35 21

Just as speed and accuracy on straight copy are highly prized, so 40 24
is the ability to process with efficiency a wide variety of documents 44 27
that are used for both personal and business needs. Another term of 49 29
directed practice will push you to higher skill in both areas. 53 32

gwam 3′ | 1 | 2 | 3 | 4 | 5 |
5′ | 1 | 2 | 3 |

220d ▶ 25 Prepare for Measurement

plain full sheets

Problem 1
Table with Source Note

Key the table at the right; leave 12 spaces between columns.

Problem 2
Table with Totals

Rekey Problem 1; add amounts in each column, and key the total for each column.

Total words: 80

Problem 3
Table with Rulings

Rekey Problem 2 with horizontal rulings.

Total words: 109

References: pp. 346, 349, 350

			words
TREMONT CONSTRUCTION COMPANY			6
Wholesale Division			10
State	Sales	Income Tax Paid	20
Alabama	$ 938,849.65	$ ~~18,472~~ 26,742	26
Arizona	1,342,770.12	55,263	32
Connecticut	964,504.78	93,134	38
~~Montana~~ Florida	~~729,166.24~~ 815,679.22	~~64,760~~ 56,406	43
North Carolina	858,332.60 ⇅	21,089 ⇅	50
Utah	1,182,927.93 ⇅	33,475 ⇅	55
~~Washington~~ Wisconsin	814,293.89	75,791	60
________________			64
Source: 1986 Income Tax Returns.			71

Lesson 221 Keyboarding/Prepare for Measurement

221a ▶ 5 Conditioning Practice

each line twice SS (slowly, then faster); then a 1′ writing on line 4

alphabet 1 Jack is bedazzled with sixty-five quality computer printing functions.
figures 2 When 538,924 people were surveyed, 67 out of 100 answered all 9 items.
fig/sym 3 That sign read: 2,859 used* plus 1,347 new items are 90% and 67% off!
speed 4 If paid right, a proficient maid may tidy the shelf and shake the rug.

| 1 | 2 | 3 | 4 | 5 | 6 | 7 | 8 | 9 | 10 | 11 | 12 | 13 | 14 |

221b ▶ 8 Improve Keyboarding Skill

1. Set tabs 6 spaces apart, starting at left margin.

2. Key lines 1-12 once as shown.

3. Take a 1′ writing on line 11, then on line 12; find *gwam* on each writing.

tabulator
1 any 950 fix 104 men 892 wire 4365 rule 7223 kick 3071
2 can 661 qua 349 pet 856 soar 2916 zoom 8402 open 7344

shift keys
3 Ms. Wakui selected Maria, Clyde, Karla, Jose, Ellen, Isaac, and Harry.
4 J.R. may see Colorado Springs, Glacier Park, or the Hawaiian Islands.

shift lock
5 Their book PERSONAL ACHIEVEMENTS was a best-seller for over 13 months.
6 Teachers find THE BALANCE SHEET and CENTURY 21 REPORTER quite helpful.

figures
7 His exam scores of 54, 63, 82, and 91 boosted his class average to 70.
8 My 9-digit social security number, 428-63-5170, has nearly 3,800 uses.

special symbols
9 A stock brief* indicated that 650 stocks ranged from 27 1/8 to 69 3/4.
10 All 790 items (*) are discounted at 1/2, 5/8, or 3/4 off for 26 weeks.

speed
11 I may keep the bicycle by the shanty at the lake, then go to the dock.
12 The big ruby is right for the shape of the hand, but it is a bit pale.

| 1 | 2 | 3 | 4 | 5 | 6 | 7 | 8 | 9 | 10 | 11 | 12 | 13 | 14 |

73c ▶ 35
Check Formatting Skills: Letters

1 plain full sheet
2 letterheads (LM pp. 83-86)
correction supplies

Problem 1
Personal-Business Letter

Using your own return address, format and key the letter on a plain sheet. Use a 60-space line; place date on line 15.

words

(Your return address) August 25, 19-- Mrs. Alice Lindsay, Director Kilmer 18
Youth Camp P.O. Box 575 Tapoco, NC 28780-8514 Dear Mrs. Lindsay 31

Thank you very much for giving me the opportunity to work in your office 46
this summer. It was an excellent experience, and I enjoyed working for 60
money instead of grades! 66

Although I missed a few of the activities others enjoyed, I felt sort of special 82
being able to work with you, the other directors, and the counselors. I'm 97
sure the trade-off was worthwhile. 104

I'll be returning to Kilmer next summer. If you found my work satisfactory, 119
perhaps you will permit me to work for you again. With another year of 134
training, I should be prepared to use the new word processor you expect to 149
have by then. 152

Cordially yours (Your name) 158

Problem 2
Business Letter

letterhead; 60-space line; current date on line 15; prepare an envelope; correct errors

Problem 3
Business Letter

Use Problem 2 directions, but address the letter to:

Mr. Henry S. Ho
Senior Class President
Midtown School of Business
4800 Wilshire Boulevard
Los Angeles, CA 90010-2253

Supply an appropriate salutation.

Miss Paula Nicols, President Business Education Club Waverly Academy 14
of Business 800 S. Rolling Road Baltimore, MD 21228-7801 Dear Miss 27
Nicols 29

Thank you for giving me the opportunity to tell you the main things we look 44
for in entry-level office workers. 51

First, we look for graduates who have specific skills we need: in keyboard- 66
ing, word processing, accounting, filing, and so on. A personal data sheet 82
will usually provide such information. 90

Next, we seek people who show pride in themselves -- those who dress appro- 104
priately and are well groomed and who speak positively and forcefully about 119
their educational background and related experiences. Usually these behav- 134
ior patterns are observed in the job interview. 144

Finally, we seek people who show evidence that they can work well with 158
others. An effective application letter and data sheet will identify group 174
activities in which the applicant has participated successfully and in what 189
roles. 190

People with these qualifications have at least the potential to develop into 206
valuable members of an office staff. 213

Sincerely yours Arnold J. Hoffman, Director Personnel Department xx 227

220a ▶ 5
Conditioning Practice

each line twice SS (slowly, then faster); than a 1′ writing on line 4

alphabet 1 Get quick feedback on the six jingle prizes given for your major work.
figures 2 The vote was 317 to 248; only 565 of the 950 registered persons voted.
fig/sym 3 He asked, "How does a 14.6% bond yield a $58,290 return in 37 months?"
speed 4 Lend a quantity of pens to the girls so they may make a big city sign.

| 1 | 2 | 3 | 4 | 5 | 6 | 7 | 8 | 9 | 10 | 11 | 12 | 13 | 14 |

220b ▶ 12
Improve Keyboarding Control

each line twice SS (slowly, then faster); DS between 6-line groups

adjacent-key reaches
1 weigh power yule trods opinion ask oil rebuild polka sport condemn hew
2 bulky treaty | opera suit | wet yucca | triumphant reporter | buys new options
3 Support for her weird plan was spoiled when a sulky patron opposed it.

direct reaches
4 vroom ump eczema musty brisk gravy myrrh censure nutty hypo unaffected
5 YMCA celebrity | btu units | myriad of hypotheses | NY and VT | grand echelons
6 No doubt the bright ecru nylon was unique for my mundane office walls.

one-hand words
7 craze kiln fever honk debt link grass mommy swear onion tease null web
8 Yukon cafe | pink sweater | oil free | union card | minimum debate | poppy seeds
9 I was served a yummy plum treat at noon in a deserted cafe on a knoll.

shift keys
10 Kasba Apulia Oxbow Diver Iquitos Nzega Epila Usak Vladimir Ywathit Qom
11 Fort MacMahon | Soap Lake | Glen Island | Roche Harbor | El Palmito | Flat Woods
12 Jan Wloch, Toby Yale, Zola Kane, and Bob Iwen won Good Conduct medals.

220c ▶ 8
Check Language Skills

plain sheet

1. Read the letter message at the right, noting corrections that need to be made.

2. Format the letter in block style. Address it to:

Miss Carmen Velaquez
Computer Programs, Inc.
13240 Heights Boulevard
Sunnyvale, CA 94086-7559

Use the current date; supply an appropriate salutation and complimentary close. Use your name as the writer.

As you key the body, correct all errors.

(¶1) Your advertizement in our hometown newspaper the weekly chronicle has prompted me to right you for more information about your companys Computer software products. I am mainly interested in your business related software.

(¶2) I would like a accounting program for balancing my checkbook a dictionary program for checking spelling and a mailing-list program to prepare mailing lables. Also send me you current brochure anouncing your new product's.

(¶3) If their is a supplyer of you soft ware in my area please supply the companys name and address. I would like to have a demonstration of the product's before bying them.

74a ▶ 5 Conditioning Practice

each line twice SS (slowly, then faster); if time permits, a 1′ writing on line 4

alphabet 1 The vote forced the town board to combine six zoning projects quickly.

figures 2 She wired them $365 on May 29 for the items ordered on Invoice 401827.

fig/sym 3 Su & Wong's order (#21473) for 850 sets of 6-ply NCR paper came May 9.

speed 4 It is their duty to sign the amendment if he is to handle the problem.

| 1 | 2 | 3 | 4 | 5 | 6 | 7 | 8 | 9 | 10 | 11 | 12 | 13 | 14 |

74b ▶ 45 Check Formatting Skills: Reports

4 plain full sheets
correction supplies

Problem 1
Two-Page Unbound Report

Format and key the report. Add page number at top of second page. Correct marked errors and any errors you make as you key.

Proofreader's Marks

- ∧ insert
- ⁀‿ close up
- ℓ delete
- # space
- ❝ ❞ quotation marks
- / lc lowercase
- ∧, insert comma
- ∿ transpose
- ⊙ period
- ≡ capitalize

words

HUMAN RELATIONS AT WORK 5

The term "human relations" means simply "all interactions 16
among two or more people" (Higins, 1982, 4). The term aplies 29
equally in family, business, and other organizational settings. 44
Of the definitions of "work," the most com monly used one is 57
offered by Buttel (1985,25): Labor, task, or duty that gives 70
one the accustomed means of livelihood." 78

Human relations consists of gettingalong with others on 94
the job: with supervisers, with peers, and subordinates. Vir- 108
tually all busness operations are group activities that demand 121
team work of the people who make up the group. Without team- 134
work--each one contributing his share of effort in the right 148
way--the goals of the group activity are not met. From the 163
personal stand point, it means learning to fit in, to do one's 176
share, and to be recognized as a valued member of the team. 190

As a beginning worker, learning to do the job assigned 201
seems the most important imediate goal. Just as important is 217
to learn the status of people around you, the code of behavior 231
in your work area, what treatment others expect from you and 244
how you can fit yourself into the work group. 259
266
<u>Supervisors and Other Superiors</u> 278

First learn who has some control of the work you do. Let 291
them guide you into the work patterns they wish you to follow, 304
the formality or informality of the relationship they want to 316
maintain with you, and the chain of command you are to follow 329
to seke help and resolve problems (Reynolds, 1983, 24). 340

219c ▶ 8 Check Language Skills

1. Read the ¶ at the right, noting errors that need to be corrected.

2. Key the ¶, making the needed corrections. Correct any errors you make as you key the copy.

The plane paper copyer in my office can not be repaired because a old worn part is no longer avalable. It is hour Service representatives opinion that we should replase the copyer with a newer Modes especially now that we are useing heavier paper for copying. In addition he believes the copyers badly worn feed mechanism are causing the paper jam's when copying onto our company' stationary.

219d ▶ 25 Prepare for Measurement

plain full sheets

Problem 1
Unbound Report

Prepare the copy at the right as a 2-page unbound report with side headings.

Problem 2
Simplified Memo

Using the first and last ¶s of the report at the right (without the side headings), prepare a simplified memo to Earlene Sampson, Vice President. The memo is from Jesse Wilson, Research and Development Director. Use the title of the report as the subject line; use today's date. Change the last sentence of ¶ 1 to read: The A & F targeted areas for upgrading are summarized in the attached report.

Total words: 167

Problem 3
Leftbound Report

Rekey the report in Problem 1 as a leftbound report. Change the side headings to ¶ headings. Prepare a cover page. The report was prepared by the Division of Research and Development; use today's date.

References: pp. 279, 284, 324

words

A SUMMARY REPORT OF AUTOMATION AND TECHNOLOGY 9
Allen & Fauver Manufacturing 15

Automation, mainly associated with computer technology, presently af- 29
fects the jobs of ninety percent of all Allen & Fauver employees. Within the 44
next ten years, the total work force will be involved directly with computer- 60
related operations of the company. The A & F targeted areas for upgrading 75
are summarized in this report. 81

Networking, Communications, and Data Bases 98

Local area networks (LANs) are used extensively for materials and sup- 112
plies ordering, transfer, and inventory; for nearly all information process- 127
ing; and for intercompany communications (electronic message system). 141
Teletype, facsimile, electronic mail, and video conferencing are contributing 157
to higher productivity among the company's branch offices. There is less 171
rekeying of information, faster information retrieval from remote locations, 187
and less time loss for intercompany travel. 196

Microforms have replaced most paper records. Excellent data bases 209
exist for virtually all company needs. Tie-ins to national geographical infor- 225
mation sources are needed to expand future markets. 235

Computer Aided Design and Manufacturing 251

CAD/CAM operations are cutting production time by at least a third. 265
While the number of design changes per job has increased, both designers 280
and buyers are benefiting from graphically viewing the finished product 294
before costly manufacturing is started. The accessibility to simulations of 309
product designs is making marketing easier and more cost effective. Re- 324
peat business has tripled in the last two years. Also, CAD/CAM workers 338
seem to be highly motivated, creative, and productive. 349

Robotics and Artificial Intelligence 364

Robots are being used in most assembly-related operations. Although 377
not totally cost effective, laser scanners, video image analyzers, and other 393
automated equipment have contributed to better quality control. The distri- 408
bution accuracy of the robot-controlled, automated parts centers has reduced 423
waste and minimized reinventorying. Expert systems are being used for 437
creating and checking computer configurations; however, artificial intelli- 452
gence applications virtually are untapped. 461

Long-Term Goals 467

The long-range automation and technology goals of A & F must encom- 480
pass two basic premises: 1. Future productivity will be linked to state-of- 495
the-art automation being integrated into all A & F operations. 2. Market 510
competitiveness will be contingent upon developing human resources for 524
innovation and change within an expanding technology. 535

words

Peers 342

Coworkers at your level of employment are a second group 356
you should study. Learn to distinguish between those who are 370
officious and those who are helpful valued members of hte 383
work group in the eyes of other workers. Be courteous to all, 399
but pattern your behavor after those who have the ear of their 414
supervisors. 417

Subordinates 422

Those whose job level is higher than that of others must 434
learn to show courtesy toward and respect for such people. 447
Give directions clearly to avoid having subordinates do over 460
work needlessly. Show appreciation for work. If criticism 473
and correction are required, inform the worker in private. 484
rather than in front of other workers. 492

In summary, human relations requires an "all for one and 504
one for all attitude. It means that all pull to gether fore 516
a common goal and each member aids and supports every other 531
member in all ways possibel. 537

Problem 2
Reference Page

REFERENCES 2

QS

Bittel, Lester R. What Every Supervisor Should Know 5th ed. 21
New York: McGraw-Hill Book Company, 1985. 30

Daggett, Willard R. The Dynamics of Work. Cincinnati: South- 47
Western Publishing Co., 1984. 53

Higgins, James M. Human Relations Concepts and Skills. New 72
York: Random House, 1982. 78

Reynolds, Carolyn. Dimensions in Professional Development. 98
2d ed. cincinnati: South-Western Publishing Co., 1983. 109

Problem 3
Title (Cover) Page

218c ▶ 25 Prepare for Measurement

2 plain full sheets
1 letterhead (LM p. 213)

Problem 1
Letter in Block Format
(plain full sheet)
Key the letter at the right in block format, open punctuation.

Problem 2
Letter in Modified Block Format
(plain full sheet)
Rekey the letter in Problem 1 in modified block format, open punctuation.

Problem 3
Letter in Modified Block Format, Indented ¶s
(executive-size letterhead [LM p. 213])
Rekey the same letter in modified block format, indented ¶s, mixed punctuation.

References: pp. 272, 306, 313

words

Current date Mrs. Louise McDonald Fabrics of America Marshall, MO 14
65340-5751 Dear Mrs. McDonald Subject: COTTON PERCALINE FABRICS 25

(¶ 1) It is our pleasure to announce the arrival of several new fabrics we 39
think you will want to stock for your customers. These fabrics, all cotton 54
percaline, come in 86 different solids, stripes, and prints. 66

(¶ 2) As you know, cotton fabrics lost their popularity when customers 79
discovered the easy-care characteristics of polyester. Then, when manufac- 94
turers began combining the fine qualities of natural fibers with the easy- 109
care synthetic materials, a revolution in the clothing industry took place. 124
Now with improved cotton percaline, designers all over the world are find- 139
ing exciting new ways of presenting high fashion in clothing. 152

(¶ 3) A color brochure with samples of several of our percaline cotton fabrics 166
is enclosed. Call us collect or use the form in the brochure for ordering 181
these quality fabrics. You will find they sell themselves. 194

Very truly yours TYSON FABRIC MANUFACTURERS Max Tyson, President 207
Enclosure 208/**220**

Lesson 219 Keyboarding/Prepare for Measurement

219a ▶ 5 Conditioning Practice

each line twice SS (slowly, then faster); then a 1′ writing on line 4

alphabet 1 Jagged, unevenly blemished pottery is fixed quickly with zineb liquid.
figures 2 Telephone discounts of 34 to 87 percent are offered in 106,295 cities.
fig/sym 3 She paid $4.78 for #2 spuds, $3.69 for #1 rice, and $1.50 for a roast.
speed 4 The big problem with the amendment is the land endowment for the firm.

| 1 | 2 | 3 | 4 | 5 | 6 | 7 | 8 | 9 | 10 | 11 | 12 | 13 | 14 |

219b ▶ 12 Improve Keyboarding Speed

1. Each line once as shown; push for speed.
2. A 1′ writing on each of lines 8, 10, and 12; find *gwam* on each writing.

space bar 1 if he | or me | for us | so it is | to do an | of the six | he may own | why she did
2 If the wish of the man is to own the land, he may pay for the big map.

home/3d rows 3 quote it | poor eye | outer route | your worry | pretty wet | tie rope | to irrupt
4 People were pretty rude to the weary writer who quietly quoted poetry.

home/1st rows 5 Mexican men/women, comic babble, mnemonic name, navy velvet, buzz box.
6 Fox, mink, and/or zebra are common animals in Nevada and Montana zoos.

stroke response 7 I wax | my average | after him | carefree opinion | in red ink | on a devastated
8 Fujio was scared as a junky car swerved on oily grass in a hilly area.

word response 9 lame duck | firm turns | do the work | by a dorm | laugh with us | soap six pans
10 A chapel down by the lake is all right for an authentic ivory antique.

combination response 11 a feasible form | an unfit blend | maybe he owns it | the statement of title
12 The humble man withdrew the great case due to the city audit problems.

| 1 | 2 | 3 | 4 | 5 | 6 | 7 | 8 | 9 | 10 | 11 | 12 | 13 | 14 |

Lesson 75 Measure Straight-Copy and Table Skills

75a ▶ 5 Conditioning Practice

each line twice SS (slowly, then faster); if time permits, a 1′ writing on line 4

alphabet 1 Al criticized my six workers for having such quick tempers on the job.

figures 2 FOR URGENT CALLS: Fire, 561-3723; Police, 461-7022; Doctor, 841-5839.

fig/sym 3 Terms on Devlin & Arnold's order dated 4/6 for $587.90 are 2/10, n/30.

speed 4 It is the wish of all of us to lend a hand to the visitor to the city.

| 1 | 2 | 3 | 4 | 5 | 6 | 7 | 8 | 9 | 10 | 11 | 12 | 13 | 14 |

75b ▶ 10 Check Keyboarding Skill: Straight Copy

1. A 3′ writing on ¶s 1-2 combined; find *gwam*, circle errors.
2. A 1′ writing on ¶ 1, then on ¶ 2; find *gwam* and circle errors on each.
3. Another 3′ writing on ¶s 1-2 combined; find *gwam*, circle errors.

all letters used | A | 1.5 si | 5.7 awl | 80% hfw |

	gwam 3′	5′
Few people have enough time to accomplish everything they desire.	4	3
Those who appear to accomplish many of the things they attempt to do	9	5
make choices regarding the most valuable uses of their time. They set	14	8
up a series of major and minor goals and allocate their time to these	18	11
goals on the basis of relative value in terms of time requirement.	23	14
First, determine exactly what it is you desire to have or to do.	27	16
Next, analyze your behavior or actions to see whether they are helping	32	19
or hindering your progress toward your objectives. On the basis of	37	22
this self-analysis, devise a plan for time use that is unique to your	41	25
own situation. Practice self-management until it becomes a habit.	46	27

gwam 3′ | 1 | 2 | 3 | 4 | 5 |
5′ | 1 | 2 | 3 |

75c ▶ 35 Check Formatting Skills: Tables

2 half sheets; 1 full sheet
correction supplies

Problem 1
Two-Column Table with Main Heading and Source Note

half sheet, long edge at top, 6 spaces between columns

WHO BENEFITS FROM SOCIAL SECURITY		words
		7
Retired workers	46.0 million	13
Disabled workers	10.0 million	19
Children of disabled workers	8.0 million	27
Children of deceased workers	5.0 million	35
Spouses of retired workers	2.5 million	43
Widows and widowers	1.5 million	49
____________		52
Source: Social Security Administration.		60

Unit 46 Lessons 218-221

Learning Goals

1. To improve basic skills in keyboarding, language knowledge, and document production.
2. To prepare for measurement of skills in language usage, in keying straight copy, and in preparing letters, memos, reports, tables, message-reply forms, invoices, and purchase orders.

Machine Adjustments

1. Paper guide at *0*.
2. Margin sets: 70-space line for drills; as appropriate for document production.
3. Spacing: SS drills; DS between drill groups; as appropriate for document production.

Lesson 218 Keyboarding/Language Skills

218a ▶ 5 Conditioning Practice

each line twice SS (slowly, then faster); then a 1′ writing on line 4

alphabet 1 A jovial boy serves wonderful pretzels from a huge, exquisite kitchen.
figures 2 Of the 9,358 employees, 1,407 are managers and 26 are vice presidents.
fig/sym 3 Roth & Bean (8306 Todd Ave.) made $751 million on 294 shares of stock!
speed 4 If the box is big and the shape is right, both antique panels may fit.

| 1 | 2 | 3 | 4 | 5 | 6 | 7 | 8 | 9 | 10 | 11 | 12 | 13 | 14 |

218b ▶ 20 Improve Keyboarding Skill: Guided Writing

1. A 3′ writing on ¶s 1-2 combined; find *gwam*.
2. A 1′ writing on ¶ 1; find *gwam* to establish your base rate.
3. Add 2-6 words to Step 2 *gwam*; use this as your goal rate.
4. Take three 1′ speed writings on ¶ 1, trying to reach your quarter-minute checkpoints as the guides (1/4, 1/2, 3/4, time) are called.
5. Follow Steps 2-4 for ¶ 2.
6. Repeat Step 1. Compare *gwam* on the two 3′ writings.
7. Record on LM p. 3 your better 3′ *gwam*.

all letters used | A | 1.5 si | 5.7 awl | 80% hfw |

gwam 3′

In the years to come, quality office workers with good basic skills 5 62
will continue to be in high demand. Employers in most organizations will 9 67
seek out employees who have a good knowledge base in English grammar and 14 72
usage, an ability to speak and write well, and accurate proofreading 19 76
skills. Priority will be given to people who can think through a task, 24 81
plan the best way to do it, and then ably and skillfully complete it. 28 86

Getting the job done in a cost-effective manner is a primary goal of 33 90
most companies. Employees wanting to move up the ladder and advance in 38 95
an office career must be efficient and productive. They must exhibit a 43 100
good balance of skills. That is, office workers must be dependable, be 47 105
able to work accurately under pressure, be very flexible in learning new 52 110
things and ways of doing tasks, and be able to set priorities each day. 57 114

gwam 3′ | 1 | 2 | 3 | 4 | 5 |

75c (continued)

Problem 2
Two-Column Table with Main and Secondary Headings and Source Note

half sheet; long edge at top; 20 spaces between columns

		words
SURVIVAL RATES OF CANCER VICTIMS		7
(Five Most Common Types)		12
Lung	13%	13
Breast	75	15
Colonic	53	18
Prostatic	71	20
Rectal	49	22
__________		25
Source: American Cancer Society.		32

Problem 3
Three-Column Table with Three Levels of Headings and Source Note

full sheet; 10 spaces between columns

			words
TOP STATES IN DEFENSE PRODUCTION			7
($ Value and % of State Industrial Production)			16
State	$ Value	% IP	23
California	63.1 billion	7.9	29
Texas	24.6 billion	4.4	33
New York	21.7 billion	4.3	38
Virginia	16.5 billion	10.4	44
Florida	13.8 billion	4.6	49
__________			52
Source: Data Resources, Inc.			58

Problem 4

If you complete all tables before time is called, repeat Problem 1.

OPTIONAL EVALUATION: Language Skills

Capitalization and Number Expression

1. Read the two ¶s given at the right; mentally note needed changes in capitalization and number expression.
2. Key the ¶s, making the needed changes; correct any errors you make as you key.

commerce clearing house, in a usa today story on august fourteenth, 1985, reports that many states are raising sales taxes. oklahoma, for example, has raised sales tax from three % to 3.25%. connecticut's 7.5% sales tax rate is the usa's highest. 21 states plus the district of columbia impose sales taxes of 5% or more. 5 states have no sales tax, so far.

gasoline taxes, too, are on the increase. texas has raised its tax by 5 cents a gallon; arkansas, by four cents; and tennessee, by 3 cents. the state of washington has the highest gasoline tax -- 18 cents a gallon -- followed by minnesota at seventeen cents a gallon.

213b-217b (continued)

Document 8 (continued)

Ms. Hart: Check for accuracy the figures in the "Number Trained" column of the table before you format the table. Refer back to the preceding listing; total the number of participants by company or division. The totals should equal those shown in the "Number Trained" column. Correct any figure that is wrong.

At the end of the report, insert the complete current date and your initials as reference.

IPI COMPANY/Division

	Number Trained
IPI (Corporate)	38
IPI-Gas/Oil Exploration & Development	39
IPI-Gas/Oil Operations & Production	30
IPI-Pipeline Drilling and Operations	36
IPI-Royalty Interests	27
IPI-Chemicals	43
IPI-Real Estate Investments	14
IPI-Retail Gas	0
Total participation in training programs	229

Document 9

Ms. Hart: Please compose a memo in Simplified format to Mr. Humphries. Make carbon copies of the memo for the TCs. Send a copy of the Monthly Training Report with the memo to Mr. Humphries. Compose a subject line for the memo.

Please draft a short memo to Mr. Humphries about the monthly training report you just prepared. Tell him we can discuss the report at his convenience if he wishes further explanation of our activities. Be sure a cover page has been prepared for the report before attaching it to the memo. Send blind copies of the memo along with the report to our Training Coordinators.

Lessons 76-100

PHASE 4

Improve Keyboarding and Formatting Skills

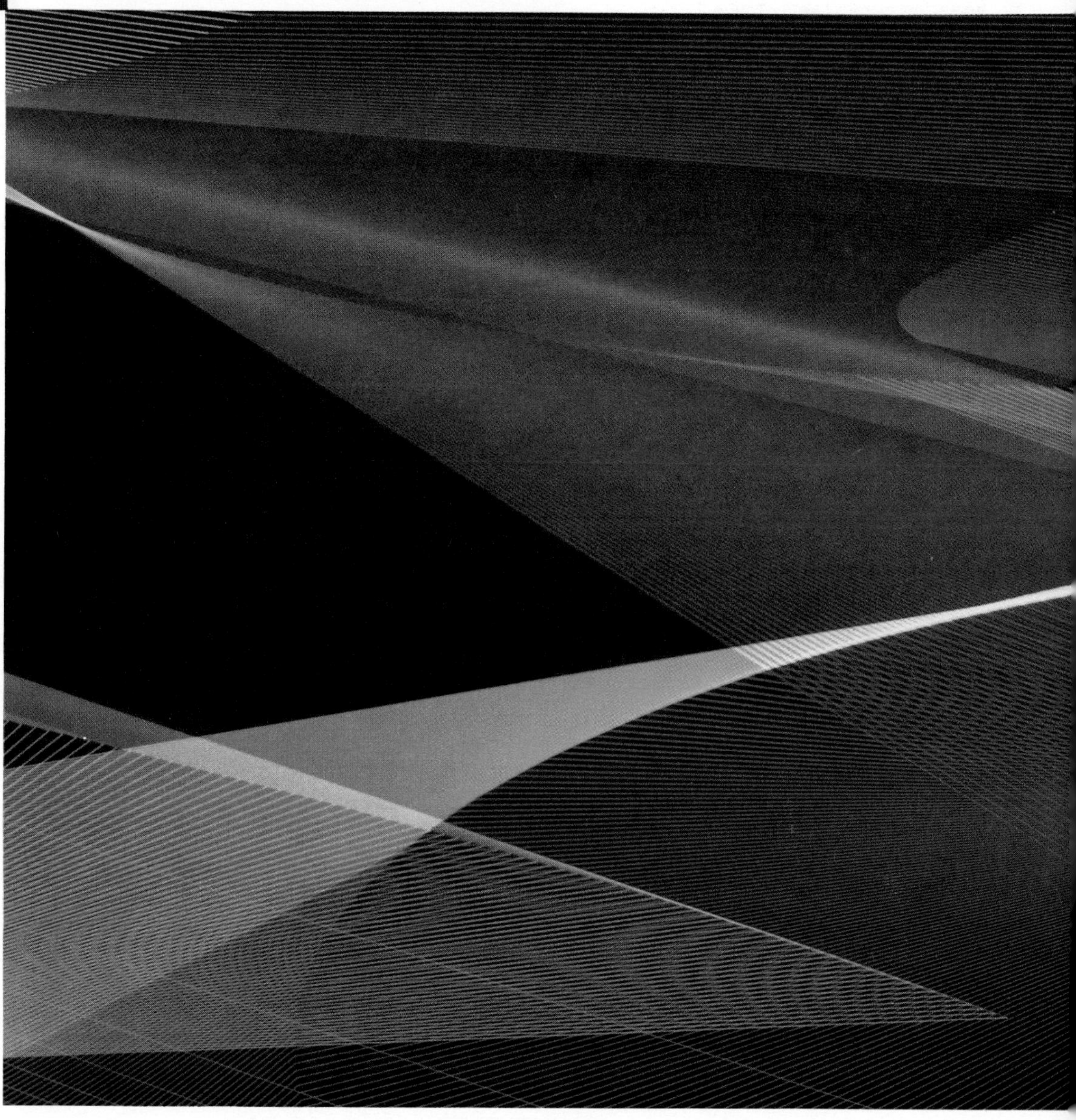

Here are the Key Steps to improving keyboarding skill:

1. Position: Maintain proper hand-and-finger position.

2. Purpose: Give a purpose to all keyboarding practice.

3. Practice: Use alternating levels of practice speed when keyboarding drill lines -- slowly, then faster, etc.

4. Goals: Set daily and weekly goals -- emphasize improvement.

The 25 lessons of Phase 4 will help you:

1. Refine technique patterns.

2. Build keyboarding skill to new levels.

3. Review Cycle 1 applications.

4. Improve skill on rough-draft and script copy.

5. Improve basic language skills.

6. Improve formatting and production skill on letters.

213b-217b (continued)

Document 8 (continued)

Ms. Hart: When formatting the trainer/participant listing, a tab stop at the center may be most efficient for handling the second column (i.e., the list of participants by company). Double-space above and below each trainer's name; single-space items beneath each trainer's name.

Divide the first and second pages in an appropriate place for ease of reading the report (i.e., between units of text or items.)

The Office Assistant III course was offered during the latter part of the month.

Assistant III. ~~This course~~ *It* was well received by the ~~first class of~~ 15 IPI executive assistants who ~~took the course during the latter part of the month~~ *participated in the nine sessions*.

TRAINER AND COURSE	~~#~~ *(sp.)* OF PARTICIPANTS BY COMPANY
Martha Hart	
Trainer Refresher	4 - IPI
Manager to Assistant	11 - IPI
John Haimes	
Interviewing Skills	13 - IPI-Chemicals
Supervisor Specialist	14 - IPI-Real Estate Invest.
	8 - IPI-Royalty Interests
Communication Skills	19 - IPI-O/G Expl. & Devel.
Helen Jackson	
Effective Writing Skills	*10 - IPI-Royalty Interests*
	18 - IPI-Chemicals
	9 - IPI-Pipe. Drilling Oper.
Inter. WP Applications, A	~~19~~ *9* - IPI-Royalty Interests
Inter. WP Applications, B	13 - IPI-Chemicals
Fred Robertson	
~~Staff~~ *Office* Assistant I~~I~~	21 - IPI-O/G Expl. & Devel.
Adv. WP Applications	6 - IPI
Office Assistant III	15 - IPI
Vicki Thiesen	
IPI Office Procedures	2 - IPI
	4 - IPI-O/G Oper. & Prod.
Effective Number Skills	26 - IPI-O/G Oper. & Prod.
	27 - IPI-Pipe. Drilling Oper.

(¶) Training participation by company (~~see~~ *refer to the* table below) does not reflect the total number of individuals who received training. Multiple reporting generally occurs when ~~some~~ *a few* employees attend more than one Training Department course during the month.

(report continues on next page)

Unit 15 Lessons 76-80

Learning Goals

1. To improve or refine technique and practice patterns.
2. To transfer improved technique patterns to straight-copy keyboarding.
3. To keyboard and format short reports.
4. To increase speed on straight, statistical, rough-draft, and script copy.

Machine Adjustments

1. Paper guide at *0*.
2. Paper bail rolls at even intervals across page.

Use:

*70-space line and single spacing for drills; DS below each SS group of drill lines
*70-space line and double spacing for ¶ timings of more than 1 minute
*5-space ¶ indention

Lesson 76 Keyboarding/Technique Skills

76a ▶ 5 Conditioning Practice

each line twice (slowly, faster); as time permits, repeat selected lines

alphabet 1 Just work for improved basic techniques to maximize keyboarding skill.
figures 2 Type 1 and 2 and 3 and 4 and 5 and 6 and 7 and 8 and 9 and 10 and 123.
adjacent key 3 Did Opal Klen make Quin aware that he was to operate the new computer?
speed 4 He or she may work with us to make a profit for the eighty city firms.

| 1 | 2 | 3 | 4 | 5 | 6 | 7 | 8 | 9 | 10 | 11 | 12 | 13 | 14 |

76b ▶ 15 Improve Techniques: Keystroking

each line twice (slowly, faster); as time permits, repeat selected lines

Home row Emphasize curved, upright fingers, wrists low; quiet hands.

1 fjfj fjfj dkdk dkdk slsl slsl a;a; a;a; a;sldkfj a;sldkfj a;sldkfj jak
2 a jag; a flag; a glass; add a dash; half a jag; add half a flask; lash
3 All lads had half a glass. Ask Sal to add a salad. Sasha had a sash.
4 Dad or Sara had half a dish of salad. Ask Dallas to add half a glass.

Third row Emphasize quick, snap strokes; finger reaches; quiet hands.

5 y yj u uj i ik o ol p p; t tf r rf e ed w ws q qa qpa; wosl eidk rufj;
6 I wrote your quote; you were to try to type it; your typewriter; query
7 Terry wrote our quarterly report; he wrote a witty query to the paper.
8 You were to try to quote proper etiquette to Peter while at the party.

Bottom row Emphasize curved, upright fingers; finger reaches; quiet hands.

9 n nj m mj , ,k . .l / /; b bf v vf c cd x xs z za aza six can vim box,
10 one man and woman; six bison and a zebu; boxes of zinc oxide in a cave
11 Vic Mann can move six or seven boxes of zinc to the cave for Anna Bax.
12 Five or six men can fix many zinc boxes for Maxwell Benjamin Cozzmann.

Document 7 (continued)

seminars (the third Thursday of Febuary, April, June, August and October).

(¶) Inform me immediately of any of the programs information ins is incorrect. I will need all basic program changes (speakers and titles of presentations) by Friday of next week. Training coordinators responsable for coordinating the respective seminars are seen under the seminar dates.

DS

Miss Thiesen: Make the attached table a part of the memo. The seminar dates were changed so many times I left them out of my draft of the table. Please complete the table by filling in the day and year for each seminar. Check the calendar for the third Thursday of the months listed.

OFFICE UPDATE SEMINAR SERIES SCHEDULE

DS

Date and TC	Topic	Speaker
Feb. Vicki Thiesen	Teleconferencing at IPI	Toshi Nozaki IPI Computer Services
Apr. Fred Robertson	Productivity in Networking	Judith C. Boyle Tech Net Co., Inc.
June Vicki Thiesen	Communicating with Computers (...or Computer Jargon)	Vincent Carlyle SW California State University
Aug. John Haimes	What Artificial Intelligence Means to Your Job	Gustavo Santana Rockworth Research and Development
Oct. Helen Jackson	The Office of 2010	Tina Parks, Career Consultants, Inc.

Document 8

Ms. Hart: Please prepare this "Monthly Training Report" of last month's activities performed by our staff. Center the month (last month) and year a double space below the report title on the first page. This same month and year should be keyed in the first ¶ of the report and on the cover page.

(¶) Training conducted by Training Department personnel during the (month, year) past month is summarized below by trainer, type of courses, and number of IPI company participants. Total training course enrollment was 229, up 2.1 percent from the previous month.

(¶) The focus of the "Trainer Refresher" course was to prepare our Training Coordinators to teach a new nine-session course entitled Office

(report continues on next page)

76c ▶ 15 Measure Basic Skill: Straight Copy

1. Two 5′ writings; *find gwam*.
2. Proofread; circle errors.
3. Record better *gwam* rate on your rate record sheet (LM, p. 3).

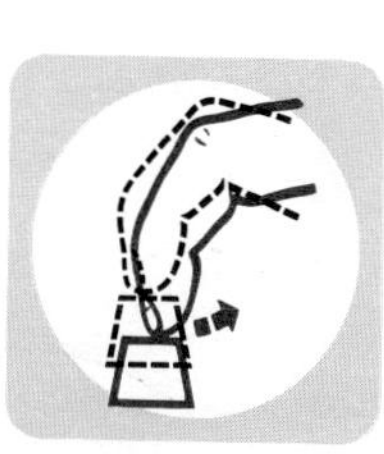

Snappy keystroking

Quick spacing

all letters used	A	1.5 si	5.7 awl	80% hfw

	gwam 3′		5′
In the lessons of this unit, try to refine your technique patterns	4	3	48
and to improve your overall keyboarding speed by at least six words a	9	5	51
minute. You can accomplish this goal if you work with a purpose and key-	14	8	54
board the various drills at alternating levels of speed. In a signifi-	19	11	57
cant research study, students who followed this plan made greater speed	24	14	60
gains than those who did not. Just remember that it is important to	28	17	62
maintain proper hand-and-finger position, to use snappy keystroking with	33	20	65
the striking action in the fingers, to space quickly after each word,	38	23	68
and to make an immediate return at the end of each line.	41	25	70
You will understand, too, the importance of the several other basic	46	27	73
techniques given in this unit. For example, you will learn to avoid	51	30	76
unnecessary motions, such as bouncing hands and arms, moving hands up	55	33	79
and down the keyboard, as well as the problem of looking away from the	60	36	82
textbook copy. The real secret of high-speed keyboarding is to keep your	65	39	85
hands and wrists very relaxed and let your fingers manipulate the keys.	70	42	87
If you do these things every time you keyboard, you will be amazed with	75	45	90
your speed growth.	76	46	91

gwam 3′ | 1 | 2 | 3 | 4 | 5 |
5′ | 1 | 2 | 3 |

76d ▶ 15 Improve Basic Skill: Straight Copy

1. Add 4 to 8 words to your 76c *gwam* rate. **Goal:** To reach a new high-speed rate.
2. Two 1′ guided writings on ¶ 1 of 76c at your new goal rate as the 1/4′ guide is called.
3. A 2′ guided writing on ¶ 1. Try to maintain your 1′ goal rate.
4. Repeat Step 2, using ¶ 2.
5. Repeat Step 3, using ¶ 2.
6. A 3′ writing using both ¶s. **Goal:** To maintain your new speed rate for 3′.

213b-217b (continued)

Document 6 (LM pp. 205-209)

Ms. Hart: Prepare letters to each of last week's seminar speakers. Use block format, open punctuation. Use their business cards for addresses.

Fred Robertson: The seminar title is **"Professionalism and Office Politics"**; the speakers and titles are as follows:

Rosella Stevenson: **"The Political Games People Play"**

R. J. Bloomfield: **"The Hidden Agenda of the 'White Space' on the Organizational Chart"**

Paul Lehman: **"Professional Politics -- What's Legal in the Office."**

Dear (insert name of seminar speaker)

(¶) Thank you for speaking at our recent seminar, Office Politics and Professionalism (Check with Fred Robertson on exact title). Your presentation on (see Fred Robertson for speech titles which were somewhat different than were publicized in our brochure) was informative, interesting, and motivational— in one word, excellent!

(¶) Please accept the enclosed honorarium of $250 with our sincere appreciation of your contribution to our staff development program. On the basis of the comments we received from participants, this seminar was one of the best-received programs we have offered to IPI employees.

Sincerely

MS. ROSELLA STEVENSON
NEWS EDITOR

THE DAILY GAZETTE

2804 PINEBROOK
AUSTIN, TX 78755-3961
(512) 452-4165

College of Business Administration

Albuquerque University

R. J. Bloomfield, Ph.D.

61 College Avenue
Albuquerque, NM 87109-4150
(505) 298-2647 Ext. 131

Paul F. Lehman, Managing Partner

Lehman, Conners, & Anderson
Attorneys-at-Law

874 Dunlavy Street
New Orleans, LA 70119-0146 *(505) 822-0900*

Document 7 (LM p. 211)

Miss Thiesen: Prepare this memo in our standard inter-office memo form. Send the memo to Ms. Hart; send copies to the TCs. Choose an appropriate subject for the memo.

(¶) The Office Update seminar sereis is shapping up well. The IPI 18the Floor Amphetheater has been reserved for each of the profram. However due to the unavailability of the Amphitheater from 11:30 a.m. to 1 p.m. on Tuesdays, I have reserved it between those hours on Thursdays. Note below the schedule of the

(memo continues on next page)

77a ▶ 5 Conditioning Practice

each line twice (slowly, faster); as time permits, repeat selected lines

alphabet 1 Quick disposal of hazardous toxic waste is governed by major controls.
figures 2 Jan sold 14 rings, 293 clips, 56 watches, 158 clocks, and 70 tie pins.
space bar 3 If they go to the city and sign the form, I may pay them for the work.
speed 4 He may go with me to the big city by the lake to do the work for them.

| 1 | 2 | 3 | 4 | 5 | 7 | 8 | 9 | 10 | 11 | 12 | 13 | 14 |

77b ▶ 20 Improve Technique: Keystroking and Response Patterns

1. Lines 1-4: Each word 3 times (slowly, faster, top speed); when bell rings, complete word, return, and continue.

2. Lines 5-8: Each phrase 3 times (slowly, faster, top speed); when bell rings, complete word, return, and continue.

3. Lines 9-12: Each sentence 3 times (slowly, faster, top speed).

4. As time permits, keyboard lines 5-8 from dictation.

Goal: High speed keyboarding response (think and key each word or word group as a whole).

Finger reaches, quiet hands

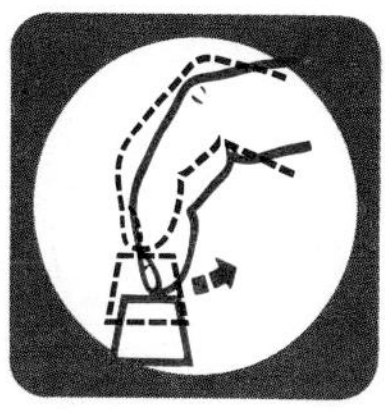
Snappy keystroking

Quick spacing

Emphasize fast finger reaches with hands quiet, wrists low and relaxed.

balanced-hand words
1 quay wow eye rut tie yen urn irk own pep aid sod for got hay jay kayak
2 lap and six did fob big ham jam kale land zoa cod vow but nap man lane
3 with they them make then when also work such form than wish paid their
4 them such form right amble amend cubic augment entitle formal downtown

Emphasize high-speed phrase response.

balanced-hand phrases
5 and the|and then|and if they|and if they go|pay for the work|sign them
6 the world of work|make it right|when they sign the form|they may go to
7 sign the form|sign the form for them|the right title for the city firm
8 fight for the land|pay a penalty to the city|dismantle the oak antique

Emphasize high-speed word-level response; quick spacing.

balanced-hand sentences
9 The map of the ancient land forms may aid them when they work with us.
10 Sign the right title forms for the big city firm and then do the work.
11 Pay for the work and then go to the city to sign the usual title form.
12 He may go to visit the ancient chapel and sit by an antique oak chair.

| 1 | 2 | 3 | 4 | 5 | 6 | 7 | 8 | 9 | 10 | 11 | 12 | 13 | 14 |

77c ▶ 10 Transfer Improved Response Patterns

1. Two 1′ writings on each of Lines 9-12 of 77b above.

Goal: With each timed repetition, to increase speed by 4 or more words.

To reach this goal, keep your hands quiet and relaxed and let the fingers do the keystroking.

213b-217b (continued)

Document 5

Ms. Hart: Use Simplified Memo format on plain paper for this informal memo to Training Coordinators about the Office Update seminar. In my haste to get this memo out to the TCs, I have not had time to proofread my copy. Please correct any errors you find. Choose an appropriate subject for the memo.

(¶) Because of the strong possibility that some changes will be made in our departments training priorities, I met with the HRD Director today specifically to discuss the Office Update programs we have planned over the next year for IPI corporate office supervisers and staff. Mr. Humphries reassured me that we should not altar our plans regarding the five Office Update luncheon seminars.

(¶) Consequently, procede with your assignments on the series and send formal confirmation letters to speakers. Do we need additional speakers for any of the seminars? We should try to get the publicity brochure to our printing department within the month to give us enough time to inform staff of the seminar series.

(¶) If we can get good attendence at the first seminar I believe we will have more requests then we can handle for the remaining programs.

77d ► 15 Format a Short Report: Rough-Draft Script Copy

full sheet

1. Prepare as an unbound report. Use 1″ side margins.

2. Use main heading: **THE TYPEWRITTEN REPORT**

QS (quadruple-space) below heading.

3. Proofread finished copy; correct errors.

(Refer to page 93, Cycle 1, if you need to review unbound report format.)

words

Many students In preparing the written work 13
for their classes, often prepare a first draft 18
which is then revised. This revision of the 26
*work lead*s *to improvement in quality of the* 36
report or other written work. Some students 45
may write the initial ~~*first*~~ *draft and then make* 53
what ever corrections are needed directly *on the* 63
handwritten copy so that it looks very 71
similar to this rough-draft script copy 79
from which you are now keyboarding. How- 87
ever, after you have learned to keyboard, 95
you can save time by ~~*if*~~ *keyboarding the* 103
initial draft before revising it. This 111
initial draft should be ~~*done as*~~ *double-* 117
spaced to make it easier to read and revise. 126
As amazing as it may seem, studies 133
indicate ~~*show*~~ *that students get higher grades on* 142
typewritten papers than on *hand written* 150
papers. All of us are impressed with the 158
neatness and easier-to-read characteristics 167
of typed copy. Teachers are no exception. 176
You can earn better grades, then, if you 184
will just take extra time to revise care- 192
fully your written work and type it in good 201
form before submitting it to your teachers. 210

Lesson 78 Keyboarding/Report Skills

78a ► 5 Conditioning Practice

each line twice (slowly, faster); as time permits, repeat selected lines

alphabet 1 Ivory silk jacquard banners marked new zoo paths leading to fox cages.

figures 2 Listed were 78 jackets, 293 blankets, 140 kits, 56 lamps, and 8 tires.

continuity 3 Purposeful repetition leads to rapid improvement of stroking patterns.

speed 4 She may go down to the ancient city by the lake to do the work for me.

| 1 | 2 | 3 | 4 | 5 | 6 | 7 | 8 | 9 | 10 | 11 | 12 | 13 | 14 |

213b-217b (continued)

Document 4 (continued)

Special Instructions: A double space below the last line of the entire text, key **Revised:** and the **current date**. Include your initials as reference a double space below the dateline.

The following activities will be pursued by ~~staff of the~~ the Training Department staff to carry out the purposes of the Department:

1. The Training Department will provide ~~a variety of~~ in-house training ~~activities~~ courses, programs, workshops, and seminars ~~for~~ to office staff for personnel development as outlined in Section 4.3 of the IPI Policy and Procedures Manual.

2. Training will ~~focus on~~ provide ~~providing~~ office employees opportunities for ~~with an opportunity~~ to:

   a. upgrade existing knowledges, skills, and competencies;

   b. develop new skills and applications based on new office technologies which should result in more efficient work procedures; and

   c. apply advanced applications by completing, in a supervised environment, regular work assignments for maximum transfer of training to the work setting.

3. Training will be provided to employees on a request basis (either by the employee or by the employee's supervisor or department manager) and will be scheduled in cooperation with the applicant's respective department. A "Request for Training" form must be completed by the applicant and signed by the employee's department manager. The Training Department will process each completed application, determine acceptance or rejection of the request, and return it to the applicant's department. If training is denied, a reason for the rejection will be noted on the application.

5. The Training Department will develop, publish, and circulate to all divisions a quarterly newsletter, THE EXECUTIVE OFFICE, announcing programs, courses, seminars, and other activities of the ~~Training~~ department.

4. Annually, the Training Department will develop, publish, and circulate an ~~annual~~ EDUCATION AND TRAINING brochure, ~~BROCHURE~~ FOR OFFICE PERSONNEL, describing the services and resources of the department.

78b ▶ 15
Improve Technique: Response Patterns

each line 3 times (slowly, faster, top speed); as time permits, repeat selected lines

Goal: To reduce time interval between keystrokes (read ahead to anticipate stroking pattern).

Technique goals

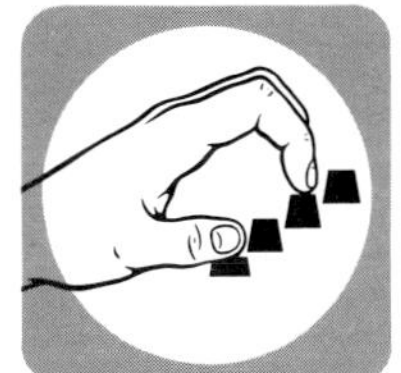
Fingers curved and upright

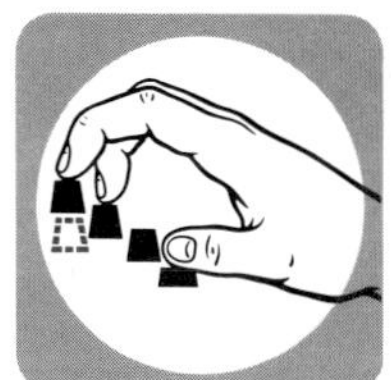
Finger keystroking action; hands quiet

Emphasize curved, upright fingers; finger-action keystroking.

one-hand words

1 as in at my be no we on up are you get him was oil dear only were upon
2 date look data pull best link area jump card lump rate hook case water
3 after union state imply great pupil staff nylon extra plump react jump

Emphasize independent finger action; quiet hands.

one-hand phrases

4 you are|my case|in my opinion|were you|great pupil|extra jump|are upon
5 after taxes|were you only|my address|minimum decrease|exaggerated poll
6 only after you were|exaggerated opinion|estate tax|you are in|you read

Emphasize continuity; finger action with fingers close to keys.

one-hand sentences

7 In my opinion, estate taxes decreased only after Junko asserted facts.
8 Only after Wes stated my exaggerated opinion were oil taxes decreased.
9 Only after Ki acted on my reserved opinion were water rates decreased.

| 1 | 2 | 3 | 4 | 5 | 6 | 7 | 8 | 9 | 10 | 11 | 12 | 13 | 14 |

78c ▶ 15
Transfer Improved Response Patterns: Guided Writing

1. Three 1′ writings (at a controlled rate with a minimum of waste motion); find *gwam*.
2. Add 4 words to best rate; determine ¼′ goal rates.
3. Three 15″ writings; try to equal or exceed ¼′ goal rate.
4. Three 30″ writings; try to equal or exceed ½′ goal rate.
5. Three 1′ guided writings at goal rate.
6. As time permits, take additional 1′ writings to increase speed.

Technique goals

Fingers well curved

Fingers upright

It is no exaggeration [4] to say that [8] the decrease in [12] rainfall has resulted in [16] water reserves [20] which are far below [24] the average required for [28] safety. We were [32] told to refer this [36] water problem to [40] the committee for attention. [44] New plans [48] probably will be [52] drafted after this committee has [56] made a [60] minimum study of the [64] water problem.

213b-217b (continued)

Document 4

Ms. Hart: I have made a few changes in the Training Department Services' section of the IPI Resource Guide. Please redo this section of the Guide in the basic format of the edited copy using IPI's standard leftbound report format.

Special Instructions: Set tab stops for efficiency in keying the single-spaced, indented text taken from the IPI Policy Manual. Double-space between numbered and lettered subsections.

Because this document will become part of the IPI Resource Guide, it does not require a cover page. The IPI Resource Guide section and page number should be centered one inch from the bottom of each page. (Page 1 is **VI-1**; page 2 is **VI-2**; etc.) Headings are not used on second and subsequent pages; thus, the text of all pages except the first should begin on line 6.

Try to plan your pages to avoid dividing text between two pages -- unless a unit of text or a paragraph is long enough to permit two or more lines to be placed on both pages. The handwritten footnote refers to the *IPI Policy Manual* quotation. When you know on which page the quotation will be completed, place the footnote at the bottom of that page. Because the Manual never has more than one footnote per page, use an asterisk (*) as a reference symbol. IPI uses standard guides for footnote indention, spacing, and placement.

Training Department Services DS

Training Department, Human Resources Division
INTERCONTINENTAL PETROLEUM, INC. QS

~~The~~ services provided to ~~personnel~~ employees of the IPI corporation through the Training Department, Human Resources Division, are described below. All Training Department resources are available to IPI ~~employees~~ personnel within the general guidelines outlined in the Intercontinental Petroleum, Inc. Policy and Procedures Manual. It states:

4.3 Training Department Services

Services provided by the Training Department, Human Resources Division, Intercontinental Petroleum, Inc., shall be as follows:

4.3.1. To provide training opportunities for office personnel (including office supervisors and, to a limited degree, department managers) within the IPI corporate: group

a. to upgrade knowledges, skills, and competencies for increasing efficiency and productivity in processing corporation information, and

b. to foster personal and professional growth and development through pride in work and job satisfaction.

4.3.2 To coordinate all training activities and to publicize training opportunities among the IPI companies.*

* From the Intercontinental Petroleum, Inc., Policy and Procedures Manual. Section 4.3: Division Services, Training Department, Revised 1987.

(document continues on next page)

78d ▶ 15 Format a Short Report: Statistical Rough-Draft Copy

full sheet

1. Prepare as an unbound report. Use 1″ side margins.

2. Use main heading:

THE QUEST FOR SPEED

QS below heading.

3. Proofread finished copy; correct errors.

(Refer to page 93, Cycle 1, if you need to review unbound report format.)

, = comma
{ } = parentheses

	gwam 1′	3′
Cheeta*hs*, the fastest of land naimals, can run withbursts of	12	4
speed up to 60 miles per hour *(mph)*. During *the* 1984 olympics, Carl Lewis	27	9
won the 100-meter dash in 9.99 seconds, the equivalent of about	40	13
22.38 mph. specially-built racing cars have travelled at *speeds over* 200	55	18
mph. In the quest for speed, however, we had have to mvoe from	68	22
the ground *to the air*. Jet aircraft, for example, cruising at altitudes of ~~over~~	83	28
35,000 *to 47,000* feet, fly at equivalent ground speeds ~~of some~~ *from* 535 *8* to ~~650~~ *1,600*	98	32
mph. contrast htese speeds with the super sonic speed of the	110	37
Concorde which can fly at a *s*peed of 1,300 mph when ~~it is~~ cruising	122	41
at an altitude of 57,000 feet.	127	42
Moving in to outer space, the speed of the space shuttle is	12	46
18,400 mph, or 5.1 miles per ~~hour~~ *second*. The space shuttle can orbit	25	51
the earth in 1 hour, ~~10~~ *21* seconds. Could it fly from Los Angeles	38	55
to San Francisco {358 *statute* miles} in 1 minute, 10 seconds. In the	52	60
physical realm, the speed of sound at sea level is approximately	65	64
1,100 feet per second. {persons have often used this *approximation* to judge	80	69
the distance of a lightening bolt. For example, if you see a	92	73
flash of lightening and approximately 3 seconds elapses before you	105	77
hear the clap of thunder, the lighting bolt was *about 3,000* ~~3,300~~ feet from	119	82
the point where you observed it.} None of these speeds, however,	132	86
can compare with the speed of light, *which travels 186,300 miles*	145	91
per second.	147	91

Lesson 79 Keyboarding/Technique Skills

79a ▶ 5 Conditioning Practice

each line twice (slowly, faster); as time permits, repeat selected lines

alphabet 1 Five or six quizzes dealt with the judicial problems in Greek history.

figures 2 The 1987 inventory included 30 office chairs, 46 desks, and 25 tables.

finger action 3 An extra plump polo pony jumped over barriers with ease and good form.

speed 4 It is the duty of the chair to key their amendment to the proxy forms.

| 1 | 2 | 3 | 4 | 5 | 6 | 7 | 8 | 9 | 10 | 11 | 12 | 13 | 14 |

79b ▶ 15 Improve Basic Skill: Statistical Rough-Draft Copy

70-space line

1. Two 1′ writings on ¶ 1 of 78d above; find *gwam*.

2. Repeat Step 1 using ¶ 2.

3. Two 3′ writings using both ¶s; find *gwam*.

4. Record better 3′ rate.

213b-217b (continued)

Document 3 (LM p. 203)

Ms. Hart: Please prepare this memo in final form. Use "Training Coordinators" in the TO line. Send a copy of the memo to each of the training coordinators (TCs).

Special Instructions: In ¶ 3, list the numbered items; SS each item, but DS between items. For efficiency, do not indent listed items.

SUBJECT: **Staff Meetings with HRD Director**

As you know, Mr. Rodney Humphries was recently appointed Director of our Human Resources Division. He met with the HRD Department Managers this morning and outlined several measures he wishes to implement to improve communications among our HRD units and, ultimately, to promote stronger IPI human resources development through expanded activities for employees.

Mr. Humphries' first priority is to meet with staff in each of the HRD five Departments. The Training Department staff ~~will~~ meet with him next week on Wednesday at 3:30 p.m. Since our Department has been targeted for increased activity over the next two years, he also wants to meet with us on a bi-weekly basis to reassess, and possibly further develop, our long-range training goals. The day and time for these bi-weekly ~~meetings~~ will be ~~determine~~ at the Wednesday meeting.

In preparation for our first meeting with Mr. Humphries, please compile documents and information pertaining to the following items: 1. Your revised training schedules for the past three months. 2. Your scheduled training activities for the next six months (with part-time staff assignments). 3. Your specific assignments with ~~respect~~ to our ~~training~~ priorities for the next two years.

Ms. Hart: Note that I have attached the Training Department's section of the IPI Resource Guide to which I refer here.

Also, please review the attached copy of the IPI Resource Guide relating to Training Department Services. You will recall ~~that~~ we ~~did a major revision to this~~ section ~~of the~~ of the Guide two years ago. Are there changes in our services (other than the minor ~~changes~~ I have made) which would warrant revision ~~to~~ the Guide ~~at the time~~?

I am sure Mr. Humphries will want to discuss both our current and long-range plans ~~of~~ meeting IPI employee training needs.

79c ▶ 15 Improve Techniques: Response Patterns/ Space Bar

1. Lines 1-3: Each phrase 3 times; key for speed; when bell rings, complete word or divide it at syllable point, return, and continue typing.

2. Lines 4-6: Each sentence 3 times; key for speed.

3. Lines 7-9: Each line 3 times; space quickly after each word and key next word without pausing.

Color bars (____) under words indicate *word* response. Read and type these words or word groups for speed.

Color dots (. . .) under words indicate *letter* response. Read and type these words letter by letter.

Technique goal

Quick spacing with down-and-in motion of right thumb

Emphasize combination or variable response patterns.

phrases

1 and the date| for the address| refer to their address| gave the statement

2 for him| they were| their date| hand weave| she saw| right union| to the tax

3 after the data| are you right| world opinion| address the ancient problem

Emphasize combination or variable response patterns.

sentences

4 Send a statement of the case to the union for an opinion on the taxes.

5 They gave the statement to the union at the address shown on the card.

6 World opinion is a factor in addressing the ancient problem of growth.

Emphasize quick, down-and-in spacing motion with right thumb.

phrases/ sentences

7 and the| and the| and the| and the| and the| and the| and the| and the| and to

8 pay them when they| pay them when they work| pay them when they work for

9 They may pay them when they try to help Jim clean the old storm drain.

79d ▶ 15 Transfer Improved Techniques: Guided Writing

1. Three 1′ writings; find *gwam*.

2. Add 4 words to best rate; determine 1/4′ goal rates.

3. Three 15″ writings; try to equal or exceed 1/4′ goal rate.

4. Three 30″ writings; try to equal or exceed 1/2′ goal rate.

5. Three 1′ guided writings at goal rate.

6. As time permits, take additional 1′ writings.

Goal: To increase speed still more.

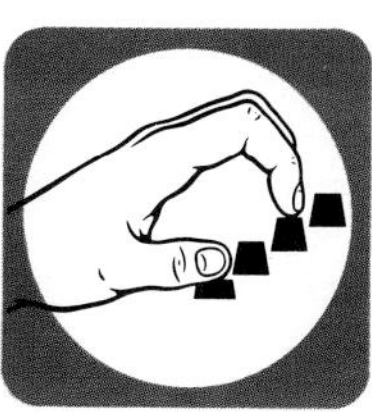

Fingers well curved, upright

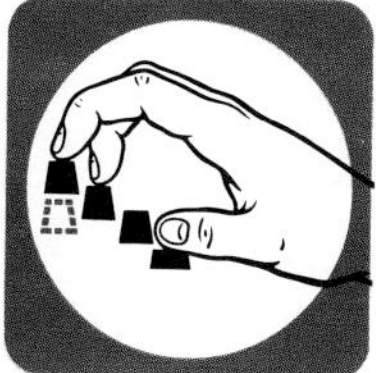

Quick, snap keystroke; finger action only

They may send the statement to the address listed on the card. The union requested that they do this and that the case be referred to the court for further action. The court has promised to consider all the facts and the other data of the case. The court will probably be able to give us their decision by the end of this month.

213a-217a ▶ 5 Conditioning Practice

Key the lines as many times as you can in 5′ at the beginning of each work period during the simulation.

alphabet 1 Vexed hostages were blindfolded as hijackers quietly zipped moneybags.

figures 2 Over 735 major companies will need 289,600 top office workers in 1994.

fig/sym 3 A #92-08 ROM chip is 31% cheaper ($51.67) than a #25-40 chip ($74.89).

speed 4 If they do the audit, they may risk their right to a land entitlement.

| 1 | 2 | 3 | 4 | 5 | 6 | 7 | 8 | 9 | 10 | 11 | 12 | 13 | 14 |

213b-217b ▶ 45 Office Job Simulation

Note: As you complete each document in this simulation, record the information required on the Word Processing Log Sheet you prepared in Unit 44, 212b, p. 361.

Document 1 (LM p. 199)

Ms. Hart: Please format this memo to send to Vicki Thiesen, Training Coordinator. Use our standard memo form. Include titles with names in the heading lines.

SUBJECT: **Office Update Seminars**

(¶) What is the current status of the Office Update Seminars we are planning for IPI corporate office staff? Have all five speakers been scheduled for the program? Have any of the topics changed?

(¶) Several department managers indicated to me that they want all of their office personnel to attend the luncheon seminars. One even suggested bringing in a temporary receptionist to cover for his office staff--others agreed.

(¶) To accommodate as many people as possible, check on the availability of the main amphitheater for the seminars.

Document 2 (LM p. 201)

Ms. Hart: Please prepare this letter addressed to Mr. Mike Peters. I've written the address on the copy. Use our usual letter format. I'd like a photocopy of the letter sent to the address shown below:

Mrs. Carlota Romero
Houston Chapter AATDM
President
717 East Kingsway Road
Houston, TX 77043-2959

SUBJECT: REQUEST FOR JOURNAL COPIES

Special Instructions: Usually I prefer closing my letters with "Sincerely" followed by my name and title. But for this letter I want to use "Membership Chair, AATDM Houston Chapter" as my title.

Send to: MIKE PETERS, EXECUTIVE DIRECTOR
AMERICAN ASSOCIATION OF TRAINING AND
DEVELOPMENT MANAGERS
7943 NORTH COMPTON ROAD
RESTON, VA 22019-5706

(¶) The AATDM flyers you recently sent to me will be most useful in our annual campaign for recruiting new AATDM local chapter members. The Houston chapter now boasts 78 members, but we would like to increase our membership to at least 100.

(¶) It is much easier to recruit new members when we place the Association's magazine and other timely information in their hands. Consequently, please send us 50 copies of The AATDM Journal--the most recent issues would be most appreciated.

(¶) I look forward to seeing you at the annual AATDM Convention in Chicago next summer.

Lesson 80 Keyboarding/Report Skills

80a ▶ 5 Conditioning Practice

each line twice (slowly, faster); as time permits, repeat selected lines

alphabet 1 Jay Wilkert utilized complex formulas for solving this unique problem.

figures 2 The new book contains 926 illustrations, 475 forms, and 1,380 figures.

quiet hands 3 Many union members will expect to receive a maximum salary adjustment.

speed 4 The key to proficiency is to name the right goals, then work for them.

| 1 | 2 | 3 | 4 | 5 | 6 | 7 | 8 | 9 | 10 | 11 | 12 | 13 | 14 |

80b ▶ 10 Format a Short Report: Rough-Draft Copy

full sheet

1. Prepare as an unbound report. Use 1" side margins.
2. Use main heading: **KEYBOARDING SKILL**

QS below heading.

3. Proofread finished copy; correct errors.

(Refer to page 93, Cycle 1, if you need to review unbound report format.)

	gwam 1'	3'
During this decade, it has been predicted that over 70	12	4
percent of the polulation of hte United States will operate a	24	8
keyboard of some kind in thier day-to-day activities. Your	37	12
transfer of your keyboarding skill will, in all probability, be	51	17
a computer key board. You will learn the meaning of such terms	64	21
as bit, byte, chip, CPU, dish, program, and modem. Otrher com-	77	26
puter words will become a part of your vocabulary. But best of	90	30
all, you will learn through and with a computer. You may use a	102	34
microcomputer, for example, to help you improve your skills	121	40
and communication.		
Many persons will have personal computers in their homes.	12	44
These personal computers will be portable. Some time ago, a	25	48
copany the in computer industry announced its so-called "computer	38	53
on a chip," a single chip that incorporates all a computer's cir-	56	59
cuitry on one stamp-size block of silicon. Another computer com-	69	63
pany has develped a chip the size of a collar button that has	83	68
half a million circuits on it. Still naother innovation is bubble	98	73
memory, designed to hold hundreds of thousands bits of information	112	77
in a chip even when the power is off. Indeed, the future of	124	82
computers continues to be exciting.	131	84

80c ▶ 10 Improve Basic Skill: Rough-Draft Copy

70-space line

1. Two 1' writings on ¶ 1 of 80b above.
2. Repeat Step 1 using ¶ 2.
3. A 3' writing using both ¶s.
4. Find and record 3' *gwam*.

Unit 45 Lessons 213-217

Learning Goals

1. To apply keyboarding, formatting, and language knowledge and skills at levels expected of a beginning office worker.

2. To produce with minimum direction and assistance a variety of business documents of high quality within a reasonable time.

Machine Adjustments

1. Paper guide at *0*.

2. Margin sets: 70-space line for warmup drill; as appropriate for document production.

3. Spacing: SS drills; as appropriate for document production.

INTERCONTINENTAL PETROLEUM, INC.: A TRAINING DEPARTMENT SIMULATION

Before you begin processing the documents in this unit, read carefully the information at the right.

Make notes of any standard procedures that you think will save you time during the completion of the simulation.

Daily Work Plan

Conditioning practice .... 5′
Document production .... 45′

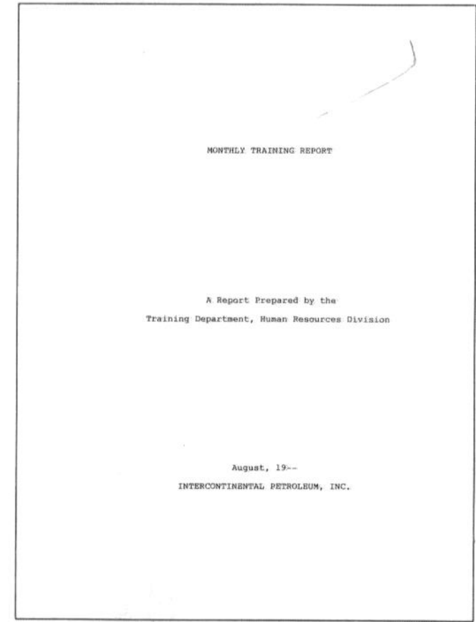

MONTHLY TRAINING REPORT

A Report Prepared by the
Training Department, Human Resources Division

August, 19--
INTERCONTINENTAL PETROLEUM, INC.

Cover Page

Work Assignment

Intercontinental Petroleum, Inc., is a large oil and gas corporation made up of fifteen subsidiary companies with offices and operations in several countries. You are employed at IPI's corporation headquarters, One Corporate Plaza South, Houston, TX 70064-3952.

As an entry-level employee, you are classified as an Office Assistant I. When you complete your probation and training period at IPI, you will be eligible for promotion to an Office Assistant II.

The Training Department at IPI is one of five departments in the Human Resources Division. You will work under the direct supervision of Ms. Martha Hart, Training Manager. Ms. Hart's staff includes four training coordinators; John Haimes, Helen Jackson, Fred Robertson, and Vicki Thiesen; three Office Assistant IIIs; and you.

The Training Department is responsible for developing and providing training for office supervisors and other office staff in the IPI companies. Your primary role will be to process routine office documents relating to the department's training activities. You will format memos, letters, tables, and reports.

Most original source documents are prepared in handwritten or rough-draft form by Ms. Hart or the training coordinators. Since Ms. Hart assigns all work to the four office assistants, submit your completed documents to her for her approval or signature. Do your best on each work assignment so you will deserve a favorable rating leading to a promotion!

The office-assistant work center is well equipped with a computer terminal, text editing equipment, and other automated electronic devices. As available and appropriate, use the Center's equipment and resources for completing your work assignments.

The following excerpts from the Information Processing Manual of IPI should be helpful to you in processing documents for the Training Department. Also, you may rely on your other desk resources such as *Century 21 Keyboarding, Formatting, and Document Processing*, Fourth Edition. Special instructions, when needed, will accompany the documents you will be processing.

Excerpts from IPI Information Processing Manual

Interoffice correspondence usually is prepared on IPI interoffice communications forms. In some situations, Simplified Memo format on plain paper may be specified. You are to supply your reference initials and notations for any copies and attachments or enclosures. Use the current date in all correspondence unless directed to do otherwise.

Letters usually are prepared on IPI letterheads. The preferred IPI letter format is modified block style with blocked paragraphs, open punctuation, and a subject line. Other formats may be specified for special circumstances.

Reports are prepared on plain paper. Unless otherwise specified, use leftbound format. Title lines are centered on the line of writing beginning on line 10 of the first page. The text begins on the fourth line space below the title.

On page 2 and subsequent pages, the page number is entered on line 6 at the right margin. The text continues a double space below.

A cover page is prepared for each report. It includes the report title, the statement **"A Report Prepared by the"** followed by department and division names, the date of the report, and the IPI company name. All lines are centered on the line of writing. (See the cover page format at the left.)

Professional proofreading is vital at IPI. Examine, check, and correct all your completed documents very carefully so they reflect the high image of IPI.

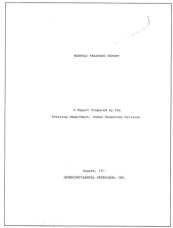

80d ▶ 10
Improve Techniques: Shift Keys/Return

1. Lines 1-3: Each line 3 times (slowly, faster, top speed).

2. Lines 4-10: As directed in copy; work for speed.

Technique cue

Manual Return: Use a quick flick-of-hand motion to return carriage.

Electric Return: Make a quick, little-finger reach to the return key.

shift keys — Emphasize little finger reach; keep other fingers in keyboarding position.

left 1 **Ja Ja Ja Jan Jan Jan; Jan McNeil, President of McNeil, Inc., resigned.**

right 2 **F; F; Flo Flo Flo; Dot Ride visited Denver, Cheyenne, and Sioux Falls.**

both 3 **Flo James, Jack Dowd, and Mario Diaz visited London, Rome, and Berlin.**

Emphasize quick return and start of new line. ↓ tab: center + 10

4 tab ——————→ **and the**

5 **lake** ——— tab ———→ **and the**

6 **work** ——— tab ———→ repeat 3 times

7 tab ——————→ **A quick return**

8 **at the end of a line** ——— tab ———→ **with an immediate start**

9 **of the new line** ——— tab ———→ **will help you reach**

10 **new speed goals.** ——— tab ———→ repeat 3 times

80e ▶ 15
Measure Basic Skill: Straight Copy

two 5′ writings; find *gwam*; circle errors; record better rate

all letters used | A | 1.5 si | 5.7 awl | 80% hfw

	gwam 3′	5′	
Are you now keyboarding with stationary hands? Are your wrists	4	3	53
low and relaxed but off the border of the keyboard? Do you endeavor	8	6	56
to keep your fingers well curved and upright and execute all keyboard	13	8	59
reaches with the fingers only? Do you space quickly after every word	18	11	61
and begin the next word immediately? At line endings, do you make the	23	14	64
return quickly with an immediate start of the new line? Do you remember	28	17	67
to keep your fingers close to the keys when operating the keyboard? Do	33	19	70
you activate every key with a snap stroke made by the correct individual	37	22	73
finger? If you can answer in the affirmative to these questions, you	42	25	76
should be making an effective growth in speed.	45	27	77
As you remember, your objective in this writing is to increase your	50	30	80
overall speed by at least six words a minute. If you followed carefully	54	33	83
the purpose given for each technique activity, and then made a diligent	59	35	86
effort to make a refinement in your technique pattern and to eliminate	64	38	89
all unproductive motions as you operated the keyboard, you should reach	69	41	92
this objective. If you do not increase your speed by at least six words	73	44	95
a minute, you may want to make a concerned evaluation of your keyboard-	78	47	97
ing form, and then do again selected technique drills given in the lessons	83	49	100
of this unit.	84	50	101

gwam 3′ | 1 | 2 | 3 | 4 | 5 |
5′ | 1 | 2 | 3 |

Lesson 212 Prepare for a Simulation

212a ▶ 5 Conditioning Practice

1. Each line twice SS.
2. Take as many 1′ writings on line 4 as time permits.

alphabet 1 Jake was very delighted to have the exact number sequence for a prize.
figure 2 The final 25 answers to the 90-point quiz are on pages 31, 46, and 78.
underline 3 Before leaving for work, Rufus reads The New York Times and USA Today.
speed 4 Go to the firm for the title to the auto and then to the city auditor.

| 1 | 2 | 3 | 4 | 5 | 6 | 7 | 8 | 9 | 10 | 11 | 12 | 13 | 14 |

212b ▶ 10 Prepare a Log Sheet for Use in the Simulation of Unit 45

Prepare for photoduplicating a Weekly Log Sheet on which you will record all jobs you complete in the simulation in Unit 45.

Key the log illustrated at the right on 8 1/2″ × 11″ paper with top, bottom and side margins of about 1″. Use a pen or pencil to draw the vertical lines.

WORD PROCESSING LOG SHEET

Operator's Name ____________________ For Week of __________

Document No.	Originator	Document Description	Begin Time	End Time	Production Time	Total Lines*

*Count each line regardless of length (including any titles or subtitles). Count 3 lines for the opening lines of a letter and 3 lines for the closing lines. Count 4 lines for letter envelopes; 1 line for COMPANY MAIL envelopes.

212c ▶ 35 Prepare for a Simulation

In the simulation you will complete in Unit 45, you will format/process a variety of documents similar to those you have done during the school term. From the list at the right, choose and practice selected problems before you start Unit 45.

Letters (plain paper)
page 274, 155b, Problem 2
page 276, 156b, Problem 3
page 316, 182c, Problem 2

Reports (plain paper)
page 280, 159c, Problem 1
page 283, 160c, Problem 1

Tables (plain paper)
page 346, 201c, Problem 1
page 347, 202c, Problem 1
page 351, 206b, Problem 1

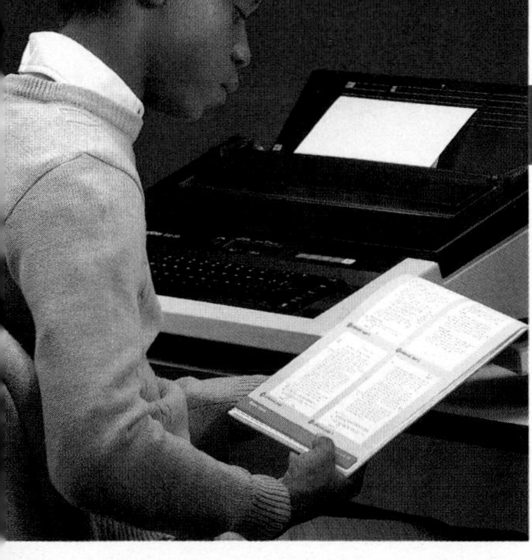

Unit 16 Lessons 81-85

Learning Goals

1. To review and improve basic application skill for preparing tables, personal/business letters, and reports.

2. To improve language and word-division skills.

3. To maintain and improve techniques and basic skills.

Machine Adjustments

1. Paper guide at *0*.

2. Paper bail rolls at even intervals across page.

Use:

*70-space line and single spacing for drills; DS below each SS group of drill lines

*70-space line and double spacing for ¶ timings of more than 1 minute

*5-space ¶ indention

Lesson 81 Center/Language Skills

81a ▶ 5 Conditioning Practice

each line twice (slowly, faster); as time permits, repeat selected lines

alphabet 1 Max just amazed that Portland crowd by kicking five quick field goals.

learning* 2 two, 2; fifty, 50; four thirty-two, 432; three, one twenty-four, 3,124

home row 3 Dashall Kagal added all glass sales as Jeff Ladd added all jade sales.

speed 4 He or she may go with us to the city to do the work for the big firms.

| 1 | 2 | 3 | 4 | 5 | 6 | 7 | 8 | 9 | 10 | 11 | 12 | 13 | 14 |

*Read, think, and keyboard figures in combination sequences, as possible.

81b ▶ 30 Recall Centering Skills

Problem 1
half sheet, long edge at top

1. DS copy; determine vertical placement.

2. Center problem vertically and each line horizontally (Reference: page RG 10).

Problem 2
Repeat Problem 1 on full sheet.

BASIC COMPUTER TERMINOLOGY

CPU: Central Processing Unit

ROM: Read-Only Memory

RAM: Random-Access Memory

DOS: Disk Operating System

Problem 3
half sheet, long edge at top

DS; center problem vertically and horizontally (*name of each language to be centered on separate line*).

(Problem 4 on page 142)

SOME COMPUTER LANGUAGES

Basic | Logo | Pascal | Smalltalk | Cobol | Fortran | Forth

211b (continued)

Problem 2
Purchase Order

words

Futura Computer Systems PURCHASE ORDER

42 Cannon Drive • Santa Barbara, CA 93105-2233 • (805) 925-1125

DELGADO'S OFFICE PRODUCTS — Purchase Order No.: B28 781 7

1735 ORANGEWOOD AVENUE — Date: September 25, 19-- 15

WINTER HAVEN FL 33880-1452 — Terms: 2/10, n/30 23

Shipped Via: Johnson Freight 26

Quantity	Description/Stock Number	Price		Per	Total		words
10	Post-It Notes, 5"x3" Pad (B19-435)	1	00	ea	10	00	36
1	Rolodex Swivel Files (B18-285)	30	35	ea	30	35	48
1	Heavy-Duty Stapler (B18-266)	45	30	ea	45	30	56
2	E-Z Mark Porcelain Board (B67-482)	34	20	ea	68	40	69
4	See-Thru Clear Tape, 2" (B30-104)	3	50	ea	14	00	79
					168	05	80

By Sidney Jacobson 83

Problem 3
Invoice

Centek Office Systems, Inc. 400 Garfield Avenue, Aurora, IL 60506-9250, (312) 797-8822 — INVOICE

IWASAKI JEWELERS — Date: July 2, 19-- 6

365 NORTH 600 WEST — Customer 10

PROVO UT 84601-2635 — Order No.: AA 367-173 16

Terms	Shipped Via	Our Order No.	Date Shipped	words
10/1, n/30	Cruz Transport, Inc.	483 AJ 621	7/21/--	26

Quantity	Description/Stock No.	(Unit Price)		(Amount)		words
2	CJ-2000 Telephone {63C15}	49	99	99	98	34
1	CJ-2100 Telephone {54C54}	39	99	39	99	42
1	Touch-A-Matic {73C72}	139	99	139	99	49
1	Record-A-Call Cassette (24D88)	169	99	169	99	58
5	Modualr Line Cord {95A10}	6	99	34	95	67
				484	90	68
	Sales Tax			26	67	72
				511	57	73

Problem 4

Reformat the invoice in Problem 3, making these changes:

Change our order number to **387 JB 381**.

Change the cost for the CJ-2000 telephone to **$59.99** per unit. The sales tax is **5.5%**. Make all other necessary changes.

81b (continued)

Problem 4

half sheet, long edge at top

1. DS copy; determine vertical placement.

2. Center problem vertically and each line horizontally.

DS > CENTERING STEPS

Find horizontal center of paper:
add scale reading at left edge of paper
to scale reading at right edge of paper;
divide sum by 2 to find center point.
From center point, backspace 1 space for
each 2 letters and spaces in line; ignore any
odd letter; start line at ending point.

81c ▶ 15

Improve Language Skills: Grammar

full sheet; 1" top margin; 60-space line

Study/Learn/Apply/Correct Procedures

1. STUDY explanatory rule.

2. Key line number (with period); space twice, then key the LEARN sentence(s) DS, noting rule application.

3. Key the line number (with period); space twice, then key the APPLY sentence(s) DS, selecting the word (in parentheses) needed to make the sentence(s) correct.

4. As your teacher reads the correct sentence(s), show in pen or pencil any corrections that need to be made in your copy.

5. Rekey any APPLY sentence containing an error, CORRECTING the error as you key. Place the corrected sentence in the space below the APPLY sentence containing the error.

SINGULAR VERBS

Use a singular verb with a singular subject.

Learn 1. The tree has lost its leaves.
Apply 2. A careless driver (is, are) dangerous to pedestrians.

Use singular verbs with indefinite pronouns (each, every, any, either, neither, one, etc.) used as subjects.

Learn 3. Everyone is doing well in this class.
Apply 4. Each of us (is, are) ready to help you.

Use a singular verb with singular subjects linked by *or* or *nor*. Exception: If one subject is singular and the other is plural, the verb agrees with the closer subject.

Learn 5. Either my sister or my brother is to do the work.
Learn 6. Neither the teacher nor the students are here.
Apply 7. Neither the book nor the magazine (is, are) being used.
Apply 8. Either the girl or her parents (is, are) to help us.

Use singular verbs with collective nouns (committee, team, class, jury, etc.) if the collective noun acts as a unit.

Learn 9. The committee is meeting with the president.
Learn 10. The class has been dismissed.
Apply 11. The jury (has, have) returned its verdict.
Apply 12. The board (is, are) in session.

Lesson 211 Evaluation: Forms Processing

211a ▶ 5 Conditioning Practice

1. Each line twice SS.
2. Take as many 1′ writings on line 4 as time permits.

alphabet 1 The very flabby men by the hexagon-shaped building were quizzing Jack.
fig/sym 2 To reach their 1987 quota, they have to sell 50 trucks and 2,346 cars.
long reaches 3 The minimum number of boys necessary for the musical ceremony is five.
speed 4 I wish to pay for the bushel of corn when she is paid for the bicycle.

| 1 | 2 | 3 | 4 | 5 | 6 | 7 | 8 | 9 | 10 | 11 | 12 | 13 | 14 |

211b ▶ 45 Measure Document Production Skill: Forms

Time Schedule
Plan and Prepare .... 5′
Timed Production .... 30′
Proofread and Correct Errors ... 7′
Compute *n-pram* .... 3′

1. Arrange supplies (LM pp. 189-195), second sheets, carbon paper, eraser.
2. Make 1 cc of each problem.
3. When directed to begin, key for 30′ from the following problems, correcting all errors neatly. Proofread before removing the problems from the machine.
4. Compute *n-pram* for the 30′ period.
5. Turn in all problems in order shown.

Problem 1
Purchase Requisition

Futura Computer Systems
42 Cannon Drive • Santa Barbara, CA 93105-2233 • (805) 925-1125

PURCHASE REQUISITION

words

Deliver to: Marc Hemsley   Requisition No. BJ 1783 4
Location: Suite 689   Date March 12, 19-- 9
Job No. 78396   Date Required April 15, 19-- 13

Quantity	Description	words
10	Post-It Notes, 5" x 3" Pad	19
1	Rolodex Swivel Files, 5" x 3" Card	27
1	Heavy-Duty Stapler	31
2	E-Z Mark Porcelain Board, 18" x 24"	38
4	See-Thru Clear Tape, 2"	44

Requisitioned by: Rebecca Silverstein 47

Problems 2-4 are on page 360.

82a ▶ 5
Conditioning Practice

each line twice (slowly, faster); as time permits, repeat selected lines

alphabet 1 With care and vigor, Kim Bass uniquely played the sax for a jazz trio.

figures 2 twelve thirty-four, 1234; fifty, six seventy-eight, 50,678; ninety, 90

3d row 3 A witty reporter wrote quips without error for reports for your paper.

speed 4 Pay them for their work and then go with us to the city for the forms.

| 1 | 2 | 3 | 4 | 5 | 6 | 7 | 8 | 9 | 10 | 11 | 12 | 13 | 14 |

82b ▶ 15
Improve Language Skills: Grammar

full sheet, 1″ top margin; 60-space line

Key the lines as directed in 81c, p. 142.

SINGULAR VERBS (continued)

Use singular verbs with the pronouns *all* and *some* (as well as fractions and percentages) when used as subjects *if* their modifiers are singular. Use plural verbs *if* their modifiers are plural.

Learn 1. All the food is gone.
Learn 2. All of the supplies were lost or misplaced.
Apply 3. Some of the work (is, are) done.
Apply 4. All of us (is, are) present.

Use a singular verb when number is used as the subject and is preceded by *the*; however, use a plural verb if *number* is preceded by *a*.

Learn 5. The number of persons requesting information has increased.
Learn 6. A number of visitors are here for the tour.
Apply 7. The number who can qualify for work (is, are) small.
Apply 8. A number of persons (has, have) left for the day.

PLURAL VERBS

Use a plural verb with a plural subject.

Learn 9. The trees have lost their leaves.
Apply 10. The boxes (is, are) in the storage room.

Use plural verbs with compound subjects joined by *and*.

Learn 11. The dog and the cat are in the kennel.
Apply 12. The principal and the superintendent (is, are) here.

209c (continued)

Problem 2
Invoice

Prepare the invoice shown at the right. Proofread; circle errors.

Problem 3
Invoice

Reformat the invoice of Problem 2, making these changes:

Change quantity of **Daisy Wheel -- Gothic 12** from **3** to **2**. Make all necessary changes.

Add to the invoice items **1 Daisy Wheel -- Elite 12**; stock no. -- **(AA 485)**; unit price of **$18.49**.

Centek Office Systems, Inc. 400 Garfield Avenue, Aurora, IL 60506-9250, (312) 797-8822 — **INVOICE**

		words
YOUR WORD PROCESSING CO	Date: April 15, 19--	8
685 MAIN STREET	Customer Order No.: 390 A 481	11
RICHLAND WA 99352-1865		18

Terms	Shipped Via	Our Order No.	Date Shipped	words
6/14, n/30	K & K Lines, Inc.	68792 AQ	5/15/--	27

Quantity	Description/Stock No.	(Unit Price)	(Amount)	words
1	Daisy Wheel - Courier 10 (AA 483)	18.49	18.49	36
1	Daisy Wheel - Courier 12 (AA 484)	18.49	18.49	46
2	Daisy Wheel - Script 12 (AA 492)	18.49	36.98	55
3	Daisy Wheel - Gothic 12 (AA 498)	18.49	55.47	64
1	Daisy Wheel - Orator 10 (AA 503)	18.49	18.49	74
			147.92	75
	Sales Tax		11.69	77
			159.61	78

Lesson 210 Review: Forms Processing

210a ▶ 5 Conditioning Practice

1. Each line twice SS.
2. Take as many 1′ timed writings on line 4 as time permits.

alphabet 1 Jan Metzger may pick her quota of extra grapes before leaving at dawn.

figures 2 Checks outstanding as of August 24, 1987, include Numbers 357 and 360.

adjacent-key 3 Lois was very sad when we opposed plans for selling juice at the pool.

speed 4 Drew Tory and eight men may dismantle the sign by the downtown chapel.

| 1 | 2 | 3 | 4 | 5 | 6 | 7 | 8 | 9 | 10 | 11 | 12 | 13 | 14 |

210b ▶ 45 Build Sustained Document Production Skill: Forms

Time Schedule

Plan and Prepare .... 5′
Timed Production .... 30′
Proofread and Correct Errors ... 7′
Compute *n-pram* .... 3′

1. Make a list of problems to be formatted/processed:
page 355, 207c, Problem 2
page 356, 208c, Problem 2
page 358, 209c, Problem 2
page 358, 209c, Problem 3
2. Arrange supplies (LM pp. 181-187), second sheets, carbon paper, eraser.
3. Make 1 cc for each problem.
4. When directed to begin, key for 30′ from the list of problems, correcting all errors neatly. Proofread before removing the problems from the machine.
5. Compute *n-pram* for the 30′ period.
6. Turn in problems in the order listed.

82c ▶ 30 Recall Table Formatting

Problem 1

half sheet; long edge at top

1. Center problem vertically and horizontally in proper table format.
2. DS table.
3. Decide how many spaces to leave between columns for best appearance.

COMPUTER tERMINOLOGY

micro chip	graphics
software	main frame
data base	automation
terminal	bug
disk drive	flawchart

Problem 2

full sheet

1. Center problem vertically and horizontally; DS table.
2. Decide how many spaces to leave between columns.
3. DS above and DS below the divider line (1½" long).

Note. SS and key table notation the width of the table.

WORD DIVISION REVIEW*

(Preferred Division Points at Ends of Lines)

knowl-edge	mathe-matics
study-ing	area
oper-ate	highly
planned	enough
sum-mer	run-ning
starter	begin-ning

*If a word is written without hyphens, it cannot be divided.

Problem 3

half sheet, long edge at top

1. Center vertically and horizontally; DS table.
2. Decide how many spaces to leave between columns.
3. Key the words without the periods that show syllabic division.

As time permits, repeat Problem 3; full sheet. Show by hyphens preferred division points for each word at end of a line. Assume bell rings on the first letter of each word.

WORDS FREQUENTLY MISSPELLED

ac·com·mo·date	li·brar·y	scis·sors
an·swer	li·cense	sep·a·rate
change·a·ble	min·i·a·ture	ser·geant
e·quipped	mis·spell	su·per·sede
fa·mil·iar	mort·gage	syn·o·nym
lab·o·ra·tor·y	oc·curred	ven·geance

209a ▶ 5
Conditioning Practice

1. Each line twice SS.
2. Take as many 1′ writings on line 4 as time permits.

alphabet	1	Seven major questions were from the psychology textbook by Fitzgerald.
fig/sym	2	Oki traveled 1,023 miles in March, 965 miles in April, and 748 in May.
outside reaches	3	Polly and Ward are very anxious to oppose Sally in the quiz on Africa.
speed	4	Make a formal amendment so they can vie for a civic proficiency title.

| 1 | 2 | 3 | 4 | 5 | 6 | 7 | 8 | 9 | 10 | 11 | 12 | 13 | 14 |

209b ▶ 15
Improve Tabulating Technique

70-space line

1. Clear tab stops.
2. Starting at left margin, set 4 tab stops 11 spaces apart.
3. Key the copy once, tabulating from column to column.
4. Take as many 2′ writings as time permits to improve tabulating skill.

					gwam 2′	
$497.53	95%	#8749	(101)	$77.28	3	28
$511.24	87%	#1902	(922)	$43.56	6	31
$763.10	66%	#3122	(133)	$15.98	9	34
$122.69	12%	#3564	(342)	$62.70	12	37
$330.85	34%	#5375	(510)	$61.14	16	40
$258.98	10%	#6496	(976)	$20.12	19	43
$649.07	26%	#7810	(475)	$57.35	22	47
$804.76	37%	#1028	(867)	$43.34	25	50

209c ▶ 30
Format/Process Invoices

(LM pp. 175-179)

Problem 1
Invoice

Prepare the invoice shown at the right. Follow placement/spacing guides shown in color. Proofread; circle errors.

Centek Office Systems, Inc.
400 Garfield Avenue
Aurora, IL 60506-9250
(312) 797-8822

INVOICE

Tab

		words
CHIANG DECORATORS	Date: June 20, 19--	6
201 TOWNE HOUSE ROAD	Customer	11
HAMDEN CT 06514-4562	Order No.: 58 BB 6741	17

Terms	Shipped Via	Our Order No.	Date Shipped	words
9/12, n/30	Smith Transit, Inc.	2 596-81	6/20/--	26

Quantity	Description/Stock No.	(Unit Price)	(Amount)	words
1	12-Digit Desktop Calculator (87Z01)	88 95	88 95	36
2	10-Digit Desktop Calculator (76Z82)	48 95	97 90	46
1	Type-O-Graph Typewriter (65X84)	245 97	245 97	55
1	Cabinet and Safe Combination (71Q49)	117 49	117 49	65
5	Graph Paper 8 1/2" x 11" (01P97)	5 99	29 95	75
	Set tab 1 or 2 spaces from rule		DS	
			580 26	76
	Sales Tax		43 52	78
			DS	
			623 78	79
Approximate center	Indent 3 spaces	Tab	Tab	

Problems 2 and 3 are on page 358.

Letter/Language Skills

83a ▶ 5

Conditioning Practice

each line twice (slowly, faster); as time permits, repeat selected lines

alphabet 1 Quickly, zealous Gene Fox jumped over the big hurdles to win the race.

figures 2 ninety-eight, 98; one, seven eighty, 1,780; fifteen thirty-four, 1534.

bottom row 3 Manny Cox and Ada Nixon helped me move six zinc boxes from the cavern.

speed 4 The six busy men may go down to the field to fix an authentic antique.

| 1 | 2 | 3 | 4 | 5 | 6 | 7 | 8 | 9 | 10 | 11 | 12 | 13 | 14 |

83b ▶ 35

Format and Key Personal/Business and Business Letters

4 full sheets

Problem 1

Using your home address in the opening lines, and your name in the closing lines, format the letter in personal/business style (see p. 75) to:

Mr. Mark Gray
Director, Camp Paiviki
c/o Crippled Children's Society
7120 Franklin Avenue
Los Angeles, CA 90046-1211

Use block style, open punctuation. Use a 50-space line and start your address on line 17. Supply all necessary parts for letters (salutation, complimentary close, and your printed name).

Problem 2

Arrange Problem 2 in block style, open punctuation (see p. 75). Use a 60-space line; begin dateline on line 19. Supply an appropriate salutation.

Problems 3 and 4

Format and key the letters as directed for Problem 1.

Problem 1

April 10, 19-- (¶ 1) I wish to apply for the job as counselor at Camp Paiviki, your summer camp for handicapped children.
(¶ 2) During the past two summers, I have worked as an aide in the Crippled Children's Summer Camp Day Program in (give name of your city). I taught arts and crafts and assisted with the swimming program.
(¶ 3) The supervisor of these summer programs, Mrs. Marilyn Graves, said she would be happy to recommend me. Her phone number is (use your area code) 285-3976.

Problem 2

May 9, 19-- (Use your name and home address) (¶ 1) Because Mrs. Graves speaks so highly of your work with handicapped children in the Summer Camp Day Program, I am prepared to offer you a summer job as counselor at Camp Paiviki. You will be working with children in the 9-12 age group.
(¶ 2) If you accept this job offer, I'd like to have you report for work on the afternoon of June 20. I am enclosing a map showing the location of Camp Paiviki in Crestline, California. We will work out the details of clothes you should bring after I hear from you.
Sincerely yours|Mark Gray, Director|jr|Enclosure

Problem 3

May 13, 19-- (¶ 1) Your letter offering me a position as counselor at Camp Paiviki arrived today. I am happy to accept your offer.
(¶ 2) As you requested, I shall report for work on the afternoon of June 20.

Problem 4

August 30, 19-- (¶ 1) Thank you for the opportunity to be a counselor at Camp Paiviki this summer. It was a new and wonderful experience for me to work so closely with handicapped children. Their optimistic approach to life is an example that I shall follow.
(¶ 2) I enjoyed, too, the opportunity to become so well acquainted with you and the rest of your staff. Thanks, again.

208c ▶ 30 Format/Process Purchase Orders

(LM pp. 169-173)

Problem 1
Purchase Order

Prepare the purchase order shown at the right. Follow placement/spacing guides shown in color. Proofread; circle errors.

words

Futura Computer Systems
42 Cannon Drive • Santa Barbara, CA 93105-2233 • (805) 925-1125

PURCHASE ORDER

Tab | Tab

BENNETT'S OFFICE SUPPLY
1135 PITTMAN DRIVE
MISSOULA MT 59803-2462

Purchase Order No.: BZ 3972 6
Date: April 19, 19-- 10 16
Terms: 2/10, n/30 18
Shipped Via: Western Freight 21

Quantity	Description/Stock Number	Price		Per	Total		words
1	Computer Cabinet (FB4199)	298	47	ea	298	47	30
2	Low-Standing Bookcase (FB9840)	198	95	ea	397	90	40
2	Two-Drawer File (FB4481)	169	49	ea	338	98	48
1	Lateral File (FB8305)	259	99	ea	259	99	56
1	Executive Desk, 24" x 54" (BK7498)	429	49	ea	429	49	68
↑ Approximate center	↑ Set tab 1 or 2 spaces from rule	↑ Tab			1,724	83	70
					↑ Tab		

By Caleb Rosenberg 73

Problem 2
Purchase Order

Prepare the purchase order as you did in Problem 1. Add the figures in the total column and enter the total under the column.

Problem 3
Purchase Order

Rekey the purchase order of Problem 2, making the following changes:

Alphabetize entries in description column.

Decrease order for **File Folders** to **50**. (Change total column)

Include **75 Diskette Labels (BK6140)** with other items being ordered. They sell for **7 cents** apiece.

Futura Computer Systems
42 Cannon Drive • Santa Barbara, CA 93105-2233 • (805) 925-1125

PURCHASE ORDER

DELGADO'S OFFICE PRODUCTS
1735 ORANGEWOOD AVENUE
WINTER HAVEN FL 33880-1452

Purchase Order No.: 848-T-16 7
Date: October 9, 19-- 15
Terms: 3/10, n/30 23
Shipped Via: Carlson Freight 26

Quantity	Description/Stock Number	Price		Per	Total		words
1	Digital Postal Scale (FB4199)	79	95	ea	79	95	35
1	Chart Tape, 1/8" x 324" (FB9840)	1	99	ea	1	99	45
10	Flexible Disks, S.S./D.D. (FB4481)	2	95	ea	29	50	55
15	W. P. Ribbons, 5/16" x 60' (FB8305)	4	95	ea	74	25	66
100	Assorted File Folders (BK7498)		10	ea	10	00	76

By Sylvia Lathman 78

83c ▶ 10
Improve Language Skills: Grammar

full sheet; 1″ top margin; 60-space line

Key as directed in 81c, p. 142.

OTHER VERB GUIDES

If there is confusion whether a subject is singular or plural, consult a dictionary.

Learn 1. The data in your report are interesting.
Learn 2. The world news is encouraging.
Learn 3. The alumni are meeting today.
Apply 4. (Is, Are) the alumni meeting today?
Apply 5. Parentheses (is, are) used in these guides.

When used as the subject, the pronouns I, we, you, and they, as well as plural nouns, require the plural verb *do not* or the contraction *don't*.

Learn 6. They do not want to attend the meeting.
Learn 7. The scales don't work properly.
Apply 8. I (don't, doesn't) think the way you do.
Apply 9. The samples (don't, doesn't) match.

When used as the subject, the pronouns, he, she, it, as well as singular nouns, require the singular verb *does not* or the contraction *doesn't*.

Learn 10. She doesn't want to go with you.
Learn 11. The scale doesn't work properly.
Apply 12. It (don't, doesn't) matter; use either style.
Apply 13. The computer (don't, doesn't) work.

Lesson 84 Outline/Report Skills

84a ▶ 5
Conditioning Practice

each line twice (slowly, faster); as time permits, repeat selected lines for extra credit

alphabet 1 This bright jacket has an amazing weave and is of exceptional quality.
figures 2 The invoice covered 1,398 lamps, 476 chairs, 270 desks, and 115 sofas.
shift key 3 Jane Dodd, President of O'Brien, McNeil & Webber, is in New York City.
speed 4 If it is so, then she may go with me to the city by a lake to do work.

| 1 | 2 | 3 | 4 | 5 | 6 | 7 | 8 | 9 | 10 | 11 | 12 | 13 | 14 |

84b ▶ 10
Format and Key an Outline

full sheet; 50-space line

Begin on line 12; space parts of outline properly (see p. 94).

YOUR CAREER

I. CHOOSING A CAREER
  A. Assess Personal Abilities and Interests
  B. Determine Society's Needs
    1. Growth rates of occupations
    2. Possible future trends
  C. Obtain Career Counseling and Guidance
  D. Match Talents with Opportunity
II. PREPARING FOR YOUR CAREER
  A. Need for Formal Education
  B. Need for Specialized Education
  C. Need for On-the-Job Training

207c (continued)

Problem 2
Purchase Requisition

Prepare the purchase requisition shown at the right. Proofread; circle errors.

Problem 3
Purchase Requisition

Repeat the purchase requisition of Problem 2, making the following changes:

Alphabetize entries in description column.

Decrease order for **File Folders** to **50**.

Include **75 Diskette Labels** with the other items being requisitioned.

Futura Computer Systems
42 Cannon Drive • Santa Barbara, CA 93105-2233 • (805) 925-1125

PURCHASE REQUISITION — words

Deliver to: *Eloisa Soto* — Requisition No. *B5873* — 4

Location: *Room 324* — Date *October 21, 19--* — 9

Job No. *76841* — Date Required *November 10, 19--* — 13

Quantity	Description	words
1	*Digital Postal Scale*	18
1	*Chart Tape, 1/8" x 324"*	23
10	*Flexible Disks, Single Side/Double Density*	32
15	*Word Processing Ribbons, 5/16" x 60'*	40
100	*Assorted Color-Coded File Folders*	48

Requisitioned by: *Dora Carter* — 50

Lesson 208 — Language Skills/Purchase Orders

208a ▶ 5 Conditioning Practice

1. Each line twice SS.
2. Take as many 1′ writings on line 4 as time permits.

alphabet 1 Judge Brown quickly seized the important map from the chief executive.

figures 2 He bettered his .325 batting average of 1980 when he hit .364 in 1987.

long words 3 Her efficiency in computer programming languages is very questionable.

speed 4 Sue may go to the firms to handle the audit and aid with both socials.

| 1 | 2 | 3 | 4 | 5 | 6 | 7 | 8 | 9 | 10 | 11 | 12 | 13 | 14 |

208b ▶ 15 Improve Language Skills

Line: 60 spaces

1. Read the ¶ at the right, noting where errors should be corrected.
2. Key the ¶ on a 60-space line. Listen for the warning bell as a signal to return, divide a word, or add a short word to the line.
3. Check your corrections with your teacher.
4. Prepare a final copy with all errors corrected.

If you are planing on writeing an excellent report you must beable to define three key concept. These three concepts enclude word processing data processing and infromation processing. Word Procesing can be defined as the transformation of ideas and information into writen comunication. Data processing are the process of changeing raw facts or data into useable infomation. Information processing is a knewer term use to encompas both word processing and data processing. If you can describe these two concept you report should be an excellent one.

84c ▶ 35
Format and Key Report with Textual Citations

full sheets; center heading on line 10 (pica) or line 12 (elite); DS ¶s, indent first line 5 spaces; SS quotations of 4 or more lines, indenting 5 spaces from side margins.

Arrange report in unbound report format (see p. 93, if necessary). Correct errors if directed to do so by your teacher.

Margins:
side: 1″
bottom: at least 1″

Place page numbers on line 6 in upper right-hand corner of second and additional pages. DS below page number and continue text.

Note. You are not expected to complete the report in this lesson; additional time is provided in Lesson 85.

Guide. Make two light pencil marks at the right edge of your paper: One 1″ from the bottom and another ½″ above the 1″ mark, as a page-end reminder; or use page-line gauge provided on LM. p. 7.

Note. Center the first line of poem; start remaining lines at this point.

Note. The ellipsis, indicating omission of words from a quotation, is keyed by alternating 3 periods and spaces (. . .) or 4 (. . . .), if the end of a sentence is included in the quotation.

FRIENDSHIP

At some time in our lives, each of us has tossed a pebble into a pool and then watched the ever-increasing concentric circles radiate out from a common center--the point where the pebble entered the water. Our relationships with others are similar; they can be seen as existing on various levels--concentric circles radiating out from each of us. The people in the inner circle are our close friends. They are the people to whom we become attached by feelings of deep personal regard; they are the people we refer to as "pals, buddies, chums, sidekicks, sisters, and brothers," and other such words. As we move outward to other circles, we find our casual friends. These are the people who share a common interest with us in such things as sports, clubs, music, and the like. Still farther out in the concentric circles are acquaintances. These are the people who may or may not become our friends.

All friends start out as acquaintances, and it is from this group that we select those who eventually become close or "true" friends. But, how do we choose a friend out of a group of acquaintances? It is easy to say that friendships are built around common interests and values, but as Block (1980, 221) has noted, "That isn't enough to explain close relationships." We could list those kinds of qualities that stimulate friendships--trust, openness, good humor, sensitivity--but all of us have acquaintances who have many of these qualities but who fail to ignite in us the spark of close friendship. Over one hundred years ago, Ralph Waldo Emerson lamented that Americans too often mistake acquaintances for true friends. The implication of his statement is that we need to know what friendship is and what it is not.

What, then, is a friend? Webster's New World Dictionary (1980) defines a friend as "a person one knows well and is fond of; an intimate associate." This definition, however, still does not adequately differentiate between true friendship and casual acquaintanceship. What is the extra ingredient needed for a casual acquaintance to become a real friend? Sometimes real friendships grow out of a shared hardship. For example, a paraplegic veteran, inconsolable, said of his buddy killed in Vietnam: "We were not just fellow victims of the war, you see. He was my best friend. I loved him more than my brother" (Block, 1980, 210).

The Vietnam veteran's statement is about true or real friendship, not a casual acquaintanceship. But, perhaps Emerson came closer to defining true friendship when he said, "A true friend is somebody who can make us do what we can." And further, he said, "The only way to have a friend is to be one." The importance of Emerson's words is that they suggest that although a real friend will make us use our potential to the fullest, a friend also will require us to be a friend to keep the relationship thriving.

A real friendship, then, requires effort to develop and effort to keep alive. As a recent telephone commercial stated, we must "reach out and touch someone" if we are to develop a friendship. Fischer (1983, 74) makes an important statement about friendship, "Friends do not come for free." Just as we must work for anything worthwhile in life, we must work at our friendships. In the final analysis, as Block (1980, 13) has said, "We are each the architects of our own friendships. . . ."

Although friendships require effort to develop, they are also rewarding. As Abraham Lincoln said, "The better part of one's life consists of his friendships." Further, all of us know that our sense of well-being is often enhanced by the quality of our interpersonal relationships with friends. As a result of a friendship, we have often been influenced not only to think differently about things, but also to transform our attitudes about life. By their

207b ▶ 15 Improve Keyboarding Skill

1. Three 1′ writings on ¶ 1; find *gwam*; circle errors.

2. Practice ¶ 2 in the same way.

3. Two 3′ writings on ¶s 1-2 combined; find *gwam*; circle errors.

all letters used | A | 1.5 si | 5.7 awl | 80% hfw |

	gwam 1′	3′
Many changes have taken place in the business environment over the	13	4
past few years. The changes have been quite noticeable for today's	27	9
office help. With all of the vast strides being made in the area of	41	14
word processing, many of today's workers have had to take extra train-	55	18
ing. Persons now training to work in an office have to take a new,	68	23
revised curriculum. They have to learn how to operate new machines.	82	27
They also have to acquire extended vocabularies in order to be a part	96	32
of today's offices which use the latest technological developments.	110	37
A principal is no longer just a person primarily in charge of a	13	41
high school; in word processing terminology, the term is also used to	27	46
refer to a person who originates work. We no longer have just a type-	41	50
writer; we now have a keyboard, screen, central processing unit, and	55	55
printer. The term "menu" takes on new meaning; it can now be used to	69	60
describe a list of functions from which an operator can choose. We can	83	64
also add such words as teleprocessing, telecommunicating, and electronic	98	69
mail to a growing list of "buzz" words of a modern-day office worker.	111	74

207c ▶ 30 Format/Process Purchase Requisitions

(LM pp. 163-167); 1 cc of each form

Problem 1
Purchase Requisition

Prepare the purchase requisition shown at the right. Follow placement/spacing guides shown in color. Proofread and circle errors.

Futura Computer Systems
42 Cannon Drive • Santa Barbara, CA 93105-2233 • (805) 925-1125

PURCHASE REQUISITION (Tab)

				words
Deliver to:	Josefina Ramos	Requisition No.	A19889B	4
Location:	SSS 204	Date	July 24, 19--	9
Job No.	B 4821	Date Required	August 9, 19--	13

Quantity	Description	words
DS		
1	Computer Cabinet	17
2	Low-Standing Bookcase	22
2	Two-Drawer File	25
1	Lateral File	28
1	Executive Desk, 24" x 54"	34

Approximate center — Set tab 2 spaces from rule

Requisitioned by: Seth Katz — 36

Problems 2 and 3 are on page 355.

84c (continued)

reactions to us, friends help teach us acceptable social behavior. Further, friends, as Duck (1983, 31) has said, "help cushion our personalities and reassure us about our values as people." Even teacher-student interpersonal relationships have been found crucial to student intellectual growth. The following quote from a study by Block (1980, 178) suggests the importance of a teacher-student friendship:

> Consider the myth that students need only have intellectually resourceful and knowledgeable teachers to grow intellectually. When the data are examined, it is found that teachers who provide a sound emotional relationship with students elicit as much as five times the achievement growth over the course of a year as those who coldly pursue intellectual development.

Friendships, then, require a deep personal involvement with others, being interested in their well-being, in their unique identities, and in their perceptions of the world. Real friends like and accept us for what we are, just as we like and accept them for what they are. To build friendships, we need to be ourselves, take the risk of reaching out, and say "hello" first. We need to show we care. As Henry David Thoreau said, "The most I can do for my friend is just be his friend." Perhaps the following poem, attributed to Albert Camus, best describes the mutual acceptance and closeness that characterize real friendship:

Don't walk in front of me
I may not follow
Don't walk behind me
I may not lead
Walk beside me
And just be my friend.

Lesson 85 Report Skills

85a ▶ 5 Conditioning Practice

each line twice (slowly, faster); as time permits, repeat selected lines

alphabet 1 Very excited dolphins whizzed quickly by a mako, jellyfish, and slugs.

figures 2 Please order 1,765 pencils, 894 pens, 239 file boxes, and 90 dividers.

space bar 3 Jan and Sam may go to a spa when they come to see me in the late fall.

speed 4 She may make the goal if she works with vigor and with the right form.

| 1 | 2 | 3 | 4 | 5 | 6 | 7 | 8 | 9 | 10 | 11 | 12 | 13 | 14 |

85b ▶ 45 Format and Key Report with Textual Citations

Complete the report you began in 84c, pp. 147-148. Prepare a reference list for your report.

top margin, same as p. 1; other margins as in report; center heading; start first line of each entry at left margin; indent additional lines 5 spaces; SS each entry; DS between entries

If space permits, the reference list may be typed as a part of the last report page. Start it 4 spaces below the last report line; otherwise, use a separate page.

Note. For a longer report (2 or more pages) number the reference page. For a short report, the reference page need not be numbered.

(line 6) 5

REFERENCES

Block, Joel D. Friendship. New York: MacMillan Publishers, Co., Inc., 1980.

Duck, Steve. Friends, for Life--The Psychology of Close Relationships. New York: St. Martin's Press, 1983.

Fischer, Claude. "The Friendship Cure-All." Psychology Today, January 1983, 74-78.

Webster's New World Dictionary. 2d ed. New York: Simon and Schuster, 1980.

Unit 44 Lessons 207-212

Learning Goals

1. To develop skill in processing purchase requisitions, purchase orders, and invoices.
2. To improve tabulating skills.
3. To improve language skills.

Machine Adjustments

1. Paper guide at *0*.
2. Margins: 70 space line for drills and ¶s; as directed for problems.
3. Spacing: SS drills; DS ¶s; as directed for problems.
4. Tab sets: 5 for ¶ indention; as needed for problems.

FORMATTING GUIDES: BUSINESS FORMS

Purchase Requisition:
A form used by a person or department to request the purchasing department to order items such as supplies, services, and equipment.

Purchase Order:
A form used by the purchasing department of one company to order merchandise or services from another company.

Invoice:
A form used by one company to bill a person or another company for services or merchandise purchased from the company that sends the invoice.

Tips for Processing Purchase Requisitions, Purchase Orders, and Invoices

1. Begin the address at the tab stop set for the description column; set tab stops for other columnar items using the same stop more than once if possible.

2. SS the items in the description column beginning in the first or second space below the horizontal rule under the column headings.

3. In the total column, underline the amount for the last item; then DS and key total.

4. All items to be keyed under headings (except the items keyed under the description head) should be approximately centered under the heading. The description column items should begin 1 or 2 spaces to the right of the vertical line.

5. Business papers like these are often mailed in window envelopes (see RG 7).

Note: Total amounts in forms may be keyed with or without commas separating thousands and hundreds. Either is equally correct.

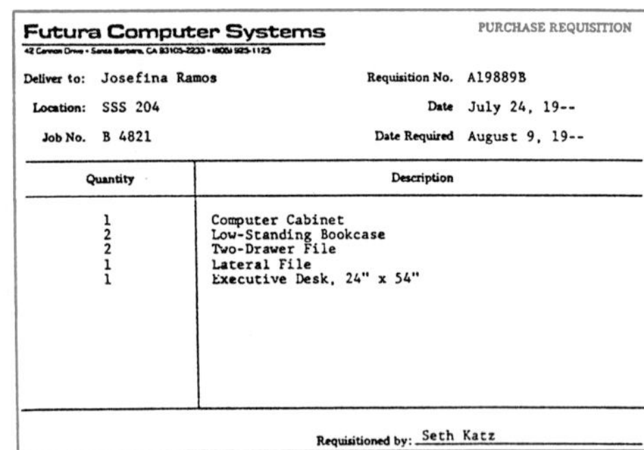

Futura Computer Systems PURCHASE REQUISITION
42 Cannon Drive • Santa Barbara, CA 93105-2233 • (805) 925-1125

Deliver to: Josefina Ramos Requisition No. A19889B
Location: SSS 204 Date July 24, 19--
Job No. B 4821 Date Required August 9, 19--

Quantity	Description
1	Computer Cabinet
2	Low-Standing Bookcase
2	Two-Drawer File
1	Lateral File
1	Executive Desk, 24" x 54"

Requisitioned by: Seth Katz

Formatted Purchase Requisition

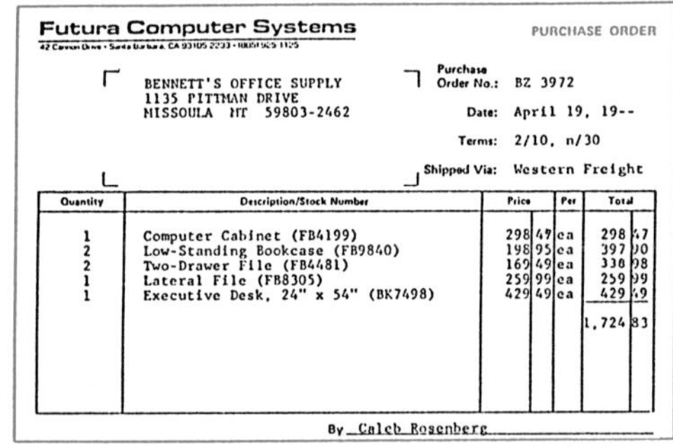

Futura Computer Systems PURCHASE ORDER
42 Cannon Drive • Santa Barbara, CA 93105-2233 • (805) 925-1125

BENNETT'S OFFICE SUPPLY
1135 PITTMAN DRIVE
MISSOULA MT 59803-2462

Purchase Order No.: BZ 3972
Date: April 19, 19--
Terms: 2/10, n/30
Shipped Via: Western Freight

Quantity	Description/Stock Number	Price	Per	Total
1	Computer Cabinet (FB4199)	298 47	ea	298 47
2	Low-Standing Bookcase (FB9840)	198 95	ea	397 90
2	Two-Drawer File (FB4481)	169 49	ea	338 98
1	Lateral File (FB8305)	259 99	ea	259 99
1	Executive Desk, 24" x 54" (BK7498)	429 49	ea	429 49
				1,724 83

By Caleb Rosenberg

Formatted Purchase Order

Lesson 207 Keyboarding Skills/Purchase Requisitions

207a ▶ 5 Conditioning Practice

1. Each line twice SS.
2. As many 1′ writings on line 4 as time permits.

alphabet 1 Liz and Jack were greatly perplexed by the sequence of amazing events.
figures 2 Joe moved to 4365 Harrison Boulevard in 1987 when he was 20 years old.
fig/sym 3 Please phone Schultz & Thiel Printing (608-735-9244) before 11:45 a.m.
speed 4 Blame Pamela for the usual problems with the proficiency of the girls.

| 1 | 2 | 3 | 4 | 5 | 6 | 7 | 8 | 9 | 10 | 11 | 12 | 13 | 14 |

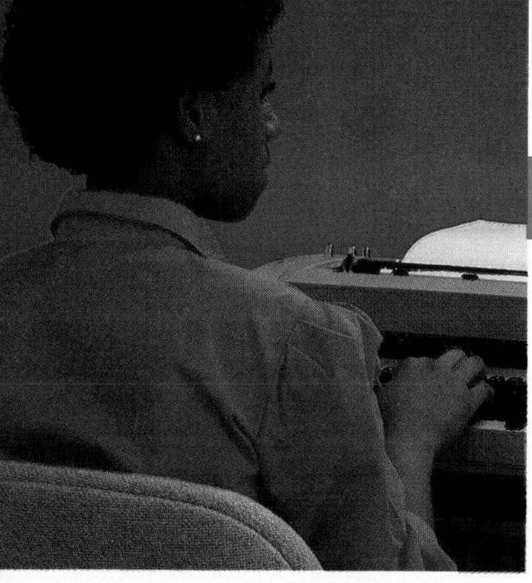

Unit 17 Lessons 86-90

Learning Goals

1. To develop and increase skill in formatting and keying letters in the modified block (blocked ¶s) and modified block (indented ¶s) styles.

2. To maintain good keyboarding technique patterns when keyboarding and doing applications.

3. To learn and apply basic language skills.

4. To do all work with a minimum of waste time and motion.

Machine Adjustments

1. Paper guide at *0*.

2. 70-space line and SS, unless otherwise directed.

SPECIAL LETTER PLACEMENT POINTS

LETTER PLACEMENT TABLE

Letter Classification	5-Stroke Words in Letter Body	Side Margins	Margin Settings		Dateline Position (from Top Edge of Paper)
			Elite	Pica	
Short	Up to 100	2″	24-78*	20-65*	19
Average	101-200	1½″	18-84*	15-70*	16
Long	201-300	1″	12-90*	10-75*	13
Two-page	More than 300	1″	12-90*	10-75*	13
Standard 6″ line for all letters**	As above for all letters	1¼″	15-87*	12-72*	As above for all letters

*Plus 3 to 7 spaces for the bell cue—*usually add 5* (see p. 78).

**Use only when so directed. Some business firms use a standard 6″ line for all letters.

Placement Table

A placement table will help you place letters properly. With time, you should learn to estimate letter length and place letters properly without using a placement aid.

Stationery

Most business letters are arranged on standard-size letterheads (8½″ × 11″) with the company name, address, and other information printed at the top.

For letters longer than 1 page, plain paper of the same size, color, and quality as the letterhead is used after the first page.

For short letters, smaller letterheads, executive-size (7¼″ × 10½″) or half-size (5½″ × 8½″), may be used; however, most letters, irrespective of length, are placed on standard-size stationery.

Placement Table Guides

1. Vertical Placement. Vertical placement of the dateline varies with letter length. If a deep letterhead prevents placing the date on the designated line, place it on the second line below the last letterhead line.

2. Letter Address and Closing Lines. The letter address is always started on the fourth line (3 blank line spaces) below the dateline. The name of the writer or originator of the letter is placed on the fourth line space below the complimentary close. It may be followed on the same line, or on the next line, by the business title of the writer.

3. Spacing Between Letter Parts. Except after the dateline and the complimentary close, double spacing is used between letter parts.

4. Special Lines. Special lines (attention, subject, company name in closing lines, etc.) or features such as a table, a list, or extra opening or closing lines may require a higher dateline placement than is shown in the placement table.

Letter Formatting Guides

Letter formatting guides are given with the style letter introduced in this unit.

Mixed Punctuation

Mixed punctuation means that a colon is used after the salutation and that a comma is used after the complimentary close.

206b (continued) words

Problem 2
Table with Source Note
full sheet; DS body; decide spaces between columns

CONSUMPTION OF MAJOR FOODS 5
(Pounds Per Person) 9

Food	Last Year	This Year	words
			19
Meats	144.5	139.4	23
Fish	13.0	16.4	26
Poultry Products	96.0	97.5	31
Fats and Oils	57.3	56.8	36
Fresh Fruits	87.3	81.4	41
Fresh Vegetables	95.2	150.9	46
Grains	128.0	130.4	51

__________ 54

Source: U.S. Agriculture Department. 62

Problem 3
Table with Mixed Column Headings
full sheet; DS body; decide spaces between columns

FINISHED GOODS SUMMARY 5

July 30, 19-- 7

Item	Labor	Materails	60% Over head	words
				20
S-1024	$328.70	$295.85	$197.22	27
S-1028	245.65	221.10	147.39	33
S-1030	172.90	155.60	103.74	38
S-1031	430.20	387.20	258.12	44
S-1032	336.55	302.90	201.93	49

Problem 4
Table with Horizontal/Vertical Rulings
full sheet; DS body; decide spaces between columns; insert horizontal and vertical rulings

U.S. FOREIGN TRADE 4
(Millions of Dollars) 8

Trade Area	Exports	Imports	words
			21
			27
			40
Western Hemisphere	$67,312	$84,467	47
Europe	63,664	53,413	51
Near East	64,822	87,170	56
Japan	20,966	37,744	60
East and South Asia	27,907	35,615	67
Oceania	5,700	3,131	71
Africa	10,271	17,770	75
			88

Lesson 86 Modified Block Letters

86a ▶ 5 Conditioning Practice

each line twice (slowly, faster); as time permits, repeat selected lines

alphabet 1 Forty big jets climbed into a hazy sky at exactly quarter past twelve.

figures 2 What is the sum of 16 7/8 and 23 3/4 and 45 1/2 and 10 8/9 and 90 1/4?

fingers 3, 4 3 Was it Polly who saw Paul quizzing Wally about eating all the loquats?

speed 4 Vivian may pay the men for the work and then go with them to the city.

| 1 | 2 | 3 | 4 | 5 | 6 | 7 | 8 | 9 | 10 | 11 | 12 | 13 | 14 |

86b ▶ 20 Problem Solving: Learn a New Letter Style

1. Arrange the letter on a plain full sheet in modified block style with blocked paragraphs, mixed punctuation.

2. Use the Letter Placement Table, page 149, to determine margins and dateline placement.

(words in body: 92)

3. When you complete the letter, make the check suggested; then make whatever corrections are needed and redo the letter in final form. Correct all errors you make in keyboarding the final draft.

4. In keying the letter, supply the missing parts:

- Address the letter to you at your home address.
- Use the current date.
- Supply an appropriate salutation.

Learning cue: The modified block style letter with blocked ¶s is arranged in the same format as the block style except that the dateline, complimentary close, and the printed or typed name are started at the horizontal center point.

(¶1) In solving problems, you will need to utilize previous learnings in new ways as you attempt to find problem solutions.
(¶2) Recall how you placed letters in block style; then make the needed modifications to arrange this letter in modified block style with blocked paragraphs.
(¶3) When you complete the letter, check your style arrangement with the style letter shown on the next page. If you arranged this letter in the style format shown there, congratulations. / Sincerely, / Robert J. Keller / jim

86c ▶ 25 Reinforcement Learning: New Letter Style

plain full sheets

Step 1

Learn the letter style

Key model letter on p. 151 in modified block style with blocked ¶s as shown (words in body: 209). Use the Letter Placement Table, p. 149.

In arranging the letter in proper format, be guided by the placement and spacing notations given in color.

Key the letter at rough-draft speed (top speed); x-out or strike over any keyboarding errors.

Step 2

Proofread and make rough-draft corrections

Proofread the letter you prepared in Step 1. Show by handwritten corrections any changes that need to be made in the copy.

Where you x'd out or struck over any words or letters, write such words correctly. In making the corrections, use the proofreader's marks you learned (Reference, p. RG 10).

Step 3

Build skill

Using your corrected rough-draft copy, redo the letter. As you key, make the corrections you have indicated in your copy.

Key on the control level and correct any errors you make. Compare your final draft with the model on p. 151. If you prepared the letter using elite type, your lines will end at different points than those in the model, but spacing between letter parts will be the same.

205b ▶ 45
Sustained Production: Tables with Leaders, Rulings, and Boxed Headings

Time Schedule
Plan and Prepare .... 5′
Timed Production .... 30′
Proofread and Correct Errors ... 7′
Compute *n-pram* .... 3′

1. Make a list of problems to be typed:
page 346, 201c, problem 2
page 347, 202c, problem 3
page 349, 203c, problem 3
page 350, 204c, problem 3

2. Arrange supplies; full sheets; half sheets; second sheets; carbon paper; eraser.

3. Make 1 cc for each problem.

4. When directed to begin, type for 30′ from the list of problems neatly. Proofread before removing the problems from the machine.

5. Compute *n-pram* for the 30′ period.

6. Turn in problems in the order listed.

Lesson 206 Evaluation: Table Processing

206a ▶ 5
Conditioning Practice

each line twice SS (slowly, then faster); then a 1′ writing on line 4

alphabet 1 Jim Cox quietly played the kazoo while waiting for his band to arrive.
figures 2 Pages 16-28 are changed to pages 20-33 and 47-59 are changed to 50-63.
fig/sym 3 Your payment of $487.69 (received on 8/13) included a discount of 25%.
speed 4 Diane and Dick paid the duty for the antique paisley rug for a chapel.

| 1 | 2 | 3 | 4 | 5 | 6 | 7 | 8 | 9 | 10 | 11 | 12 | 13 | 14 |

206b ▶ 45
Measure Production: Tables

Time Schedule
Plan and Prepare .... 5′
Timed Production .... 30′
Proofread and Correct Errors ... 7′
Compute *n-pram* .... 3′

Supplies: full sheets, second sheets; carbon paper; eraser.

Procedures: Key the problems for 30′ with 1 cc for each problem; correct errors; compute *n-pram*.

Problem 1
Table with Leaders and Total Line

full sheet; DS body; leave 20 spaces between Columns 1 & 2 and 4 spaces between Columns 2 & 3

SALES OF DRUGS AND TOILETRIES

(Millions of Dollars)

Item	Last Year	This Year	words
SALES OF DRUGS AND TOILETRIES			6
(Millions of Dollars)			10
Item	Last Year	This Year	20
Prescriptions	$14,170	$16,154	31
Analgesics	1,430	1,655	41
Cough/Cold Item	1,252	1,326	50
Vitamins	980	1,031	60
Cosmetics	3,871	4,450	69
Hair Care	4,001	4,410	79
Dental Products	1,798	1,927	89
Fragrances	1,803	1,926	98
Skin Care Products	1,447	1,685	108
Shaving Products	1,191	1,218	123
Total	$31,943	$35,782	127

ORCC Office Research & Communication Consultants

30 Lewis Road o Linfield, PA 19468-4353 o (215) 793-8264

		words in parts	total words
Dateline	Line 13 January 23, 19--	3	3
	4 line spaces (3 blank lines)		
Letter address	Mr. Scott Kirkwood, President	9	9
	Solar Corporation of America	15	15
	1160 Avenue of the Americas	20	20
	New York, NY 10036-2291	27	27
Salutation	Dear Mr. Kirkwood:	31	31
	This letter is arranged in the modified block style with blocked	13	44
	paragraphs. The only difference between this letter style and the	26	57
	block style is that the dateline and the closing lines (complimen-	40	70
	tary close and the typed or printed name of the originator of the	53	83
	letter) are started at the horizontal center point.	63	94
Body of letter	Although the block style letter is the most popular letter style	76	107
	used in the business world, the modified block style with blocked	90	120
	paragraphs is a popular second choice. As you can see, a letter	102	133
	arranged in this format presents an attractive appearance.	115	145
	Mixed punctuation (a colon after the salutation and a comma after	128	158
	the complimentary close) is used in this letter. Since the origina-	141	172
	tor's name is shown in typed format in the closing lines, only the	155	185
	initials of the typist or the word processing operator need be	167	198
	shown in the reference notation. If an enclosure is mentioned in	181	211
	the body of the letter, the word Enclosure, or Enc., is keyed or	193	224
	typed a double space below the reference notation, flush with the	206	237
	left margin.	209	240
Complimentary close	Sincerely yours,	3	243
	Kaye Banovich		
Typed name	Mrs. Kaye Banovich	6	246
Official title	Communications Consultant	11	251
Reference initials	le	12	252

Shown in pica type
1" side margins

Modified Block with Blocked Paragraphs and Mixed Punctuation

204c ▶ 35
Format/Process Tables with Horizontal and Vertical Rulings

Problem 1
Table with Horizontal Rulings

full sheet; DS body; decide spaces between columns

			words
ENROLLMENT IN PUBLIC AND PRIVATE SCHOOLS			8
Projected 1989 and 1990			13
			26
Level	**1989**	**1990**	29
			41
Kindergarten through 8			46
Public	29,447,000	30,244,000	53
Private	3,900,000	4,000,000	58
Grade 9 through 12			62
Public	11,158,000	11,023,000	69
Private	1,400,000	1,400,000	74
College			76
Public	9,636,000	9,616,000	81
Private	2,503,000	2,485,000	86
			99

Problem 2
Table with Horizontal and Vertical Rulings

full sheet; SS body; decide spaces between columns; box table by inserting vertical lines between columns

Problem 3

Repeat Problem 1 on a full sheet; SS body within grade groups; DS between grade groups.

Add the following:

Total: 1989 -- **58,044,000**
1990 -- **58,768,000**

Source: U.S. Commerce Department.

Total words: 108

				words
POPULATION OF THE U.S.				5
1980 Census				7
				21
Division	**Urban**	**Rural**	**Total**	26
				40
New England	9,269,279	3,079,244	12,348,523	48
Middle Atlantic	29,636,296	7,150,494	36,786,790	58
East North Central	30,533,879	11,148,338	41,682,217	69
West North Central	10,985,867	6,197,586	17,183,453	79
South Atlantic	24,813,020	12,146,103	36,959,123	89
East South Central	8,166,274	6,500,149	14,666,423	99
West South Central	17,434,964	6,311,852	23,746,816	109
Mountain	8,685,310	2,687,475	11,372,785	117
Pacific	27,526,133	4,273,572	31,799,705	125
				139

Lesson 205 Review: Table Processing

205a ▶ 5
Conditioning Practice

each line twice SS (slowly, then faster); then 1′ writing on line 4

alphabet 1 Dot James will be vying for prizes with her patchwork quilt next year.

figures 2 The car with License No. 580-379 parked in Space 164 in Parking Lot 2.

fig/sym 3 Our Purchase Order #470-259 was sent 3/18 and filled last week (3/26).

speed 4 Dixie did go downtown to fix the turn signal problems on the city bus.

| 1 | 2 | 3 | 4 | 5 | 6 | 7 | 8 | 9 | 10 | 11 | 12 | 13 | 14 |

87a ▶5 Conditioning Practice

each line twice (slowly, faster); as time permits, repeat selected lines

alphabet 1 Freshly squeezed grape juice was served at breakfast the next morning.

figures 2 We proofread 278 letters, 15 reports, 369 invoices, and 40 statements.

space bar 3 Many men and women may be needed to pay for the work down by the lake.

speed 4 They may make the six men pay for the ancient ornament or do the work.

| 1 | 2 | 3 | 4 | 5 | 6 | 7 | 8 | 9 | 10 | 11 | 12 | 13 | 14 |

87b ▶ 15 Improve Language Skills: Grammar

full sheet; 1" top margin; 70-space line

Study/Learn/Apply/Correct Procedures

1. STUDY explanatory rule.
2. Key line number (with period); space twice, then key the LEARN sentence(s) DS, noting rule application.
3. Key the line number (with period); space twice, then key the APPLY sentence(s) DS, selecting the word (in parentheses) needed to make the sentence(s) correct.
4. As your teacher reads the correct sentence(s), show in pen or pencil any corrections that need to be made in your copy.
5. Rekey any APPLY sentence containing an error, CORRECTING the error as you key. Place the corrected sentence in the space below the APPLY sentence containing the error.

PRONOUN AGREEMENT

Pronouns (I, we, you, he, she, it, their, etc.) agree with their antecedents *in person* (i.e., person speaking—first person; person spoken to—second person; person spoken about—third person).

Learn 1. I said I would go if I complete my work early. (*1st person*)
Learn 2. When you leave to go to the play, bring your ticket. (*2d person*)
Learn 3. Jay said that he would be taking the troop in his car. (*3d person*)
Apply 4. All persons who see the exhibit find that (they, you) are moved.
Apply 5. After you enter a dark room, (one's, your) eyes adjust slowly.

Pronouns agree with their antecedents *in gender* (masculine, feminine, and neuter).

Learn 6. Each Girl Scout has her favorite sport. (*feminine*)
Learn 7. Jack will present his lecture as soon as he arrives. (*masculine*)
Apply 8. Each boy will vote for (his, its) favorite sport.
Apply 9. The rose lost (her, its) petals within three days.

Pronouns agree with their antecedents *in number* (singular or plural).

Learn 10. The girls discussed their summer vacation. (*plural*)
Learn 11. Christina lost her book report on the way to class. (*singular*)
Apply 12. They may complete (his, her, their) assignments this week.
Apply 13. A pronoun must agree with (their, its) antecedent.

When a pronoun's antecedent is a collective noun, the pronoun may be either singular or plural depending on the meaning of the collective noun.

Learn 14. The class planned its next field trip. (*acting as a unit*)
Learn 15. The class had their pictures taken. (*acting individually*)
Apply 16. The committee has completed (their, its) report.
Apply 17. The committee met to cast (their, its) votes.

203c (continued)

Problem 2
Table Centered by Longest Item in Column

DS body; decide spaces between columns

Problem 3
Table with 2-Line Column Headings

Reformat Problem 2, converting wide headings into 2 lines as follows:

Column 2 -- **Square Miles**

Column 3 -- **Square Kilometers**

			words
AREA OF CANADA BY PROVINCES			6
Province	Square Miles	Square Kilometers	21
Newfoundland	156,650	405,720	27
Prince Edward Island	2,180	5,660	34
Nova Scotia	21,420	55,490	40
New Brunswick	28,360	73,440	46
Quebec	594,860	1,540,680	51
Ontario	412,580	1,068,580	57
Manitoba	250,950	649,950	62
Saskatchewan	251,870	652,330	68
Alberta	255,290	661,190	73
British Columbia	365,950	947,800	79

Lesson 204 Tables with Horizontal/Vertical Rulings

204a ▶ 5 Conditioning Practice

each line twice SS (slowly, then faster); then a 1′ writing on line 4

alphabet 1 The anxious woman very joyfully seized a bouquet the girls had picked.

figures 2 Flight 1096 is scheduled to depart from Gate 43 at 12:50 p.m. on 7/28.

fig/sym 3 Mr. Johnson enclosed a check (#346) for $279.80 for 15 circus tickets.

speed 4 She may keep the eight antique enamel bowls in a box by the oak chair.

| 1 | 2 | 3 | 4 | 5 | 6 | 7 | 8 | 9 | 10 | 11 | 12 | 13 | 14 |

204b ▶ 10 Learn to Format Tables with Horizontal and Vertical Rulings

Study the illustration at the right, observing the spacing between the keyed copy and the rulings. Then key the table on a full sheet, DS body; leave 10 spaces between columns. Key horizontal rulings as indicated.

Remove the page and, using a pen (preferably black ink), draw vertical rules at the midpoint between columns.

Note: When formatting tables with horizontal rulings, the most error-free method of vertical spacing is to set the machine for single spacing and return twice for double-spaced entries.

PAYROLL REPORT
DS
Research Department
SS

Name	Gross Wages	Net Wages
Dixon, Gregory	$18,295	$14,636
Greene, Helen	23,040	18,432
Melendez, Jose	20,565	16,452
Sheng, Tien	19,730	15,784

(Spacing marks in illustration: DS above and SS below column headings; DS before first entry; SS after last entry; DS after bottom ruling.)

Source: Payroll Register, December 31, 1988.

87c ▶ 30
Build Document Processing Skill: Letters

plain full sheets; modified block style, blocked ¶s; mixed punctuation; current date

Use your name and your home address (with ZIP Code) as the letter address for both problems. Supply an appropriate salutation.

Placement

Use the Letter Placement Table, page 149, to determine margins and dateline placement. The number of words in the letter body is indicated by the number in parentheses at the end of each letter.

Proofread

Proofread your finished copy. Circle all errors.

words

Problem 1

opening lines 16
(¶ 1) The question you raised about the value of keyboarding skill is one that 31
I am pleased to answer. 36
(¶ 2) In the near future, nearly everyone will need to know how to operate a 50
keyboard, whether that keyboard is a part of a microcomputer, a computer, 65
an electronic typewriter, or a word processor. According to recent fore- 79
casts, approximately 70 percent of the total population of the United States 94
will be using a keyboard in one form or another by 1993. 106
(¶ 3) Today, a microcomputer with a keyboard or keypad is being used in 119
most white-collar jobs, in educational environments, and in the home. If 134
you learn to operate a keyboard, you will have a skill that will be useful to 150
you for the remainder of your life. It is important, therefore, to learn this 165
skill well. (152) 168
Sincerely yours, | Jeff Brown, Director | Public Relations | cm 179

Problem 2

opening lines 16
One application of key boarding is the operation of a word 29
processor. Many different models of word processors are being 41
used in the business office. Some machines can perform only 54
word processing bunctions; others, sometimes called information 66
processors, can do both word and data processing. Most word and 79
information processors have simillar features: an electronic key- 92
board or key pad, a display screen, a diskette recording mechanism 114
with a disk drive, and a printer. The keyboard or keypad has a 131
standard letter and number keyboard, but it also has special func- 144
tion keys, and it may have a 10-key numeric pad, all of which are 158
a part of the total key board configuration. The special function 171
keys, enable the operator to manipulate copy on th display screen 189
in a variety of ways. Among the uses of these keys are to erase 204
delete or otherwise modify the copy. Using these keys, it is easy 217
to move, insert, edit, recall, story, or print out copy as needed 230
This suto mation of word and data processing has changed the way 243
in which office work is done, and it has increased dramatically 256
office productivity. some the of skill needed for the automated 269
office can be learned in school; still osther skills will need 283
to be developed in an on-the-job situation. (276) 297
Sincerely yours, / Jeff Brown, Director / Public Relations / cm 307

a central processing unit that may include

Lesson 203 Tables with Variable Column Headings

203a ▶ 5 Conditioning Practice

each line twice SS (slowly, then faster); the a 1′ writing on line 4

alphabet	1	Twelve jars of pink liquid froze in the extremely cold lab last night.
figures	2	Ms. Nagai should call 641-7035, Extension 528, at 9:15 a.m. on May 20.
fig/sym	3	The bag (Cat. #420) was priced at $35.68 on the May, 1987, price list.
speed	4	My neighbor at the mall may make an ornament of eight prisms for them.

| 1 | 2 | 3 | 4 | 5 | 6 | 7 | 8 | 9 | 10 | 11 | 12 | 13 | 14 |

203b ▶ 10 Recall Procedures for Centering Column Headings

Key the drills shown at the right as directed below (8 spaces between columns).

Drill 1: Center by column entries.

Drill 2: Center by column headings.

Drill 3: Center by longest item in each column, whether a heading or an entry.

Drill 1

Employee	Gross	Net
Hernandez, Alberto	$482.95	$394.30

Drill 2

Telephone Number	Number of Calls	Total Time
782-5519	4	28 min.

Drill 3

Corporation Name	Assets	Liabilities
Liang, Inc.	$138,690	$25,430

203c ▶ 35 Format/Process Tables with Column Headings of Variable Lengths

full sheets

References: p. 287, RG 11

Problem 1
Table Centered by Longest Item in Column (Whether Entry or Column Heading)

DS body; decide spaces between columns

MERCHANT FLEETS

Country	No. of Ships	Total Gross Tons	words
			3
			18
Belgium	76	1,710	22
Denmark	253	4,571	25
France	317	10,430	29
Greece	2,893	42,893	35
Italy	606	9,844	38
Japan	1,770	37,491	42
Netherlands	445	4,779	47
Norway	600	21,711	51
Sweden	221	3,254	54
United Kingdom	927	22,529	59
United States	853	15,976	64

88a ▶ 5 Conditioning Practice

each line twice (slowly, faster); as time permits, repeat selected lines

alphabet 1 Seven quiet boys extracted juicy chunks from the sizzling pot of stew.

figures 2 Will you enter Machine Nos. 12-93045 and 10-87306 on the repair cards.

shift keys 3 R.H. McNeil, of Smith, Paine & Winnet Company, is visiting in Newark.

speed 4 The maps may aid them when they do the work for the town and the city.

| 1 | 2 | 3 | 4 | 5 | 6 | 7 | 8 | 9 | 10 | 11 | 12 | 13 | 14 |

88b ▶ 10 Improve Language Skills: Punctuation

full sheet; 1" top margin; 70-space line

Key the lines as directed in 87b, p. 152; however, instead of selecting the correct word from those in parentheses, insert commas where needed.

COMMA USAGE

Use a comma after (a) introductory words, phrases, or clauses and (b) words in a series.

Learn 1. On our trip, we visited London, Paris, Rome, and Stockholm.
Apply 2. Before you leave please finish the letters reports and memos.

Do not use a comma to separate two items treated as a single unit within a series.

Learn 3. She ordered ham and eggs, toast, and coffee.
Apply 4. He ordered lox and bagels strawberries and tea.

Use a comma before short direct quotations.

Learn 5. The teacher said, "If you try, you can reach your goal."
Apply 6. The students said "We'll try."

Use a comma before and after word(s) in apposition.

Learn 7. Chris, the outgoing president, said to arrive early.
Apply 8. Jean our new president will give the report to the committee.

Use a comma to set off words of direct address.

Learn 9. I'll look forward, Casey, to seeing you at the meeting.
Apply 10. Please try Letecia to finish this work before you leave.

REMINDER:

When keying drill and problem copy, remember to use good techniques.

Fingers curved and upright

Use quick, snappy keystroking

Space quickly after each word

202b ▶ 10

Learn to Format Tables with Leaders

full sheet; SS body; decide spaces between columns; insert leaders as shown

To align leaders

Key the first line of the first column; space once; note the position of the printing point indicator (on an odd or even number); key a period, then a space alternately across the line; stop 2 or 3 spaces before the second column. On lines that follow, align the periods with those in line 1, keying on odd or even numbers.

PETTY CASH SUMMARY

Supplies Expense	$ 24.10
Miscellaneous Expense	47.85
Freight Expense	10.63
Postage Expense	18.90
Total	$101.48

202c ▶ 35

Format/Process Tables with Leaders and Column Headings

Problem 1
2-Column Table with Leaders

full sheet; DS body; decide spaces between columns; insert leaders

PER CAPITA PERSONAL INCOME		words
		5
Area	Amount	10
New England	$11,916	17
Mideast	12,087	24
Great Lakes	11,055	31
Plains	10,789	38
Southeast	9,602	45
Southwest	11,122	52
Rocky Mountains	10,754	59
Far West	12,238	66

Problem 2
3-Column Table with Leaders and Totals

full sheet; DS body

Leave 16 spaces between Columns 1 & 2; 4 spaces between Columns 2 & 3; insert leaders between Columns 1 & 2.

Note: Do not key leaders in the *Total* line.

Problem 3

half sheet, short edge at top; DS body; decide spaces between columns

Repeat Problem 1; add the following:

Source: U.S. Department of Commerce.

Total words: 73

POLLUTION ABATEMENT EXPENDITURES			7
(In Millions of Dollars)			12
Industry	Air	Water	19
Food	53.9	104.8	28
Lumber and Wood	49.2	10.5	38
Paper	168.0	86.5	48
Chemicals	335.0	322.2	59
Petroleum	440.8	131.7	68
Stone, Clay, Glass	165.1	13.8	77
Primary Metal	567.2	144.1	97
Electric Equipment	48.7	41.0	97
Transportation Equipment	209.2	60.0	107
Total	2,037.1	914.6	118

88c ▶ 35
Build Document Processing Skill: Letters

(LM pp. 11-16) or plain full sheets; correct errors; use your initials instead of xx in the reference notation

Problem 1

modified block style; indented ¶s; mixed punctuation

> **Note:** Modified block style with indented ¶s differs from modified block style with blocked ¶s only in that each ¶ is indented 5 spaces.

words

January 25, 19-- | Mrs. Jane Denny | Communications Consultant | Heald 13
Colleges, Suite 1100 | 1255 Post Street | San Francisco, CA 94109-4201 | Dear 28
Mrs. Denny: 30
(¶ 1) My employer, Mr. Henry Seurer, heard you speak at a recent conven- 43
tion. He was impressed with your comments about improving communica- 57
tion skills. He said that if I would write to you, you could give me some 72
suggestions for improving my proofreading skills. 82
(¶ 2) May I hear from you soon. I really do need your help. (63) 93
Sincerely yours, | Ms. Stacey Hunnel | Administrative Assistant | xx 106
128

Problem 2

modified block style; blocked ¶s; mixed punctuation

Indent numbered items 5 spaces from left and right margins. When keying numbered items follow this procedure:

1. Space in 5 spaces, key the figure 1, period, and two spaces. Set left margin at this point. Move right margin to left 5 spaces.

2. After keying the lines of the first item, DS, press margin release, and backspace to the point to key the figure 2. Space forward to key lines of numbered item.

3. Repeat Step 2 for remainder of numbered items. Remember to reset left and right margins for ¶ 2.

Note: Because this letter has a number of unusual parts, start date on line 12.

January 30, 19-- | Ms. Stacey Hunnel | Administrative Assistant | Seattle Office 15
Products Company | 200 Academy Place | Seattle, WA 98109-2239 | Dear Ms. 29
Hunnel: 30
(¶ 1) I'm pleased to respond to your inquiry about improving your proof- 43
reading skills. In this "high-tech" age, proofreading is an important skill. 59
All keyboarded work should be proofread before you remove it from your 73
typewriter or before you push the print key if you are using a word pro- 88
cessor. Here are some steps to follow when proofreading the letters you 102
prepare: 104

1. The first step is to check the format and placement of the letter. 119
   Employers expect keyboard operators to use accepted style and to 132
   format letters properly. 137
2. Second, check the accuracy of all figures used in the letter: in the 152
   date, in the street address, and in the letter body. 162
3. Third, check to see that all words are divided correctly at the ends 177
   of lines. 179
4. As a final step, read carefully the entire letter. As you read the letter 195
   for meaning, check to see that grammar is correct and that there are 209
   no keyboarding errors. Any errors found must be corrected. 221

(¶ 2) If you follow these proofreading steps, your proofreading skills will 235
improve. (207) 237
Sincerely yours, | Mrs. Jane Denny | Communications Consultant | xx 249
272

Problem 3

modified block style; indented ¶s; mixed punctuation

January 31, 19-- | Mr. Tom Stubbs | 3812 Raleigh Avenue | Napa, CA 94558- 14
3311 | Dear Mr. Stubbs: 18
(¶ 1) Today, we must cope with an information explosion and a technological 32
revolution. The one piece of equipment that may be revolutionizing the way 47
we live is the microcomputer. 54
(¶ 2) It is amazing what microcomputers can do. Writing efficiency--and 67
some say creativity--can be enhanced with the use of software word pro- 81
cessing programs designed for use with a microcomputer. As a communica- 95
tions device, the microcomputer can be linked online, by telephone, with an 110
extensive list of massive data banks, ranging from Dow Jones to libraries to 126
ERIC centers, as well as to various other special services. As is obvious, the 142
microcomputer can place computer power directly in our hands. 154
(¶ 3) Visit our showroom soon and see our complete line of microcomputers 168
and software packages. We know you will be pleased with our low prices. 183
(165) Sincerely yours, | Miss Virginia Whitacre | Vice President | xx 194
205

201c ▶ 30 Recall Basic Table Format

full sheets

References: p. 287, RG 11

Problem 1
3-Column Table with Totals

full sheet; DS body; 10 spaces between columns

Note: When keying tables with dollar totals, consider the dollar sign part of the intercolumn. Begin the underline under the last entry in the column at the point where the dollar sign will begin the "total" line.

CORPORATE INVESTMENTS 4

Type	Market Value	Book Value	words
Short Term	$ 825,412,000	$ 795,558,000	24
Corporate Bonds	519,340,000	608,720,000	32
Municipal Bonds	1,016,000	2,214,000	40
Common Stock	1,582,614,000	1,620,835,000	49
Real Estate	794,612,000	794,612,000	63
Total	$3,722,994,000	$3,821,939,000	71

(header line: 15 words)

Problem 2
4-Column Table with Source Note

full sheet; SS body; 6 spaces between columns

Problem 3

Repeat Problem 2; DS body; decide spaces between columns.

1983 SCHOOL ENROLLMENT IN U.S. 6

(In Thousands) 9

Age	Male	Female	Total	words
3 and 4	1,363	1,261	2,624	23
5 and 6	3,166	3,048	6,214	28
7 to 13	11,887	11,391	23,278	35
14 and 15	3,617	3,476	7,093	41
16 and 17	3,404	3,294	6,698	46
18 and 19	1,956	1,983	3,938	52
20 and 21	1,379	1,230	2,609	58
22 to 24	1,203	908	2,111	63
25 to 29	1,084	892	1,976	69

(header line: 17 words)

______________ 73

Source: U.S. Bureau of the Census. 80

Lesson 202 — Tables with Leaders and Totals

202a ▶ 5 Conditioning Practice

each line twice SS (slowly, then faster); then a 1′ writing on line 4

alphabet 1 Jeff Vorth excels at being able to complete crossword puzzles quickly.
figures 2 Her prescription No. 321-9845 was filled on 7/16 and refilled on 9/10.
fig/sym 3 The fee increased approximately 28% ($106); they will now pay $734.95.
speed 4 Half of their busy signals are kept visible and half are kept audible.

| 1 | 2 | 3 | 4 | 5 | 6 | 7 | 8 | 9 | 10 | 11 | 12 | 13 | 14 |

Lesson 89 Letter/Language Skills

89a ▶ 5 Conditioning Practice

each line twice (slowly, faster); as time permits, repeat selected lines

alphabet 1 The voluble judge quizzes expert witnesses before making any decision.
figures 2 The zoo ordered 785 birds, 4 bears, 20 bison, 9 lions, and 163 snakes.
quiet hands 3 They decided to attend the dedication when the ceremony was cancelled.
speed 4 Pam may pay the firm for the work when they sign the right audit form.

| 1 | 2 | 3 | 4 | 5 | 6 | 7 | 8 | 9 | 10 | 11 | 12 | 13 | 14 |

89b ▶ 10 Improve Language Skills: Punctuation

full sheet; 1″ top margin; 70-space line

Key as directed in 88b, p. 154.

COMMA USAGE (continued)

Use a comma to set off nonrestrictive clauses (not necessary to the meaning of the sentence); however, do not use commas to set off restrictive clauses (necessary to the meaning of the sentence).

Learn 1. The report, which you prepared, was just great.
Learn 2. The report that deals with uses of solar energy was timely.
Apply 3. Unit 13 which you prepared is well written.
Apply 4. Keyboardists who practice with a purpose make speed gains.

Use a comma to separate the day from the year and the city from the state.

Learn 5. John made the nominating speech in San Francisco, California.
Learn 6. October 12, 1492, is a special day in history.
Apply 7. (Keyboard a complete sentence giving the date, city, and state of your birth.)

Use a comma to separate two or more parallel adjectives (adjectives that could be separated by the word "and" instead of the comma).

Learn 8. A happy, excited crowd cheered the team to victory.
Learn 9. A dozen large red roses were delivered. *(comma cannot be used)*
Apply 10. The hot sticky humid air made our stay uncomfortable.
Apply 11. The key is in the small square wooden box on my desk.

Use a comma to separate (a) unrelated groups of figures which come together and (b) whole numbers into groups of three digits each. *Note:* Policy, year, page, room, telephone, and most serial numbers are keyboarded without commas.

Learn 12. During 1987, 3,285 cars were insured under Policy 23-90456.
Apply 13. In 1986 5674 students were enrolled.
Apply 14. Please call 825-2,626 if you need information on Policy #7,304.

89c ▶ 35 Build Sustained Document Processing Skill: Letters

plain full sheets

Time Schedule

Build skill .... 6′
Plan and prepare .... 4′
Timed production .... 20′
Proofread; compute *g-pram* .... 5′

1. Two 1′ writings on date through salutation of Problem 1, page 155; then two 1′ writings on complimentary close through reference notation of the problem.

2. A 20′ sustained production writings on problems listed below (make pencil notations of the pages and problems):
page 153, 87c, Problem 1
page 155, 88c, Problem 1
page 155, 88c, Problem 3

If you complete the letter problems before time is called, start over. Work on the control level; do not correct errors. When time is called, proofread each letter; circle errors. Compute *g-pram* (gross production rate a minute):

g-pram = total words ÷ 20

Unit 43 Lessons 201-206

Learning Goals:

1. To improve keyboarding skill on sentence copy.
2. To improve statistical keyboarding.
3. To improve skill in formatting business tables.

Machine Adjustments

1. Paper guide at *0*.
2. Margins: 70-space line for sentences and ¶s; as directed for problems.
3. Spacing: SS sentence drills; DS ¶s; as directed for problems.
4. Tab sets: as needed for problems.

Lesson 201 Format/Process Business Tables

201a ▶ 5 Conditioning Practice

each line twice SS (slowly, then faster); then a 1′ writing on line 4

alphabet	1	Jake Ward made up vague excuses for being late to the psychology quiz.
figures	2	Their Order 341-782 for 150 packages of Item 463 was shipped on 12/19.
fig/sym	3	The interest the bank paid on Account #47328 (as of 9/30) was $161.65.
speed	4	The man kept a pair of ducks, eight hens, and six turkeys on the land.

| 1 | 2 | 3 | 4 | 5 | 6 | 7 | 8 | 9 | 10 | 11 | 12 | 13 | 14 |

201b ▶ 15 Improve/Check Keyboarding Skill: Statistical Copy

1. Two 1′ writings on each ¶; find *gwam*, circle errors.
2. A 3′ writing on ¶s 1-2 combined; find *gwam*, circle errors.

all letters used | A | 1.5 si | 5.7 awl | 80% hfw |

gwam 3′

During the January 5, 1986, conference, the managers adopted the 4 | 52
1987 Stock Incentive Plan (the 1987 Plan). Under the 1987 Plan, stock 9 | 57
options may be awarded to employees at neither less than 50% nor more 14 | 62
than 100% of the current value of the stock on the date of award. The 18 | 66
total number of shares shall not exceed 475,000 at prices ranging from 23 | 71
$25.60 to $48.75 per share. 25 | 73

The number of shares still outstanding from the 1985 and 1986 29 | 77
incentive plans are 1,823,419 and 1,457,608, respectively, at prices 34 | 82
ranging from $20.64 to $53.18. These options are available for a period 39 | 87
not to exceed 10 years from the date of award. So it is amazing to see 44 | 91
that over 5,248 shares are still unacquired from the 1975 plan. 48 | 96

gwam 3′ | 1 | 2 | 3 | 4 | 5 |

Lesson 90 Measurement

90a ▶ 5 Conditioning Practice

each line twice (slowly, faster); as time permits, repeat selected lines

alphabet	1	Gymnasts amaze excited fans and judges with very quick leaps on beams.
figures	2	I may buy 15 jackets, 289 blankets, 74 kits, 360 lamps, and 110 tires.
fingers 3, 4	3	Wally saw six wax owls as he and Pris moved about the quaint villages.
speed	4	The city firm may make the audit when they do the work for you and me.

| 1 | 2 | 3 | 4 | 5 | 6 | 7 | 8 | 9 | 10 | 11 | 12 | 13 | 14 |

90b ▶ 7 Measure Basic Skill: Straight Copy

a 5′ writing; find *gwam*; proofread; circle errors

Emphasize: Fingers curved and upright; quick finger-action keystroking.

all letters used | A | 1.5 si | 5.7 awl | 80% hfw |

	gwam 3′		5′
Just what does it mean to be young and when is a person young? To	4	3	49
be young is perhaps a feeling or disposition, a particular manner of	9	5	52
looking at things and responding to them. To be young is never a chrono-	14	8	55
logical period or time of life, although it might be a young person	18	11	57
examining some material with fascination and pleasure or the composer	23	14	60
Verdi in his eighties writing his best opera. To be young might be a	28	17	63
person "hanging ten" on a surfboard or swinging to a musical composi-	32	19	66
tion. To be young might be Einstein in his seventies still working with	37	22	69
his field theory, sailing his boat, or playing his cherished fiddle.	42	25	71
To be young is never the monopoly of youth. It flourishes every-	46	28	74
where visionaries have stimulated our thinking or amazed us. To be young	51	31	77
in nature is quite desirable whether you are a young person, a middle-	56	33	80
aged person, or a chronologically old person. To be young should be	60	36	83
respected whether the beard is soft and curly or firm and gray. To be	65	39	85
young has no color; it seems always translucent with its own imaginative	70	42	88
light. There is no generation space between the young of any age because	75	45	91
they see things as they ought to be.	77	46	93

gwam 3′ | 1 | 2 | 3 | 4 | 5 |
5′ | 1 | 2 | 3 |

90c ▶ 8 Improve Accuracy

1. Three 1′ writings of 90b above; start second and third writings at ending point of previous writing. **Goal:** No more than 2 errors in each writing.

2. A 3′ writing on ¶s of 90b with a goal of not more than 6 errors. To do this, start slowly and gradually increase your speed as you feel relaxed. Concentrate on the copy and work with continuity.

Lessons 201-225

PHASE 9

Extend Statistical Document Processing Skills

Keyboard operators in modern offices must be able to prepare statistical documents as well as correspondence and reports with a high level of proficiency. Phase 9 (Lessons 201-225) is designed to help you develop this important job qualification. After intensive practice on table and forms formatting to develop statistical document processing skills, you will apply those skills in an office job simulation which mirrors the work of a real company.

Specifically, this unit will:

1. Build your table formatting skill to a new high level.
2. Improve your skill in processing purchase requisitions, purchase orders, and invoices.
3. Place you in a simulated office where you will process a variety of realistic documents typical of those used in modern offices.
4. Develop your ability to work with minimum directions and to use your decision-making skills.
5. Improve your language and composing skills.

90d ▶ 30
Measure Document Processing Skill: Letters

Time Schedule

Plan and prepare .... 4′
Timed production .... 20′
Proofread; compute *n-pram* .... 6′

Use letterheads (LM pp. 17-20) or plain full sheets for the letter problems. Determine placement: See table, p. 149. Correct all errors.

If you complete the letters before time is called, start over on plain sheets. Proofread your work.

Determine total words keyed. Deduct 15 words for each uncorrected error; divide remainder by 20 to determine *n-pram* (net production rate a minute). Compare your *n-pram* with your *g-pram* of 89c. If your *n-pram* is much lower, you may need to try to improve your accuracy or give attention to your error correction skill.

n-pram (net production rate a minute) = total words keyed − (15 × number of uncorrected errors) ÷ time (in minutes) of writing

words

Problem 1
modified block style; blocked ¶s; mixed punctuation

February 3, 19-- | Ms. Stacey Hunnel | Administrative Assistant | Seattle Office 15
Products Company | 200 Academy Place | Seattle, WA 98109-2239 | Dear Ms. 29
Hunnel: 30
(¶ 1) I should like to add to the suggestions I sent to you about proofread- 44
ing. Prevention or reduction of keyboarding errors will reduce the time 59
needed for the detection and correction of errors. 69
(¶ 2) How does a person prevent or reduce keyboarding errors as letters are 83
produced, and as a consequence, increase letter production rates? The first 99
step is to try to keep your eyes on the copy from which you are keyboard- 113
ing. In this way, you can avoid breaks in your keyboarding rhythm. As 127
you keyboard, keep your fingers well curved and close to the keys; space 142
quickly after each word and start the new word without a pause. When the 157
bell rings, either finish the word you are keyboarding, if this can be done in 173
a few keystrokes, or divide it with a hyphen at a proper division point. Then 188
make the return and start a new line immediately. Concentrate on the copy 203
to be keyboarded. Read ahead; think and keyboard. 214
(¶ 3) These suggestions will help you increase your letter production rates. 228
They will help you reduce keyboarding errors and thus simplify the proof- 243
reading process. Try them and see. (220) 250
Sincerely yours, | Mrs. Jane Denny | Communications Consultant | xx 262
285

Problem 2
modified block style; indented ¶s; mixed punctuation

> **Recall:** Modified block style with indented ¶s differs from modified block style with blocked ¶s only in that each ¶ is indented 5 spaces.

February 10, 19-- | Mr. Darwin Parsons, President | Domino Technology, Inc. | 14
1511 Pacific View Drive | San Diego, CA 92109-2299 | Dear Mr. Parsons: 28
(¶ 1) Planning for the future is the key element for the continuing success 42
of any business firm. To paraphrase Abraham Lincoln, you can't be sure of 57
getting there unless you determine in advance where it is you are going. 72
(¶ 2) When planning for the future of your company, the definition of goals 86
and objectives is crucial. Without that, it would not be clear when an oppor- 101
tunity was being realized, nor would we know what to do in the face of end- 116
less options. 119
(¶ 3) All this concern with the importance of planning is by way of intro- 133
ducing you to our new publication, EFFECTIVE PLANNING. This book has 147
received rave reviews from all who have read it. The content of the book is 162
described in the enclosed brochure. I know you will want to order a copy 177
for yourself and other key executives in your company. It will be an invest- 192
ment that will pay immediate dividends. (172) 200
Sincerely yours, | Miss Jackie Schaefer | Publications Department | xx | 213
Enclosure 215
236

198b-200b (continued)

Job 9
Telegram

Ms. Young-Bryge: Format the message at the right as a phoned telegram to the manager of A & S Business Essentials. Her name and address are in the card file on this page. Charge to the account of **Pro-Tech Sales Department**; use **January 13** as the date and **3:15 p.m.** as the time.

Job 10
Summary Minutes

Ms. Young-Bryge: The members of the marketing management committee have reviewed the minutes we distributed earlier. Find your copy of the minutes and key a final copy as a leftbound manuscript for my record book. Make the change indicated below.

Change: Delete **"tapes and"** in the first sentence of the second paragraph. When you have made the change, it will read **"magnetic disks."**

Job 11
Form Letters
(LM pp. 139-145)

Ms. Young-Bryge: Prepare for me this handwritten letter to send to each of the managers on the file cards shown above. Use AMS Simplified style; date each letter **January 15**.

Shipment of the three vertical files, Model E4-7000-TN, cannot be made until March 15. All other items on January 5 order (P.O. #25784) will be shipped on January 19.

A & S Business Essentials
3121 West Jefferson Street
Joliet, IL 60435-4793

Manager: Ms. Elizabeth Ford
Phone: (815) 751-8734

DCF Office Furniture and Equipment
3220 Auburn Road
Pontiac, MI 48057-2197

Manager: Dan Harris
Phone: (313) 561-7339

General Office Supply
1520 Walnut Street
Des Moines, IA 50309-3482

Manager: Bob Cherif
Phone: (515) 384-9642

Premiere Office Products
3340 North Arlington Avenue
Indianapolis, IN 46218-2592

Manager: Miss Tien Wang
Phone: (317) 262-4545

Date

(Insert name and address of addressee)

(Subject) NEW FILING PRODUCTS

(¶) I am happy to announce that Pro-Tech has added a new line of products to meet the filing needs of your customers.

(¶) Beginning March 1, 19--, Pro-Tech will be ready to ship a variety of key control systems. Included will be:

1. Color coordinated key cabinet systems capable of storing 40 to 140 keys.
2. Key control boxes for use in office desks, filing cabinets, or any place where portability is desired.
3. Key racks capable of storing 10 frequently used keys.
4. Keyboards which store up to 60 keys where security is not a concern.

(¶) An adequate number of numbered key tags, "Out Key" control tags, key control charts, and cross-reference charts are provided with each system.

(¶) I will call you soon to explain the special introductory pricing arrangement which is available to Pro-Tech's valued customers.

Unit 18 Lessons 91-95

Training Goals

1. To become familiar with the work of a word processing office.
2. To develop and increase skill in formatting and keying letters in modified block and block styles.
3. To develop and increase skill in preparing simplified memos.

Machine Adjustments

1. Paper guide at *0*.
2. Paper bail rolls at even intervals across page.

Use:

*70-space line and single spacing for drill; DS between each SS group of drill lines

*70-space line and double spacing for ¶ timings

*as directed for jobs

UNITED PROCESSING SERVICE: A CO-OP SIMULATION

Futura Computer Systems

42 Cannon Drive • Santa Barbara, CA 93105-2233 • (805) 925-1125

June 18, 19--

Mr. J. B. Brown, Executive Vice President

PROPOSED AD FOR SECRETARIES

As you know, the main problem in our headquarters office is the shortage of secretaries. Attached is the proposed ad that we would like to run soon in the Los Angeles Times. After you review it, please give me your comments.

We plan to have the ad displayed in a 6" x 6" format. The ad will carry our logo in the lower left corner. Others who have reviewed the ad believe that it will help us to attract the secretarial personnel that we so desperately need.

Adeline Acres, Advertising Director

PE

Attachment

Simplified Memo

Work Assignment

Your school in conjunction with various businesses in your community has developed a co-op program to give you actual work experience. You have been assigned to work as a keyboarding trainee for United Processing Service, which provides office services for local businesses. As a co-op trainee you will be assigned work from John McGee, General Office Manager of United Processing Service. You will be preparing mainly correspondence (letters and memorandums).

Each job assignment you receive will be accompanied by instructions stating any particular procedure(s) you will need to follow. When only minimum instructions are given, you are expected to use your own judgment. In some cases, you may be expected to correct undetected errors in grammar or punctuation that have been overlooked by the company submitting the documents.

When completed, all work should be given to your supervisor (your teacher) to examine. You, however, must judge the acceptability of your final work. You should proofread your work carefully, neatly correcting all errors, before submitting it to your supervisor.

United Processing Service has based its office manual on CENTURY 21 KEYBOARDING, FORMATTING, AND DOCUMENT PROCESSING; therefore, use the index of your textbook to check matters of placement when in doubt.

Before beginning your first job assignment, your supervisor gives you a copy of "Excerpts from the Office Manual." You are requested to review them before beginning your work.

Excerpts from the Office Manual

Simplified Memos

A simplified memorandum may be prepared on either letterhead or plain paper. It is formatted in block style with 1" side margins. Place the date on line 10 or a DS below the letterhead (if letterhead paper is used). DS below major parts of memo and below paragraphs except after the dateline and the last paragraph of the body. Quadruple-space (space down 4 times) below the date and last paragraph of the body; SS body paragraphs.

Letters

Prepare letters in either block or modified block style, depending on the request of a client. Use 1", 1½", or 2" side margins, depending on the number of words in the letter body (refer to letter placement table, page 149 of your textbook, if necessary).

Second page of letter. For letters requiring a second page, use plain paper of the same quality as the letterhead. Provide a heading on second page and leave at least a 1" bottom margin on each page. When dividing a paragraph between pages, at least 2 lines of the paragraph must appear on each page.

Heading for second page of letter. The heading for a second page of a letter is started on line 6. DS between heading and body. The two heading styles, as illustrated below, are: (1) *block style*—usually used with block letters; and (2) *horizontal style*—usually used with modified block letters.

Miss Holly Hudson
Page 2
June 15, 19--

In your new position as an account representative for Ernst and Jung Associates. The two-day orientation session will allow you to learn about the company's philosophy and purpose, as well as

Block Style Heading

Miss Holly Hudson 2 June 15, 19--

In your new position as an account representative for Ernst and Jung Associates. The two-day orientation session will allow you to learn about the company's philosophy and purpose, as well as

Horizontal Style Heading

198b-200b (continued)

Job 6
Letter to Regional Office
(LM p. 135)

Ms. Young-Bryge: Format this handwritten copy for me as a letter. Arrange the table within the letter so it is centered between the left and right letter margins. Use an appropriate salutation and complimentary close. Send the letter to:

Mr. Sabura Wakui, Manager
Pro-Tech Regional Office
122 Amity Road
New Haven, CT 06515-1466

Job 7
Letter to Regional Office
(LM p. 137)

Ms. Young-Bryge: I need the same letter with a different table sent to:

Mrs. Connie Chiodo, Manager
Pro-Tech Regional Office
90 Eureka Square
Pacifica, CA 94044-2692

Reformat the letter you just completed but substitute the last two columns of the table given below:

Present Quota	New Quota
1,160	1,275
2,300	2,545
475	535
1,920	2,134

The selling price of expanding files in the 800X series has been reduced by 20%. Sales of files in this series have declined during the last two quarters, and it is expected the lower price will reverse this downward trend.

Because of the lowered price, the regional quotas have been adjusted. The table below gives the product, the present quarterly quota, and the new quarterly quota for your region.

Product	Present Quota	New Quota
Subject File	1,209	1,340
A-Z Index File	2,200	2,415
Banker's Filing Case	450	510
Jan.-Dec. Index Files	1,759	2,007

The 20% reduction will remain in effect through June. An evaluation will be made before the end of June to determine future pricing.

Job 8
Memorandum

Ms. Young-Byrge: Process this memo for me to Mr. Batiste. Use a full sheet and simplified format.

Subject: NEW SALES REP TRAINING PROGRAM

(¶) March 6-9 have been confirmed as the dates for the training program for new sales representatives.

(¶) There will be 27 participants, and they will be notified to make travel arrangements so they can attend a reception and dinner at 6 p.m. at the Blue Royal Inn on March 5.

(¶) The formal training program will begin at 9 a.m. the next day and will end at 3 p.m. on March 9. All topics, times, and presenters have been confirmed. The agenda approved at the last Marketing Management Committee Meeting will be followed.

Excerpts (continued)

Special parts of a letter. The *subject line,* if used, informs the reader of the content of the letter; it is shown in ALL CAPS a DS below the salutation. Begin at left margin or indent to paragraph point if body paragraphs are indented.

The *company name in closing lines,* if used, is shown in ALL CAPS a DS below the complimentary close. The writer's name and title are then placed four lines below the company name.

If more than one *notation* is used in a letter, DS between them and follow this order: typist's initials, enclosure or attachment notation, copy notation, and postscript. Use the abbreviations *cc* (carbon copy) or *pc* (photocopy) for copy notations, leaving one space between the abbreviation and the name of the receiver. Omit the abbreviation (P.S.) for postscript and begin at left margin if body paragraphs are blocked or indent to paragraph point if body paragraphs are indented.

Kingsley Publishers

200 Fairway Drive • Davenport, IA 52806-1320 • (319) 642-8811

June 8, 19--

Miss Arlene Douglas
Central Business Academy
666 Walnut Street
Des Moines, IA 50309-2661

Dear Miss Douglas:

LETTER FORMATTING

Enclosed is the booklet, LETTER FORMATTING, that you asked me to send you. It illustrates and describes the letter formats most often used for business letters.

The letter you are reading is an example of the modified block style with indented paragraphs and mixed punctuation. As you can see, a colon is placed after the salutation, and a comma follows the complimentary close when using mixed punctuation. Also, the dateline and closing lines are begun at center point in all modified block letters.

This letter also illustrates the correct placement of special parts: subject line, company name in closing, enclosure notation, copy notation, and postscript. A letter rarely will use more than one or two special parts; many letters have none. We have used them merely to illustrate their placement.

Sincerely yours,

KINGSLEY PUBLISHERS

Mark Greeley, Managing Editor

bx

Enclosure

cc Joan Banks

Should you desire to place an order with us for additional copies of LETTER FORMATTING, let me know.

Special Parts of Letter

ASSEMBLING AND INSERTING CARBON PACKS

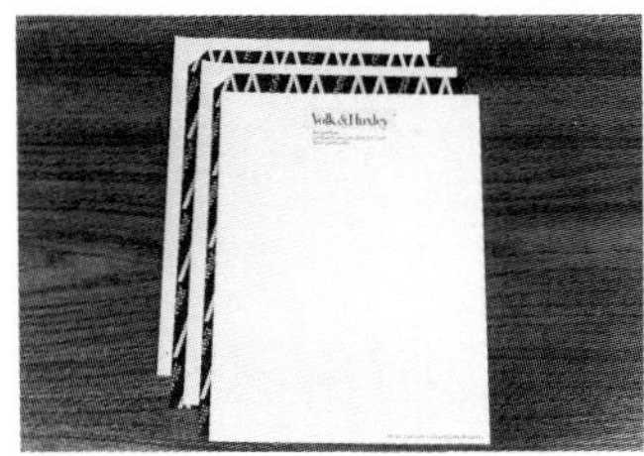

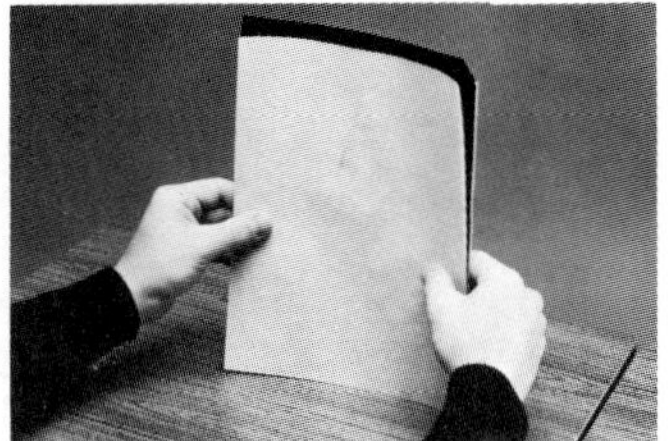

Desk-top assembly method

1. Assemble letterhead, carbon sheets (uncarboned side up), and second sheets as illustrated above. *Use one carbon and one second sheet for each copy desired.*

2. Grasp the carbon pack at the sides, turn it so that the *letterhead faces away from you, the carbon side of the carbon paper is toward you, and the top edge of the pack is face down.* Tap the sheets gently on the desk to straighten.

3. Hold the sheets firmly to prevent slipping; insert pack into typewriter. Hold pack with one hand; turn platen with the other.

Inserting the pack with a trough

To keep the carbon pack straight when feeding it into the typewriter, place the pack in the fold of a plain sheet of paper (paper trough) or under the flap of an envelope. Remove the trough or envelope when the pack is in place.

198b-200b (continued)

Job 2
Memorandum (LM p. 129)

Ms. Young-Bryge: Format material as a formal memo from me to the members of the marketing management committee. Use **MINUTES OF JANUARY 5 MEETING** as the subject.

Enclosed is a draft copy of the summary minutes of the January 5 Marketing Management Committee Meeting I prepared for you to review.

Please initial the copy after you have reviewed it, and return it to me by January 12. If you make a correction, please note the correction on the copy.
Enclosure

Job 3
Executive-Size Letters
(LM pp. 131-133)

Ms. Young-Bryge: Use the handwritten copy to process two letters for Mr. Batiste's signature. One letter is to:

Mr. Nicolas Perez, Manager
DJS Office Products
6222 Riverside Boulevard
Sacramento, CA 95831-1201

The second letter goes to:

Mrs. Emma Burns, Manager
Prestige Business Supplies
487 Prospect Avenue
Hartford, CT 05105-3902

Use executive-size stationery and make 1 cc of each letter.

(¶) Pro-Tech is pretesting a sales promotion campaign for selected products in its lateral filing cabinet group. Your office supply company has been selected to participate in this pretest campaign.
(¶) The lateral files we are promoting include two-, three-, and four-drawer cabinets from Pro-Tech's Ozwood Line. The cabinets in this line are ideal for credenzas, room dividers, or wherever space is critical.
(¶) Your Pro-Tech sales representative will contact you to explain the details and the advantages of the campaign for you and your customers. A campaign such as this is one way we can show appreciation to our valued customers. I hope you will participate.
Sincerely, Robert C. Batiste Sales Manager

Job 4
Sales Summary

Ms. Young-Bryge: Produce a final copy from the revised table shown at the right. Center the copy horizontally and vertically on a full sheet of paper.

Job 5
Sales Summary

Ms. Young-Bryge: I want you to produce a different sales report by adding a fourth column to the sales summary you just completed. Use **Difference** as the heading for the fourth column. Compute and enter in the fourth column the difference between the quarterly sales for each product. If sales have declined, enter a minus sign in front of the number.

EXPANDING FILING SYSTEMS SALES SUMMARY
~~Second~~ Third and ~~Third~~ Fourth Quarters, 19--

Product	October December	July September
Banker's Filing Case	~~1,974~~ 1,645	1,785
Subject File	~~5,011~~ 4,756	4,897
A-Z Index File	~~8,876~~ 9,011	9,412
Jan.-Dec. Index File	~~8,013~~ 6,987	7,325
Daily 1-31 Index File	~~3,886~~ 3,357	3,588
Household File	~~13,253~~ 11,750	12,751
TOTAL UNIT SALES	~~42,013~~ 37,506	39,758

91a-95a ▶ 5 (daily)

Conditioning Practice

each line twice (slowly, faster); repeat as many times as you can in 5′ at the beginning of each class period

alphabet 1 New equipment will be purchased for the key junior magazine executive.

figures 2 We received 130 chairs, 129 desks, and 75 computers on Order No. 5648.

shift key/lock 3 J. A. Hall, C. McLain, and P. Anzell are experts in BASIC Programming.

speed 4 Sign the form so the auditor may pay their men for their work with us.

| 1 | 2 | 3 | 4 | 5 | 6 | 7 | 8 | 9 | 10 | 11 | 12 | 13 | 14 |

91b-95b ▶ 45 (daily)

Job 1 (plain sheet)

all letters used | A | 1.5 si | 5.7 awl | 80% hfw |

> *From the desk of*
> *John McGee*
>
> *Please take this keyboarding test to give me a gauge of your keyboarding potential. Take two 1′ writings on each ¶ and one 5′ writing on both ¶s combined. Record your best 5′ score at the top of your paper.*
>
> *John McGee*

gwam 5′

The question that may be and often is asked by some persons is this: 3 54
What is a computer? A computer is merely a piece of equipment, much like 6 57
an electronic typewriter only much more complicated. The heart of the 9 60
computer is the microchip, or what is known as the central processing 11 63
unit. Computers are designed and programmed to process data at high 14 66
speed. With special software programs, the computer can be converted to 17 68
a word processor so that it can be used for the preparation of written 19 71
documents. The basic parts of a computer system are the keyboard, the 23 75
central processing unit, the display unit, and the printer. 25 76

Computers can be programmed to do almost any kind of a job. At the 27 79
present time, there are as many as fifty or more different programming 31 82
languages. Languages are used to change the English-like orders of a 33 85
programmer into the binary symbols–ones and zeros–which can be under- 36 88
stood by the central processing unit of the computer. BASIC is one of 39 91
the common programming languages. It has many benefits. It is very easy 42 94
to learn and to use because its English-like commands and organization 45 96
are flexible and easy to remember. During your life, you will probably 48 99
learn to use many different computer languages. It will be an exciting 51 102
adventure for you. 51 103

gwam 5′ | 1 | 2 | 3 |

198a-200a ▶ 5 (daily) Conditioning Practice

1. Each line twice SS.
2. A 1′ writing on line 4; find *gwam*.

alphabet 1 My taxi quickly weaved through a frozen back street into Tokyo, Japan.
figures 2 Of 2,350 women graduates in 1984, an M.Ed. degree was attained by 675.
fig/sym 3 The Model #234-15-97 which was reduced by 25% cost $60 instead of $80.
speed 4 A goal of the city is to own or make a bicycle lane by the giant lake.

| 1 | 2 | 3 | 4 | 5 | 6 | 7 | 8 | 9 | 10 | 11 | 12 | 13 | 14 |

198b-200b ▶ 45 (daily) Office Job Simulation

Job 1
Summary Minutes

Ms. Young-Bryge: At the right is an edited copy of the summary minutes from the last marketing management committee meeting. Prepare a copy of the minutes for distribution to the committee members. Format it as an unbound manuscript. Make one carbon copy and retain it in your files for use in a later job assignment.

SUMMARY MINUTES OF THE MARKETING MANAGEMENT COMMITTEE MEETING

January 5, 19--

All members of the committee were present at this meeting which was convened at 1:30 p.m. in Board Room c. Mr. Bryce C. Mounte, Vice President for Marketing, served as chair person and Ms. Renee Young-Bryge, Assistant Sales Manager, served as secretary.

The new-products manager reported on the status of the proposal recommending Pro-Tech begin manufacturing and distributing magnetic tapes and discs for microcomputers. The committee recommends that Pro-Tech not pursue this prosal. The committee believes resources should be allocated to increase market penetration for existing products and not used for diverisgying into what is presently a highly competititive and rapidly changing market.

The marketing research amnager reported on the need for a new computer output microfilm (com) unit. The results of a marketing research survey indicate that Pro-Tech's present COM unit will not meet the retrieval needs of businesses beyong a three-year period. The committee recommends that ProTech continue to develop a Com unit.

The advertising manager presented the design engineer's sketches and scale model of the new executive dsk-top filing system. The committee was pleased with the proposed design and recommends that it be approved put into production as soon as possible.

The committee reviewed the sales of selected groups of products and recommends that a sales promotion campaign be pretested for proucts in the lateral filing cabinet group and a price reduction be considered for products in the expanding filing systems groups.

The assistant slaes manager discussed the agenda and dates for the upcoming sales training program for new sales representatives. The committee approved the agenda and suggested that the program be conducted during the week of March if seminar rooms are available.

---

1 The survey results are abased on 55 replies from businesses with in the market of the Eastern Regional Sales Office.

2 The committee recommends the price be reduced for the 800x series if all products within the group cannot be reduced.

Job 2

From the desk of
John McGee

Joanne Cox, Vice President of United Processing Service, has prepared this draft memo describing the new policy regarding simplified memorandums in the company. Please prepare it in final form on plain paper, using the simplified style discussed in the memo. Ms. Cox asked for 1 carbon copy.

John McGee

Febuary 14, 19--

QS

Janet C. Robertson, Personnel Manager

Simplified Memorandum ALL CAPS

Sumarized here is the our policy on regarding simplified memos. We like have adopted the simplified memorandum not only for our own interoffice memorandums to be prepared within the company, but also for any memorandums which our clients request us to prepare. The only exception will be if clients request that their memorandums be prepared on their own printed forms.

We will need copies of this policy distributed to all of the current word procesors and keyboard specialists. Also, please review the feaures of this style (listed below) so that you will be able to discuss them in detail should questions arise.

1. Prepare simplified memorandums on standard letterhead or plain paper (as specified).

DS

2. Use block format with 1" side margins.

3. Place the date a double space below the last line of the letterhead or on line 10 if plain paper is used.

4. Double-space below all major parts (name of recipient, the subject line, body paragraphs, reference initials, closing notations) except below the dateline and the last paragraph of the body. Quadruple-space (space down 4 times) below the dateline and last paragraph.

5. Single-space the body; double-space between paragraphs.

6. Single-space enumerated items; leave iether a double or single space between them items.

DS

Because of its streamlined format, the simplified memorandums can be processed easily on our microcomputer or word processors. Should and any problems arise regarding this policy, please let me know.

QS

Joanne Cox, Vice Presidnt

xx

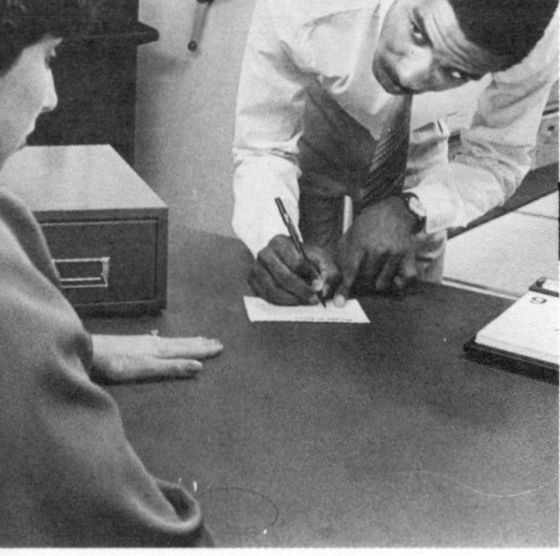

Unit 42 Lessons 198-200

Learning Goals

1. To simulate the keyboarding activities of an administrative specialist in a sales office.
2. To improve your ability to make formatting decisions without violating directions.
3. To improve your production skills by keying from unarranged, rough-draft, and script copy.

Machine Adjustments

1. Paper guide at *0*.
2. Ribbon control to use top half of ribbon.
3. Margins: 70-space line for sentences and ¶s; as required for problems.
4. Spacing: SS drills; DS ¶s; as required for problems.

PRO-TECH INC.: AN OFFICE JOB SIMULATION

Work Assignment

You are employed in the home office of Pro-Tech, Inc., a company that designs, produces, and sells filing supplies, equipment, and systems to office supply businesses throughout the United States. The home office is located at 802 North Delaware Street, Indianapolis, IN 46204-1182.

You are assigned to work for Ms. Renee Young-Bryge, Assistant Sales Manager. Ms. Young-Bryge reports to Mr. Robert C. Batiste, Sales Manager, who reports to the vice president of marketing.

The sales manager is responsible for planning, directing, and controlling the marketing functions of Pro-Tech. Ms. Young-Bryge assists the sales manager, supervises the regional sales managers, and maintains four of the company's largest sales accounts.

Your job title is Administrative Specialist to the Assistant Sales Manager. You are, however, expected to assist the sales manager on an "as needed" basis. All assignments come to you through Ms. Young-Bryge.

You are to complete assigned tasks that are managerial, secretarial, or clerical in nature. Document production tasks include summary minutes, memos, sales reports, correspondence, and telegrams.

Pro-Tech has an Office Employee's Manual which specifies the formats for reports, letters, memos, and forms. Excerpts from this manual are given at the right and are to be used to complete the tasks in this unit.

Use January 9, 19--, as the date unless otherwise directed. Carbon copies are not made unless they are requested.

OFFICE EMPLOYEE'S MANUAL

SUMMARY MINUTES are formatted as unbound or leftbound manuscripts. Page 1 top margin is 1½" for pica and 2" for elite; all other pages use 1" top margin. Bottom margin is at least 1", and left margin is 1" for unbound and 1½" for leftbound. Right margin is 1" for both unbound and leftbound. QS below the main or secondary heading; DS above and below side headings; DS the body.

STANDARD-SIZE STATIONERY requires 1" to 2" side margins depending on length of body. Begin letter address a QS below dateline. If no specific letter style is requested, use modified block style, mixed punctuation.

EXECUTIVE-SIZE STATIONERY is 7¼" by 10½". Use modified block style, mixed punctuation, and 1" side margins.

MEMOS are prepared in formal or simplified format with 1" side margins. SS the message a DS below last heading line. DS between message paragraphs.

TABLES are centered horizontally and vertically on plain paper. DS between all lines in table except use SS for multiple line column headings. The first line of the table is to begin on an even numbered vertical line.

TABLES WITHIN LETTERS are centered horizontally between the letter margins. DS above and below the title and column headings and below last line of body. SS multiple line main headings and column headings and entries in the columns.

91b-95b (continued)

Jobs 3 and 4
(LM pp. 21-24)

> **From the desk of John McGee**
> *William Turnage, President of the Wilderness Society, wishes to see this letter prepared in both modified block and block letter style. Use blocked ¶s and open punctuation with each letter and correct any errors Mr. Turnage may have overlooked. Prepare 1 carbon copy of each letter for the files.*
> John McGee

Use current date

Mr. James Bisenius
1633 East Avenue
Haywood, CA 94541-2203

Dear Mr. Bisenius

Enclosed ~~you will find~~ is your new membership decal along with your renewal notice. Although your membership in The Wilder ness Society has not expired, it will soon; and I am writing ~~ine order~~ to ask you to renew at this time. In this way, we can avoid costly membership reminders, and use our limited budget for the public good.

This ~~passed~~ past year, The wilderness Society has been very influ- ential in working to expand our nations inventory of wildlands--public lands whose need for protection has never been more ~~urgante~~ urgent.

Thank you for your continued support, a reply envelope is enclosed for your ~~conveniance~~. Convenience

Sincerely

The Wilderness Society (ALL CAPS)

(QS) William A. Turnage, President

xx Enclosure

By renewing now, you can be sure your subscription to The Living Wilderness will continue without interruption.

Job 5

> **From the desk of John McGee**
> *Prepare this hand-written memo for Carlos Lara, Head of Transportation of Fairfield Manu-facturing. He asks for simplified for-mat on plain paper.*
> John McGee

Use current date

All Employees
Transportation For Company Business } ALL CAP

(¶) The Purchasing Department has recently signed an agreement to lease a variety of cars, vans, and buses. They will be arriving within the next two weeks. (¶) When you need to use such equipment for company business, please place your request at our central garage. At least a forty-eight-hour notice will be necessary to reserve any needed transporta-tion. Your authorized budget number should be given when placing your request.

Carlos Lara, Head of Transportation
xx

197c ▶ 25
Prepare for a Simulation

1 plain full sheet
1 letterhead (LM p. 127)

1. Format the letter given at the right in modified block style, mixed punctuation, on a plain full sheet with these letter parts included:

a. Insert **CERTIFIED** as a mailing notation.

b. Use **DRESSER REPLACEMENT** as the subject line.

c. Insert the company name **LEWIS J. MEIER COMPANY** in the closing lines.

d. Add a photocopy notation identifying **Mrs. Amanda Van Telburg** as the recipient.

2. Proofread your copy, mark it for correction, and prepare a final copy on letterhead with all errors corrected.

3. Address an envelope.

Note: Words in letter parts added to the letter are included in the word count at the right of the letter.

words

July 2, 19-- 3

Ms. Wendy Grimaldi 8
1203 Hallmark Drive 12
Arlington, TX 76011-1448 18

Dear Ms. Grimaldi: 21

(¶) Thank you for bringing to our attention the prob- 35
lem that you are having with the dresser you pur- 45
chased from our Arlington dealer. It is only through 55
customer feedback that we can assure customer 65
satisfaction. 68
(¶) As you may know, warping of veneer does occur 77
occasionally despite all the quality-control efforts 87
that take place before the furniture leaves the 97
factory. When this happens, we replace the defec- 107
tive piece of furniture. Please fill out the enclosed 118
preaddressed form and mail it to Mrs. Amanda 127
Van Telburg, our Arlington branch manager, to 136
arrange a convenient time for delivery of your 146
new dresser. 148
(¶) We apologize for any inconvenience this may 157
have caused you and hope you will find this 166
arrangement satisfactory. 171

Sincerely, 174

Walter Finch 181
Customer Relations 185

xx 185
Enclosure 192/**207**

91b-95b (continued)

Job 6

From the desk of John McGee

Prepare this rough-draft memo in simplified format on plain paper. Correct any undetected errors you may find.

John McGee

All Office Personel

ELECTRONIC KEYBOARD

Here is additional informaiton about the electronac keyboard or keypad which is ~~to be~~ used with the micro computer or the word processor.

In my previous ~~letter,~~ memo I mentioned ~~to you~~ that the basic keyboard is the same as that now found on the electornic typewriter. The location of the special function keys varies according to the brand name of the manufacturer fo the keyboard or keypad. Never the less it is relatively easy to learn to use the speical functin keys. The operators manual usually gives a detailed explanation of these uses; or, if the keyboard is "user friendly," the function of a key ~~will be~~ is indicated on the key.

The key pad can be tilted from 10 to 15 degrees to accomodate the operator. Here however it is important for the operator to ~~be sure to~~ keep the keypad in proper keyboarding position for maximum keyboarding efficiency. ~~and for the reduction of keyboarding fatigue.~~

The rule to follow is this: When the tips of the fingers are on the keyboard, the base of the hand and the elbow should all be aligned with the angle of the keypad for maximum keyboarding efficiency and for reduction of keyboarding fatigue.

The attached literature will give you additional information about the keyboard or keypad. A special workshop will be offered to all interested employees in the near future.

Please review the literature before the workshop.

Marie Cortez, Director of Personnel

xx

Attachment

196d ▶ 25 Prepare for a Simulation

1. Copy the list shown below:
p. 283, 160c, Problem 1
p. 331, 191b, Problem 3
p. 333, 193b, Problem 2

2. Review the features of the various problems and select for practice the one(s) on which you need most practice.

3. As time permits, format other problems on the list or format from unarranged copy another similar problem.

Stationery Needs:
plain full sheets

Lesson 197 Keyboarding Skills/Prepare for Simulation

197a ▶ 5 Conditioning Practice

1. Each line twice SS.
2. A 1′ writing on line 4; find *gwam*. Repeat if time permits.

alphabet 1 Crazy Jake determined what represented an exact quorum before leaving.
figures 2 The May 27, 1986, shipment included 50 typewriters and 34 calculators.
fig/sym 3 The toll free number (1-800-234-6759) can be used to buy a 1988 issue.
speed 4 Make them pay us a sufficient penalty or cut the profit for the cycle.

| 1 | 2 | 3 | 4 | 5 | 6 | 7 | 8 | 9 | 10 | 11 | 12 | 13 | 14 |

197b ▶ 20 Improve Keyboarding Skill

1. Two 1′ *speed* writings on each ¶; find *gwam* on each writing.
2. Two 5′ *control* writing on both ¶s combined; find *gwam*; circle errors.

all letters used | A | 1.5 si | 5.7 awl | 80% hfw |

Text	gwam 1′	5′	
The model office employee is in the eyes of the beholder. What	13	3	52
one boss would view as the model employee may not be viewed as the model	27	5	55
employee by another boss. However, there are many traits that most em-	42	8	58
ployers would agree are necessary for the exceptional office worker to	56	11	61
possess. A listing of desirable traits of office workers would include	70	14	64
the words reliable and professional. Reliability means more than just	84	17	66
being at work each day. It means that the person can be counted on to	99	20	69
do the job to the best of his or her ability. A professional person	112	22	72
is one that always strives to create a positive image.	123	25	74
The list of traits could be further expanded to require good oral	13	27	77
and written communication skills and teamwork capability. A person with	28	30	80
good communication skills creates a good image for the firm for which	42	33	82
he or she works. Just as important, this person creates a good atmos-	44	36	85
phere for office workers. A person who is a good teamworker can best	70	39	88
be described as one who feels that the success of the company is more	84	41	91
important than personal success. This person recognizes that a job is	98	44	94
a joint effort with other workers and that the company can succeed as	112	47	97
a group; but as an individual, a person may occasionally fail.	124	49	99

gwam 1′ | 1 | 2 | 3 | 4 | 5 | 6 | 7 | 8 | 9 | 10 | 11 | 12 | 13 | 14 |
5′ | 1 | 2 | 3 |

91b-95b (continued)

Job 7

(LM pp. 25-30)

From the desk of
John McGee

Jeff Brown, Division Manager of Centek Office Systems, Inc., wants three letters prepared for the three regional managers of his company. Their names and addresses are listed below. Use modified block style, indented ¶s, and mixed punctuation. Use current date and supply an appropriate salutation and complimentary close. Mr. Brown will sign each letter. The three names and addresses are:

Mrs. Judith Marx, Manager
Centek Office Systems, Inc.
Western Regional Office
303 Kings Lane
Santa Maria, CA 93454-0091

Mr. Alberto Valdez, Manager
Centek Office Systems, Inc.
Eastern Regional Office
2900 Revere Avenue
Manchester, NH 03103-2211

Mrs. Carmen Torres, Manager
Centek Office Systems, Inc.
Southern Regional Office
450 Crest Lane
Lakeland, FL 33803-1021

John McGee

(¶) When we meet next month at the divisional meeting, we will be discussing various printers on the market and the budget allocations each regional division will be given to purchase such printers. There will be various manufacturers on hand to answer any questions you may have about such acquisitions. In the paragraphs below, I have outlined some basic characteristics of the types of printers we will be examining.

(¶) Dot matrix printers--those that use a combination of dots on the paper to form the letters or characters--can print copy at high speed. The speed is usually listed in characters per second (cps). A high-speed dot matrix printer can produce copy at a rate of 400 characters per second, the equivalent of 80 five-stroke words. With such high-speed printers, the dots are visible and the quality of print is poor. Letter-quality daisy wheel printers are also available. The printing speed varies from 10 to 50 cps. These printers cost much more than matrix printers.

(¶) Two other technologies--laser and ink jet--can give letter-quality print at extremely high speeds, but such printers may be too expensive for regional budgets. With the first method, a laser beam scorches images onto regular paper. With the second, spurts of ink controlled by a magnetic field are shot onto the paper to form the characters.

(¶) Please familiarize yourself with the enclosed booklets. I will send information about the display unit soon.

195c ▶ 25
Prepare for a Simulation

1. Copy the list shown below:
p. 292, 168c, Problem 3
p. 307, 176b, Problem 1
p. 308, 177b, Problem 1

2. Review the features of the various problems and select for practice the one(s) on which you need most practice.

3. As time permits, format other problems on the list or format from unarranged copy another similar problem.

Stationery Needs:
half sheet
executive-size letterhead (LM p. 123)
message reply memo (LM p. 125)

Lesson 196 — Language Skills/Prepare for Simulation

196a ▶ 5
Conditioning Practice

1. Each line twice SS.
2. A 1′ writing on line 4; find *gwam*. Repeat if time permits.

alphabet 1 Jacob Cruz kept extremely quiet when he received his first gold medal.
figures 2 The index slipped 1.79 points to 86.34 as sales hit 13,725,000 shares.
fig/sym 3 The contract (4/15, n/30) allowed a $2,876 discount if paid by June 9.
speed 4 When did the widow make the eighty formal gowns for the downtown firm?

| 1 | 2 | 3 | 4 | 5 | 6 | 7 | 8 | 9 | 10 | 11 | 12 | 13 | 14 |

196b ▶ 10
Improve Language Skills

full sheet; 70-space line

Key the paragraph shown at the right, selecting the correct word choice. Verify your copy with your teacher.

Mr. Whitehill, the (principal, principle), invited Miss Schantz to be his guest at the noon luncheon (meating, meeting). Dr. Janet Banks, an excellent speaker, has been scheduled to talk (preceding, proceeding) lunch. She is an (eminent, imminent) school psychologist who lost her (cite, sight, site) in a car accident several years ago. After her last speech, the audience paid her the supreme (compliment, complement) by giving her a standing ovation. She has a very positive (effect, affect) on all those who (hear, here) her speak.

196c ▶ 10
Improve Keyboarding Technique

1. Each line once as shown.
2. A 1′ writing on each of lines 3, 6, and 9. Find *gwam* on each writing.
3. If time permits, practice slower lines again.

Shift keys

1 July|San Jose|Monday|Rhode Island|Easter|Kentucky Derby|Miami Dolphins
2 United States of America|the Fourth of July|United States Marine Corps
3 Eva Lopez, Maria Ruiz, Ana Cruz, and Mario Ortiz are from Puerto Rico.

Shift lock

4 first place TODD FLYNN, second place ERIN BROCK, third place ADA SCOTT
5 the book GONE WITH THE WIND the play KING LEAR or the magazine REDBOOK
6 Emi read TO KILL A MOCKINGBIRD in April and THE SUN ALSO RISES in May.

Space bar

7 up win me see we can do may up the no top by key as ask he her low did
8 very fun sum say sun foam day noon room money men ream lay pan jam hay
9 Jan will be back in the city by noon so that she can play in the band.

| 1 | 2 | 3 | 4 | 5 | 6 | 7 | 8 | 9 | 10 | 11 | 12 | 13 | 14 |

91b-95b (continued)

Job 8

(plain paper)

From the desk of John McGee

Please prepare this second page of a letter for Ms. Stephanie Whitt--the first page has already been keyboarded. Use block style, blocked ¶s, and open punctuation.

John McGee

Miss Barbara Perez
Page 2
Current date

¶ Further, I'd like to alert you to another of Women In Business' Saturday Conferences for Women. On Saturday, November 14, the conference will be concerned with the topic "Stress Management." Morning speakers will be followed by a buffet luncheon; the afternoon will be devoted to group discussion. The complete agenda is described in the enclosed brochure.

¶ Also, plan now to be with your colleagues in Chicago for the October National Conference. A number of key speakers (see enclosure) will speak on a variety of topics which address current issues affecting today's business woman. Please fill out the reservation request card as soon as possible to assure your registration.

¶ We look forward to seeing you for these upcoming programs.

Sincerely

Ms. Stephanie Whitt
Executive Director

xx

Enclosures

194c ▶ 10
Improve Keyboarding Technique

1. Each line twice SS.
2. A 1′ writing on line 2, then on line 4, and then on line 6.

letter response	1	awarded you | bare minimum | based on my opinion | state reserve | extra award
	2	In my opinion, state taxes on gas are best set at a minimum base rate.
word response	3	to the | of them | may go | it may | to it | with them | when they go | for the | of a
	4	Jane may lend the six men the bus she owns if they go to the big lake.
combination response	5	for you | up to date | in such | to be | to see | if you go | was the | was with him
	6	Jo addressed a statement to the panel on the effects of minimum taxes.

| 1 | 2 | 3 | 4 | 5 | 6 | 7 | 8 | 9 | 10 | 11 | 12 | 13 | 14 |

194d ▶ 20
Improve Keyboarding Skill

1. Two 1′ *speed* writings on each ¶; find *gwam* on each writing.
2. Two 5′ *control* writings on both ¶s combined; find *gwam*; circle errors.

all letters used | A | 1.5 si | 5.7 awl | 80% hfw |

	gwam 1′	5′	
To be successful in business, one must develop effective listening	13	3	46
skills. Many authorities in the field of listening believe we will	27	5	48
retain approximately a fourth of what we hear. This suggests that we	41	8	51
have a very low level of proficiency when it comes to the art of listen-	55	11	54
ing. Ineffective listening is usually the result of poor habits. We	70	14	57
have to want to listen before we can actually do so. Most people would	84	17	60
agree that listening is work and that a majority of us have a tendency	98	20	63
to be lazy when it comes to quality listening.	107	21	65
There are several points that set a good listener apart from a poor	14	24	67
one. Good listeners generally listen for facts and for a sense of where	28	27	70
the speaker is going. They do not have prior biases about the subject	42	30	73
matter or toward the speaker. On the other hand, poor listeners allow	57	33	76
things to draw their attention and distract them from what is being said.	72	36	79
They judge the speaker's mannerisms and physical appearance rather than	86	39	82
concentrate on the message. They believe they already know what is	100	41	85
going to be said and will only half listen.	108	43	86

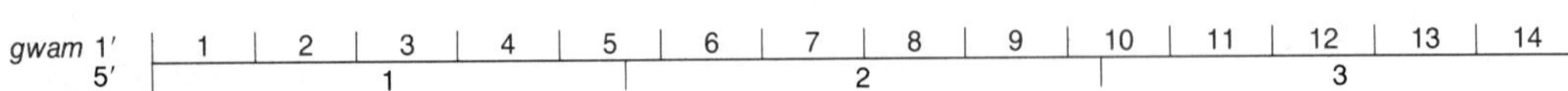

Lesson 195 Keyboarding/Prepare for Simulation

195a ▶ 5
Conditioning Practice

1. Each line twice SS.
2. A 1′ writing on line 4; find *gwam*. Repeat if time permits.

alphabet	1	Before leaving, Jerome quickly ordered the six pizzas with everything.
figures	2	Rooms B208, B45, and B376 are reserved for the conference on the 19th.
fig/sym	3	The interest (14.75%) on the loan would amount $2,036.89 each year.
speed	4	He owns an antique enamel duck, an ancient ivory lamb, and a clay fox.

| 1 | 2 | 3 | 4 | 5 | 6 | 7 | 8 | 9 | 10 | 11 | 12 | 13 | 14 |

195b ▶ 20
Improve Keyboarding Skill

Practice 194d, above, as directed there.

1′ Goal: To increase speed by at least 3 *gwam*.

5′ Goal: To reduce errors to no more than 8 in 5 minutes.

91b-95b (continued)

Job 9

(LM pp. 31-36)

From the desk of John McGee

Mr. Brown wishes this two-page letter prepared as soon as possible. Use modified block style, blocked ¶s, and open punctuation. Refer to the Office Manual before keying the second-page heading. You may wish to put a light pencil mark at the right edge of your paper (about $1\frac{1}{2}$" from the bottom) to remind yourself when to end the first page. Prepare an original copy for each of these addresses:

Mrs. Judith Marx, Manager
Centek Office Systems, Inc.
Western Regional Office
303 Kings Lane
Santa Maria, CA 93454-0091

Mr. Alberto Valdez, Manager
Centek Office Systems, Inc.
Eastern Regional Office
2900 Revere Avenue
Manchester, NH 03103-2211

Mrs. Carmen Torres, Manager
Centek Office Systems, Inc.
Southern Regional Office
450 Crest Lane
Lakeland, FL 33803-1021

John McGee

Use current date
Add address and salutation

As I promised, or monitor of

Here is the information on the display unit--a basic component a microprocessor or a word processing system. Please review this information beofre the divisional meeting. We will need to order the monitors at the same time we order printers.

television

The display unit is much like a screen. If a word processing software package is used with a microcomputer, or if a word processor is being used, the display shows the operator the lines that have been keyboarded. Some monitors have only 40 characters per line--but most have 80 characters. This is a basic necessity if the unit is to be used efficiently for word processing. Vertically a good montior should display at least 25 lines of text. Some units can display a full page. Still others monitors have a control line which shows the horizontal keystroke number and the number remaining on the page.

selecting of vertical lines

In a display unit, yoiu may have a choice of three types. The cheapest unit is the monochromatic monitor, which works well for word processing. Some operators find green and white displays easier to read than black-and-white displays. So-called composite color monitors are considered best for games and graphics. Composite refers to the way the colors are mixed. In the more expensive range, we have the RGB mon;itors. These monitors can produce truer colors and sharper printed images than is true for the composite model.

Another referred to as

~~An additional~~ key to a monitor's quality is bandwidth, measured in megahertz (MHz). Bandwidth indicates the frequency level that the monitor can handle. As MHz increase, the resolution becomes better. A monitor's resolution is measured also by what is known as the pixel count. Pixels are tiny pictures elements that combine to form the image that appears in on the screen. Again, the more pixels there are, the sharper the resolution. A color monitor's pixel count should be listed on the specification sheet accompanying the monitor. Furhter, the specification sheet should state how many vertical lines--comprised of pixels--will fit on its screen.

relatively

Finally, a monitor should be glare free. Keyboard operators who use monitors sometimes complain of eyestrain. With a nonglare screen the operator is less apt to experience eyestrain.

information which I have supplied here

I hope the ~~description~~ has given you some basic information about printers and monitors now available. Feel free to call me should you have any questions before the divisional meeting.

I look forward to seeing you there.

Sincerely

Jeff Brown, Division Manager

xx

Unit 41 Lessons 194-197

Learning Goals

1. To improve straight-copy keyboarding speed and accuracy.
2. To improve language skills.
3. To improve skill in formatting and keying a variety of business documents.

Machine Adjustments

1. Paper guide at *0*.
2. Ribbon control to use top half of ribbon.
3. Margins: 70-space line for sentences and ¶s; as required for problems.
4. Spacing: SS drills; DS ¶s; as required for problems.

Lesson 194 Improve Keyboarding/Language Skills

194a ▶ 5 Conditioning Practice

1. Each line twice SS.
2. A 1′ writing on line 4; determine *gwam*. Repeat if time permits.

alphabet 1 Everyone except Zelda thought Marquis was playing the befuddled joker.
figures 2 Between April 3, 1979, and March 2, 1986, Dane traveled 145,600 miles.
fig/sym 3 On May 27 (1958) he received his social security number (520-89-1346).
speed 4 If she turns in the six problems to the panel, she may go to the lake.

| 1 | 2 | 3 | 4 | 5 | 6 | 7 | 8 | 9 | 10 | 11 | 12 | 13 | 14 |

194b ▶ 15 Check Language Skills

60-space line

1. Read line 1, noting where corrections are needed.
2. Key the line including numbers, making the needed corrections.
3. Read and key the remaining lines in the same way.
4. Check the accuracy of your work with your teacher. As time permits, rekey any line in which you made errors.

1. The fourth of july is a special day for most americans.
2. Larry Paula and Karl will repeat their Freshman year.
3. On jan. 24 1948 he arrived in harpers ferry iowa.
4. The attorney was supposed to be here on monday May 17.
5. Rebecca ordered 2 dresses, but she received only 1.
6. The methodist Church is located at 1488 yorkton Ave..
7. A talented german author wrote <u>a return from yesterday</u>.
8. Northwestern bank will be open from 9 A.M. to 5:30 P.M.
9. Jonathan the boy next door works at mcIntyre library.
10. Joe, felipe, and chi spent the day at Huntington beach.
11. Flutie the winner of the heisman trophy will be here.
12. He was given a 15% discount for paying so early.
13. 8 people were injured in the accident West of town.
14. Miss. Sanchez, governor Jones, and dr. Chang were there.
15. Write to Mr. Mike Baker 414 Main street Paris maine.
16. Barbara was born on April 15, 1949 at Craig Colorado.
17. As the Treasurer receives the checks he deposits them.
18. If you will look on P. 18 you will find the answers.

Unit 19 Lessons 96-98

Learning Goals

1. To refine your keyboarding technique patterns.
2. To increase your speed and improve your accuracy.
3. To increase your straight-copy rate.
4. To improve language skills.
5. To improve proofreading skills.

Machine Adjustments

Paper guide at *0*.

Use:

*70-space line and single spacing for drills; DS below each SS group of drill lines

*70-space line and double spacing for ¶ timings of more than 1 minute

*as directed or needed for other copy

Lesson 96 Keyboarding/Language Skills

96a ▶ 5 Conditioning Practice

each line twice (slowly, faster); as time permits, repeat selected lines

alphabet 1 A travel expert frequently amazed them with talks about jungle dances.

figures 2 Please ship Order 1750 for 36 word processors, 49 desks, and 28 lamps.

shift key 3 J.A. Hall, P.C. McLain, and Anzel Paul work for Steinmann & Company.

speed 4 It is the duty of the eight men to fix the bicycle for the city firms.

| 1 | 2 | 3 | 4 | 5 | 6 | 7 | 8 | 9 | 10 | 11 | 12 | 13 | 14 |

96b ▶ 5 Improve Accuracy/ Force Speed

1. Two 1′ writings on line 1 of 96a. **Goal:** Not over 2 errors in each writing.
2. Two 1′ writings on line 4 of 96a. **Goal:** To force speed to a new level.

96c ▶ 10 Improve Language Skills: Punctuation

full sheet; 1″ top margin; 70-space line

Study/Learn/Apply/Correct Procedures

1. STUDY explanatory rule.
2. Key line number (with period); space twice, then key the LEARN sentence(s) DS, noting rule application.
3. Key the line number (with period); space twice, then key the APPLY sentence(s) DS, making changes to correct sentence(s).
4. As your teacher reads the correct sentence(s), show in pen or pencil any corrections that need to be made in your copy.
5. Rekey any APPLY sentence containing an error, CORRECTING the error as you key. Place the corrected sentence in the space below the APPLY sentence containing the error.

EXCLAMATION MARK

Use an exclamation mark after emphatic exclamations and after phrases and sentences that are clearly exclamatory.

Learn 1. What a beautiful view!
Apply 2. That was a great game.

QUESTION MARK

Use a question mark at the end of a sentence that is a direct question; however, use a period after a request that appears in the form of a question.

Learn 3. Do you know how to program a microcomputer?
Learn 4. Will you please see me after this class.
Apply 5. Will you please try to complete the report before the meeting.
Apply 6. Did you finish all the reports.

HYPHEN

Use a hyphen to join compound numbers from twenty-one to ninety-nine.

Learn 7. Their ages ranged from twenty-three to seventy-six.
Apply 8. Spell out these numbers as you keyboard them: 42, 66, and 91.

193b ▶ 145
Measure Production Skill: Special-Type Communications

Time Schedule

Plan and Prepare .... 5′
Timed Production .... 30′
Proofread and Correct Errors ... 7′
Compute *n-pram* .... 3′

2 forms (LM pp. 119-121)
2 plain full sheets

1. Arrange forms, second sheets, carbon paper, and envelopes. Make 1 cc of each problem on plain paper.

2. Work for 30′ when directed to begin; correct errors neatly before removing paper.

3. Compute *n-pram*; turn in completed work in problem number order as given below.

Problem 1
Formal Memorandum (LM p. 119)
Format/process the memo given at the top of the page.

Problem 2
Simplified Memo (plain full sheet)
Format/process the memo of Problem 1 in simplified style on a plain full sheet.

Problem 3
News Release (LM p. 121)
Format/process the copy given at right as a news release.

words

TO: Britt Seymore, Administrative Specialist FROM: Paul C. Copley, Build- 12
ings and Grounds DATE: November 15, 19-- SUBJECT: Temporary Parking 23
Permit 24

(¶ 1) The director of human resources has notified me that you should have 38
an assigned parking space while you are recovering from your knee surgery. 53

(¶ 2) I have assigned you to Space #25 in Parking Lot C. The space is near 67
the building in which you work. You may begin using the parking space 82
tomorrow, and it will be assigned to you for the next nine weeks. If you 96
are not fully recovered by that time, please contact me and I will arrange 111
an extension for you. 116

tap 116

RELEASE 2
ON RECEIPT 4

(¶ 1) Pittsburgh, November 15, 19--. The Western Area Chamber of Com- 16
merce held its Annual Recognition Banquet at Treetops Country Club on 30
November 13. The evening was highlighted by giving recognition to two 45
outstanding leaders from the community. 53

(¶ 2) Mrs. Elinor Avadellas, a business education teacher at Western Senior 67
High School, was recognized as this year's outstanding educator for her 81
service to the Western School System and to the local community. Mrs. 95
Avadellas has taught at Western for the past 15 years. During this time, 110
she has directed an active business education advisory committee and has 125
served as faculty advisor for Western's student chapter of the Future Busi- 140
ness Leaders of America Club. Mrs. Avadellas serves on the Western Town- 154
ship Planning Council and is an executive board member of and a coach in 169
the Western Soccer Club. 174

(¶ 3) Mr. Bruce Herold, the controller for Good's Department Store, was rec- 188
ognized as this year's outstanding business leader. Mr. Herold serves as 202
chairperson of the Western Redevelopment Industrial Council, which has 216
been instrumental in influencing many businesses to locate in the new West- 231
ern Shopping and Office Complex. Bruce Herold serves on the executive 245
board of the local Junior Achievement organization and chairs JA's scholar- 260
ship committee. 263

Denise Caton 266

tap 266

Problem 4
Phoned Telegram (plain full sheet)
Format/process on a plain sheet the telegraph message given at the right.

PHONED TELEGRAM Telegram November 15, 19--, 10:45 a.m. Miss Leslie 13
Morgan, Account Manager Collins Computer Equipment, Inc. 7504 Cy- 26
press Drive Humble, TX 77396-1473 33

Verification of phone order for three 160CPS Top-Line Printers. Each printer 49
is to have Courier 10, Artisan 10, and Letter Gothic 12 print wheels. Use P. O. 65
#27934 for invoicing. Ship for agreed upon December 10 delivery date. 79
Send maintenance agreement options for review. 88

Henry Ferris, Purchasing Agent West Hills Health Care Center 101

tap 101

96d ▶ 15
Measure Basic Skill: Straight Copy

1. Two 5′ writings; find *gwam*.

2. Proofread; circle errors.

3. Record better *gwam* rate on your rate record sheet.

Quarter-Minute Checkpoints

gwam	1/4′	1/2′	3/4′	1′
24	6	12	18	24
28	7	14	21	28
32	8	16	24	32
36	9	18	27	36
40	10	20	30	40
44	11	22	33	44
48	12	24	36	48
52	13	26	39	52
56	14	28	42	56
60	15	30	45	60
64	16	32	48	64
68	17	34	51	68
72	18	36	54	72
76	19	38	57	76
80	20	40	60	80

all letters used | A | 1.5 si | 5.7 awl | 80% hfw |

	gwam 2′	3′	5′
One of the key advances in computer technology during the last	6	4	3
thirty years has been the growth of small computers, which are versatile,	14	9	4
reliable, and quite easy to use. Known as microprocessors, these com-	21	14	8
puters on a chip of silicon no larger than the tip of a finger are the	28	19	11
heart of microcomputers. They can process, store, retrieve, and pass on	35	23	14
millions of pieces of information. Such computers are making low-cost	42	28	17
computer power available in the home, in the business office, and in our	49	33	20
schools. As has often been said, they are an idea whose time has come.	57	38	23
Expectations for the uses of the microcomputer are almost without	7	42	25
end. Microcomputers in cars have the job of checking mechanical func-	14	47	28
tions as well as the speed. Microcomputers and a few other items built	21	52	31
into typewriters have become word processing systems. The high speed of	28	56	34
the computer along with the ability of the computer for pattern recogni-	35	61	37
tion has made possible talking as well as speech recognition machines.	42	66	40
Also, machines that read books aloud are now in wide use by the visually	50	71	43
handicapped. Many new changes have come about in the field of medicine,	57	76	45
and you should realize the effect that the microcomputer has had and	64	80	48
will have in the future on your life as well as on the lives of others.	71	85	51

gwam 3′ | 1 | 2 | 3 | 4 | 5
5′ | 1 | 2 | 3

96e ▶ 15
Improve Basic Skill: Straight Copy

1. Add 4 to 8 words to your 96d *gwam* rate. **Goal:** To reach a new high-speed rate.

2. Two 1′ guided writings on ¶ 1 of 96d at your new goal rate as the 1/4′ guides are called.

3. A 2′ guided writing on ¶ 1. Try to maintain your 1′ rate.

4. Repeat Step 2, using ¶ 2.

5. Repeat Step 3, using ¶ 2.

6. A 3′ writing using both ¶s. **Goal:** To maintain your new speed rate for 3′.

191c ▶ 15
Improve Language Skills

full sheet
line: 60 spaces

1. Read line 1, noting where corrections are needed.

2. Key line 1, making needed changes; also correct any errors you make as you key the line.

3. Read and key lines 2-15 in the same manner.

4. Check the accuracy of your sentences with your teacher; rekey any lines that are in error.

1. joe and me is going to sues meeting in room 1,001.
2. the census takers data was used by morse's group.
3. the heat effected our teams performance in todays win.
4. the rough draft memo were discussed among tom and syd.
5. the team made less out of bounds tackels this week.
6. the hand painted vase remained stationery on anns desk.
7. he don't like to be given a out of class assignment.
8. i felt sad before i took the end of term english test.
9. tom said "lets all go;" mary replied "i cannot".
10. jims on line computer were used fore five hours work.
11. i past mr smiths most resent pop english quizz.
12. sue morse's button is lose, i hope she don't loose it.
13. their the club members who went to the forth meeting.
14. the book "Now is the Time" was resently reviewed in Time.
15. the schools principle will revue the absence polisy.

Lesson 192 — Review: Memos/News Releases/Telegrams

192a ▶ 5
Conditioning Practice

Practice the lines of 193a below.
Follow the directions given there.

192b ▶ 45
Sustain Production: Special-Type Communications

Time Schedule

Plan and Prepare	5′
Timed Production	30′
Proofread and Correct Errors	7′
Compute *n-pram*	3′

1. Make a list of problems to be keyed:

p. 325, 188b, Problem 1
p. 327, 189b, Problem 1
p. 329, 190b, Problem 1
p. 331, 191b, Problem 1

2. Arrange memo forms (LM pp. 115-117), plain sheets, and carbon paper (1 cc for each problem).

3. Work for 30′ when directed to begin; follow directions given for each problem; correct all errors neatly, proofreading carefully before removing a problem from the machine.

4. Compute *n-pram*; then turn in completed work arranged as listed in Step 1.

Lesson 193 — Evaluation: Memos/News Releases/Telegrams

193a ▶ 5
Conditioning Practice

1. Each line twice SS.

2. A 1′ writing on line 4; determine *gwam*. Repeat if time permits.

alphabet 1 A lumberjack carefully blazed an exact path by the quiet virgin woods.
figures 2 The farmer had 176 cows, 9 horses, 385 turkeys, 40 sheep, and 23 pigs.
fig/sym 3 I bought six 160′ rolls of #74 wire at $9.83/roll less a 25% discount.
speed 4 An auditor may work for the city firm to handle a key civic amendment.

| 1 | 2 | 3 | 4 | 5 | 6 | 7 | 8 | 9 | 10 | 11 | 12 | 13 | 14 |

97a ▶ 5 Conditioning Practice

each line twice (slowly, faster); as time permits, repeat selected lines

alphabet 1 Frank Carr puzzled over Meg's interest in the exquisitely written job.

figures 2 In 1987, we had 36 office chairs, 42 office desks, and 50 work tables.

one-hand words 3 In fact, a star at rear stage rested as eager casts regarded only him.

speed 4 It is their duty to go downtown to do the work for the six busy firms.

| 1 | 2 | 3 | 4 | 5 | 6 | 7 | 8 | 9 | 10 | 11 | 12 | 13 | 14 |

97b ▶ 5 Improve Accuracy/Force Speed

1. Two 1′ writings on line 1 of 97a. **Goal:** Not over 2 errors in each writing.

2. Two 1′ writings on line 4 of 97a. **Goal:** To force speed to a new level.

97c ▶ 15 Improve Techniques: Keystroking/Response Patterns/Rhythm

1. Lines 1-6 twice (slowly, faster).

2. Lines 7-12 three times (slowly, faster, top speed).

3. Two 1′ writings on line 10 for speed.

4. Two 1′ writings on lines 11 and 12 for control.

Emphasize fast finger-action keystroking; quiet hands.

third row 1 qua wow with end eke rut for the dot yam jay us usual if it is of pals

first row 2 zoa xyster cod economy vie five bog fob tub name man comb vow but exam

finger emphasis 3 qaza wsxs edcd rfvf tgbg yhnh yjmj ik,k ol.l p;/; aqua aza six wise p;

"b" reach 4 The bright baby boys babbled with joy as the abbey cobbler hurried by.

"y" reach 5 Jay Young may try to carry the yummy yellow yams to their yacht today.

"z" reach 6 Zestful quizzical quiz kids dizzily zigzagged around a buzzing bazaar.

Emphasize high-speed response patterns.

7 and if they|and if they go with me|and if they go with me to the firms

8 she did the work|she did the work for them|six men did the work for me

9 he may go|he may go with them|he may go with them and me to their city

10 If he is to do their work for them, then he may go with me to the bog.

Emphasize variable rhythm; finger-action keystroking.

11 Send the statement on the monopoly case to the union at their address.

12 Ask him to restate the nylon problem as the statement was exaggerated.

| 1 | 2 | 3 | 4 | 5 | 6 | 7 | 8 | 9 | 10 | 11 | 12 | 13 | 14 |

97d ▶ 5 Improve Language Skills: Punctuation

full sheet; 1″ top margin; 70-space line

Follow directions as given in 96c, page 168.

HYPHEN (continued)

Use a hyphen to join compound adjectives preceding a noun they modify as a unit.

Learn 1. The Book-of-the-Month Club lists this book.

Apply 2. The out of bounds catch stopped our first down drive.

Use a hyphen after each word or figure in a series that modifies the same noun (suspended hyphenation).

Learn 3. All 6-, 7-, and 8-foot boards were used during construction.

Apply 4. Please check the rates on first, second, and third class mail.

Lesson 191 Telegraphic Messages/Language Skills

191a ▶ 5
Conditioning Practice

1. Each line twice SS.
2. A 1′ writing on line 4; find *gwam*. Repeat if time permits.

alphabet 1 The children zipped very quietly away from the extremely boring jokes.
figures 2 Mary had 1,578 drinks, 649 hot dogs, and 320 candy bars for the stand.
sym 3 Ty O'Neil said, "I will give you $1 for each * you find in my report."
speed 4 The men may rush to visit the cozy island to fish for cod and panfish.

| 1 | 2 | 3 | 4 | 5 | 6 | 7 | 8 | 9 | 10 | 11 | 12 | 13 | 14 |

191b ▶ 30
Format Telegraphic Messages

3 plain full sheets

Problem 1

1. Read the information about telegraphic messages on page 324.
2. Note the placement and spacing guides shown in color on the message at the right. Margin: 60-space line.
3. Prepare a copy of the telegram on plain paper; make 1 cc; correct errors.

Problem 2

Reformat the telegram in Problem 1 and address it to:

Ms. Nell Vogel, Sales Manager
Computer Sales and Consultants
2269 Paxton Street
Harrisburg, PA 17111-1037
(717) 784-3256

Change the class of service to **Night Letter.**

Total words: 97.

words

center on line 12 PHONED TELEGRAM 3
QS

Telegram 8
DS
AMEL International 9
DS
November 7, 19--, 2:30 p.m. 14
DS
Mr. Ying Huang, Marketing Manager 21
Microcomputer Hardware and Software, Inc. 30
1948 Florida Avenue 34
Johnstown, PA 15902-3306 39
(814) 555-4343 42
DS
Request prices, delivery schedules, and maintenance agreements 54

for 12 micros to be connected to REALTIME 995 mini with RTOS 67

operating system. Micros must run Letterrite and Spreadrite 79

software using CROS operating system. 87
DS
Aida Fernandez, Word Processing Supervisor 95
Tokay Chemicals 98
DS
ssr 99

Problem 3

Format/process the telegram shown at the right; 1 cc; correct errors.

PHONED TELEGRAM Mailgram November 7, 19--, 3:30 p.m. Dr. Anne 12
Landino, President Ohio Business Education Association 2210 East 25
Avenue Lorain, OH 44052-3222 Thank you for inviting me to the 38
reception for past recipients of the Ohio Outstanding Business Teacher 52
Award. I would enjoy very much visiting with many of my colleagues 65
and meeting many of the younger business teachers, but poor health 79
prevents me from making such a demanding trip. Give my best wishes 93
to all the members and my congratulations to this year's recipient. 107
Have an excellent conference! 113
Anita Barber, 1967 Award Recipient 120

97e ▶ 10 Improve Control: Guided Writing

1. A 2′ writing (at a controlled pace with fingers curved; quiet hands).
2. Find *gwam*. Subtract 4 from your *gwam* rate. Find 1/4′ goals for 1′ writings at new goal rate.
3. Two 1′ writings at goal rate as 1/4′ guide is called. Work for accuracy; no more than 1 error in each writing.
4. Another 2′ writing for control. Maintain goal rate.

	gwam 2′	
Failure to concentrate on the copy to be keyboarded often causes	6	48
errors. Looking from the copy to the screen, to the paper in your ma-	13	55
chine, or at your fingers causes still other errors. Faulty techniques	21	62
are another major contributing factor. To reduce errors, concentrate	28	69
on the copy, keep your fingers curved and upright in keyboarding posi-	35	76
tion, and then let your fingers do the keyboarding. Try it and see.	41	83

97f ▶ 10 Improve Basic Skill: Straight Copy

Two 3′ writings on 96d, p. 169. Emphasize control.

Goal: No more than 6 errors in each writing.

Lesson 98 Keyboarding/Language Skills

98a ▶ 5 Conditioning Practice

each line twice (slowly, faster); as time permits, repeat selected lines

alphabet 1 As a freezing wave hit them, the explorers quickly adjusted the beams.
figures 2 I reviewed 127 books, 364 magazines, 50 newspapers, and 189 pamphlets.
ny, un, ce, br 3 Many persons were uncertain about swimming under the old brick bridge.
speed 4 She may lend the ancient city map to us if the city pays for the work.

98b ▶ 10 Improve Language Skills: Punctuation

full sheet; 1″ top margin; 70-space line

Follow directions as given in 96c, p. 168.

COLON

Use a colon to introduce an enumeration or a listing.

Learn 1. Please bring the following: a typewriter, a book, and paper.
Apply 2. Add these items to your grocery list bread, butter, and eggs.

Use a colon to introduce a question or a long direct quotation.

Learn 3. The question is this: Are you using good techniques?
Apply 4. This is my concern, Did you really study for the test?

Use a colon between hours and minutes expressed in figures.

Learn 5. The program will start promptly at 7:30 p.m.
Apply 6. Does United Flight 1104 leave at 915 or 1015 a.m.?

Palmero, Skonsi, Alvarez, & Hall

225 Nicollet Avenue, Minneapolis, MN 55401-1924 (612) 434-7888 • Public Relations Department

words

RELEASE 2
ON RECEIPT 4

Minneapolis, November 5, 19--. The law firm of Palmero, Skonsi, 17
Alvarez, & Hall is planning to construct a Technology Law Center 29
south of Minneapolis at 25504 Wycliffe Road in order to serve the 41
many high technology firms which located in that area. 51

The center will specialize in areas such as copyrights, con- 63
tractual agreements, import/export regulations, and new business 78
formation for the high tech businesses in the Minneapolis area. 90
Donald Vuckovich, a managing partner in the firm, stated "This 103
Technology Law Center is a new concept in the legal services field, 115
and the firm is convinced the center will benefit the many high 131
tech businesses in the area as well as entice many others to locate 145
near Minneapolis" 149

A ground breaking ceremony for the Center will be held in two 161
weeks and construction is scheduled for completion within 9 months. 176
In addition to the many legal services available, the center will 188
serve as a place where clients of Palmero, Skonsi, Alvarez, & Hall 201
from cities can meet with many area business leaders and will be 218
the site of several forums on technology and the law. Attorney 231
Vuckovich will operate the center He will be assisted by six at- 244
tornies, two paralegal assistants, and two legal administrative 257
specialists. 259

Ms. Jo-Ann Herrod 263

bas 264

News Release in Rough Draft

98c ▶ 15
Measure Basic Skill: Straight Copy

two 5′ writings; find *gwam*; circle errors; record better rate

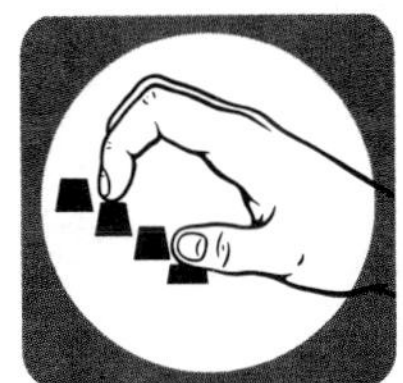
Fingers curved

Keystroke

Spacing stroke

all letters used | A | 1.5 si | 5.7 awl | 80% hfw |

	gwam 3′		5′
As you read copy for keyboarding, try to read at least a word or,	4	3	44
better still, a word group ahead of your actual keyboarding point. In	9	5	47
this way, you should be able to recognize the keystroking pattern needed	14	8	50
as you learn to keyboard balanced-hand, one-hand, or combination word	19	11	52
sequences. The adjustments you make in your speed will result in the	23	14	55
variable rhythm pattern needed for expert keyboarding. It is easy to	28	17	58
read copy correctly for keyboarding if you concentrate on the copy.	32	19	61
When you first try to read copy properly for keyboarding, you may	37	22	63
make more errors, but as you learn to concentrate on the copy being read	42	25	66
and begin to anticipate the keystroking pattern needed, your errors will	47	28	69
go down and your keyboarding speed will grow. If you want to increase	51	31	72
your keyboarding speed and reduce your errors, you must make the effort	56	34	75
to improve during each and every practice session. If you will work to	61	37	78
refine your techniques and to give a specific purpose to all your prac-	66	39	81
tice activities, you can make the improvement.	69	41	82

gwam 3′ | 1 | 2 | 3 | 4 | 5
5′ | 1 | 2 | 3

98d ▶ 20
Improve Speed/Accuracy: Straight Copy

1. Add 4 words to your *gwam* rate of 98c. Take two 1′ guided writings at this new goal rate on each ¶ of 98c.

2. Two 3′ writings on the ¶s of 98c. In each writing, try to improve your speed and/or your accuracy, according to your need.

3. If time permits, take a 5′ writing with a goal of improvement.

190a ▶ 5 Conditioning Practice

1. Each line twice SS.
2. A 1′ writing on line 4; find *gwam*. Repeat if time permits.

alphabet 1 A quartet performed while an exciting jazz band kept very steady time.
figures 2 In 4 years, Robert scored 1,598 points, 723 rebounds, and 206 assists.
fig/sym 3 I bought Model #237 for $168.95 (less 40%) from A & B Sales this week.
speed 4 Eight girls laud the rhapsody of the bugle corps in the island chapel.

| 1 | 2 | 3 | 4 | 5 | 6 | 7 | 8 | 9 | 10 | 11 | 12 | 13 | 14 |

190b ▶ 35 Format News Releases

Problem 1 (LM p. 109)
1. Read the information about news releases on page 324.
2. Prepare a final copy of the model news release on page 330.

Problem 2 (LM p. 111)
Format and key a rough-draft copy of the news release given at the right.

Problem 3 (LM p. 113)
Proofread and mark for correction your copy of Problem 2; then prepare a final copy with errors corrected.

words

RELEASE 2
ON RECEIPT 4

(¶ 1) Baltimore, November 5, 19--. In a restructuring of its senior manage- 18
ment team, Maxwell Nash has named Clara Buford vice president of admin- 32
istrative systems and services. Mrs. Buford has been with Maxwell Nash as 47
an administrative manager for the past five years. 57

(¶ 2) James Childs, President of Maxwell Nash Corporation, stated, "This 70
position has been created to ensure that Maxwell Nash takes advantage of 85
the technological advances which are revolutionizing office work." Vice 100
President Buford will be responsible for deciding office systems and proce- 114
dures for Maxwell Nash. Maxwell Nash Corporation has been a pioneer in 129
networking office information systems throughout its regional offices, and 144
the creation of this senior-level management position demonstrates the com- 159
pany's commitment to improving the office environment. Mrs. Buford indi- 173
cated she plans to evaluate the existing word and data processing operations, 189
communication services, and records management systems. 200

(¶ 3) Mrs. Buford majored in administrative management at Southland Col- 213
lege and has completed graduate study in business administration at Young 228
University. She resides in Eastmont with her husband Robert and her two 243
daughters, Amy and Leslie. 248

William Vlonick 251

tjs 252

190c ▶ 10 Improve Language Skills: Composing

1. Read the ¶s at the right.
2. Complete the two statements below the ¶s by composing a double-spaced ¶ for each.
3. Correct your copy; then key the copy in final form on a full sheet of paper.

From time to time most people reflect on their personal and professional priorities and set short- and long-range goals to provide meaningful direction to their lives.

The goals set should not be too easy or too difficult to reach. Goals which are too easy do not allow a person to experience the feeling of fulfillment that comes with success. Goals which are too difficult to attain may result in a person experiencing the negative effects of failure.

Statement: Upon graduation from high school, I would like to ....

Statement: Five years from now, I would like to ....

SOUTH-WESTERN
PUBLISHING CO.

Unit 20 Lessons 99-100

Evaluation Goals

1. To measure and help you evaluate your overall keyboarding skill.

2. To help you identify areas of needed improvement.

Machine Adjustments

Use:

*70-space line and single spacing for drills; DS below each SS group of drill lines

*70-space line and double spacing for ¶ timings of more than 1 minute

*as directed or needed for other copy

Lesson 99 Evaluate Keyboarding/Language Skills

99a ▶ 5 Conditioning Practice

each line twice (slowly, faster); as time permits, repeat selected lines

alphabet 1 The unique weave of the blue-gray jacket pleased many zealous experts.

figures 2 Is the total charge on Order No. 2384, dated July 10, \$57.69 or \$5.76?

adjacent keys 3 Opal asked them to weigh and polish a brass pot prior to its delivery.

speed 4 The maps may aid them when they do the work for the town and the city.

| 1 | 2 | 3 | 4 | 5 | 6 | 7 | 8 | 9 | 10 | 11 | 12 | 13 | 14 |

99b ▶ 15 Check Language Skills: Grammar/Punctuation

full sheet; DS; 1" top margin; 70-space line

1. Keyboard each sentence, including the sentence number, period, and two spaces. Choose the correct word in the parentheses or insert correct punctuation as you keyboard the line.

2. As your teacher reads the corrected sentences to you, circle the number of any sentence in which you have made an error.

3. Reinsert your paper, align it, and rekey correctly any sentence in which you made an error in the blank space below the sentence.

Awareness cue: Remember to reset margin when you reach Figure 10.

1. One of the persons (is, are) here for the interview.
2. Jim and John (is, are) going to the theater to see the musical.
3. Neither the teacher nor the students (has, have) left the school.
4. Neither of the men (is, are) here to do the work.
5. Each of the boys (is, are) doing (his, their) work.
6. Some of the students (is, are) in Room 1134.
7. He (don't, doesn't) like the cafeteria food.
8. They, too, (don't, doesn't) like the cafeteria food.
9. Neither Marc nor Greg (has, have) completed (his, their) report.
10. The committee (has, have) completed (its, their) report.
11. All the books (is, are) new.
12. The number of books in the library (has, have) been increased.
13. The box (is, are) in the storage room.
14. A number of students (has, have) registered for the new program.
15. The data (seems, seem) to be incorrect.
16. Each of the girls (has, have) (her, their) favorite sport.
17. The class planned (its, their) prom.
18. Somsara and Robert (don't, doesn't) have (his or her, their) books.
19. If you go to the market please get milk bread and eggs.
20. He was born in Denton Texas on April 18 1956.
21. During 1987 1249 applications for patents were filed.
22. Seventy six applications were received for the twenty three jobs.
23. These are the items you will need a workbook pencil and pad.
24. A first class ticket is more expensive than a coach class ticket.
25. The teacher said This is my best class.

189b (continued)

words

John Quintana *begin on line 6* 497
Page 2 *9* 498
April 28, 19-- 501

capabilities possible, including *error* correction, deletion and inser- 515
tion of copy, along with the capability to rearrange copy and to 528
change format of copy in memory. They say that the system chosen 542
must also be able to merge form paragraphs to build new documents, 555
must have global search and replace capability, must be albe to 568
format coapy with justified right margins, and, if possible, should 581
have memory capacity to allow for spelling verification *and word division.* 596

Does this sould like a tall order for nay WP system? Please think 612
over our needs and see if you can match them up to any word process- 625
ing systems that are now on the market. I would like to meet with 639
you sometime the week of May 24, and you can give me your findings 652
then. I will meet with the executive officers of the company on 665
August 6 to present a final proposal for a word processing system, 679
and I would like to have your findings included *in that report.* 692

Yoriko Mozaki, Information Systems Manager 700

edo 701

Page 2 of Interoffice Memorandum

189c ▶ 10 Improve Language Skills

full sheet
70-space line

Key the ¶ shown at the right. As you key, select the correct word from the words in parentheses. If time permits, proofread your copy, mark errors for correction, and key the ¶ from your corrected copy. Correct errors you make as you key.

(There/Their) has been (sum/some) discussion about the (past/passed) 9
practice of permitting (any one/anyone) of the employees to borrow (least/ 22
leased) equipment from the office. The (principal/principle) concern of the 34
officers is that they do not want to be responsible for equipment which (per- 50
sonal/personnel) may (loose/lose). At (it's/its) (later/latest) meeting, the 57
(board/bored) of officers introduced a motion to establish a policy whereby 71
each employee is (liable/libel) for equipment on (lone/loan). The motion was 84
followed by (farther/further) discussion (between/among) the four officers. 95
They discussed (whether/weather) employees should be required to provide 108
proof of insurance before being (allowed/aloud) to borrow equipment. This 121
idea was not (adapted/adopted) as part of the motion, and the original mo- 134
tion (passed/past). 136

99c ▶ 20 Format a Short Report from Statistical Rough-Draft Copy

full sheet

1. Prepare as an unbound report. Use 1" side margins.
2. Use main heading: **A LOOK AT OUR POPULATION** QS below heading.
3. Indent 5 for ¶s.
4. Proofread copy before removing it from the machine; correct any errors you find.
5. Evaluate and grade your work in terms of neatness and correct division of words at ends of lines.

all figures used | A | 1.5 si | 5.7 awl | 80% hfw |

gwam 5'

country
The total population of our ~~nation~~ is continuing to grow. 2
Itis estimated that our poplation will grow from some 230 mil- 5
lion in 1981 to 268 million in the year 2000, and ~~that~~it will 7
a factor
reach an all-time high of 309 million in 2050. ~~An element~~ con- 10
tributing to hte population increase isthe fact that we are 12
living longer
~~growing older~~. Adequate exercise, good nutrition, and better 15
to our longer longevity
health care are contributing factors. At the turn of the 18
average
century, the life expectancy was only 49 years. today the average 21
life expectancy has increased to 70.7 years for males and to 23
78.3 years for fe males. By the year 2005, life expectancy 26
for and to 81.3 for females
will increase to 73.3 years males. 28
country
The total population of our ~~nation~~, too, is groing older. In 31
median
1970, the age of our population was 27.9 years; in 1980, it was 34
30.2 years; by 1990, it is projected to be 32.8 years; and by 36
approximately
the year 2000, the estimated median age will increase to 35.5 39
indicates
years. This "graying of America," as it has been called, ~~shows~~ 42
that the proportion ofour poulation 65 years and over will 45
in crease from 26.2 million in 1981 to 35.1 million in the year 47
2000, with a startling jump to 67.0 million in 2050. additionally, 50
it means that we will have to discover new ways to 51
use the unique talent and wisdom that are characteristic 54
of the older person. 55

99d ▶ 10 Evaluate Technique

each line 3 times; repeat as time permits (Make a self-evaluation of keyboarding technique; compare with your teacher's evaluation.)

↓ tab set (60)

tab and return 1 and start of the new line. ——— tab ———→ Try to make a quick return (Repeat three times)

keystroking and space bar 2 If they do the work for us, then I may pay them if they sign the form.

shift keys 3 Ms. Sue McCray, President of Dalton & O'Brien, Inc., lives in Chicago.

continuity and variable rhythm 4 Send these forms and the statement to them at the address on the card.

| 1 | 2 | 3 | 4 | 5 | 6 | 7 | 8 | 9 | 10 | 11 | 12 | 13 | 14 |

189a ▶ 5 Conditioning Practice

1. Each line twice SS.
2. A 1′ writing on line 4; find *gwam*. Repeat if time permits.

alphabet 1 Zero visibility kept private jets from whisking to an exotic quietude.
figures 2 Lu cooked 367 hamburgers, 408 hot dogs, and 19 turkeys for 25 parties.
symbol 3 The * and # are key codes on telephones made by Nu Phones, Inc. (NPI).
speed 4 Alan paid for the eight bushels of corn and the pair of giant turkeys.

| 1 | 2 | 3 | 4 | 5 | 6 | 7 | 8 | 9 | 10 | 11 | 12 | 13 | 14 |

189b ▶ 35 Format Simplified Memos

Problem 1
2 plain full sheets

1. Read the information about simplified memos on page 324.
2. Study the placement of the heading for the second page of a simplified memo on page 328.
Note: This second-page heading format may be used for simplified memos, formal memos, and letters.
3. Prepare a copy of the simplified memo shown at the right and on page 328.

Problem 2
2 plain full sheets
Prepare another copy of the memo shown at the right and on page 328, but address it to **Shirley Puryear, Director of Office Operations.**

words

April 29, 19-- 3
QS
John Quintana, Director *of Data Processing* 12

RESULTS OF SURVEY OF WORD PROCESSING NEEDS 18

the heads and *each*
I have met with supervisors in departments in the company to 34
discuss their word processing needs. What follows is a summary 47
of the word processing needs of the various departments and 59
some thoughts on the type of equipment that may meet those 71
needs. I would like you to review this material and share with 83
me any suggestions you may have equipment that fit our needs. 102
about the type of *will best*

Whatever word processing system we choose will have to handle 114
all word processing jobs in the company. As long as we have 126
only one system, only one set of manuals will have to be pro- 138
duced and any WP operator will be able to operate any piece of 151
equipment in the company. This system will be used primarily 163
to produce letters, memorandums, and reports; but it must also 176
have the ability to produce forms and tabular copy and will 188
occasionally be called upon to produce line and bar graphs. 200

and department heads told
All supervisors ~~tell~~ me that they make their documents within 217
their departments and would like to continue doing so. This 229
finding leads me to believe that a decentralized WP system may 241
be superior to one that is centralized. With a decentralized 254
system, equipment could be set up in clusters in various de- 266
partments throughout the company. This arrangement would put 278
the equipment in the hands of the WP spacialists in the vari- 290
ous departments. The flexibility of a decentralized system 302
would allow us to shift equipment according to changing needs. 319
also *by the company* *among departments*

The system that is chosen will be required to store a large 334
amount of data in memory. If a centralized system is chosen, 347
it must be capable of storing a large number of prerecorded 359
letters, forms, and other data that can be reused with variable 372
changes. If a decentralized system is chosen, it must have *can* 384
storage, such as disks, that be kept in specific departments 397
where the stored material will be used. With *a* decentralized 409
system, ~~however,~~ we will have to keep very detailed records. 420
The records will be used by all departments, and the data 445
listed in them will be shared among departments. 455

should show where specific data and documents are kept in memory and

polled *that the*
All people agreed ~~whatever~~ system we choose should include 468
text editors with CRT visual display screens. They all ex- 480
pressed that the system should have the widest text editing 494
the desire

continued on next page

100a ▶ 5
Conditioning Practice

each line twice (slowly, faster); as time permits, repeat selected lines

alphabet 1 These children were amazed by the quick, lively jumps of the gray fox.
fig/sym 2 The 468 copies (priced at $3.75 each) may be shipped on July 19 or 20.
fingers 3, 4 3 Did Sid say if Ada saw the several polo ponies near the old mill pond?
speed 4 Dudley and the auditor did their work and may wish to sign their form.

| 1 | 2 | 3 | 4 | 5 | 6 | 7 | 8 | 9 | 10 | 11 | 12 | 13 | 14 |

100b ▶ 15
Measure Basic Skill: Statistical Rough Draft

Two 5′ writings on 99c, p. 174; find *gwam*; circle errors; record better rate. Compute your percent of transfer by dividing your 100b rate by your straight-copy rate on 98c, p. 172.

100c ▶ 30
Measure Document Processing Skill: Letters

Time Schedule

Plan and prepare .... 4′
Timed production .... 20′
Proofread; compute *n-pram* .... 6′

1. Use letterheads (LM pp. 39-44) or plain full sheets; adjust margins according to letter length.

Letter 1: Modified block, blocked ¶s; mixed punctuation; correct errors.

Letter 2: Block style, open punctuation; correct errors.

Letter 3: If time permits, format Letter 1 with indented ¶s.

2. When time is called, proofread your completed work; mark any uncorrected errors; deduct 15 words for each uncorrected error. Compute *n-pram*.

Letter 1 words

Current date | Dr. L. W. Evans | Jones Graduate School of Education | 300 14
Agnew Avenue | Los Angeles, CA 90045-3116 | Dear Dr. Evans: 27
(¶ 1) I was pleased to have the opportunity to discuss with you your skill 40
learning/writing research proposal when you were in the office last week. I 55
believe the formal proposal you left with me will receive favorable attention 71
by our Board and that it will be considered for funding. 82
(¶ 2) So that I will be able to answer Board questions, I need to know your 96
rationale for the use of the typewriter in the writing program that you out- 111
lined in your proposal. The Board is scheduled to meet at the end of next 126
month. (101) 128
Sincerely yours, | Miss Jan Gilcrest | Vice President-Secretary | xx | 140
159

Letter 2

Current date | Miss Jan Gilcrest | Vice President-Secretary | The Windsor Foun- 14
dation | 1510 Michigan Avenue | Los Angeles, CA 90033-3600 | Dear Miss 28
Gilcrest 30
(¶ 1) It is my belief that a new approach to the teaching of writing is 43
needed. I suggest that the typewriter can be used effectively to teach writ- 59
ing and other skills needed by everyone. Why the typewriter? First of all, 74
if students are to learn to write, it is clear that we need more powerful inter- 90
vention strategies than are presently being used. Students learn to write by 106
writing, and the typewriter is the most effective writing tool we presently 121
have. Its use in helping students improve their writing or composition skills 137
represents an alternative learning strategy that has great promise. 150
(¶ 2) Handwriting is a cumbersome and slow process. It is relatively easy for 165
most persons to learn to keyboard at least two or three times faster than 180
they can handwrite. All students, therefore, can get much more writing 194
practice as they use the typewriter for their writing. 205
(¶ 3) In addition, a knowledge of and proficiency in the use of the typewriter 220
keyboard has many values -- in writing, in computer applications, in using 235
word processing equipment, and in the employment marketplace. 247
(¶ 4) Please let me know if you need any other information. Thanks, again, for 262
your interest and help. (237) 267
Sincerely yours | L. W. Evans | Professor of Education | xx | 278
301

Maxwell Nash Corporation

2502 Sycamore Avenue Baltimore, MD 21219-1331 Interoffice Communication

words

TO: Isabel Garcia 3

FROM: Sidney Cross, Assistant to Personnel Director 12

DATE: November 3, 19-- 16

SUBJECT: Insurance Benefit Package 21

DS

As we discussed in your orientation session yesterday, Maxwell Nash 34
Corporation does provide insurance benefits for its full-time em- 47
ployees. The insurance plans for which you are eligible are: 60

DS

1. Medical, hospital, and major medical insurance covering the 72
prevailing fees charged by participating physicians, hospitals, 85
and other health agencies. Employees may elect to participate 98
in this insurance plan. 103

DS

2. Life insurance including basic life, accidental death, and dis- 116
memberment coverage at a rate of two times the employee's regu- 129
lar annual salary. Employees may elect to participate in this 142
insurance plan. 145

DS

3. Disability insurance which becomes effective 90 days after the 159
beginning of a disability. This insurance provides monthly 171
payments equal to 60 percent of the employee's regular salary 183
up to a maximum of $1,800 per month. Participation in this 196
insurance plan is required of all employees. 205

DS

4. Dental insurance covering the entire or a portion of the pre- 218
vailing fees charged by participating dentists for dental work 230
which is covered in the plan. Employees may elect to partici- 243
pate in this insurance plan. 249

DS

Maxwell Nash will pay 90 percent of the cost of the premium for 262
each of these four insurance plans. Employees pay the remaining 275
10 percent through payroll deductions. 283

DS

Please decide within the next 15 days which of the three voluntary 246
plans in which you will participate. If you need additional infor- 309
mation, contact Mark Harmon in the personnel department. 321

DS

sjc 321

Formal Memorandum

Lessons 101-125

PHASE 5

Extend Document Processing Skills

The 25 lessons of Phase 5 continue the emphasis on improving your keyboarding and document processing skills. The lessons are designed to help you:

1. Further refine your keyboarding techniques as you make applications of your keyboarding skill.
2. Improve and extend your document formatting skills on simple and complex tables and on reports that include footnotes as well as textual citations (the modern method of showing reference citations).
3. Increase your basic language-skill competency.
4. Increase your keyboarding speed and improve your control.
5. Improve your proofreading competency.

188a ▶ 5 Conditioning Practice

1. Each line twice SS.
2. A 1′ writing on line 4; find *gwam*. Repeat if time permits.

alphabet 1 The zeal of the exquisitely jeweled woman can be vital for good parks.

figures 2 Flight 378 will depart in 90 minutes with a crew of 15 and 246 riders.

fig/sym 3 Jo said, "Buy Model #2389 or #4761 at a 50% discount at Smith & Sons."

speed 4 A goal of the eighty men in the firm is to make a big profit downtown.

| 1 | 2 | 3 | 4 | 5 | 6 | 7 | 8 | 9 | 10 | 11 | 12 | 13 | 14 |

188b ▶ 35 Format Formal Memorandums

Problem 1
Formal Memo (LM p. 105)

1. Read the information about formal memos on page 324.
2. Study the model memo on page 326.
3. Prepare a copy of the model memo on page 326.

Problem 2
Formal Memo (LM p. 107)
Format and key the memo shown at the right.

Problem 3 (LM p. 107)
Prepare another copy of the memo shown at the right, but address it to:
Sally Almedo, Sales Department WP Supervisor

words

TO: Vicente Sanchez, Legal Department WP Supervisor FROM: Cynthia 11
Romita, Word Processing Manager DATE: November 3, 19-- SUBJECT: AMS 22
Conference 24

I will be attending the Administrative Management Society's annual conven- 39
tion in Chicago next month. Throughout the three-day conference, over 200 54
vendors will be displaying the latest office equipment and supplies. There 69
will be numerous vendors of word processing equipment and software appli- 83
cation packages among the exhibitors. 91

If you want me to obtain information, prices, or specifications on any spe- 106
cific pieces of equipment or software packages, please send me the appro- 120
priate information by the end of this month. This may be an excellent 134
opportunity to identify optical character readers and laser printers which 149
could be considered for purchase during the next fiscal year. 162

sjc 163

188c ▶ 10 Improve Language Skills

full sheet
line: 60 spaces

As you read and key the paragraph, correct any errors in capitalization, spelling, word choice, punctuation, etc., that you find. If you make any errors as you key, correct those, too. Check your work with your teacher; then as time permits, rekey the paragraph.

Office Mail Envelope

INTER-OFFICE USE ONLY--DO NOT MAIL
Use Every Line in Order

Name	Name	Name ....
Dept.................	Name	Name ....
Name	Name	Name ....
Dept.................	Dept.................	Dept.................

In small company's, interoffice memorandums of a routime nature are 13
ruted simply by checing or circling the anme of the addressee in the head- 28
ing. When the kontent of a memo is confidintial, a office mail envelop are 44
used. The adrress on an office mail envelop should include the addressees 59
personnel title, name, and busniess title, or name of department. If plane 74
unmarked envelops (as oppossed to colored envelopes) are used COMPANY 88
MALE is shone in all capitles in the postage location. 99

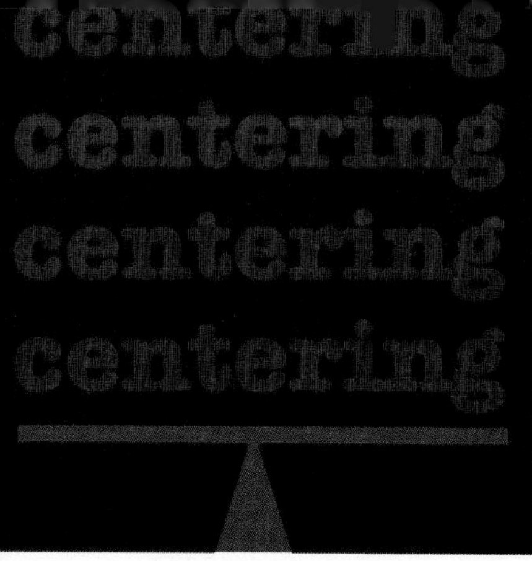

Unit 21 Lessons 101-105

Learning Goals

1. To improve skill in formatting material in table (tabulated) form.
2. To improve spelling and word-use skills.
3. To improve language skills (punctuation).

Machine Adjustments

1. Paper guide at *0*.
2. 70-space line and SS, or as directed.
3. Line-space selector on *1*, or as directed.
4. Paper bail rollers set to divide paper into thirds, or fourths, if your machine has three rollers.

FORMATTING GUIDES: TABLES

Table Spacing Summary

Double-space (DS):

1. Below all heading lines.
2. Above and below column headings.
3. Column entries when so directed.
4. Above and below source note ruling separating column entries from source notes.
5. Above column TOTALS, when used.

Single-space (SS):

1. Column entries when so directed.
2. Multiple-line column headings.

Vertical Placement

Step 1: Count all lines to be used in table (including all blank line spaces).

Step 2: Subtract this figure from total lines available on sheet. **Note.** Most machines have six line spaces to the vertical inch; therefore, paper 8 1/2″ × 11″ has 66 vertical line spaces (11 × 6).

Step 3: Divide remainder by 2 to determine the number of the line on which to key the main heading. If a fraction results, disregard it. If the number that results is

EVEN, space down that number from the top;
ODD, use next lower even number.

Note. This means that the main heading of a table will always begin on an even number.

Horizontal Placement of Columns Using Backspace-from-Center Method

Step 1: Move margin stops to ends of scale and clear all tab stops.

Step 2: From the horizontal center of sheet, backspace once for each 2 strokes in the longest line in each column (carry over to the next column any extra stroke at the end of a column but ignore any extra stroke at the end of the last column); then, backspace once for each 2 spaces to be left between columns. **Note.** As center point of paper 8 1/2″ wide, use 42 for pica; 51 for elite.

Step 3: Set left margin stop at point where backspacing ends.

Step 4: From the left margin stop, space forward once for each stroke in the longest line in the first column, and once for each space to be left between the first and second columns. Set a tab stop at this point for the start of the second column. Continue procedure for any additional columns.

lines used

WORDS FREQUENTLY MISSPELLED

occurrence	permissible	privilege
conscientious	acknowledgment	conscious
supersede	questionnaire	precede
consensus	category	restaurant
accommodate	maintenance	benefited

____

Source: Shell and Schmidt, DPE JOURNAL, 1984.

Spacing Between Columns

As a general rule, leave an even number of spaces between columns (4, 6, 8, 10, or more). **Note.** The number of spaces to be left between columns is governed by the space available, the number of columns needed for the table, and the ease of reading the table.

Column Headings

When used, column headings are often centered over the columns. **Note.** If a table contains single-line column headings and also column headings of two or more lines, the bottom line of each multiple-line heading is placed on the same line as the single-line heading(s).

Computer Placement

Key longest line in first column, plus spaces to be left between first and second columns; then key the longest line of second column. Continue procedure for any additional columns. When line is completed, press CENTER key, then set margin stop and tab stops at points indicated. Delete trial line; then key the table using stops determined with trial line.

Unit 40 Lessons 188-193

Learning Goals

1. To format and key interoffice memorandums in formal and simplified styles.
2. To arrange and key news releases.
3. To arrange and key telegraphic messages.
4. To reinforce skills on formatting with carbon copies.
5. To reinforce language skills.

Machine Adjustments

1. Paper guide at *0*.
2. Ribbon control to use top half of ribbon.
3. Margins: 70-space line for sentences and ¶s; as required for problems.
4. Spacing: SS drills; DS ¶s; as required for problems.

FORMATTING GUIDES: MEMOS AND NEWS RELEASES

Interoffice memorandums are "stripped-down" versions of letter messages and are used to convey information among individuals within a company. They omit the address, personal titles, salutation, and complimentary close. Memorandums may be prepared in either of two formats: formal style and simplified style.

Half-page Formal Memo

Maxwell Nash Corporation
2502 Sycamore Avenue Baltimore, MD 21219-1331 Interoffice Communication

TO: Britt Seymore, Administrative Specialist

FROM: Paul C. Copley, Buildings and Grounds

DATE: November 15, 19--

SUBJECT: Temporary Parking Permit

The director of human resources has notified me that you should have an assigned parking space while you are recovering from your knee surgery.

I have assigned you to Space #25 in Parking Lot C. The space is near the building in which you work. You may begin using the parking space tomorrow, and it will be assigned to you for the next nine weeks. If you are not fully recovered by that time, please contact me and I will arrange an extension for you.

tap

Simplified Memo

Maxwell Nash Corporation
2502 Sycamore Avenue Baltimore, MD 21219-1331 Interoffice Communication

November 5, 19--

All Branch Employees

FEASIBILITY STUDY TO BE CONDUCTED

A feasibility study will be conducted to determine what type of word processing equipment should be purchased for each secretarial work station within the branch office.

Patricia Mueller, Word Processing Specialist, will conduct an orientation session for all employees on November 15 at 3:30 p.m. in Conference Room A. She will present the objectives and schedule of the feasibility study.

Yoriko Nozaki, Branch Manager

sjc

News Release

News releases announce to newspapers or to individuals items of special interest. A news release should always designate a place and time for release of the news. See illustration on page 330.

Interoffice Memorandums

Formal style. Formal memorandums are prepared on full- or half-sheet forms with printed headings (see model memo on page 326). Such memos use block format and 1-inch side margins. The headings *TO:*, *FROM:*, *DATE:*, and *SUBJECT:* are printed in the left margin so that data used in the heading and the message can begin 2 spaces to the right of the headings (at the margin stop set for the 1-inch left margin).

Memo headings are double-spaced, and a double space separates the last heading line from the memo message. The message is single-spaced; a double space is left between paragraphs. The machine operator's initials are placed at the left margin a double space below the memo message.

Simplified style. Simplified memorandums are prepared on plain paper or on standard company letterheads. Simplified memorandums contain no preprinted or keyed headings. Simplified memos are prepared in block format with 1- or 1 1/2-inch side margins and follow these placement/spacing guides:

Date: plain paper, line 10; letterhead, a double space below the letterhead.

Addressee's Name: on the 4th line space below the date.

Subject: in ALL-CAPS or cap-and-lowercase a double space below the addressee's name.

Body: a double space below the subject line; single-spaced with a double space between paragraphs.

Writer's Name: on the 4th line space below the last line of the memo message.

Operator's Initials: a double space below the writer's name.

News Releases

The heading for a news release may be preprinted on a special form, or it may be typed or computer generated on letterhead stationery or plain paper. In either case, the heading usually occupies the first 1 1/2 to 2 inches of the sheet. The message or body of the news release is begun on the fourth line space below the preprinted or keyed heading. Side margins of 1 inch are used. Paragraphs are double-spaced; the first line of each paragraph is indented 5 spaces. The first paragraph begins with the place and time of release.

The name of the writer of the release is placed on the fourth line space below the message at the left margin. The machine operator's initials, when used, are placed a double space below the writer's name.

Telegraphic Messages

Some messages are telephoned to Western Union for transmission. Messages to be "phoned in" are prepared on plain paper. The following formatting guides govern the preparation of phoned telegrams (also see page 331):

Line Length: 60 spaces

Heading: *PHONED TELEGRAM* centered on line 12.

Class of Service (Telegram, Night Letter, Mailgram, Phone-A-Gram): shown at left margin on 4th line space below heading.

Name of Account to be Charged (if not that of sender): shown at left margin a DS below class of service.

Filing Date and Time of Message: a DS below class of service (or account to be charged, if used).

Address (including telephone number if known): single-spaced block form a DS below date.

Message: a DS below date; DS in block style.

Name and Title of Sender: a DS below message, followed on next line by company name.

Operator's Initials: a DS below company name.

101a ▶ 5 Conditioning Practice

each line 3 times (slowly, faster, in-between rate); as time permits, repeat selected lines

alphabet 1 Baryshnikov freely executed with ease the amazingly quick dance jumps.

fig/sym 2 Order 4 color #710 monitors, 6 IBM-POs, 89 Lotus 1-2-3s, and 5 modems.

rhythm 3 Please make the address corrections on all the old computer printouts.

speed 4 The right goal is to work for proficiency when a key problem turns up.

| 1 | 2 | 3 | 4 | 5 | 6 | 7 | 8 | 9 | 10 | 11 | 12 | 13 | 14 |

101b ▶ 20 Problem Solving: Table Formatting

Check solutions with placement cues given below problems.

Problem 1
3-Column Table

full sheet; DS data; 6 spaces between columns; dividing line, 1 1/2"

Problem 2
Build Skill

Repeat Problem 1 on half sheet, long edge at top; DS data; 6 spaces between columns.

Problem 3
Build Skill

Repeat Problem 1 on half sheet; short edge at top; DS data; 4 spaces between columns.

Learning cue: To find horizontal center of half sheet with short edge at top: Add scale reading at left edge of sheet to scale reading at right edge of sheet and divide by 2.

lines used

WORDS FREQUENTLY MISSPELLED

			words
WORDS FREQUENTLY MISSPELLED			6
occurrence	permissible	privilege	12
conscientious	acknowledgment	conscious	20
supersede	questionnaire	precede	26
consensus	category	restaurant	32
accommodate	maintenance	benefited	39
________________ DS			43
DS Source: Shell and Schmidt, DPE JOURNAL, 1984.			52

Vertical Placement of Table

Formula: $\frac{\text{lines available} - \text{lines used}}{2} = X$ if X has a fraction, drop it; if X (the resulting number) is:
EVEN, space down that number;
ODD, use next lower even number.

Full sheet

$\frac{66 - 15}{2} = 25.5$ (Begin on line 24.)

Half sheet (long edge at top)

$\frac{33 - 15}{2} = 9$ (Begin on line 8.)

Half sheet (short edge at top)

$\frac{51 - 15}{2} = 18$ (Begin on line 18.)

Horizontal Placement of Table

Backspace from center of paper 1 space for each 2 strokes in longest line of each column, carrying over to next column any odd stroke. Ignore any odd stroke at end of last column. Then backspace 1 space for each 2 strokes to be placed between columns.

co|ns|ci|en|ti|ou|sa|ck|no|wl|ed|gm|en|tr|es|ta|ur|an + 3 + 3 *(2 + 2 for Problem 3)*

Set left margin stop; then space forward to determine tab stops for Columns 2 and 3.

187b ▶ 45
Measure Production Skill: Letters with Special Features

Time Schedule
Plan and Prepare .... 5′
Timed Production .... 30′
Proofread and Correct Errors ... 7′
Compute *n-pram* .... 3′

3 letterheads (LM pp. 97-101)

1. Arrange letterheads, second sheets, carbon paper, and envelopes. Make 1 cc of each problem.

2. Key for 30′ when directed to begin; correct errors neatly; proofread carefully before removing each letter from the machine.

3. Compute *n-pram*; turn in completed work arranged in sequence given below.

Problem 1
Letter with Special Features

Key letter in modified block style with indented ¶s and mixed punctuation. Begin date on line 15; use 1″ side margins; address envelope.

Problem 2
AMS Simplified Letter

Key date on line 13; use 1½″ side margins; address envelope.

words

Current date CERTIFIED Ms. Dana Roberts Your Word Processing Center 14
685 Main Street Richland, WA 99352-2217 Dear Ms. Roberts 26
COMPUTER SUPPLIES AND SERVICES 32

(¶ 1) We appreciate your interest in M & H Computer Supplies and are 45
pleased to enclose a copy of our catalog along with a current price list and 60
coupon for 20 percent off your first purchase. 69

(¶ 2) We offer an extensive array of computer supplies and accessories. If 83
you are not fully satisfied with your purchase, you may return the goods 98
within 30 days for a full refund. 105

(¶ 3) If you need to receive your supplies quickly, you can order by using our 119
"800" number. This toll-free number, 1-800-632-2841, is available between 134
8:30 a.m. and 7:30 p.m. 139

Sincerely yours M & H COMPUTER SUPPLIES Ms. Victoria Mendez Sales 152
Manager xx Enclosures Catalog Price List Discount Coupon 164/**181**

July 14, 19-- Mrs. Faye Kenwood Sales Division Manager Office Systems, 14
Inc. 4567 Edgewood Boulevard Omaha, NE 68128-1845 ITINERARY FOR 27
WEEK OF JULY 20-24 31

(¶ 1) Because of recent neglect, my assigned territory is one of our weaker 45
territories. However, I think it has excellent potential. 57

(¶ 2) I have made appointments with all of our regular customers in the cities 71
listed below, and I hope to have time to make additional contacts in each 86
city. Here is my itinerary for July 20-24. 95

1. July 20, Kimball, Nebraska 101
2. July 21, Scottsbluff and Gering, Nebraska 111
3. July 22, Torrington, Wyoming 117
4. July 23, Newcastle, Wyoming 124
5. July 24, Chadron, Nebraska 130

(¶ 3) I am looking forward to working in this area. At the district meeting 144
in Lincoln on July 28, I will be able to give you a detailed assessment of our 160
potential in these cities. 165

MS. MARIA PAGAN, SALES REPRESENTATIVE xx 173/**195**

Problem 3
Informal Government Letter

Use 1″ side margins; ALL CAP letter address for a window envelope.

Date: November 5, 19-- Reply to Attn of: GSA Subject: Educational Mate- 8
rials To: Mrs. Claudia Kolfax Federal Reserve Bank of Chicago 230 South 21
LaSalle Street Chicago, IL 60690-2486 29

(¶ 1) Here is a copy of a unit of instruction which was developed by our edu- 43
cational division. "Your Credit Rights" could be used by your branch with 58
only minor changes. 62

(¶ 2) We appreciate your sharing your units with our branch and hope that 76
the enclosed unit will be of value to personnel in your educational division. 91

RICHARD J. GRUBER Educational Division Manager Enclosure 103
GSA:RJGruber:xx 11-5-19-- 107

101c ▶ 15 Check Learning: Composition

full sheet; 1″ top, side, and bottom margins

Compose complete sentence answers to the questions listed here. If necessary, refer to the *Table Formatting Guides* on page 177 and 178.

Number your answers as you keyboard them. SS the lines of each answer; DS between answers. X-out or strike over any keyboarding errors you make as you compose.

1. How many line spaces are available on a full sheet (8 1/2″ × 11″)?
2. How many line spaces are available on a half sheet with the long edge at top?
3. How many line spaces are available on a half sheet with the short edge at top?
4. What governs the number of spaces to be left between columns?
5. In your own words, give the steps to follow to determine the vertical placement of a table.
6. In your own words, give the steps to follow in using the backspace-from-center method to determine the horizontal placement of columns.
7. When column entries are double-spaced and a source note ruling is used, how many blank line spaces are left above and below the ruling?
8. How do you find the horizontal center of a sheet of any size?

101d ▶ 10 Improve Language Skills: Punctuation

full sheet; 1″ top margin; 70-space line

Study/Learn/Apply/Correct Procedures

1. STUDY explanatory rule.

2. Key line number (with period); space twice, and key LEARN sentence(s) DS, noting rule application.

3. Key APPLY sentence(s) DS, placing parentheses around the proper words or numbers to make the sentence(s) correct.

4. As your teacher reads the correct sentences, show in pen or pencil any corrections that need to be made in your copy.

5. Rekey any APPLY sentence containing an error, CORRECTING the error as you keyboard. Key the corrected sentence in the space below the APPLY sentence containing the error.

PARENTHESES

Use parentheses to enclose parenthetical or explanatory matter and added information. (Commas or dashes also may be used.)

Learn 1. Enclosed are the contracts (Exhibits A and B).
Apply 2. Nichols' memoirs published by Delta Pi Epsilon are interesting.

Use parentheses to enclose identifying letters or figures in lists.

Learn 3. Check these techniques: (1) keystroking and (2) spacing.
Apply 4. She emphasized two key factors: 1 speed and 2 control.

Use parentheses to enclose figures that follow spelled-out amounts when added clarity or emphasis is needed.

Learn 5. The balance due on the note is five hundred dollars ($500).
Apply 6. I bequeath to my son the sum of five thousand dollars $5,000.

Use parentheses to enclose a name and date used as a reference.

Learn 7. Learning stamps you with its moments (Welty, 1984).
Apply 8. In writing, no rules prevail except to avoid monotony Lanham, 1979.

185c (continued)

words

opening lines 34

Problem 3
Informal Government Letter
window envelope

Key the informal government letter shown at the right using the following information:

Date: **August 29, 19--**
Reply to Attn of: **DNR**
Subject: **Area Forester/ Ranger Position**
To: **MR ROBERT AMUNDSON ASSISTANT AREA FORESTER/ RANGER DEPARTMENT OF NATURAL RESOURCES P O BOX 220 PARK FALLS WI 54552-7359**
Closing Lines:
MISS JANICE K. SESSIONS
Examination Coordinator
DNR:JKSessions:xx 8-29-19--

¶ Your oral examination for the position of Natural Resource 46
Supervisor II (Area Forester/Ranger) has been scheduled 57
for Wednesday, September 25, at 10:30 a.m. Please 67
report to the Department of Natural Resources, 1110 Frederick 80
Avenue, Saint Joseph, Missouri, for the examination. 90
¶ Upon your arrival, you will be given specific instruc- 101
tions concerning the oral examination procedure. Following 113
the instruction period, a copy of the exam questions will 124
be given to you. You will be allowed 15 minutes to prepare 136
your response to the questions before going before the 147
board. 149
¶ Thank you for your interest in the St. Joseph Branch 159
of the Department of Natural Resources. If you should have 171
questions prior to the oral examination, please contact me 183
at 861-781-3511. 187

closing lines 202

Lesson 186 Review: Special Letter Forms

186a ▶ 5 Conditioning Practice

Practice the lines of 187a, below, as directed there.

186b ▶ 45 Sustain Production: Letters with Special Features

Time Schedule

Plan and prepare	5′
Timed Production	30′
Proofread and Correct Errors	7′
Compute *n-pram*	3′

1. Make a list of problems to be completed:
p. 314, 181c, Step 3
p. 317, 183c, Step 3
p. 319, 184c, Step 4
p. 321, 185c, Problem 2

2. Arrange plain sheets or letterheads (LM pp. 89-95); second sheets; carbon paper. Make 1 cc for each problem; address envelopes where directed.

3. Work for 30′ when directed to begin; follow directions given for each problem; correct all errors neatly, proofreading carefully before removing a letter from the machine.

4. Compute *n-pram*; then turn in completed work, arranged in the order listed in Step 1.

Lesson 187 Evaluation: Special Letter Forms

187a ▶ 5 Conditioning Practice

1. Each line twice SS.
2. A 1′ writing on line 4; determine *gwam*. Repeat if time permits.

alphabet 1 The kind of quartz watch Gordon Dejon purchased is extremely valuable.
figures 2 There were 154 seniors, 297 juniors, 160 sophomores, and 238 freshmen.
fig/sym 3 The 1987 estimate on the home was $64,500 (a 23% jump over last year).
speed 4 Vivian, the rich widow, may pay the maid to dismantle the big bicycle.

| 1 | 2 | 3 | 4 | 5 | 6 | 7 | 8 | 9 | 10 | 11 | 12 | 13 | 14 |

102a ▶ 5 Conditioning Practice

each line 3 times (slowly, faster, in-between rate); as time permits, repeat selected lines

alphabet 1 Will Jim realize that excellent skill develops by refining techniques?

figure 2 Just call 1-800-645-3729 for complete information on software systems.

one hand 3 Only after I stated my adverse opinion were better grades agreed upon.

speed 4 If they do the work for the city and me, he may spend the day with me.

| 1 | 2 | 3 | 4 | 5 | 6 | 7 | 8 | 9 | 10 | 11 | 12 | 13 | 14 |

102b ▶ 30 Problem Solving: Table Formatting

Problem 1
2-Column Table

full sheet; DS data; 16 spaces between columns

Learning recall: length of dividing line.

Learning cue: Reset tab stop for Column 2 after keying Item 2.

Problem 2
Build Skill

Repeat Problem 1 on half sheet, short edge at top; SS data; 10 spaces between columns.

Learning cue: Remember to DS above and below divider line even though the body is single-spaced.

		words
LEADING CAUSES OF DEATH		5
(Approximate Percent of Total Deaths)		12
Heart disease	49.6	16
Cancer	29.9	19
Stroke	8.6	21
Accidents	5.3	24
Pulmonary disease	2.8	28
Pneumonia and influenza	2.6	34
Diabetes	1.7	37
Liver disease	1.6	40
Atherosclerosis	1.5	44
Suicide	1.3	47
________________		50
Source: Vital Statistics.		56

Problem 3
2-Column Table

full sheet; DS data; center vertically and horizontally; 20 spaces between columns

Note. Save problem to use in 102c, p. 181.

WORDS WITH SIMILAR PRONUNCIATION		7
BUT DIFFERENT MEANINGS (HOMONYMS)		14
stationary	stationery	18
their	there	20
blue	blew	22
whether	weather	26
would	wood	28
do	due; dew	30
deer	dear	32
sight	cite; site	36
advice	advise	38
farther	further	42
lose	loose	44
principal	principle	48
real	reel	50
two	to; too	52

185a ▶ 5 Conditioning Practice

1. Each line twice SS.
2. A 1′ writing on line 4; determine *gwam*. Repeat if time permits.

alphabet	1	Jane packed the very beautiful quilt from Wyoming in an oversized box.
figures	2	Her 1987 license plate number, 230H 43R65, was recorded as 230H 43S65.
fig/sym	3	The gold bracelet (#538-641) and the gold ring (#709-128) are on sale.
speed	4	The haughty neighbor kept half of the handiwork down by the city dock.

| 1 | 2 | 3 | 4 | 5 | 6 | 7 | 8 | 9 | 10 | 11 | 12 | 13 | 14 |

185b ▶ 10 Compose at the Keyboard

full sheet; 70-space line

1. Compose as directed.
2. Using proofreader's marks, edit your composition for clarity of thought and accuracy of keying.

Compose a list of five or more goals you would like to accomplish in the next six months. The goals may include keyboarding goals, school-related goals, and/or personal goals.

185c ▶ 35 Build Skill on AMS and Informal Government Letters

3 letterheads (LM pp. 83-87); arrange letterheads, carbon sheet, second sheets; make 1 cc of each letter; correct errors; address envelope for AMS letter

Problem 1
AMS Simplified Letter
date: line 19
margins: 1½″
address envelope

	words
April 9, 19-- Miss Karla Shultz 2943 Thurber Place Tucson, AZ 85705-7355	15
MARCH BILLING ERROR	19
(¶ 1) Thank you for bringing the error on your March bill to our attention so	33
quickly.	35
(¶ 2) Your March 15 purchases had been keyed as $397.38 when the amount	48
should have been $379.38. We have corrected the error and will credit your	63
account for the $18.	67
(¶ 3) We appreciate your business and are eager to continue serving you.	81
For the inconvenience caused you, we are enclosing a coupon for $5 off on	96
your next purchase.	100
MRS. SARA GILL, ACCOUNTING MANAGER xx Enclosure	109/**121**

Problem 2
Informal Government Letter
Margins: 1″
ALL-CAP letter address for window envelope

Date: July 27, 19-- Reply to Attn of: GSA Subject: User Satisfaction Survey	9
To: MRS MARY VAN SLYKE BOX 783 GRAND JUNCTION CO 81501-2935	20
(¶ 1) Since early 1985, the General Services Administration has implemented	34
several changes in its policies and procedures. The Grand Junction Branch	49
of the General Services Administration is compiling data on the degree of	64
user satisfaction with these changes. Your assistance in evaluating these	79
changes will tell us if we have taken steps in the right direction.	92
(¶ 2) Please take a few minutes today to complete the enclosed questionnaire	107
and return it in the stamped addressed envelope. Responses will be kept in	122
strict confidence.	126
(¶ 3) Your assistance in this study will help us better meet our users' needs.	140
MS. MARTHA R. JAMISON Director Enclosure GSA:MRJamison:xx 7-27-19--	154

Problem 3 is on next page.

102c ▶ 15
Improve Language Skills: Composition

70-space line; SS sentences; DS between sentences; full sheet

From the list of words given in Problem 3, p. 180, use as many as you can in complete sentences. If you can use two or more homonyms in the same sentence, do so, as in the example given below.

Example: He remained in a stationary position as he distributed the stationery.

Lesson 103 Simple Table/Language Skills

103a ▶ 5
Conditioning Practice

each line 3 times (slowly, faster, in-between rate); as time permits, repeat selected lines

alphabet 1 After a wild jump ball, the guards very quickly executed a zone press.

fig/sym 2 The 0-384 MC costs $196.75, and the 300/1200 Baud modem costs $265.89.

shift key 3 Ryan read the articles "Fatigue," "How to Relax," and "Saving Energy."

speed 4 A big firm kept half of the men busy with their work down by the lake.

| 1 | 2 | 3 | 4 | 5 | 6 | 7 | 8 | 9 | 10 | 11 | 12 | 13 | 14 |

103b ▶ 35
Problem Solving: Table Formatting

Problem 1
2-Column Table

full sheet; DS data except where more than one title is given with a name; SS such titles with a DS above and below the group of titles; 16 spaces between columns; space forward twice after each period given with each number; center column headings over columns

Learning cue: To center column headings shorter than column entries follow these steps:

1. Determine placement of columns in usual way.

2. From column starting point, space forward once for each two strokes in longest entry. From this point, backspace once for each 2 strokes in column heading.

3. Keyboard and underline column heading.

Problem 2
Build Skill

Repeat Problem 1 with 8 spaces between columns.

		words
IMPORTANT READINGS FOR THE HUMANITIES		8
(Ranked in Order of Importance)		14
Name	Title	18
1. Shakespeare	Macbeth; Hamlet	24
2. American Historical Documents	Declaration of Independence	34
	Constitution	39
	Gettysburg Address	43
3. Twain	Huckleberry Finn	48
4. Bible	Old and New Testaments	55
5. Homer	Odyssey; Illiad	60
6. Dickens	Great Expectations	66
	A Tale of Two Cities	70
7. Plato	The Republic	75
8. Steinbeck	Grapes of Wrath	81
9. Hawthorne	The Scarlet Letter	88
10. Sophocles	Oedipus	92
11. Melville	Moby Dick	97
12. Orwell	1984	102
13. Thoreau	Walden	106
14. Frost	Collected Poems	112
15. Whitman	Leaves of Grass	117
______________		121
Source: National Endowment for the Humanities, Washington, DC,		134
1984.		135

GENERAL SERVICES ADMINISTRATION

WASHINGTON, DC 20008-7667

words

DATE: February 18, 19-- 4
DS

REPLY TO ATTN OF: GSA 4
DS
symbol for originating office

SUBJECT: Format for the Informal Government Letter 13
TS

TO: MR FERNANDO SANCHEZ 17
DEPARTMENT OF HEALTH & HUMAN SERVICES 25
812 NORTH 7TH STREET 29
KANSAS CITY KS 66101-6763 34

Set left margin 2 spaces to right of headings.

1" side margin

Start body on 6th line below *To*:

This letter shows the format for preparing letters for agencies of 48
the United States government. This format speeds up the prepara- 61
tion of correspondence and saves effort, time, and materials. The 74
following features of the format aid keyboard operations. 86

a. All elements except the first line of lettered items are 98
blocked at the left margin. This block style minimizes the use of 111
the space bar, the tabulator set, and the tabulator bar or key. 124

b. Salutations and complimentary closes are omitted in in- 136
formal government letters. They may be used, however, in formal 149
government letters to any individual on a personal or private mat- 162
ter (notices of serious illness, letters of condolence, etc., where 176
warm and personal feeling is paramount), or where protocol or tra- 189
dition dictates. 192

c. The address is positioned to be visible after insertion 204
into a window envelope; thus, an envelope need not be addressed. 217

3 blank line spaces

MRS. TOMOKO MATSUMI 221
Director of Communications 227
DS

2 Enclosures: 230
Revised Style Manual 234
Tips for Effective Writing 239
DS

GSA:TMatsumi:xx 2-18-19-- ← on carbon copy only 244

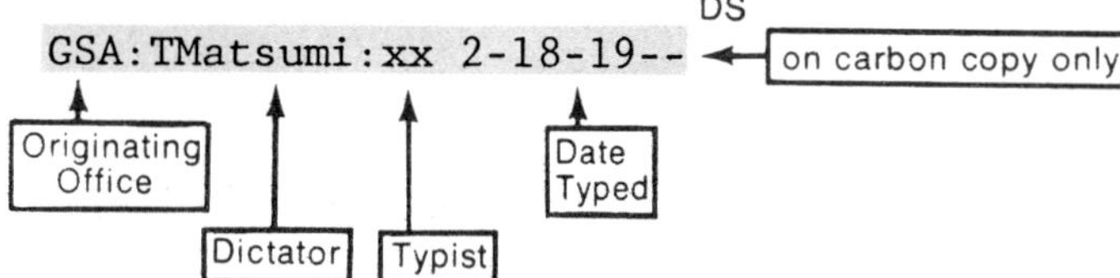

Informal Government Letter

103b (continued)

Problem 3
2-Column Table

half sheet, long edge at top; DS data; 12 spaces between columns

Alertness cue: Reset tab stop for Column 2 as needed; or, remember to space forward.

Problem 4
Build Skill

Repeat Problem 3 on half sheet, short edge at top; DS data; 6 spaces between columns.

Note. When % signs or $ signs appear in the body of a table, they are keyed in the intercolumns; therefore, do not count them as parts of columns.

SUGAR CONTENT OF SELECTED FOODS		words
(Mean percentage of sugar)		12
Live-savers mints (assorted)	68.6%	18
Chocolate (plain)	56.0	23
Chocolate creme cookies and	40.2	30
Dry cereals breakfast	25.1	35
Icecream products	15.1	40
Soft drinks	4.3	43
Canned juices	2.5	47
________________		51
Source: Newburn, E. Cardiology, 2d ed.		59

(Title line: 6 words)

103c ▶ 10
Improve Language Skills: Punctuation

full sheet; 1″ top margin; 70-space line

1. STUDY explanatory rule.
2. Key line number (with period); space twice, and then key the LEARN sentence(s) DS, noting rule application.
3. Key the line number (with period); space twice, then key the APPLY sentence(s) DS, making changes needed to correct each sentence.
4. As your teacher reads the correct sentence(s), show in pen or pencil any corrections that need to be made in your copy.
5. Rekey any APPLY sentence containing an error, CORRECTING the error as you key. Place the corrected sentence(s) in the space below the APPLY sentence containing the error.

UNDERLINE

Use an underline to indicate titles of books and names of magazines and newspapers. (Titles may be keyed in ALL CAPS without the underline.)

Learn 1. The book Learning How to Think was condensed in Reader's Digest.
Apply 2. I read the review of Any Child Can Write in the Los Angeles Times.

Use an underline to call attention to special words or phrases (or use quotation marks). **Note:** Use a continuous underline (see preceding rule) unless each word is to be considered separately, as shown below.

Learn 3. She asked us to spell separate, privilege, and stationery.
Apply 4. He misspelled supersede, concede, and proceed.

QUOTATION MARKS

Use quotation marks to enclose direct quotations. **Note:** When a question mark applies to the entire sentence, it is typed outside the quotation marks.

Learn 5. The teacher asked, "Did you do your homework?"
Learn 6. Was it Emerson who said, "To have a friend is to be one"?
Apply 7. He quoted Zinsser, Writing is the logical arrangement of thought.
Apply 8. Did Shakespeare say, All the world is a stage?

Use quotation marks to enclose titles of articles, poems, songs, television programs, and unpublished works like dissertations and theses.

Learn 9. Please read the poem "The Road Not Taken" by Robert Frost.
Apply 10. They enjoyed watching the TV series Dallas.

184a ▶ 5 Conditioning Practice

1. Each line twice SS.
2. A 1′ writing on line 4; find *gwam*. Repeat if time permits.

alphabet 1 Kay Mendoza will purchase the very exquisite gold jewelry from Robert.
figures 2 Joy received 560 votes; Mary, 427; and Gail, 381 in the 1987 election.
fig/sym 3 He had two sisters (Sue 8/7/65, Jo 4/1/73) and a brother (Tom 9/3/70).
speed 4 He may dismantle both the docks by the lake, or he may burn them down.
| 1 | 2 | 3 | 4 | 5 | 6 | 7 | 8 | 9 | 10 | 11 | 12 | 13 | 14 |

184b ▶ 8 Format Features of Informal Government Letter

Study the information at the right. Relate each point to the model letter shown on page 320.

Formatting Guides: Informal Government Letter

Side Margins. The informal government letter uses side margins of 1 inch (1″).

Headings. Printed headings on informal government letterheads indicate where certain items of information are to be entered: *Date:, Reply to Attn of:, Subject:,* and *To:*. With margins set for 1″, the entries opposite these headings will align with the left margin of the body of the letter.

Address. When window envelopes are used, use the ALL-CAP nonpunctuated form of address. If regular envelopes are used, either the ALL-CAP or the cap-and-lowercase form may be used for the letter address.

Body. If regular envelopes are used, start the body a TS below the last line of the letter address. If window envelopes are used, begin the address at least 6 lines below the *To:* line.

Closing lines. The writer's name in ALL CAPS is placed on the fourth line space (QS) below the last line of the body. The writer's title is shown in cap-and-lowercase letters on the next (SS) line.

Enclosure notation lines are single-spaced a double space below the writer's title. A reference line (showing the initials of the originating office, the name of the dictator, the initials of the machine operator, and the date) is shown a double space (DS) below the last line of the enclosure notation. *The reference line appears only on the carbon copy.*

To show reference on carbon copy only:
1. Position printing point at the left margin.
2. Insert slip of paper (not flimsy) between the ribbon and the original copy.
3. Key in the notation and remove the slip of paper.

184c ▶ 25 Informal Government Letters

2 letterheads (LM p. 79-81); arrange letterheads, carbon sheets, and second sheets

1. Study the model letter shown on page 320; review features with your teacher.
2. Format the letter on a letterhead (1 cc), following cues shown in the illustration.
3. Circle errors; check copy for correct style.
4. Rekey the model letter as directed in Step 2 with errors corrected, but address the letter to:

MS JUANITA VARGAS
DEPARTMENT OF PUBLIC WORKS
100 NASHUA STREET
BOSTON, MA 02114-5468

Note: Letters prepared on the government agency form shown on p. 320 are mailed in window envelopes. Folding procedures for such letters are described and illustrated on RG 7.

184d ▶ 12 Compose at the Keyboard

full sheet; 70-space line

1. Key the ¶ shown at the right.
2. Compose another ¶ as directed.
3. Using proofreader's marks, edit your composition for clarity of thought and accuracy of keying.

After graduation from high school, students have many decisions to make. One of those decisions that has to be made is whether or not to continue their education. Compose a short paragraph indicating what your plans are following graduation from school. Give reasons for your choice.

104a ▶ 5 Conditioning Practice

each line 3 times (slowly, faster, in-between rate); as time permits, repeat selected lines

alphabet	1	Fools won't likely adopt the unique economizing objectives of experts.
fig/sym	2	Here are the prices: #300/1200, $455; #3878, $695; and #515/20, $159.
long words	3	Systems engineers had complete responsibility in space communications.
speed	4	Vivian may sign the amendment form if they do their work for the city.

| 1 | 2 | 3 | 4 | 5 | 6 | 7 | 8 | 9 | 10 | 11 | 12 | 13 | 14 |

104b ▶ 35 Problem Solving: Table Formatting

Problem 1
Table with Centered Column Headings

full sheet; DS data; 8 spaces between columns; center headings over columns

Column Heading Centering Formula: Forward space 1 for 2 in longest column line; backspace 1 for 2 in heading to be centered.

SOME ENDANGERED SPECIES

Common Name	Location	words
		5
		13
Bald eagle	USA	16
Black-footed ferret	Western USA	22
Blue whale	Pacific Ocean	27
California condor	California	33
Dusky seaside sparrow	Florida	39
Gray wolf	Northern USA	44
Ivory-billed woodpecker	USA	49
Kirtland's warbler	Eastern USA	55
Manatee	Florida	59
Whooping crane	Canada, USA	64

________________ 67

Source: U.S. Department of Interior, Washington, 77
DC. 78

Problem 2
Table with Centered Column Headings

full sheet; DS data; 8 spaces between columns; center column headings

Problem 3
Build Skill

As time permits, repeat Problem 2, half sheet, long edge at top; 6 spaces between columns; SS data; block column headings. **Note:** For Problems 2 and 3, DS between source notes.

WORLD'S LARGEST METROPOLITAN AREAS 7

(In Descending Order) 11

1900	1950	2000*	
			17
London	New York	Mexico City	23
New York	London	Sao Paulo	28
Paris	Tokyo	Tokyo	31
Berlin	Paris	New York	36
Chicago	Shanghai	Shanghai	41
Vienna	Chicago	Peking	45
Tokyo	Los Angeles	Rio de Janeiro	52
Leningrad	Berlin	Bombay	57
Philadelphia	Moscow	Calcutta	63
Manchester	Philadelphia	Jakarta	69

________________ 73

Source: World Almanac. 78

*Projected data: The Christian Science Monitor, August 7, 95
1984, p. 19. 98

words

Begin all major lines at left margin

December 5, 19-- 3

Begin address 3 blank line spaces below date

Miss Julia Seidenberg 7
Word Processing Manager 12
Modern Office Assistants 17
4822 Claymore Road 21
Houston, TX 77024-8336 26

Omit salutation

Subject line in all capital letters; triple-space above and below it

AMS SIMPLIFIED LETTER FORMAT 32

We are using the simplified letter format recommended by 43
the Administrative Management Society; it is formatted 54
as follows: 56

Begin enumerated items at left margin; indent unnumbered items 5 spaces

1. Use block format. 60

2. Start the address on the fourth line below the date. 72

3. Omit the salutation and complimentary close. 82

4. Always use a subject heading, shown in ALL CAPS, a 93
triple space below the address; triple-space below 103
the subject line to start the body of the letter. 113

5. Begin enumerated items at the left margin; indent 124
unnumbered items five spaces. 130

6. Show the writer's name and title in ALL CAPS on the 140
fourth line space below the body of the letter. 150

7. Lowercase reference initials (operator's only) a 161
double space below the writer's name. Double-space 171
between enclosure notations, carbon copy notations, 181
and postscripts (if used). 187

We all like the efficiency of the AMS letter format. 197

Omit complimentary close

Writer's name and title in ALL CAPS at least 3 blank line spaces below letter body

MARIO GARCIA, ADMINISTRATIVE SUPPORT SUPERVISOR 207

eb 207
230

AMS Simplified Letter

104c ▶ 10
Improve Language Skills: Punctuation

full sheet; 1″ top margin; 70-space line

Key as directed in 103c, p. 182.

QUOTATION MARKS (continued)

Use quotation marks to enclose special words or phrases used for emphasis, or for coined words (words not in dictionary usage).

Learn 1. My problem is that I have "limited resources" and "unlimited wants."
Apply 2. His speech was liberally sprinkled with you knows.

Use a single quotation mark (the apostrophe) to indicate a quotation within a quotation.

Learn 3. She said, "We must take, as Frost suggests, the 'different road.' "
Apply 4. I wrote, "We must have, as Tillich said, the courage to be."

SEMICOLON

Use a semicolon to separate two or more independent clauses in a compound sentence when the conjunction is omitted.

Learn 5. To be critical is easy; to be constructive is not so easy.
Apply 6. We cannot live on past glory we must strive to improve.

Use a semicolon to separate independent clauses when they are joined by a conjunctive adverb (however, consequently, etc.).

Learn 7. You exceeded the speed limit; consequently, you were stopped.
Apply 8. I cannot help you however, I know someone who can.

Lesson 105 Simple Table/Language Skills

105a ▶ 5
Conditioning Practice

each line 3 times (slowly, faster, in-between rate); as time permits, repeat selected lines

alphabet 1 The kind queen received extra jewels from a dozen brave young pirates.
fig/sym 2 The #5346 item will cost McNeil & Company $921.78 (less 10% for cash).
adjacent key 3 Did Bert Werty say he would join Robert or Lasiter before he departed?
speed 4 Eighty of the men may work for the island firms if they make a profit.

| 1 | 2 | 3 | 4 | 5 | 6 | 7 | 8 | 9 | 10 | 11 | 12 | 13 | 14 |

105b ▶ 35
Problem Solving: Table Formatting

Problem 1
2-Column Table

half sheet, long edge at top; DS data; 6 spaces between columns

Alertness cue: Space forward twice after height Items 1, 2, 4, and 5 in Column 1.

(Problem 2 on next page)

NORMAL WEIGHT RANGE

		words
		4
Men	Women	8
5′6″ = 142 lbs.	5′0″ = 100 lbs.	14
5′8″ = 154 lbs.	5′2″ = 110 lbs.	21
5′10″ = 166 lbs.	5′4″ = 120 lbs.	27
6′0″ = 178 lbs.	5′6″ = 130 lbs.	34
6′2″ = 190 lbs.	5′8″ = 140 lbs.	40

182c (continued)

Problem 3
Letter with Special Features

modified block style, open punctuation; address envelope

Insert the numbered information about the letter copy into the corresponding numbered places within the letter.

1. **Mr. James Groble**
   Commodore Life
   Insurance Co.
   3900 Wisconsin Avenue
   Washington, DC 20016-6648
2. **Impromptu Speaking**
3. **Monday, July 2,**
4. **10**
5. **9:30**

Problem 4

If time permits, proofread Problem 3, mark errors for correction, and prepare a final copy with all errors corrected.

words

June 1, 19-- | CERTIFIED | (1) | Dear (insert appropriate salutation) | FBLA 29
LEADERSHIP CONFERENCE 33

(¶ 1) Thank you for agreeing to judge the (2) event at the National FBLA 49
Leadership Conference at the Washington Hilton on July 2-5. We are look- 64
ing forward to working with you. 70

(¶ 2) A copy of the guidelines for the event is enclosed. The event is sched- 84
uled for (3) at (4) a.m. Would it be possible for you to meet me in Suite 16 of 103
the Hilton at (5) a.m.? At that time, I will further explain the event to you 119
and give you the necessary forms. 125

(¶ 3) If you have any questions or need further information before the con- 139
ference, please call me at 703-860-3334. 147

Sincerely | Mrs. Cindy Brown | Conference Director | xx | Enclosures | Guide- 161
lines | Reservation Form | cc Ed Fogler 168

We would enjoy having you as our luncheon guest at 11:45. Please return the 184
enclosed reservation by June 15. 190

Lesson 183 AMS Letters/Composing

183a ▶ 5 Conditioning Practice

1. Each line twice SS.
2. A 1′ writing on line 4; determine *gwam*. Repeat if time permits.

alphabet 1 The king and queen expressed joy about Fulton's moving west to Zurich.

figures 2 Jan's Floral sold 197 roses, 245 carnations, and 86 daisies on May 30.

fig/sym 3 Rose's electric bill is $58.70 (973 KWH at .056 plus $4.21 state tax).

speed 4 Diane may blame the fight on the problems with the title for the auto.

| 1 | 2 | 3 | 4 | 5 | 6 | 7 | 8 | 9 | 10 | 11 | 12 | 13 | 14 |

183b ▶ 15 Compose at the Keyboard

full sheet, 70-space line

1. Key the ¶ shown at the right.
2. Compose another ¶ as directed.
3. Using proofreader's marks, edit your composition for clarity of thought and accuracy of keying.

You are currently completing Cycle 3 of Century 21 Keyboarding, Formatting, and Document Processing. How would you respond if one of your friends who had never had a class in keyboarding were to ask you to give your opinion about whether he or she should take such a course? Give your response and justification.

183c ▶ 30 Learn to Format Letters in AMS Simplified Style

plain full sheet
letterhead (LM p. 77)
margins: 1½″
date: line 15

1. Study the AMS letter on page 318; then format and key the letter on a plain sheet.
2. Proofread; circle errors; check copy for correct style.
3. Review AMS features; then format on a letterhead the letter on page 318 to send to:

Ms. Sandra Kingman
Word Processing Specialists
3845 Kushtaka Circle
Anchorage, AK 99504-1937

Correct any errors you make as you key the letter.

105b (continued)

Problem 2
3-Column Table

half sheet, long edge at top; SS 2-line items in Col. 1, indenting second line 3 spaces; DS between items; 8 spaces between columns; SS source lines

Reminder: Col. 1 heading is started a DS below secondary heading.

{ } = parentheses

¬ = comma

RACIAL AND ETHNIC MINORITIES IN U.S.A. IN 1980 — words 9

{Percent of Total population} — words 15

Group	Number	%	words
			21
Blacks	26¬487¬000 (7 corrected to 8)	11.7	25
Hispanics	14¬606¬000	6.5	30
Asians and			33
Pacific Islands	3¬501¬000	1.5	39
Indians¬ Eskimos¬			43
Aleuts	1¬418¬000	0.6	47

__________________ 51

Source: Bureau of Census¬ Supplementary Reports¬ 66
May 1981. 68

105c ▶ 10
Improve Language Skills: Punctuation

full sheet; 1" top margin; 70-space line

Key as directed in 103c, p. 182.

SEMICOLON (continued)

Use a semicolon to separate a series of phrases or clauses (especially if they contain commas) that are introduced by a colon.

Learn 1. These are the sales figures: 1987, $5,678,342; 1988, $6,789,020.
Apply 2. The new officers are: Dee O'Brien, President Jay Ford, Secretary.

Place the semicolon *outside* the closing quotation mark; the period, *inside* the quotation mark.

Learn 3. Mrs. Jane spoke on "Building Speed"; Mr. Paul, on "Accuracy."
Apply 4. He said, "Don't use sarcasm;" she said, "I'll try".

APOSTROPHE

Use an apostrophe as a *symbol* for *feet* in billings or tabulations, or as a *symbol* for *minutes*. (The quotation mark may be used as a *symbol* for *inches* or *seconds*.)

Learn 5 Please deliver ten 2″ × 4″ × 10′ pine boards to my address.
Apply 6. He ran the mile in 3 min. 54 sec. The room is 12 ft. 6 in. × 18 ft.

Use an apostrophe as a symbol to indicate the omission of letters or figures (as in contractions).

Learn 7. Each July 4th, we try to renew the "Spirit of '76."
Apply 8. Use the apostrophe in these contractions: isnt, cant, youll.

Lesson 182 Letters with Special Parts/Language Skills

182a ▶ 5
Conditioning Practice

1. Each line twice SS.
2. A 1′ writing on line 4; find *gwam*. Repeat as time permits.

alphabet 1 Joaquin realized he could skirt the awful bumps by driving extra slow.
figures 2 A 1984 model costs more than a 1976 by approximately 25 to 30 percent.
fig/sym 3 He was born at 2:05 a.m. (3/16/87) and weighed 9 pounds and 14 ounces.
speed 4 Henry was the big man with the ancient rifle to the right of the bush.

| 1 | 2 | 3 | 4 | 5 | 6 | 7 | 8 | 9 | 10 | 11 | 12 | 13 | 14 |

182b ▶10
Improve Language Skills

full sheet; 70-space line

Key the ¶ shown at the right, selecting the correct words from those in parentheses. Verify your corrected copy with your teacher.

(Every one; Everyone) of the students should be able to finish the examination before the game at (3 p.m.; 3 p.m. o'clock; 3 o'clock). (There; Their) exams will be returned on (March 16; March 16th). If (any one; anyone) is not satisfied with the grade he or she (receive; receives), please have her or him discuss it with (I; me). (To; Too; Two) exams were turned in last week with (no; know) name. (Whose; Who's) going to claim them?

182c ▶ 35
Format Letters with Special Parts

3 plain full sheets
margins: 1″
date: line 13

Problem 1
Block Style Letter, Open Punctuation

Send letter to:

Ms. Vicky Tokheim
Jefferson High School
3871 Arlington Avenue
Minneapolis, MN 55443-1846

Supply an appropriate salutation; use your initials as reference.

Problem 2
Modified Block Style Letter, Block ¶s, Open Punctuation

Reformat Problem 1, adding photocopy notation to **Miss Mildred Crocker** and the following postscript:

If there is any further information that I can provide, please contact me at 715-836-4320.

Problem 3 is on next page.

words

words in opening lines 22

August 1, 19-- | SPECIAL DELIVERY | Subject: BUSINESS EDUCATION AND 33
ADMINISTRATIVE MANAGEMENT DEPARTMENT 40

(¶ 1) Thank you for your interest in attending Holybrook College at Macon, 54
Georgia. We are proud of our Business Education and Administrative Man- 68
agement Department and are always eager to share information about it. 83

(¶ 2) Currently, we offer three majors within the Department: a Business 96
Education major, an Administrative Management major, and a Secretarial 110
Administration major. The Business Education major is designed to prepare 125
students for teaching careers at the secondary level. The Administrative 140
Management major is designed to prepare students with all the necessary 155
front-line supervisory skills to manage the administrative support of an orga- 170
nization. The last major, Secretarial Administration, is designed to prepare 186
students for careers in the office. 193

(¶ 3) I am enclosing brochures on each of the programs along with the col- 207
lege catalog. 209

Sincerely yours | Norbert Hodges, Chairperson | Enclosures | Business Educa- 223
tion Brochure | Administrative Management Brochure | Secretarial Adminis- 237
tration Brochure | College Catalog 243

Improve Keyboarding: Speed and Control

Use the two sets of paragraphs to increase your skill. Follow the procedure below.

1. Take two 1′ speed writings on each of the three ¶s in a set; find *gwam* and circle errors on each writing.

2. Take two 1′ control writings on each of the three ¶s in a set. Pace yourself so that you can key for 1′ with no more than 2 errors.

3. Take a 5′ writing on the three ¶s combined; find *gwam*, circle errors.

all letters used | A | 1.5 si | 5.7 awl | 80% hfw |

gwam 1′ | 5′

Knowing that there are sixty seconds in every minute and sixty min- 13 | 3 | 49
utes in each hour, we should be able to schedule our activities into the 28 | 6 | 52
available time without difficulty. Why, then, do so many people end up 42 | 8 | 55
rushing around in a frenzy, trying to meet deadlines? The answer is in 56 | 11 | 58
the psychological nature of time. When we are enjoying ourselves, time 71 | 14 | 61
seems to fly away; but time spent on tedious jobs seems endless. 85 | 17 | 64

Do you ever "goof off" for an hour or more with a television program 14 | 20 | 66
or a visit on the telephone and discover later that you haven't actually 28 | 23 | 69
enjoyed your leisure? Each nagging little vision of homework or chores 43 | 26 | 72
to be completed always seems to result in taking the edge off your plea- 57 | 28 | 75
sure. And you still have to complete whatever you postponed--probably 71 | 31 | 78
in a hurry. 74 | 32 | 78

If you fit the situation above, don't waste valuable time feeling 13 | 34 | 81
guilty; for you have lots of company. What you should feel is cheated-- 28 | 37 | 84
out of leisure that you didn't enjoy and study time that didn't produce 42 | 40 | 87
results. Check with your companions who always seem ready for a good 56 | 43 | 90
time but are also ready for unexpected quizzes. The secret is in the 71 | 46 | 92
budgeting of your time. 74 | 47 | 93

gwam 1′
5′
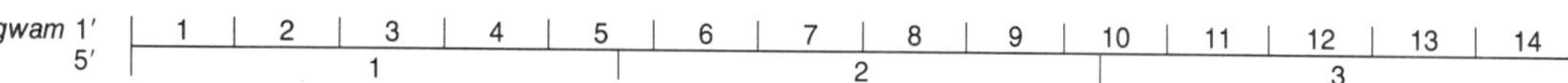

all letters used | A | 1.5 si | 5.7 awl | 80% hfw |

Although the path to success is usually lengthy, you can make it 13 | 3 | 46
shorter if you will start at the beginning of your business career to 27 | 5 | 49
develop two important skills. The first is the ability to see and to 41 | 8 | 52
solve problems; the second, the ability to gather facts and arrange them 56 | 11 | 55
in logical order, from which you can draw the correct conclusions. 69 | 14 | 57

Surely you can recall occasions when you devoted many hours, even 13 | 16 | 60
days, to striving unsuccessfully for a goal, and then you happened to see 28 | 19 | 63
the difficult problem from a new viewpoint. Perhaps you exclaimed to a 43 | 22 | 66
friend or yourself, "Now I see what the problem is!" And once identified, 57 | 25 | 69
the problem was easily solved. As you begin work on a project, make your 71 | 28 | 72
initial step that of seeing the actual problem. 81 | 30 | 73

To solve problems, use all effectual means to get the data that you 14 | 33 | 76
will need. Books and magazine articles give facts and expert opinions, 28 | 36 | 79
and a request by mail or phone may offer added aid. Enter the data on 42 | 38 | 82
cards, divide the cards into logical groups, review the work, and apply 57 | 41 | 85
common sense to reach conclusions that the data support. 68 | 44 | 87

gwam 1′
5′
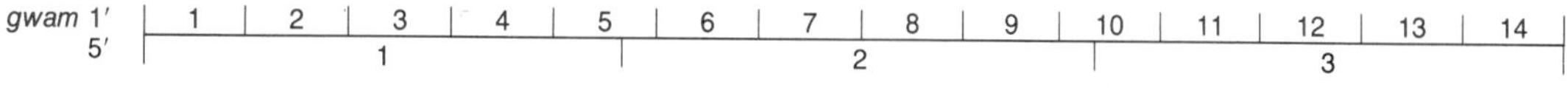

		words in parts	total words
	February 7, 19--	3	3
Mailing notation	CERTIFIED	5	5
Attention line	Jensen Manufacturing Company	11	11
	Attention Ms. Carmen Rodriguez	17	17
	3829 Harrison Boulevard	22	22
	Ogden, UT 84404-6390	27	27
	Ladies and Gentlemen:	31	31
Subject line	MANAGERIAL SEMINARS	35	35
	We are planning to offer our managerial seminars in the Ogden area	13	48
	again this year. Because of the excellent response to last year's	27	62
	seminar, two seminars are being scheduled for your area this year.	40	75
	The first seminar, "The Impact of Your Nonverbal Communication,"	54	89
	will be held on June 18 at the Civic Center Inn. The second one	67	102
	is tentatively scheduled for September 6 at the Morris Convention	80	115
	Center. Some aspect of interpersonal communication will be the	93	128
	main focus of the second seminar.	99	134
	I asked Ms. Worthington, our convention coordinator, to include	112	147
	you on our mailing list. You should receive the brochure for the	125	160
	first seminar by the middle of March. We look forward to working	139	174
	with employees of the Jensen Manufacturing Company	149	184
	Sincerely,	2	186
Company name in closing lines	STERLING COMMUNICATIONS, INC.	8	192
	Joshua Schuricht		
	Joshua Schuricht	12	196
	Public Relations Manager	17	201
	jh	17	201
Listed enclosures	Enclosures	19	203
	Request Form	22	206
	Fact Sheet	24	208
Copy notations	pc Ms. Fern Worthington	29	213
	Mr. Jay Kummerfeld	33	217
Postscript	If you need additional brochures, please complete the enclosed	45	229
	request form.	48	232
			255

Letter with Special Features

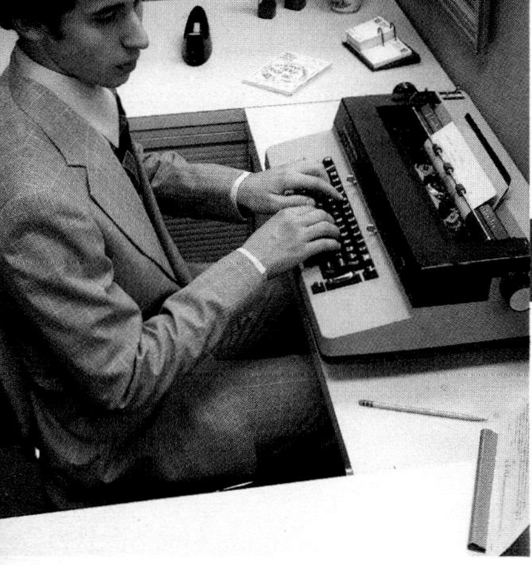

Unit 22 Lessons 106-110

Learning Goals

1. To improve skill in formatting complex tables.
2. To improve spelling and word-use skills.
3. To increase straight-copy skill.
4. To improve language skills (punctuation).

Machine Adjustments

1. Paper guide at *0*.
2. 70-space line and SS, or as directed.
3. Line-space selector on *1*, or as directed.
4. Paper bail rollers in proper position.

Lesson 106 Complex Table/Language Skills

106a-110a ▶ 5 (daily)
Conditioning Practice

each line 3 times (slowly, faster, in-between rate); as time permits, repeat selected lines

(In each new lesson, try to increase your speed and control.)

alphabet 1 Joan Zadik, who was piqued by Gail's rude manner, left very excitedly.

fig/sym 2 The new pool (19′ wide × 26′ long × 8′ deep) will cost but $14,235.70.

direct reaches 3 Cecil brought a number of bright nylon flags to a big center ceremony.

speed 4 Big profit is born with a busy hand, a key focus, and proficient work.

| 1 | 2 | 3 | 4 | 5 | 6 | 7 | 8 | 9 | 10 | 11 | 12 | 13 | 14 |

106b ▶ 10
Improve Language Skills: Punctuation

full sheet; 1″ top margin; 70-space line

Study/Learn/Apply/Correct Procedures

1. STUDY explanatory rule.
2. Key line number (with period), space twice, and key LEARN sentence(s) DS, noting rule application.
3. Key APPLY sentence(s) DS, making changes needed to correct sentences.
4. As your teacher reads the corrected sentences, show in pen or pencil any corrections that need to be made in your copy.
5. Rekey any APPLY sentence(s) containing an error, CORRECTING the error as you key. Key the corrected sentence in the space below the APPLY sentence containing the error.

APOSTROPHE (continued)

Use an apostrophe *plus s* to form the plural of most figures, letters, and words (6's, A's, five's). In market quotations, form the plural of figures by the addition of *s only.*

Learn 1. Your f's look like 7's. Boston Fund 4s are due in 2005.

Apply 2. Cross your ts and dot your is. Sell United 6's this week.

To *show possession,* use an apostrophe *plus s* after a (a) singular noun and (b) a plural noun which does not end in s.

Learn 3. The boy's bicycle was found, but the women's shoes were not.

Apply 4. Childrens toys are on sale; buy the girls bicycle.

To *show possession,* use an apostrophe *plus s* after a proper name of one syllable that ends in s.

Learn 5. Please pay Jones's bill for $675 today.

Apply 6. Was it Bess' hat, Ross' shoes, or Chris' watch that was lost?

To *show possession,* use *only* an apostrophe after (a) plural nouns ending in s and (b) a proper name of more than one syllable which ends in s or z.

Learn 7. The girls' counselor will visit the Adams' home.

Apply 8. The ladies handbags were found near Douglas Restaurant.

Lesson 181 Letters with Special Parts

181a ▶ 5 Conditioning Practice

1. Each line twice SS.
2. A 1′ writing on line 4; find *gwam*. Repeat if time permits.

alphabet 1 The majestic spring bouquet of dark yellow azaleas was very expensive.

figures 2 The Chargers won the game by a score of 138 to 107 before 24,596 fans.

fig/sym 3 Thomas sold 30 (15%), Dwayne sold 78 (39%), and Timothy sold 92 (46%).

speed 4 The amendment by the girl was cut down by the eight rich, haughty men.

| 1 | 2 | 3 | 4 | 5 | 6 | 7 | 8 | 9 | 10 | 11 | 12 | 13 | 14 |

181b ▶ 15 Learn to Place and Space Special Letter Parts

2 plain full sheets
margins: 1½″
date: line 15

1. Study the material on page 313; check each placement point with the model letter on page 313 or 315.
2. On a full sheet, arrange and key the opening lines of Drill 1, beginning on line 15 from top edge.
3. After keying the subject line, return 12 times to key the closing lines.
4. Do Drill 2 in the same way.

Drill 1: Block Format

October 16, 19--

REGISTERED

Fleming & Thatcher, Ltd.
Attention Mr. J. Evan Smythe
Marketing Division
5149 Heather Court
Asheville, NC 28804-2645

Ladies and Gentlemen

AUTOMATED WORD PROCESSING SYSTEM

Space down 12 times (using INDEX or RETURN) to allow for body of letter.

Sincerely yours

CRAFTRONICS, INCORPORATED

Mylam R. Liggett, Sales Manager

tjc

pc Janice P. Cooley
Robert C. Lang

Drill 2: Modified Block Format

October 16, 19--

Mr. Todd K. Richardson
Harvard Arms, Suite 1650
755 Breezewood Drive
Pittsburgh, PA 15237-3428

Dear Mr. Richardson

AUTOMOBILE POLICY 482710-A

Space down 12 times (using INDEX or RETURN) to allow for body of letter.

Sincerely yours

Ms. Lurlene Hill
Assistant Manager

lbj

Enclosures: Policy 482710-A
Rider to Policy

If you have further questions about your policy, contact Mike Jones (412-801-3895) in your district.

181c ▶ 30 Format Letters with Special Parts

2 plain full sheets
1 letterhead (LM p. 75)
margins: 1″
date: line 13

1. Study the letter on page 315, noting the placement and spacing of special parts.
2. On plain paper, copy the letter, spacing the special parts correctly.
3. Proofread your copy, mark it for correction, and rekey it in final form on letterhead paper.
4. If time permits, take a 2′ writing on opening lines (date through subject line); then a 2′ writing on closing lines (complimentary close through postscript).

106c ▶ 25
Improve Basic Skill: Straight Copy

1. Take two 1′ speed writings on each paragraph.

2. Take two 3′ writings on ¶s combined; proofread and circle errors; find *gwam*. Record better score.

3. Take two 5′ writings on ¶s combined; proofread and circle errors; find *gwam*. Record better score.

all letters used | A | 1.5 si | 5.7 awl | 80% hfw |

	gwam 3′	5′	
In the word-processing area of work, there is now an increasing	4	3	55
demand for persons who can key with speed on their machines. Keyboarded	9	5	58
errors are not as relevant as they were in the past because of the ease	14	8	61
of correction of such errors with the modern electronic equipment now in	19	11	64
use in many modern-day offices. Along with the speed of keyboarding, the	24	14	67
next most relevant factor is good proofreading skill. A keyboard opera-	29	17	70
tor must be able to proofread the copy well and to spot and correct any	33	20	73
errors that were made. Developing good proofreading skill is not very	38	23	75
easy. Proofreading is learned through zealous effort and much practice.	43	26	78
An individual can become a speedy keyboard operator after an ample	47	28	81
amount of practice. The most important element in building speed is	52	31	84
learning to keyboard with requisite technique or good form patterns.	57	34	87
Good form means that the fingers are kept curved over the keys and the	61	37	89
keystroking action is limited to the fingers. The hands and arms should	66	40	92
be kept in a quiet position. An expert operator also should try to learn	71	42	95
to space quickly after each word and to begin the next word without a	76	45	98
pause or stop. To do this, the expert operator learns to read slightly	81	48	101
ahead in the copy while it is being keyed to anticipate just the right	85	51	104
keystroking or response patterns.	88	53	105

gwam 3′ | 1 | 2 | 3 | 4 | 5
5′ | 1 | 2 | 3

106d ▶ 10
Preapplication Drills

Drill 1
Column Headings Longer Than Column Entries

1. If column headings are longer than column entries, first center and key the column headings horizontally (in this drill leave 4 spaces between headings).

2. Then DS, center, and set margin and tab stops for the longest column entry under each heading. Use forward-space, backspace method.

Study Each Word	Pronounce by Syllables	Capitalize Trouble Spots
mathematics	math-e-mat-ics	mathEmatics

Endangered Mammals	Known Distribution
Manatee	Florida

(Drill 2 on next page)

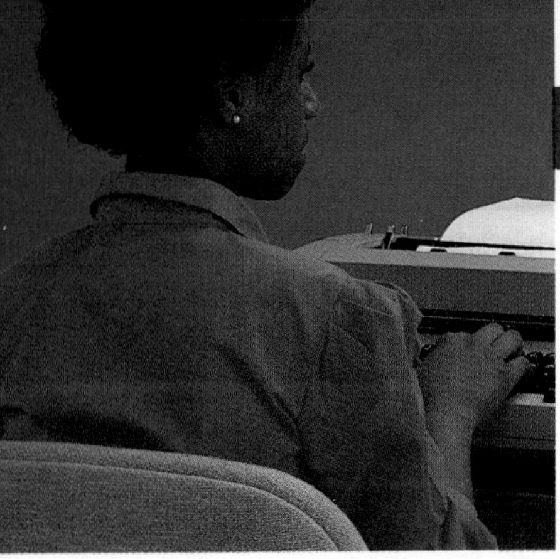

Unit 39 Lessons 181-187

Learning Goals

1. To develop keyboarding skill on business letters with special features.

2. To develop keyboarding skill on letters in the AMS simplified style.

3. To develop keyboarding skill on informal government letters.

4. To improve skill in composing at the keyboard.

5. To assess and improve language skills.

Machine Adjustments

1. Paper guide at *0*.

2. Ribbon control to use top half of ribbon.

3. Margins: 70-space line for sentences and ¶s; as required for problems.

4. Spacing: SS drills; DS ¶ activities; as directed for problems.

FORMATTING GUIDES: LETTERS WITH SPECIAL PARTS

Sterling Communications, Inc.

February 7, 19--

CERTIFIED

[illegible]
Attention Ms. Carmen Rodriguez
3829 Harrison Boulevard
Ogden, UT 84404-6390

Ladies and Gentlemen:

MANAGERIAL SEMINARS

We are planning to offer our managerial seminars in the Ogden area again this year. Because of the excellent response to last year's seminar, two seminars are being scheduled for your area this year.

The first seminar, "The Impact of Your Nonverbal Communication," will be held on June 18 at the Civic Center Inn. The second one is tentatively scheduled for September 6 at the Morris Convention Center. Some aspect of interpersonal communication will be the main focus of the second seminar.

I asked Ms. Worthington, our convention coordinator, to include you on our mailing list. You should receive the brochure for the first seminar by the middle of March. We look forward to working with employees of the Jensen Manufacturing Company.

Sincerely,

STERLING COMMUNICATIONS, INC.

Joshua Schuricht

Joshua Schuricht
Public Relations Manager

jh

Enclosures
   Request Form
   Fact Sheet

pc Ms. Fern Worthington
   Mr. Jay Kummerfeld

If you need additional brochures, please complete the enclosed request form.

Letter with Special Parts

Mailing Notation

A mailing notation (which indicates a special postal service such as CERTIFIED, REGISTERED, SPECIAL DELIVERY, or AIRMAIL) is placed at the left margin a DS below the date. A DS separates it from the first line of the letter address.

Attention Line

If a letter is addressed to a company, the address *may* include an attention line (the second line of the address) to call the letter to the attention of a specific person, department, or job title. When a letter is addressed to a company (whether or not an attention line is included), the salutation *Ladies and Gentlemen* is typically used.

Subject Line

Some companies use a subject line to announce the subject about which a letter is written and to aid in filing correspondence. A subject line is often placed a DS below the salutation, but some companies prefer to place it a DS above the salutation. It may begin at the left margin, begin at paragraph point when paragraphs are indented, or be centered over the body of the letter. For sake of efficiency, begin it at the left margin unless otherwise specified.

Company Name in Closing Lines

When the company name is used in the closing lines, it is placed a DS below the complimentary close (at the left margin in block style letters; beginning at center point in modified block style letters). A quadruple space (QS) separates it from the writer's keyed name.

Listed Enclosures

When enclosures are to be listed, place Enclosures at the left margin a DS below the reference initials. Listed enclosures may be formatted in one of two ways. List the enclosures SS 3 spaces from the left margin, as shown in Model 1 at the left; or, follow the word Enclosures with a colon and 2 spaces and list each enclosure (as shown on p. 314).

Copy Notation

When a copy notation is used, place the letters cc (carbon copy) or pc (photocopy) at the left margin a DS below the reference initials (or enclosure notation, if any). The person's name follows cc or pc separated by one space. If more than one name is shown, they are listed SS.

Postscript

A postscript (a message added at the end of a letter) is placed a DS below the last of the reference lines. It is blocked at or indented from the left margin, to agree with the paragraphing of the letter. The abbreviation P.S. is no longer widely used.

Drill 2
Long and Short Column Headings

1. If a table has both long and short column headings, center items according to the longest item in each column, whether a column heading or a column entry.

2. In this drill, use backspace-from-center method to set left margin and tab stop using longest column item. Leave 4 spaces between columns.

Name	Location
Grizzly Bear	USA
Bald Eagle	USA
Brown Pelican	USA

Lessons 107-110 Complex Tables

107b-110b ▶ 45 (daily) Format Complex Tables

In the time period for each lesson, try to complete as many problems as possible, pages 189-193. Unless otherwise directed, center tables using the longest column item, whether a heading or entry.

Problem 1
3-Column Heading

half sheet, long edge at top; DS data; 12 spaces between Cols. 1 and 2; 6 spaces between Cols. 2 and 3; block column headings;
Learning cue: DS between 2-line main heading.

AVERAGE COST IN CENTS PER MILE TO OWN AND OPERATE A NEW CAR			words
			6 12
Car Size	1978	1983	19
Subcompact	22.5	34.6	23
Compact	24.8	43.3	27
Mid-Size	28.7	45.5	31
Intermediate	28.9	49.6	35
Standard	32.3	55.4	39
AVERAGE	27.5	45.7	42

Problem 2
2-Line Column Headings

half sheet, long edge at top; DS data, but SS column headings; 6 spaces between columns

Learning cue: When you space forward, 1 for 2, for longest column entry, note center point of column for use in centering column headings.

IMPROVE YOUR SPELLING			4
Study Each Word	Pronounce by Syllables	Capitalize Trouble Spots	10 24
environmental	en-vi-ron-men-tal	enviRONmenTAL	33
existence	ex-ist-ence	ExistENCE	40
guarantee	guar-an-tee	gUARanTEE	46
incidentally	in-ci-den-tal-ly	incidenTALLY	55
miniature	min-i-a-ture	miniATURE	61
miscellaneous	mis-cel-la-ne-ous	misCELLanEOUS	70
omission	o-mis-sion	omisSION	76
pursue	pur-sue	PURsue	80

Problem 3
Long Column Headings

full sheet; DS data; 4 spaces between columns (review directions, page 188, if necessary).

IMPROVE YOUR SPELLING			4
Study Each Word	Pronounce by Syllables	Capitalize Trouble Spots	29
address	ad-dress	aDdress	34
analyze	an-a-lyze	anaLYZE	40
believe	be-lieve	belIEve	45
convenience	con-ven-ience	convenIence	52
courtesy	cour-te-sy	COURteSY	58
disease	dis-ease	disEASE	63
eligible	el-i-gi-ble	eligIble	69
equipped	e-quipped	equipPed	75
judgment	judg-ment	juDGMent	80
mortgage	mort-gage	morTgage	86
occurred	oc-curred	oCCuRRed	91
unforgettable	un-for-get-ta-ble	unforgetTABLE	100

180b (continued)

Problem 1
Letter on Executive-Size Stationery (LM p. 67)

modified block style, open punctuation; 1 cc on plain sheet; address an envelope

Problem 1 words

September 15, 19-- Mrs. Donna Newhart 2403 Lincoln Road Anderson, IN 14
46011-1517 Dear Mrs. Newhart 20

(¶ 1) I am delighted to welcome you, on behalf of the Board of Governors, 33
to charter membership in the Executives Club. The enclosed membership 47
card provides you with all privileges offered by the Club. It also entitles 63
you to nonresident membership at the more than 100 prestigious private 77
clubs throughout the country with which we have associate privileges. 91
These city, country, athletic, and resort clubs offer the finest in dining, 106
entertaining, fitness, and recreational facilities. 117

(¶ 2) All associate clubs are totally private and will not accept cash or credit 132
cards. Your charges will be billed through the Executives Club. Although 147
reservations are suggested, the presentation of your membership card is the 162
only credential needed at these clubs. 170

(¶ 3) If you have questions about any phase of the Executives Club's opera- 184
tions, please contact me. 189

Sincerely yours Mrs. Tien Chiang Vice President, Membership xx 200

Enclosure 201/**213**

Problem 2
Message/Reply Memo
(LM p. 69)

1 cc on plain sheet; address a COMPANY MAIL envelope

Problems 3 and 4
Letters from Form Paragraphs (LM pp. 71-73)

block style, open punctuation; current date; supply salutation and complimentary close; use **Mrs. Lois Russell, Sales Manager** in closing lines; 1 cc on plain sheet; address an envelope

1. Copy the addresses and ¶ numbers (see below) for the two letters.
2. Turn to page 310 and prepare the letters from the form paragraphs.

Problem 3
Mr. John Lee
900 E. Broad Street
Richmond, VA 23219-2814
Use ¶s 1.3, 2.3, and 3.2
Total words: 128

Problem 4
Mrs. Maria Hernandez
2241 Reynolds Road
Winston-Salem, NC 27106-1927
Use ¶s 1.1, 2.2, and 3.1
Total words: 153

Problem 2

TO: Mrs. Ruth Schurtter Director of Publicity 157 Administration Build- 13
ing DATE: September 15, 19-- SUBJECT: Copy for News Release 22

(¶ 1) It occurred to me that you might like to have some preliminary infor- 36
mation concerning the opening of our branch plant in Topeka. Many details 51
still must be worked out, but the following personnel assignments may prove 66
of interest: 69

Branch Manager	Miss Rhena Carlock	76
Sales Manager	Mr. John Portella	82
Warehouse Manager	Mr. Anthony DeLeo	89

(¶ 2) Just as soon as other details are finalized, I shall send them to you for 104
use in the preparation of future news releases. 114

SIGNED: Raymond Gupta, Secretary 119

(REPLY) DATE OF REPLY: September 17, 19-- 123

(¶) Thank you for providing information about persons assigned to the 136
new branch plant in Topeka. I shall prepare a news release for inclusion 151
in next Sunday's newspaper editions. For the grand opening, I should like 166
to prepare more comprehensive releases for regional television and news- 180
paper coverage. I appreciate your memo; the information you provided is 195
newsworthy. 197

SIGNED: Ruth Schurtter 200/**216**

Problem 4
3-Column Table

full sheet; DS data; 12 spaces between columns

Learning cue: Remember to TS to Col. 1 heading; DS above and below divider line.

Alertness cue: Set tab stop for the digit in each column that requires the least forward and backward spacing. To align figures, space forward ▶ or backward ◀ as necessary.

words

POPULATION OF UNITED STATES, 1790-1980 8

(In Millions) 11

12

Year	Population	Percent Increase	words
			22
1790	3.9	—	24
1810	7.2	84.6%	27
1830	12.9	79.2	30
1850	23.2	80.0	33
1870	38.6	66.4	36
1890	63.0	63.2	39
1910	92.2	46.3	42
1930	123.2	33.6	45
1950	151.3	22.8	49
1970	203.3	34.4	52
1980	226.5	11.4	55

______________ 59

Source: World Almanac, 1985, pp. 248-249. 67

Problem 5
Unarranged Table

Arrange table in proper format; full sheet; DS data; 12 spaces between columns; SS source note and key full width of table.

Main heading: WORLD POPULATION, 30-2000 A.D. 6

Secondary heading: (In Millions) 9

Column headings: Year / Population / Percent Increase 11 20

Year	Population	Percent Increase	words
30	250	—	23
1650	545	118.0%	26
1700	623	14.3	29
1750	728	16.7	33
1800	906	24.5	36
1850	1,171	29.2	39
1900	1,608	37.3	42
1940	2,170	35.0	45
1950	2,501	15.3	49
1960	2,986	19.4	52
1970	3,610	20.9	55
1980	4,478	24.0	58
1990	5,326	18.9	61
2000	6,246	17.3	65

______________ 68

Source: Woytinsky and Woytinsky, 1953; United Na- 78
tions Population Studies, 1984. 84

Lesson 179 Review: Letters and Memos

179a ▶ 5 Conditioning Practice

each line twice SS (slowly, then faster); DS between 2-line groups; if time permits, rekey selected lines

alphabet 1 Vince Paquette wrote exactly six new books for judging home-size gyms.

figures 2 The members were assigned into study groups of 60, 51, 48, 37, and 29.

3d row 3 potato query error were quote retort territory porter profiteer retire

speed 4 I kept the eight worn sign panels for the coal firm on the big island.

| 1 | 2 | 3 | 4 | 5 | 6 | 7 | 8 | 9 | 10 | 11 | 12 | 13 | 14 |

179b ▶ 5 Carbon-Pack Assembly and Error-Correction Tips

1. Assemble letterhead, carbon sheets (uncarboned side up), and second sheets as illustrated above. *Use one carbon and one second sheet for each copy desired.*

2. Grasp the carbon pack at the sides, turn it so that the *letterhead faces away from you, the carbon side of the carbon paper is toward you, and the top edge of the pack is face down.* Tap the sheets gently on the desk to straighten.

3. Hold the sheets firmly to prevent slipping; insert pack into typewriter. Hold pack with one hand; turn platen with the other.

Error correction

Different methods may be used in making corrections: lift-off paper, correction fluid (liquid paper), eraser, etc. Use the method recommended by your teacher. Be certain that corrections are made neatly on original and all copies.

179c ▶ 40 Build Sustained Document Processing Skills: Managerial Correspondence

Time Schedule

Plan and Prepare .... 3′
Timed Production .... 30′
Proofread and correct errors ... 5′
compute *n-pram* .... 2′

letterheads and forms (LM pp. 61-65); plain full sheets; carbon sheet

1. Make a list of problems to be keyed

p. 307, 176b, Problem 2
p. 308, 177b, Problem 2
p. 310, 178b, Problem 1

2. Arrange letterheads and plain sheets for efficient handling. Make 1 cc of each problem; address envelopes.

3. Work for 30′. Follow directions given for each problem. Proofread each sheet carefully before removing it from the machine. Correct errors neatly. If you finish before time is called, begin with Problem 1 and rekey on plain sheets as much as possible in the time remaining.

4. Compute *n-pram*:

$$\frac{\text{total words} - \text{penalty*}}{\text{time (30')}}$$

*Penalty is 15 words for each uncorrected error.

5. Turn in problems arranged in the order given in Step 1.

Lesson 180 Evaluation: Letters and Memos

180a ▶ 5 Conditioning Practice

each line twice SS (slowly, then faster); DS between 2-line groups; if time permits, rekey selected lines

alphabet 1 Twenty zealous workers made craft exhibits for quaint Camp Jungleview.

figures 2 The four school lecture halls seat 290, 385, 46, and 71, respectively.

one-hand 3 jump loin pool join milky racer trader crafts wasted decrease greatest

speed 4 They may make the six men go to the coalfield to dig for coal to burn.

| 1 | 2 | 3 | 4 | 5 | 6 | 7 | 8 | 9 | 10 | 11 | 12 | 13 | 14 |

180b ▶ 45 Measure Document Processing Skills

Time Schedule

Plan and Prepare .... 3′
Timed Production .... 30′
Proofread and correct errors ... 5′
compute *n-pram* .... 2′

letterheads and forms (LM pp. 67-73); plain full sheets; carbon sheet

1. Arrange letterheads and forms for efficient handling.

2. Keyboard/format for 30′ the problems provided on page 312.

3. Proofread; correct errors neatly. Circle uncorrected errors found in final check.

4. Compute *n-pram*.

5. Turn in problems in order given.

Problem 6
Unarranged "Special" Table

Arrange table in proper format; full sheet; DS data; 12 spaces between columns (see note).

Note. In arranging some tables horizontally on a sheet, it may be necessary to use judgment to avoid an off-center appearance of data. In this table, use longest column entry (excluding column headings) to determine horizontal placement. The Column 3 heading is then centered over the longest entry in that column.

Use 2-line main heading:

PRINCIPAL PARTS OF TROUBLESOME IRREGULAR VERBS

Problem 7

Repeat Problem 6 on half sheet, short edge at top; DS data; 8 spaces between columns. Key column entries as you did in Problem 6.

Present	Past	Past Participle	words in heading 9
			20
see	saw	seen	23
do	did	done	25
go	went	gone	28
break	broke	broken	32
choose	chose	chosen	36
drink	drank	drunk	39
eat	ate	eaten	42
freeze	froze	frozen	46
give	gave	given	49
know	knew	known	53
ring	rang	rung	55
run	ran	run	58
speak	spoke	spoken	61
swim	swam	swum	64
take	took	taken	68
write	wrote	written	72

Problem 8
5-Column Table

full sheet; DS data; SS source note; leave 6 spaces between Col. 1 and Col. 2; then, use the following intercolumn spacing between columns: 2-4-2.

Alertness cue: % signs are keyed in intercolumns; see note, page 182.

REASONS OF FRESHMEN FOR ATTENDING COLLEGE 8

(Percent of Total Respondign) 14

Reasons	1984	Rank	1971	Rank	
					24
Bet a better job	75.7%	1	73.8%	1	31
Learn more about things	72.3	2	-	-	38
Makre more moneoy	67.8	3	49.7	4	44
Gain general education	65.1	4	59.5	3	52
Meet new and interesting people	56.1	5	45.1	5	61
Prepare for graduate school	47.9	6	34.5	6	69
Improve reading/study skills	41.6	7	22.2	9	80
Become a more cultured person	33.8	8	28.9	7	89
Parental pressure	31.7	9	22.9	8	96
Get away from home	11.1	10	-	-	102
Could not find a job	5.3	11	-	-	109
Nothing better to do	2.0	12	2.2	11	116
Learn more about my interests	-	-	68.8	2	125
Contribute more to my community	-	-	18.7	10	134

_______________ 138

Soucre: American Council on Education/UCLA, The American Freshmen National Norms, 1971, p. 43; 1984, p. 46. 154 167

178a ▶ 5 Conditioning Practice

each line twice SS (slowly, then faster); DS between 2-line groups; if time permits, rekey selected lines

alphabet 1 Bev Mixon worked the zones adjacent to five exquisite new playgrounds.

figures 2 Jose paid $4,896.75 on May 23 for nine items purchased on February 10.

1st & 3d rows 3 music quiz vortex numbers review vestment initiate youngster murmurous

speed 4 They may pay the panel to handle the work for all of the fight claims.

| 1 | 2 | 3 | 4 | 5 | 6 | 7 | 8 | 9 | 10 | 11 | 12 | 13 | 14 |

178b ▶ 45 Learn to Process Letters from Form Paragraphs

letterheads/envelopes (LM pp. 55-59)

1. Use block style with open punctuation for all form-paragraph letters. Use current date for each letter; supply an appropriate salutation and complimentary close; address envelopes; circle errors.

2. All letters are to be signed by Ricardo Perez, Marketing Manager.

Problem 1

Send a letter to:
Mrs. Essie Mitamura
501 Biltmore Avenue
Asheville, NC 28801-2552

Use ¶s 1.1, 2.1, and 3.1
Total words: 153

Note: When a table appears within a letter, center the table horizontally within the margins of the letter. DS above and below the table; SS the table. Decide spacing between columns.

Problem 2

Send a letter to:
Mr. James Collins
806 Madison Avenue
Memphis, TN 38103-6421

Use ¶s 1.2 (insert name Mr. Khary Payton), 2.2, and 3.2.
Total words: 163

Problem 3

Send a letter to:
Miss Christiana Lim
736 Market Street
Chattanooga, TN 37402-1628

Use ¶s 1.1, 2.2, and 3.2.
Total words: 160

¶1.1 Thank you for writing to inquire about our real estate developments in Florida. I am pleased to learn of your interest, and I am certain that we have some projects which you may find attractive.

¶1.2 I am delighted to know that (insert name) suggested that you write to inquire about real estate developments in Florida. It is always gratifying to know that we are recommended to others by our former clients.

¶1.3 It is always pleasant to hear from someone interested in low-risk, profitable real estate developments.

¶2.1 We now have underway three developments in scenic and potentially strong growth areas:

Fort Myers Area	Condominiums
North Naples Area	Commercials
West Palm Beach	Residentials

Each development has distinctive features which we feel will create immediate and widespread interest for investors.

¶2.2 We are involved in construction of many types, attempting to provide diversified opportunities for persons having a variety of investment interests. All of our projects are located in extremely attractive and strategic locations.

¶2.3 For investors interested in residential housing in the form of multiple-unit apartment buildings, we have some very enticing propositions worthy of serious and immediate consideration.

¶3.1 Thank you for your inquiry. I look forward to the opportunity of showing you some of our fascinating projects.

¶3.2 Thank you for your letter. I am looking forward to the opportunity of showing you some of our development projects and to the possibility of your investing with us.

Problem 9
5-Column Table

full sheet; DS data; 4 spaces between columns

Alertness cue: Set tab stop for the digit in each column that requires the least forward and backward spacing. To align figures, space forward ► or backward ◄ as necessary.

Note: Total lines are usually indented three spaces.

words

A LOOK AT THE EARTH 4

Continents	Area (Sq. Mi.)	Percent of Earth	Population*	Percent World Total	words
					7
					30
Asia	16,999,000	29.7	2,850,567,000	59.9	38
Africa	11,688,000	20.4	531,000,000	11.2	46
North America	9,366,000	16.3	395,000,000	8.3	56
South America	6,881,000	12.0	264,000,000	5.5	65
Europe	4,017,000	7.0	696,433,000	14.6	73
Australia	2,911,000	5.2	15,500,000	0.3	81
Antarctica	5,100,000	8.9			86
*Estimated World Population			4,762,000,000		95

_______________ 98

Source: <u>World Almanac</u>, 1985, p. 625. 108

Problem 10
Unarranged Table

Arrange table in attractive format on full sheet. Spacing suggestion: 2 spaces between columns.

Learning cue: Backspace once from tab stops for underline that precedes totals; start total figures at this point.

Main heading: METHODS OF ERROR CORRECTION USED IN THE BUSINESS OFFICE 11

Column headings:

Method	Letters	Memos	Reports	Forms	Tables	Total Use	words
							12
							30
Lift-off	57%	58%	50%	48%	48%	57%	36
Electronic correction	16	16	18	12	16	16	44
Correction fluid	13	13	22	24	25	13	51
Chalk-back paper	11	11	7	8	7	11	58
Eraser	2	1	2	6	3	2	63
Other method	1	1	1	2	1	1	77
Totals	100%	100%	100%	100%	100%	100%	84

_______________ 87

Source: Guffey and Erickson, <u>Monograph 136</u>, South-Western Publishing Co., Cincinnati, Ohio, 1981, p. 13. 103 111

Problem 11
Unarranged Table

Arrange table in attractive format on full sheet.

Main heading: NATIONAL STUDY OF LETTER VARIABLES 7

AS USED IN THE BUSINESS OFFICE 13

Column headings: <u>Variable</u> / <u>Percent</u> 20

Variable	Percent	words
Length of letter		23
125 words or less	57%	27
126-225 words	26	31
226-325 words	9	34
Two or more pages	8	38
Line length		41
Standard 6-inch line	54	46
Other line lengths	46	50
Two-letter state abbreviation in address	30	58
Columnar material in letter	11	65

_______________ 69

Source: Guffey and Erickson, <u>Monograph 136</u>, South-Western Publishing Co., Cincinnati, Ohio, 1981, p. 24. 81 92

MESSAGE REPLY MEMO

Webster Manufacturing Co.
9543 Edmund Drive
St. Louis, MO 63114-5270

MESSAGE

words

TO Dr. Mabel C. Wright 4
Campbell, David, and Wright 13
442 Quincy Street, SE 18
Topeka, KS 66603-3245 26

DATE September 7, 19--

SUBJECT Order Clarification
File No: GP-580624 32

We are pleased to have your order of September 5, for two 1/2" x 25" 46
x 36" glass table tops. When processing your order, we found that 59
you did not specify the type of finish you want around the edges of 73
the glass. Since the tops are quite large and very heavy, I recom- 86
mend that you have a "flat polish" finish for both pieces of glass. 100
This will give you an attractive finish without having severe angles 114
around the work surface. 119

We shall proceed with your order as soon as you indicate the type of 133
finish you prefer. Delivery from the mill should be within three weeks 147
after they receive the work order. You should have the tops by October 1 162
if we receive your clarification within the next few days. Thanks for 176
your business. 179

SIGNED Jane E. Truax, President 184

REPLY

DATE September 10, 19-- 188

Our preference is to have the edges of the new table tops more rounded 202
than those having the "flat polish" finish you suggest. While we appre- 217
ciate your recommendation, we like the "pencil-type" finish illustrated 231
in your Product Catalog F-47. Please revise our order to show a pencil 245
finish on both table tops. I should like to have them delivered no later 260
than October 5. 264

SIGNED Mabel C. Wright 265
283

Message/Reply Memo

Problem 12
Special Table

half sheet, long edge at top; SS and DS data as shown in table; 10 spaces between columns; add following source note:

Source: Rand Youth Poll, December 1983.

(Total words: 53)

			words
AVERAGE WEEKLY INCOMES			5
OF 2,500 U.S. TEENAGERS			10
	Allowance	Earnings	17
13-15 Years			21
Boys	$11.35	$11.40	25
Girls	11.70	11.90	29
16-19 Years			34
Boys	$21.80	$31.65	37
Girls	22.05	32.5~~6~~5	41

Problem 13
Unarranged Table: Learning Transfer

full sheet; SS and DS data in a form similar to table of Problem 12 above; 8 spaces between columns; use 2-line main heading: **MEAN EARNINGS OF MEN AND WOMEN/ BY EDUCATIONAL ATTAINMENT**; use secondary heading: **(Persons With Income, Aged 18 and Over).**

			in heading 19
	Men	Women	23
Elementary School			30
Less than 8 years	$ 8,910	$ 4,333	36
8 years	11,481	4,897	41
High School			45
1-3 years	11,056	4,988	50
4 years	14,375	6,750	54
College			57
1-3 years	14,791	7,188	62
4 years or more	23,833	10,696	68
______________			71
Source: Bureau of the Census, Current Population			85
Reports, 1981.			89

Problem 14
Unarranged Table

Arrange table in attractive format on full sheet. Use main heading: **DOES PRODUCTION STOP AS WE GET OLDER?**

Use secondary heading: **(Some Noteworthy Achievements).** Block column headings.

		in headings 14
Age	Achievement	20
85	Grandma Moses wrote her autobiography	28
82	Goethe wrote FAUST	32
79	Benjamin Franklin appointed chief	40
	executive of Pennsylvania	45
76	Margaret Chase Smith served 24th	52
	year as U. S. Senator	57
72	Katharine Hepburn won an Academy	64
	Award for ON GOLDEN POND	69
72	Verdi composed OTHELLO	74

Lesson 177 Message/Reply Memos

177a ▶ 5 Conditioning Practice

each line twice SS (slowly, then faster) DS between 2-line groups; if time permits, rekey selected lines

alphabet 1 Six or seven quiet campers played with amazing skill at Lake Bojekiff.

figures 2 She posted keyboarding rates of 90, 81, 72, 63, and 54 for the timing.

3d row 3 oppose require porter wire treat were order upper reword terror retort

speed 4 They may disown their endowment and amend their title to the big auto.

| 1 | 2 | 3 | 4 | 5 | 6 | 7 | 8 | 9 | 10 | 11 | 12 | 13 | 14 |

177b ▶ 45 Learn to Format Message/Reply Memos

3 message/reply forms (LM p. 49-53); plain sheets for carbon copies; envelopes for COMPANY MAIL

Read the information about message/reply memos on p. 306 and follow procedures given.

Problem 1

Format and process the model memo shown on p. 309. Make 1 cc on a plain sheet; circle errors. Address envelope.

Problem 2

Format and process the memo at top, right, as directed in Problem 1. Address COMPANY MAIL envelope.

words

TO: Miss Fabiola Balza, Director Human Resource Development 301 12
Administration Building DATE: September 8, 19-- SUBJECT: Personnel 22
Selection 24

(¶ 1) At its September 3 meeting, the Board of Directors decided to open two 39
branch operations within the next six months. The locations selected are 53
Independence, Missouri, and Topeka, Kansas. Both communities appear to 68
have excellent growth potential for our type of business. 80

(¶ 2) By the end of this month, I want you to prepare from our list of expe- 94
rienced personnel a list of individuals who have credentials which merit 108
favorable consideration for transfer to our new facilities. I am especially 124
interested in finding individuals who have particularly strong backgrounds 139
in warehousing and shipping. We have already selected our supervisory and 154
managerial staffs. SIGNED: David Kim, Vice President 162

(REPLY) DATE OF REPLY: September 11, 19-- 166

(¶ 1) I shall have the list you requested no later than September 20. Would it 181
be helpful for me to indicate on that list the geographic areas in which the 197
employees live? Perhaps identifying the residence locations for each em- 211
ployee will prove helpful when you consider final assignments. 224
SIGNED: Fabiola Balza 227/**246**

Problem 3

Format and process the memo at the right as directed in Problem 1. Address COMPANY MAIL envelope.

TO: Mrs. Bessie Williams Director of Training 495 Training Center 12
DATE: September 8, 19-- SUBJECT: Scheduling Employee Training 22

(¶ 1) To prepare for our anticipated moves into our two new branch opera- 35
tions, it is imperative for some of our key personnel to be updated on mat- 50
ters relating to their assignments. I should like to have you at the first 65
opportunity enter the following employees in the training programs shown: 80
Ms. Mattie Todd, Inventory Control; Mr. Donald Brummett, Warehouse Man- 95
agement; and Ms. Valerie Beauvier, Marketing Channels. 106

(¶ 2) I shall appreciate learning from you the dates each training session will 120
be scheduled. Thank you. SIGNED: Larry Rogers, Controller 131

(REPLY) DATE OF REPLY: September 12, 19-- 135

(¶) We are now in the process of preparing schedules for all training pro- 149
grams to be offered during the next three-month period. The sessions of 163
particular interest to you should begin in about three weeks and meet three 178
days a week (Mondays, Wednesdays, and Thursdays) for six weeks. As soon 193
as the completed schedule is printed, I shall send you a supply. 206

SIGNED: Bessie Williams 209/**224**

Unit 23 Lessons 111-118

Learning Goals

1. To improve your manuscript and report keyboarding skill.
2. To improve language skills (sentence structure).
3. To improve straight-copy keyboarding skills.

Machine Adjustments

1. Paper guide at *0*.
2. 70-space line and DS, unless otherwise directed.
3. Line space selector on *2* or as directed.

FORMATTING GUIDES: REPORTS

ELECTRONIC DATA/WORD PROCESSORS

Electronic data and word processors have become a way of life. Almost every area of business and many facets of our personal lives have felt their impact.

> Computers are such awesome machines! Their blinking lights . . . produce a mystique that results in both admiration and distrust. . . . But whether we like or dislike them, we cannot ignore them.[1]

Recent technological advances have produced microcomputers and increased the speed of processing words and data. Government agencies, banks, retailers, schools, and homes have found uses for these mystical wonders. For example:

1. after-hour electronic banking
2. automatic scoring devices in bowling alleys
3. electronic controls in home appliances
4. electronic check-out devices in supermarkets
5. electronic information displays in cars
6. electronic patient records in hospitals

Although "fourth generation computers" have personal and business disadvantages as well as advantages, there is little doubt that these mystical devices will have increasing impact on our daily lives in the years to come. "Computers are essential tools of today's society. . . . Everyone, today, needs to understand them."[2]

[1] Louis E. Boone and David L. Kurtz, Contemporary Business (Hinsdale, IL: The Dryden Press, 1976), p. 450.

[2] David R. Adams, Gerald E. Wagner, and Terrence J. Boyer, Computer Information Systems (Cincinnati: South-Western Publishing Co., 1983), p. 26.

Report with Footnotes

Spacing

Reports or manuscripts may be either single- or double-spaced. Double-space school reports, formal reports, and manuscripts to be submitted for publication. Indent the first line of paragraphs 5 spaces. Single-space quoted material of 4 or more lines, indenting 5 spaces from left and right margins. DS above and below quotation.

Margins (Unbound and Leftbound Reports)

Top	Place main heading on: line 10 (pica) line 12 (elite)
Side	1″ left and right margins for unbound 1 1/2″ left and 1″ right margins for leftbound
Bottom	At least 1″ on all pages

Headings and Subheadings

Main heading. Center the main heading in ALL CAPITALS over the *line of writing*. Follow by a quadruple space. **Note:** To find the horizontal center for a leftbound report, add the figures at the left and right margins and divide by 2.

Side headings. Begin side headings at left margin, underline, and capitalize the first letter of all main words. DS above and below side headings.

Paragraph headings. Begin paragraph headings at paragraph indention point, underline, and follow by a period. Capitalize the first letter of the first word.

Reference Notations

Footnotes. If used, place footnotes at the bottom of the page on which the quoted reference appears. Use a divider line (1 1/2″ long) to separate the textual material from the footnotes. DS above and below the divider line. Indent first line of each footnote to the paragraph point and key superior figure about 1/2 line space above footnote line. SS footnotes, but DS between them.

Number footnotes consecutively throughout a report, using superior numbers (raised about 1/2 line space) to refer to the numbered footnotes at the bottom of the page. In planning the placement of footnotes, allow at least a 1 inch bottom margin below footnotes on all pages except the last. Place the footnotes on the last page a DS below the divider line, which separates the footnotes from the report. Footnotes must be arranged in a consistent and acceptable form throughout a report (see illustration on page 199).

Textual citations. Reference citations also may be keyboarded as a part of the text of a report (see page 93). When this is done, footnotes are not used; instead the references are cited by enclosing the author's surname, year of publication, and the page number in parentheses. For example:

(Roberts, 1987, 34)

If the author's name is used in the text of the report, the citation need only include the year and page number. If a reference has no author, the first two or three words of the title are used in place of the author's name. Full information for the textual citations is given in the Reference List at the end of the report.

Page Numbers

The first page may or may not be numbered. The number, if used, is centered and placed on line 62. For second and subsequent pages, place page numbers on line 6 approximately even with the right margin.

Lesson 176 Executive Letters

176a ▶ 5 Conditioning Practice

each line twice SS (slowly, then faster); DS between 2-line groups; if time permits, rekey selected lines

alphabet 1 Hazel Wayman spoke to five adults about judging the aquatic exercises.

figures 2 Julio keyed this figure drill many times today: 487, 139, 50, and 26.

double letters 3 puppy funny assess smooth deepen bubble flurry success illegal repress

speed 4 The handy robot may work for us and make a handle for the antique box.

| 1 | 2 | 3 | 4 | 5 | 6 | 7 | 8 | 9 | 10 | 11 | 12 | 13 | 14 |

176b ▶ 45 Learn to Format Letters on Executive-Size Stationery

letterheads/envelopes (LM pp. 43-47)

1. Read information about executive-size stationery on p. 306 and follow the formatting procedures given there.

2. Use modified block style, open punctuation, for each letter; address envelopes; circle errors.

Problem 1

Format and process the letter shown at the right; use current date.

words

(current date) Miss Mildred Hillenbrand 3907 N. Kessler Boulevard 13
Indianapolis, IN 46208-3842 Dear Miss Hillenbrand 24

(¶ 1) On behalf of the Board of Governors, it is my pleasure to invite you to 38
become a Charter Member of the newly formed Executives Club. This Club 52
is dedicated to providing its members and their guests with superior facili- 68
ties and personal services to help meet their business and social entertain- 83
ment needs. 85

(¶ 2) The Executives Club is located on the top floor of the Hoosier Towers 98
Building at 100 West Washington Street, a convenient location providing a 114
spectacular view of downtown Indianapolis and surrounding countryside. 128
Its quarters include a spacious lounge, elegant dining room, informal grill, 144
and many private dining rooms. 150

(¶ 3) Enclosed is an Executives Club Directory in which you will find infor- 164
mation dealing with the organization and operation of the Club. A list of 179
affiliate and associate clubs in which members may enjoy out-of-town privi- 194
leges is also enclosed. 199

(¶ 4) To accept this invitation, please complete and return the enclosed ac- 213
ceptance form to the Club Secretary. 220

Sincerely yours Leroy Hoffman Chairperson xx Enclosures 3 232/**248**

Problem 2

Format and process the letter shown at the right; use current date.

Problem 3

If time permits, rekey Problem 1, but address it to:

Mrs. Minnie Surian
621 N. Michigan Avenue
South Bend, IN 46601-2614

Provide an appropriate salutation.

(current date) Mr. Dominic Petrucci 2075 North Fairview Drive Columbus, 15
IN 47201-1525 Dear Mr. Petrucci 21

(¶ 1) I am pleased to have your inquiry about the availability of private din- 36
ing rooms of the Executives Club for personal and/or business entertaining. 51
We are uniquely equipped to handle the type of meeting you described, and 66
we shall be happy to try to accommodate you, provided we can work out a 80
mutually satisfactory agreement. 87

(¶ 2) We have a total of 15 private dining rooms of various sizes and appoint- 101
ments. The following ones may interest you: Cardinal, seating capacity of 117
40; Hoosier, seating capacity of 25; Speedway, seating capacity of 15. 131

(¶ 3) Please plan to visit the Club at your earliest convenience so we can dis- 146
cuss your plans and try to reach some decisions concerning details. 159

Sincerely yours Willie Adams Club Manager xx 168/**182**

111a ▶ 5
Conditioning Practice

each line 3 times (slowly, faster, in-between rate); as time permits, repeat selected lines

alphabet 1 The qualified expert analyzed water from seventy cracked jugs by noon.

fig/sym 2 After May 5, Al's new address will be 478 Pax Avenue (ZIP 92106-1593).

adjacent key 3 To permit emotion to control action seriously limits positive results.

speed 4 He did the work for us, but the city paid for it with their endowment.

| 1 | 2 | 3 | 4 | 5 | 6 | 7 | 8 | 9 | 10 | 11 | 12 | 13 | 14 |

111b ▶ 15
Improve Language Skills: Kinds of Sentences

full sheet; 1" top margin; 70-space line; DS

1. Study the definitions and explanatory guides.

2. Keyboard the learn sentences DS, noting the application of the guidelines.

3. Compose sentences as directed DS. Number each sentence.

SENTENCES

Phrases are groups of related words used as subjects, adjectives, or adverbs. They do not express a complete thought and cannot stand alone. Most phrases consist of a preposition and a noun or pronoun.

Clauses, on the other hand, have both a subject and a verb; they are either *independent* or *dependent*. An independent clause forms the principal unit of the sentence; it expresses a complete thought and can stand alone. Even though it has both a subject and a verb, a dependent clause does not express a complete thought and cannot stand alone. It needs the independent clause to make sense.

Learn 1. She came from a small town. *(phrase)*

Learn 2. I laughed when I heard him tell the story. *(independent clause)*

Learn 3. I laughed when I heard him tell the story. *(dependent clause)*

Apply (Number and compose three sentences that contain: 1. a phrase; 2. an independent clause; 3. a dependent clause.)

SIMPLE SENTENCE

A *simple sentence* contains a single independent clause. A simple sentence may have as its subject more than one noun or pronoun and as its predicate more than one verb.

Learn 7. Juan has a new bicycle. *(single subject and single predicate)*

Learn 8. Juan and his brother have a new bicycle. *(subject with two nouns)*

Learn 9. Juan washed and polished his bicycle. *(predicate with two verbs)*

Learn 10. Juan and his brother washed and polished his bicycle. *(subject with two nouns and predicate with two verbs)*

Apply (Number and compose four simple sentences that contain(s): 1. single subject and single predicate; 2. subject with two nouns; 3. predicate with two verbs; and 4. subject with two nouns and predicate with two verbs.)

Unit 38 Lessons 176-180

Learning Goals

1. To build skill in processing letters requiring executive-size stationery.

2. To build skill in processing message-reply memos.

3. To build skill in processing form-paragraph letters.

4. To build production skills on managerial correspondence.

Machine Adjustments

1. Margins: 70-space line for drill copy; as directed for each problem copy.

2. Spacing: SS drill lines with DS between groups; space problems as directed or required.

STANDARD FORMATTING GUIDES: MANAGERIAL CORRESPONDENCE

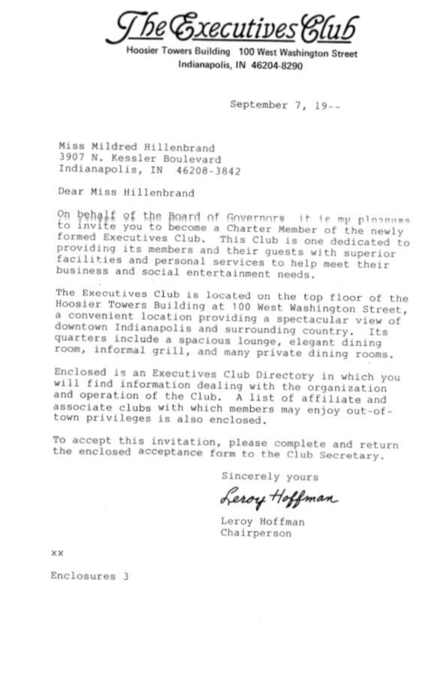

The Executives Club
Hoosier Towers Building 100 West Washington Street
Indianapolis, IN 46204-8290

September 7, 19--

Miss Mildred Hillenbrand
3907 N. Kessler Boulevard
Indianapolis, IN 46208-3842

Dear Miss Hillenbrand

On behalf of the Board of Governors, it is my pleasure to invite you to become a Charter Member of the newly formed Executives Club. This Club is one dedicated to providing its members and their guests with superior facilities and personal services to help meet their business and social entertainment needs.

The Executives Club is located on the top floor of the Hoosier Towers Building at 100 West Washington Street, a convenient location providing a spectacular view of downtown Indianapolis and surrounding country. Its quarters include a spacious lounge, elegant dining room, informal grill, and many private dining rooms.

Enclosed is an Executives Club Directory in which you will find information dealing with the organization and operation of the Club. A list of affiliate and associate clubs with which members may enjoy out-of-town privileges is also enclosed.

To accept this invitation, please complete and return the enclosed acceptance form to the Club Secretary.

Sincerely yours

Leroy Hoffman

Leroy Hoffman
Chairperson

xx

Enclosures 3

Executive-size letter 7¼″ × 10½″

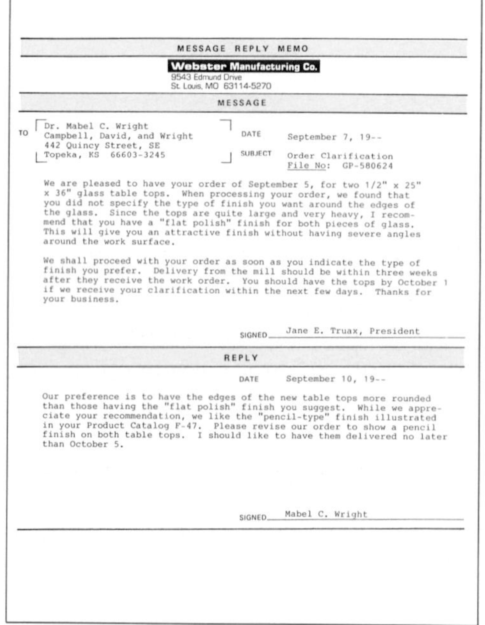

MESSAGE REPLY MEMO

Webster Manufacturing Co.
9543 Edmund Drive
St. Louis, MO 63114-5270

MESSAGE

TO Dr. Mabel C. Wright
Campbell, David, and Wright
442 Quincy Street, SE
Topeka, KS 66603-3245

DATE September 7, 19--

SUBJECT Order Clarification
File No: GP-580624

We are pleased to have your order of September 5, for two 1/2" x 25" x 36" glass table tops. When processing your order, we found that you did not specify the type of finish you want around the edges of the glass. Since the tops are quite large and very heavy, I recommend that you have a "flat polish" finish for both pieces of glass. This will give you an attractive finish without having severe angles around the work surface.

We shall proceed with your order as soon as you indicate the type of finish you prefer. Delivery from the mill should be within three weeks after they receive the work order. You should have the tops by October 1 if we receive your clarification within the next few days. Thanks for your business.

SIGNED Jane E. Truax, President

REPLY

DATE September 10, 19--

Our preference is to have the edges of the new table tops more rounded than those having the "flat polish" finish you suggest. While we appreciate your recommendation, we like the "pencil-type" finish illustrated in your Product Catalog F-47. Please revise our order to show a pencil finish on both table tops. I should like to have them delivered no later than October 5.

SIGNED Mabel C. Wright

Message/reply memo 8½″ × 9¼″

STANDARD FORMATTING PROCEDURES

Executive-Size Stationery (7¼″ × 10½″)

Style. Any business-letter style may be used -- block, modified block, or modified block with indented paragraphs.

Margins: Use one-inch (1″) side margins.

Dateline: Place the date on line 11.

Spacing: Leave three blank lines (space down 4 lines) between the date and the address, and between the complimentary close and the keyed (or printed) name of the sender. Separate all other parts by a double space.

Message/Reply Memos

Forms: Special forms, generally in triplicate (3 copies) and "carbonized," are used. The forms may be either ruled or unruled and are used to exchange messages either within or outside a company. The data required are keyed next to the preprinted headings. The sender keys the message in the "Message" portion of the form. The addressee replies in the "Reply" portion of the form. No reference initials are needed. The original copy and one carbon copy are sent to the recipient; one carbon copy is retained in the file of the originator. The original copy is returned to the sender when the "Reply" has been keyed. Generally, window envelopes are used, requiring no envelope addressing. When regular envelopes are used for in-house mailing, the words COMPANY MAIL are keyed in all capital letters in the upper right-hand corner (stamp location).

Style: Use block style for all entries.

Spacing: Leave 3/4″ side margins. Key required data opposite the headings on "Message" portion of memo; then double-space (DS) to begin the body of the "Message." (If a file number is used in the message/reply memo, it may be keyed under the subject line a single space (SS) below.) On the "Reply" portion of the memo, key the date and double-space (DS) to begin the body of the "Reply."

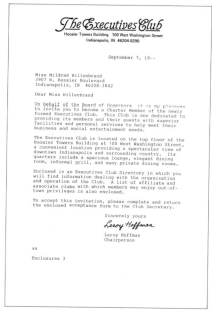

111c ▶ 30
Format and Key an Unbound Report

Key an unbound report from rough-draft copy.

full sheets; DS the ¶s; 5-space ¶ indention; SS the definitions, but DS between them (*as indicated*)

Follow standard directions for keying unbound manuscript and paragraph headings as given on p. 194. Stay alert.

Compuer Terminology) center in ALL CAPS QS

Any new technology quickly develops a set of terms that are peculiar to that new technology. The field of computer systems is no exception ot his generalized statement. As computers have e volved, such terms as bits, bytes, compatibility data bases, debug, hard copy, icons, and modems have evolved. Important to computer literacy is to have a knowledge of such terms. The purpose of this report is to give a vocabulary or selected glossary of computer terms that will help computer operators with many of the mroe common tersm. The selected glossary is shown below. DS

BASIC. Beginner's All-purpose Symbolic Instruction Code--a procedure-oriented computer language.

BAUD. A measurement of transmission rates expressed as "bits per second" or bps. Abbreviation of Baudot. DS

Bit. The smallest binary unit for storing data.

Bug. Mistake.

Byte. A term used to indicate a measureable potion of consecutive binary digits, e.g., and 8- bit or 6-bit byte.

Compatability. The ability of one type of computer system to share information or to communicate with another type of computer.

Cathode-Ray Tube (CRT). Tv-like screen for displaying data.

Computer Program. A set of instructions which directs a computer to perform a sequence or series of task in order to produce a desired result.

Data base. Organized system of data files.

Debug. To test a program to determine if it works.

Diskdrive. A device on which a disk can be mounted for use with a comptuer.

(continued on next page)

Lessons 176-200

PHASE 8

Build Skill in Document Processing

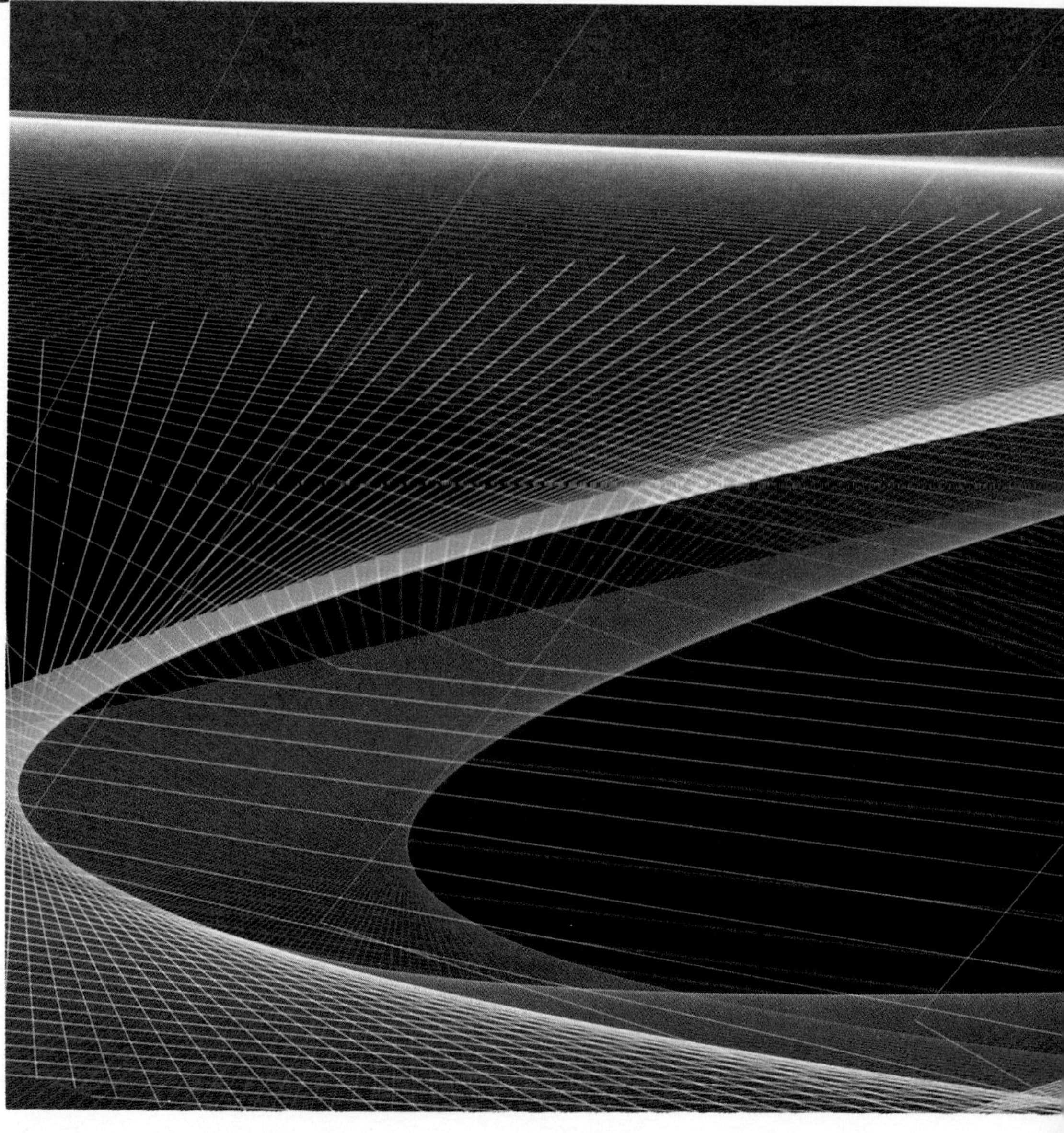

Modern offices require employees to have high skill in keyboarding as well as efficient skills in formatting, text-editing, and document processing. In this phase, you will build and reinforce all of these important office skills while planning, organizing, and making decisions relating to realistic office jobs. Specifically, the objectives of Phase 8 are:

1. To develop formatting/processing skills in handling managerial correspondence and letters with special features.

2. To develop formatting/processing skills on special-type communications, such as memos, news releases, and minutes.

3. To improve keyboarding/language skills.

4. To develop and strengthen integrated production skills.

DOS. Disk Operating System.

Disk, floppy. An oxide coated plasic disk which can be used for magnetically sorting information.

Flow charting. The processs of graphically showing the detailed steps in the solution of a problem.

GIGO. "Garbage In, Garbage Out"--an expression used to describe a poor program or when inappropriate data is ~~inputer,~~ inputted.

Graphics. The use of diagrams or other writen symbols and visual displays.

Hard copy. A printed copy of machine output in a ~~good~~ visually readable form.

Icon. A visual image on the display or screen indicating a computer function, such as a miniature file drawer for storage and retrieval.

Input. Information or data transferred or to be transferred from an external source into the internal storage of a computer.

K {Kilo}. Abbreviation denoting ~~24~~ 1,024 Bytes.

Menu. A numbered list of choices from which a selection can be made in using a computer.

Modem. A device which converts data from a form which is compatible with data processing equipment to a form which is compatible with transmission facilities, and vice versa.

Output. Information that is produced as a reult of processing data.

Printer. Device used for printing of information prepared on a computer.

RAM. "Random Access Memory"--a type of computer memory in which data may be "written in" or "read out."

Scrolling. Moving lines displayed on a terminal screen either up or down.

Software. Programs written for computer systems.

Word processing. The processing, manipulation, and storage of information needed in the preparation of written communications.

This glossary of computer terms is not intended to be all-inclusive. Other terms, and new terms which evolve, will become a part of the basic vocabulary of anyone who learns to use a computer in school, in the home, or in the business world.

commands, you will be ready to learn the editing commands in Part 5.

When you have finished Part 4, you will have learned how to create a docuement; and you may wish to make some changes in it. Part 5 describes the editing commands that allow you to do so. We recommend that you go through the exercises** at the end of Part 5 before continuing through the formatting commands.

In Part 6, default formatting values--those already set in the program--are explained, and directions are given for changing those values. The KEY systems allow maximum flexibility in formatting documents. Practice exercises are included at the end of this section.

Before printing a document, KEYspell may be used to locate spelling and typergraphical errors. Directions for using KEYspell, as well as directions for adding and deleting words to and from the dictionery so you can tailor this part of the program to your specialized vocabulary, are given in Part 7.

The Programmer's Notes in Part 8 were written to answer frequently asked questions by programmers. It is technical in nature and may be omited by nontechnical users.

The final part of the manual is a complete index to facilitate ease and speed in using this document as a reference.

<u>Part 3: KEYteach</u>

Most of the directions for KEYteach are included in the program and will appear on your screen. Only those items about which we think you may need additional explanation or for which we have some special tips will be listed here. So, insert the teach disk in Drive 1, turn your system on, and wait for the first set of instructions on your screen.

<u>Using the cursor</u>. The cursor is the square blinking light that you see on your screen. Its purpose is to show you on what line and space the next character you key will be located. The two cursor control keys on your KEY 6000 are located on the top row of the numeric keypad. They are the keys with arrows indicating the directions of cursor movement that they control. For example, the cursor key on the right side of the numeric keypad will move the cursor either right or left. The shift key must be used simaltaneously to move the cursor to the left. Similarly, the cursor key on the left side of the numeric keypad will move the cursor either up or down {requires shift}.

<u>Creating a document</u>. If you hear a beep while keying your document name, do not become alarmed. You have made an error in the document name, but that can be easily corrected. Just move the cursor to the position of the error and key the correction.

**Written by Ken Stevens, a long-time KEY user.

112a ▶ 5
Conditioning Practice

each line 3 times (slowly, faster, top speed); as time permits, repeat selected lines

alphabet 1 Liquid oxygen fuel was used to give this big jet rocket amazing speed.

fig/sym 2 We bought a 144″ × 96″ drapery, priced at $128.95, on sale for $63.70.

first row 3 Vince named his baby Zana, Ben named his Maxinc, and I named mine Ann.

speed 4 If they do the work for us, they then may go to the lake with the men.

| 1 | 2 | 3 | 4 | 5 | 6 | 7 | 8 | 9 | 10 | 11 | 12 | 13 | 14 |

112b ▶ 10
Improve Language Skills: Kinds of Sentences

1. STUDY explanatory rules.

2. Key line number (with period); space twice, and key LEARN sentence(s) DS, noting rule application.

3. Number and key APPLY sentence(s) DS as directed.

COMPOUND SENTENCE

A compound sentence contains two or more independent clauses connected by a coordinating conjunction (and, but, for, or, nor).

Learn 1. Brian Yaeger likes to hike, and Beau James likes to swim.
(contains two independent clauses)

Learn 2. A fire is crackling in the fireplace, the skiers are relaxing, and dinner is being prepared. *(contains three independent clauses)*

Apply (Number and compose two compound sentences.)

COMPLEX SENTENCE

A complex sentence contains only one independent clause but one or more dependent clauses.

Learn 5. The book that you gave Juan for his birthday was lost.
(dependent clause is in color)

Learn 6. If I were you, I would speak to Paul before I left.
(dependent clauses are in color)

Apply (Number and compose two complex sentences.)

112c ▶ 35
Format and Key a Leftbound Report with Footnotes

full sheet

Review the general guidelines for keying leftbound reports and footnotes on page 194. Then, key model on page 199, following the guidelines given there.

Correct errors if your teacher so directs.

Note. The model on page 199 is shown in pica type; if you are keying in elite, your line endings will be different, but your spacing will be the same.

Learning Guide: When formatting manuscripts with footnotes, a simple procedure to remind you to leave a 1″ bottom margin is to do the following:

Make a light pencil mark at the right edge of the sheet 1″ from the bottom. As you key each footnote reference number, add another pencil mark 1/2″ above the previous one. In this way, you will reserve about 3 line spaces for each footnote at the bottom of the sheet. Erase marks when you have completed the page.

If you have a page line gauge (LM, p. 7), use it.

To position the footnote reference figures: Turn the platen forward a half space if your machine has vertical half spacing; use the automatic line finder and turn the platen forward a half space on machines that do not have vertical half spacing.

<u>KEYspell</u>.* One of the enhancements of KEY Word Processing is KEYspell, which is used to find your typographical and spelling errors. KEYspell is a 20,000-word dictionary; and if that is not enough, you can add up to 1,000 more words that are unique to your vocabulary. KEYspell is actually a part of the KEY Word Processing program, so it is no longer necessary to change disks when you are ready to do a spelling check.

<u>KEYteach</u>. What better way can there be to learn to use KEY Word Processing than to let the computer assist in the instruction? KEY-teach introduces you to the basics of word processing and gives you step-by-step directions for using all of the commands in the main menu. Oops! Here we go using "computereze" again. KEYteach will even explain what a main menu is.

The KEY Word Processing system is one of the most powerful on the market, yet it is easy to learn and simple to use. The amount of memorization needed for learning to use the program is minimal and the help command is always available when you do forget. How-ever, once you have mastered the system, there are several shortcuts that you may select. The program provides alternatives to fit the needs of our numerous users.

<u>Part 2: How to Use This Manual</u>

This manual provides a detailed reference for using KEY Word Processing, including KEYspell and KEYteach. It is divided into the following parts:

1. Welcome to KEY
2. How to Use This Manual
3. KEYteach
4. KEY Main Menu Commands
5. KEY Editing Commands
6. KEY Formatting Commands
7. KEYspell
8. Programmers Notes
9. Index

Once you have read the first two parts, you are ready to start learning some of the basics of word processing and the main commands of menus. KEYteach is an excellent place to start, particularly if this is your first experence with a word processing program. How-ever, if you are all ready familiar with word processing terms and concepts, you may elect to by pass the teach program and learn how to use the main menu by going directly to Part 4.

If you use KEYteach, and we highly recommend that you do, you may then use Part 4 for later reference. It duplicates the information included in Part 3, KEYteach, but omits the practice exercises. When you feel reasonably comfortable with the main menu

*Also available as a separate program.

Line 10 (pica)
Line 12 (elite)

ELECTRONIC DATA/WORD PROCESSORS

QS

1½" left margin

1" right margin

Electronic data and word processors have become a way of life. Almost every area of business and many facets of our personal lives have felt their impact.

Indent quotation 5 spaces from left and right margins.

> Computers are such awesome machines! Their blinking lights . . . produce a mystique that results in both admiration and distrust. . . . But whether we like or dislike them, we cannot ignore them.[1]

Recent technological advances have produced microcomputers and increased the speed of processing words and data. Government agencies, banks, retailers, schools, and homes have found uses for these mystical wonders. For example:

Indent enumerated items 5 spaces from left and right margins.

1. after-hour electronic banking
2. automatic scoring devices in bowling alleys
3. electronic controls in home appliances
4. electronic check-out devices in supermarkets
5. electronic information displays in cars
6. electronic patient records in hospitals

Although "fourth generation computers" have personal and business disadvantages as well as advantages, there is little doubt that these mystical devices will have increasing impact on our daily lives in the years to come. "Computers are essential tools of today's society. . . . Everyone, today, needs to understand them."[2]

DS

____

DS

[1]Louis E. Boone and David L. Kurtz, Contemporary Business (Hinsdale, IL: The Dryden Press, 1976), p. 450.

DS

[2]David R. Adams, Gerald E. Wagner, and Terrence J. Boyer, Computer Information Systems (Cincinnati: South-Western Publishing Co., 1983), p. 26.

(at least 1" bottom margin)

Leftbound Report with Footnotes

171b-175b (continued)

Job 8 (full sheets)
Report, Title Page, Table of Contents

Maxine Jackson, the office manager, has asked you to work on the revision of the manual to accompany an update of KEY Word Processing, which is software developed for the KEY 6000 series. She knows that you will not be able to complete the manual during your week in this job, but she hopes you can complete the pages assigned.

1. Process the report for binding at the left. Main heading: **KEY WORD PROCESSING**; secondary heading: **PC-6000 Series**. Correct any errors you may find.

2. Prepare a title page containing the following information:

KEY WORD PROCESSING
PC-6000 Series
Version 3.1
KEY Office Systems
1246 State Street
Kansas City, KS 66102-1824

3. Prepare a rough draft copy of the Table of Contents for the portion of the manual that you process. Proofread and mark errors using proofreader's marks (see RG p. 10). Then prepare the copy in final form for binding at the left.

Part 1: Welcome to KEY

Your selection of a KEY Series 6000 computer can create an amazing new world for you. The KEY is a powerful tool that may be used to organize, process, and, manage information; or it may become your most poplar entertainment center. Regardless of whether you work or play at your KEY 6000, you will find that some understanding of "computerese," the terms used to communicate in the computer world will be helpful.

The KEY 6000 computer is known as the hardware and built into the hardware is one kind of software known as the operating system. All computers have an operating system which acts somewhat as a traffic director by keeping the electrical signals moving in the right way and alloting space to the various kinds of memory. Another kind of soft ware is a program that you may develop or purchase that gives the computer instructions for doing specific tasks such as word processing or balancing your checkbook. The software, or program that is described in this manual is designed for the specific task of word processing.

KEY Word Processing is the program that turns your Series 6000 KEY computer into an electronic typewriter. This application software allows you to do some rather amazing things with the Series 6000. You can add, delete, move and copy text--and much much more in a matter of seconds, something that you always wished you could do with your regular typewriter. The dridgery of having to rekey material that has been revised or rearranged is gone forever.

113a ▶ 5
Conditioning Practice

each line 3 times (slowly, faster, top speed); as time permits, repeat selected lines

alphabet 1 The winning team just broke every existing record for playing bezique.

fig/sym 2 Is Check #1576 for $48.90, dated May 23, made out to McNeil & O'Brien?

adjacent key 3 If we are to oppose the oppressive restriction, we must do so quietly.

speed 4 It is a civic duty to handle their problem with proficiency and rigor.

| 1 | 2 | 3 | 4 | 5 | 6 | 7 | 8 | 9 | 10 | 11 | 12 | 13 | 14 |

113b ▶ 10
Improve Language Skills: Kinds of Sentences

Follow standard directions given with 111b, p. 195.

COMPOUND-COMPLEX SENTENCE

A compound-complex sentence has at least two independent clauses and one or more dependent clauses. (*In the examples below, the independent clauses are in color.*)

Learn 1. He will go with us if you do his work, but you must do the work today.

Learn 2. In Carmel, we spent the morning looking for oil paintings that we would like, but we were unsuccessful.

(*Note that Sentence 2 is introduced by the phrase, "In Carmel."*)

Apply (Number and compose two compound-complex sentences.)

113c ▶ 35
Format and Key Leftbound Report with Footnotes

full sheets; DS the ¶s; set tab for 5-space ¶ indention; SS and indent quotations of 4 or more lines 5 spaces from left and right margins

MICROCOMPUTERS QS

Microcomputers have now become commonplace. They are used by business offices for information processing, by schools for various educational activities, by medical doctors to interact with medical databases, by attorneys to research case data, and by individuals in the home to perform a variety of special tasks. In schools and in homes, microcomputers have become one of this decade's most potent tools. Yet without software to direct them how to perform, computers can be simply expensive boxes with blank faces. Conversely, with carefully designed software packages or tied into extensive knowledge databases, computers can be exciting, stimulating, and effective tools for directing learning.

The key question is: Will the computer take over the business of education with neither teachers nor schools being necessary? The answer is an emphatic No! Computers just cannot provide the many types of learning experiences that can be offered in schools by human teachers. Cornish says:

> . . . teachers will continue to be needed in the future and so will schools. Teachers will provide

171b-175b (continued)

Job 5 (full sheet)
Table

Sheila Sanders needs to have this table prepared to submit to Philip Rice, her manager. Use the following headings:

Main heading: **CLIENT CONTACTS MADE BY SHEILA SANDERS**; Secondary heading: **Week Ending (fill in last Friday's date)**; Column 1: **Name of Client;** Column 2: **Length of Visit;** Column 3: **Contact Mode**

Gary L. Sawatzky	1.5 hrs.	My office
Cynthia Grossman	10 min.	Telephone
Barbara Schlosser	25 min.	Telephone
Gilbert Wagner	2 hrs.	Their office
Carl C. Cook	2.25 hrs.	Their office
Jana Washburn	1.75 hrs.	Their office
Paula Murphy	1 hr.	My office
Robyn O'Connor	45 min.	Telephone
Eric Daniels	1.5 hrs.	Their office
Kelly Miller	2.5 hrs.	Their office

I need this table as soon as possible for a conference with Mr. Rice this afternoon. Thank you. Sheila

Job 6 (LM p. 31)
Compose a Letter

Compose a letter to Jeanine Daniels from Deborah Matsuo. A note indicating the information to be included in the letter is shown at the right.

Send letter to Jeanine Daniels saying I am glad she can accept the Baker job. Ask if she can come next Thursday or Friday (insert correct date) for a meeting with Baker. There are early and late direct flights between Dallas/Fort Worth and Kansas City, or we can make a hotel reservation for her. We'll meet her at the airport. Let us know travel plans.

Job 7 (full sheets)
Tables

Using the information from the catalog page at the right, prepare two price quotations for Frank Randall. The main title of each table should be **"Price Quotation for (fill in company name)."** One company is Standard Office Supply, and the other is Morton Associates, Inc. Use **"Effective Through December 31, 19--"** as a secondary heading. Be sure to add the 10% discount note at the bottom of each.

The items to be listed on each price quotation are on Frank's notes at the left of the catalog information. Arrange each table so that item numbers are in numerical sequence and match description and unit price on catalog page.

STANDARD OFFICE SUPPLY
PC-4001A
PC 4031A
PC 4041A
PC 4025A
4054M
6704X
7210X

MORTON ASSOCIATES, INC.
PC-4001A
PC 4031A
PC 4041A
PC 4024A
PC 5026A
4051M
6402X
8401X

Frank

Item No.	Description	Unit Price*
PC-4001A	Microprocessor	$2,895
PC-4031A	Input/Output Unit	589
PC-4041A	Dual Disk Drive	416
PC-4024A	Dot Matrix Printer	325
PC-4025A	Daisy Wheel Printer	895
PC-5026A	Color Graphics Printer	475
4051M	Color Monitor	325
4054M	B/W Monitor	195
8401X	Glare Guard	95
6402X	Data Entry Station	185
6704X	Power Surge Strip	70
7210X	Printer Stand	195

*10% discount on orders over $5,000.

113c (continued)

> leadership, gently guiding (students) in the right direction and counseling them when difficulties occur. Schools will provide a safe environment in which (students) can engage in many types of learning experiences.[1]

Two very important technologies in education will be video and computer systems. Videotapes and videodisks will make it possible for master teachers to produce effective learning programs that can teach almost any subject. These programs will be designed to capture the interest of the learner. Students will be able to check out videotapes from school libraries, and they will be able to use them in special instructional cubicles located in the school or in their homes if they have a videotape player. These new technologies will help to make education much more effective than it has been in the past. Students will learn material faster, and teachers will have more time to deal with individual student learning problems.[2] Beechhold supports the view that the computer in the classroom can have positive enhancing effects; if used correctly, he feels that computers can be an invaluable aid to the creative teacher in the educational process.[3]

Another question frequently raised about computers is the following: Can computers be so programmed that they will have a type of artificial intelligence (AI) comparable to human intelligence? If so, it would mean that computers would have to define and organize the vast amount of knowledge that we have stored in the 100 billion nerve cells, known as "neurons," that make up our brains. These neurons, when stimulated, fire electromechanical impulses across the microscopic gaps called "synapses" at the rate of thousands per second. This is what "thinking" is all about, and so far even highly sophisticated computers cannot do that kind of thinking. Nor do they possess the ordinary sort of knowledge that is called "common sense." Common sense, together with language skills, seems to define the essence of what it means to be human and to have human intelligence.[4]

---

[1] Edward Cornish, "Computer Can't Replace the Teacher," Los Angeles Times, 10 May 1985, Part V, p. 2.

[2] Cornish, p. 2.

[3] Henry F. Beechhold, "Computerized Classroom Visions," PC, May 28, 1985, pp. 303-305.

[4] Frank Rose, Into the Heart of the Mind (New York: Harper & Row, 1984), pp. 12-23.

Nevertheless, microcomputers and the new technology are having and will continue to have a profound effect on everything we do, whether in school, in ~~our~~ workplaces, or in ~~our~~ homes.

171b-175b (continued)

Job 2 (LM p. 27)
Letter

This letter was prepared by Deborah Matsuo and should be sent to Jeanine Daniels at the address shown in 154b, p. 273. Use her first name in the salutation. Correct any errors you may find.

Last week at our regional office automation conference, I visited with Joan Thompson of besco Systems. She indicated that you have just completed a project for them and that they are most pleased with the organizational structure you recommended. Now I am wondering if you would like to do a similar job for a company that I am working with here in Kansas City.

For the past month, I have been working with the Baker Mini-Storage firm to determine its office automation needs. During my study of Baker's home office here in Kansas City and 14 branch offices throughout the Southwest, it has become apparent to me that the present organizational structure is not working well. Baker represents the usual story of a company that started small about five years ago and enjoyed rapid growth and success. However, this success story will be short-lived, I predict, unless it does something soon to add order to the chaos {the term used by Baker's president} in which it now operates.

I believe that, working together, we can provide the kind of help that Baker needs. If office procedures can be modified and the organization is restructured at the same time that an automated office system is implimented, I think Baker will see an immediate improvement in productivity.

Mona Schooley, our educational specialist, is working with me on this assignment; and we would like to have you join us if you can start within the next two weeks.

Job 3 (full sheet)
Table

The copy at the right is a portion of a page from the manual from one of our printers. David Martin needs it prepared in table form for one of his clients. The only directions he left are those on the note attached to the page.

Full sheet; omit rulings. Heading: PRINT SIZES

Thanks. Dave

Ch/Line	Ch/Inch	Remarks
136	17	Condensed characters
68	8.5	Condensed enlarged characters
80	10	Pica-pitch characters
40	5	Pica-pitch enlarged characters
96	12	Elite-pitch characters
48	6	Elite-pitch enlarged characters

Job 4 (LM p. 29)
Letter

Process the letter of Job 1 again with the changes shown at the right. Address it to:

Charles Rathbun Office Manager Star Heating and Air Conditioning 421 Anglum Drive Hazlewood, MO 63042-2243

¶1 - Change KEY 8000 to KEY 6000.

¶2 - Change Thursday to Wednesday.
Change David Martin to Sheila Sanders.

¶3 - Add (913) at beginning of telephone no.

P.A.R.

114a-118a ▶ 5 (daily)

Conditioning Practice

each line 3 times (slowly, faster, top speed); as time permits, repeat selected lines

alphabet	1	Fine cooks brought piquant flavor to exotic foods with zesty marjoram.
fig/sym	2	The purchase price is $14,573.89 plus 6% sales tax and 20% excise tax.
space bar	3	Try to do the work for Jim and then go with me to the city for a week.
speed	4	Sight the visitor, turn the dial to the right, and focus the eye lens.

| 1 | 2 | 3 | 4 | 5 | 6 | 7 | 8 | 9 | 10 | 11 | 12 | 13 | 14 |

114b-115b ▶ 15

Measure and Improve Keyboarding Skill: Straight Copy

two 3′ writings; then one 5′ writing

Goal: To maintain 3′ rate for 5′.

Proofread; circle errors; record better 3′ and 5′ rates.

all letters used | A | 1.5 si | 5.7 awl | 80% hfw |

	gwam 3′	5′	
What does it mean to be a good manager and a good leader? Early in	4	3	52
life you learned to manage yourself, your time, and your energies so that	9	6	55
you could accomplish a given task in a given period of time. This is the	14	9	58
initial requirement of a good manager. As you learned self-management	19	11	60
skills, you probably developed leadership skills. A good leader has a	24	14	63
deep respect and just concern for others. He or she can bring out the	29	17	66
best in others by seeking out and encouraging others to develop to their	33	20	69
fullest potentials.	35	21	70
This type of self-confidence may develop from a conscientious effort	39	24	72
to determine one's abilities and weaknesses and zealously to do something	44	27	75
about them. It is tempered by experience and by the acquisition of a	50	29	78
sense of oneself in relation to others and to the world. Next, a good	54	32	81
leader and a good manager needs to plan carefully, to determine the	58	35	84
chance of success or failure of an act, and to give much thought to a	63	38	87
course of action before making a decision to proceed. Such a person is	68	41	89
concerned with a vision of a future that is worthy of achievement. Good	72	43	92
management and good leadership skill, then, is that intangible ability to	77	46	95
motivate yourself and others to perform beyond the ordinary.	81	50	98

gwam 3′ | 1 | 2 | 3 | 4 | 5 |
5′ | 1 | 2 | 3 |

171a-175a ▶ 5
Check Equipment

Each day before you begin work on the jobs, check your equipment to see that it is in good working order by keying the paragraph at least twice (first slowly, then faster).

All letters and figures used

Ken was recognized as the high-scoring player in 20 of their 38 games. He scored just over half the points last week (57), which made a total of 1,469 for the season. His "extra" effort resulted in quite a bonus paid to all of the men, a big surprise both to the men and to Ken too.

| 1 | 2 | 3 | 4 | 5 | 6 | 7 | 8 | 9 | 10 | 11 | 12 | 13 | 14 |

171b-175b ▶ 45
An Electronic Office System Simulation

Study the information on p. 298 before starting the simulation and refer to it as needed throughout the processing of the jobs. Correct any errors you may find.

Job 1 (LM p. 25)
Letter

This letter is from **Philip A. Rice**, who is the sales manager.

Address letter to:

Mrs. Karen K. Moretti
Administrative Systems Manager
H & S Designs, Inc.
P.O. Box 2001
Kansas City, KS 66110-3468

Please process this letter and Job 4 immediately. M.J.

Your request for a ~~computer~~ demonstration [of our office system] next week is one that we can easily accomodate. Your busness is one that (we believe) can profitably use several of the software applications that the KEY 8000 system supports, and we are pleased to have the oppertunity to discuss your needs with you.

Since you sugested that ~~Wednesday~~ [Thursday] afternoon would be the best time for you, we would like to schedule David Martin, our sales representative for ~~130 pm~~ [1:30 p.m.]. It would be ideal if he could spend about (2) [sp.] hours with you and the other persone[n]l who ~~you expect to~~ [will] be frequent users of this system.

It will take about ~~thirty~~ [30] minutes for ~~Henry~~ [Dave] to set up the equipment, so you may wish to schedule the demonstration to begin at 2 ~~oclock~~ [p.m.]. If for some reason these plans need to be changed just call me at 722-4448. The group size should be limited to about (6) [sp.] people.

114c-115c ▶ 30
116b-117b ▶ 45
118b ▶ 25

Format and Key Leftbound Report with Textual Citations

full sheets; center heading over line of writing; DS ¶s; 5 space ¶ indention; errors corrected

Use margins and spacing as given for leftbound report on model page 199, and in guidelines, page 194.

Show page numbers on second and additional pages in upper right corner.

Note. You are not expected to complete the manuscript in this lesson; additional time is provided in Lessons 115-118.

The textual citation form of reference notation is to be used (*as illustrated in manuscript*). This is the preferred form to use in manuscripts prepared for publication.

Guide: Make a light pencil mark at the right edge of the sheet 1″ from the bottom and another 1/2″ above the 1″ mark as a page-end reminder; or, use the page-line gauge provided in LM, p. 7.

IMPROVE YOUR WRITING — Center

QS

All of us have a need to write no mat t er what we do in life. Writing well is a problem that has concerned our schools since their beginning. This report emphasizes the general principles that lead to good writing or composing.

What Is Writing?

Sometime ago, the National Council of Teachers of English formed a Committee on Writing Standards to try to find out what good writing is all about. The Committee (1979, 220) has given us a definition of writing that is still useful: "Writing is the process of selecting, combining, arranging, and developing ideas in effective sentences, paragraphs, and often longer units of discourse."

"Good writing," according to the American Psychological Association (1967, 15), "is clear, precise, unambiguous, and economical."

When you or I ~~set~~ sit down to write, we tend to follow the writing process that the Committee on Writing Standards spoke about. Thoughts and ideas flow from the words we use, with the words forming sentences and the sentences growing into paragraphs. The process may be difficult at first, but it becomes easier with time and practice. Eventually, we not only learn to put our ideas ~~on~~ onto paper, but we learn to put those ideas in a form that effectively conveys what we mean to the reader. The reader reverses the process: decoding print into words and words into thought.

Good writing is not a set of rules of writing to be memorized. And this issue creates one of the problems of writing. It is often easier to ~~teach~~ learn codified rules than to learn how to write; it is often easier to learn about language than to learn how to use language. Goodlad (1984, 205) supports this point when he indicates that more emphasis

(continued on next page)

Unit 37 Lessons 171-175

Learning Goals

To integrate the knowledge and skills reviewed and acquired in Phase 7 in:

1. processing documents.
2. detecting errors.
3. applying communication skills.
4. making decisions.

Documents Processed

1. letters
2. tables
3. report
4. table of contents
5. title page

KEY OFFICE SYSTEMS: AN ELECTRONIC OFFICE SYSTEM SIMULATION

Unit 37 is designed to give you a close parallel to working in a real office. Assume that you are presently employed part time by KEY Office Systems to do general office tasks, such as answering the telephone, photocopying, filing, and formatting/keyboarding. You will soon be completing a course of study in secretarial education and would like to have a full-time position with KEY. One of the full-time secretaries will be on vacation for a week, and Mrs. Jackson, the office manager, has asked you to fill this position for that week. You regard this as a great opportunity to show Mrs. Jackson and the other personnel for whom you will work that you are qualified to fill such a position.

Here are some directions and tips that will help you succeed in this assignment:

1. Use the current date on correspondence.
2. Supply appropriate opening and closing lines for correspondence, being careful to follow all of the guidelines given below and the particular preferences of some of the people for whom you will work. Supply appropriate personal titles (Mr., Dr., Ms., Mrs., Miss) in the opening lines by looking at previous correspondence to/from that person or by using your judgment. If you cannot determine the appropriate title for a woman, use Ms. In the salutation, use the addressee's personal title and last name unless directed to use a first name.
3. Use your reference initials and supply enclosure notation(s), if needed.
4. Use your judgment for letter styles and formatting problems except when specific directions are given in these guidelines, with the problem, or with individual preferences.
5. Be particularly alert to correct errors in punctuation, capitalization, spelling, and consistency (for example, "KEY" appears in ALL CAPS when referring to the company or a product made by the company). All of the personnel for whom you will be working will be depending on you to detect and correct all such errors.

During this week you will be working for the personnel listed below. The titles that you will need for processing their work are included. In addition, two of them have special preferences concerning their letter styles and the complimentary close to be used.

Your immediate supervisor is:

Mrs. Maxine Jackson
Office Manager

The sales personnel are:

Philip A. Rice
Sales Manager
He prefers modified block letter style with mixed punctuation. The complimentary close that he likes is "Sincerely yours."

Ms. Sheila Sanders
Sales Representative

David Martin
Sales Representative

Frank L. Randall
Sales Representative

The business consultants are:

Miss Deborah Matsuo
Office Systems Analyst
She prefers block letter style with open punctuation. She likes a complimentary close of "Sincerely." She uses the personal title "Miss" in the closing lines of her letters.

Dr. Mona Schooley
Educational Specialist

in writing needs to be given to self-expression and creative thought, rather than to learning basic language use skills and mastering mechanics -- capitalization, punctuation, parts of speech, and the like. And yet, we must emphasize good sentence structure if what we write is to have meaning.

Further, writing is difficult because it differs greatly from our spoken English. Graves and Hodge (1979, 17) point up this difference as follows:

> ...there are everywhere obvious differences between written and spoken English. A speaker reinforces his meaning with gestures and vocal inflections, and if people he addresses still do not understand, they can ask for further explanations; whereas a writer, not enjoying either of these advantages, must formulate and observe certain literary principles if he wishes to be completely understood.

Since the writer must rely solely on the written language to get the ideas across to the audience, he or she must write effectively. Written English, unlike spoken English, often has only one shot at getting the reader's interest and attention. And so, we must give it our best shot!

Why Writing Is Important

Writing helps us review and revise our ideas as we think through what it is we want to write. Professor Carlos Baker highlights an important aspect of writing: "Learning to write is learning to think" (Cross, 1979, 226). Dr. S. I. Hayakawa, a semanticist deeply concerned with the meaning of language, says much the same thing when he tells us, "You just don't know anything until you can write it" (Cross, 226).

Writing helps us remember things and so makes us better learners; it contributes to our success, not only in school but also in our jobs and careers. It is a necessary and important skill to master if we are to function in the modern culture.

Further, as pointed out by the Committee on Writing Standards, "Writing can be a deeply personal act of shaping our perceptions of the world and our relationships to people and things in that world" (1979, 220). Writing can be an important means of self-discovery, of finding out what we believe and know.

Some Suggestions to Help You Improve Your Writing

Good writing seems to grow best when all four elements of discourse (listening, speaking, reading, and writing) are constantly woven together. For example, a history class utilizes the elements of discourse when students read textbooks, listen to historical accounts, discuss events, and write reports and essays.

1. Listening. Listening is one of the primary ways we learn: Without listening and learning, we would have little to say in our writing. Our first experiences in listening occur when we are babies. Through these early experiences, we assimilate a vast amount of information in a short time, making it possible to relate to the world and to learn the basics of communication skills. Later, in school, we learn still more as ideas are discussed. Listening is crucial to learning, and thus, crucial to the writing process.

2. Speaking. We can't listen for long without speaking. Basic to good writing is being able to verbalize well -- to put our thoughts into words effectively. Just as we have a "voice" in the classroom when we express our opinions, so do we have our own unique "voice" in our writing. As we learn to convey our thoughts with facility when speaking with others, we find that conveying those same opinions in our writing becomes easier.

3. Reading. Most of us can improve our writing by reading, especially if we read good prose. As we read, we should note how an author captures our attention with words -- words that may stir the imagination. We should study how an author chooses to put these words together to form sentences (sentence structure) for a desired effect. A good writer takes care to choose words with just the correct shade of meaning. He or she takes care to create the best sentence structure. Note how the two authors quoted below have effectively used words and sentence structure to bring about a desired effect. The first author, wishing to capture "present action," uses short sentences and repetition for effect. The second author uses parallel phrases, lists, and figurative language to create a sense of the mysterious or unknown.

(continued on next page)

170b, (continued)

Problem 3 (half sheet, full sheet)

1. Take a 10′ writing on the table at the right on a half sheet, long side up; SS body; 6 spaces between columns. Use the following column headings:

Column 1: **Company**
Column 2: **Home Office**
Column 3: **Telephone Number**

2. If you finish the table before time is called, begin again on a full sheet DS.

3. After time is called, proofread the 3 problems and correct errors.

			words
TOLL-FREE TELEPHONE NUMBERS			6
FOR CUSTOMER PROBLEMS AND COMPLAINTS			13
			words in heading 28
Boswell Electronics	Miami, FL	800-897-2464	36
Continental Enterprises	Cincinnati, OH	800-984-8354	46
Cornerstone Developers	New York, NY	800-663-0433	56
H & M Supplies, Inc.	Atlanta, GA	800-284-1127	65
Unity Associates, Inc.	Los Angeles, CA	800-776-0234	75

170c ▶ 8 Evaluate Straight-Copy Skill

1. Take a 5′ writing; determine *gwam* and errors.

2. Compare with your score for 158b, p. 277.

3. Record on LM p. 3 for comparison in Lesson 153c, p. 271.

all letters used | A | 1.5 si | 5.7 awl | 80% hfw |

gwam 3′ | 5′

If you are one of those persons who sits around just waiting for 5 | 3 | 57
a prized promotion to happen to you, possibly you should examine the 9 | 5 | 60
situation and determine if some alternative action might be appropri- 14 | 8 | 63
ate. If you know you are capable and qualified, then you should view 18 | 11 | 65
your present job as one in which to demonstrate what you can do rather 23 | 14 | 68
than waiting silently for another opportunity to come your way. 27 | 16 | 71

It takes more than just hard work to bring about success. You may 32 | 19 | 73
know a person who has worked very hard but nevertheless has failed. 36 | 22 | 76
The person in this spot likely did not realize that goals must be set 41 | 24 | 79
and a belief developed in the ability to reach them. Being successful 46 | 27 | 82
requires great energy, and putting energies into motion can be a stimu- 50 | 30 | 85
lating experience. 52 | 31 | 86

Dreaming of great accomplishments is important if you organize 56 | 33 | 88
your life to allow adequate time to pursue those dreams. To do so, 61 | 36 | 91
you must adjust your life to eliminate trivial tasks. For example, 65 | 39 | 93
people sometimes accept busywork as being of worth when they should 70 | 42 | 96
make a quick appraisal of what is really important to them. The real 74 | 44 | 99
goal is to find out what you want most out of life. 78 | 47 | 101

Without specific goals, it is easy to rationalize lack of drive 82 | 49 | 104
on a job. Therefore, the first step is to set specific goals; the 87 | 52 | 106
next step required is to adjust your mental attitude about success. 99 | 55 | 109

gwam 3′
5′

> There was a tug on the line. Nick pulled against the taut line. It was his first strike. Holding the now living rod across the current, he brought up the line with his left hand. The rod bent in jerks, the trout pumping against the current. Nick knew it was a small one. He lifted the rod straight up in the air. It bowed with the pull (Hemingway, 1970, 201).

> It is not difficult to discover the unknown animal. Spend a day in the tropical forest of South America, turning over logs, looking beneath bark, sifting through the moist litter of leaves, followed by an evening shining a mercury lamp on a white screen, and one way and another you will collect hundreds of different kinds of small creatures. Moths, caterpillars, spiders, long-nosed bugs, luminous beetles, harmless butterflies disguised as wasps, wasps shaped like ants...(Attenborough, 1979, 1).

Reading, too, can help us develop our vocabularies, and good vocabularies increase our potentials as writers. In our reading, when we come across words we don't know, we should look them up in a dictionary and then add them to our vocabularies. In order to write, we must use words, and we can't use words we don't have in our vocabularies.

The dictionary, too, can help us pick the right word or the precise word to express thoughts and help us learn to write what we mean. As you study words in the dictionary, you will note that some words are pronounced the same but are spelled differently, e.g., "bare" and "bear." "Bear," used as a noun can mean "a large, furry animal"; it may mean "a person who is clumsy, rude, or gruff"; or it may mean "a person who believes prices on the stock market are going to decline." Used as a verb, "bear" has still other meanings: "to bear fruit," "to support or hold up," "to tolerate," and so on. What we learn as we use the dictionary is that the English language, as William Zinsser has stated, "is rich in words that convey an exact shade of meaning" (1983, 100).

In your reading, learn how to use your library, since it contains the best written words of our culture. As you study and learn the meanings of words, singulars and plurals of nouns, tenses and modes of verbs, the right places to put punctuation, and ways to arrange sentences to show what goes with what, your writing will improve.

4. <u>Writing</u>. That we "learn to write by writing" is an accepted truism; but as Zinsser (1983, 100) has said: "Writing is a deeply personal process, full of mystery and surprise. No two people go about it in exactly the same way." Some writers write carefully and methodically -- their writing is in an almost finished form from the very beginning. Other writers, and this would include most of us, dash off a first draft not caring too much whether it conforms with the mechanics of good English. Research in writing reveals that the "process of writing" (getting thoughts on paper) is the key element; the "product of writing" (the final copy) can be taken care of in the editing and revision phase of writing and that comes later in the learning-to-write cycle.

It may be well to remember that different writing approaches are used for different purposes. There is no one best way to write. The best approach is most often determined by what you are writing. Often, for example, it is necessary to plan carefully what you want to say in a paper before writing it. This is especially true for research papers. Some writers outline what they want to say and then write from the outline. In the research paper, much of the hard work is in the planning, but it must be done if you are to write well. As you make your plan, you can write key ideas and their supporting statements on 6″ × 4″ or 8″ × 5″ cards. You can give a topic to each card, arrange the cards in logical order of presentation, and write your paper from the cards. Walshe (1979, 54-56) lists these steps in the writing process:

*Selection of a topic

*Pre-writing preparation, including planning

*Draft writing

*Editing, rewriting, with feedback and evaluation from your peer group

*Final writing, publication, or sharing

Use a typewriter or a word processor in preparing your first draft of any writing. Writing on a typewriter or a word processor is the first step in improving the efficiency of writing. Double-space your copy to make it easier to proofread, edit, and revise.

(continued on next page)

170b, (continued)

Problem 2 (2 full sheets)
Leftbound Report

1. Take a 10′ writing on the report at the right DS. Determine correct placement of headings.

2. If time is called before you finish the report, move immediately to Problem 3. If you finish the report before time is called, begin the report again in unbound style.

words

AVERY INDUSTRIAL PARK PROJECT 6
Lawn Sprinkler System 10

Our guidelines for lawn sprinkler systems must be strictly observed 24
throughout the implementation of this project. Any deviations requested 39
must be approved in writing by the project supervisor. 50

Specific Materials Required 61

Rotary sprinkler heads. The rotary sprinkler heads will be G50,* or 79
approved equal. The sprinklers will be the pop-up type with positive gear 94
drive to give coverage in either a full circle or a part circle. 107

Lawn spray heads. The lawn spray heads will be P34,* or approved 124
equal. The heads will be nonadjustable nozzles with fixed orifices. The 138
heads will have adjustable risers. 146

Shrub spray heads. The shrub spray heads will be S100,* or approved 163
equal. These heads will also be the type that are nonadjustable with fixed 178
orifices. They will be compatible with the lawn spray heads used on the 193
project. The direction of the heads that spray in part circles will be con- 208
trolled by turning the nozzle. 214

Approved equal heads must have flow rates and pressure requirements 228
within 5 percent of those specified. 235

General Guidelines 243

The contractor will furnish all materials and labor required to provide 257
a complete irrigation system as specified by the drawings and these guide- 272
lines. In general, the project consists of the complete installation of the 287
following equipment: 291

1. yard piping 295
2. control valves, heads, and controls 303
3. system controller 307

The contractor will stake all head locations and indicate the type of head 323
to be used at each location. Before trenching is begun, the project super- 337
visor must approve the locations and head types. After the equipment has 352
been installed but before the holes are covered, the project supervisor will 367
again inspect the project and give approval to proceed. 378

The contractor will clean out all lines, adjust all valves and heads, regu- 393
late all control equipment, and leave the whole system in complete working 408
order. The contractor will also be responsible for fully explaining the opera- 424
tions of the system to maintenance personnel before final approval is given. 439
General operating instructions and manuals and all tools needed to operate 455
and adjust the system will be left with maintenance personnel upon final 469
approval of the project. 474

________________ 478

*Manufactured by Automatic Sprinkler Division of Moore Industries. 491

5. Preparing the final draft. After many experiences in writing, and as your writing begins to take shape, it is necessary to move to the final phase. All writing needs careful editing and revision. Hemingway is said to have made thirty-nine revisions of the ending of his best seller, A FAREWELL TO ARMS. Mario Puzo, author of the top selling novel of the 1970's, THE GODFATHER, states categorically that "rewriting is the whole secret to writing" (Walshe, 1979, 55).

When you are ready to edit and revise your writing, here are some suggestions that may be helpful:

a. Underline words, phrases, and/or sentences you may want to change or eliminate. (Remove words, phrases, or sentences that really aren't needed.)
b. Use active verbs rather than passive verbs. As Zinsser says, "Passive verbs are the death of clarity and vigor" (1983, 101).
c. Check the sentences. Are they in logical and sequential order? Sentences come in a variety of shapes and sizes which are useful so long as they add interest, not confusion, to your writing. A good suggestion for all writers: Keep your sentences short. Zinsser cautions, "Don't try to make a sentence do too many jobs -- you only confuse the reader and make your writing difficult to follow" (1983, 100).
d. Read your paper aloud. How does it sound? Does it flow smoothly? Is it unified and coherent?

When you edit your work, it is helpful to have your classmates, or others, evaluate and react to your writing. Professor Richard Lanham of UCLA suggests the use of the "CBS Style," CBS standing for Clarity, Brevity, and Sincerity. In writing, he warns us to avoid the "Official or Bureaucratic Style," which often characterizes government publications. To see his point, we have only to read this statement which was written several years ago after the Three Mile Island nuclear accident: "It would be prudent to consider expeditiously the provision of instrumentation that would provide an unambiguous indication of the level of fluid in the reactor vessel." If we translate this statement from the "Bureaucratic Style," it would probably read something like this: We need accurate measuring devices.

When you edit your writing, first check for the more obvious errors -- errors in spelling, grammar, and punctuation. Check to make sure that you have avoided the pitfalls of misplaced modifiers, incorrect verb usage, and fragmented or run-on sentences. Then check your sentence style. Look for long and involved sentences that could be improved by removing nonfunctional words or by dividing them into two shorter sentences. Make sure all words are used correctly in a sentence and that you have not repeated yourself. Stay away from the kind of "confusing wording" we often see in signs on office building doors, such as: EMERGENCY EXIT ONLY -- NOT TO BE USED UNDER ANY CIRCUMSTANCES. (If a door cannot be used under any circumstances, it cannot be used at all!) In other words, check to make sure that what you have said in your writing is logical and makes sense. If you are to convince your reader, what you say must be reasonable and must be supported with convincing evidence. When you have done all or at least some of these things, your paper is ready for the final draft.

Summary Statement

Now what about your writing style? The basic requirement of writing style is to follow the elementary rules of grammar and good usage. Other than that, writing is unique with each of us. Words arranged in one manner in a sentence are capable of stirring the reader deeply. The same words rearranged only slightly may be impotent. Lincoln's Gettysburg Address and the Declaration of Independence are examples of words arranged effectively. Arranged in any other way, the Gettysburg Address or the Declaration of Independence would not be nearly so effective.

The question of writing style, as is true for writing improvement, has no single answer. Each of us must develop a writing style that is unique to us. But we must start somewhere, and that somewhere is to start by writing.

169d, (continued)

Drill 3
Table with Column Headings

1. Take a 3′ writing using the following directions: half sheet, long side up; SS body; 6 spaces between columns. Use following column headings:

Column 1: **Orchestra**
Column 2: **Conductor**
Column 3: **Manager**

Circle errors.

2. Take a 3′ writing using the following directions: full sheet; DS body; 4 spaces between columns. Circle errors.

Note: Review Formatting Guides for Tables on page 287.

			words
SELECTED MAJOR SYMPHONY ORCHESTRAS			7
OF THE UNITED STATES			11
		words in heading	22
Atlanta Symphony	Robert Shaw	Stephen Sell	30
Chicago Symphony	Sir George Solti	John Edwards	39
Pittsburgh Symphony	Andre Previn	Marshall Turkin	49
St. Louis Symphony	Leonard Slatkin	Joan Briccetti	59
Syracuse Symphony	Christopher Keene	Eleanor Shopiro	70
______________			73
Source: American Symphony Orchestra League.			82

Lesson 170 Evaluation: Letters/Tables/Reports

170a ▶ 5 Conditioning Practice

each line twice SS (slowly, then faster); DS between 2-line groups; if time permits, rekey selected lines

alphabet 1 Kazi helped by exclaiming very loudly for Quin to jump away to safety.
figures 2 The 32 cars, 47 jeeps, and 16 trucks, or 95 units, are due in 80 days.
third row 3 To equip with either pretty pottery or pewter is your request to Pete.
speed 4 The formal amendment is a penalty and is no aid to the downtown firms.

| 1 | 2 | 3 | 4 | 5 | 6 | 7 | 8 | 9 | 10 | 11 | 12 | 13 | 14 |

170b ▶ 37 Check Document Production Skill: Letter, Report, Table

Time Schedule

Plan and Prepare .... 2′
Timed Production
Problem 1 .... 10′
Problem 2 .... 10′
Problem 3 .... 10′
Proofread and Correct Errors ... 5′

Problem 1 (plain full sheet)

Block Style Letter with Open Punctuation

1. Take a 10′ writing on the letter at the right in proper format. Add your reference initials and an enclosure notation.

2. If time is called before you finish the letter, move immediately to Problem 2.

Note: Check accuracy of format of a block style letter on RG 6.

words

January 18, 19-- Dr. Frank D. Russell College of Business Administration 15
Victory Hills University Tempe, AZ 85287-3426 Dear Dr. Russell 27

(¶ 1) Dr. R. B. Jackson has indicated to us that you are experienced in con- 41
ducting professional development seminars on the subject of organizational 56
communications. After reviewing a description of your two-day seminar, 71
which was sent to us by Dr. Jackson's office, we are sure that you are just 86
the person who can present the kind of program we need. 97

(¶ 2) We believe that it is important for both the office personnel of our com- 112
pany and their immediate supervisors to participate in this seminar; there- 126
fore, the times available are somewhat limited. Would it be possible for you 142
to present your two-day program at our company headquarters, 800 Carver 156
Road, Tucson, AZ 85284-3119, on either March 2 and 3, March 21 and 22, or 171
April 14 and 15? 175

(¶ 3) If the enclosed contract is satisfactory, fill in the program dates and 189
sign and return one copy to us. We will appreciate hearing from you as soon 205
as possible so that we can notify those who are interested in attending. 220

Sincerely yours Ms. Jean Parker Training Director 229

118c ▶ 20 Format and Key a Reference List and a Title Page

Problem 1

Format and key a reference list from the copy below. The top margin is the same as page 1 of the report; the other margins are the same as for the leftbound report. Center heading over line of writing; start first line of each entry at left margin; indent additional lines 5 spaces; SS each entry; DS between entries.

Line 6 11

REFERENCES

QS

American Psychological Association. <u>Publication Manual</u>. 2d ed. Washington, DC: American Psychological Association, 1974.

Attenborough, David. <u>Life on Earth</u>. Boston: Little, Brown and Company, 1979.

Committee on Writing Standards, The National Council of Teachers of English. "Standards for Basic Skills Writing Programs." <u>College English</u>, October 1979, 220-222.

1½" left margin

Cross, Donna W. <u>Word Abuse</u>. New York: Coward, McCann & Geoghegan, Inc., 1979.

1" right margin

Goodlad, John I. <u>A Place Called School</u>. New York: McGraw-Hill Inc., 1984.

Graves, Robert, and Alan Hodge. <u>The Reader Over Your Shoulder</u>. New York: Random House, 1979.

Hemingway, Ernest. <u>In Our Time</u>. New York: Charles Scribner's Sons, 1970.

Lanham, Richard. UCLA Writing Project Lecture, 1979.

Walshe, R. D. "What's Basic to Teaching Writing?" <u>The English Journal</u>, December 1979, 51-56.

Zinsser, William. <u>Writing With a Word Processor</u>. New York: Harper & Row, 1983.

Problem 2

Format and key a title page for the leftbound report. Using the center point for a leftbound report:

a. Center title on line 16.

b. Center and key your name 8 DS's below title; DS and center the name of your school.

c. Center and key the current date 8 DS's below the name of your school.

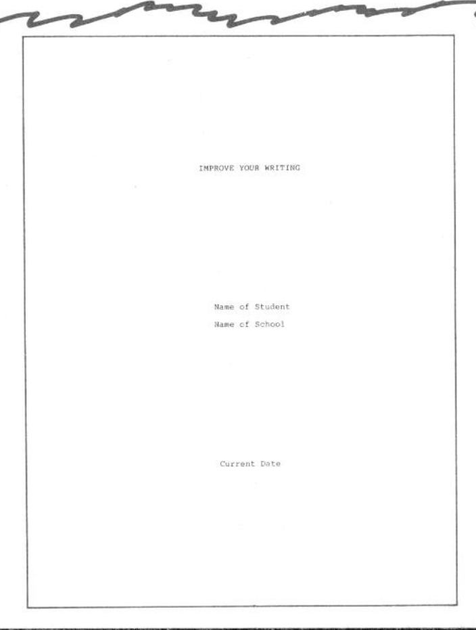

IMPROVE YOUR WRITING

Name of Student

Name of School

Current Date

169d ▶ 30

Drill on Document Production: Letter, Report, Table

plain full sheets

Drill 1

Modified Block Style Letter with Mixed Punctuation

1. Take three 1′ writings in letter form on opening lines (date through salutation); try to improve by 1 or 2 words with each timing.

2. Take three 1′ writings in letter form on the closing lines (complimentary close through enclosures); try to improve by 1 or 2 words with each timing.

3. Take a 3′ writing in letter form on the complete letter; proofread and circle errors.

Note: Check accuracy of format of modified block style letter on RG 6.

Drill 2

Reports

1. Take a 3′ writing on the report at the right in leftbound format. Proofread and circle errors.

2. Take a 3′ writing on the report in unbound format. Proofread and circle errors.

Note: Check accuracy of format of a leftbound report on RG 8.

Drill 3 is on next page.

	words parts	total
June 15, 19-- Mr. Jim Greenwold, President Greenwold Managerial Pro-	13	13
grams, Inc. P.O. Box 52920 Tulsa, OK 74152-1518 Dear Mr. Greenwold	27	27
(¶ 1) Ms. Peggy Carpenter has applied for a position as office systems ad-	13	41
ministrator and has listed you as a reference. She indicated that she held a	29	56
similar position with your company for two years.	39	66
(¶ 2) Your evaluation of Ms. Carpenter's qualifications will help us in making	54	81
a decision about employing her. You will notice that Ms. Carpenter has	68	95
given permission to keep her file confidential, and you may be assured that	83	111
we will treat your reference in a confidential manner.	95	122
(¶ 3) Will you please complete the enclosed form and return it to us in the	109	136
enclosed envelope. If you wish to discuss Ms. Carpenter's qualifications for	124	151
this position with me, please call at 743-2837. We appreciate your assistance.	140	167
Sincerely Mrs. Beverly Freeman Human Resource Director xx	12	179
Enclosures	14	181

EMPLOYEE INSURANCE BENEFITS 6

This description of employee insurance benefits is a summary only and is 20
not intended to include details. Additional information is available in the 36
Employee Benefits Handbook.* 47

Life Insurance 53

Life insurance is provided for all employees and includes dismember- 66
ment provisions and double indemnity for accidental death. During the first 81
31 days of employment, no medical examination will be required of em- 95
ployees enrolling in the life insurance program. 105

Regular life insurance. The regular life insurance is for an amount val- 124
ued at approximately 1 1/2 times the annual salary of the employee. The 138
premium for regular life insurance is paid by the company. 150

Optional life insurance. Additional life insurance up to the amount of 169
$50,000 is available on an optional basis, and premiums are deducted from 184
the checks of the employees each month. 192

Liability Insurance 200

Liability insurance is provided for employees against claims resulting 214
from actions taken while performing company-related duties. The policy 229
covers bodily injury, libel, and destruction of property, as well as punitive 244
damages, bail bond, and legal defense. 252

Long-Term Disability Insurance 265

Long-term disability insurance for salary continuance is available for 279
employees who work 30 or more hours per week. For employees who choose 293
to enroll in the plan, the company will pay two-thirds of the cost of the 308
monthly premium and the remaining third will be deducted from the checks 323
of the employees. 326

_______________ 330

*A copy of the Employee Benefits Handbook is available from the 348
Human Resource Management Office. 355

Unit 24 Lessons 119-123

Learning Goals

1. To refine and improve your basic keyboarding techniques.
2. To increase your speed and improve your accuracy on basic skill copy.
3. To improve composing skills.

Machine Adjustments

1. Paper guide at *0*.
2. 70-space line and SS unless otherwise directed.
3. Line-space selector on 2 (DS) for all timed writings of more than 1′.

Lesson 119 Keyboarding Technique/Speed

119a ▶ 5 Conditioning Practice

each line 3 times (slowly, faster, in-between rate); as time permits, repeat selected lines

alphabet 1 Just strive for maximum progress by quickly organizing the daily work.

fig/sym 2 Al Jones's order (#30-967) included 248 desks, 15 chairs, and 9 lamps.

space bar 3 If what you say is so, then they should find the work very easy to do.

speed 4 If they do the work for us, I may go to the lake and then to the city.

| 1 | 2 | 3 | 4 | 5 | 6 | 7 | 8 | 9 | 10 | 11 | 12 | 13 | 14 |

119b ▶ 15 Letter Emphasis: Refine Techniques/Improve Control and Speed

each line 3 times (slowly, faster, top speed)

Minimum standard: To complete all lines as directed in 15′.

Extra credit: All lines beyond minimum standard.

Goal: To keep hands quiet with keystroking action limited to the fingers.

Emphasize: Continuity and rhythm with curved, upright fingers.

a As Ada and Anna ate bananas and apples, an aardvark ate many fat ants.

b Bobby bounced a big, bright rubber ball by the babbling abbey cobbler.

c A crane cackled crazily as a raccoon captured the newly hatched chick.

d Don decided on the dark, dreary day to deliver a dog to dad's address.

e Every technique refinement leads to greatly elevated speed rate gains.

f Fifi ate five freshly fried falafels at the fast food efficiency cafe.

g Gregg and Reggie built a garish gargoyle for the gigantic garden gate.

h The highlight of the hike was when Hugh served ham and chips at lunch.

i If it is his to give, I will aid each individual in finding six pails.

| 1 | 2 | 3 | 4 | 5 | 6 | 7 | 8 | 9 | 10 | 11 | 12 | 13 | 14 |

119c ▶ 15 Transfer Refined Techniques and Increased Speed: Guided Writing

1. Two 1′ writings; find *gwam*.
2. Add 4 words to better rate; determine 1/4′ goals.
3. Two 15″ writings; try to equal or exceed 1/4′ goal.
4. Two 30″ writings; try to equal or exceed 1/2′ goal.
5. Two 1′ guided writings at goal rate.
6. Two 1′ speed writings.

Recognize that the primary element of high-speed keyboarding is to (4, 8, 12) try to type or keyboard with good form and refined technique patterns. (16, 20, 24) In each of the lessons of this unit, your goal should be to fix your (28, 32, 36, 40) mind on the principal keyboarding elements: finger-action keystroking, (44, 48, 52, 56) quick spacing after every word, and a fast return with a very quick (60, 64, 68) start of the new line. (72, 74)

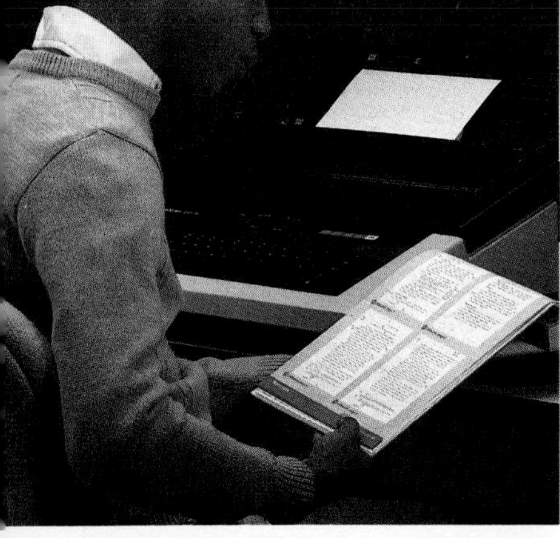

Unit 36 Lessons 169-170

Learning Goals

1. Improve straight-copy skill.
2. Review formatting guidelines for letters, reports, and tables.
3. Drill on parts of letters, reports, and tables to improve speed.
4. Check language skills.

Machine Adjustments

1. Margin sets: 70-space line or as directed.
2. Spacing: SS sentences; DS ¶s; or as directed.

Lesson 169 Review: Letters/Tables/Reports

169a ▶ 5 Conditioning Practice

each line twice SS (slowly, then faster); DS between 2-line groups; if time permits, rekey selected lines

alphabet 1 Kimberly exerted great vigor in her careful quest to win major prizes.

figures 2 Our sales were $168,000 in 1987, but sales should be $253,000 by 1994.

third row 3 Petite Terry used quite proper etiquette to outwit her poor tired pop.

speed 4 They held no blame for their goof, but he did make them pay a penalty.

| 1 | 2 | 3 | 4 | 5 | 6 | 7 | 8 | 9 | 10 | 11 | 12 | 13 | 14 |

169b ▶ 10 Improve Keyboarding Skill: Guided Writing

1. Take a 1′ writing on the ¶ for speed; determine base rate (*gwam*).
2. With guides called at ¼′ intervals, take two more 1′ writings on the ¶; note ¼′ checkpoints before each writing to increase speed by 2-6 *gwam* (see table, p. 270). **Goal:** 2-6 words faster on each writing.
3. Deduct 4-6 *gwam* from top speed and note new ¼′ checkpoints. With ¼′ guides called, take three 1′ writings on the ¶ for control. **Goal:** 2 or fewer errors per minute.

all letters used | A | 1.5 si | 5.7 awl | 80% hfw |

There is no objection to the fast and easy way of doing essential, routine things, of course; but doctors tell us that the increasing time spent in sedentary activity is impairing our physical and mental health. They tell us to use more of our leisure time for active things. For example, walk more, ride less; take a zestful swim instead of sunbath; take part in athletic activities instead of merely sitting and viewing them. They request that we work toward a better balance between sitting and acting.

169c ▶ 5 Improve Language Skills

As you key the ¶ at the right, correct errors in spelling, punctuation, capitalization, and any keying errors you find. Check your corrected copy with the first ¶ of the letter in Problem 1, 170b, p. 295.

Dr R.B. Jackson has indicate to us that your are expereinced in conducting profesional develupment seminars on the subjects of organisational comunications. After reviewing a descripton of your two-day semniar, which was send to us by dr jacksons office we are sure that you are just the purson who can present the kind of programm we need.

119d ▶ 15
Measure and Evaluate Basic Skill: Straight Copy

two 3′ writings; then one 5′ writing

Goal: To maintain 3′ rate for 5′.

Proofread; circle errors; record better 3′ rate and 5′ rate.

After each writing, make a self-evaluation of your technique patterns; reduce rate slightly if you made more than 10 errors.

all letters used | A | 1.5 si | 5.7 awl | 80% hfw

	gwam 3′	5′	
Several important elements affect fatigue and eyestrain when a	4	2	48
computer is operated. A computer monitor should be exactly positioned so	9	5	51
you can look directly at it, and there should be little or no reflection	14	8	54
from it. The keyboard should be placed in a position that is very com-	19	11	57
fortable for you as you are operating it. A good guide is to place the	24	14	60
keyboard so that the tips of the fingers, the base of the hand, and the	28	17	63
lower arm are in alignment with the angle of the keyboard. This position	33	20	66
of the keyboard results in reduced operating fatigue.	37	22	68
Another key requirement in relation to position of the keyboard is	41	25	71
the need of an adjustable, comfortable chair which may help to make it	46	28	73
easy to operate the keyboard and view the monitor. Still another impor-	51	30	76
tant element is the color of the screen. Some workers have selected an	56	33	79
amber color; others maintain that green produces much less stress and is	60	36	82
easier on the eyes. In addition, the copy on the screen must be easy	65	39	85
to read. Size of print is important, but of greater importance is the	70	42	88
intensity of the print on the screen, a condition of the number of dots	75	45	91
that comprise each letter.	76	46	92

gwam 3′ | 1 | 2 | 3 | 4 | 5 |
5′ | 1 | 2 | 3 |

Lesson 120 Keyboarding/Composing Skills

120a ▶ 5
Conditioning Practice

each line 3 times (slowly, faster, in-between rate); as time permits, repeat selected lines

alphabet 1 Liza picked several exquisite flowers which grew by the jungle swamps.

fig/sym 2 Order the 38#, 56#, and 79# packages (untaped) from J. C. Burl & Sons.

adjacent key 3 A sad reporter reported the disaster as he gave his opinion of causes.

speed 4 If he signs the right forms, the auditor may augment the usual profit.

| 1 | 2 | 3 | 4 | 5 | 6 | 7 | 8 | 9 | 10 | 11 | 12 | 13 | 14 |

120b ▶ 15
Improve Basic Skill: Straight Copy

1. Add 4 to 8 words to your 119d *gwam* rate. **Goal:** To reach a new speed level.

2. Two 1′ writings on ¶ 1, 119d, above. Try to reach goal rate.

3. A 2′ writing on ¶ 1. Try to maintain your 1′ rate (2′ *gwam* = total words ÷ 2).

4. Repeat Step 2, using ¶ 2.

5. Repeat Step 3, using ¶ 2.

6. A 3′ timed writing using both ¶s. **Goal:** To maintain your new speed rate for 3′.

168b ▶ 10
Evaluate Straight-Copy Skill

1. A 5′ writing on both ¶s of 158b, p. 277.

2. Determine *gwam* and number of errors.

3. Compare with original score made in 158b.

4. Record on LM p. 3 for comparison in Lesson 170.

168c ▶ 35
Evaluate Document Production: Tables

Time Schedule

Plan and Prepare .... 3′
Timed Production .... 25′
Proofread and Correct Errors .. 5′
Compute *n-pram* .... 2′

Problem 1

full sheet

Format the table shown at the right; DS body; 8 spaces between columns.

SELECTED INVENTIONS AND INVENTORS			words
FROM 1642 TO 1872			
			7
			10
Adding machine	1642	Blaise Pascal	17
Stain for straw hats	1716	Sybilla Masters	25
Calculating machine	1823	Charles Babbage	35
Paper bag folding machine	1870	Margaret Knight	43
Vacuum processor for canning	1872	Amanda T. Jones	53

Problem 2

half sheet, long edge at top

Format the table shown at the right; SS body; center by longest item (heading or entry) in each column; 10 spaces between columns.

WESTERN STATES, CAPITALS, AND 6

DATE ENTERED UNION 10

State	Capital	Year	17
Arizona	Phoenix	1912	21
California	Sacramento	1850	26
Nevada	Carson City	1864	31
Oregon	Salem	1859	35
Washington	Olympia	1889	40

Problem 3

half sheet, short edge at top

Format the table shown at the right; 4 spaces between columns; SS or DS body as you prefer.

OFFICE SYSTEMS UNITS 4

(1987-88) 6

Description	Clock Hours	Number Students	9 / 19
Accounting	60	48	22
Business Law	45	25	26
Data Processing	60	48	31
Economics	45	32	34
Records Management	15	50	39
Keyboarding	60	85	42
Typewriting	60	68	46

Problem 4

full sheet

Format the table shown at the right; 6 spaces between columns; SS or DS body as you prefer.

PROPOSED PLANT SPECIMENS 5

Doctors' Building 9

Common Name	Botanical Name	Quantity	22
Live Oak	Quercus virginiana	2	28
Willow Oak	Quercus phellos	3	34
Frasers Photinia	Photinia fraseri	10	41
Italian Jasmine	Jasminum humile	4	48
Common Periwinkle	Vinca minor	50	55

Bonus

1. At the conclusion of the 25′ production time, you will have 7′ to proofread again, correct any errors you find or rekey if errors cannot be corrected, and compute *n-pram*. This step must be completed accurately before credit for bonus problem may be earned.

2. If time remains, rekey Problem 4.

120c ▶ 15
Letter Emphasis: Refine Techniques/Improve Speed and Control

each line 3 times (slowly, faster, top speed)

Minimum standard: To complete all lines as directed in 15′.

Extra credit: All lines beyond minimum standard.

Goal: To keep hands quiet with keystroking action limited to the fingers.

Emphasize: Continuity and rhythm with curved, upright fingers.

j A jungle jaguar jabbed a paw into the jelly jug as Jon ate the jicama.
k Kiku and Jack packed a deck keg with krill as Khmer packed a knapsack.
l Lilly and Polly will fill the old pail with nails for a lake dwelling.
m Mamie may recommend that Sammy move to Maine to maintain a maple farm.
n Nancy was naive to think that Ann's name would be on the nylon banner.
o Otto often looked for gold in the old gold mine near Golden, Colorado.
p At a political party, Pepe supplied popular apple and pineapple punch.
q Quen quickly and quietly queued up to buy quince jam in a quaint town.
r Roberta worked four hours before the morning train arrived from Rugby.

| 1 | 2 | 3 | 4 | 5 | 6 | 7 | 8 | 9 | 10 | 11 | 12 | 13 | 14 |

120d ▶ 15
Composing at the Keyboard: Improve Writing Skill

full sheet; DS copy

1. Prepare a rough draft. Compose a paragraph describing an orange. A paragraph usually has a single main idea (topic sentence) with supporting details. To help you, use the following sentence as your topic sentence:

An orange is a reddish-yellow colored fruit which belongs to the citrus family.

Continue your paragraph by describing the size, shape, texture, and smell of an orange. Then tell what happens when you peel an orange. Describe the peeled orange and the taste of the segments when they are eaten.

2. Prepare the final draft. Make any needed corrections in your rough-draft paragraph; then prepare a final draft. Use as the heading: AN ORANGE.

Lesson 121 Keyboarding/Composing Skills

121a ▶ 5
Conditioning Practice

each line 3 times (slowly, faster, in-between rate); as time permits, repeat selected lines

alphabet 1 Patient quarriers uncovered famous Greek bronzes with onyx-jewel eyes.
fig/sym 2 Lorenzo & Son wrote Check #403 for $310.99 and Check #573 for $862.42.
3d row 3 A reporter tried to write a witty story of Peter Piper for your paper.
speed 4 He may hand me the clay and then go to the shelf for the die and form.

| 1 | 2 | 3 | 4 | 5 | 6 | 7 | 8 | 9 | 10 | 11 | 12 | 13 | 14 |

121b ▶ 5
Build Basic Skill: Control/Speed

1. Two 1′ writings, line 1 of 121a. Emphasize accuracy.

2. Two 1′ writings, line 4 of 121a. Emphasize speed.

Lesson 167 Sustained Production: Tables

167a ▶ 5 Conditioning Practice

each line twice SS (slowly, then faster); DS between 2-line groups; if time permits, rekey selected lines

alphabet	1	Zack Goss, a quiet hockey player, waved joyfully to many excited boys.
figures	2	Questions 18, 27, 40, and 59 are from Chapter 3, but 6 and 28 are not.
shift/lock	3	NASA received 12 packages of parts C.O.D., but others were sent F.O.B.
speed	4	Doris cut the risk and got eight firms up to their usual profit goals.

| 1 | 2 | 3 | 4 | 5 | 6 | 7 | 8 | 9 | 10 | 11 | 12 | 13 | 14 |

167b ▶ 10 Improve Keyboarding Skill: Guided Writing

1. A 1′ writing to establish base rate.
2. Two 1′ writings for speed with quarter-minute checkpoints noted and guides called. (see Table, p. 270). **Goal:** 2-6 words faster on each writing.
3. Deduct 4-6 words from top speed; then note checkpoints. Two 1′ writings for control with guides called. **Goal:** 2 or fewer errors a minute.
4. A 3′ writing. **Goal:** 6 or fewer errors.

all letters used | A | 1.5 si | 5.7 awl | 80% hfw |

	gwam 3′	
If you are considering college, you may need to seek advice from	4	36
just a few individuals who have some conception of your ability and	9	41
potential to succeed, such as your teachers, counselors, and parents.	13	45
They may assist you in making the complex decision of whether to attend	18	50
and, if so, where and what to study. In the final analysis, though,	23	54
you must answer these questions by analyzing your goals and interests.	27	59
At this phase in life, you must make an honest appraisal of yourself.	32	64

gwam 3′ | 1 | 2 | 3 | 4 | 5 |

167c ▶ 35 Sustained Document Production: Tables

format/key each table as directed; proofread; correct errors

Time Schedule

Plan and Prepare .... 5′
Timed Production .... 25′
Proofread and Correct Errors .... 5′
Compute *n-pram* .... 2′

1. Make list of problems to be produced:
   page 288, 164b, Problem 1
   page 288, 164b, Problem 3
   page 289, 165b, Problem 1
   page 289, 165b, Problem 2
   page 290, 166c, Problem 1
2. Arrange paper and correction materials for easy access. Produce as many tables as you can in 25′. Proofread and correct errors before removing letters from machine.
3. After 25′ timing, proofread again and correct errors or rekey.
4. Determine *n-pram* and number of errors; turn in work arranged in order listed in Step 1.

Lesson 168 Evaluation: Tables

168a ▶ 5 Conditioning Practice

each line twice SS (slowly, then faster); DS between 2-line groups; if time permits, rekey selected lines

alphabet	1	Meg executed her jumps quickly to win the bronze medal for that event.
figures	2	Our team won by scores of 102 to 95, 87 to 64, 93 to 82, and 73 to 71.
fig/sym	3	He said, "Ship 40 #84 posts, listed at $76.39 less 15% cash discount."
speed	4	A visitor to the island dug up the authentic ivory tusk by the shanty.

| 1 | 2 | 3 | 4 | 5 | 6 | 7 | 8 | 9 | 10 | 11 | 12 | 13 | 14 |

121c ▶ 15
Letter Emphasis: Refine Techniques/Improve Speed and Control

each line 3 times (slowly, faster, top speed)

Minimum standard: To complete all lines as directed.

Extra credit: All lines beyond minimum standard.

Goal: To keep hands quiet with keystroking action limited to the fingers.

Emphasize: Continuity and rhythm with curved, upright fingers.

s Susana was asked to assist us at the session assigned to us in Shensi.

t Tagett tossed that battered ball into the butter tub without thinking.

u Your unusual number of unused rubber jugs should be used at our union.

v Vivian's vivid vocalization of her vowels gave her varied jobs for TV.

w Wild winter wind will whip powerful waves with force over the wharves.

x The extra xeroxed copies of next week's taxes would have vexed Xerxes.

y You may buy yesterday's yield of yams any day; why not buy them today.

z Zestful Zabrze, eluding tacklers, dizzily zigzagged into the end zone.

alphabet While Izzy performed exciting jokes, I recited various quaint ballads.

| 1 | 2 | 3 | 4 | 5 | 6 | 7 | 8 | 9 | 10 | 11 | 12 | 13 | 14 |

121d ▶ 15
Transfer Refined Techniques and Improved Control: Guided Writing

1. Two 1′ timed writings; find *gwam*; circle errors.
2. Deduct 4 words from better rate; determine 1/4′ goals.
3. Two 15″ writings; try to reach goal and to keyboard without error.
4. Two 30″ writings; try to reach goal and to keyboard without error.
5. Four 1′ guided writings at goal rate. **Goal:** Each writing with not more than 2 errors.

Every time you operate the keyboard, make the use of good techniques (12) your goal. This is the way to build your keyboarding efficiency to its (28) highest possible level. Keyboarding efficiency is needed if you are to remain competitive in the world of work, and if you are to use the sophis- (56) ticated equipment now in use in the technological society in which we live and work. (74)

121e ▶ 10
Composing at the Keyboard: Improve Writing Skill

full sheet; DS copy

1. **Prepare a rough draft.** Compose a narrative paragraph (tells a story) or two on some fond childhood memory. Do this: Jot down some ideas you want to relate. Arrange ideas in a logical sequence and compose paragraph(s) using your outline.
2. **Prepare the final draft.** Make any needed corrections in your rough-draft copy; then prepare a final draft. Use as the heading:

A CHILDHOOD MEMORY

Lesson 122 Composing/Report Skills

122a ▶ 5
Conditioning Practice

each line 3 times (slowly, faster, in-between rate); as time permits, repeat selected lines

alphabet 1 The reporters quickly recognized the vexing problems of judging flaws.

fig/sym 2 Use the toll-free number (1-800-632-4759) to call Brown & Jordon, Inc.

shift key 3 Mary Flood, Jack E. Langs, and B. M. Quaile work for O'Brien & Kearns.

speed 4 They may do the problems for us when the city auditor signs the forms.

| 1 | 2 | 3 | 4 | 5 | 6 | 7 | 8 | 9 | 10 | 11 | 12 | 13 | 14 |

166a ▶ 5 Conditioning Practice

each line twice SS (slowly, then faster); DS between 2-line groups; if time permits, rekey selected lines

alphabet 1 Jo expects quality work from the dozen members of the executive group.

figures 2 Purchase Order 89016, sent to 475 East 132 Street, was mailed June 28.

fig/sym 3 Over any 3- to 6-year period from 1984 to 2005, she expects a 7% gain.

speed 4 He did tie the turkey to the dock by the fish he got in the city lake.

| 1 | 2 | 3 | 4 | 5 | 6 | 7 | 8 | 9 | 10 | 11 | 12 | 13 | 14 |

166b ▶ 15 Reinforce Formatting of Column Headings

Review centering of column heads in formatting guides on p. 287 and RG 11. Then format the drills at the right as directed; leave 10 spaces between columns for each drill.

Drill 1
Center by column entries.

Drill 2
Center by column headings.

Drill 3
Center by longest item in each column, whether heading or entry. This procedure should be used unless otherwise directed.

Drill 1

Delegate	Vocation	Birthplace
Barbara Jordan	Political leader	Houston, Texas

Drill 2

Date of Purchase	Price	Warranty
1/5/87	$58	90 days

Drill 3

Title	Date of Appointment	Date of Tenure
Professor	1970	1985

166c ▶ 30 Document Production: Tables

format/key each table as directed; proofread; correct errors

Problem 1
full sheet
Format the table shown at the right; DS body; center by longest item in each column, whether heading or columnar entry; 8 spaces between columns.

Problem 2
half sheet, long edge at top
Format the table shown at the right; SS body; 10 spaces between columns.

Problem 3
If time permits, rekey Problem 1 on a half sheet, long edge at top; SS body; make other formatting decisions.

words

CAPITALS AND LAND AREA OF 5
DS
SELECTED CANADIAN PROVINCES AND TERRITORIES 14
DS

Province or Territory	Capital	Land Area in Square Miles	words
			18 / 32
Newfoundland	St. John's	143,510	38
Nova Scotia	Halifax	20,400	44
Saskatchewan	Regina	220,350	49
British Columbia	Victoria	358,970	56
Yukon Territory	Whitehorse	184,930	63

(SS between heading lines; DS after headings)

INVENTORY OF TOOLS 4
DS
Twin Oaks Project 7
DS

Description	Present Supply	Future Need	words
			10 / 20
Brace	4	5	22
Drill -- electric	7	10	26
Drill -- hand	7	3	29
Hammer	10	15	32
Keyhole saw	7	9	35

(SS between heading lines; DS after headings)

122b ▶ 20
Key a Report from Statistical Rough-Draft Copy

full sheet; DS copy

1. Format as unbound report. Center main heading:

IMPORTANCE OF KEYBOARDING EFFICIENCY

2. Indent 5 for ¶s.

3. Correct errors. **Goal:** To produce report with maximum keyboarding efficiency: good techniques, continuity of keyboarding, few or no waste motions.

all letters used | A | 1.5 si | 5.7 awl | 80% hfw |

	gwam 3'	5'
words in heading	2	1
Keyboarding efficiency is a big part of the *information* produc-	7	4
tion *process,* and *it affects as well the* flow of information in the ~~technological society~~ *high-tech world*	12	7
in which ~~we~~ *you and I* live. A re cent study of *the use of the* keyboard~~ing~~ in	17	10
business ~~offices~~ *firms* in this country shows that key board	20	12
~~operators~~ *workers* (typists, word processing ~~operators~~ *workers*, stenos,	24	14
~~and~~ secretaries*, and the like*) give 30% of their total keyboarding time	28	17
~~producing~~ *to* letters, 20% to reports, 19% to memos, 13% to	32	19
forms, and 10% ~~producing~~ *to* tables. The ~~remainder~~ *rest* of their	35	21
~~keyboarding~~ time (8 ~~percent~~ *%*) in a day is given to key-	37	22
boarding such ~~items~~ *things* as messages, envelopes, itineraries,	41	24
minutes, press releases, ~~and the like.~~ *as well as other items.*	44	26
Quality time studies ~~reveal~~ *show* that the average word	47	28
processing operator may use 8.17 minutes just to finish	51	31
a letter of 176 words, a net ~~keying~~ *keyboarding* rate of about 21.5	55	33
words a minuet. ~~An~~ *This* operator may be ~~able to type~~ *capable of typing a* letter	59	36
~~material~~ at a rate of ~~about~~ 40 words a minuet, but, when	62	37
all otehr things ~~relating~~ *which relate* to the completion of a letter	66	40
are included (placement, proof reading, correcting spell-	70	42
ing *and keyboarding errors*, and time lost--pauses, looking up *from* copy *and* finding palace	76	45
in copy, *and* checking keyboarding point), the net ~~production~~	79	47
rate ~~falls drammatically~~ *is much lower*. Business people are now ~~putting~~ *giving*	83	50
~~increased emphasis on the importance of the~~ *a great deal of their attention to* keyboarding	86	51
efficiency and are ~~requiring that~~ *looking for* keyboarding operators	89	54
~~be~~ *who are* able to type at 70 to 80 words or more a minute so as	93	56
to expand data flow and minimize the costs of information	97	58
~~processing or producing business communications~~ *production.*	98	59

Lesson 165 Three-Column Tables

165a ▶ 5 Conditioning Practice

each line twice SS (slowly, then faster); DS between 2-line groups; if time permits, rekey selected lines

alphabet 1 Peg quickly viewed the exotic flowers in the zoo but enjoyed them all.

figures 2 Martinez bought the 1934 coupe and the 1927 roadster for only $58,065.

shift/lock 3 AT&T offered their DATAPHONE II for the purpose of network management.

speed 4 The busywork is a penalty, but it may entitle me to sit on the panels.

| 1 | 2 | 3 | 4 | 5 | 6 | 7 | 8 | 9 | 10 | 11 | 12 | 13 | 14 |

165b ▶ 45 Document Production: Tables

format/key each table as directed; proofread; circle errors

Problem 1

half sheet, long edge at top

Format the table shown at the right; SS body; 10 spaces between columns; use 2 lines for main heading.

			words	gwam 2'
ZIP CODE AND POPULATION OF ALASKAN URBAN AREAS DS			9	5
OF OVER 5,000 PEOPLE DS			13	7
(1980 Census) DS			16	8
Anchorage	99502	173,017	21	11
Eielson AFB (u)*	99702	5,232	27	14
Fairbanks	99701	22,645	31	16
Juneau	99801	19,528	35	18
Kenai Peninsula Borough	99611	25,282	42	21
Ketchikan	99901	7,198	47	24
Sitka	99835	7,803	50	25
DS ____________________ DS			54	27
*(u) means place is unincorporated.			63	31

Problem 2

full sheet

Format the table shown at the right; DS body; 8 spaces between columns.

Problem 3

half sheet, short edge at top

Rekey Problem 2 arranged alphabetically by last name; leave 4 spaces between columns. Ann-Margret is alphabetized as "A."

Problem 4 (skill building)

1. If time permits, determine vertical and horizontal placement for Problem 1; then take a 2' writing on the table.
2. Repeat for Problem 2.

ENTERTAINMENT PERSONALITIES			6	3
(Where and When Born) DS			10	5
Bill Crosby	Phildelphia, PA	7/12/37	17	9
Debbie Boon	Hackansack, NY	9/22/56	25	12
Desi Arnez	Santiago, Cuba	3/02/17	32	16
Evie Turnquist	Rahway, NJ	3/28/16	39	19
Woody Alan	Brooklyn, NY	12/01/35	45	23
Betty Furnes	New York, NY	1/03/06	53	26
Julie Andrews	Walden, England	10/01/35	60	30
David Snow	Tenterden, England	4/07/39	68	34
Ann-Margaret	Stockhome, Sweden	4/28/41	76	38

122c ▶ 15
Improve Basic Skill: Statistical Rough-Draft

Two 3′ writings on ¶s of 122b, p. 212; then one 5′ writing.
Goal: To maintain 3′ rate for 5′. Proofread; circle errors; record better 3′ rate and 5′ rate.

122d ▶ 10
Composing at the Keyboard: Improve Writing Skill

full sheet; DS copy; indent 5 for ¶s

Keyboard the quotation by Hemingway given in the upper-left column, p. 205; then compose a second ¶ in which you try to imitate the writing style of Hemingway.

If time permits, do the same for the Attenborough quotation, p. 205.

Lesson 123 — Keyboarding Speed/Accuracy

123a ▶ 5
Conditioning Practice

each line 3 times (slowly, faster, in-between rate) as time permits, repeat selected lines

alphabet	1	The queerly boxed package of zinc mixtures was delivered just in time.
fig/sym	2	The sale price of P165/8OR138 -- a steel-belted radial tire -- is $172.94.
variable rhythm	3	Did he send a statement to the firm at their new address on that date?
speed	4	He may sign the usual form by proxy if they make an audit of the firm.

| 1 | 2 | 3 | 4 | 5 | 6 | 7 | 8 | 9 | 10 | 11 | 12 | 13 | 14 |

123b ▶ 22
Improve Basic Skill: Speed-Forcing Drill

1. Each line twice at top speed; then:
2. In each set, try to complete each sentence on the call of 15″, 12″, or 10″ timing as directed. Force speed to higher levels as you move from line to line.
3. Move from Set 1 to Set 2 to Set 3 as you are able to complete the lines in the time allowed.
4. Two 1′ speed-forcing timings on lines 1e, 2e, and 3e. Compare rates.
5. Take additional 1′ timings on the sentence or sentences on which you made your lowest rate(s).

		gwam 15″	12″	10″
	Set 1: High-frequency balanced-hand words emphasized.			
1a	He may also make me go with them to do their work.	40	50	60
1b	They may sign the right amendment form for the auditor.	44	55	66
1c	The firm may make a profit if the men do a quantity of work.	48	60	72
1d	It is their wish to do the right problem and then visit the city.	52	65	78
1e	Both of them may go with me when I go to a city to sign the six forms.	56	70	84
	Set 2: High-frequency combination-response patterns emphasized.			
2a	Send a copy of the statement to me with the check.	40	50	60
2b	Please send the statement to them at their new address.	44	55	66
2c	Nearly all the information enclosed with this report is new.	48	60	72
2d	The quality of the special individual items now in stock is high.	52	65	78
2e	You and I were to go there to do the work before the end of this week.	56	70	84
	Set 3: High-frequency one-hand words emphasized.			
3a	After you rate him, read only a few reserve cases.	40	50	60
3b	After you state a minimum tax rate, give averages only.	44	55	66
3c	Jon regrets that you were referred to him for a tax opinion.	48	60	72
3d	After you state a few tax rates, will you set a tax reserve rate?	52	65	78
3e	In my opinion, you were to refer only a few extra oil tax cases to me.	56	70	84

| 1 | 2 | 3 | 4 | 5 | 6 | 7 | 8 | 9 | 10 | 11 | 12 | 13 | 14 |

Lesson 164 Two-Column Tables/Composing

164a ▶ 5 Conditioning Practice

each line twice SS (slowly, then faster); DS between 2-line groups; if time permits, rekey selected lines

alphabet 1 Greg Mackey planned to relax and review the book just before the quiz.

figures 2 Pages 4, 89, 320, and 576 need corrections; but page 471 has no error.

fig/sym 3 Sheng & Co. paid $2,178.94 for a Model #56230 copier for their office.

speed 4 He may fight for the amendment if he owns all of the land by the lake.

| 1 | 2 | 3 | 4 | 5 | 6 | 7 | 8 | 9 | 10 | 11 | 12 | 13 | 14 |

164b ▶ 30 Document Production: Tables

format/key each table as directed; proofread and circle errors

Problem 1

full sheet

Format the table shown at the right vertically and horizontally; DS body; 4 spaces between columns.

SPACING MEASUREMENTS FOR KEYBOARDING/FORMATTING		words
	DS	10
Elite (12-pitch) spaces to a horizontal inch	12	19
Pica (10-pitch) spaces to a horizontal inch	10	29
Elite spaces to an 8 1/2″ line (full sheet)	102	38
Pica spaces to an 8 1/2″ line (full sheet)	85	48
Elite spaces to a 5 1/2″ line (half sheet, short side up)	66	60
Pica spaces to a 5 1/2″ line (half sheet, short side up)	55	72
Vertical lines to an 11″ sheet	66	79
Vertical lines to a 5 1/2″ sheet (half sheet)	33	88
Vertical lines to an 8 1/2″ sheet (half sheet, short side up)	51	101

Problem 2

half sheet, long edge at top

Format the table shown at the right vertically and horizontally; SS body; 10 spaces between columns.

Problem 3

half sheet, short edge at top

If time permits, rekey Problem 2; decide spacing between columns; DS body.

Selected Noted Jazz Artists	DS	6
Dave Brubeck	Piano	9
Tommy Dorsey	Trombone	14
Ella Fitzgerald	Singer	18
Benny Goodman	Clarinet	23
Mary Lou Williams	Piano	28

164c ▶ 15 Improve Language Skills: Composing

1. Select a career in which you think you will be happy. In at least 3 ¶s, discuss 2 or more skills that are necessary for success in that career and ways by which you might acquire them.

2. Compose at the keyboard in DS format; ignore keyboarding errors; if necessary, x-out copy and continue keyboarding.

3. Edit your copy; then, format and key it in final form as an unbound report on a full sheet. Use MY CHOSEN CAREER as the heading.

123c ▶ 8
Improve Accuracy: Common Errors

each line 3 times at a control rate

Goal: Not over 1 error in each line. As time permits, repeat any line on which you made an error.

Emphasize quiet hands and curved, upright fingers.

adjacent-key and long-reach errors

1 A number of economic reports predict a bright outlook for the economy.

2 In my opinion, few errors of the covert type were made by the officer.

Emphasize concentration on copy and continuity of typing.

vowel-confusion errors

3 A thief stole a pie from my neighbor during the weird but quiet storm.

4 I tried to seize the foreign piece before it was weighed by the chief.

Emphasize down-and-in spacing with thumb curved and close to space bar.

spacing errors

5 If he is to do the work for us, she may not be able to work with them.

6 Many men and women may share my interest in an exhibit of pop artists.

123d ▶ 15
Measure Basic Skill: Straight Copy

two 5′ writings; find *gwam*; circle errors; record better rate

all letters used | A | 1.5 si | 5.7 awl | 80% hfw

	gwam 3′		5′
Information is made up of words, numbers, and symbols that convey	4	3	40
knowledge which can be used in many ways. The mass of information we	9	5	42
have is expanding at a rapid rate. It has caused a paperwork explosion.	14	8	45
One of the major results is a revolution in the way information is pro-	19	11	48
cessed in the office. The most widely used term for such work is word	23	14	51
processing. It is a system that involves workers who are educated to	28	17	54
use specific procedures and electronic equipment.	32	19	56
A word originator dictates or writes input that a word processing	36	22	58
worker types on electronic equipment. It is stored in the system for	41	24	61
later use. The system makes it easy to record, store, recall, and revise	46	27	64
information. For instance, name and address lists can be recalled from	50	30	67
a memory bank to be changed or to send bills, fliers, and other notices.	55	33	70
As you can see, a sizable amount of information stored in the system	60	36	73
can be used in many ways.	62	37	74

gwam 3′ | 1 | 2 | 3 | 4 | 5

5′ | 1 | 2 | 3

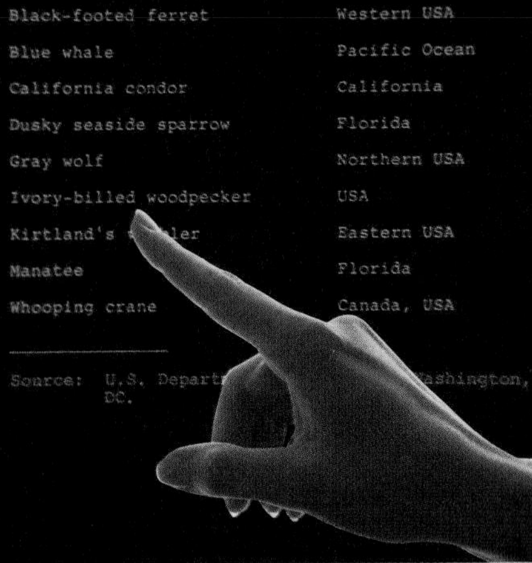

Unit 35 Lessons 164-168

Learning Goals

1. Assess and reinforce knowledge of table format.
2. Improve efficiency in processing tables.
3. Improve composing skill at the keyboard.
4. Increase straight-copy speed and control.

Kinds of Tables Processed

1. Tables with 2 and 3 columns.
2. Tables with main headings, secondary headings, and column headings.
3. Script and rought-draft tables.

FORMATTING GUIDES: TABLES

Full sheet

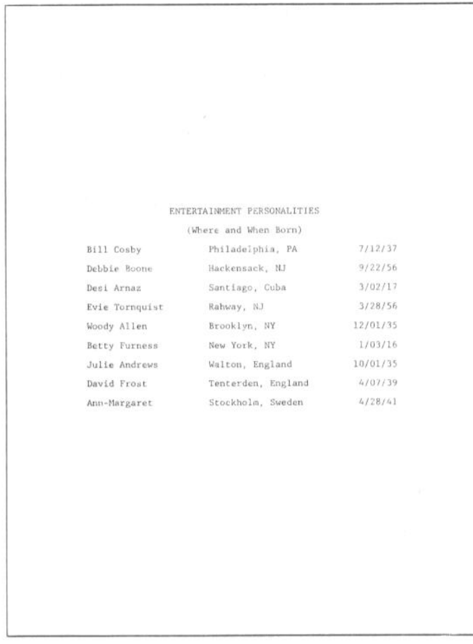

ENTERTAINMENT PERSONALITIES

(Where and When Born)

Bill Cosby	Philadelphia, PA	7/12/37
Debbie Boone	Hackensack, NJ	9/22/56
Desi Arnaz	Santiago, Cuba	3/02/17
Evie Tornquist	Rahway, NJ	3/28/56
Woody Allen	Brooklyn, NY	12/01/35
Betty Furness	New York, NY	1/03/16
Julie Andrews	Walton, England	10/01/35
David Frost	Tenterden, England	4/07/39
Ann-Margaret	Stockholm, Sweden	4/28/41

Half sheet, long edge at top

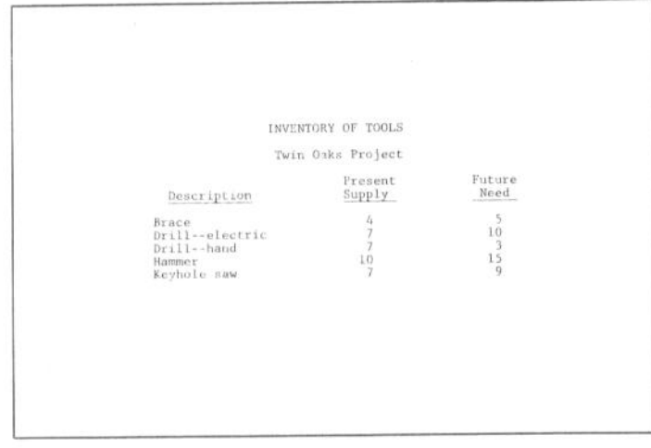

INVENTORY OF TOOLS

Twin Oaks Project

Description	Present Supply	Future Need
Brace	4	5
Drill--electric	7	10
Drill--hand	7	3
Hammer	10	15
Keyhole saw	7	9

Half sheet, short edge at top

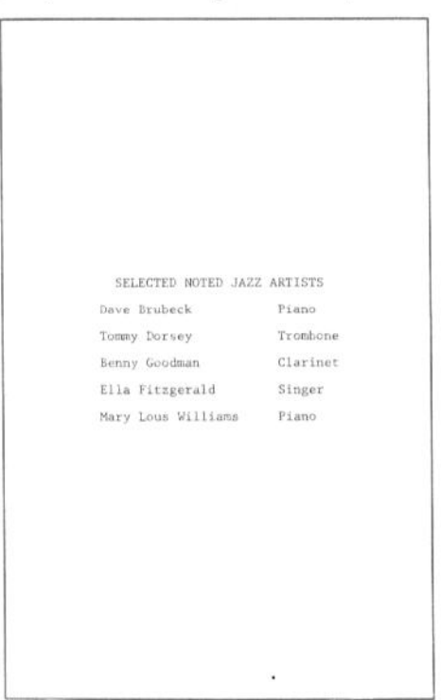

SELECTED NOTED JAZZ ARTISTS

Dave Brubeck	Piano
Tommy Dorsey	Trombone
Benny Goodman	Clarinet
Ella Fitzgerald	Singer
Mary Lous Williams	Piano

To format tables, you must know how to center vertically (up and down) and horizontally (across the page).

Vertical Centering

Tables are keyed on sheets so that the top margin and the bottom margin are approximately equal. Approximately half of the lines of the table are placed above the vertical center of the sheet and approximately half are placed below the vertical center.

To determine the line on which to key the main heading, do the following:

1. Count the total lines, including blank lines.
2. Subtract the total lines from lines available (66 for full sheet; 33 for half sheet, long edge at top; 51 for half sheet, short edge at top).
3. Divide the remainder by 2 to determine the number of the line on which to start. If a fraction results, disregard it. If the number that results is even, space down that number from the top edge of your paper. If the number is odd, use next lower number.

Tables that are placed slightly above vertical center are sometimes said to be in "reading position." This placement seems to make a more attractive placement.

Horizontal Centering

Tables should be placed horizontally so that an equal number of blank spaces appear in the left and right margins. Half the number of characters and spaces in the lines of the table should be to the left of the horizontal center point of the sheet and half should be to the right of the center point.

Spacing between columns of tables varies depending upon the number of columns to be centered. For ease of centering, leave an even number of spaces between columns.

The line length for the illustration in the next column above is 39 spaces. Half of those spaces (19) should be placed to the left of center and half (20) to the right of center.

center ↓

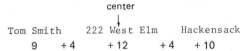

Tom Smith		222 West Elm		Hackensack
9	+ 4	+ 12	+ 4	+ 10

Note: The number of spaces in the longest line of each column is shown; the number of spaces between columns is 4. Total = 39

Use these steps to center horizontally:

1. Clear all margin and tab stops.
2. Find exact horizontal center on any size paper by adding the typewriter or printer scale reading at the left and right edges of the paper and dividing the total by 2.
3. Backspace from center point once for each 2 strokes in the longest line of each column, then once for each 2 spaces between columns. Ignore a single stroke at the end of backspace process. Set left margin stop.
4. Space forward once for each stroke in the longest line in the first column plus once for each space between Columns 1 and 2; set tab stop at this point for Column 2; repeat the procedure for the remaining columns.

Horizontal Centering of Columnar Headings

Columnar headings are generally centered over their respective columns. To center a heading over a column:

1. Determine the longest item in the column, whether columnar heading or columnar entry.
2. Determine the center point of the column by spacing forward once for each 2 characters and spaces in the longest item. If an odd or leftover stroke occurs at the end of the longest item, do not space forward for it.
3. From the center point of the column, backspace once for each 2 characters and spaces in the columnar heading. Begin heading where the backspacing ends.

SOUTH-WESTERN
PUBLISHING CO.

Unit 25 Lessons 124-125

Measurement Goals

1. To evaluate your table formatting and keyboarding skill.

2. To evaluate your report formatting and keyboarding skill.

Machine Adjustments

Make the usual machine adjustments as required for various activities.

Lesson 124 Evaluate Table Skills

124a ▶ 5 Conditioning Practice

each line 3 times (slowly, faster, in-between rate); as time permits, repeat selected lines

alphabet 1 Most companies emphasize extra valuable jobs for good quality workers.

fig/sym 2 This rug (12′ × 13′6″) was $481.50, but it is now on sale for $317.90.

shift key 3 The salespersons are from Dow & Co., J. & B. Products, and Lynn & Son.

speed 4 When they pay for the land, they may sign the audit form for the firm.

| 1 | 2 | 3 | 4 | 5 | 6 | 7 | 8 | 9 | 10 | 11 | 12 | 13 | 14 |

124b ▶ 45 Evaluate Table Formatting and Problem-Solving Skill

In this activity, you will be evaluated on your ability to arrange and keyboard tables. Only minimum directions are given. You are to make any needed decisions as to placement.

Problem 1

full sheet; DS data; correct errors

		words
Main heading:	TEN LARGEST COUNTRIES	4
	IN TERMS OF POPULATION	9
Secondary heading:	(In Millions)	12

Country	Population	words
People's Republic of China	1,042.0	24
India	762.2	26
Soviet Union	278.0	30
United States	238.9	34
Indonesia	168.4	37
Brazil	138.4	40
Japan	120.8	42
Bangladesh	101.5	45
Pakistan	99.2	48
Nigeria	91.2	51

__________________ 55

Source: Population Reference Bureau, Inc., Wash- 63
ington, DC, 1985. 68

Problems continued on page 216.

162b (continued)

words

Education for enrichment. Since enrichment education is often regarded 606
as being over and above the required or expected, it is a "natural" for an in- 621
dependent learning setting. One skill that is not typically taught in regular 637
elementary classes and that can be taught effectively by CAI is keyboarding. 653
Since keyboarding skill is essential to the efficient operation of the com- 668
puter and since most teachers in elementary schools are not familiar with 682
keyboarding teaching techniques, it seems particularly appropriate for 696
CAI. However, caution should be observed in selecting the learning pack- 711
age, as there are numerous programs available but few that apply sound 725
keyboarding learning principles. 732

Secondary Education 739

CAI has a place in almost every subject offered in the high school. In addi- 755
tion, there are numerous subject matter applications that students should 769
learn to perform on the computer rather than manually. The applications 784
range from those in vocational classes to those in general education classes. 801
Quite possibly the subject area with the greatest potential for computer 814
usage is business education. By some estimates, as high as 80 percent of all 830
applications on the computer are business related. 840

Postsecondary and Adult Education 853

Several colleges and universities now require entering students to purchase 869
computers for use throughout their tenure at the institution. Those that do 884
not require the individuals to own computers provide ample exposure to 898
computer usage so that graduates are comfortable with the technology when 912
they enter their respective careers. 920

Many individuals, though, who are already into their careers have not had 935
the opportunity to interact with computers. Businesses recognize this defi- 950
ciency and are quickly correcting it through training and development 964
programs designed for this purpose. 971

It seems apparent that there are no age or ability barriers to the potential of 987
computers as educational tools and as aids in performing tasks. Even the 1002
video games that are popular with both children and adults have some skill 1017
development and educational value. 1024

Lesson 163 Leftbound/Topbound Reports

163a ▶ 5 Conditioning Practice

Repeat 162a, p. 284.

163b ▶ 30 Leftbound Report

Continue 162b, pp. 285-286, until finished.

163c ▶ 15 Improve Formatting: Topbound Reports

2 full sheets

1. Key the main heading and ¶ 1 of 162b-163b as a topbound report (use page line gauge, LM p. 8).

2. Key a portion of the second page of a topbound report as follows: Begin with paragraph heading "Education for enrichment"; complete two lines only; operate return 20 times (DS mode); continue keying beginning with the side heading "Postsecondary and Adult Education"; complete the number of lines needed to finish page 2, including the page number.

3. Proofread; circle errors.

124b (continued)

Problem 2
full sheet; DS data; correct errors

words

Main heading: KEYBOARDING TASKS PERFORMED 6

ACCORDING TO JOB CLASSIFICATIONS 12

Secondary heading: (Percent of Keyboarding Time) 18

	Typist	Steno.	Secretary	W.P.O.*	Other**	words
						32
Letters	21%	27%	32%	32%	23%	36
Reports	16	20	19	24	21	39
Memos	12	19	22	14	13	42
Forms	29	11	11	7	24	45
Tables	9	13	9	15	8	48
Other	13	10	7	8	11	55
Totals	100%	100%	100%	100%	100%	61

____________________ 65

*Word Processing Operators. 70
**Workers with titles other than those listed. 79

Problem 3
full sheet; DS data; block headings; correct errors

Main heading: LARGEST PARKS LOCATED WITHIN 6

THE LIMITS OF AMERICAN CITIES 12

Column headings: Name of Park / City / Acres 21

Name of Park	City	Acres	words
Fairmont Park	Philadelphia	3,845	27
Griffith Park	Los Angeles	3,761	34
Pelham Bay Park	New York City	2,117	41
Rock Creek Park	Washington	1,800	48
Balboa Park	San Diego	1,400	53
Forest Park	St. Louis	1,380	59
Washington Park	Cleveland	1,212	65
Lincoln Park	Chicago	1,185	71
Golden Gate Park	San Francisco	1,107	78
Belle Isle Park	Detroit	985	84

____________________ 87

Source: National Recreation and Parks Association, Washington, DC. 98 101

If time permits, repeat as many problems as possible for extra credit. Make these changes:
Problem 1, half sheet, short edge at top
Problem 2, half sheet, short edge at top
Problem 3, half sheet, long edge at top, SS data

Lesson 125 Evaluate Report Skills

125a ▶ 5 Conditioning Practice

each line 3 times (slowly, faster, in-between rate); as time permits, repeat selected lines

alphabet 1 Visitors did enjoy the amazing water tricks of six quaint polar bears.
fig/sym 2 Order #3-170 (May 24) from Smith & Co. totals $58.69, less 2/10, n/30.
long words 3 These laboratories specialize in solid-state space propulsion systems.
speed 4 Their men may do the work for us and the city if she pays them for it.

| 1 | 2 | 3 | 4 | 5 | 6 | 7 | 8 | 9 | 10 | 11 | 12 | 13 | 14 |

162b ▶ 45
Document Production: Leftbound Report

Process the copy at the right as a leftbound report DS. Space and key side and paragraph headings according to standard guides; indent paragraphs appropriately. Also, format a reference page, title page, and table of contents for the report. Use the information below to prepare the reference page:

"B. F. Skinner: Computers Can Cure What's Wrong in American Education."
InfoWorld
Peggy Zientara
February 6, 1984, 23.

"Keyboarding Instruction in Elementary School."
Business Education Forum
Patricia L. Headley
December 1983, 18-19.

"Something Old, Something New: Trainers and Computer-based Learning."
Training and Development Journal
John R. Eldridge and Warren A. Boyd, Jr.
December 1983, 57-61.

"Microcomputers in the Business Classroom."
The Balance Sheet
Kathryn M. Pearce
May/June 1984, 35-36.

"Special Tools for Special Kids."
Teaching, Learning, Computing
Eve G. Freeman
December 1983, 54-57.

Proofread and correct errors.

words

COMPUTERS IN EDUCATION 5

The widespread availability of computers today has led to their use in almost 20
all phases of our personal and our professional lives. It is not surprising, 36
therefore, that computers have become an aid in the educational process, 50
not only in the formal educational environment, but also in people's personal 66
learning efforts as well as in businesses' employee training and development 81
programs. 84

One of the major problems, though, in attempting to use computers for edu- 99
cational purposes is the violation of sound principles of learning in much of 114
the software. Individuals selecting educational software should evaluate the 129
program for the same appropriate instructional methods that B. F. Skinner 144
stated about his teaching machine in an interview with Zientara (1984, 23): 160
". . . teaching should incorporate individual, interactive instruction and should 176
give the student immediate feedback." In addition, other well-founded 190
teaching/learning practices that would be used in the traditional classroom 206
setting can and should be applied in the software. 216

Elementary Education 224

While computer-aided instruction (CAI) can be of value with all aspects of 239
elementary education, it can perhaps add more to what is already being 253
accomplished in areas outside the regular classes. Two such areas are spe- 268
cial education and education for enrichment. 277

Special education. Special education teachers are quick to point out that 296
computers are aids and not meant to replace the teacher and other success- 311
ful methods. They suspect, though, that "their students feel comfortable 325
with the machines because they make no value judgments and never get 339
impatient when repeating a lesson for the umpteenth time," reported Free- 354
man (1983, 54). Computers, therefore, help to overcome the human element 368
of teaching that involves boredom with and/or lack of time for repetition. 384

Equally important is the capability of compensating for physical handicaps 399
through the uses of various devices to operate the computer. These include 414
mouthsticks, toesticks, and headwands which may be used to operate the 428
keyboard. In addition, voice-entry terminals may be used by those who are 443
unable to use the keyboard. 449

There are numerous reports of physically handicapped individuals who have, 464
through the computer, encountered successes that they have never before 478
experienced. One such example was a 48-year-old deaf-mute man whose 492
speech was understood for the first time in his life. The computer was able 507
to assimilate his sounds and reproduce the words which the sounds repre- 522
sented. This accomplishment was possible because: "Once a word is typed 536
into a computer equipped with a voice recognition board, and repeated aloud, 552
the computer is able to reproduce the word in print when it hears the sound 567
again" (Freeman, 1983, 57). These kinds of experiences are laden with emo- 582
tion and are rewarding. 587

(continued on next page)

125b ▶ 45

Evaluate Report Formatting Skill

Arrange copy in unbound manuscript form; DS; number second and additional pages in upper right corner; correct errors if so directed.

PREPARING A TERM PAPER

Preparing a term paper for a class requirement can be an ordeal, or it can be an enjoyable learning experience. Here are some suggestions that may make your experience easier and help you produce a winning term paper.

Select a Topic

If a topic for your term paper isn't assigned to you, try to select a topic which may be of interest to you or that will further your knowledge about a particular field. Once you've decided on a topic, read a general overview about it in an encyclopedia or a specialized reference book. This overview should give a history of your topic, acquaint you with many of the definitions relating to your topic, and highlight those aspects you may wish to research further. In addition, it will pinpoint major controversies and problems dealing with your topic and will usually contain references that will give you new leads to follow.

Locate and Summarize Information About Your Topic

Once you have some general knowledge about your topic, you will want to locate and examine more detailed data. Look in books, periodicals, abstracts, newspapers, and government documents. Also, personal interviews with knowledgeable persons may be a rich source of information.

After locating and reading your source material, you will need to take detailed notes on the material. Most persons like to use cards (6″ × 4″ or 8″ × 5″) for their notations and summaries. You may wish to use one set of cards for necessary reference information (author, title, publisher, city, and date of publication) and another for summaries and quotations. When compiling your reference information, be sure to record accurately and completely all needed information.

Good note taking is essential for producing a good research paper. Do not try to write down everything you read but rather select only the key points that you think you might later use. Further, you will not want your paper to be a string of quotations; therefore, learn to paraphrase main ideas from your sources, quoting directly only the information you feel is of major importance. Taylor describes what he found that good summarizers often did:

> The successful (summarizers)...(saw) objectively how the pieces were organized--the introduction, key points, and the conclusion. They knew where to look for meaning....In addition, the successful summarizers read each article four or five times to make sure they understood what the author had said (1984, 390-391).

Write and Edit Your Paper

The central purpose of a reference paper should be clear in your mind before you have finished investigating all your resources. When you have gathered a sufficient amount of material to put your topic in focus, it is time to formulate a thesis statement. Your thesis statement--the main idea or statement of purpose--makes a claim about a topic. Usually this claim will argue a specific position, analyze a problem, or explain a situation.

Organize your reference cards and prepare an outline. Read through your cards so that you will have a working knowledge of the information you have compiled. Sort your cards into piles, using the title headings on each card as a guide. Working from your cards, prepare an outline showing the order in which you wish to present your material. Each point in the outline should contribute in some way to the central idea or thesis.

Prepare a rough draft. Use your notes and your outline to prepare a rough draft. It should include an introductory paragraph (which contains your thesis statement), the body of your paper (substantive content which supports your thesis), and a conclusion. You should also, as Corder suggests, "Make certain that you are thoroughly familiar with your material before you begin to write. You should have the information on your note cards so well in mind that you can write rapidly and with confidence once you start" (1978, 425).

Edit and revise your rough draft and prepare the final copy. Consult a standard English grammar handbook to help you correct any usage errors. You may also want to incorporate into your paper any suggestions made by persons who have read your rough draft. Make other changes which you think will improve your paper. Then, prepare the final draft. A neatly keyboarded double-spaced report is an added plus when you submit your work for evaluation by your teacher. In preparing your final draft, you may wish to incorporate some of the suggestions given in Unit 23, Lessons 111-118, of this book.

After following the above suggestions, you should have a winning term paper!

(Lesson 125 is continued on next page.)

Lesson 161 Title Page/Contents Page

161a ▶ 5 Conditioning Practice

each line twice SS (slowly, then faster); DS between 2-line groups; if time permits, repeat selected lines

alphabet 1 Many workers can be lax and lazy about quotas if the job is depriving.

figures 2 I placed a Model 4026 microcomputer in Room 382 at 156 West 79 Street.

shift/lock 3 Neva belongs to ASLA, Lois belongs to NBEA, and Bruno belongs to ASTD.

speed 4 Shamrocks and an iris may be visible on the land by an ancient chapel.

| 1 | 2 | 3 | 4 | 5 | 6 | 7 | 8 | 9 | 10 | 11 | 12 | 13 | 14 |

161b ▶ 30 Document Production: Reports

Problem 1
Title Page and Table of Contents

1. Study the models and prepare a title page and table of contents for 159c, Problem 1, p. 280.

2. Insert leaders in the table of contents by alternating periods and spaces, noting whether you start the periods on an odd or even space.

3. Proofread; circle errors.

Problem 2
Title Page and Table of Contents

Prepare a title page and table of contents for 160c, Problem 1, p. 283.

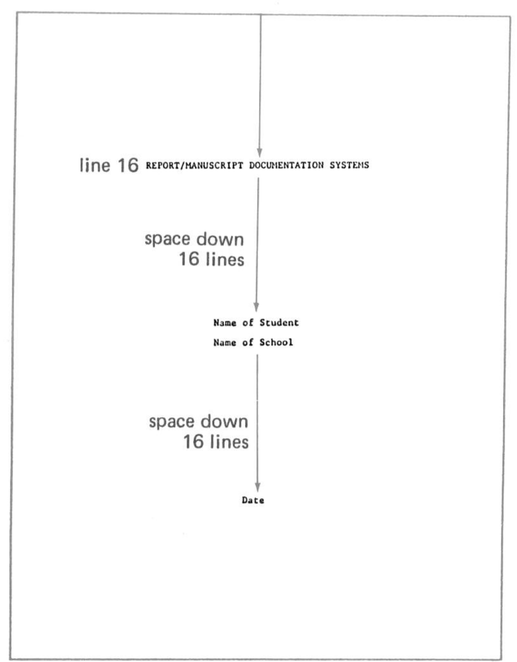

Unbound title page

line 10 (10-pitch)
line 12 (12-pitch)

TABLE OF CONTENTS

QS

Footnotes with Bibliography 1

indent 5 spaces Historic method 1

Difficulties 1

Endnotes 1

Textual Citations with Reference List 2

Unbound table of contents

161c ▶ 15 Improve Language Skills: Compose at Keyboard

Identify two things that you consider to be your greatest time wasters. Compose a ¶ on each one explaining what the time waster is, why it is a problem for you, and how you might eliminate it.

1. Compose at the keyboard in DS format; ignore keying errors; if necessary, x-out copy and continue keying.

2. Edit your copy; then rekey it in final form on a full sheet.

Lesson 162 Leftbound/Topbound Reports

162a ▶ 5 Conditioning Practice

each line twice SS (slowly, then faster); DS between 2-line groups; if time permits, repeat selected lines

alphabet 1 Zeb expressed a sense of humor even by joking in a calm and quiet way.

figures 2 Jo looked at Section 25 on page 179 instead of Section 48 on page 360.

symbols 3 "Yeah!" shouted Pedro's big brother as Pedro marched across the stage.

speed 4 The girls may dig for antique ivory and bowls by a shanty at the lake.

| 1 | 2 | 3 | 4 | 5 | 6 | 7 | 8 | 9 | 10 | 11 | 12 | 13 | 14 |

125b (continued)
Prepare a Reference Page

REFERENCES

Corder, Jim W. Handbook of Current English. 5th ed. Glenview, IL: Scott, Foresman and Company, 1978.

Taylor, Karl K. "Teaching Summarization Skills." Journal of Reading, February 1984, 390-391.

ENRICHMENT ACTIVITY: Timed Writing

Increase Your Keyboarding Speed and/or Improve Your Control

1. Take a 3′ timed writing. Find *gwam*; circle errors.

2. *If you made six or fewer errors* in the Step 1 writing, take a 2′ guided writing on each ¶; work for increased speed. **Goal:** To increase your speed 2-4 *gwam*.

If you made more than 6 errors in the Step 1 writing, follow Step 3.

3. Take a 2′ guided writing on each ¶ for improved control. Reduce your Step 1 rate by 4 *gwam*. **Goal:** To keyboard with not over 2 errors a minute.

4. Take five 1′ writings on each ¶; *start each new writing at the end of the previous writing.* Try to maintain your rate for either speed or control (according to your needs) for the second and succeeding writings. *Example*: If you keyboarded to the 40-word mark in the first 1′ timed writing, you should try to get to the 80 word mark in the second timed writing since you will start it at the 40-word mark, etc.

5. Take a 5′ timed writing on both paragraphs. **Goal:** To maintain your Step 4 rate for the 5′ writing. Find *gwam*; circle errors.

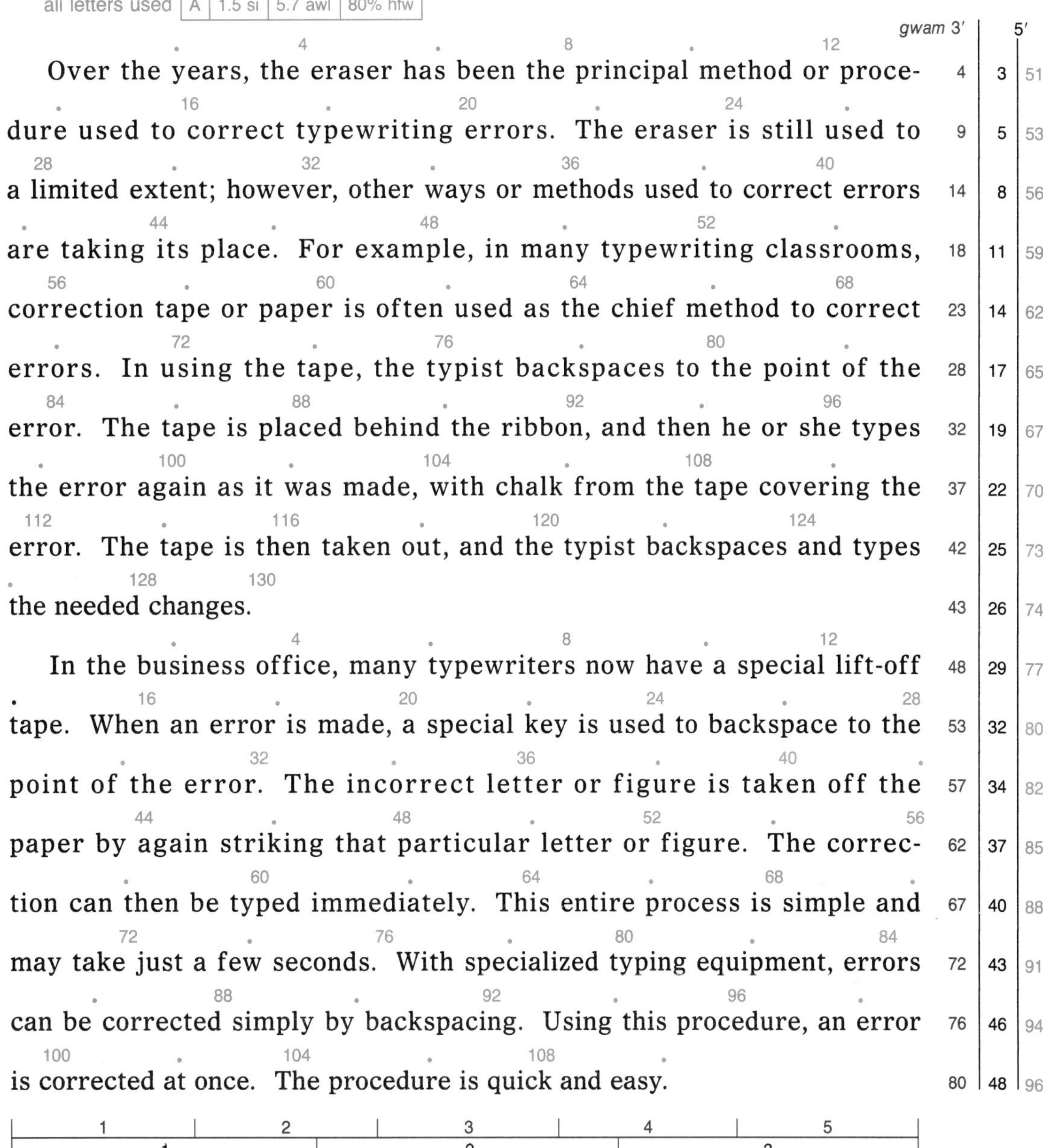

all letters used | A | 1.5 si | 5.7 awl | 80% hfw

gwam 3′ | 5′

Over the years, the eraser has been the principal method or proce- 4 3 51
dure used to correct typewriting errors. The eraser is still used to 9 5 53
a limited extent; however, other ways or methods used to correct errors 14 8 56
are taking its place. For example, in many typewriting classrooms, 18 11 59
correction tape or paper is often used as the chief method to correct 23 14 62
errors. In using the tape, the typist backspaces to the point of the 28 17 65
error. The tape is placed behind the ribbon, and then he or she types 32 19 67
the error again as it was made, with chalk from the tape covering the 37 22 70
error. The tape is then taken out, and the typist backspaces and types 42 25 73
the needed changes. 43 26 74

In the business office, many typewriters now have a special lift-off 48 29 77
tape. When an error is made, a special key is used to backspace to the 53 32 80
point of the error. The incorrect letter or figure is taken off the 57 34 82
paper by again striking that particular letter or figure. The correc- 62 37 85
tion can then be typed immediately. This entire process is simple and 67 40 88
may take just a few seconds. With specialized typing equipment, errors 72 43 91
can be corrected simply by backspacing. Using this procedure, an error 76 46 94
is corrected at once. The procedure is quick and easy. 80 48 96

gwam 3′ | 1 | 2 | 3 | 4 | 5
5′ | 1 | 2 | 3

160c ▶ 30 Document Production: Reports

Problem 1
Leftbound Report with Footnotes

Review the directions for formatting leftbound reports on p. 279 and 282. Then process the report DS; proofread; circle errors.

words

ERGONOMICS AND THE BUSINESS OFFICE 7

Ergonomics, simply defined by Springer as "the study of humans at 20
work,"[1] has become a topic of popular interest and concern in recent years. 36
To be more specific, ergonomics deals with the compatibility of people and 51
the other properties in their work environment. According to Popham, 65
"...ergonomics integrates both the physiological and psychological factors 80
involved in creating an effective work area."[2] It includes, therefore, the 95
office furniture and equipment; the physical layout; and procedures such 110
as the organization and method of work in the office as well as the worker's 125
attitude toward computer software he or she must use. 136

Physical Factors 143

While there are several physical factors that affect workers' produc- 157
tivity, two of the more common ones are the office chair and the video dis- 171
play terminal (VDT). Since most office personnel perform their tasks from 186
a seated position, it is obvious that the chair is the foundation of the work- 202
station. The widespread use of the video display terminal--sometimes for 217
long periods of time--in today's office makes the VDT another apparent 231
source of ergonomics attention. 237

Office chairs. Since office personnel vary so greatly in size, it is impera- 255
tive that office chairs be adjustable. While most chair seats can be moved 270
up or down, most often it is difficult to do and sometimes requires special 286
tools. The ideal is the office chair designed for easy adjustments of both 301
the seat and back so that users can alter their positions as tasks change or 316
fatigue occurs. 320

VDTs. Problems with VDTs vary from screen glare to posture strain. 334
Glare can be remedied by the use of window coverings, recessed or indirect 349
lighting, and screens that tilt and turn. Designs that separate the keyboard 365
and screen aid both of these problems. 373

Psychological Factors 381

Among the psychological factors that influence worker comfort is the 395
worker's perception of software he or she may use. Even some ergonomi- 409
cally alert people have not considered software to be an ergonomic issue. 424
However, "friendly" software that is designed to be readily usable and that 439
is documented for understanding by nontechnical users is just as much a 454
part of ergonomics as are the hardware and furniture. 465

______________ 469

[1]T. J. Springer, "Ergonomics: The Real Issues," Office Administration 483
and Automation, May 1984, p. 69. 493

[2]Estelle L. Popham, Rita Sloan Tilton, J. Howard Jackson, and J Marshall 507
Hanna, Secretarial Procedures and Administration (Cincinnati: South- 521
Western Publishing Co., 1983), p. 31. 527

Problem 2
Bibliography

Prepare a bibliography for Problem 1 using the information in the footnotes plus the references listed at the right that were used for general information.

"Ergonomics: The Human Factor."
Output
Tom McCusker
March 1981
24-27

"Reports from the Ergonomics Frontiers."
Office Administration and Automation
Walter J. Presnick
October 1983, 40-44

"Developers Apply Psychology."
InfoWorld
Peggy Watt
March 5, 1984
37-38

Lessons 126-150

PHASE 6

Process Special Documents

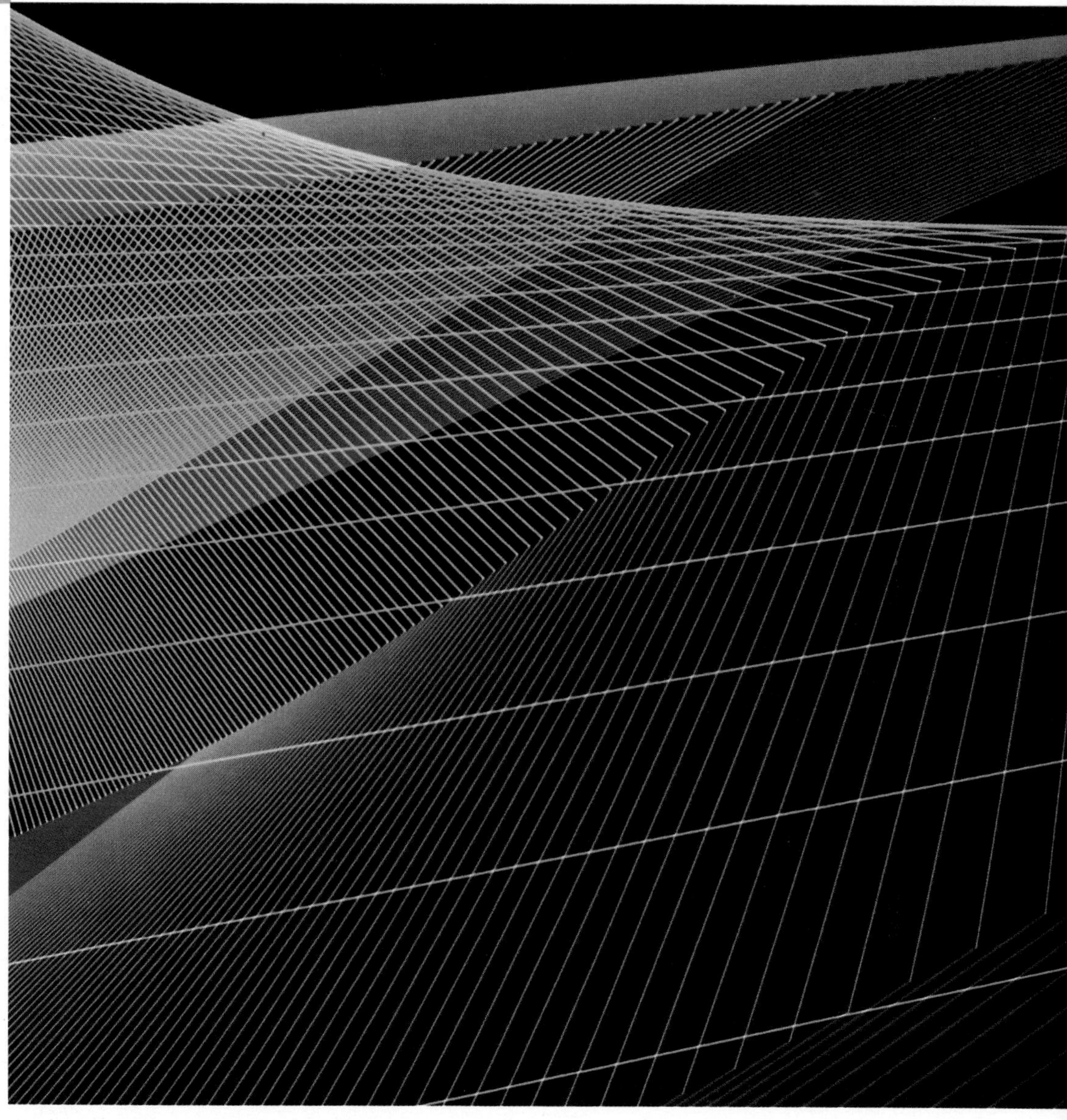

The primary goals of Phase 6 are to continue the development of your skill in processing documents and to integrate the knowledge and skills you acquired in Phases 4 and 5. You will learn to format correspondence with special features, various kinds of forms, and office employment documents. You will compose employment documents for your own personal use.

The specific objectives of Phase 6 are to improve, develop, and/or measure the following competencies:

1. Straight-copy speed and accuracy.
2. Production of documents such as letters with special features, forms, and employment documents.
3. Decision-making skills.
4. Language skills.

159c (continued)

Problem 3
Unbound Report with Explanatory Note

When an explanatory note or footnote appears on a partially filled page, the divider line and explanatory footnote may be placed either immediately following the body of the report or at the bottom of the page, leaving a 1″ bottom margin. Use the page line gauge, LM p. 8, as an aid in placing explanatory footnotes at the bottom of the page.

words

Employee Insurance Eligibility 6

All group insurance policies are underwritten by the National 19
Insurance Company. 23

Eligible Employees and Dependents 36

An eligible employee is defined as a company employee who is 48
employed at least 75 percent of the time for a period of not less 61
than 12 consecutive calendar months. The eligible dependents 74
include the legal spouse of the insured, unmarried children 86
under the age of 19 years, and unmarried children who are full- 98
time students at an accredited college or university.* 110

Effective Date of Coverage 120

Policy coverage will become effective on the first day of the 133
calendar month following the date of application. If the 144
insurance application is made after payroll closeout, a double 157
deduction from the next paycheck will be made. 166

______ 170

*Definition of "dependent" may be altered in some cases. 181

Lesson 160 Leftbound Reports with Footnotes

160a ▶ 5 Conditioning Practice

each line twice SS (slowly, then faster); DS between 2-line groups; if time permits, repeat selected lines

alphabet 1 Zack did fly quite a way by private plane just for the extra meetings.

figures 2 Al's ZIP Code in Cincinnati, Ohio, is 45236-7819; Sue's is 45207-2763.

symbols 3 Lu's aunt (her mother's sister) was secretary-treasurer of B & B Club.

speed 4 It is their duty to fight for the amendment and risk their own profit.

| 1 | 2 | 3 | 4 | 5 | 6 | 7 | 8 | 9 | 10 | 11 | 12 | 13 | 14 |

160b ▶ 15 Improve Footnote Formatting

1. Review information on formatting footnotes on p. 279.

2. Set margins for leftbound report.

3. Determine the line on which to begin typing (near bottom of page) in order to leave a 1″ bottom margin. Use page line guage, LM p. 8.

4. Key these last two lines of the page plus the footnotes in correct format.

5. Proofread and circle errors.

greater to satisfy human interface requirements and to meet productivity goals in a real-world business environment."[3]

______

[2]Jorday Gold, "How Fast Are you Really communicating?" Personal Computing july 1984 p. 149.

[3]Robert C. Natale, Networking Micros, Computerworld 13 July 1934 p. 61.

Unit 26 Lessons 126-129

Learning Goals

1. To learn to format and process letters with special features: mailing notation, attention line, subject line, company name in closing lines, multiple enclosures, copy notations, and postscripts.
2. To learn to format letter addresses with long lines.
3. To improve production speed.
4. To compose and edit paragraphs.

Machine Adjustments

1. Paper guide at *0*.
2. Paper bail rolls at even intervals across page.
3. Margins: 70-space line for drill lines and timed paragraphs; as needed for letters.
4. Spacing: SS for drill lines and letters, unless otherwise directed. DS for timed paragraphs.

FORMATTING GUIDES: CORRESPONDENCE WITH SPECIAL FEATURES

Although not frequently used, several special features may be used in business letters. These features are illustrated in the model letter on page 221. In some cases, alternative formats for special parts are correct (for example, the subject line may be placed in various positions). The simplest and most efficient formats, however, are illustrated in this unit.

Mailing notations (REGISTERED, CERTIFIED, SPECIAL DELIVERY, or AIRMAIL) begin at the left margin in ALL CAPS a double space below the dateline and a double space above the first line of the letter address. (Note: AIRMAIL is used only on foreign mail.)

An *attention line* may be used if the first line of the letter address is a company name. Place the attention line on the second line of the letter address. Some examples are:

Attention Mrs. Susan Jay, Manager
Attention Mr. Edward Jackson
Attention Office Manager

When a letter is addressed to a company, the correct salutation is "Ladies and Gentlemen," even though an attention line may name an individual.

Place the *subject line* a double space below the salutation. If the body paragraphs are blocked, block the subject line at left margin. If the body paragraphs are indented, indent the subject line or center it. The word "Subject" may be used. If used, follow the word "Subject" by a colon and two spaces before completing the subject line.

When used, place *company name* a double space below the complimentary close in ALL CAPS. QS (quadruple-space) to signature line.

Place *enclosure notation* a double space below reference initials. If multiple enclosures are referred to in the letter, follow the word "Enclosures" with a colon and two spaces and list each enclosure.

Enclosures: Order Forms
Price List

A *photocopy* or *carbon copy* notation indicates that a copy of the letter is being sent to someone other than the addressee. Use "pc" (*photocopy*) or "cc" (*carbon copy*) followed by the name of the person(s) to receive a copy. Place copy notation a double space below Enclosure, if used, or the reference line if there is no enclosure.

pc James C. Smith
Cynthia J. Maxon
Julio Sanchez

A *postscript* is an additional paragraph that may be added after a letter has been completed. It is the last item in the letter. Place a double space below the preceding item, and begin at same paragraph point (indented or blocked) as the body paragraphs.

Long lines in the letter address are carried to the next line and indented three spaces.

In both the letter address and closing lines, *professional titles* may be placed on the same line as the name separated by a comma or placed on the following line without a comma.

Ms. Anna Cox, Office Manager
or
Ms. Anna Cox
Office Manager

Use the form which gives the best balance and attractiveness.

Note. When several special features are used in a letter, the dateline may be raised to present a more attractive appearance on the page. Generally, raise the dateline one line for each two special-feature lines used.

words

Endnotes 259

When using endnotes as recommended by the Modern Language Associa- 272
tion (1977, 28-31), the sources are listed in the order cited in the Endnote sec- 288
tion at the end of the paper. This method is simpler to use than the footnote 304
method. However, both the endnote and footnote methods require the use of 319
superior (raised) figures at the point of reference in the text, which cannot 334
be accommodated by some of the electronic printers in use today. There- 349
fore, the MLA recommendation (1984, 161-63) was revised to use brief paren- 363
thetical citations in the text and a bibliography at the end of research papers. 380
With this procedure, endnotes are used only for explanatory purposes. 394

This newer MLA-recommended method of documentation is similar to the 408
author-date method used in this report and described below as textual cita- 423
tions with reference list. 428

Textual Citations with Reference List 443

When using the textual citation method, the surname of each author, 457
the publication date, and page number(s) (if appropriate) of the material 472
cited are given in the text. Then a reference list arranged alphabetically 487
by authors' names appears on a separate page at the end of the paper. This 502
method is strongly recommended by Seybold and Young in The Chicago 518
Manual of Style (1982, 400) because it is simple and efficient to produce on 536
both the typewriter and electronic printer. 545

Problem 2
Reference Page

Process the reference page at the right for the Problem 1 report using the same margins as for Problem 1 (unbound report).

Note that references are arranged in alphabetical order by authors' last names. See RG 9 for illustrations of references having an editor rather than author or having neither author nor editor.

Note: When two or more works by the same author are listed, repetition of the author's name is unnecessary. Instead, a line the length of the last name of the first author listed, followed by a period, is substituted.

REFERENCES 2

Gilbaldi, Joseph, and Walter S. Achtert. MLA Handbook for 17
Writers of Research Papers, Theses, and Dissertations New 40
York: Modern Language Association, 1987. 49

________. MLA Handbook for Writers of Research Papers New York: 71
Modern Language Assocaition 1984. 78

Seybold, Catharine and Bruce Young. The Chicago Manual of Style. 97
13th ed. Chicago: The Unibersity of Chicago Press, 1982. 109

Turabian, Kate L. A Manual for Writers of Term Papers, Theses 131
and Dissertations. 4th ed. Chicago: The University of 146
Chicago press 1973. 150

(Problem 3 is on next page.)

words in parts | total words

Line 12 March 15, 19-- 3 3
DS

Mailing notation REGISTERED 5 5
DS

Hildebrand, Kemp, Fitzgerald, Milton, 12 12
Fenton, and Associates, Inc. 18 18
Attention line Attention Mr. Richard C. Hrbacke 25 25
124 North Broad Street 29 29
Philadelphia, PA 19107-2218 35 35
DS

Ladies and Gentlemen: 39 39
DS

Subject line Subject: Everett-Cox Agreement 46 46
DS

The enclosed draft has been prepared in accordance with 11 57
our understanding of the verbal agreements that your 22 68
clients, Cecil and Ann Cox, made with Cynthia E. Everett 33 79
on March 8, 19--. Would you please review this document, 45 91
mark any changes that you believe should be made, and 56 101
return the draft to me within the next week. 65 111

In addition to the Agreement draft, we are sending a copy 76 122
of the Mortgage Release for the property in question. 87 133
You will note that this document was filed on March 1, 98 144
19--. I believe this resolves one of the issues discussed 110 156
on March 8. 113 158

To help you in responding to this request, we also are 124 169
sending copies of this material to Mr. and Mrs. Cox. 134 180

Sincerely, 2 182
DS

Company name FREEMAN AND HOLT 6 186
QS

Andrea Colson

Ms. Andrea Colson 11 191
Attorney-at-Law 14 194
DS

xx 15 195
DS

Enclosure notation Enclosures: Agreement Draft 21 201
Mortgage Release 24 204
DS

Copy notation pc Cecil and Ann Cox 28 208
DS

Postscript Should you determine that major changes need to be made, 42 220
please call me immediately. 45 225

Letter with Special Features

159a ▶ 5 Conditioning Practice

each line twice SS (slowly, then faster); if time permits, repeat selected lines

alphabet 1 My green velour blazer is quite tawdry for a dinner jacket in Phoenix.
figures 2 Flight 486 will leave 15 minutes before Flight 270 arrives at Gate 39.
shift/lock 3 Station KBEX plays jazz music all night; Station KMEG stops at 11 p.m.
speed 4 She is the heir to the usual big profit the firms make for the panels.

| 1 | 2 | 3 | 4 | 5 | 6 | 7 | 8 | 9 | 10 | 11 | 12 | 13 | 14 |

159b ▶ 15 Improve Reference Page Formatting

1. Review formatting guides for reports on page 279 and the model on RG 9.

2. Arrange references at the right in alphabetical order.

3. Key the references as a reference page in correct format; set margins for an unbound report; use 4 as the page number.

4. Proofread; circle errors.

REFERENCES

Panko, Raymond R. "Electronic Mail: The Alternatives." Office Administration and Automation, June 1984, 37-40, 43.

Katzan, Jr., Harry. Office Automation: A Manager's Guide. New York: AMACOM Book Division, 1982.

Ricks, Betty R., and Kay F. Gow. Information Resource Management. Cincinnati: South-Western Publishing Co., 1984.

Thiel, Carol Tomme. "Training Starts with Top-Down Acceptance." Infosystems, May 1984, 60-64.

159c ▶ 30 Document Production: Reports

Problem 1
Unbound Report with References

1. Key the report at the right in unbound format DS.

2. Proofread; circle errors.

words

REPORT/MANUSCRIPT DOCUMENTATION SYSTEMS 8

When a writer of a report or manuscript uses the work of others to sup- 22
port statements made or to give credibility to the paper, credit should be 37
given to the sources used. This is done by documentation, usually using one 53
of the three following methods: footnotes with a bibliography, endnotes, and 68
textual citations with a reference list. 77

Footnotes with Bibliography 88

Historic method. The historic method of documentation has been to use 105
footnotes at the bottom of pages on which references appear. Then, at the 120
end of the report, all references cited in the footnotes or used simply for 135
general information are arranged alphabetically on a separate page called 150
the bibliography. This method is described by Turabian (1973, 132-143). The 165
most recent edition of The Chicago Manual of Style modifies the system 185
(1982, 400-05). 188

Difficulties. There are difficulties with using footnotes. Lines needed at 206
the bottom of pages to accommodate footnotes must be estimated. Copy must 222
be reformatted when footnotes are added or deleted. Footnotes must be re- 236
formatted to create a bibliography. Therefore, a more efficient system, end- 251
notes, came into use. 256

(continued on next page)

Lesson 126 Letters with Special Features/Composing

126a ▶ 5 Conditioning Practice

each line twice SS (slowly, then faster); DS between 2-line groups; if time permits, repeat selected lines

alphabet 1 Kay revealed her expert qualities as a jazz artist by coming with Fay.

figures 2 In my classes, I have 6 students at 7:30, 52 at 9:30, and 84 at 10:30.

adjacent key 3 As we agreed, the new shop we build will serve the fashionable people.

speed 4 Nancy and Nema may pay the busy auditor a visit to amend a formal bid.

| 1 | 2 | 3 | 4 | 5 | 6 | 7 | 8 | 9 | 10 | 11 | 12 | 13 | 14 |

126b ▶ 25 Format Documents: Letters with Special Features

Review the formatting guides for correspondence with special features on p. 220.

Problem 1 (plain paper)

Format and key the letter on p. 221, giving careful attention to the placement of the special features. Proofread and circle errors. Keep the copy to use as a model in the next lesson.

Problem 2 (plain paper)

If time permits, repeat the letter on p. 221 with the changes listed at the right. Proofread and circle errors.

Addressee: Loper and Martinez, Attorneys-at-Law, Attention Ms. Mary Struble
(same street and city address)
Sender: Mrs. Kaye Payne
Attorney-at-Law

126c ▶ 10 Formatting Drill: Letter with Special Features

plain paper

1. Two 1′ writings in correct letter format on opening lines (date through ¶ 1) of letter on page 221. Concentrate on correct placement of letter parts.

2. Two 1′ writings in correct letter format on closing lines (¶ 3 through postscript). Concentrate on correct placement of letter parts.

3. A 3′ writing in correct letter format on the complete letter. Concentrate on correct format.

126d ▶ 10 Language Skills: Compose at Keyboard

plain paper; 1″ side margins

1. Compose at the keyboard 1 or 2 paragraphs on one of the topics shown at right. DS paragraph(s); ignore typographical errors. If necessary, x-out copy and continue keying.

2. Edit your copy, marking corrections and changes to improve sentence structure and organization.

Topics:

My Plans Following Graduation
My Ideal Job
My Life Five Years From Now
Why I Need Good Keyboarding Skills
How the Computer Affects My Life
How Composing at the Keyboard Can Save Time

Lesson 127 Letters with Special Features

127a ▶ 5 Conditioning Practice

each line twice SS (slowly, then faster); DS between 2-line groups; if time permits, repeat selected lines

alphabet 1 Vicki's quick signal was for Perry to come and judge the zany exhibit.

figures 2 Flights 329 and 475 will be replaced by Flights 168 and 420 next week.

adjacent key 3 Oliver hoped to please a few vacationers with a choice mountain guide.

speed 4 Sofia may end the problem if she pays the big penalty and the tax due.

| 1 | 2 | 3 | 4 | 5 | 6 | 7 | 8 | 9 | 10 | 11 | 12 | 13 | 14 |

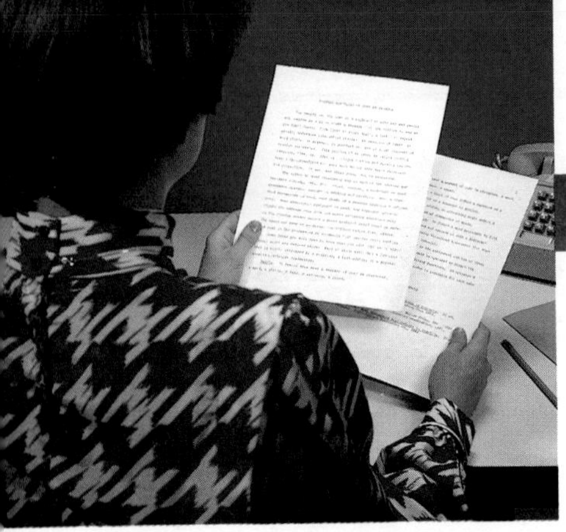

Unit 34 Lessons 159-163

Learning Goals

1. Assess and improve knowledge of report formats.
2. Improve productivity level in processing reports.
3. Get experience in composing at the keyboard.

Documents Processed

1. Unbound and leftbound reports
2. Reference pages
3. Title pages
4. Tables of contents

FORMATTING GUIDES: REPORTS

REPORT FORMATS

PLACEMENT/SPACING		UNBOUND		LEFTBOUND		TOPBOUND	
		Pica	Elite	Pica	Elite	Pica	Elite
CENTERPOINT:		42	51	45	54	42	51
TOP MARGIN:	FIRST PAGE Place heading on .... QS below heading. No page number is necessary.	line 10	line 12	line 10	line 12	line 12	line 14
	SECOND AND SUCCEEDING PAGES Place page number on ...	line 6 at right margin	line 6	line 6 at right margin	line 6	line 62 bottom center	line 62
	Continue body of report on line	8	8	8	8	10	10
BOTTOM MARGIN:	ALL PAGES	1″ 6 lines	1″	1″ 6 lines	1″	1″ 6 lines	1″
LEFT MARGIN:	ALL PAGES Inches .... Spaces	1″ 10	1″ 12	1½″ 15	1½″ 18	1″ 10	1″ 12
RIGHT MARGIN:	ALL PAGES	All report styles use a 1″ right margin.					
SPACING MODE:		Body of a report is usually DS, but may be SS.					

FOOTNOTES AND EXPLANATORY NOTES

Plan vertical spacing for footnotes and explanatory notes. Save 2 lines for divider line and spacing below it, 3 or 4 lines for each note, and 6 lines for bottom margin. After completing the last line of text, DS and key a 1½″ divider line. DS below divider line to begin the first line of the note. SS each note; DS between notes. Indent 5 spaces to begin the first line of a note; begin second and succeeding lines at the left margin.

On a partially filled page, footnote(s) may immediately follow the report body or may be placed at the foot of the page.

REFERENCE PAGE

Use the same margins as for the first page of the report. SS references; DS between them. Begin the first line of each reference at the left margin; indent second and succeeding lines 5 spaces.

TABLE OF CONTENTS

Use the same margins as for the first page of the report. Usually, list side and paragraph headings as report sections. Key the side headings DS beginning at the left margin; DS above and below a listing of paragraph headings. Key the page number of each report heading at the right margin; connect the heading to the page number by leaders.

TITLE PAGE

Center each line of a title page horizontally; key the title of the report on line 16 in ALL CAPS; space down 16 lines and key the name of the student in caps and lowercase; SS; key the name of the department, school, or section; space down 16 lines; key the date of the report.

127b ▶ 25
Improve Formatting Skill: Short Letters with Special Features

plain paper; proofread and circle errors; supply current date, salutation, complimentary close, and special features as directed

Problem 1

modified block format; blocked ¶s; mixed punctuation

Special features:

AIRMAIL
Subject: Moving Arrangements
Enclosures: Transportation Request/Change-of-Address Form

words in body: 94
total words: 144

Dr. Neal Esposito | Isar Strasse 22 | D-6082 WALLDORF | GERMANY, FED REP OF
(¶ 1) Your transfer to the Boston Regional Office will be simplified if you will complete the enclosed Transportation Request and Change-of-Address Form that I have enclosed. Please return them to the personnel office within two weeks so we can issue airline tickets for you and your family well in advance of the time of your departure.
(¶ 2) We hope that your experiences during your three years in Walldorf have been rewarding; however, we understand your desire to return home.
Fred R. Stevens | Director of Personnel

Problem 2

modified block format; blocked ¶s; mixed punctuation

Special features:

Attention Ms. Vera Patton
Company name in closing lines: ELAND MANUFACTURING, INC.
pc Martha Cullen, Senior Vice President

Postscript: Also, please bring your lightest weight portable printer to demonstrate.

words in body: 100
total words: 164

Baker and Smith, Inc. | 821 West Forbes Avenue | Pittsburgh, PA 15219-5505 |
(¶ 1) Thanks for sending the booklets which describe the various brands and models of microcomputers that you sell. We have thoroughly reviewed the material and would like to schedule demonstrations for the Elon 220 and the PEC 8021.
(¶ 2) After checking the schedules of the four employees most interested in seeing the demonstrations, I find that next Thursday afternoon or Friday morning will be the best time for us. Are either of these times convenient for you?
(¶ 3) Please call us to set up an appointment.
Terry Peck, Manager

Problem 3

block format; open punctuation

Special features:

Attention Mr. Lyndon Sommer
Subject: Managing Change Seminar
Enclosures: Program Outline/Registration Forms

Postscript: Note the 10 percent discount if you send three or more participants.

words in body: 91
total words: 161

Southwestern-Continental Airfreight Co., Inc. | 486 San Jacinto Street | Houston, TX 77002-1134 |
(¶ 1) A detailed outline of our Managing Change Seminar is enclosed to help you determine if this program is appropriate for your middle managers. From our discussion last week, I believe that it is; however, I will be happy to work with you in tailoring an individualized program for your company if you prefer.
(¶ 2) Several registration forms are enclosed and should be returned within the next week if you wish to send participants to our next open seminar.
Alan Conners | Program Director

Problem 4

block format; open punctuation

Special features:

Subject: Meeting Room for May 3, 19--
Company name in closing lines: BELMONT HOTELS, INC.

words in body: 57
total words: 104

Mrs. Kim Matsumoto, President / Matsumoto, Inc. / 586 East Broad Street / Columbus, OH 43215-1913
(¶1) We have reserved the Phoenix Room for your use on the afternoon of May 3. We shall be happy to provide coffee, soft drinks, and refreshments of cheese and fruit. Please have your guests register at the front desk upon their arrival.
(¶2) Thank you for selecting the Belmont once again!
Ms. Lara Howard / Conference Director

158c ▶ 35
Evaluate Document Production: Business Letters

Time Schedule

Plan and prepare .... 3′
Timed production .... 25′
Proofread; compute *n-pram* .... 7′

1. Arrange letterheads (LM p. 17-21), plain full sheets, and correction materials for easy access. Produce as many letters as you can in 25′. Proofread and correct errors before removing letters from machine.

2. After time is called (25′), proofread again and correct errors or repeat letter. If time remains after correcting/repeating, key bonus letter.

4. Compute *n-pram*.

Problem 1 (LM p. 17)
Block Style Letter, Open Punctuation

Problem 2 (LM p. 19)
Modified Block Style Letter, Block ¶s, Mixed Punctuation

Problem 1 — words

September 25, 19-- Mr. Robert M. Pickens Director of Human Resources 14
Community National Bank P.O. Box One Gainesville, FL 32602-8621 27
Dear Mr. Pickens 30

(¶ 1) Your participation in our seminar on Understanding Leadership Styles 44
will result, we believe, in some positive changes for you and your com- 58
pany. This is the feedback that we get over and over again from those who 73
have attended the program. 79

(¶ 2) So that your Leadership Style Profile can be processed before the semi- 93
nar, would you please ask five business associates to complete the enclosed 108
instruments and mail them to us in the envelopes that are also enclosed. We 123
need to receive them by October 8, 19--. 131

(¶ 3) We look forward to seeing you on October 12 at 8:30 a.m. 143

Sincerely yours Ms. Sheila K. Weigand Vice President xx Enclosures 156/**179**

Problem 2

October 28, 19-- Ms. Sheila K. Weigand Vice President A & J Learning 14
Systems 488 West Fourth Street Jacksonville, FL 32202-1529 Dear Sheila 28

(¶ 1) The Understanding Leadership Styles Seminar that I attended on Octo- 42
ber 12-15 was all that you promised and more. The program addressed the 56
subject in much greater depth than any other I have attended. Furthermore, 72
there were several concepts that I had not considered before which I think 87
will be quite useful. 91

(¶ 2) I have discussed this program with several of the officers in the bank, 105
and some of them expressed an interest in attending it. In fact, it appears 121
that there may be enough demand to offer the program on an in-house 134
basis. I believe you mentioned that it is cost effective to offer this as an 150
in-house program if there are 12 or more participants. 161

(¶ 3) Would you please submit a proposal to conduct this program for us. If 175
possible, I would like to present it at our monthly meeting on November 10. 190
If you have questions as you prepare the proposal, please call me at (904) 205
336-5221. 207

Sincerely Robert M. Pickens Director of Human Resources xx 219/**241**

Problem 3 (LM p. 21)
Modified Block Style Letter, Indented ¶s, Mixed Punctuation
Date letter **November 5, 19--**; use letter address and closing lines (except change enclosures to enclosure) as shown in Problem 1.

Problem 4 (plain full sheet)
Repeat Problem 2 if you finish before time is called.

Bonus (plain full sheet)
If time remains after correcting/repeating, repeat Problem 3 on a plain full sheet.

Problem 3 — *words in opening lines* 27

Dear Bob ¶ Thanks for the opportunity to do business 37
with you. I think you will find the enclosed 46
proposal to be detailed and complete; but if 55
you do need more information, just give me a call. 66
¶ I look forward to working with Community 74
National Bank on the Understanding Leadership 83
Styles Seminar. 86

words in closing lines 99

127c ▶ 20
Formatting Drill: Letter with Special Features

plain paper; modified block format; open punctuation

1. A 5′ writing on the letter to establish a base rate. If you finish before time is called, start over.

2. Find *gwam*. Use this rate as your goal rate. From the table below, find quarter-minute checkpoints; mentally note these figures in opening lines through ¶ 1.

3. Take three 1′ guided writings on the opening lines through ¶ 1. Leave proper spacing between letter parts.

4. Repeat Steps 2 and 3, but begin with ¶ 3 and continue through closing lines.

5. Take another 5′ writing on the letter. Try to maintain your new goal rate.

Quarter-Minute Checkpoints

gwam	1/4′	1/2′	3/4′	1′
24	6	12	18	24
28	7	14	21	28
32	8	16	24	32
36	9	18	27	36
40	10	20	30	40
44	11	22	33	44
48	12	24	36	48
52	13	26	39	52
56	14	28	42	56
60	15	30	45	60
64	16	32	48	64
68	17	34	51	68
72	18	36	54	72
76	19	38	57	76
80	20	40	60	80

	gwam 5′	
June 3, 19-- SPECIAL DELIVERY C. M. Moore Company Attention Office	3	42
Manager 409 East 14 Street Oakland, CA 94612-4401 Ladies and Gentlemen	5	45
Subject: EDM Copiers	6	46
(¶ 1) It was a pleasure to visit with your associate, Robby Kerr, last	9	48
week at our exhibit at the Office Systems Convention in San Francisco.	12	51
Robby indicated that you are in the process of selecting a new copying	15	54
machine and that two of our models appear to fit your needs -- Models	17	57
1403 and 8645.	18	57
(¶ 2) The enclosed brochure explains in detail the special features of	20	60
both our 1400 series and our 8600 series. Further, the great news is	23	63
that we can offer these copiers at last year's prices for all orders	26	65
received before July 1 (as indicated on the enclosed price list).	29	68
(¶ 3) May we help you make your selection of an EDM Copier.	31	70
Sincerely EDM OFFICE SYSTEMS Bill Newell Vice President xx Enclo-	34	73
sures: Brochure Price List pc Robby Kerr postscript Our representative,	37	76
Kyle Stabler, will call you next week to see how we can be of assistance.	39	79

Lesson 128 Letters with Special Features/Composing

128a ▶ 5
Conditioning Practice

each line twice SS (slowly, then faster); DS between 2-line groups; if time permits, repeat selected lines

alphabet 1 Jeff seized every chance to make progress to quash unwanted tax bills.

symbols 2 Shelley's article -- her second one -- entitled "Job Interviews" is great.

direct reach 3 After writing many checks, I put a number of them under my brown book.

speed 4 He may wish to aid the sick with their problems if they wish such aid.

| 1 | 2 | 3 | 4 | 5 | 6 | 7 | 8 | 9 | 10 | 11 | 12 | 13 | 14 |

128b ▶ 10
Language Skills: Compose at Keyboard

plain paper; 1″ side margins

Repeat 126d, p. 222, but select a different topic from the one you selected earlier or select a topic of your choice to be approved by your teacher.

157c ▶ 10 Paragraph Guided Writing

1. Three 1′ writings for speed with quarter-minute checkpoints noted and guides called on 2nd and 3rd writings (see Table, p. 270). **Goal:** 2-6 words faster on each writing.

2. Three 1′ writings for control with quarter-minute checkpoints noted and guides called. Deduct 4-6 words from top speed; then note checkpoints. **Goal:** 2 or fewer errors a minute.

3. A 3′ writing. Compare *gwam* and errors with 155d.

all letters used | A | 1.5 si | 5.7 awl | 80% hfw

gwam 3′

It is very probable that you will be chosen to perform the job of 4 | 32
a manager of some kind. If so, you will be expected to set goals that 9 | 37
are long term, intermediate term, and short term. Therefore, you must 14 | 41
organize a variety of resources that may involve people, equipment, and 18 | 46
materials to help accomplish these goals. Getting the right mix of 23 | 50
these resources will partially determine your success as a manager. 27 | 55

gwam 3′ | 1 | 2 | 3 | 4 | 5 |

Lesson 158 Evaluation: Keyboarding/Letter Skills

158a ▶ 5 Conditioning Practice

each line twice SS (slowly, then faster); DS between 2-line groups; if time permits, repeat selected lines

alphabet 1 Quincy knows how to analyze and to explain every job the firm designs.
figures 2 The building at 3425 West 187 Street has 130,695 square feet of space.
fig/sym 3 Val's aunt (age 42) and May's uncle (age 69) contributed $1,875 (30%).
speed 4 The man they got to fix their bicycle for the big city social is Juan.

| 1 | 2 | 3 | 4 | 5 | 6 | 7 | 8 | 9 | 10 | 11 | 12 | 13 | 14 |

158b ▶ 10 Evaluate Straight-Copy Skill

1. A 5′ writing on both ¶s.
2. Determine *gwam* and number of errors.
3. Compare with score in 153c.
4. Record on LM p. 3 for comparison in Lesson 168.

all letters used | A | 1.5 si | 5.7 awl | 80% hfw

gwam 3′ | 5′

Good keyboarding skill is very important, as it is needed in jobs 4 | 3 | 41
that utilize the computer. Most office jobs today require some use of 9 | 5 | 44
the computer, and several call for working a major portion of the day 14 | 8 | 46
at a terminal. Therefore, the person who can keyboard by touch, that 18 | 11 | 49
is, without looking at the keys, can perform much more efficiently than 23 | 14 | 52
the one who is constantly looking for the next key. The time spent to 28 | 17 | 55
learn to keyboard properly will return big dividends. 31 | 19 | 57

However, people who recognize how important it is to improve 36 | 21 | 59
productivity will not be satisfied with just knowing the location of 40 | 24 | 62
keys by touch. They will want to extend their skill by acquiring a 45 | 27 | 65
high level of speed and a proper level of control. They realize that 49 | 30 | 68
they have the potential to input three, four, or even five times more 54 | 32 | 70
information by improving their skill beyond the knowledge level of key 59 | 35 | 73
locations; and this can make a big difference in performance each day. 63 | 38 | 76

gwam 3′ | 1 | 2 | 3 | 4 | 5 |
5′ | 1 | 2 | 3 |

128c ▶ 35
Build Sustained Document Processing: Letters with Special Features

plain paper; proofread; correct errors

Time Schedule
Plan and prepare .... 3′
Timed production .... 25′
Proofread and correct errors ... 7′

1. Make a list of problems to be processed:
page 222, 126b, Problem 2
page 223, 127b, Problem 2
page 223, 127b, Problem 3
page 223, 127b, Problem 4
Bonus: page 224, 127c

2. Arrange paper and correction materials for easy access. Process as many letters as you can in 25′. Proofread and correct errors before removing letters from machine.

3. After 25′ timing, proofread again and correct errors or rekey. If time remains after correcting/rekeying, process the bonus letter.

4. Determine number of problems and number of errors; turn in work, arranged in order listed in Step 1.

Lesson 129 Letters with Special Features

129a ▶ 5
Conditioning Practice

each line twice SS (slowly, then faster); DS between 2-line groups; if time permits, repeat selected lines

alphabet 1 Zack expressed some vague ideas on equality while a few jested boldly.
symbols 2 Iba & Kane Co. (located on Elm Street) sells hunting/fishing licenses.
direct reach 3 Annually, Myra goes to a ceremony to celebrate many of these advances.
speed 4 Jane's big wish is to sit in a chair on the dock by the lake and fish.

| 1 | 2 | 3 | 4 | 5 | 6 | 7 | 8 | 9 | 10 | 11 | 12 | 13 | 14 |

129b ▶ 10
Evaluate Straight-Copy Skill

1. A 5′ writing on both ¶s.
2. Find *gwam* and number of errors.
3. Compare to score in Lesson 123d, page 214.
4. Record on LM p. 3.

all letters used | A | 1.5 si | 5.7 awl | 80% hfw |

	gwam 1′	5′	
Many firms feel that their employees are their most valuable re-	13	3	45
sources. Excellent companies realize that people working toward common	27	5	48
goals influence the success of the business. They are also aware of the	42	8	51
need to hire qualified people and then to create a work environment to	56	11	54
allow the people to perform at their highest potential. Firms which	70	14	56
believe that the main job of managers is to remove obstacles that get	84	17	59
in the way of the output of the workers are the firms that do, in fact,	98	20	62
achieve their goals.	102	20	63
Not only do executives and managers in the most successful firms	13	23	65
admit to themselves the value of their employees, but they also reveal	27	26	68
this feeling to their workers. They know that most people enjoy being	41	29	71
given credit for their unique qualities. They also know that any action	56	32	74
on their part that aids the workers in realizing their own self-worth	70	34	77
will lead to a higher return for the firm, since such people are self-	84	37	80
motivated. When leaders do not have to be occupied with employee moti-	98	40	82
vation, they can devote their energy to other vital tasks.	110	42	85

gwam 1′ | 1 | 2 | 3 | 4 | 5 | 6 | 7 | 8 | 9 | 10 | 11 | 12 | 13 | 14 |
5′ | 1 | 2 | 3 |

156b (continued)

Problem 2 (LM p. 11)
Modified Block Letter with Indented ¶s
open punctuation; supply an appropriate salutation and enclosure notation

Problem 3 (LM p. 13)
Modified Block Letter with Blocked ¶s
Key Problem 2 in modified block style, blocked ¶s, open punctuation. Supply an appropriate salutation; address the letter to:
Mr. Henry M. Curtis
Personnel Manager
T. D. Martin Company
1485 West Douglas Avenue
Wichita, KS 67213-7365
Words in opening lines: 27

	words parts	total
Current date Mr. Mark J. Cyr, Manager Marketing Department Ogden Ma-	14	14
chinery Company 8124 Highway 24, NW Topeka, KS 66618-7856	29	29
(¶ 1) Making the right selection of individual workstations is indeed difficult,	15	44
and I can understand your dilemma. This is an important decision, and	29	58
there are many alternatives to consider. I believe the material in the pack-	45	73
age I am sending today will be helpful.	53	81
(¶ 2) As you requested, a reading list is included with priorities marked in	67	95
red. In addition, the booklet of guidelines that I developed will likely raise	83	111
some points that you have not yet considered.	92	120
(¶ 3) My consulting fee is $75/hour as shown on the enclosed statement.	105	134
Sincerely Kurt J. Santos Office Systems Consultant xx	13	147 / 169

156c ▶ 10 Drill on Document Production: Letter Parts

plain full sheets

1. Three 1′ writings in letter form on opening lines (date through salutation) of 156b, Problem 2. Try to improve by 1 or 2 words with each timing.

2. Three 1′ writings in letter form on the closing lines (complimentary close through enclosure). Try to improve by 1 or 2 words each time.

3. A 3′ writing in letter form on the complete letter (plain full sheet). Determine *gwam*; compare with rates from 154c and 155c.

156d ▶ 10 Reinforce Communication Skills: Decision Making

1. Review word-division guides on RG 5.

2. Key the words in a single column, inserting hyphens at all acceptable points of word division. Use a dictionary if necessary; correct errors.

3. Circle any hyphens at less than desirable word-division points, even though they do not violate a rule.

Example ⟶ situ-ation

situ-ation	geography	quite
approximately	classroom	tagging
everything	automobile	criticism
statement	magazine	dilemma
available	among	misspell
through	carat	pastime
into	faster	optical

Lesson 157 Letters

157a ▶ 5 Conditioning Practice

each line twice SS (slowly, then faster); DS between 2-line groups; if time permits, repeat selected lines

alphabet 1 Fifty big jets climbed into a hazy sky at exactly quarter past twelve.
figures 2 Here are their ages: Ida, 18; Emi, 25; Kay, 39; Jim, 60; and Ann, 47.
direct reaches 3 Bring annually any offers received to serve on my arbitration council.
speed 4 Their theory is to form the right social goals to handle key problems.

| 1 | 2 | 3 | 4 | 5 | 6 | 7 | 8 | 9 | 10 | 11 | 12 | 13 | 14 |

157b ▶ 35 Sustained Document Production: Business Letters

Time Schedule
Plan and prepare .... 3′
Timed production .... 25′
Proofread; compute *n-pram* .... 7′

1. Make a list of problems to be produced:
page 273, 154b, Problem 2
page 274, 155b, Problem 2
page 274, 155b, Problem 3
page 275, 156b, Problem 1
Bonus: page 273, 154b, Problem 1

2. Arrange plain full sheets, letterhead (LM p. 15), and correction materials for easy access. Produce as many letters as you can in 25′. Proofread and correct errors before removing letters from machine.

3. After time is called (25′), proofread again and correct errors or repeat letter. If time remains after correcting/repeating, key bonus letter.

4. Compute *n-pram*; turn in work arranged in order listed in Step 1.

129c ▶ 35
Evaluate Document Processing: Letters with Special Features

Time Schedule

Plan and prepare .... 3′
Timed Production .... 25′
Proofread and correct errors ... 7′

LM pp. 61-66; supply current date, salutation, complimentary close, and special features as directed; proofread and correct errors

Problem 1

modified block format; blocked ¶s; mixed punctuation

Special features:

REGISTERED
Attention Mr. George All
Subject: 401(k) Profit-Sharing Plan
Company name in closing lines: FINANCIAL ADVISORS, INC.
Enclosures: 401(k) PLANS/ ADMINISTERING 401(k) PLANS
pc Mr. Dale Grimes

words in body: 132
total words: 217

Mueller, Huddleston, Osberghaus, Schroeder, and Triplett | 586 Riverside Avenue | Jacksonville, FL 32202-8301

(¶ 1) Companies like yours are always looking for ways to offer greater benefits to their employees, and one that I recommend for your consideration is the 401(k) Profit-Sharing Plan. This plan is practical for large organizations such as yours, and many Fortune 500 companies are already offering it to their employees as a type of retirement plan.

(¶ 2) The 401(k) offers several advantages over an IRA. They are explained in the enclosed booklet entitled 401(k) PLANS. The second enclosure explains the requirements of the employer in administering the plan.

(¶ 3) If you have questions about this plan, call me; and we can set a time to get together for a discussion.

Mrs. Carry Lorenzo, President | postscript If you wish, I can provide a list of local firms that offer 401(k)'s.

Problem 2

block format; open punctuation

Special features:

Attention Human Resources Manager
Company name in closing lines: BUSINESS NEWSLETTER SERVICE
Enclosure: Reservation Card

words in body: 149
total words: 225

Oki & Fong Office Systems | 486 South Second Street | Macon, GA 31201-4910
Subject: Winning at Organizational Politics

(¶ 1) Office politics are a part of every organization; and as much as you might like to ignore them, it would not be wise to do so. Perhaps you wish that the employees in your company could concentrate solely on doing their jobs; however, you are well aware that hard work alone cannot protect your workers from various kinds of political hazards.

(¶ 2) Our monthly newsletter entitled WINNING AT ORGANIZATIONAL POLITICS provides an effective educational program. It creates an awareness of the various aspects of office politics and suggests how to deal with them in a manner that will result in a win-win situation.

(¶ 3) Return the enclosed reservation card and start distributing ten copies of WINNING AT ORGANIZATIONAL POLITICS to your employees each month.

Miss Elaine McLaurin, President postscript If you are not completely satisfied, you may cancel within three months for a total refund.

Problem 3

Decide letter and punctuation style.

Send letter by SPECIAL DELIVERY to:

Mr. Kenneth K. Mattison
Executive Vice President
Brentwood Inns
2186 North Main Street
Santa Ana, CA 92706-6214

words in body: 107
total words: 156

Subject: Portfolio of Designs

(¶ 1) A portfolio of my work will be sent to you under separate cover by priority mail. It will be marked for special delivery, so I believe it will arrive by the date that you requested.

(¶ 2) Since I am sending several pieces of original work, I would like to have the portfolio returned after you have completed your review.

(¶ 3) I shall be pleased to submit a proposal for your project and can begin the work within the month. I am looking forward to hearing from you after you have received and reviewed my portfolio.

Cordially yours | OFFICE DESIGNS, INC. | Mrs. Jessica Martinez

Problem 4

Repeat Problem 1 on plain paper if you finish before time is called.

155c ▶ 10 Drill on Document Production: Letter Parts

plain full sheets

1. Three 1′ writings in letter form on opening lines (date through salutation) of 155b Problem 3. Try to improve by 1 or 2 words with each timing.

2. Three 1′ writings in letter form on the closing lines (complimentary close through enclosure). Try to improve by 1 or 2 words each time.

3. A 3′ writing in letter form on the complete letter (plain full sheet). Compare with 154c rate; record *gwam* for future comparisons.

155d ▶ 10 Reinforce Straight-Copy Keyboarding Skill

1. Three 1′ writings for speed. **Goal:** improve rate by 1 or 2 words with each timing.

2. Three 1′ writings for control. **Goal:** not more than 2 errors a minute.

3. A 3′ writing; record *gwam* and errors for comparison with 157c.

all letters used | A | 1.5 si | 5.7 awl | 80% hfw |

	gwam 1′	3′	
A manager is one who achieves a goal or objective by guiding other	13	4	27
people. We may think a manager is required to work in a business; but	28	9	32
homemakers, teachers, and leaders of youth organizations are examples	42	14	37
of managers, too, as they seek to secure results through others. Many	56	19	42
people who do not consider themselves to be managers in fact are.	69	23	46

gwam 1′ | 1 | 2 | 3 | 4 | 5 | 6 | 7 | 8 | 9 | 10 | 11 | 12 | 13 | 14 |
3′ | 1 | 2 | 3 | 4 | 5 |

Lesson 156 Modified Block Letters/Word Division

156a ▶ 5 Conditioning Practice

each line twice SS (slowly, then faster); DS between 2-line groups; if time permits, retype selected lines

alphabet 1 Zackary quoted poetry expertly to win the job from seven great rivals.

figures 2 On June 30, Li paid for 28 scarves and 16 hats with Check Number 4759.

shifting 3 Will Laura and Irene go to Fort Myers before Tod and Cory leave there?

speed 4 They may work to cut and shape their lens to make it fit my right eye.

| 1 | 2 | 3 | 4 | 5 | 6 | 7 | 8 | 9 | 10 | 11 | 12 | 13 | 14 |

156b ▶ 25 Document Production: Business Letters

Review envelope addressing procedures (RG 4) and error correction procedures (RG 12). Judge the length of the letters to set margins; proofread and correct errors; prepare envelopes.

Problem 1 (LM p. 9)
Modified Block Letter with Indented Paragraphs

Use current date, mixed punctuation, and the following letter address:

Mr. Kurt J. Santos
Office Systems Consultant
1425 West Elmwood Avenue
Kansas City, KS 66103-1862

Use an appropriate complimentary close.

words

words in opening lines 21

Dear Mr. Santos ¶ Within the next few months, we 30
plan to add several desk-top workstations for 39
individual use in my department. In our investigation 51
of what is available, we have found the options to be 61
almost unlimited. Now we are completely confused 71
and need some advice from an expert. 79
¶ Could you please recommend some reading 87
material that would be helpful. Also, do you have 97
written guidelines for making such decisions? If so, 108
may we purchase a copy? 113
¶ Please send us a statement for this service, 122
along with information concerning the fees you 131
will charge should we need more help. 140
Mark J. Cyr, Manager xx 146

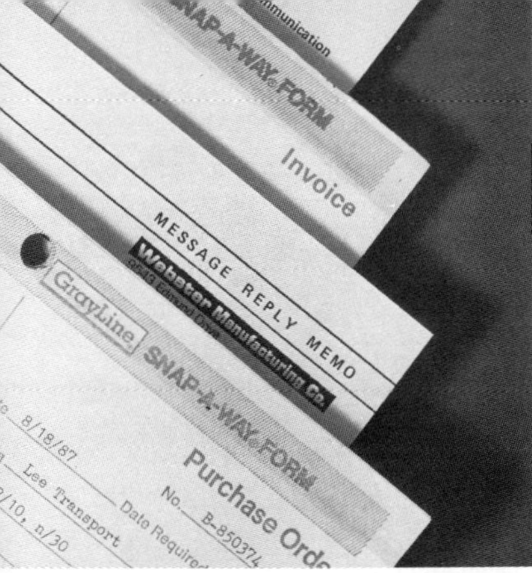

Unit 27 Lessons 130-134

Learning Goals

1. Improve stroking rate.
2. Format and process formal and simplified memorandums.
3. Format and process special forms.
4. Improve language skills.
5. Format and process documents on lined forms.

Machine Adjustments

1. Paper guide at *0*.
2. Margins: 70-space line for drills; as directed for problems.
3. Spacing: as directed.

FORMATTING GUIDES: FORMS AND SPECIAL DOCUMENTS

MATHAS EQUIPMENT COMPANY
INTEROFFICE COMMUNICATION
210 CADDY LANE JOLIET, IL 60435-3322

TO: Joe R. Marshall, Administrative Assistant

FROM: Beverly K. Nesser, Executive Vice President

DATE: Current date

SUBJECT: Formation of Productivity Committee

As you know, one of the major company objectives this year is to evaluate the productivity of our office in order to determine if and how our productivity may be improved. To address this objective, we have decided to appoint a committee consisting of members from each department as well as members from the various organizational levels.

I believe that your input as a member of this committee will be very valuable since you have demonstrated considerable creativity in solving problems in the past. This committee needs people who are visionary and unafraid of change, and you fit that description.

Are you willing to serve on this important committee? Please let me know as soon as possible.

xx

cc Denise Mendez

COMPANY MAIL

Mr. Joe R. Marshall, Administrative Assistant
Personnel Department

Formal Memo and Company Envelope

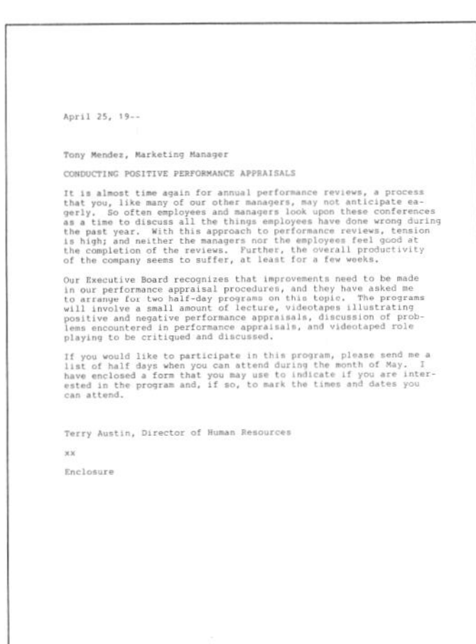

April 25, 19--

Tony Mendez, Marketing Manager

CONDUCTING POSITIVE PERFORMANCE APPRAISALS

It is almost time again for annual performance reviews, a process that you, like many of our other managers, may not anticipate eagerly. So often employees and managers look upon these conferences as a time to discuss all the things employees have done wrong during the past year. With this approach to performance reviews, tension is high; and neither the managers nor the employees feel good at the completion of the reviews. Further, the overall productivity of the company seems to suffer, at least for a few weeks.

Our Executive Board recognizes that improvements need to be made in our performance appraisal procedures, and they have asked me to arrange for two half-day programs on this topic. The programs will involve a small amount of lecture, videotapes illustrating positive and negative performance appraisals, discussion of problems encountered in performance appraisals, and videotaped role playing to be critiqued and discussed.

If you would like to participate in this program, please send me a list of half days when you can attend during the month of May. I have enclosed a form that you may use to indicate if you are interested in the program and, if so, to mark the times and dates you can attend.

Terry Austin, Director of Human Resources

xx

Enclosure

Simplified Memo

Interoffice Memorandums

Communications within an organization are often formatted as memorandums rather than as letters. Two styles of the interoffice memorandum are commonly used. The *formal memorandum* is processed on a form having special printed headings. The *simplified memorandum* is prepared on plain paper without headings.

Formatting guides for the interoffice memo are listed below.

1. Use either a half or full sheet.
2. Use block style.
3. Use approximately 1″ side and bottom margins.
4. Omit personal titles (Miss, Mr., Ms., Dr., etc.) on memo, but include them on the company envelope.
5. Omit salutation and complimentary close.
6. SS the body, but DS between ¶s.
7. Use special colored envelopes. If unavailable, use plain envelope with COMPANY MAIL printed in the usual stamp position. Include on the envelope the receiver's personal title, name, and business title; also, include receiver's department (see illustration at left).

Formal memorandum. Begin heading information 2 spaces to the right of printed headings (as shown on page 229). Note that headings are printed in the 1-inch left margin so that the lines of the heading data and the message can begin at the 1″ left margin setting. A memo may be sent to more than one individual; if so, each name is included on the same line as the "To:" heading. DS between all parts of the formal memorandum.

Simplified memorandum. Begin the date on line 6 for a half sheet and line 10 for a full sheet. DS between all parts of the simplified memo, *except* below date and the last ¶ of the body. Quadruple-space (QS) below the dateline and last ¶ of body.

Special Forms (See models on pp. 231-232.)

Purchase requisitions, purchase orders, invoices, and other similar documents are prepared on printed forms. Although forms vary from company to company, well-designed forms allow the keyboard operator to follow the general guidelines listed below.

1. Set left margin stop so that items are approximately centered in the Quantity column of purchase requisitions, purchase orders, and invoices. (This stop is also used to begin the *Deliver to* block of Purchase Requisitions.)
2. Set a tab stop to begin the Description items of Purchase Requisitions and to begin the address and Description items of Purchase Orders and Invoices. (The address must be placed so that all of it shows through the window of a window envelope; items in the Description column should begin 1 or 2 spaces to the right of the vertical rule.)
3. Set a tab stop for keying information in the upper right-hand area of the form (1 or 2 spaces to the right of printed items). This stop may also be used to key items in the Price column, or an additional stop may be set for that purpose.
4. Set additional tab stops for aligning and keying items in remaining column(s).
5. SS column entries, beginning on the first or second space below the horizontal rule under the column headings.
6. If the form lists prices and totals, position monetary amounts so that cent figures fall to the right of the vertical rules. Use of commas to indicate thousands in figure columns is optional.
7. Underline the last figure in the Total column; then, DS before keying the total amount.
8. Tabulate and key across the form rather than keying all items column by column.

154d ▶ 10
Reinforce Communication Skills; Decision Making

1. Examine these sentences for commonly confused words. Use a dictionary if needed.

2. Key the sentences (including number) DS, correcting the words that are misused. Also correct your typographical errors.

1. What affect did your advice have on the selection they choose?
2. What course of action did the Core of Engineers take about the cite?
3. What is the fare if less than three people go on the trip?
4. It is plain to see that you can easily peal the piece of fruit.
5. What roll did you play in getting the overdo book to the library?
6. She seamed rather quite during the recent disagreement.
7. He sales steaks at a price that is too low according to most sellers.
8. Did you doze before the announcement or just faint when you herd it?
9. She had a rite to a forth of the estate, but she waved it.

Lesson 155 Modified Block Letters

155a ▶ 5
Conditioning Practice

each line twice SS (slowly, then faster); DS between 2-line groups; if time permits, repeat selected lines

alphabet 1 Jobe watched the foxy old goat quickly zip over those mountain ledges.

figures 2 Those club members read 54 plays, 163 books, and 207 articles in 1987.

direct reaches 3 Any debts assumed must produce mutual trust between debtor and lender.

speed 4 The dog bit the girl, but a panel may blame a man for the dog's fight.

| 1 | 2 | 3 | 4 | 5 | 6 | 7 | 8 | 9 | 10 | 11 | 12 | 13 | 14 |

155b ▶ 25
Document Production: Business Letters

proofread and circle errors

Problem 1 (plain full sheet)
Short Letter
modified block style, mixed punctuation

	words parts	total
Current date State Board of Landscape Architects 528 West 20 Street Little	15	16
Rock, AR 72206-3642 Ladies and Gentlemen	23	24
(¶ 1) After considerable discussion, the State Board of Architects has de-	14	38
cided to decline your offer to share an office in Little Rock. Your proposal	29	53
would provide several benefits to us; however, we expect to need all of our	44	68
space within the next six months to a year.	52	77
(¶ 2) I am enclosing a brochure from an office locator service and hope that	66	91
they may be able to assist you in locating your office.	77	103
Cordially Allen J. Turner President xx Enclosure	10	112

Problem 2 (plain full sheet)
Average-Length Letter
modified block style, open punctuation

	words parts	total
Current date Mrs. Claire Riolo, Chair State Board of Landscape Architects	15	15
528 West 20 Street Little Rock, AR 72206-3642 Dear Mrs. Riolo	28	28
(¶ 1) In a recent visit, Mr. Allen Turner indicated your interest in locating an	15	43
office of the State Board of Landscape Architects in Little Rock. My busi-	30	58
ness is to assist people with needs similar to yours, and I would like to work	46	74
with you.	48	76
(¶ 2) If you will complete the enclosed form describing your space, furniture	62	90
and equipment, and office personnel requirements, we will locate an office	77	105
that fits your specific needs. At the present time, we have a number of	92	120
office listings, and we may just have what you need.	102	130
(¶ 3) Please call me if you have questions about completing the form.	115	143
Sincerely yours Ms. Diane Epley, President xx Enclosure	11	154

Problem 3 (plain full sheet)
Key Problem 1 in block style, open punctuation. Address the letter to:

Secretary
Trio Design Society
521 Garrison Avenue
Fort Smith, AR 72901-6482

Supply an appropriate salutation; in ¶ 1, change **State Board of Architects** to **State Board of Landscape Architects;** change signature line to **Lane Elswick, President.**

Total words in letter: 112

130a ▶ 5 Conditioning Practice

each line twice SS (slowly, then faster); DS between 2-line groups; if time permits, repeat selected lines

alphabet	1	As Gay kept varied time for him on the drums, Jacques blew a jazz sax.
figures	2	I shall buy 230 dresses, 197 suits, 185 hats, and 364 pants at market.
fig/sym	3	The dress is $238.46, and the coat is $598.70 (includes 15% discount).
speed	4	If they keep the busybody busy with the work, then my problem may end.

| 1 | 2 | 3 | 4 | 5 | 6 | 7 | 8 | 9 | 10 | 11 | 12 | 13 | 14 |

130b ▶ 10 Improve Basic Skill: Speed-Forcing Drill

The columns at the right of the sentences show the rate at which you are keying if you complete each sentence the number of times indicated at the top.

1. From lines 1-12, select a speed-goal rate from the columns at the right.

2. Using the sentence at the left of that speed rate, take a 1′ writing, trying to complete the sentence the number of times indicated at the top of the column.

3. If in the first writing you reach your speed goal, select the next higher speed rate from the columns. Take additional 1′ writings until you reach the new goal rate. Continue to increase your goal with each new achievement.

4. From lines 13-21, select a goal rate equal to your highest rate on lines 1-12.

5. Repeat Steps 2-4 above.

6. Take a 1′ writing on line 22; record your rate to compare in Lessons 131 and 133.

	Balanced hand	times per minute to type sentence 4	6	8
1	Sue also works for an auditor.	*gwam* 24	36	48
2	The robot turns right to do work.	26	40	53
3	Ana may go to the big lake to fish.	28	42	56
4	Pay the city for the visual aid I got.	30	46	61
5	The haughty man paid a buck for the pen.	32	48	64
6	The visit by the chap got rid of a problem.	34	52	69
7	The eye may focus to the right of the chapel.	36	54	72
8	A widow may sign both of the audit forms in pen.	38	58	77
9	An amendment may entitle me to pay for their fuel.	40	60	80
10	Make their oak shelf and hang it by their oak mantle.	42	64	85
11	Make idle chaps of the city do their work to keep busy.	44	66	88
12	The goal is to make a big profit so we may keep the land.	46	68	91
	Combination			
13	I saw the eight autos go downtown after he left.	38	58	77
14	The wild deer and turkey on the land are so plump.	40	60	80
15	We paid high duty on the case of food we sent by air.	42	64	85
16	My social sorority had their rituals in an aged chapel.	44	66	88
17	The beggar greeted him as he passed the field by the city.	46	70	93
18	If you have a cataract on the eye, it may impair your sight.	48	72	96
19	The fable was of a cat with a beard and a big dog with red fur.	50	76	101
20	Bob agrees that we may make a great profit if we handle the deal.	52	78	104
21	If you do withdraw the endowment, we may have to end a good program.	54	82	109
22	The sun on an area of icy trees seems to create a land of enchantment.	56	84	112
23	The agreement on exactly what was to be in the chapter was news to us.	56	84	112
24	The defacement of authentic artwork adds to our problems as officials.	56	84	112

| 1 | 2 | 3 | 4 | 5 | 6 | 7 | 8 | 9 | 10 | 11 | 12 | 13 | 14 |

Lesson 154 Block Letters

154a ▶ 5 Conditioning Practice

each line twice SS (slowly, then faster); DS between 2-line groups; if time permits, retype selected lines

alphabet 1 Buzz just got a taxi off to a very quiet place marked on his worn map.

figures 2 On March 23 I traveled 1,075 miles; on July 29 I traveled 1,468 miles.

shifting 3 I have lived in South Carolina, Hawaii, Maryland, Florida, and Kansas.

speed 4 May is the chair of their panel and turns problems into profit for it.

| 1 | 2 | 3 | 4 | 5 | 6 | 7 | 8 | 9 | 10 | 11 | 12 | 13 | 14 |

154b ▶ 25 Document Production: Business Letters

Review the formatting guides for business letters on p. 272; then process the letters; proofread and circle errors.

Problem 1 (plain full sheet)
Short Letter
block style, open punctuation

	words: parts	total
September 12, 19-- Dr. Jeanine Daniels Management Consultant Post and	14	14
Post, Inc. P.O. Box 833145 Richardson, TX 75083-2436 Dear Dr. Daniels	28	28
(¶ 1) You were recommended to us by Betty Martinez of the Ross-Jordan	13	41
Company as one who is well qualified to work with us in restructuring our	27	55
organizational design. We feel that a change is needed at this time because	43	71
of our rapid growth over the past two years and the addition of some rather	58	87
sophisticated technology.	63	92
(¶ 2) Our top management has identified this as a high-priority assign-	76	105
ment. If you are interested in working with us on this project, we would like	92	121
to meet with you soon.	96	125
Sincerely Miss Joan Thompson Vice President xx	9	135

Problem 2 (plain full sheet)
Average-Length Letter
block style, open punctuation

	words: parts	total
September 14, 19-- Miss Joan Thompson Vice President Besco Systems,	14	14
Inc. 428 West Ninth Street Dallas, TX 75208-4864 Dear Miss Thompson	27	27
(¶ 1) Your request for immediate assistance with the restructuring of your	14	41
organization comes at a good time for me, since I have just completed a	28	56
commitment. While I have two proposals outstanding, both are fortunately	43	70
somewhat flexible as to the starting date.	52	79
(¶ 2) Before we visit, I would like to have copies of your last three Annual	66	93
Reports. Also, would it be possible to get a list or summary of the technol-	81	109
ogy that you have added within the past two years.	91	119
(¶ 3) I will call you on September 16 to arrange an appointment. My sched-	105	133
ule is open all day on September 20, during the morning on September 22,	120	147
and during the afternoon on September 23.	128	156
Sincerely yours Dr. Jeanine Daniels Management Consultant xx	12	168

Problem 3 (plain full sheet)
Repeat Problem 1 addressed to:
Mr. Joseph Burke, President
Burke Consulting, Inc.
721 Lindsey Street
Denton, TX 76201-1854
Supply an appropriate salutation. Words in opening lines: 25.

154c ▶ 10 Drill on Document Production: Letter Parts

plain full sheets

1. Three 1′ writings in letter form on opening lines (date through salutation) of 154b, Problem 1. Try to improve by 1 or 2 words with each timing.

2. Three 1′ writings in letter form on the closing lines (complimentary close through initials). Try to improve by 1 or 2 words each time.

3. A 3′ writing in letter form on the complete letter (plain full sheet). Record *gwam* for future comparisons.

130c ▶ 35 Format Documents: Interoffice Memorandums

Study the Formatting Guides for interoffice memorandums and company envelopes on p. 227.

Problem 1
Formal Memorandum
(LM p. 67)

Format and key the memorandum from the model copy below. Proofread and circle errors. Prepare a company envelope to:

Ms. Patricia Hamilton
Sales Representative
Sales Department

words

SALT LAKE
SUPPLY COMPANY **Interoffice Communication**

TO: Patricia Hamilton, Sales Representative 8

FROM: Albert C. Chung 11

DATE: April 25, 19-- 14

SUBJECT: Sales Presentation for Product X-38 21

We have had several requests for a session on how to present Product 35
X-38 successfully to our clients. Since your sales of this product 49
have been unusually high, would you be in charge of a two-hour 61
program on this topic at our regional sales conference next month. 75

You may have complete freedom, Pat, on how to conduct the program. 89
Just let me know what equipment and/or assistance you need, and we 102
will be glad to help. 105

xx 107
121

Problem 2
Formal Memorandum
(LM p. 69)

Format and key the memo to Joe R. Marshall, Administrative Assistant, from Beverly K. Hesser, Executive Vice President. Use current date. Supply an appropriate subject line. Add your reference initials and send one cc to Denise Mendez. Prepare a company envelope (address to Personnel Department). Proofread and correct errors.
(words in heading lines: 27)
(total words: 172/**187**)

(¶1) As you know, one of the major company objectives this year is 40
to evaluate the productivity of our office in order to determine 53
if and how our productivity may be improved. To address 64
this objective, we have decided to appoint a committee 75
consisting of members from each department as well as 86
members from the various organizational levels. 95
(¶2) I believe that your input as a member of this com- 105
mittee will be very valuable since you have demonstrated 117
considerable creativity in solving problems in the past. This 129
committee needs people who are visionary and unafraid 140
of change, and you fit that description. 149
(¶3) Are you willing to serve on this important committee? 159
Please let me know as soon as possible. 167

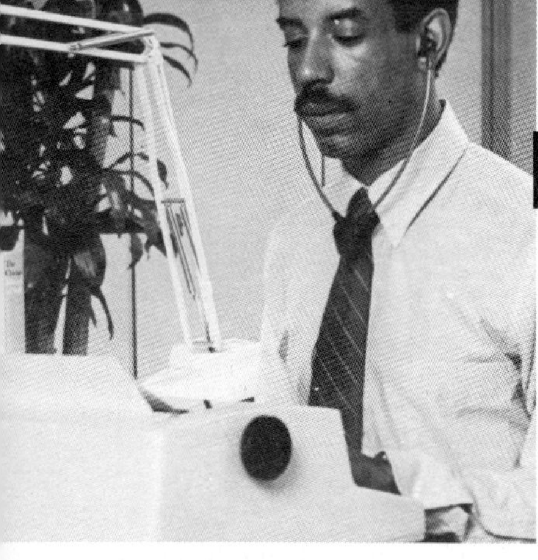

Unit 33 Lessons 154-158

Learning Goals

1. Inventory and reinforce knowledge of letter format.
2. Improve productivity level in processing letters.
3. Reinforce production from script copy.
4. Reinforce straight-copy keyboarding skill.
5. Reinforce decision making and communication skills.

Machine Adjustments

1. Margin sets: 70-space line or as directed.
2. Spacing: SS sentences; DS ¶s; or as directed.

FORMATTING GUIDES: BUSINESS LETTERS

A&J Learning Systems
488 West Forsyth Street Jacksonville, FL 32202-1529 (904) 381-2789

September 25, 19--

Mr. Robert H. Pickens
Director of Human Resources
Community National Bank
P.O. Box One
Gainesville, FL 32602-8621

Dear Mr. Pickens

Your participation in our seminar on Understanding Leadership Styles will result, we believe, in some positive changes for you and your company. This is the feedback that we get over and over again from those who have attended the program.

So that your Leadership Style Profile can be processed before the seminar, would you please ask five business associates to complete the enclosed instruments and mail them to us in the envelopes that are also enclosed. We need to receive them by October 8, 19--.

We look forward to seeing you on October 12 at 8:30 a.m.

Sincerely yours

Ms. Sheila K. Weigand
Vice President

xx

Enclosures

Block style;
open punctuation

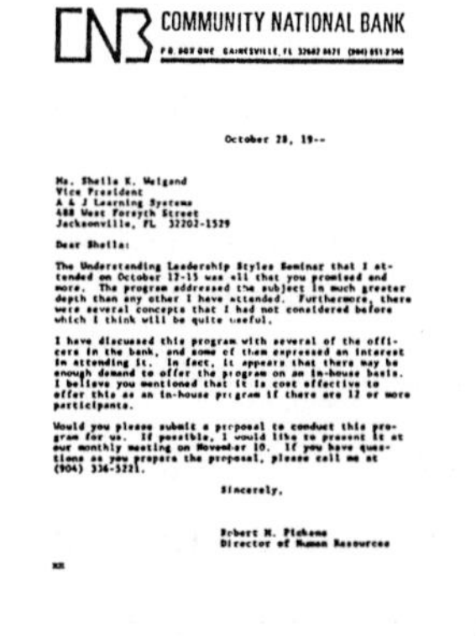

CNB COMMUNITY NATIONAL BANK

October 28, 19--

Ms. Sheila K. Weigand
Vice President
A & J Learning Systems
488 West Forsyth Street
Jacksonville, FL 32202-1529

Dear Sheila:

The Understanding Leadership Styles Seminar that I attended on October 12-15 was all that you promised and more. The program addressed the subject in much greater depth than any other I have attended. Furthermore, there were several concepts that I had not considered before which I think will be quite useful.

I have discussed this program with several of the officers in the bank, and some of them expressed an interest in attending it. In fact, it appears that there may be enough demand to offer the program on an in-house basis. I believe you mentioned that it is cost effective to offer this as an in-house program if there are 12 or more participants.

Would you please submit a proposal to conduct this program for us. If possible, I would like to present it at our monthly meeting on November 10. If you have questions as you prepare the proposal, please call me at (904) 336-5221.

Sincerely,

Robert H. Pickens
Director of Human Resources

xx

Modified block;
mixed punctuation

Guides for All Letters

1. The placement of the dateline varies depending upon the letter length. Use the letter placement table on page 149 (or below) as a guide. Follow the dateline with 4 returns (3 blank line spaces).
2. Most letters are addressed to an individual, in which case the salutation should include that person's name. The salutation of a letter addressed to a company, even if an attention line is used, should be "Ladies and Gentlemen," and the salutation of a letter addressed to an unidentified person such as "Office Manager" should be "Dear Sir or Madam." DS above and below the salutation.
3. The complimentary close is placed a DS below the last line of the body of the letter.
4. The signer's typed name is placed on the fourth line space below the complimentary close or company name, if one is used (operate return 4 times, leaving 3 blank line spaces).
5. The title of the signer may be either on the line with the name, separated by a comma, or on the next line (no comma), depending on length of the name and title.
6. Place reference initials a DS below the signer's name and/or title at the left margin. Only the keyboard operator's initials (lowercase) are needed for reference when the signer's name is included in the closing lines.
7. Place the enclosure notation (when used) a DS below the reference initials.

Letter Styles

Block Style. All lines begin at the left margin, including all opening lines, message lines, and closing lines. This letter style is simple and efficient to use and is recommended for frequent use.

Modified Block Style. The modified block style differs from the block style in that the date, complimentary close, and signer's typed name and title begin at the center point of the paper. Set a tab stop at the center point to speed alignment.

Paragraphs in modified block style may either be blocked at the left or indented. Usually a 5-space paragraph indention is used, but a few companies prefer a 10-space indention.

Punctuation Styles

Open Punctuation. No punctuation follows the salutation or complimentary close.

Mixed Punctuation. A colon follows the salutation and a comma follows the complimentary close.

Either open or mixed punctuation may be used with any of these letter styles; however, open punctuation is most often used with the block style letter. Many people use open punctuation, unless otherwise directed, because of efficiency.

Letter Placement

Length	*Margins*	*Dateline*
Short	2″	19
Medium	1½	16
Long	1″	13

130c (continued)

Problem 3
Simplified Memorandum
(plain full sheet)

Format and key the memorandum at the right as a simplified memo. Proofread and circle errors.

Problem 4
Formal Memorandum
(LM p. 71)

Repeat Problem 3 as a formal memorandum. Prepare a company envelope (address to Marketing Department). (total words: 287)

words

April 25, 19-- 3
QS

Tony Mendez, Marketing Manager 9
DS

CONDUCTING POSITIVE PERFORMANCE APPRAISALS 18
DS

It is almost time again for annual performance reviews, a process that you, 33
like many of our other managers, may not anticipate eagerly. So often 47
employees and managers look upon these conferences as a time to discuss 62
all the things employees have done wrong during the past year. With this 76
approach to performance reviews, tension is high; and neither the managers 91
nor the employees feel good at the completion of the reviews. Further, the 107
overall productivity of the company seems to suffer, at least for a few weeks. 123

Our Executive Board recognizes that improvements need to be made in our 137
performance appraisal procedures, and they have asked me to arrange for 151
two half-day programs on this topic. The programs will involve a small 166
amount of lecture, videotapes illustrating positive and negative performance 181
appraisals, discussion of problems encountered in performance appraisals, 196
and videotaped role playing to be critiqued and discussed. 208

If you would like to participate in this program, please send me a list of half 224
days when you can attend during the month of May. I have enclosed a form 239
that you may use to indicate if you are interested in the program and, if so, 255
to mark the times and dates you can attend. 264
QS

Terry Austin, Director of Human Resources 272
DS

xx 273
DS

Enclosure 274

Lesson 131 Keyboarding Skills/Business Forms

131a ▶ 5 Conditioning Practice

each line twice SS (slowly, then faster); DS between 2-line groups; if time permits, repeat selected lines

alphabet 1 Zack quit going fox hunting, so we can provide him with a job all day.

figures 2 The 24 students lost 13 of the 97 textbooks and 85 of the 460 pencils.

fig/sym 3 Mark's car insurance (effective 6/21/87) went from $335.50 to $409.75.

speed 4 Name an auditor to handle the problems and pay the city for this work.

| 1 | 2 | 3 | 4 | 5 | 6 | 7 | 8 | 9 | 10 | 11 | 12 | 13 | 14 |

131b ▶ 10 Improve Basic Skill: Speed-Forcing Drill

1. Repeat 130b, p. 228, Steps 1-5.

2. Take a 1′ writing on line 23; compare with rate in Lesson 130.

3. Record score on your paper to compare in Lesson 133.

153c ▶ 15
Assess Straight-Copy Keyboarding Skill

1. Two 5′ writings on ¶s 1-3 combined.

2. Determine *gwam*; circle errors.

3. Compare with score in 151c.

4. Record the better score of the two writings on LM p. 3 for comparison in Lesson 158.

all letters used | A | 1.5 si | 5.7 awl | 80% hfw

gwam 5′

Almost all business problems can be attributed in some way to a 3 61
lack of good communication. When exchanges of communication in an orga- 5 64
nization break down, the group cannot operate as a team. It becomes 8 67
more difficult for people to do their jobs, as they may not have all of 11 70
the information they need. Also, individuals may not comprehend their 14 72
role in relation to the goals of the company. The result is that the 17 75
quality of the product suffers, and demand for it begins to decline. 20 78

We usually think of communications as being in either written or 22 81
oral form. However, there are many ways by which we communicate, some 25 83
of which are equally as important as written and oral forms. For exam- 28 86
ple, facial and eye expressions give clues that alert people use to 31 89
judge the hidden meaning of words or to judge the reaction of a person 33 92
to words that are spoken. People who can zero in on these and other 36 95
signals have a more thorough message than they would from words alone. 39 97

One other way of communicating that is not recognized by most peo- 42 100
ple is listening. The person who has excellent listening skill enjoys 44 103
the benefit of a higher level of understanding of what is said. This 47 106
quality helps a person not only to gain more information but also to 50 108
gain more goodwill from co-workers, as the good listener gives a feeling 53 111
of caring about what others have to say. So good listening skill can 56 114
be just as helpful as good speaking, writing, and nonverbal skills. 58 117

gwam 5′ | 1 | 2 | 3 |

153d ▶ 10
Assess Language Skills: Decision Making

SS sentences; DS between groups of sentences

1. Examine the 3 groups of sentences for errors in spelling (lines 1-3), punctuation (4-6), and capitalization (7-9).

2. Key each sentence, correcting these language errors. Also, correct any typographical errors you make.

1 Two occurrences of typagraphical errers are permissable.
2 James was well equiped for hunting, which he did ocasionally.
3 After the argument, they were seperated until they appologized.

4 Jack said "As you know school ends on May 25 1987."
5 The beautiful, brown dog won a second-place prize.
6 Will you please hand me a pen two paper clips and a rubber band.

7 Labor day is always on monday, but Independence day varies.
8 Chris served as Secretary of the spanish club last year.
9 "Do you know," asked Julio, "If sam plans to go to st. louis?"

131c ▶ 25 Process Special Forms

Study the Formatting Guides for processing purchase requisitions, purchase orders, and invoices on p. 227.

1 cc; proofread carefully and correct errors.

Problem 1
Purchase Requisition
(LM p. 73)

Key purchase requisition as shown at right.

words

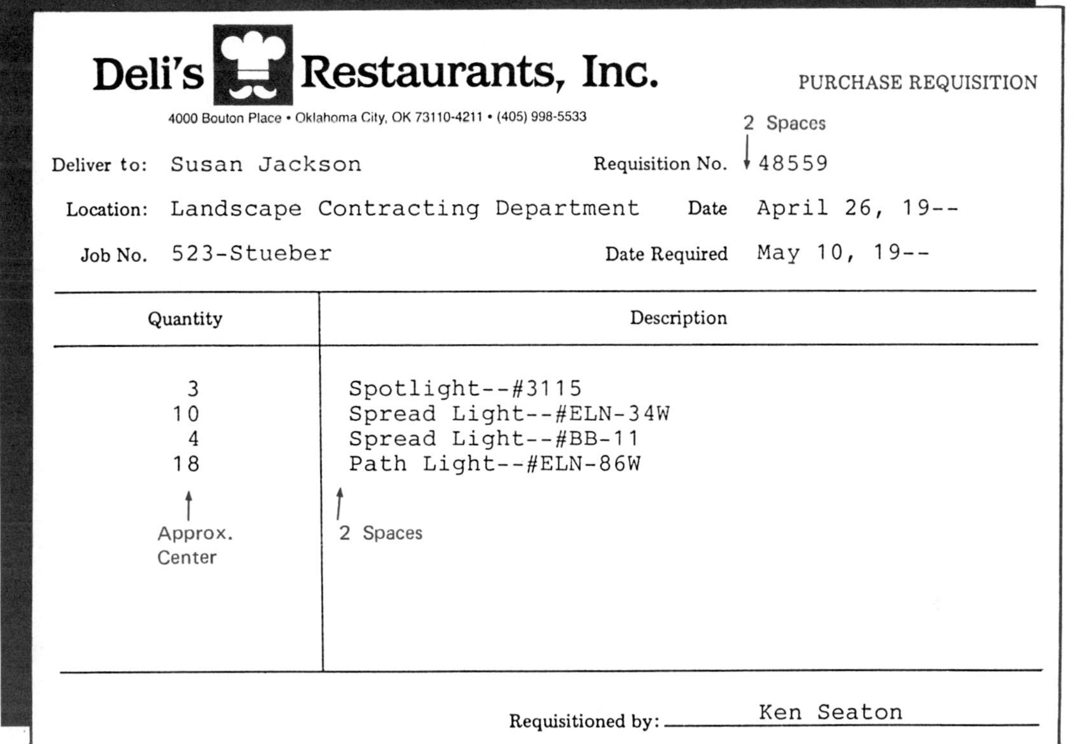

Deli's Restaurants, Inc.
4000 Bouton Place • Oklahoma City, OK 73110-4211 • (405) 998-5533

PURCHASE REQUISITION

2 Spaces

Deliver to: Susan Jackson — Requisition No. 48559 — 4

Location: Landscape Contracting Department — Date April 26, 19-- — 14

Job No. 523-Stueber — Date Required May 10, 19-- — 19

Quantity	Description	words
3	Spotlight--#3115	23
10	Spread Light--#ELN-34W	28
4	Spread Light--#BB-11	33
18	Path Light--#ELN-86W	37
Approx. Center	2 Spaces	

Requisitioned by: Ken Seaton — 39

Problem 2
Purchase Order
(LM p. 75)

Key purchase order as shown at right.

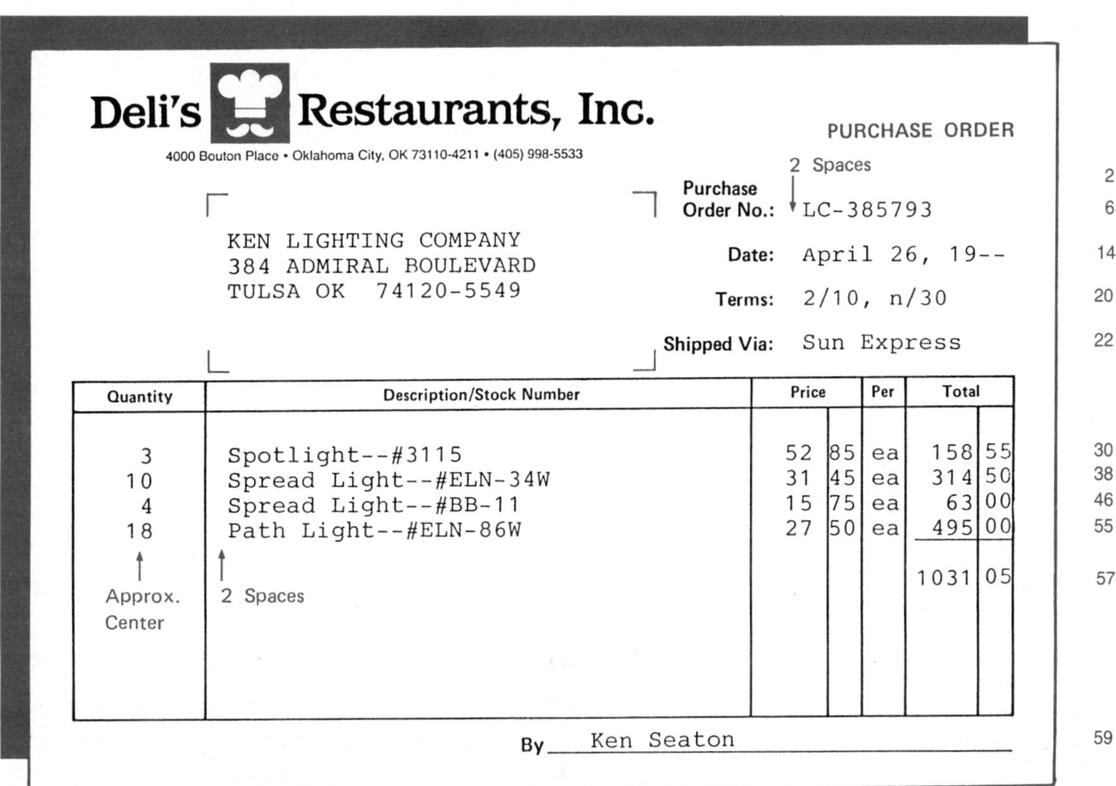

Deli's Restaurants, Inc.
4000 Bouton Place • Oklahoma City, OK 73110-4211 • (405) 998-5533

PURCHASE ORDER

2 Spaces

Purchase Order No.: LC-385793 — 2, 6

KEN LIGHTING COMPANY
384 ADMIRAL BOULEVARD
TULSA OK 74120-5549

Date: April 26, 19-- — 14

Terms: 2/10, n/30 — 20

Shipped Via: Sun Express — 22

Quantity	Description/Stock Number	Price	Per	Total	words
3	Spotlight--#3115	52 85	ea	158 55	30
10	Spread Light--#ELN-34W	31 45	ea	314 50	38
4	Spread Light--#BB-11	15 75	ea	63 00	46
18	Path Light--#ELN-86W	27 50	ea	495 00	55
				1031 05	57
Approx. Center	2 Spaces				

By Ken Seaton — 59

153a ▶ 5 Conditioning Practice

each line twice SS (slowly, then faster); DS between 3-line groups; if time permits, repeat selected lines

alphabet 1 Jacky required experts for evidence that my material was a big hazard.

figures 2 In 1896 the population was only 752,043, but by 1987 it was 2,460,350.

fig/sym 3 Of all my items, 75% (or 3/4) cost over $20; 16% cost between $80-$90.

speed 4 The rich pair may also make an endowment of the chapel and land to us.

| 1 | 2 | 3 | 4 | 5 | 6 | 7 | 8 | 9 | 10 | 11 | 12 | 13 | 14 |

153b ▶ 20 Improve Keyboarding Skill: Guided Writing

1. A 3′ writing on ¶s 1-2 combined; determine *gwam*.

2. A 1′ writing on ¶1; determine *gwam* to establish your base rate.

3. Add 2-6 words to Step 2 *gwam;* use this as your goal rate.

4. From the table below, find quarter-minute checkpoints; note these figures in ¶1.

5. Take three 1′ speed writings on ¶1, trying to reach your quarter-minute checkpoints as the guides (¼, ½, ¾, time) are called.

6. Follow Steps 2-5 for ¶2.

7. Repeat Step 1. Compare *gwam* on the two 3′ writings.

8. Record on LM p. 3 your better 3′ *gwam.* Compare to 3′ *gwam* rates you got in 152d and 151b.

gwam	¼′	½′	¾′	1′
32	8	16	24	32
36	9	18	27	36
40	10	20	30	40
44	11	22	33	44
48	12	24	36	48
52	13	26	39	52
56	14	28	42	56
60	15	30	45	60
64	16	32	48	64
68	17	34	51	68
72	18	36	54	72
76	19	38	57	76
80	20	40	60	80
84	21	42	63	84
88	22	44	66	88
92	23	46	69	92
96	24	48	72	96
100	25	50	75	100

all letters used | A | 1.5 si | 5.7 awl | 80% hfw |

gwam 3′

Office productivity refers to the ratio of office input, or the 4
cost of equipment, office space, supplies, and labor, to the output of 9
the office work force. The ability of an organization to increase out- 14
put at a faster rate than operating costs are rising is vital to its 18
success and possibly to its survival. Most people agree that improving 23
productivity is crucial, but the puzzle is how to go about doing so. 28
Perhaps the first step is to dispel the myth that many people believe-- 33
that is, they must work harder to exceed their present rate of produc- 37
tion. The better idea is that they must work smarter at their jobs, 42
not harder. 43

To determine how to work smarter, one might first analyze the daily 47
routine to see if some tasks that are being done manually might be 52
performed more efficiently with the aid of technology. Through office 56
automation, many jobs can be done more quickly and more accurately. 61
Often, information that is complete and up to date can be provided only 66
through automated systems, as some information becomes obsolete by the 71
time it can be produced manually. However, care must be exercised to 75
assure that automation is not used to generate too much of the wrong 80
kind of data as has sometimes been the case. 83

gwam 3′ | 1 | 2 | 3 | 4 | 5 |

131c (continued)

Problem 3
Invoice
(LM p. 77)

Key invoice as shown at right.

Problem 4
Invoice
(LM p. 79)

Repeat Problem 3 changing the quantities to 6, 10, 6, and 3. Calculate the total column. Add 6% sales tax.

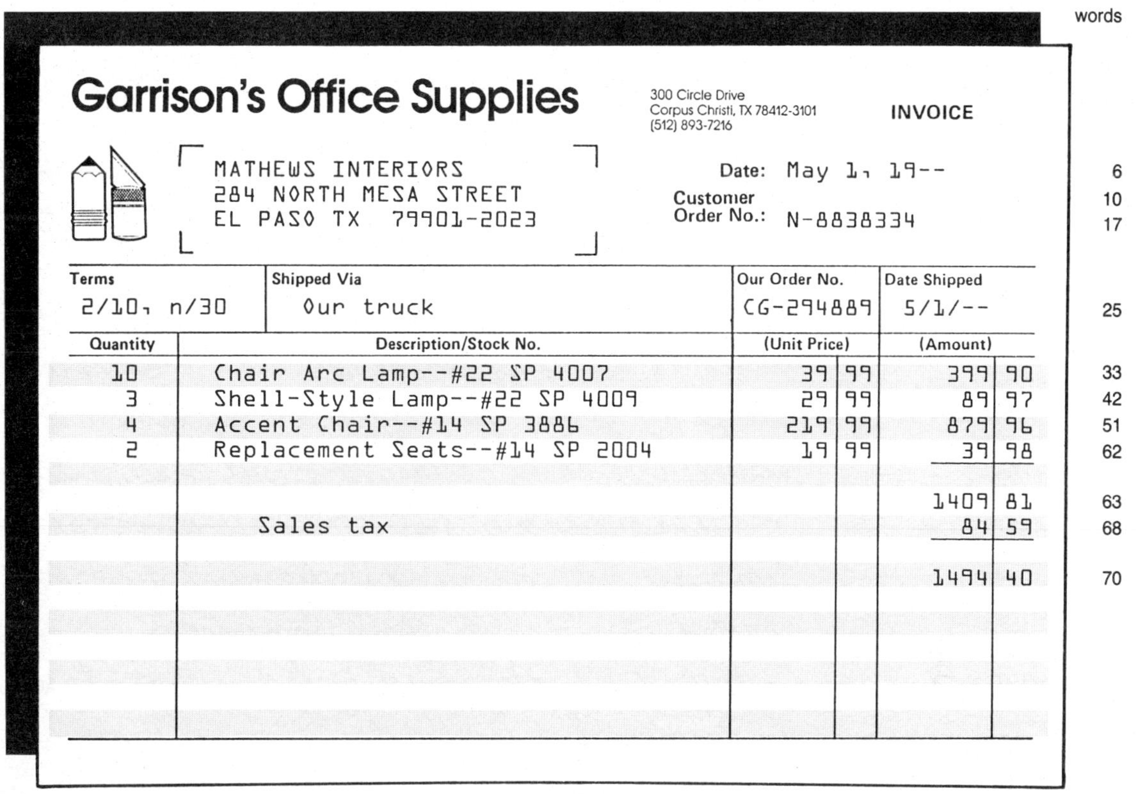

words

Garrison's Office Supplies
300 Circle Drive
Corpus Christi, TX 78412-3101
(512) 893-7216

INVOICE

MATHEWS INTERIORS
284 NORTH MESA STREET
EL PASO TX 79901-2023

Date: May 1, 19-- 6
Customer Order No.: N-8838334 10 17

Terms	Shipped Via	Our Order No.	Date Shipped	words
2/10, n/30	Our truck	CG-294889	5/1/--	25

Quantity	Description/Stock No.	(Unit Price)	(Amount)	words
10	Chair Arc Lamp--#22 SP 4007	39 99	399 90	33
3	Shell-Style Lamp--#22 SP 4009	29 99	89 97	42
4	Accent Chair--#14 SP 3886	219 99	879 96	51
2	Replacement Seats--#14 SP 2004	19 99	39 98	62
			1409 81	63
	Sales tax		84 59	68
			1494 40	70

131d ▶ 10 Language Skills: Learn Commonly Misspelled Words

70-space line; SS

1. Key the first word as shown in the example. Capital letters show the portion commonly misspelled.

2. Repeat Step 1 for each of the other words in the list.

3. From dictation, key each word 3 times in lowercase letters with the book closed.

(This procedure is recommended for any words you may have trouble spelling.)

Example

aCross aCross aCross across across across

aCross	noticEable
aLL riGHt	oCCaSion
benEfiTed	pamPHlet
embaRRaSS	recoMMend
juDGment	transfeRRed

Lesson 132 Spelling/Business Forms

132a ▶ 5 Conditioning Practice

each line twice SS (slowly, then faster); DS between 2-line groups; if time permits, repeat selected lines

alphabet 1 Just after Max passed the quiz on keyboarding, we left for a vacation.

figures 2 On June 30, 1987, shipments of 52 boxes of paper and 64 books arrived.

fig/sym 3 The new contract (#64382) will assure 75% of the workers a $109 raise.

speed 4 The field hand may work to fix the problems with the dock by the lake.

| 1 | 2 | 3 | 4 | 5 | 6 | 7 | 8 | 9 | 10 | 11 | 12 | 13 | 14 |

152c ▶ 15
Assess Script-Copy Skill

1. Two 1′ writings on each ¶ for speed; determine *gwam*.

2. One 1′ writing on each ¶ for control; circle errors.

3. One 3′ writing on ¶s 1-3 combined; determine *gwam* and circle errors.

	gwam 1′	3′
The firm that does well is one in which management	10	3
clearly understands the mission of the organization. Goals	22	7
are set to reflect the mission, and objectives are written in	35	12
definite terms so that they can be observed and measured.	46	15
Moreover, all staff know how their jobs contribute to	57	19
company goals. The staff are quite aware of what is	68	23
expected of them as they go about their daily activities.	80	27
The managers of this firm recognize that if expecta-	10	30
tions are not communicated, much time and effort are	21	34
wasted. For example, if an employee must question what	32	37
is important, the majority of time may be spent in trying	44	41
to decide what to do. In this instance, very little	54	45
work is finished and what is may not be correct. A	65	48
reprimand for such low output, though, may seem unjust	76	52
and lead to tension between staff and managers.	86	55
When relationship tension develops, the problems	10	58
become even more complex. Such tension becomes a further	21	62
barrier to open discussions, and both quantity and quality	33	66
of work suffer. Major effort is now needed to build trust	45	70
or just to minimize the lack of it. So the manager	55	74
who is aware of the situations that cause problems, who	67	78
can look ahead to see problems arising, and who can	78	81
avoid them is the one who is most prized.	86	84

152d ▶ 15
Improve Script-Copy Skill

1. Set a goal for either speed or control. Work for control (accuracy) if you exceeded 6 errors on the 3′ writing in 152c; otherwise, work for speed.

2. Take two 1′ writings on each of the 3 ¶s in 152c above.

3. Take a 3′ writing on ¶s 1-3 combined; determine *gwam*, circle errors.

4. Compare your 3′ score with the 3′ score recorded for 151b.

5. Record on LM p. 3 your 3′ *gwam* to compare with your 3′ *gwam* in 153b.

132b ▶ 10
Language Skills: Learn Commonly Misspelled Words

70-space line; SS

1. Key the first word as shown in the example. Capital letters show the portion commonly misspelled.

2. Repeat Step 1 for each of the other words in the list.

3. From dictation, key each word 3 times in lowercase letters with the book closed.

(This procedure is recommended for any words you may have trouble spelling.)

Example

```
amONg amONg amONg among among among
```

amONg	elIgIble
calendAr	grAtEful
coMMiTment	pErcEIve
defInIte	precEDe
desirAble	simIlar

132c ▶ 10
Preapplication Drill: Key on Ruled Paper

(plain full sheet)

1. Use the underline key to key a line 4 inches long (40 pica spaces; 48 elite spaces).

2. Center and key your full name on the line.

3. Study the proximity of the letters in your name to the underline. Only a slight space should separate the letters from the underline. Downstem letters (p, y, q, g, etc.) may touch the line.

4. Remove paper from machine.

5. With a pencil and ruler (or other straight edge), draw 3 horizontal lines 4″ long and 1/2″ apart.

6. Insert the paper and use the variable line spacer to align for keying the copy shown below. You may check the alignment by setting the ribbon control in stencil position and keying a downstem letter. This letter should be near or barely touch the line.

If it does not, make needed adjustments in the position of the paper.

7. Key the information below on lines, leaving 15 spaces between columns.

```
Mary Hargrove              Muncie
Mark Hauser                Gary
Terry Sumpter              Kokomo
```

132d ▶ 25
Keyboard on Ruled and Unruled Forms

Problem 1
Index Cards
(LM p. 81)

Key an index card from the model at right using same format as shown. Key 2 more index cards from information provided below.

Mr. Juan Guazero, President
Highland Industries, Inc.
200 Boyce Road
New Orleans, LA 70121-8809
(504) 932-1000

HOME BEAUTIFUL MAGAZINE
Attention Joanne Langley
90 Connally Avenue
Jacksonville, FL 32209-5530
(904) 655-2290

```
MILLER, JANE (DR.)

Dr. Jane Miller
200 Watson Road
Jackson, MS  39212-1110

(601) 439-2210
```

151c ▶ 15
Improve Straight-Copy Keyboarding Skill

1. Set a goal of either speed or control. Work for control (accuracy) if you exceeded 6 errors on the 3′ writing in 151b; otherwise, work for speed.

2. Take two 1′ writings on each of the 3 ¶s in 151b.

3. Take a 5′ writing on ¶s 1-3 combined. Determine *gwam*; circle errors.

4. Record on LM p. 3 your 5′ *gwam* to compare with your *gwam* in Lesson 153.

151d ▶ 15
Assess Keyboarding Response Patterns

each line twice SS; DS between 2-line groups; repeat difficult lines as time permits

letter 1 we no ad up be oil act pop get lip best upon area loop vest only trade
word 2 of is am he do sir key big wit she cork when them make fish soap visit
combination 3 at by my me tag vow pin tug far busy pink fuel beef cocoa plump visual

letter 4 as in|wet cat|oil pump|saw deer|look sad|wet case|wage war|pull uphill
word 5 to tow|an eye|got sick|so tight|cut down|visible lake|their own theory
combination 6 am ill|aged man|icy knoll|with zest|torn kimono|red signal|minimum aid

letter 7 We deserved a badge, as we defeated a ragged lion on a deserted knoll.
word 8 Did the six girls amend their work or do they risk a rigid city audit?
combination 9 If they fear defacement, they may hang their artwork only in the hall.

| 1 | 2 | 3 | 4 | 5 | 6 | 7 | 8 | 9 | 10 | 11 | 12 | 13 | 14 |

Lesson 152 Keyboarding Skills

152a ▶ 5
Conditioning Practice

each line twice SS (slowly, then faster); DS between 2-line groups; if time permits, repeat selected lines

alphabet 1 Fritz and Peggy will back the council vote on the major tax questions.
figures 2 Juan counted 28 pencils, 43 pens, 69 erasers, 71 clips, and 50 stamps.
fig/sym 3 Jun sold 29 spools of ribbon for $1.06/yd. (45% less than 378 others).
speed 4 Orlando owns the six sick ducks in the eighth pen, and he is so sorry.

| 1 | 2 | 3 | 4 | 5 | 6 | 7 | 8 | 9 | 10 | 11 | 12 | 13 | 14 |

152b ▶ 15
Improve Keyboarding Response Patterns

each line twice SS; DS between 2-line groups; repeat difficult lines as time permits

letter
1 him tax mop far ply care milk bear jump cease holly verse mummy drawer
2 join him|serve you|taste bad|plump beggars|minimum wage|my pink rabbit
3 As we feared waste, we treated aged cedar trees on vast test acreages.
4 Only rare rate decreases were stated in test data cases in my opinion.

word
5 man due she pays dusk goals slap rigid tight spend world orient handle
6 may fit|is apt to|oak chair|their amendment|burn the ham|the big whale
7 The height and shape of the panels form a visual problem for the firm.
8 Cory may turn to pen pals for an authentic element to a social ritual.

combination
9 vow are rush limp ivory farce shape imply civic profit minimum visible
10 no risk|the basement|see the cobwebs|to get treatment|upset the airman
11 It was up to you to get all the facts and to base the opinion on them.
12 With regard to estate taxes, did he agree with my auditor's statement?

| 1 | 2 | 3 | 4 | 5 | 6 | 7 | 8 | 9 | 10 | 11 | 12 | 13 | 14 |

132d (continued)

Problem 2
Activity Log
(LM p. 83)

Prepare an activity log from the handwritten copy at the right. Fill in the time elapsed column in minutes. Correct errors.

ACTIVITY LOG

Date 5-18 Name Margaret Roderick

Code	Started	Finished	Elapsed	Remarks
P	7:35	8:05		
A	8:05	8:30		Talked w/6 people
V	8:35	8:50		Tod Miller
T	8:50	9:15		Returned 5 calls
V	9:15	9:25		Michelle Kopecky
C	9:30	10:30		Productivity
RM	10:35	11:05		
AM	11:10	11:55		8 letters
O	12:00	1:25		Lunch--Dick Martin

A Assigning tasks to subordinates
R Reading professional journals
RM Reading mail
AM Answering mail
C Committee meetings/conferences

T Telephone
V Visitor
P Planning
O Other

Problem 3
Formal Memorandum
(LM p. 85)

Format and key the memo to Kevyn Slovak from Chris L. Hoy. Use current date. Supply an appropriate subject line. (words in heading lines: 13)

words

At your convenience, Kevyn, I would like to visit with you 25
about a research project that I believe we should consider 37
for next year. It would involve a number of people from 48
your area; therefore, your input is essential. Please call 60
me as soon as you can. 66

Problem 4
Purchase Order
(LM p. 87)

1 cc; correct errors; complete total column

To: TGC PLAY EQUIPMENT
14106 FIVE POINTS ROAD
CLEVELAND OH 44181-7771
Order No.: PE-47804
Date: Current
Terms: Net/30
Ship Via: Vey Lines
(total words: 62)

Quantity	Descriptions/Stock Nos.	Price
2	Big "J" Gym Set--#74568N	219.99
3	4-Activity Swing Set--#78421N	289.98
1	Big Slider--#76218N	159.99
1	Crazy Slide--#75248N	125.00

Jack Benson, Purchasing Agent

Unit 32 Lessons 151-153

Learning Goals

To assess and improve:

1. Keyboarding techniques.
2. Straight-copy keyboarding speed and accuracy.
3. Skill in keyboarding from script copy.
4. Decision making and language skills.

Machine Adjustments

1. Margin sets: 70-space line.
2. Spacing: SS sentence drills; DS ¶s; or as directed.

Lesson 151 Keyboarding Skills

151a ▶ 5 Conditioning Practice

each line twice SS (slowly, then faster); DS between 2-line groups; if time permits, repeat selected lines

alphabet 1 Pam realized the rock exhibit was judged as being of very low quality.

figures 2 Invoice No. 58126 was paid on May 3, and No. 47901 was paid on June 8.

fig/sym 3 Vi's first book (published in 1984) earned a 20% royalty of $9,853.76.

speed 4 The duel is to be at dusk by the town chapel if they wish to go to it.

| 1 | 2 | 3 | 4 | 5 | 6 | 7 | 8 | 9 | 10 | 11 | 12 | 13 | 14 |

151b ▶ 15 Assess Straight-Copy Keyboarding Skill

1. Two 1′ writings on each ¶ for speed; determine *gwam*.
2. One 1′ writing on each ¶ for control; circle errors.
3. A 3′ writing on ¶s 1-3 combined; determine *gwam*, circle errors.
4. Record on LM p. 3 your 3′ *gwam* to compare with your 3′ *gwam* on 152d.

all letters used | A | 1.5 si | 5.7 awl | 80% hfw |

	gwam 3′	5′	
In an era of more awareness of the need for higher productivity,	4	3	45
offices are trying to improve employee self-management skills. Among	9	5	47
them is improved skill in managing time. Business has come to realize	14	8	50
that even though all of us have exactly the same amount of time, some	18	11	53
seem to achieve much more than others. Some question just why that is.	23	14	56
Actually, there are many aspects of time management to consider.	28	17	59
One is that individuals who are good time managers employ a variety of	32	19	61
techniques to help them maximize their time resource and complete more	37	22	64
jobs. Most of these techniques are simple to use, and most people have	42	25	67
adequate skills to use them. We just need to apply them more often.	47	28	70
Possibly the most crucial requirement of a practical time manage-	51	31	73
ment plan is the conclusion to take command. Each person does govern	56	33	75
the use of his or her own time just as each person is responsible for	60	36	78
that behavior. This concept is not a complex one if we keep the notions	65	39	81
of control and responsibility in mind as we analyze each circumstance.	70	42	84

gwam 3′ | 1 | 2 | 3 | 4 | 5 |
5′ | 1 | 2 | 3 |

Lesson 133 Keyboarding Skills/Business Forms

133a ▶ 5
Conditioning Practice

each line twice SS (slowly, then faster); DS between 2-line groups; if time permits, repeat selected lines

alphabet 1 At Jaxton Zoo, they may hear ducks quack, wolves bark, and pigs fight.

figures 2 I planted 138 rose bushes, 57 crape myrtles, 40 lilacs, and 269 bulbs.

fig/sym 3 Styles #70-A and #93-C (see page 24 of the catalog) cost $186.50 each.

speed 4 Lem is the name visible on the visor of the big cycle, for he owns it.

| 1 | 2 | 3 | 4 | 5 | 6 | 7 | 8 | 9 | 10 | 11 | 12 | 13 | 14 |

133b ▶ 10
Improve Basic Skill: Speed-Forcing Drill

1. Repeat 130b, p. 228, Steps 1-5.

2. Take a 1′ writing on line 24.

3. Compare with rate in Lessons 130 and 131.

133c ▶ 35
Build Sustained Document Processing: Forms and Special Documents

(LM p. 85)
(LM pp. 89-94)
company envelopes for formal memos; correct errors

Time Schedule

Plan and prepare .... 3′
Timed production .... 25′
Proofread and correct errors ... 5′
Compute *n-pram* .... 2′

1. Make a list of problems to be processed:
page 229, 130c, Problem 1
page 229, 130c, Problem 2
page 230, 130c, Problem 3
page 231, 131c, Problem 2
page 232, 131c, Problem 3

2. Arrange forms, supplies, and correction materials for easy access. Process as many problems as you can in 25′. Proofread and correct errors before removing problems from machine.

3. Compute *n-pram* for problems completed. Turn in work, arranged in order listed in Step 1.

Net production rate a minute **(n-pram)** = **(total words keyed − penalty*) ÷ time**
*Penalty is 15 words for each uncorrected error.

Lesson 134 Measure Form Processing Skills

134a ▶ 5
Conditioning Practice

each line twice SS (slowly, then faster); DS between 2-line groups; if time permits, repeat selected lines

alphabet 1 Buz will make a quick trip next Monday to judge five recipes for fish.

figures 2 Dale drove 376 miles on 18 gallons of gas and 459 miles on 20 gallons.

fig/sym 3 The 326 numbers in the table add up to $190.87 (45% of overall total).

speed 4 The city may cut their payment to an endowment, and a fight may ensue.

| 1 | 2 | 3 | 4 | 5 | 6 | 7 | 8 | 9 | 10 | 11 | 12 | 13 | 14 |

134b ▶ 10
Figure and Tab-Key Drill

three 1′ writings and two 2′ writings; 65-space line; set tab stops and 10-space intervals

Concentrate on figure locations; quiet hands; quick tab spacing.

							words
3601	5702	4803	7904	5704	9506	4607	7
6208	7909	9401	6911	8512	6813	8914	14
9015	5716	8617	6818	4719	8520	9621	21
9722	4823	6924	8725	9426	8627	7528	28
5029	5730	8531	6132	7033	2734	4735	35
6936	9637	1838	5839	6540	7341	7842	42
1	2	3	4	5	6	7	

Lessons 151-175

PHASE 7

Inventory Keyboarding and Formatting Proficiency

The primary goal of Phase 7 is to assess and improve keyboarding skills you have previously acquired. The first unit concentrates on basic skills. The next three units concentrate on document formatting and production; namely, letters, reports, and tables. These units are then followed by a drill unit on both basic keyboarding and the production of documents. The last unit is a simulation designed to integrate skills.

The specific objectives of Phase 7 are to assess and improve the following competencies:

1. Straight-copy keyboarding speed and accuracy.

2. Keyboarding from script and rough-draft copy.

3. Production of documents such as letters, reports, and tables.

4. Decision-making skills.

5. Language skills.

6. Techniques that contribute to keyboarding productivity.

134c ▶ 35
Measure Document Processing: Forms/Special Documents

Time Schedule

Plan and prepare .... 3′
Timed production .... 25′
Proofread and correct errors ... 5′
Compute *n-pram* .... 2′

1 cc for forms; proofread and correct errors

Problem 1
Purchase Order
(LM p. 95)

Use the information at the right to prepare a purchase order.

Problem 1 words

HIGH-TECH INC
1408 WASHINGTON BOULEVARD
DETROIT MI 48226-9433

		words
Purchase Order No.:	TEL-468201	2
Date:	May 2, 19--	8
Terms:	2/10, n/30	15
Shipped Via:	Main Express	22

Quantity	Description/Stock No.	Price	Total	words
3	Automatic Memory Dialer -- #32-289	57.75/ea	173.25	33
2	Pocket Tone Dialer -- #32-132	54.95/ea	109.90	42
4	Phone Amplifier -- #32-274	47.50/ea	190.00	51
2	Tone Dialer with Memory -- #32-134	34.95/ea	69.90	61
3	Amplified Headset -- #32-289	33.75/ea	101.25	70
1	Office Monitor -- #32-146	189.95/ea	189.95	78
Prepared by: Carl Quintana			834.25	85

Problem 2
Invoice
(LM p. 97)

Use the information at the right to prepare an invoice. Add 6% sales tax ($28.29) to total.
(total words: 79)

Problem 2

BAKER AUDIO SYSTEMS
1401 SOUTH HAVANA STREET
AURORA CO 88012-7712

		words
Date:	May 4, 19--	2
Cust. Order No.:	361482	8
Terms:	2/10, n/30	15
Shipped Via:	Bear Express	22
Our Order No.:	HG-46184	24
Date Shipped:	4/24/--	26

Quantity	Description/Stock No.	Price	Total	words
2	Surface Mount Speaker -- #16-1741	58.95	117.90	35
3	6″ × 9″ 3-Way Speaker -- #42-1241	25.95	77.85	44
1	Graphic Stereo Equalizer -- #16-1756	89.95	89.95	54
4	AM/FM Stereo Antenna -- #16-1284	8.99	35.96	63
3	AM/FM Radio -- #16-1664	49.95	149.85	70
			471.51	75

Problem 3
Formal Memorandum
(LM p. 99)

Key a formal memorandum from the information at the right and the information listed below.

To: The Council on Education
From: Karen Rosenfeld, Director of Education
Date: Current
Subject: Continuing Education Proposal

Problem 4
Simplified Memorandum
(LM p. 101)

Using the information supplied above, rekey Problem 3 as a simplified memo.

Problem 3 words in heading 22

(¶ 1) A new copy of the Continuing Education Proposal is enclosed. You will 36
notice that a few minor changes have been made, among them being the 50
addition of a table of contents for easy reference. 60
(¶ 2) Ed has reviewed the proposal and has suggested that it be divided into 75
two parts -- one that describes in detail the changes we are proposing in the 90
program and one that describes the new budget we will be establishing. 104
(¶ 3) Since I anticipate that you will have other changes you wish to incorpo- 118
rate in the proposal, I shall wait to hear from you and then make all of the 134
changes at one time. May I have your comments within the next two weeks. 149
xx | Enclosure 151

150c (continued)

An increasing number of people are giving attention to the importance of 615
physical health to their productivity and goal achievements. They realize 630
that being physically fit enables them to function more effectively in today's 646
dynamic world. Many companies are beginning to implement physical fit- 660
ness programs within their companies, since they, too, realize the impor- 674
tance of their employees' physical health to their job productivity. The 689
primary areas that individuals and companies should examine if they wish 704
to influence physical fitness are proper diet, exercise, and sufficient rest. 720

On the other hand, mental health may be influenced by such things as 733
living in the present and maintaining balance in our lives. Living in the past 749
is unrealistic, and living in the future may mean looking forward to things 765
that will never happen. The people who constantly say, "Someday, I'll..." 780
will probably never do the many things that they had intended to do. Setting 796
realistic daily or weekly goals will help people achieve the more dramatic 811
and greater goals in life. Equally important is to maintain an appropriate 826
balance between work and play. Whatever people's hobbies or forms of en- 840
tertainment, it is important that a certain amount of time be given to these 856
"play" activities. It is important to give the mind a rest from daily work 871
routines. 873

Identifying and Eliminating Sources of Stress 891

Many of life's events can be controlled by people, but many others are 905
outside the realm of control. To aid in preventing stress, people should peri- 921
odically analyze and evaluate the stress-producing events in their lives. If 937
the number is high, people should strive to eliminate the stress-producing 952
events that they can. By eliminating stress-causing events wherever possible, 967
people can deal more effectively with those events beyond their control. 982

The first step in the evaluation process is to identify the sources of stress 998
because only after identification can action be taken. Several aids are avail- 1013
able in literature and from professionals which will aid in the detection of 1029
specific sources of stress. Questionnaire-type forms may be helpful in deter- 1044
mining what particular aspects of a job or an organization may be causing 1059
stress to employees. For example, people may feel stress about their job 1074
positions because their roles at work are ambiguous or because there is 1088
some conflict concerning their roles. Or stress may be caused by the lack 1103
of opportunity for career development. Additional causes of job stress may 1118
be related to the climate or structure of the organization. Responses to spe- 1134
cially designed questionnaires help to determine the specific problems that 1149
cause stress and if they can be eliminated. 1158

Recognizing Alternatives 1168

All too often stress is compounded if people feel trapped in a situation. 1183
Sometimes people feel helpless to change a situation. It is a great relief, 1198
though, to realize that alternatives are often available. If one cannot elimi- 1214
nate a stress-producing event, it is important to look for alternative ways 1229
of dealing with the event or alternative ways of transforming a situation 1244
so that it will be less stressful. Options are usually available; one just has 1260
to determine what they are and to assume responsibility for the alternatives 1275
they elect. 1277

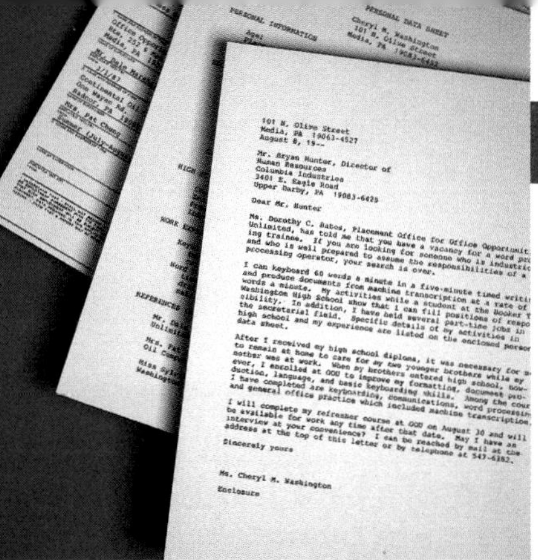

Unit 28 Lessons 135-138

Learning Goals

1. To learn guidelines for preparing a data sheet, application letter, application form, and follow-up letter.
2. To apply guidelines for preparing employment documents.
3. To compose and process personal employment documents.
4. To improve language skills through composing activities.

Machine Adjustments

1. Paper guide at *0*.
2. Paper bail rolls at even intervals across page.
3. Margins: 70-space line (drill lines) or as directed.
4. Spacing: as directed.

FORMATTING GUIDES: DATA SHEET, APPLICATION LETTER, APPLICATION FORM, AND FOLLOW-UP LETTER

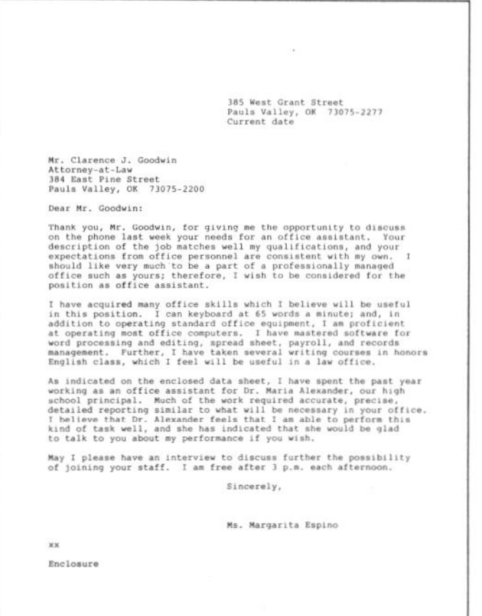

385 West Grant Street
Pauls Valley, OK 73075-2277
Current date

Mr. Clarence J. Goodwin
Attorney-at-Law
384 East Pine Street
Pauls Valley, OK 73075-2200

Dear Mr. Goodwin:

Thank you, Mr. Goodwin, for giving me the opportunity to discuss on the phone last week your needs for an office assistant. Your description of the job matches well my qualifications, and your expectations from office personnel are consistent with my own. I should like very much to be a part of a professionally managed office such as yours; therefore, I wish to be considered for the position as office assistant.

I have acquired many office skills which I believe will be useful in this position. I can keyboard at 65 words a minute; and, in addition to operating standard office equipment, I am proficient at operating most office computers. I have mastered software for word processing and editing, spread sheet, payroll, and records management. Further, I have taken several writing courses in honors English class, which I feel will be useful in a law office.

As indicated on the enclosed data sheet, I have spent the past year working as an office assistant for Dr. Maria Alexander, our high school principal. Much of the work required accurate, precise, detailed reporting similar to what will be necessary in your office. I believe that Dr. Alexander feels that I am able to perform this kind of task well, and she has indicated that she would be glad to talk to you about my performance if you wish.

May I please have an interview to discuss further the possibility of joining your staff. I am free after 3 p.m. each afternoon.

Sincerely,

Ms. Margarita Espino

xx

Enclosure

Application Letter

Special care should be given to the preparation of all employment documents. Such documents will most likely be the first impression you make on a prospective employer; they may also determine whether an interview will be granted to you. Thus, it is important to use extra care in preparing these documents.

Make sure that each document you prepare is neat in appearance, is correct grammatically, and presents both accurate and appropriate information. It is also important to follow exactly the specific directions that are given and to answer all relevant questions.

Prepare application documents on a keyboard with the possible exception of the application form. You may be asked to complete the application form at the time of the interview, in which case it may be prepared with a pen. Always use high-quality paper when preparing your data sheet and application letter.

Data Sheet

In most cases, a data sheet should be limited to one page. The information presented usually covers five major areas: personal information (*your name, address and telephone number*), education, school activities, work experience, and references. It may also include a section listing community activities and hobbies and/or special interests.

Top, bottom, and side margins may vary depending on the length of the data sheet. The specific format may also vary with personal preference. In general, the most important information is presented first, which means that a person who has been out of school for several years and has considerable work experience may place that information before educational background information. References, however, are usually the last item on the page.

Always get permission from the people on your reference list before using their names. Also, keep them informed about the jobs that you apply for and the specific skills that are important in qualifying you for each job.

Application Letter

An application letter is a personal business letter and includes the sender's return address, as shown in the model at the left. The letter should be limited to one page.

The first paragraph of an application letter contains a "you" message. It may point out something positive that the sender knows about the company or someone who works for the company. Worked into this paragraph may be information about how you learned of the opening. Conclude the paragraph with a statement indicating the specific position for which you are applying (or the kind of position you desire if you are sending a letter to determine if an opening is available in your area).

The next one or two paragraphs are "I" paragraphs. They should state how you are uniquely qualified for the job in question and why you should be hired. You may elaborate on the information on your data sheet -- mentioning that the data sheet is enclosed -- and explain how the experiences listed there qualify you for the job. This information, though, must go beyond just repeating what is on the data sheet. It explains the significance of your activities and experiences for the position you are seeking.

The final paragraph is a "request for action." It specifically asks for an interview and tells when you are available for an interview.

Follow-Up Letter

The follow-up letter is a thank you for being given an interview. If you can honestly do so, give positive impressions of the company and the people you met. Indicate that you would like an offer and provide a courteous ending to the letter.

150c ▶ 37
Evaluate Document Processing Skill: Reports

Time Schedule

Plan and prepare .... 4′
Document processing .... 25′
Proofread and correct errors ... 6′
Compute *n-pram* .... 2′

Problem 1
Unbound Report

Format and key the first page of the report at right in unbound report style.

Problem 2
Leftbound Report

Beginning with page 2, continue the report at right in leftbound style.

Bonus

1. At the conclusion of the 25′ production time, you will have 6′ to proofread again, correct any errors you find, or rekey if errors cannot be corrected. This step must be completed accurately before credit for bonus problem may be earned.

2. If time remains, rekey Problem 1 in leftbound style.

words

JOB STRESS 2

Coping with Stress 6

The rapid rate of change in the business environment leads to the poten- 20
tial for increased levels of job stress. This potential becomes a reality, 35
though, only if office personnel allow it to do so. People who have learned 51
to cope effectively with situations that could increase stress to unproductive 67
levels are the people who can function most successfully in today's business 82
world. 84

People vary greatly in their abilities to cope with stress. Some people 98
seem to accept change and undesirable problems that may arise with little 113
noticeable effect on their ability to perform on the job. At the other ex- 128
treme are those whose job performance seems to suffer by even the most 142
insignificant events. Fortunately, people can raise their tolerance for stress 158
if they wish to do so. By gaining a proper perspective toward problems and 173
by keeping physically and mentally healthy, it is much easier to cope with 188
stress. In addition, by eliminating sources of stress that can be eliminated 204
and by recognizing that often alternatives to problems exist, we can learn to 219
have some control over stress-producing situations. 230

Gaining a Proper Perspective 241

Some people seem to look upon almost all of life's events with a negative 256
viewpoint. Even when something good happens, their most immediate 270
thoughts are pessimistic. They worry about how the good event may be 284
taken away from them or how it will probably lead to some other undesirable 299
occurrence. On the other hand, some people find good in almost any situ- 313
ation. These people have a unique talent for "turning lemons into lemon- 328
ade." They look at a negative situation and realize that the situation could 343
be worse. Further, they immediately look for ways to solve a problem. By 358
using energy to eliminate a bad situation instead of wasting energy worrying 374
or being negative, positive people often turn a problem into an opportunity. 389

Further, Dr. Denis E. Whitley indicates that there is a causal relationship 404
between people's perspectives and what actually occurs in people's lives. 419
He suggests that people move toward their currently dominant thoughts. 434
Thus, those with negative thoughts move in a negative direction; those with 449
positive thoughts move in a direction that leads to the achievement of their 464
goals. In other words, people's perspectives are a great determining factor 480
of their futures. 484

In conclusion, individuals must realize that only they can control their 498
own minds, and a problem is only a problem if they perceive it to be one. If 514
people refuse to regard a situation as a problem, it ceases to be one. 528

Keeping Physically and Mentally Healthy 544

Both physical and mental health influence people's ability to cope with 558
stress. In addition, physical and mental health are interrelated. Physically 574
healthy people are more likely to be mentally healthy; likewise, mentally 589
healthy people are more likely to be physically healthy. 601

(continued on next page)

MARGARITA ESPINO
385 West Grant Street
Pauls Valley, OK 73075-2277
(405) 273-3591
QS

EDUCATION

Senior at Pauls Valley High School
High School Diploma, pending graduation
Majors: Business and English
Grade Average: 3.48; upper 15% of class

SCHOOL ACTIVITIES

Student Council President, senior year; member for 3 years

Member of National Honor Society, junior and senior years

Pen and Quill Secretary (literary writing club), senior year; member for 2 years

Junior Class Treasurer (handled budgeting, bookkeeping, and bills for junior-senior banquet and prom)

WORK EXPERIENCE

Office assistant to high school principal 24 hours a week during senior year; kept attendance reports, typed correspondence, filed, and helped with bookkeeping for athletic programs.

Director of own lawn mowing service for three years; solicited customers, scheduled work, purchased and maintained equipment, mowed lawns, and hired assistants.

REFERENCES (by permission)

Ms. Betty Jo Markley, Computer Instructor, Pauls Valley High School, P.O. Box 874, Pauls Valley, OK 73075-2278

Mr. Franklin J. Reeves, Loan Officer, First National Bank, 416 North Main Street, Pauls Valley, OK 73075-2309

Dr. M. J. Alexander, Principal, Pauls Valley High School, P.O. Box 874, Pauls Valley, OK 73075-2278

Data Sheet

149c (continued)

words

Problem 3
half sheet, short edge at top; SS body; 4 spaces between columns

			words
	SALES REPORT		3
	(Quarter Ending June 19--)		8
		Increase/	10
Office	Sales Volume	Decrease	21
Atlanta	$ 64,186	up	25
Dallas	87,241	up	29
Kansas City	26,424	down	33
Little Rock	14,861	down	38
New Orleans	56,743	up	43
Omaha	12,166	down	46
Santa Fe	26,841	up	50
Springfield	48,236	up	54
Tulsa	33,885	up	61
Total	$370,583	up	64

Problem 4
full sheet; DS body; decide spacing between columns

Bonus

1. At the conclusion of the 25′ production time, you will have 6′ to proofread again, correct any errors you find, or rekey if errors cannot be corrected. This step must be completed accurately before credit for bonus problem may be earned.

2. If time remains, rekey Problem 2 on a full sheet, DS, decide spacing between columns.

			words
BUSINESS DEPARTMENT COURSE OFFERINGS			7
Spring 1987			10
Course Name	No. of Sections	Total Enrollment	14
Accounting	9	224	26
Computer Literaacy	6	136	29
Computer Programming	3	77	34
Economics	5	133	39
Information/Word Processing	6	118	43
Keyboarding/Typewriting	12	335	49
Office Practice	2	47	56
		1,070	61
Tot al	43	~~7700~~	64

Lesson 150 Evaluation: Keyboarding/Report Skills

150a ▶ 5 Conditioning Practice

each line twice SS (slowly, then faster); DS between 2-line groups; if time permits, repeat selected lines

alphabet 1 The new professor gave six quizzes in math by the second week of July.

figures 2 Our 1987 inventory lists 362 diskettes, 40 computers, and 15 printers.

fig/sym 3 If the cost is $3,548.19 (less 20%), I can save $709.64 by buying now.

speed 4 An auditor may sign the forms to pay for half of the eight oak panels.

| 1 | 2 | 3 | 4 | 5 | 6 | 7 | 8 | 9 | 10 | 11 | 12 | 13 | 14 |

150b ▶ 8 Check Straight-Copy Skill

1. Take a 5′ writing on 148b, page 260.

2. Find *gwam* and number of errors.

3. Record score. Compare score with 148b and 149b.

Lesson 135 Personal Data Sheet/Composing

135a ▶ 5 Conditioning Practice

each line twice SS (slowly, then faster); DS between 2-line groups; if time permits, repeat selected lines

alphabet 1 Jan's views quickly became fogged and hazy during the perplexing exam.
figures 2 Terry bought 293 rings, 485 watches, 601 bracelets, and 749 necklaces.
3d row 3 The trusted reporter tried quietly to wire her top story to our paper.
speed 4 If they sign the forms, any proficient auditor can handle the problem.

| 1 | 2 | 3 | 4 | 5 | 6 | 7 | 8 | 9 | 10 | 11 | 12 | 13 | 14 |

135b ▶ 45 Prepare Data Sheets

plain paper; 1″ side margins

Problem 1

Format and key the data sheet shown on page 238.

Problem 2

Compose at the machine a rough-draft data sheet for yourself using the one on page 238 as a model (also, see guidelines on page 237, if necessary). Edit; then make a final copy.

Lesson 136 Application Letter/Composing

136a ▶ 5 Conditioning Practice

each line twice SS (slowly, then faster); DS between 2-line groups; if time permits, repeat selected lines

alphabet 1 Galena may have to think hard about just a few complex quiz questions.
figures 2 Our last order, dated May 30, was for Part No. 2974 and Part No. 1586.
adjacent key 3 Ophelia's and Polonius' performances in a serious rendition were good.
speed 4 If Shana pays for fuel for the auto, then she may go to town to visit.

| 1 | 2 | 3 | 4 | 5 | 6 | 7 | 8 | 9 | 10 | 11 | 12 | 13 | 14 |

136b ▶ 45 Prepare Application Letters

plain full sheets; 1 cc; modified block format; blocked ¶s; mixed punctuation; proofread and correct errors

Problem 1

Format and key the application letter for Ms. Margarita Espino. Study the guidelines and model illustration (p. 237); use personal-business letter format and begin return address on line 11. (See data sheet, p. 238, for Ms. Espino's return address.)

(words in return address: 10)

Problem 2

Compose at the keyboard a rough-draft letter applying for a job that you have seen advertised in the newspaper or one you have actually heard about and would like to do. In the latter case, include a short description of the job and how you learned about it. Edit your letter; then process it in final form.

words

Current date | Mr. Clarence J. Goodwin | Attorney-at-Law | 384 East Pine 24
Street | Pauls Valley, OK 73075-2200 | Dear Mr. Goodwin: 35

(¶ 1) Thank you, Mr. Goodwin, for giving me the opportunity to discuss on 49
the phone last week your needs for an office assistant. Your description of 64
the job matches well my qualifications, and your expectations from office 79
personnel are consistent with my own. I should like very much to be a part 94
of a professionally managed office such as yours; therefore, I wish to be 109
considered for the position of office assistant. 119

(¶ 2) I have acquired many office skills which I believe will be useful in this 133
position. I can keyboard at 65 words a minute; and, in addition to operating 149
standard office equipment, I am proficient at operating most office com- 164
puters. I have mastered software for word processing and editing, spread 178
sheet, payroll, and records management. Further, I have taken several 193
writing courses in honors English class, which I feel will be useful in a 207
law office. 210

(¶ 3) As indicated on the enclosed data sheet, I have spent the past year 224
working as an office assistant for Dr. Maria Alexander, our high school prin- 239
cipal. Much of the work required accurate, precise, detailed reporting simi- 254
lar to what will be necessary in your office. I believe that Dr. Alexander 269
feels that I am able to perform this kind of task well, and she has indicated 285
that she would be glad to talk to you about my performance if you wish. 299

(¶ 4) May I please have an interview to discuss further the possibility of join- 314
ing your office staff. I am free after 3 p.m. each afternoon. 327

Sincerely, | Ms. Margarita Espino | xx | Enclosure 335

Lesson 149 Evaluation: Keyboarding/Table Skills

149a ▶ 5 Conditioning Practice

each line twice SS (slowly, then faster); DS between 2-line groups; if time permits, repeat selected lines

alphabet 1 Not to be jeopardized, Max moved quickly away from the burning bushes.

figures 2 Flight 798 with 16 to 20 irate hostages was due to arrive at 3:45 p.m.

fig/sym 3 Please add a tax of 5% to Sales Slip #3479 to make a total of $268.10.

speed 4 The girls got a big quantity of the profit of the firm for their work.

| 1 | 2 | 3 | 4 | 5 | 6 | 7 | 8 | 9 | 10 | 11 | 12 | 13 | 14 |

149b ▶ 8 Check Straight-Copy Skill

1. Take a 5′ writing on 148b, page 260.

2. Find *gwam* and number of errors.

3. Record score. Compare score with 148b.

149c ▶ 37 Evaluate Document Processing Skill: Tables

Time Schedule

Plan and prepare .... 4′
Document processing .... 25′
Proofread and correct errors ... 6′
Compute *n-pram* .... 2′

Problem 1

full sheet; DS body; 8 spaces between columns

			words
EQUIPMENT INVENTORY			4
Maintenance Department			9
		Estimated	11
Item	Quantity	Value	19
Electric Rotary Mower	1	$150	25
Commercial-Duty Mower	3	700	30
Lawn Thatcher	1	80	34
Lawn Sweeper	2	220	38
Lawn Roller	2	180	41
Electric Weedwhacker	2	75	46
Electric Blower	1	55	51
Edger-Trimmer	2	120	54

Problem 2

half sheet, long edge at top; SS body; 8 spaces between columns

				words
LONG DISTANCE PRICING SCHEDULE				6
Rate per Minute				9
			Night/	11
Mileage	Day	Evening	Weekend	21
1-50	0.2037	0.1368	0.0912	26
51-124	0.3510	0.2268	0.1512	32
125-292	0.3618	0.2268	0.1512	38
293-430	0.4400	0.2310	0.1540	43
431-1910	0.4920	0.3129	0.2090	49
1911-3000	0.5831	0.3465	0.2371	55
3001-4250	0.6035	0.3560	0.2478	61
4251-5750	0.6212	0.3759	0.2573	67

(Problem 3 is on next page.)

Lesson 137 Application Form/Composing

137a ▶ 5 Conditioning Practice

each line twice SS (slowly, then faster); DS between 2-line groups; if time permits, repeat selected lines

alphabet 1 Lucy scored very high on every major botany quiz taken except for two.

figures 2 Ki passed out 43,570 pamphlets at 26 meetings in 19 towns in 8 months.

direct reach 3 Greg's voice echoed in the museum after he became unnecessarily angry.

speed 4 Lana may work and fight with vigor to handle a giant fish in the lake.

| 1 | 2 | 3 | 4 | 5 | 6 | 7 | 8 | 9 | 10 | 11 | 12 | 13 | 14 |

137b ▶ 45 Prepare Application Forms

(LM p. 109-112)

Problem 1

Format and key the application form on p. 241, being especially careful in proofreading and correcting errors.

Problem 2

Study the headings and questions on the application form. Make notations to complete an application form if you were applying for the job you wrote about in 136b, Problem 2, p. 239. Then prepare a final application form with your own data as if you were applying for the position. Use the extra form on LM p. 111.

Lesson 138 Follow-Up Letter/Composing

138a ▶ 5 Conditioning Practice

each line twice SS (slowly, then faster); DS between 2-line groups; if time permits, repeat selected lines

alphabet 1 Zed Loy was exceedingly jovial at making his quota before his partner.

figures 2 The group ate 259 hot dogs, 186 hamburgers, 370 colas, and 42 pickles.

space bar 3 Al and his son may try to tell us why they have not yet cut your bush.

speed 4 The goal of both of the panels is to halt all of their civic problems.

| 1 | 2 | 3 | 4 | 5 | 6 | 7 | 8 | 9 | 10 | 11 | 12 | 13 | 14 |

138b ▶ 45 Prepare Follow-Up Letters

plain full sheets; 1 cc; modified block format; blocked paragraphs; open punctuation; proofread and correct errors

Problem 1

Format and key the follow-up letter at the right. It is to Mr. Goodwin from Margarita Espino (see 135b, Problem 1, and 136b, Problem 1). Use current date and supply missing letter parts.

Problem 2

Study the guidelines for follow-up letters on p. 237. Assume that you interviewed for the job you applied for in 136b, Problem 2. Compose your follow-up letter; edit and prepare final copy.

words

opening lines 35

(¶ 1) Thank you, Mr. Goodwin, for the opportunity to discuss with you your 49
needs for an office assistant and my qualifications for that position. I ap- 64
preciate your thorough explanation of the objectives of your firm, and Ms. 79
Benson was especially helpful in outlining the details of the job. 93

(¶ 2) After visiting with you and Ms. Benson, meeting your office staff, and 107
seeing your facilities, I am even more enthusiastic about joining your firm. 123
I believe that my education, experiences, and ability to learn quickly qualify 138
me for this position; and I think working under Ms. Benson's supervision 153
would be a pleasure. Furthermore, I look upon your organization as one 167
which will provide me with an opportunity for career growth; and that is 182
important to me. 186

(¶ 3) I look forward, Mr. Goodwin, to becoming a part of your office team. 200

closing lines 206

148c ▶ 37
Evaluate Document Processing Skill: Letters

Time Schedule

Plan and prepare .... 4′
Document processing .... 25′
Proofread and correct errors ... 6′
Compute *n-pram* .... 2′

1 cc; correct errors; address envelopes

Problem 1
(LM p. 127)
block format; open punctuation

Problem 2
(LM p. 129)
modified block format; blocked ¶s; open punctuation

Problem 3
(LM p. 131)
modified block format; indented ¶s; open punctuation

Problem 4
(LM p. 133)
modified block format; blocked ¶s; open punctuation

Repeat Problem 2 with these changes:
Holt & Holt
Attention Office Systems Manager
P.O. Box 1847
Montclair, NJ 07042-2199
(words including envelope count: 183)

Bonus

1. At the conclusion of the 25′ processing time, you will have 6′ to proofread again, correct any errors you find, or rekey if errors cannot be corrected. This step must be completed accurately before credit for the bonus problem may be earned.

2. If time remains, rekey Problem 1 in modified block format, blocked ¶s, and mixed punctuation, on plain paper.

Problem 1 — words

May 3, 19-- Mr. Clark M. Pruett Pruett, Inc. P.O. Box 3033 Bend, OR 14
97702-9322 Dear Mr. Pruett Subject: Publication Committee Audit 27

(¶ 1) The three copies of the audit requested by the Board of Trustees con- 40
cerning the activities of the Publication Committee are enclosed. I have 55
sent one copy to Leigh Cozier and would like for you to make any other dis- 70
tributions that you consider appropriate. 78
(¶ 2) On the morning of May 22, I will report directly to the Board to discuss 93
this audit in detail. Since you were instrumental in preparing this year's 108
audit, could you also plan to attend the meeting. We will meet at 10:30 a.m. 124
in Room 203. 127
(¶ 3) If you cannot attend the meeting, will you please let me know as soon as 141
possible so that I can reschedule it. 149

Sincerely HTM ASSOCIATES Ronald D. Martin, Vice President xx Enclo- 162
sures pc John T. Baker, President There will be a luncheon at Nobel's 176
directly following the meeting, and you are cordially invited to join us. 191
205

Problem 2

June 25, 19-- Office Systems Manager Energy Alternatives, Inc. 13186 14
North Sunset Boulevard Renton, WA 98056-8871 Dear Sir or Madam 27

(¶ 1) Many office systems managers are beginning to realize that the depend- 40
ability of their office copiers significantly affects their productivity. They 56
recognize that frequent breakdowns are causing bottlenecks and worker 70
frustration. 73
(¶ 2) For this reason, many progressive offices have switched to the new LAN 87
copier. The LAN 650 is reliable and produces high-quality copies. Each docu- 103
ment to be copied is read electronically and adjustments are made automati- 118
cally to ensure a clear, clean copy every time. 127
(¶ 3) May we have our representative call you to set up a demonstration and 141
explain how you can get better copies at a lower cost. 153

Cordially LAIR OFFICE MACHINES Ms. Dana R. Lipke Sales Manager xx 166
186

Problem 3

July 3, 19-- REGISTERED Ms. Roberta Sanchez 488 North Murray Avenue 14
Anderson, SC 29621-7722 Dear Ms. Sanchez 22

(¶ 1) The agreement between you and Forrest W. Wilcox has been prepared 35
according to our understanding of your instructions of last Tuesday. You 50
will notice that Mr. Wilcox has signed each of the three enclosed copies. 65
(¶ 2) If you agree with all of the terms set forth in this document, would you 80
please sign the three copies enclosed and return two of them to me by regis- 95
tered mail. One copy is for your files. 103
(¶ 3) If there are any points that you question, would you please call me 117
as soon as possible for clarification. We would appreciate hearing from you 132
immediately because Mr. Wilcox is eager to complete this agreement. 146

Sincerely yours Susan Yamada Attorney-at-Law xx Enclosures 157
173

APPLICATION FOR EMPLOYMENT

PLEASE PRINT WITH BLACK INK OR USE TYPEWRITER — *AN EQUAL OPPORTUNITY EMPLOYER*

NAME (LAST, FIRST, MIDDLE INITIAL)	SOCIAL SECURITY NUMBER	CURRENT DATE
Espino, Margarita	448-38-5940	May 18, 1987

ADDRESS (NUMBER, STREET, CITY, STATE, ZIP CODE)	HOME PHONE NO.
385 West Grant Street, Pauls Valley, OK 73075-2277	(405) 273-3591

REACH PHONE NO.	U.S. CITIZEN? YES NO	DATE YOU CAN START
	X YES	May 25, 1987

ARE YOU EMPLOYED NOW?	IF SO, MAY WE INQUIRE OF YOUR PRESENT EMPLOYER?
Yes	Yes

TYPE OF WORK DESIRED	REFERRED BY	SALARY DESIRED
Office Assistant	Mr. Samuel Crampton	$ open

IF RELATED TO ANYONE IN OUR EMPLOY, STATE NAME AND POSITION

	YES	NO	IF YES, EXPLAIN
DO YOU HAVE ANY PHYSICAL CONDITION THAT MAY PREVENT YOU FROM PERFORMING CERTAIN KINDS OF WORK?		X	
HAVE YOU EVER BEEN CONVICTED OF A FELONY?		X	

EDUCATION

	EDUCATIONAL INSTITUTION	LOCATION (CITY, STATE)	DATES ATTENDED FROM MO.	FROM YR.	TO MO.	TO YR.	DIPLOMA, DEGREE, OR CREDITS EARNED	CLASS STANDING (CHK QUARTER) 1	2	3	4	MAJOR SUBJECTS STUDIED
COLLEGE												
HIGH SCHOOL	Pauls Valley High	Pauls Valley, OK	9	83	5	87	Diploma	X				Bus./Eng.
GRADE SCHOOL							X	X	X	X	X	X
OTHER												

LIST BELOW THE POSITIONS THAT YOU HAVE HELD (LAST POSITION FIRST)

1. NAME AND ADDRESS OF FIRM	DESCRIBE POSITION RESPONSIBILITIES
Pauls Valley High School P.O. Box 874 Pauls Valley, OK 73075-2278	Kept attendance reports, typed corres- pondence, and helped with bookkeeping for athletic programs.
NAME OF SUPERVISOR: Dr. M. J. Alexander, Principal	
EMPLOYED (MO-YR) FROM: 8/86 TO: 5/87	REASON FOR LEAVING: Graduation

2. NAME AND ADDRESS OF FIRM	DESCRIBE POSITION RESPONSIBILITIES
Directed my own lawn mowing service.	Solicited customers, scheduled work, purchased and maintained equipment, mowed lawns, and hired assistants.
NAME OF SUPERVISOR:	
EMPLOYED (MO-YR) FROM: 4/84 TO: present	REASON FOR LEAVING: Continues to operate on limited basis.

3. NAME AND ADDRESS OF FIRM	DESCRIBE POSITION RESPONSIBILITIES
NAME OF SUPERVISOR:	
EMPLOYED (MO-YR) FROM: TO:	REASON FOR LEAVING:

I UNDERSTAND THAT I SHALL NOT BECOME AN EMPLOYEE UNTIL I HAVE SIGNED AN EMPLOYMENT AGREEMENT WITH THE FINAL APPROVAL OF THE EMPLOYER AND THAT SUCH EMPLOYMENT WILL BE SUBJECT TO VERIFICATION OF PREVIOUS EMPLOYMENT, DATA PROVIDED IN THIS APPLICATION, ANY RELATED DOCUMENTS, OR RESUME. I KNOW THAT A REPORT MAY BE MADE THAT WILL INCLUDE INFORMATION CONCERNING ANY FACTOR THE EMPLOYER MIGHT FIND RELEVANT TO THE POSITION FOR WHICH I AM APPLYING, AND THAT I CAN MAKE A WRITTEN REQUEST FOR ADDITIONAL INFORMATION AS TO THE NATURE AND SCOPE OF THE REPORT IF ONE IS MADE.

Margarita Espino
SIGNATURE OF APPLICANT

Application for Employment Form

SOUTH-WESTERN PUBLISHING CO.

Unit 31 Lessons 148-150

Measurement Goals

1. To evaluate straight-copy speed and control.
2. To evaluate document processing skill.

Documents Processed

1. Letters
2. Tables
3. Reports

Lesson 148 Evaluation: Keyboarding/Letter Skills

148a ▶ 5 Conditioning Practice

each line twice SS (slowly, then faster); DS between 2-line groups; if time permits, repeat selected lines

alphabet 1 Jackie Dexter gave his music classes a pop quiz while Faye was absent.

figures 2 In 1987, we bought 46 textbooks, 20 workbooks, and 35 placement tests.

fig/sym 3 Al's stores (1987 data) hired 1,623 clerks at a minimum rate of $4.50.

speed 4 They wish to make six big signs to make the title visible to the town.

| 1 | 2 | 3 | 4 | 5 | 6 | 7 | 8 | 9 | 10 | 11 | 12 | 13 | 14 |

148b ▶ 8 Check Straight-Copy Skill

1. A 5′ writing on all ¶s.
2. Find *gwam* and number of errors.

all letters used | A | 1.5 si | 5.7 awl | 80% hfw |

Text	gwam 3′	5′	
The technology used in most business organizations today makes it	4	3	45
quite needless to rekey a document. Also, there is no economic justi-	9	5	48
fication for ever recording a letter, for example, more than one time.	14	8	51
This is possible, of course, only if the person who first writes the	18	11	54
letter, as well as any other person who may edit or revise it, has	23	14	56
keyboarding skill. It is plain to see that one who is not able to	27	16	59
keyboard by touch is handicapped in her or his ability to communicate	32	19	62
efficiently, and this creates a business problem.	35	21	64
If the communication system of a business firm does not run effi-	40	24	66
ciently and smoothly, the flow of information is hampered. If the flow	44	26	69
of information lags, executives and others who make dozens of critical	49	29	72
decisions each day may not have the information that they require in	54	32	75
order to do their jobs well. In some cases, getting this information	58	35	78
a day late or maybe just an hour late can cause serious problems and	63	38	80
can be costly. An efficient and effective flow of information is crit-	68	41	83
ical in a complex and competitive business world.	71	43	85

gwam 3′ | 1 | 2 | 3 | 4 | 5 |
5′ | 1 | 2 | 3 |

The two sets of paragraphs on this page are counted internally for 1′ guided and unguided writings. In addition, the paragraphs at the bottom of the page are counted for 3′ and 5′ timed writings. They may be used at any time additional drills and/or timed writings are desired.

Straight-Copy Drill

1. A 1′ writing on the ¶ at the top to establish a base rate.

2. Add 4-8 words to base rate to set goal rate. Note quarter-minute checkpoints.

3. Three 1′ writings on the ¶, trying to achieve goal rate each quarter minute as guides are called. Set goal rate higher each time the goal is achieved.

4. Note quarter-minute checkpoints for base rate established in Step 1 above.

5. Three 1′ writings at reduced speed for control.

Goal: Not more than one error a minute. Reduce speed if necessary.

Quarter-Minute Checkpoints

gwam	1/4′	1/2′	3/4′	Time
16	4	8	12	16
20	5	10	15	20
24	6	12	18	24
28	7	14	21	28
32	8	16	24	32
36	9	18	27	36
40	10	20	30	40
44	11	22	33	44
48	12	24	36	48
52	13	26	39	52
56	14	28	42	56
60	15	30	45	60

Timed Writings

Two 3′ or 5′ writings on the ¶s at the right. Find *gwam* and errors. Record the better of the 3′ and 5′ writings. Compare 5′ score with score of 129b, page 225.

all letters used | A | 1.5 si | 5.7 awl | 80% hfw

It is well-known that computer systems are now widely accepted as tools that organizations use to run and manage office affairs. As a tool, the system must be maintained just as the tools of a builder, for example, must be maintained. A wide variety of technical people is needed to establish and support a system; this need has created a demand for a number of different kinds of specialists. Some of these specialists are needed to design and care for the hardware or equipment; others are needed to develop and maintain software or programs.

---

all letters used | A | 1.5 si | 5.7 awl | 80% hfw

	gwam 3′		5′
The experts who design, build, and modify computer equipment are	4	3	48
known to us as computer engineers. An advanced mastery of both the areas	9	6	51
of electronics and mechanics is needed by these people if they are to do	14	8	54
their jobs properly. From the first day a system is installed, a busi-	19	11	57
ness must begin to upgrade the new system; the new system must be adapted	24	14	60
to the needs of each individual business, and continuous improvements	28	17	63
must be made if optimum results are to be realized. Thus, a computer	33	20	65
engineer's job does not end once the system is installed, and her or his	38	23	68
expertise is important if the system is going to work.	42	25	70
There are two kinds of software experts. The ones who deal with the	46	28	73
programs that control only the operation of the computer are the computer	51	31	76
scientists; also, they set up the programs that make sure that the equip-	56	34	79
ment gives valid results. Those who develop the programs to process the	61	37	82
data are the application programmers; they also write the codes that	65	39	85
instruct a computer to perform the given tasks and solve the various	70	42	88
problems. The skills of both kinds of experts are needed to make sure	74	45	90
the system works.	76	46	91

gwam 3′ | 1 | 2 | 3 | 4 | 5
5′ | 1 | 2 | 3

147c ▶ 10
Check Straight-Copy Skill

1. A 5′ writing on all ¶s.
2. Find *gwam* and number of errors.

all letters used | A | 1.5 si | 5.7 awl | 80% hfw

	gwam 3′	5′
Choosing a career is not an easy task, but it is a significant	4	2
decision that requires careful consideration. It is important to think	9	5
about the education that you will need in order to attain expertise in	13	8
the exact field that may interest you. Also, you should consider	18	11
the income you will realize after you have finished your schooling. You	23	14
may wish to ask yourself if the rewards will exceed the amount of energy	28	17
and time that will be required in the process of getting prepared for	33	20
a chosen career. Furthermore, you should consider if you are suited to	37	22
the career chosen. If you wished to be a teacher, for example, you	42	25
might contemplate the points below.	44	27
There are some traits that are desirable in a teacher, and one	48	29
should possess many of them before entering the profession. For example,	53	32
excellent teachers should be interested in the exact needs of each indi-	58	35
vidual student as well as the needs of a class as a whole. The quiet	63	38
student in the back row should be given as much attention as the rowdy	67	41
student in the front row. An expert teacher will be capable of recog-	72	43
nizing the unique qualities possessed by each student and helping each	77	46
student to develop important traits.	80	48
An adept teacher must have many insights into the learning process.	84	50
Even if we do not know all of the cause and effect relationships, we do	89	53
know that students learn more if they are treated in certain ways. For	94	56
example, we recognize that learners react to praise better than reproof.	99	59
Also, there is no question that learners who do a job well initially	103	62
will do even better when confronted with another task. Further, learners	108	65
who are given feedback about the accuracy of their work do better than	113	68
if they are given little or no feedback.	116	69
Gathering information about the skills that are required in a	120	72
designated field before you make a career choice is very important.	124	75
Also, spending the time initially looking into various aspects of a	129	77
career that may interest you will reap rewards in the long run. In	133	80
addition, it will allow you to make the right choice.	137	82

Unit 29 Lessons 139-143

Learning Goals

To integrate the knowledge and skills acquired in Cycle 2 in:

1. processing documents.
2. detecting and correcting errors.
3. applying language skills.
4. making decisions.

Documents Processed

1. Memorandums and letters (one- and two-page)
2. Report
3. Table
4. Special documents: index cards, ruled form, menu, and announcement

WOLF CREEK LODGE: AN OFFICE JOB SIMULATION

Ms. Ada Perez
Page 2
June 1, 19--

addition, we maintain a staff of qualified individuals who thoroughly enjoy entertaining children. Each person on staff was carefully screened because we realize how important quality child care is to parents.

Last, we haven't forgotten that teenagers require their "special" brand of entertainment. That is why we have hired Betsy Barnes, a full-time youth director, who is responsible for keeping teenagers happy. From rowboating to horseback riding to backpacking hikes, Betsy has planned a wide variety of activities. And, judging from the volume of fan mail that Betsy has received this past year, I would say she has made quite a hit with teenagers. Another benefit from the teenage program is the lasting friendships that continue long after the vacation at Wolf Creek is over.

We hope these details are helpful to you as you continue to plan your vacation. If we can answer questions or be of assistance in any way, do let us know. You can reach us at 1-800-227-8800.

Sincerely

Paul R. Skidmore
Lodge Director

xx

Enclosures: 2 Brochures
Sample Menu
Announcement

Second Page of Letter with Blocked Second-Page Heading

John Smith	Vocalist
Maxine Freeland . .	Pianist

Aligned Leaders Between Columns

Work Assignment

Wolf Creek Lodge is a large vacation resort located in a scenic area near Pagosa Springs, Colorado. It offers a wide variety of activities, facilities, and services for single and family vacations. Although the lodge rents units on a single-night basis, most of their summer business results from guests who stay at least a week.

You have been hired to work as an office assistant for Wolf Creek Lodge. As such, you will work directly under the supervision of Ms. Roberta Callahan, Office Manager, who will assign to you various keyboarding tasks. You will prepare an assortment of documents (letters, memos, tables, menus, and announcements) for Ms. Callahan and other individuals at the lodge. You are expected to correct any undetected errors (whether in spelling, punctuation, and/or capitalization) which Ms. Callahan or others at the lodge have overlooked. Also, the finished document must be technically correct with all typographical errors neatly corrected.

Before beginning your first assignment, Ms. Callahan asks you to read "Excerpts from the Office Procedures Manual."

Excerpts from the Office Procedures Manual

While Wolf Creek Lodge uses a standard format for letters and memos (see below), most other formatting decisions are made by office personnel. You are expected to use good judgment in attractively arranging such documents as menus, tables, and announcements.

Letters and memorandums. Most letters are signed by Mr. Skidmore, Lodge Director. Memos, however, may be prepared for the signature of several different lodge employees. Use your reference initials and an enclosure notation, if needed, when preparing letters and memos. Use block format and open punctuation for all letters; use simplified memo format for all memos. Prepare one *cc* and company envelope unless otherwise directed.

Second page of letter. When keying two-page letters, use block format for second-page headings. Begin heading on line 6, flush with the left margin; supply receiver's name, page number, and date (see illustration at left).

Form letters. Wolf Creek Lodge often uses form letters to correspond with potential guests, since they have such a large mailing list. Stock paragraphs (standardized text known as boilerplate) will be written, and the keyboard operator will be instructed as to which appropriate paragraphs are needed for a particular letter. In some cases, you will be instructed to select an appropriate phrase from those suggested to adapt your letter to the receiver of a letter.

If you are using a manual, electric, or an electronic typewriter, key subsequent letters from the letter you have just prepared if the same paragraphs are used. This way you can proofread the previous letter while keying. All materials should be proofread twice to make sure the material is error free. If, on the other hand, you are using a word processor, and if the copy has been stored correctly, then you have to proofread only the variable material to make certain that it is error free.

Leaders. At times, documents need leaders to help the reader's eyes horizontally align material presented in columns (see example at left). Leaders are made by alternating periods and spaces between columns.

When keying leaders, space once after the first item in the first column. Then alternate periods and spaces to a point 2 or 3 spaces before beginning of second column. To help align periods, note on the line-of-writing scale whether the first period is keyed on an odd or even number, and then place all subsequent periods accordingly.

147b (continued)

Problem 3
Leftbound Report

Format and key page 1 of the report at the right as a leftbound report.

Problem 4
Unbound Report

Beginning where you stopped at the end of Problem 3, format and key the remainder of the copy as page 2 of an unbound report.

Bonus

1. At the conclusion of the 25′ production time, you will have 6′ to proofread again, correct any errors you find, or rekey if errors cannot be corrected. This step must be completed accurately before credit for the bonus problem may be earned.

2. If time remains, rekey Problem 1 in modified block style, blocked ¶s, and open punctuation.

words

AN INFORMATION SYSTEM 4
Common Elements 8

For information processing to occur, an information system must be devel- 22
oped. The essential elements of such a system are the people, procedures, 37
equipment, and data. 42

People 44

An information system is developed as a tool or a support for the individuals 60
who will use it. Users give an information system a purpose, and most 74
people associated with an information system will be users. Other people 89
associated with an information system are those who develop the hard- 102
ware and software and those people who specialize in systems design and 117
programming. 120

Procedures 124

Procedures consist of instructions and directions. Instructions tell the com- 139
puter what to do to achieve the desired results, and directions tell users 154
how to accomplish the desired results with the hardware and software being 169
used. Instructions are given in the form of computer programs, and direc- 187
tions are written in the form of procedures manuals. 195

Computer programs. Programs are the instructions that are written in 212
English-like statements to control the processing done by the machine. 226
They must be written in a specific format to be read by the computer and 241
translated into machine language (through a different program that is a part 256
of the operating system) before processing can occur. 267

Procedures manuals. For people to use programs successfully, they must 285
be guided through appropriate steps to make the program work. This is 300
accomplished through a manual that gives directions for preparing input 314
data, for setting up the computer to run or process the data, and for setting 330
up the computer for output data. 336

Equipment 340

Equipment consists of the computer and what is known as peripherals. 354
Peripherals are devices such as keyboards, VDTs,* disk or tape drives, and 369
printers and other output devices. 376

Data 378

The very reason for the existence of an information system is to handle data. 394
Data must be controlled in such a way to assure that it is accurate, safe, and 410
secure. The control system provides a means of checking output data peri- 424
odically to verify its quality. In addition, stored files must be protected 440
from disasters such as fires, floods, and tornadoes as well as theft. 454

Finally, an appropriate environment, sometimes with special air condition- 469
ing, must be provided to assure proper operation of equipment and to save 483
and protect data media. 488

________________ 492

*VDT stands for video display terminal. 500

139a-143a ▶ 5 (daily)

Each day before you begin work on the problems (139b-143b), check your equipment to see that it is in good working order by typing the paragraph at the right at least twice (first slowly, then faster).

Val's keyboarding speed is quite high now. She increased from 60 gwam to 85 gwam (a gain of 29.41%) in just 37 days. Her extra practice has "paid off," as her employer recognizes her exceptional level of skill. She keys with proficiency all of the rush work of the eight officials.

| 1 | 2 | 3 | 4 | 5 | 6 | 7 | 8 | 9 | 10 | 11 | 12 | 13 | 14 |

139b-143b ▶ 45 (daily)
Work Assignments

Job 1
Employee Record Forms
(LM p. 113)

Obtain information from the application forms and complete Employee Record Forms for three new employees. You will need the following additional information:

OWENS: employed 6/1/19--
Notify: Mr. or Mrs. Ralph Owens
(303) 422-8640

WILLIAMS: employed 5/20/19--
Notify: Mrs. Mary Jane Williams
(303) 390-6897

LIN: employed 5/25/19--
Notify: Mr. Thomas Ryan
(303) 921-8847

Thanks. Roberta Callahan

APPLICATION FOR EMPLOYMENT
AN EQUAL OPPORTUNITY EMPLOYER
PLEASE PRINT WITH BLACK INK OR USE TYPEWRITER

NAME (LAST, FIRST, MIDDLE INITIAL)	SOCIAL SECURITY NUMBER	CURRENT DATE
Owens, Sarah J.	440-85-8840	March 3, 19--

ADDRESS (NUMBER, STREET, CITY, STATE, ZIP CODE)	HOME PHONE NO.
P.O. Box 322, Monte Vista, CO 81144-7321	(303) 422-8640

REACH PHONE NO.	U.S. CITIZEN?	DATE YOU CAN START
	X YES NO	May 28, 19--

ARE YOU EMPLOYED NOW? IF SO, MAY WE INQUIRE OF YOUR PRESENT EMPLOYER?

APPLICATION FOR EMPLOYMENT
AN EQUAL OPPORTUNITY EMPLOYER
PLEASE PRINT WITH BLACK INK OR USE TYPEWRITER

NAME (LAST, FIRST, MIDDLE INITIAL)	SOCIAL SECURITY NUMBER	CURRENT DATE
Williams, Rex J.	522-86-4968	May 1, 19--

ADDRESS (NUMBER, STREET, CITY, STATE, ZIP CODE)	HOME PHONE NO.
386 West First Street, South Fork, CO 81154-8820	(303) 390-6897

REACH PHONE NO.	U.S. CITIZEN?	DATE YOU CAN START
	X YES NO	May 15, 19--

ARE YOU EMPLOYED NOW? IF SO, MAY WE INQUIRE OF YOUR PRESENT EMPLOYER?

APPLICATION FOR EMPLOYMENT
AN EQUAL OPPORTUNITY EMPLOYER
PLEASE PRINT WITH BLACK INK OR USE TYPEWRITER

NAME (LAST, FIRST, MIDDLE INITIAL)	SOCIAL SECURITY NUMBER	CURRENT DATE
Lin, Yang	522-80-3854	April 2, 19--

ADDRESS (NUMBER, STREET, CITY, STATE, ZIP CODE)	HOME PHONE NO.
975 West 18 Avenue, Pagosa Springs, CO 81147-6311	(303) 447-8028

REACH PHONE NO.	U.S. CITIZEN?	DATE YOU CAN START
	X YES NO	May 15, 19--

ARE YOU EMPLOYED NOW? IF SO, MAY WE INQUIRE OF YOUR PRESENT EMPLOYER?

146d ▶ 5
Check Language Skills: Verb Agreement

half sheet; 60-space line; SS

Key the sentences at the right (including number) selecting the correct word choice from the words in parentheses. Use the dictionary if necessary.

1. I have (swam, swum) three laps every day this week.
2. I (saw, seen) in the paper that you have (wrote, written) a book.
3. Mike (drank, drunk) two cokes while Amy (eat, ate) her lunch.
4. Jan has (spoke, spoken) of the beauty of the (froze, frozen) lake.
5. Betty has (went, gone) to check on the (broke, broken) window.
6. The data that you submitted (is, are) not accurate.
7. Either Susan or her friend (is, are) here.
8. The number of people requesting information (is, are) small.
9. Neither Doris nor Richard (is, are) willing to accept credit.
10. A number of people (is, are) expected to attend the game.

Lesson 147 — Prepare for Evaluation: Sustained Production

147a ▶ 5
Conditioning Practice

each line twice SS (slowly, then faster); DS between 2-line groups; if time permits, repeat selected lines

alphabet 1 Jackie Quatman will realize her big desire to pole-vault by next fall.

figures 2 Kathrine had swum 26 laps by 12:39 p.m. today and 78 laps by 4:05 p.m.

symbols 3 Is the high-priced suit (the blue one--not the red one) Vi's favorite?

speed 4 The orient is a rich land of enchantment, and a visit is Nancy's goal.

| 1 | 2 | 3 | 4 | 5 | 6 | 7 | 8 | 9 | 10 | 11 | 12 | 13 | 14 |

147b ▶ 35
Build Sustained Document Processing Skill: Letter, Table, Report

Timed Schedule

Plan and prepare .... 3′
Timed production .... 25′
Proofread and correct errors ... 5′
Compute *n-pram* .... 2′

plain paper; correct errors

Problem 1
Letter

block style; open punctuation

Supply current date, salutation, subject line **(office space)**, complimentary close, enclosure notation, and carbon copy notation to Mr. Tom Blake. (Words supplied by student are included in word count.)

words

State Board of Engineers Attention Ms. Tracy Lambert, President P.O. 17
Box 1999 Athens, GA 30603-7731 34
(¶ 1) The State Board of Designers has decided to decline your proposal 48
to share our office space, although the decision was a difficult one. 62
The arrangement would have provided us with several benefits; however, 76
we anticipate that our office activity will continue to increase and 96
we will have a shortage of office space. 98
(¶ 2) The enclosed brochure is for an office locator service. They have 112
a good reputation for assisting organizations such as yours. 124
Lee K. Kirk postscript Please let us know your new address when it is 140
available. 147

Problem 2
Table

Full sheet; make all other decisions.

NATIONAL ASSOCIATION FOR BUSINESS TEACHER EDUCATION 10

Past Presidenst 14

Years Served	Name	State	
			22
1985-87	Thomas B. Duff	Minnesota	29
1983-58	Paul H. Steagall, Jr.	Virginai	37
1979-83	Lloyd W. Bartholeme	Utah	43
1977-79	Harry H. Jasinski	South Dakota	51
1975-77	Mearl R. Guthrie	Ohio	57
1973-75	Z. S. Dickerson, Jr.	Virginia	65
1971-73	Lawrence W. Erickson	Califonria	73
1969-71	T. Jaems Crawford	Indiana	80

139b-143b (continued)

Job 2
Index Cards
(LM p. 115)

Here is a list of names and addresses of guests who made reservations today. Prepare index cards for our information file. See the attached card for format.

r.c.

MERCER, CARY AND CRYSTAL (MR. AND MRS.)

Mr. and Mrs. Cary Mercer
2643 West Quail Avenue
Phoenix, AZ 85027-9977

Home: (602) 499-4577
Office: (602) 466-2016

Children: Bob 7; Karen 5; Previous Guest: No; Week: June 8-15

Dr. Jack R. Gomez 920 Harmon Street Birmingham, MI 48009-4320 Home: (313) 440-8124 Office: (313) 447-9967 Child: John 16 Previous Guest: 7 consecutive years Week: July 13-20

Mr. and Mrs. Gene Munson (Lois) 1486 West Catalpa Drive Baton Rouge, LA 70815-4733 Home: (504) 887-2114 Office: (504) 886-2338 Children: None Previous Guest: 4 times Week: June 22-29

Mr. and Mrs. Roger Guinn (Cindy) 1486 East Cornell Avenue Englewood, CO 80110-6255 Home: (303) 462-8841 Office: (303) 899-6521 Children: Rob 4, Elizabeth 2 Previous Guest: No Week: June 15-22

Ms. Ada Perez 1741 North First Street Fort Smith, AR 72901-7312 Home: (501) 772-4118 Office: (501) 772-6403 Children: Marcus 14, Paula 7 Previous Guest: No Week: July 17-August 3

146b ▶ 20
Build Straight-Copy Skill

1. A 3′ writing on all ¶s combined to establish base rate. Find *gwam*.

2. Add 4-6 words to base rate to establish goal rate. Note quarter-minute checkpoints in ¶ 1.

3. Two 1′ writings on ¶ 1 trying to match or exceed goal rate.

4. Repeat Steps 2 and 3 for ¶s 2, 3, and 4.

5. A 3′ writing on all ¶s combined. Compare with *gwam* achieved in Step 1.

Quarter-Minute Checkpoints

gwam	1/4′	1/2′	3/4′	1′
24	6	12	18	24
28	7	14	21	28
32	8	16	24	32
36	9	18	27	36
40	10	20	30	40
44	11	22	33	44
48	12	24	36	48
52	13	26	39	52
56	14	28	42	56
60	15	30	45	60
64	16	32	48	64
68	17	34	51	68
72	18	36	54	72
76	19	38	57	76
80	20	40	60	80

all letters used | A | 1.5 si | 5.7 awl | 80% hfw |

gwam 3′

Quite often the major stress in landscape and site plans is on only 4
the natural forces with all too much being assumed as to the needs of 9
people. One must realize that dozens of complex social and psychological 14
factors are known about our human needs. These factors should be given 19
much thought in the designing of houses, of recreation space, and of 24
other use areas in order to provide a more conflict-free setting. 28

Even though much is known about our social needs in general, it is 32
essential for a designer to recognize the wants of the region where 37
a job is to be done. Much data may be gained by using a questionnaire 42
to survey attitudes, facts, and opinions. However, in the end, judgment 47
must be based on these results along with some direct observation, as 51
people do not always express honest answers. 54

There is one other way by which design form can be matched with 58
the needs and desires of the people of an area. With this plan residents 63
build their own environments, parks, playgrounds, and even housing or 68
at least participate in these projects. Because the quality of the concept 73
is limited by the experiences of the people, the role of the designer is 78
to present options and to help analyze them. 81

In addition to social wants, we realize that we have psychological 85
needs that differ from time to time. We have some needs some of the 90
time and other needs at other times; so we must beware of the danger of 95
quickly developing an exact design form just to satisfy or fulfill tempo- 100
rary wants. The design process should identify some of the fundamental 104
demands to be satisfied and should make sure that the design does so. 109

gwam 3′ | 1 | 2 | 3 | 4 | 5 |

146c ▶ 20
Build Document Processing Skill: Report

plain paper; proofread and circle errors

1. Process the copy at the right as a leftbound report. Insert headings listed below.

Main heading: HUMAN NEEDS IN DESIGN

Side heading: (above ¶ 2): Social Needs

Paragraph heading (¶ 2): Determining by questionnaire.

Paragraph heading (¶ 3): Determining by resident participation.

Side heading (above ¶ 4): Psychological Needs

139b-143b (continued)

Job 3
Form Letters
(LM pp. 117-124)

Please prepare letters and envelopes for Mr. Paul R. Skidmore, Lodge Director, to be sent to the families for whom you just prepared index cards. Use today's date (June 1, 19--) for each letter.

Use the form paragraphs listed beside each name. In some cases, you will need to select the appropriate phrase from those suggested in parentheses.

GOMEZ -- 2, 3, 7, 9
MUNSON--3, 5, 9
GUINN--1, 3, 4, 5, 6, 8
PEREZ--1, 4, 5, 6, 7, 8

Use personal titles and last names in the salutation except for the Munsons. Use their first names, i.e., Dear Gene and Lois.

List appropriate items in an enclosure notation if enclosures are to accompany the letter. For example:

Enclosures: 2 Brochures
Sample Menu

The longer letters may need to be processed as two-page letters. Use plain full sheets for second page of letter. Thanks.

r.c.

(¶1) Your vacation at Wolf Creek Lodge will be one that you *(and your family) (and your son) (and your daughter)* will recall as one of the most enjoyable vacations you have ever taken. How can I make this statement with such confidence? It is because people like you have been sharing their vacations with us for the past 30 years, and they tell us repeatedly that their memories of Wolf Creek Lodge liner long after they have returned home. In fact, they tell us that their enjoyable memories of Wolf Creek are frequently the subject of "Remember the time when . . . " stories.

(¶2) WELCOME BACK TO WOLF CREEK LODGE!

(¶3) Looking forward to a vacation and planning that vacation is almost as much fun as the vacation itself. So let us help you with the planning by describing what your fun-filled vacation will be like this summer at Wolf Creek Lodge. We've retained the most popular "old" events--our "get-acquainted" party soon after you arrive, the guest talent show, and the "Back to Nature" lectures and field trips, and much more. In addition, we've expanded our offerings to include an overnight camp-out in the mountains, a fabulous dinner show, and an old-fashioned barbecue with entertainment by a western band.

(¶4) The two enclosed brochures describe in detail the wide variety of services and activities at the lodge and in the surrounding community. Whether you are looking for fun and action or peace and tranquillity, you will find it at Wolf Creek. The lodge is surrounded by acres of woods which are accessible by foot or bicycle; and, on the north side of our lake, you will find the secllusion you are longing for.

(¶5) Naturally, an important part of every successful vacation is good, nutritional food offered at affordable prices. We have enclosed a sample menu (for the Garden Restaurant), which will give you an idea of the tasty, nutritional meals we offer at the lodge. You will notice, also, that we have not forgotten appetizers in planning the menu! Meal tickets for any of our three restaurants may be purchased at a 10 epercent discount if purchased at least one week in advance. Also, tickets for our dinner show may be purchased at a discount when you register (see enclosed announcement for details of discount and description of the show). Although we welcome you to dine at any of our restaurants, every unit is equipped with a complete kitchenette if you prefer the casual meal at home.

(¶6) As a parent of *(a young child) (young children)*, you may be interested in our child-care services. Form 1 to 5 p.m. each afternoon, the lodge provides for "parents' time out." Our playgound is equipped to entertain children from 1 to 12 years of age, and our experienced staff is committed to seeing that children enjoy their vacation too. In adddition, we maintain a staff of qualified individuals who thoroughly enjoy entertaining children. Each person on staff was carefully screened because we realize how important quality child care is to parents.

(continued on page 247)

145d ▶ 25
Build Document Processing Skill: Tables

Review table formatting guides on pages 177-178, if necessary.

plain paper; proofread and circle errors; center by longest item, whether column entry or column heading.

Drill 1: Center columns; leave 6 spaces between columns.

Drill 2: Center columns; leave 8 spaces between columns.

Drill 1

Movie	Stars	Name of Director
Airplane II The Sequel	Robert Hays, Julie Hagerty	Ken Finklemen

Drill 2

Year	Prize Winner	Country
1982	Kenneth G. Wilson	U.S.

Drill 3: Center on half sheet, long edge at top; decide intercolumn spacing; SS body.

Drill 4: Center on full sheet; 8 spaces between columns; DS body.

Drill 5: Center on half sheet, short edge at top; 4 spaces between columns; DS body.

Drills 3, 4, 5

REGIONAL SALES DS
(In millions) DS

Region	Sales This Year	Sales Last Year SS DS
Southwestern	$ 1.6	$ 1.4
Southeastern	1.8	1.8
Northwestern	2.1	2.0
Northeastern	.6	.5
Central	3.0	2.8 DS
Total	$ 9.1	$ 8.5

Lesson 146 Prepare for Evaluation: Reports

146a ▶ 5
Conditioning Practice

each line twice SS (slowly, then faster); DS between 2-line groups; if time permits, repeat selected lines

alphabet 1 Exemplary jobs quite often have been done by a caring, zealous worker.

figures 2 In 1987, Al took 20 courses and made the grade point average of 3.645.

symbols 3 "Joel!" she exclaimed, "where is your brother's new three-piece suit?"

speed 4 Their problem is to make the girls sign the forms or pay for the work.

| 1 | 2 | 3 | 4 | 5 | 6 | 7 | 8 | 9 | 10 | 11 | 12 | 13 | 14 |

(¶7) Last, we haven't forgotten that teenagers require their "special" brand of entertainment. That is why we have hired Betsy Barnes, a full-time youth director, who is responsible for keeping teenagers happy. From row boating to horseback riding to backpacking hikes, Betsy has planned a wide variety of activities. And, judging from the volume of fan mail that Betsy has received this past year, I would say that she has made quite a hit with teenagers. Another benefit from the teenage program is the lasting friendships that continue long after the vacation at Wolf Creek is over.

(¶8) We hope these details are helpful to you as you continue to plan your vacation. If we can answer questions or be or of assistance in any way, do let us know. You can reach us at 1-800-227-8800.

(¶9) We are eager to have you *(and your children) (and your son--use name) (and your daughter--use name)* as our guest(s). Do let us know if we can be of assistance in any way.

Job 4
Dinner Show Announcement
(plain sheet)

> Please prepare this announcement to photocopy for enclosure in the letters you have just completed. Align items in second column at the left. Thanks.
> r.c.

THE RIVERSIDE ROOM
Dinner Show

For the Week of
June 15 - 21
(SS)

Dinner Music . . . . Lou Springer
Master of Ceremonies . . . . Eric Sampson
Hula Dancing . . . . The Polynesian Dancers
Fort Lewis College
Durango, CO

Music and Humor . . . . The Gold Rushers
Comedian . . . . Steven Baird
Dance Band . . . . The Gold Rushers

(QS)

Adults: $18*
Children under 12: $10*

Dinner: 6:30 - 8 p.m.
Show Time: 8 - 10 p.m.
Dancing: 10:30-midnight

*Price includes Hawaiian Buffet and show, including tax. Gratuities are not included. (SS)

145b ▶ 5
Check Language Skills: Homonyms

half sheet; 60-space line; SS

Key the sentences at the right (including number) selecting the correct word choice from the words in parentheses. Use the dictionary if necessary.

1. Susan gave Nancy a box of (stationary, stationery) for Christmas.
2. (Their, There) are several good reasons for the delay.
3. The (due, dew) made the grass quite wet.
4. I love you, (deer, dear), for your kindness during my illness.
5. Some people seem to have lost (sight, site) of the value of time.
6. Did you (lose, loose) $5 or $10 yesterday?
7. The (principle, principal) reason for the loss is obvious.
8. Jim ran much (further, farther) than Paul in the race.
9. Do you know (weather, whether) Jane will be here soon?
10. I would like to go, (two, to, too), if you don't mind.
11. How did you (advice, advise) the students about going to college?
12. The wind (blew, blue) fiercely last evening.

145c ▶ 15
Improve Skill on Statistical Copy

1. Take a 3′ writing on all 3 ¶s to establish a base rate. Find *gwam*.

2. Take two 1′ writings on each ¶ trying to improve rate with each timing.

3. Take another 3′ writing on all 3 ¶s and compare *gwam* with the first 3′ writing.

all letters used | A | 1.5 si | 5.7 awl | 80% hfw |

	gwam 1′	3′
The Grand Canyon National Park, which is located in Arizona, was	13	4
established as a national park on February 26, 1919. However, additional	28	9
land was absorbed by the park as late as 1975, making a total acreage	42	14
of just over 1.2 million. This unique exposure of rock is 217 miles long	57	19
and from 4 to 18 miles wide. During recent years, it has been seen by	71	24
about 2,840,000 people each year.	78	26
Another beautiful national park is the Great Smoky Mountains Na-	13	30
tional Park. It has an acreage of about 273,550 in North Carolina and	27	35
about 241,206 in Tennessee, for a total of over 500,000. It was ap-	41	39
proved on May 22, 1926, and established for full development in 1934.	55	44
The diverse plant life is quite beautiful and is seen by over 11 million	69	49
persons each year.	73	50
Fascinating in even a different way and older and larger than any	13	55
of the other national parks, Yellowstone was established in 1872. Its	27	59
more than 2,219,000 acres cover parts of three states. It has over	41	64
10,000 geysers, dozens of majestic falls, canyons, and quiet wildlife	55	69
areas. People from all over the world come to it in numbers that exceed	70	73
2,487,000 each year.	74	75

gwam 1′	1	2	3	4	5	6	7	8	9	10	11	12	13	14
3′	1			2			3			4			5	

139b-143b (continued)

Job 5
Menu
(plain sheet)

> Here is a rough draft of the menu we need for 6/17. I've marked changes and errors, but you may find additional errors that I've overlooked. Please prepare a final copy to photocopy and enclose with letters I will be sending to guests.
> r.c.

GARDEN RESTURANT

June 17, 19--
6 - 10 p.m.

DS

THE BEGINNING

To tanelize your taste buds - a petite assortment of canpes, cheeses, and reslishes

Plus your choice of:
Spinach and Bacon Salad
Fresh Fruit Salad
*Gazpacho

ENTREES

*Chicken Orental - served in a sauce of mushroms and a special blend of herbs and spices, over a bed of white rice, with stir-fried vegetables.

*Beef Pot Roast (au juis) - served with twice-baked potato and asparagus tips in cheese sauce.

*Golden Glazed Ham - served with orange slices and garnish, fresh green beans, and parsley new potatoes.

THE FINALE

*Fresh Blueberries With Whipped Cream
Cheese Cake with or without Cherry Topping
German Chocolate Cake

Beverages — All CAP
Coffee (Regular or Expresso)
Tee (Iced or Hot)
Milk

Bread and Butter — ALL CAP
Bread Basket of asorted fresh baked rolls and breads

CHILDREN'S Menu (Under 12)

Western Burger - a juicy, old-fashioned hamburger served with country fries, choice of dessert and beverage

Fried Chicken - a drum tick and wing browed to perfection, mashed potatoes, gravy, green beans, and beverage

*House specialties

144c ▶ 25 Build Document Processing Skill: Letters

plain full sheets; 1cc; correct errors

Take a 20′ timing on the problems below. Determine number of problems completed and number of uncorrected errors.

Problem 1
block format; open punctuation

Problem 2
modified block format; indented ¶s; mixed punctuation

Letter address:
Ms. Dana Forman
Vice President of Finance
E & M Production, Inc.
6501 West Sunset Boulevard
Los Angeles, CA 90028-7711

Subject line:
Overdue Account with Station Video, Inc.

Amount: $1,864.25
(total words: 199)

Problem 3
block format; open punctuation

Repeat Problem 1 substituting the information below.

Letter address:
Mr. Berl M. Rebenar, President
Otto Home Improvements
2109 East Russell Street
Covington, KY 41014-8882

Subject line:
Overdue Account with Cam Outdoor Lighting

Amount: $895.00
(total words: 200)

words

Current date | CERTIFIED MAIL | Mr. Frederick Mayo, President | 12
Reinier Scientific Enterprises | 45 South Penn Street | 22
Allentown, PA 18105-2295 | Dear Mr. Mayo | Subject: 32
Overdue Account with Franklin Chemical Company | 42
(¶1) This letter represents our final attempt to collect 52
your overdue account with Franklin Chemical Company. 63
Unless your remittance is received within five days 73
from receipt of this letter, we shall have no alternative 85
but to place your account with an attorney for collection. 97
(¶2) The files of the Credit Bureau are available to banks 108
and other financial institutions throughout the United 119
States. To keep your record with the Bureau as favorable 130
as possible, please send a check for $2,856.44 in full 141
payment of your account. You will find an itemized 152
statement enclosed. | Sincerely yours | ELLIS CREDIT BUREAU | 163
Ms. Maria Duvall | Manager of Collections | xx | Enclosure | 173
cc Franklin Chemical Company | If you have sent your 184
check, please verify with us that we have received 194
it in order to protect your credit. 201

Lesson 145 Prepare for Evaluation: Tables

145a ▶ 5 Conditioning Practice

each line twice SS (slowly, then faster); DS between 2-line groups; if time permits, repeat selected lines

alphabet 1 Your math quiz was given on Monday to all future juniors except Becky.
figures 2 Flight 374 will be arriving at either Gate 28 or Gate 29 at 10:56 p.m.
fig/sym 3 B & C's has 20# paper for $3.58 and 16# paper for $2.74 (a 9% saving).
speed 4 When the eight towns amend the six bills, then their problems may end.

| 1 | 2 | 3 | 4 | 5 | 6 | 7 | 8 | 9 | 10 | 11 | 12 | 13 | 14 |

139b-143b (continued)

Job 6
Table
(full sheet)

> Please prepare this list to send to Betsy Barnes, Director of Youth Activities. Alphabetize the list by surnames and check for errors I may have overlooked.
> r.c.

LIST OF TEENAGERS

June 15-~~22~~ 21

Name	Hometown	Age
Karla Zorba	Albuquerque, NM	16
Jeffrey Grimsley	Kansas City, KS	13
Neal Butler	Omaha, NE	17
Janet Brewer	Tulse, OK	14
Brian Manzer	Denver, CO	~~17~~ 18
Tien Su	~~Moab, UT~~ Houstan, TX	19
Chri~~s~~t Porter	Tompeka, KS	17
Nicole Jordan	Minneaspolis, ~~MP~~ MN	15
Don ~~Reeder~~ Rentear	Peublo, CO	16
Teresa Weaver	Santa Fe, NM	14
Victor Lopez	Austin, TX	15
~~Lynn~~ Ann Hoyer	~~Pullman, WV~~ Seatle, WA	~~23~~ 13

Job 7
Simplified Memo
(LM p. 125)

> Please prepare this memo to Betsy Barnes, Director of Youth Activities, to accompany the list of teenagers you just prepared. Let me sign the memo when you have finished. Use today's date: June 2.
> r.c.

LIST OF TEENAGERS FOR WEEK OF JUNE 15-21

¶ At the suggestion of Paul Skidmore, I have prepared a list of the presently registered teenagers who will be here during the week of June 15-21. We thought that it might be helpful for you to have this information in advance, along with ages and hometowns, so that you can plan activities for the week.

¶ As soon as you have finalized your list of activities, could you please send me a copy.

Attachment

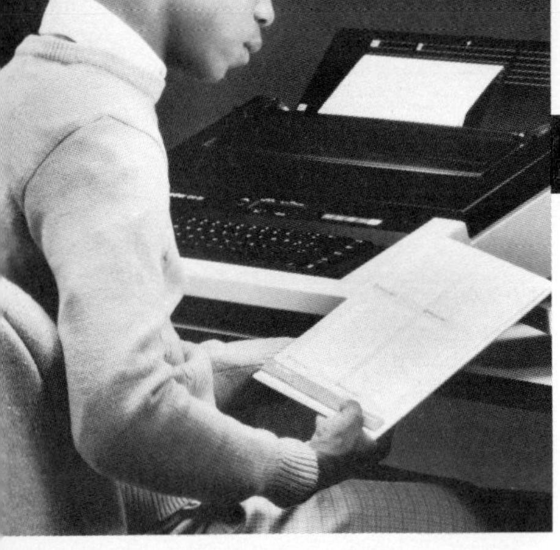

Unit 30 Lessons 144-147

Learning Goals

1. To improve straight-copy skill.
2. To review and improve skill on letters, tables, and reports.
3. To improve language skills.

Machine Adjustments

1. Paper guide at *0*.
2. Paper bail rolls at even intervals across page.
3. Margins: 70-space line for drill lines and timed paragraphs; as needed or directed for other problems.
4. Spacing: SS for drill lines and letters. DS for timed paragraphs and reports.

Lesson 144 Prepare for Evaluation: Letters

144a ▶ 5 Conditioning Practice

each line twice SS (slowly, then faster); DS between 2-line groups; if time permits, repeat selected lines

alphabet 1 Jack quickly opened the exits when the fire alarm gave a warning buzz.

figures 2 The population was 6,453 in 1987, which was an increase of 20 percent.

fig/sym 3 If we pay by May 7, we can save $659.48 with their terms (2/10, n/30).

speed 4 Their amendment will aid the panel of men and the auditor of the firm.

| 1 | 2 | 3 | 4 | 5 | 6 | 7 | 8 | 9 | 10 | 11 | 12 | 13 | 14 |

144b ▶ 20 Build Speed: Letters

plain paper; modified block format; blocked ¶s; open punctuation

1. A 5′ writing on the letter to establish a base rate. If you finish before time is called, start over.
2. Find *gwam*. Use this rate as your goal rate. Turn to page 242 to find quarter-minute checkpoints if necessary; note these figures in opening lines through ¶ 1.
3. Take three 1′ guided writings on the opening lines through ¶ 1. Leave proper spacing between letter parts.
4. Repeat Steps 2 and 3, but begin with ¶ 3 and continue through closing lines.
5. Take another 5′ writing on the letter. Try to maintain your new goal rate.

gwam 5′

May 28, 19-- SPECIAL DELIVERY Department of Office Administration 3 | 36

Attention Dr. Milton Baker Ohio Valley College 800 Noel Drive Spring- 5 | 38

field, OH 45506-3312 Ladies and Gentlemen Subject: Summer Conference 8 | 41

(¶ 1) Participating in your summer conference last week was an educational 11 | 44

and enjoyable experience for me. The program was well-planned, and your 14 | 47

faculty extended a special welcome to me. 16 | 49

(¶ 2) As you requested, I am sending brochures related to our records 18 | 51

management software. These are being sent by special delivery in hopes 21 | 54

that you will have time to consider them for your summer session. 24 | 57

(¶ 3) I look forward to working with you again as you plan future pro- 26 | 59

fessional programs. Sincerely B & C OFFICE TECHNOLOGY Mrs. Jan S. 29 | 62

Holton Vice President xx Enclosures pc Dr. Ray Camp, Dean Postscript 31 | 64

Receipts for my expenses are also enclosed. 33 | 66

139b-143b (continued)

Job 8
Unbound Report
(full sheets)

I have edited this information to be given to guests when they register at the lodge. Would you please check to make sure I have not overlooked any errors; then, process this material in unbound report format.
r.c.

center — WOLF CREEK LODGE ACTIVITIES

help plan OS
To ~~aid~~ you ~~with~~ your vacation so that you can have a fun-filled week let me reveiw the many options available to you. If we fail to mention something you had in mind, please tell us so that we can assist in making this your most memorable vacation ever.

Weekly Scheduled Activiites

You will want to decide soon which of thes(e) activiites you wish to participate in, since some fo them require reservations.

Get-acquainted burnch. You should not miss this opportunity ~~the chance~~ to get to know our toher guests before you begin ~~start~~ the weeek. On sunday from 11 a.m. to 2 p.m., you may attend a free bu(f)fet brunch. This buffet will introduce you to the excellant cuisine you can expect to enjoy for the week and will give you the opportunity to meet other guests and sign up for several exciting events occuring du(r)ing the week.

Dinner show. A flyer announcing the dinner show for the week is in your# room. This is an event you won't want to miss!

Overnight camp-out. For those who enjoy sleeping under the stars, we hav(e) a camp-out in the mountains on wednesday evnings--again, weather permitting. We will cook our "catch"; but just in case the big one gets away, we will take along adequate provisions. Fishing lisense will be provided by the lodge. Call the main desk (ext. 613) if you wish to register.

Outdoor barbeque (c). Each tuesday evening at 6 p.m. (weather permitting), we have an old-fashioned barbecue in the pavilion by the lake. A western band accompanies the festivities; and after ap(p)etites have been satiated, we clear the deck for dancing until 11:30 p.m. The cost is $18 for adults and $7 for children under 12; we need reservations by noon on Monday.

Guest talent show. Our guests started this function five years ago, and we have contined to do it by popular demand. The show usually consists of various musical songs with dance roudtines; however, short skits or a play is sometimes opted for by our guests. The "stars" perform on Saturday eveings.

Daily Activities

For those who like to throw away the watch during vacation time, most of the activities can be elected without notice.

"Nature activities." Field trips, nature walks, lectures, films, and other "nature activities" are scheduled several times a week. Watch the bulletin board in the lobby for specific information. In addition, we have designed nature trails that are accessible by foot or bicyle. You will find maps for our various trails in the loby; or if you are adventurous, take an uncharted hike thorugh the woods.

Beaches. the beach on the north side of the lake has been the quiet area. It is reserved for those who like to read write paint, or just day dream in tranquility while enjoying the sun. If you like action, the south beach is for you. Three volleyball nets are in place, and you can check out volleyballs from the Health Club and spa. Paddle boats and row boats are available for a nominal fee. Radios or tother distractions are not permitted onthe north side of the lade.

Pools. The out door pool is for general use during the summer monts, while the indoor pool is reserved for planned activities such as swiming lessons and water exercise sports. Let us know if you or family memembers are interested in swimming lessons so that we can make the necessary arrangements.

Health club and spa. Visit this area early in the week to see the many activities offered at the club and spa; they are too numerous to describe here. We have to mention, though, the installation of whirlpool baths and a new exercise room (with the latest body-building equipment).

If all of this is not enough, just tell us what is missing and we will do our best to provide it.

CAPITALIZATION GUIDES

Capitalize

1 The first word of every sentence and the first word of every complete direct quotation. Do not capitalize (a) fragments of quotations or (b) a quotation resumed within a sentence.

She said, "Hard work is necessary for success."
He stressed the importance of "a sense of values."
"When all else fails," he said, "follow directions."

2 The first word after a colon if that word begins a complete sentence.

Remember this: Work with good techniques.
We carry these sizes: small, medium, and large.

3 First, last, and all other words in titles of books, articles, periodicals, headings, and plays, except words of four letters or less used as articles, conjunctions, or prepositions.

Century 21 Keyboarding "How to Buy a House"
Saturday Review "The Sound of Music"

4 An official title when it precedes a name or when used elsewhere if it is a title of distinction.

President Lincoln She is the Prime Minister.
The doctor is in. He is the treasurer.

5 All proper nouns and their derivatives.

Canada Canadian Festival France French food

6 Days of the week, months of the year, holidays, periods of history, and historic events.

Sunday Labor Day New Year's Day
June Middle Ages Civil War

7 Seasons of the year only when they are personified.

icy fingers of Winter the soft kiss of Spring

8 Geographic regions, localities, and names.

the North Upstate New York Mississippi River

9 Street, avenue, company, etc., when used with a proper noun.

Fifth Avenue Avenue of the Stars Armour & Co.

10 Names of organizations, clubs, and buildings.

Girl Scouts Commercial Club Trade Center

11 A noun preceding a figure except for common nouns such as *line*, *page*, and *sentence*, which may be keyed with or without a capital.

Style 143 Catalog 6 page 247 line 10

NUMBER EXPRESSION GUIDES

Use words for

1 Numbers from one to ten except when used with numbers above ten, which are typed as figures. Note: It is common business practice to use figures for all numbers except those which begin a sentence.

Was the order for four or eight books?
Order 8 shorthand books and 15 English books.

2 A number beginning a sentence.

Fifteen persons are here; 12 are at home sick.

3 The shorter of two numbers used together.

ten 50-gallon drums 350 five-gallon drums

4 Isolated fractions or indefinite amounts in a sentence.

Nearly two thirds of the students are here.
About twenty-five people came to the meeting.

5 Names of small-numbered streets and avenues (ten and under).

1020 Sixth Street Tenth Avenue

Use figures for

1 Dates and time, except in very formal writing.

May 9, 1982 10:15 a.m.
Ninth of May four o'clock

2 A series of fractions.

Key 1/2, 1/4, 5/6, and 7 3/4.

3 Numbers preceded by nouns.

Rule 12 page 179 Room 1208 Chapter 15

4 Measures, weights, and dimensions.

6 ft. 9 in. tall 5 lbs. 4 oz. 8 1/2″ × 11″

5 Definite numbers used with the percent sign (%); but use *percent* (spelled) with approximations in formal writing.

The rate is 15 1/2%.
About 50 percent of the work is done.

6 House numbers except house number One.

1915-42d Street One Jefferson Avenue

7 Sums of money except when spelled for extra emphasis. Even sums may be keyed without the decimal.

$10.75 25 cents $300
seven hundred dollars ($700)

BASIC GRAMMAR GUIDES

■ Use a singular verb

1 With a singular subject.

The weather is clear but cold.

2 With an indefinite pronoun used as a subject (each, every, any, either, neither, one, etc.).

Each one is to bring a pen and paper.
Neither of us is likely to be picked.

3 With singular subjects linked by *or* or *nor*. If, however, one subject is singular and the other is plural, the verb should agree with the closer subject.

Either Jan or Fred is to make the presentation.
Neither the principal nor the teachers are here.

4 With a collective noun (*committee*, *team*, *class*, *jury*, etc.) if the collective noun acts as a unit.

The jury has returned to the courtroom.
The committee has filed its report.

5 With the pronouns *all* and *some* (as well as fractions and percentages) when used as subjects *if* their modifiers are singular. Use a plural verb *if* their modifiers are plural.

All of the books have been classified.
Some of the gas is being pumped into the tank.

6 When *number* is used as the subject and is preceded by *the*; however, use a plural verb if *number* is preceded by *a*.

The number of voters has increased this year.
A number of workers are on vacation.

■ Use a plural verb

1 With a plural subject.

The blossoms are losing their petals.

2 With a compound subject joined by *and*.

My mother and my father are the same age.

■ Negative forms of verbs

1 Use the plural verb *do not* (or the contraction *don't*) when the pronoun *I*, *we*, *you*, or *they*, as well as a plural noun, is used as the subject.

We don't have a leg to stand on in this case.
The scissors do not cut properly.
I don't believe that answer is correct.

2 Use the singular verb *does not* (or the contraction *doesn't*) when the pronoun *he*, *she*, or *it*, as well as a singular noun, is used as the subject.

She doesn't want to attend the meeting.
It does not seem possible that winter's here.

■ Pronoun agreement with antecedents

1 Pronouns (*I*, *we*, *you*, *he*, *she*, *it*, *their*, etc.) agree with their antecedent *in person* -- person speaking, first person; person spoken to, second person; person spoken about, third person.

We said we would go when we complete our work.
When you enter, present your invitation.
All who saw the show found that they were moved.

2 Pronouns agree with their antecedents *in gender* (feminine, masculine, and neuter).

Each of the women has her favorite hobby.
Adam will wear his favorite sweater.
The tree lost its leaves early this fall.

3 Pronouns agree with their antecedents *in number* (singular or plural).

A verb must agree with its subject.
Pronouns must agree with their antecedents.
Brian is to give his recital at 2 p.m.
Joan and Carla have lost their homework.

4 When a pronoun's antecedent is a collective noun, the pronoun may be either singular or plural depending on whether the noun acts individually or as a unit.

The committee met to cast their ballots.
The class planned its graduation program.

■ Commonly confused pronoun sound-alikes

it's (contraction): it is; it has
its (possessive adjective): possessive form of *it*

It's good to see you; it's been a long time.
The puppy wagged its tail in welcome.

their (pronoun): possessive form of *they*
there (adverb/pronoun): at or in that place/used to introduce a clause
they're (contraction): they are

The hikers all wore their parkas.
There are several reasons for that result.
They're likely to be late because of the snow.

who's (contraction): who is; who has
whose (pronoun): possessive form of *who*

Who's been to the movie? Who's going now?
I chose the one whose skills are best.

PUNCTUATION GUIDES

■ Use an apostrophe

1 As a symbol for *feet* in billings or tabulations or as a symbol for *minutes*. (The quotation mark may be used as a symbol for *seconds* and *inches*.)

12′ × 16′ 3′ 54″ 8′6″ × 10′8″

2 As a symbol to indicate the omission of letters or figures (as in contractions or figures).

can't wouldn't Spirit of '76

3 Add *s* to form the plural of most figures, letters, and words. In market quotations, form the plural of figures by the addition of *s* only.

6's A's five's ABC's Century Fund 4s

4 To show possession: Add the *apostrophe and s* to (a) a singular noun and (b) a plural noun which does not end in *s*.

a man's watch women's shoes boy's bicycle

Add the *apostrophe and s* to a proper name of one syllable which ends in *s*.

Bess's Cafeteria Jones's bill

Add the *apostrophe only* after (a) plural nouns ending in *s* and (b) a proper name of more than one syllable which ends in *s* or *z*.

boys' camp Adams' home Melendez' report

Add the *apostrophe* after the last noun in a series to indicate joint or common possession of two or more persons; however, add the possessive to each of the nouns to show separate possession of two or more persons.

Lewis and Clark's expedition
the manager's and the treasurer's reports

■ Use a colon

1 To introduce an enumeration or a listing.

These are my favorite poets: Shelley, Keats, and Frost.

2 To introduce a question or a long direct quotation.

This is the question: Did you study for the test?

3 Between hours and minutes expressed in figures.

10:15 a.m. 4:30 p.m.

■ Use a comma (or commas)

1 After (a) introductory words, phrases, or clauses and (b) words in a series.

If you can, try to visit Chicago, St. Louis, and Dallas.

2 To set off short direct quotations.

She said, "If you try, you can reach your goal."

3 Before and after (a) words which come together and refer to the same person, thing, or idea and (b) words of direct address.

Clarissa, our class president, will give the report.
It was good to see you, Terrence, at the meeting.

4 To set off nonrestrictive clauses (not necessary to the meaning of the sentence), but not restrictive clauses (necessary to the meaning).

Your report, which deals with the issue, is great.
The girl who just left is my sister.

5 To separate the day from the year and the city from the state.

July 4, 1986 New Haven, Connecticut

6 To separate two or more parallel adjectives (adjectives that could be separated by the word "and" instead of the comma).

a group of young, old, and middle-aged persons

Do not use commas to separate adjectives so closely related that they appear to form a single element with the noun they modify.

a dozen large red roses a small square box

7 To separate (a) unrelated groups of figures which come together and (b) whole numbers into groups of three digits each (however, *policy*, *year*, *page*, *room*, *telephone*, and most *serial numbers* are shown without commas).

During 1986, 1,750 cars were insured under Policy 806423.
page 1042 Room 1184 (213) 825-2626

■ Use a dash

1 For emphasis.

The icy road -- slippery as a fish -- was a hazard.

2 To indicate a change of thought.

We may tour the Orient -- but I'm getting ahead of my story.

3 To introduce the name of an author when it follows a direct quotation.

"Hitting the wrong key is like hitting me." -- Armour

4 For certain special purposes.

"Well -- er -- ah," he stammered.
"Jay, don't get too close to the --." It was too late.

PUNCTUATION GUIDES, continued

Use an exclamation mark

1 After emphatic interjections.

Wow! Hey there! What a day!

2 After sentences that are clearly exclamatory.

"I won't go!" she said with determination.
How good it was to see you in New Orleans last week!

Use a hyphen

1 To join compound numbers from twenty-one to ninety-nine that are keyed as words.

forty-six fifty-eight over seventy-six

2 To join compound adjectives before a noun which they modify as a unit.

well-laid plans five-year period two-thirds majority

3 After each word or figure in a series of words or figures that modify the same noun (suspended hyphenation).

first-, second-, and third-class reservations

4 To spell out a word or name.

s-e-p-a-r-a-t-e G-a-e-l-i-c

5 To form certain compound nouns.

WLW-TV teacher-counselor AFL-CIO

Use parentheses

1 To enclose parenthetical or explanatory matter and added information.

The amendments (Exhibit A) are enclosed.

2 To enclose identifying letters or figures in lists.

Check these factors: (1) period of time, (2) rate of pay, and (3) nature of duties.

3 To enclose figures that follow spelled-out amounts to give added clarity or emphasis.

The total contract was for six hundred dollars ($600).

Use a question mark

At the end of a sentence that is a direct question; however, use a period after a request in the form of a question.

What day do you plan to leave for Honolulu?
Will you mail this letter for me, please.

Use quotation marks

1 To enclose direct quotations.

He said, "I'll be there at eight o'clock."

2 To enclose titles of articles and other parts of complete publications, short poems, song titles, television programs, and unpublished works like theses and dissertations.

"Sesame Street" "The Next Twenty Years"
"Out Where the West Begins" "Living"

3 To enclose special words or phrases, or coined words.

"limited resources" "Murphy's Law"

Use a semicolon

1 To separate two or more independent clauses in a compound sentence when the conjunction is omitted.

To err is human; to forgive, divine.
It is easy to be critical; it is not so easy to be constructive.

2 To separate independent clauses when they are joined by a conjunctive adverb (*however*, *consequently*, etc.).

I can go; however, I must get excused.

3 To separate a series of phrases or clauses (especially if they contain commas) that are introduced by a colon.

These officers were elected: Lu Ming, President; Lisa Stein, vice president; Juan Ramos, secretary.

4 To precede an abbreviation or word that introduces an explanatory statement.

She organized her work; for example, putting work to be done in folders of different colors to indicate degrees of urgency.

Use an underline

1 With titles of complete works such as books, magazines, and newspapers. (Such titles may also be typed in ALL CAPS without the underline.)

<u>Century 21 Shorthand</u> <u>New York Times</u> <u>TV Guide</u>

2 To call attention to special words or phrases (or you may use quotation marks). **Note:** Use a continuous underline unless each word is to be considered separately.

Stop keying <u>when time is called</u>.
Spell these words: <u>steel</u>, <u>occur</u>, <u>separate</u>.

WORD-DIVISION/LETTER-PLACEMENT/ZIP CODE ABBR.

Word-division guides

1 Divide words between syllables only; therefore, do not divide one-syllable words. **Note:** When in doubt, consult a dictionary or a word division manual.

through-out pref-er-ence em-ploy-ees
reached toward thought

2 Do not divide words of five or fewer letters even if they have two or more syllables.

into also about union radio ideas

3 Do not separate a one-letter syllable at the beginning of a word or a one- or two-letter syllable at the end of a word.

across enough steady highly ended

4 You may usually divide a word between double consonants; but, when adding a syllable to a word that ends in double letters, divide after the double letters of the root word.

writ-ten sum-mer expres-sion excel-lence
will-ing win-ner process-ing fulfill-ment

5 When the final consonant is doubled in adding a suffix, divide between the double letters.

run-ning begin-ning fit-ting submit-ted

6 Divide after a one-letter syllable within a word; but when two single-letter syllables occur together, divide between them.

sepa-rate regu-late gradu-ation evalu-ation

7 When the single-letter syllable *a*, *i*, or *u* is followed by the ending *ly*, *ble*, *bly*, *cle*, or *cal*, divide before the single-letter syllable.

stead-ily siz-able vis-ible mir-acle
cler-ical but musi-cal practi-cal

8 Divide only between the two words that make up a hyphenated word.

self-contained well-developed

9 Do not divide a contraction or a single group of figures; try to avoid dividing proper names and dates.

doesn't $350,000 Policy F238975

Letter-placement points

Paper-guide placement

Check the placement of the paper guide for accurate horizontal centering of the letter.

Margins and date placement

Use the following guide:

5-Stroke Words in Letter Body	Side Margins	Dateline
Up to 100	2″	19
101-200	1½″	16*
Over 200	1″	13

*Dateline is moved up 2 line spaces for each additional 25 words.

Horizontal placement of date varies according to the letter style.

Address

The address begins on the fourth line (3 blank line spaces) below the date. A personal title, such as Mr., Mrs., Miss, or Ms., should precede the name of an individual. An official title, when used, may be placed on the first or the second line of the address, whichever gives better balance.

Two-page letters

If a letter is too long for one page, at least 2 lines of the body of the letter should be carried to the second page. The second page of a letter, or any additional pages, requires a proper heading. Either the block or the horizontal form may be used for the heading; each is followed by a double space.

Second-page headings

(begin on line 6)

Block form

```
Mr. J. W. Smith
Page 2
June 5, 19--
```

Horizontal form

```
   Mr. J. W. Smith        2        June 5, 19--
```

Attention line

An attention line, when used, is placed on the second line of the letter address.

Subject line

A subject line is placed on the second line (a double space) below the salutation. It may be either centered or keyed at the left margin.

Company name

Occasionally the company name is shown in the closing lines. When this is done, it is shown in *all capital letters* 2 lines (a double space) below the complimentary close. The modern practice is to omit the company name in the closing lines if a letterhead is used.

Typed/Printed name/official title

The name of the person who dictated the letter and his/her official title are placed 4 lines (3 blank line spaces) below the complimentary close, or 4 lines below the company name when it is used. When both the name and official title are used, they may be placed on the same line or the official title may be placed on the next line below the typed/printed name.

Unusual features

Letters having unusual features, such as tabulated material, long quotations, or an unusual number of lines in the address or the closing lines, may require changes in the settings normally used for letters of that length.

ZIP Code abbreviations

Alabama, AL
Alaska, AK
Arizona, AZ
Arkansas, AR
California, CA
Colorado, CO
Connecticut, CT
Delaware, DE
District of Columbia, DC
Florida, FL
Georgia, GA
Guam, GU
Hawaii, HI
Idaho, ID
Illinois, IL
Indiana, IN
Iowa, IA
Kansas, KS
Kentucky, KY
Louisiana, LA
Maine, ME
Maryland, MD
Massachusetts, MA
Michigan, MI
Minnesota, MN
Mississippi, MS
Missouri, MO
Montana, MT
Nebraska, NE
Nevada, NV
New Hampshire, NH
New Jersey, NJ
New Mexico, NM
New York, NY
North Carolina, NC
North Dakota, ND
Ohio, OH
Oklahoma, OK
Oregon, OR
Pennsylvania, PA
Puerto Rico, PR
Rhode Island, RI
South Carolina, SC
South Dakota, SD
Tennessee, TN
Texas, TX
Utah, UT
Vermont, VT
Virgin Islands, VI
Virginia, VA
Washington, WA
West Virginia, WV
Wisconsin, WI
Wyoming, WY

Modern Office Systems, Inc.
1049 Michigan Avenue, N • Chicago, IL 60611-2846 • (312) 471-2605

November 11, 19-- QS (space down 4 blank line spaces)

Mrs. Dorinda O'Neil, Director
Sooner Office Temporaries, Inc.
One Williams Center
Tulsa, OK 74172-4280 DS

Dear Mrs. O'Neil DS

The block format in which this letter is arranged has grown rapidly in popularity for business and personal letters.

Users of personal computers, word processors, and typewriters prefer block format because no tab stop settings or indenting motions are required. The result is greater efficiency. In addition, block style avoids the errors that occur in other formats when operators forget to indent certain letter parts

Changes are being made in document formats and placement to simplify the use of modern office machines and to make people more productive. The growing use of block format is just one of many such changes. Some of the other changes are described in the enclosed pamphlet. DS

Sincerely yours QS

Jeffrey T. Bellamah, Head
Work Simpification Unit DS

ke DS
Enclosure

1 Block, open

ORCC Office Research & Communication Consultants
30 Lewis Road o Linfield, PA 19468-4353 o (215) 793-8264

January 23, 19-- QS (space down 4 blank line spaces)

Mr. Scott Kirkwood, President
Solar Corporation of America
1160 Avenue of the Americas
New York, New York 10036-2991 DS

Dear Mr. Kirkwood DS

This letter is arranged in the modified block style with blocked paragraphs. The only difference between this letter style and the block style is that the dateline and the closing lines (complimentary close and the typed or printed name of the originator of the letter) are started at the horizontal center point.

Although the block style letter is the most popular letter style used in the business world, the modified block style with blocked paragraphs is a popular second choice. As you can see, a letter arranged in this format presents an attractive appearance.

Mixed punctuation (a colon after the salutation and a comma after the complimentary close) is used in this letter. Since the originator's name is shown in typed format in the closing lines, only the initials of the typist or the word processing operator need be shown in the reference notation. If an enclosure is mentioned in the body of the letter, the word Enclosure, or Enc., is keyed or typed a double space below the reference notation, flush with the left margin. DS

Sincerely yours QS

Mrs. Kaye Banovich
Communications Consultant DS

le

2 Modified block, open

ARISTOCRAT BUSINESS COMMUNICATIONS INCORPORATED
99 DECATUR STREET, NE
WASHINGTON, DC 20002-4155
(202) 684-2734

December 5, 19-- QS

Miss Julia Seidenberg
Word Processing Manager
Modern Office Assistants
4822 Claymore Road
Houston, TX 77024-8336 TS

AMS SIMPLIFIED LETTER FORMAT TS

We are using the simplified letter format recommended by the Administrative Management Society; it is formatted as follows: DS

1. Use block format.
2. Start the address on the fourth line below the date.
3. Omit the salutation and complimentary close.
4. Always use a subject heading, shown in ALL CAPS, a triple space below the address; triple-space below the subject line to start the body of the letter.
5. Begin enumerated items at the left margin; indent unnumbered items five spaces.
6. Show the writer's name and title in ALL CAPS on the fourth line space below the body of the letter.
7. Lowercase reference initials (operator's only) a double space below the writer's name. Double-space between enclosure notations, carbon copy notations, and postscripts (if used) DS

We all like the efficiency of the AMS letter format. QS

MARIO GARCIA, ADMINISTRATIVE SUPPORT SUPERVISOR DS

eb

3 AMS Simplified

April 25, 19-- QS

Tony Mendez, Marketing Manager DS

CONDUCTING POSITIVE PERFORMANCE APPRAISALS DS

It is almost time again for annual performance reviews, a process that you, like many of our other managers, may not anticipate eagerly. So often employees and managers look upon these conferences as a time to discuss all the things employees have done wrong during the past year. With this approach to performance reviews, tension is high; and neither the managers nor the employees feel good at the completion of the reviews. Further, the overall productivity of the company seems to suffer, at least for a few weeks.

Our Executive Board recognizes that improvements need to be made in our performance appraisal procedures, and they have asked me to arrange for two half-day programs on this topic. The programs will involve a small amount of lecture, videotapes illustrating positive and negative performance appraisals, discussion of problems encountered in performance appraisals, and videotaped role playing to be critiqued and discussed.

If you would like to participate in this program, please send me a list of half days when you can attend during the month of May. I have enclosed a form that you may use to indicate if you are interested in the program and, if so, to mark the times and dates you can attend. QS

Terry Austin, Director of Human Resources DS

xx DS
Enclosure

4 Simplified memo

ENVELOPES: ADDRESSING, FOLDING AND INSERTING

Addressing procedure

Envelope address

Set a tab stop (or margin stop if a number of envelopes are to be addressed) 10 spaces left of center for a small envelope or 5 spaces for a large envelope. Start the address here on Line 12 from the top edge of a small envelope and on Line 14 of a large one.

Style

Type the address in *block style*, single-spaced. Type the city name, state name or abbreviation, and ZIP Code on the last address line. The ZIP Code is typed 2 spaces after the state name abbreviation.

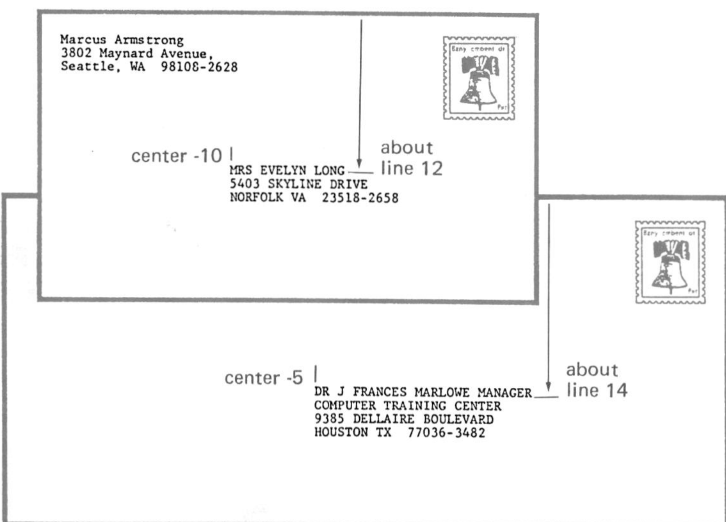

Marcus Armstrong
3802 Maynard Avenue,
Seattle, WA 98108-2628
center -10
MRS EVELYN LONG
5403 SKYLINE DRIVE
NORFOLK VA 23518-2658
about line 12
center -5
DR J FRANCES MARLOWE MANAGER
COMPUTER TRAINING CENTER
9385 DELLAIRE BOULEVARD
HOUSTON TX 77036-3482
about line 14

Addressee notations

Type addressee notations, such as *Hold for Arrival, Please Forward, Personal*, etc., a triple space below the return address and about 3 spaces from the left edge of the envelope. Type these notations in all capitals.

If an *attention line* is used, type it immediately below the company name in the address line.

Mailing notations

Type mailing notations, such as SPECIAL DELIVERY and REGISTERED, below the stamp and at least 3 line spaces above the envelope address. Type these notations in all capital letters.

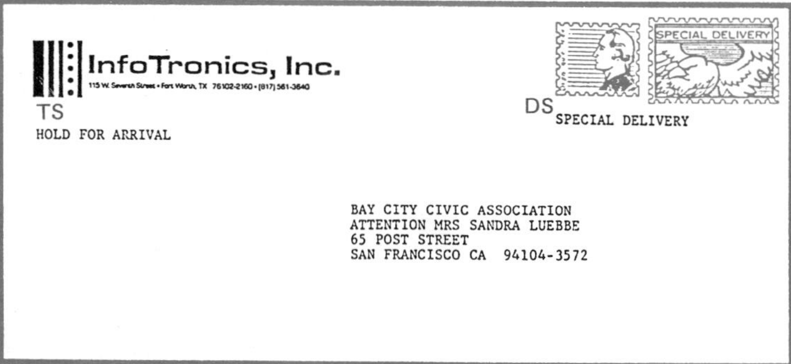

InfoTronics, Inc.
TS
HOLD FOR ARRIVAL
SPECIAL DELIVERY
DS
SPECIAL DELIVERY
BAY CITY CIVIC ASSOCIATION
ATTENTION MRS SANDRA LUEBBE
65 POST STREET
SAN FRANCISCO CA 94104-3572

Folding and inserting procedure

Small envelopes (No. 6¾, 6¼)

Step 1 With letter face up, fold bottom up to ½ inch from top.

Step 2 Fold right third to left.

Step 3 Fold left third to ½ inch from last crease.

Step 4 Insert last creased edge first.

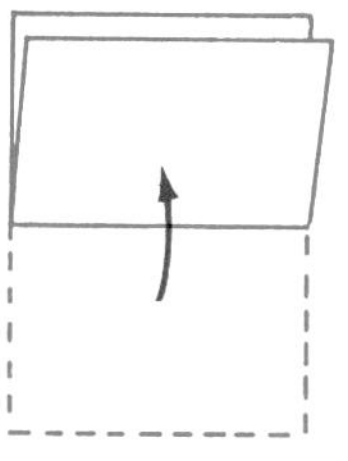
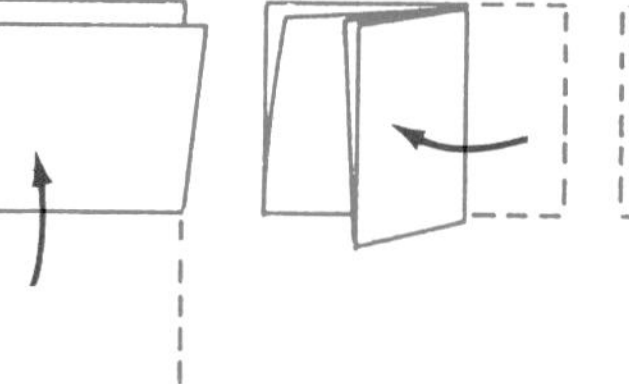
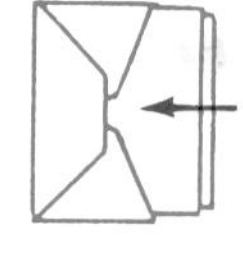

Large envelopes (No. 10, 9, 7¾)

Step 1 With letter face up, fold slightly less than ⅓ of sheet up toward top.

Step 2 Fold down top of sheet to within ½ inch of bottom fold.

Step 3 Insert letter into envelope with last crease toward bottom of envelope.

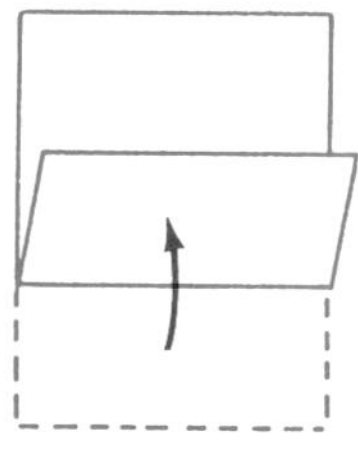
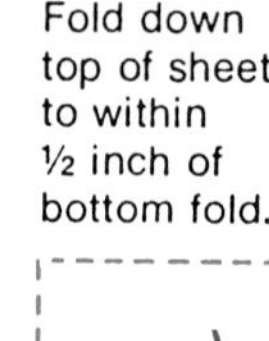
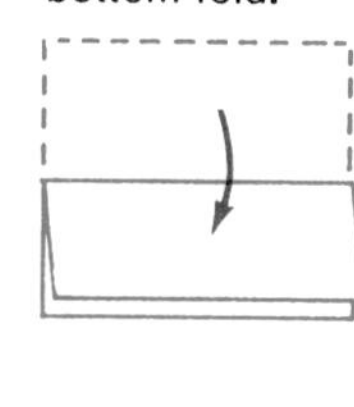

Window envelopes (letter)

Step 1 With sheet face down, top toward you, fold upper third down.

Step 2 Fold lower third up so address is showing.

Step 3 Insert sheet into envelope with last crease at bottom.

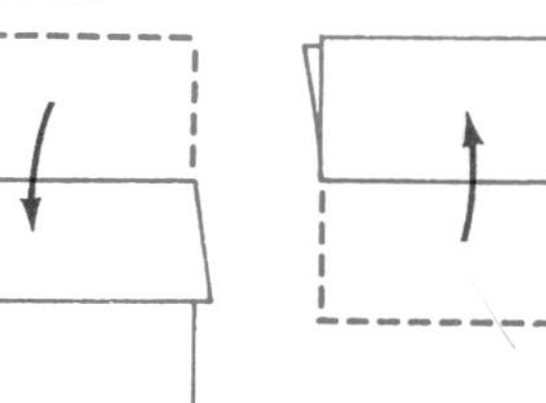
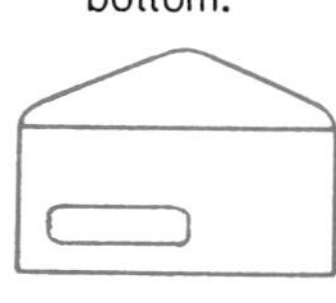

Main head

PLANNING AND PREPARING REPORTS ← line 10 pica; line 12 elite

QS

Whether written for personal or business use, a report should present a message that is well organized, stated simply, and clear in meaning (Burtness and Hulbert, 1985, 392). A report that does not meet these criteria reflects a lack of care in planning and preparation. The following suggestions will help you to plan and prepare reports that are so clear and concise that the readers will not have to puzzle over their intended meaning.

1″ 1″

DS

Side head

Planning a Report

DS

Three steps should be taken in planning a report. Selecting the topic is not merely the first step but also the most important one. It is vital that you choose a topic in which you have sufficient interest to do the necessary related reading and research. Next, it is essential that you limit the topic so that you can treat the subject adequately within the space and time limitations that have been set. Finally, you should decide upon and list in logical outline form the major ideas and the subordinate points for each idea that you want to use as support (Gonzalez et al., 1981, 499-518).

DS

Preparing the Report

DS

Three steps should be followed in preparing the report, also. The first of these is to look for data and authoritative statements to support your ideas. The next step is to prepare a rough draft of the report, organizing the data into a series of related paragraphs, each with a topic sentence to announce its major theme.

at least 1″

1 Unbound, page 1

2 line 6

line 8 The last step is to read the rough draft carefully for sequence of ideas, clarity, and accuracy and to prepare the final draft in correct form with all errors corrected. In checking for accuracy, be certain that

1. all words are spelled correctly;
2. punctuation rules have been correctly applied;
3. proper spacing follows each punctuation mark;
4. capitalization rules have been correctly applied;
5. all numbers are accurate; and
6. number expression rules have been correctly applied.

Whether the report is typed or printed, it should be neat and arranged in proper format. A neat report presented in an orderly style makes an immediate positive impression on the reader.

1″ 1″

QS

REFERENCES

QS

Burtness, Paul S., and Jack E. Hulbert. Effective Business Communication. 8th ed. Cincinnati: South-Western Publishing Co., 1985.

DS

Gonzalez, Roseann, Ruby Herlong, Mary Hynes-Berry, and Paul Pesce. Language: Structure and Use. Glenview, IL: Scott, Foresman and Company, 1981.

2 Unbound, page 2

Main head

ERGONOMICS AND THE BUSINESS OFFICE ← line 10 pica; line 12 elite

QS

Ergonomics, simply defined by Springer as "the study of humans at work,"[1] has become a topic of popular interest and concern in recent years. To be more specific, ergonomics deals with the compatibility of people and the other properties in their work environment. According to Popham, ". . . ergonomics integrates both the physiological and psychological factors involved in creating an effective work area."[2] It includes, therefore, the office furniture and equipment; the physical layout; and procedures such as the organization and method of work in the office as well as the worker's attitude toward computer software he or she must use.

1½″ 1″

DS

Physical Factors

DS

Where there are several physical factors that affect workers' productivity, two of the more common ones are the office chair and the video display terminal (VDT). Since most office personnel perform their tasks from a seated position, it is obvious that the chair is the foundation of the workstation. The widespread use of the video display terminal--sometimes

DS

DS

[1] T. J. Springer, "Ergonomics: The Real Issues," Office Administration and Automation, May 1984, p. 69.

DS

[2] Estelle L. Popham, Rita Sloan Tilton, J. Howard Jackson, and J Marshall Hanna, Secretarial Procedures and Administration (Cincinnati: South-Western Publishing Co., 1983), p. 31.

at least 1″

3 Leftbound, page 1

2 line 6

line 8 for long periods of time--in today's office makes the VDT another apparent source of ergonomics attention.

Office chairs. Since office personnel vary so greatly in size, it is imperative that office chairs be adjustable. While most chair seats can be moved up or down, most often it is difficult to do and sometimes requires special tools. The ideal is the office chair designed for easy adjustments of both the seat and back so that users can alter their positions as tasks change or fatigue occurs.

1½″ 1″

VDTs. Problems with VDTs vary from screen glare to posture strain. Glare can be remedied by the use of window coverings, recessed or indirect lighting, and screens that tilt and turn. Designs that separate the keyboard and screen aid both of these problems.

DS

Psychological Factors

DS

Among the psychological factors that influence worker comfort is the worker's perception of software he or she may use. Even some ergonomically alert people have not considered software to be an ergonomic issue. However, "friendly" software that is designed to be readily usable and that is documented for understanding by nontechnical users is just as much a part of ergonomics as are the hardware and furniture.

4 Leftbound, page 2

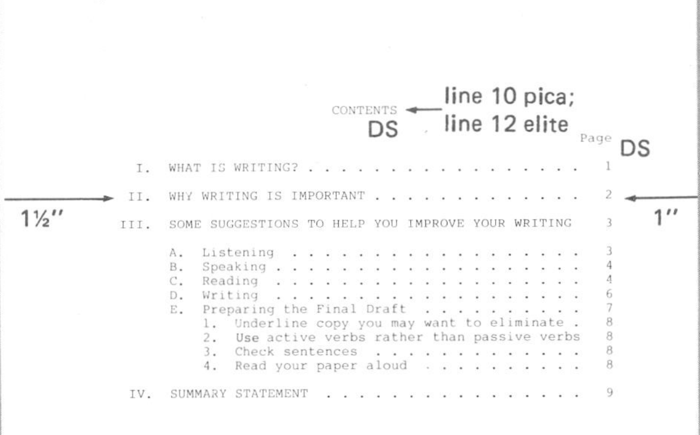

CONTENTS ← line 10 pica; line 12 elite

DS

Page DS

1½" → ← 1"

5 Leftbound, contents page

line 6

REFERENCES ← line 10 pica; line 12 elite

QS

Indent 5 →

1½" → ← 1"

American Psychological Association. Publication Manual. 2d ed. Washington, DC: American Psychological Association, 1974.

Attenborough, David. Life on Earth. Boston: Little, Brown and Company, 1979.

Committee on Writing Standards, The National Council of Teachers of English. "Standards for Basic Skills Writing Programs." College English, October 1979, 220-222.

Cross, Donna W. Word Abuse. New York: Coward, McCann & Geoghegan, Inc., 1979.

Goodlad, John I. A Place Called School. New York: McGraw-Hill Inc., 1984.

Graves, Robert, and Alan Hodge. The Reader Over Your Shoulder. New York: Random House, 1979.

Hemingway, Ernest. In Our Time. New York: Charles Scribner's Sons, 1970.

Lanham, Richard. UCLA Writing Project Lecture, 1979.

Walshe, R. D. "What's Basic to Teaching Writing?" The English Journal, December 1979, 51-56.

Zinsser, William. Writing With a Word Processor. New York: Harper & Row, 1983.

6 Leftbound, reference list (bibliography)

Main head

MEASURING PRODUCTIVITY OF OFFICE EMPLOYEES

line 12 pica; line 14 elite

QS

How much work should an office employee be expected to do in a given period of time? On what basis should an office employee be paid? These basic questions are almost impossible to answer for a number of reasons. The classification "office employee" includes hundreds of jobs. One of the major occupational categories listed in the Dictionary of Occupationl Titles is "Clerical and Sales Occupations." "Clerical occupations, which are classified in Divisions 20 through 24, include those activities concerned with preparing, transcribing, systematizing, and preserving written communications and records; distributing information; and collecting accounts" (1977, 153). The jobs listed in these divisions range from social secretary to library page. Because of the diversity of tasks performed by office employees with no standards of production, these workers traditionally have been paid on a time basis--by the hour, day, week, month, or year.

1" → ← 1"

With the adoption of word processing, attempts have been made to establish standards for those who keyboard materials. In a study conducted with word processing originators and supervisors in Tennessee, 41.3% indicated that they measured word processing production while 53.8% did not. "Typical responses regarding how production was measured included: (1) keystrokes; (2) line count; (3) number of pages; (4) weekly logs; (5) number of documents a day; and (6) quantity and quality of work" (Robinson and West, 1984,

↑ at least 1"

7 Topbound, page 1

Maxwell Nash Corporation

2502 Sycamore Avenue Baltimore, MD 21219-1331 Interoffice Communication

TO: Isabel Garcia

FROM: Sidney Cross, Assistant to Personnel Director

DATE: November 3, 19--

SUBJECT: Insurance Benefit Package DS

As we discussed in your orientation session yesterday, Maxwell Nash Corporation does provide insurance benefits for its full-time employees. The insurance plans for which you are eligible are:

1" → ← 1"

1. Medical, hospital, and major medical insurance covering the prevailing fees charged by participating physicians, hospitals, and other health agencies. Employees may elect to participate in this insurance plan. DS

2. Life insurance including basic life, accidental death, and dismemberment coverage at a rate of two times the employee's regular annual salary. Employees may elect to participate in this insurance plan.

3. Disability insurance which becomes effective 90 days after the beginning of a disability. This insurance provides monthly payments equal to 60 percent of the employee's regular salary up to a maximum of $1,800 per month. Participation in this insurance plan is required of all employees.

4. Dental insurance covering the entire or a portion of the prevailing fees charged by participating dentists for dental work which is covered in the plan. Employees may elect to participate in this insurance plan.

Maxwell Nash will pay 90 percent of the cost of the premium for each of these four insurance plans. Employees pay the remaining 10 percent through payroll deductions.

Please decide within the next 15 days which of the three voluntary plans in which you will participate. If you need additional information, contact Mark Harmon in the personnel department.

sjc

8 Memorandum Report

CORRECTION SYMBOLS/CENTERING PROCEDURES

Correction symbols

Proofreader's marks

Sometimes typed or printed copy may be corrected with proofreader's marks. The typist must be able to interpret correctly these marks in retyping the corrected copy or *rough draft* as it may be called. The most commonly used proofreader's marks are shown below.

Cap or ≡	Capitalize
⁀	Close up
↗	Delete
∧	Insert
∧ with comma	Insert comma
# or #/	Insert space
∨ with apostrophe	Insert apostrophe
∨ with quotation marks	Insert quotation marks
⊐	Move right
⊏	Move left
⊔	Move down; lower
⊓	Move up; raise
lc or /	Set in lowercase
¶	Paragraph
No new ¶	No new paragraph
‖	Set flush; align type
◯ sp	Spell out
stet	Let it stand; ignore correction
∩∪ or tr	transpose
___	Underline or italics

Centering procedures

1 Horizontal centering

1 Move margin stops to extreme ends of scale.

2 Clear tab stops; then set a tab stop at center of paper.

3 Tabulate to center of paper.

4 From center, backspace *once* for each 2 letters, spaces, figures, or punctuation marks in the line.

5 Do not backspace for an odd or leftover stroke at the end of the line.

6 Begin to key where backspacing ends.

Formula for finding horizontal center of paper

	Example
Scale reading at left edge of paper	0
+ Scale reading at right edge of paper	102
Total ÷ 2 = Center Point	102 ÷ 2 = 51

2 Spread headings

1 Backspace from center once for each letter, character, and space *except the last letter or character* in the heading. Begin to type where the backspacing ends.

2 In keying a spread heading, space once after each letter or character and 3 times between words.

3 Vertical centering

Mathematical method

1 Count lines and blank line spaces needed to type problem.

2 Subtract *lines to be used* from *lines available* (66 for full sheet and 33 for half sheet).

3 Divide by 2 to get top and bottom margins. If a fraction results, disregard it.

4 If an even number results, space down that number of times from top of sheet and key the first line. If an odd number results, use the next lower number.

Dropping fractions and using even numbers usually places copy a line or two above exact center--in what is often called *reading position*.

Formula for vertical mathematical placement

$$\frac{\text{Lines available} - \text{lines used}}{2} = \text{top margin}$$

Backspace-from-center method

Basic rule

From vertical center of paper, roll platen (cylinder) back once for each 2 lines, 2 blank line spaces, or line and blank line space. Ignore odd or leftover line.

Steps to follow:

1 To move paper to vertical center, start spacing down from top edge of paper.

a half sheet
down 6 TS (triple spaces)
− 1 SS (Line 17)

b full sheet
down 11 TS
+ 1 SS (Line 34)

2 From vertical center

a half sheet, SS or DS: follow basic rule, back 1 for 2

b full sheet, SS or DS: follow basic rule, back 1 for 2; then back 2 SS for *reading position.*

TABLE FORMATTING PROCEDURES

Prepare

1 Insert and align paper unless you are using a computer.

2 Clear margin stops by moving them to extreme ends of line-of-writing scale.

3 Clear all tabulator stops.

4 Move element carrier (carriage) or cursor to center of paper or line-of-writing scale.

5 Decide the number of spaces to be left between columns (for intercolumns) -- preferably an even number (4, 6, 8, 10, etc.).

[1] Plan vertical placement

Follow either of the vertical centering procedures explained on page RG 10.

Spacing headings. Double-space (count 1 blank line space) between main and secondary headings, when both are used. Double-space (count 1 blank line space) between the last table heading (either main or secondary) and the first horizontal line of column items or column headings. Double-space between column headings (when used) and the first line of the column entries.

Spacing above totals and source notes. Double-space (count 1 blank line space) between the total rule and the total figures. Double-space (count 1 blank line space) between the last line of the table and the 1½″ rule above the source note. Double-space (count 1 blank line space) between the 1½″ rule and the source note.

[2] Plan horizontal placement

Backspace from center of paper (or line-of-writing scale) 1 space for each 2 letters, figures, symbols, and spaces in *longest* item of each column in the table. Then backspace once for each 2 spaces to be left between columns (intercolumns). Set left margin stop where backspacing ends.

If an odd or leftover space occurs at the end of the longest item of a column when backspacing by 2's, carry it forward to the next column. Do not backspace for an odd or leftover character at the end of the last column. (See illustration below.)

Set tab stops. From the left margin, space forward 1 space for each letter, figure, symbol, and space in the longest item in the first column and for each space to be left between Cols. 1 and 2. Set a tab stop at this point for the second column. Follow this procedure for each additional column of the table.

Note. If a column heading is longer than the longest item in the column, it *may* be treated as the longest item in the column in determining placement. The longest columnar entry must then be centered under the heading and the tab stop set accordingly.

[3] Center column headings

Backspace-from-column-center method

From point at which column begins (tab or margin stop), space forward (→) once for each 2 letters, figures, or spaces in the longest item in the column. This leads to the column center point; from it, backspace (←) once for each 2 spaces in column heading. Ignore an odd or leftover space. Type the heading at this point; it will be centered over the column.

Mathematical methods

1 To the number on the cylinder (platen) or line-of-writing scale immediately under the first letter, figure, or symbol of the longest item of the column, add the number shown under the space following the last stroke of the item. Divide this sum by 2; the result will be the center point of the column. From this point on the scale, backspace (1 for 2) to center the column heading.

2 From the number of spaces in the longest item, subtract the number of spaces in the heading. Divide this number by 2; ignore fractions. Space forward this number from the tab or margin stop and key the heading.

MAIN HEADING

Secondary Heading

These	Are	Column	Heads
xxxxxx	*longest*	xxxx	xxxxx
xxxx	*item*	*longest*	xxx
xxxxx	xxxxx	*item*	*longest*
longest	xxxxxx	xxxxx	*item*
item	xxxx	xxx	xxx

lo	ng	es	t1	23	4l	on	ge	st	12	34	lo	ng	es	t1	23	4l	on	ge	st

[4] Horizontal rulings

To make horizontal rulings in tables, depress shift lock and strike the underline key.

Single-space above and double-space below horizontal rulings.

[5] Vertical rulings

On a typewriter, operate the automatic line finder. Place a pencil or pen point through the cardholder (or the typebar guide above the ribbon or carrier). Roll the paper up until you have a line of the desired length. Remove the pencil or pen and reset the line finder.

On a computer-generated table, use a ruler and pen or pencil to draw the vertical rulings.

CORRECTING ERRORS

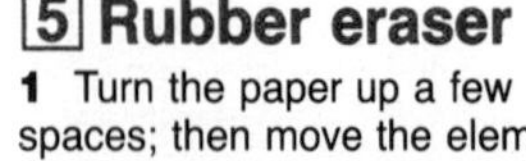

1 Electronic correction

Electronic typewriters, word processors, and computers vary in the way keystroking errors may be corrected. All, however, have a correction key that removes errors from the electronic window/screen and/or paper. Use the Operator's Manual for your machine to learn the steps for making corrections electronically.

2 Lift-off tape

1 Strike the special backspace/lift-off key to move the printing element (or carrier) to the point of the error.

2 Rekey the error exactly as you made it. In this step, the lift-off tape actually lifts the error off the page. The printing element stays in place.

3 Key the correction.

3 Correction fluid

1 Turn the paper up a few spaces to ease the correction procedure.

2 Shake the bottle; remove the applicator; daub excess fluid on inside of bottle opening.

3 Brush fluid sparingly over the entire error by a light touching action.

4 Return applicator to bottle and tighten cap; blow on the error to speed the drying process.

4 Correction paper

1 Backspace to the beginning of the error.

2 Insert the correction tape or paper strip behind the ribbon and in front of the error, coated side toward the copy.

3 Rekey the error exactly as you made it. In this step, powder from the correction paper is pressed by force into the form of the error, thus masking it.

4 Remove the correction paper; backspace to the point where the correction begins and key the correction.

Special correction paper is available for correcting errors on carbon copies.

5 Rubber eraser

1 Turn the paper up a few spaces; then move the element carrier (carriage) to the extreme right or left so that eraser crumbs will not fall into the machine.

2 Move the paper bail out of the way. Pull the original sheet forward (if a carbon copy is being made) and place a card (5″ × 3″ or slightly larger) in front of, not behind, the first carbon sheet to protect the carbon copy from smudges.

3 Flip the original sheet back and make the erasure with a hard eraser. Brush or blow the eraser crumbs off the paper.

4 Move the protective card to a position in front of the second carbon sheet if more than one carbon copy is being made. Erase the error on the first carbon copy with a soft eraser.

5 Remove the card and key the correction.

6 Correcting errors by squeezing/spreading

In correcting errors, it is often possible to "squeeze" a word into less space or to "spread" a word to fill out extra space.

Letter omitted in a word

1 Remove the word with the omitted letter.

2 Move printing element to second space after preceding word.

3 Pull half-space lever forward (or use electronic incremental backspacer) to move printing element a half space to the left.

4 Hold lever in place as you key the corrected word with the other hand.

5 Release the lever and continue keying.

Error
an omitte letter

an omitted letter
Correction

Letter added in a word

1 Remove the word with the added letter.

2 Move printing element to third space after preceding word.

3 Pull half-space lever forward (or use electronic incremental backspacer) to move printing element a half space to the left.

4 Hold lever in place as you key the corrected word with the other hand.

5 Release the lever and continue keying.

Error
a lettter within

a letter within
Correction

INDEX

INDEX, continued

SPECIAL INDEX

Alphabet sentences[1]

Figure sentences[2]

Figure/Symbol sentences[3]

Fluency (speed) sentences[4]

[1]An alphabetic sentence appears in every Conditioning practice, beginning on page 34.

[2]A figure sentence appears in most of the Conditioning practices, beginning on page 47.

[3]A figure/symbol sentence appears in many of the Conditioning practices, beginning on page 62.

[4]Beginning on page 30, an easy sentence, designed for speed building or fluency practice, appears in every Conditioning practice in the book.

Concentration drills

Guided writing copy

Models illustrated in text

Preapplication manipulative activities

Problems in rough-draft and script

Related communication activities

Skill-transfer timed writings

Straight-copy timed writings

Technique drills

Keystroking:

Machine parts:

Response patterns: